THE EMPEROR NERO'S POTTERY AND TILERY AT LITTLE LONDON, PAMBER, BY SILCHESTER, HAMPSHIRE

THE EXCAVATIONS OF 2017

THE EMPEROR NERO'S POTTERY AND TILERY AT LITTLE LONDON, PAMBER, BY SILCHESTER, HAMPSHIRE

THE EXCAVATIONS OF 2017

By Michael Fulford

With contributions by

Catherine Barnett, Catherine M. Batt, Joanna Bird, Nina Crummy, David P. Greenwood, Derek Hamilton, Sam E. Harris, Neil Linford, Paul Linford, Lisa Lodwick, Sara Machin, Nicholas Pankhurst, Andrew Payne, Jane Timby, Roger Tomlin, Peter Warry and Daniel Wheeler

Principal Illustrator: Daniel Wheeler

Britannia Monograph Series
No. 36

Published by the Society for the Promotion of Roman Studies
Senate House Malet Street London WC1E 7HU
2022

BRITANNIA MONOGRAPH SERIES NO. 36

Published by the Society for the Promotion of Roman Studies
Senate House, Malet Street, London WC1E 7HU

Britannia Monograph Series Editor: Paul T. Bidwell, OBE, FSA

This monograph was published with the aid of a grant from Paul Chadwick and the University of Reading

British Library Catalogue in Publication Data
A catalogue record of this book is available from the British Library

ISBN 978 0 907764 50 2

Cover illustrations:

Front: Kiln 4 looking south (painting © by Jenny Halstead)

Back: Trench 1 with Tile Kilns 1 and 2, view looking east

Produced by Short Run Press Ltd, Exeter

Printed in Great Britain

CONTENTS

LIST OF FIGURES

LIST OF TABLES

KEY

(1040) context number
[1181] cut feature, e.g. ditch, pit, post-hole, etc.
1155 structure, e.g. kiln

CBM ceramic building material

PREFACE

The excavations at Little London were carried out in 2017 as part of a wider project to understand better the nature of the developments which took place at Silchester (*Calleva Atrebatum*) in the first three to four decades of the Roman occupation of Britain, particularly during the reign of Nero (A.D. 54–68). Prior to modern excavations, the Roman town had produced only one example of a 'Nero tile', one stamped with the emperor's name and titles. Excavations of the forum-basilica (1980–86), Insula IX (1997–2014) and Insula III (2013–16) had produced a further eleven stamped tiles. House 1 which dominated the area under excavation in Insula IX had revealed that column fragments and blocks of Bath stone had been recycled from an earlier, demolished building into its first, otherwise timber phase, which was dated to the late first/early second century. What monumental building might have been the source of this stone? The accounts of the antiquarian excavations at Silchester gave no obvious clue to the location of the building but one possibility was a poorly understood structure in the south-east corner of Insula III which became the focus of excavation in 2013–14. Neither this, nor subsequent excavation in Insula III resolved the question of the whereabouts of the monumental building, but the finds provided further stimulus to take the enquiry in two new directions: to Little London, Pamber to explore the site of a possible tilery, where a second Nero-stamped tile was found in 1926, and the public baths of Silchester in Insula XXXIII, close to which the first Nero tile had been found found in 1903–4. The orientation of the bath-house suggested it was earlier than the late first-century date of the street grid, but fresh excavation could confirm the date and, potentially, enlarge our knowledge of the building, the materials used in its construction, how it was used and its impact on its local environment. The investigation at Little London could confirm whether or not it was the location of a tilery and, if that was the case, give insight into the scope and scale of production. Also, Little London appeared to be linked to the production of a distinctive, relief-patterned type of flue-tile — the tile used to convey the hot air from hypocausts up the walls of the room being heated and out and into the atmosphere. Confirmation of this combined with the study of examples of Little London products found beyond the kiln site also had the potential to enlarge our understanding of the reach of production.

ACKNOWLEDGEMENTS

A happy combination of circumstances led to the excavation at Little London taking place. I am extremely grateful to Stephen and Caroline Butt and the Calleva Foundation, Sir Timothy Sainsbury and the Headley Trust and to Dr Peter Warry for their financial support which made the excavation and its publication possible. I thank most warmly the Englefield Estate, its Director of Estates, Edward Crookes, and its tenant, Ben Kolosowski, for permission to carry out the excavation. I particularly thank Ben for all his help in facilitating the excavation.

The project required the particular expertise of someone experienced in the processing and classification of Roman ceramic building material. Thanks to an earlier generous grant from Peter Warry, Sara Machin had begun her PhD on the ceramic building material from Silchester in 2014 and the excavation not only provided her with invaluable source material for her research, but it benefited from her expertise in the on-site processing and classification of the excavated brick and tile, some 17,000 fragments weighing 4.5 tonnes, which reduced the assemblage to a manageable archive for permanent retention. Her contribution, with its contextualisation of the Little London industry, has been crucial to this publication. The discovery of pottery kilns was completely unexpected and I warmly thank Dr Jane Timby for taking on the publication of the resulting large and important pottery assemblage. She, in her turn, wishes to acknowledge the help of Dr Paul Tyers for his invaluable comments and discussions of her chapter.

The excavation was supervised by Nick Pankhurst and Dan Wheeler assisted by Josh Hargreaves and Bunny Waring. Dr Emma Durham, Jenni Eaton and Rory Williams Burrell managed the finds and environmental processing and archiving. Little London has also contributed to the larger Silchester Environs Project, which is co-directed by Dr Cathie Barnett and I am grateful to her for all her help in delivering the project. I particularly wish to thank Dan Wheeler for his assistance with the post-excavation and production of this publication, especially its illustration.

I warmly thank Paul Chadwick and the Society for the Promotion of Roman Studies for their generous contributions towards the cost of publication. Finally, I thank Dr Lynn Pitts for copy editing this monograph and for guiding it into print.

The archive is currently held at the University of Reading but it is intended to deposit it with the Hampshire Cultural Trust, Chilcomb House, Winchester.

Michael Fulford
Department of Archaeology
University of Reading
September 2021

CHAPTER 1

INTRODUCTION

By Michael Fulford

Silchester is unique among the towns of Roman Britain and of the western provinces more widely in having testimony of a building project or projects in the name of the emperor Nero (A.D. 54–68). The evidence for this is in the form of ceramic roofing tile stamped with his name and titles, the first example of which was found in a pit next to the public baths of the town when they were first excavated by the Society of Antiquaries of London (Hope and Fox 1905). A subsequent find from a suspected tilery at Little London, some 3 km south-south-west of the Roman town suggested local manufacture (Karslake 1926). Several more finds from excavations since 1980 in a number of locations within the town (Insulae III, IV, IX, XXX) hint that the Nero project was of some scale. The survey and excavation reported here to explore the presumed tilery paralleled further investigations within the town, particularly on the site of the public baths, to gain a better understanding of the scope and scale of the Nero project at Silchester. At the same time this research also addresses a major gap in our knowledge of an industry which produced some of the most distinctive and abundant materials associated with the Roman occupation of Britain. As Peter Warry pointed out 'Ceramic building material (CBM) frequently represents the largest proportion of the finds in Romano-British excavations, yet the relationship with the industry that supplied this material is poorly understood, particularly by comparison with our understanding of the pottery industry' (2012, 48).

While excavations, for example, in Colchester, London and Verulamium as well as at Fishbourne (W Sussex) have given valuable insights into the nature of early Roman building in the province, Little London is the earliest tilery to have been operating in the pre-Flavian period to be investigated in Britain. Besides the kiln structure itself, the excavation produced a sample of just over 17,000 pieces (4.5 tonnes) of ceramic building material of which over 10,500 pieces could be identified to form (Ch. 5). As well as revealing information about the range of products, further analysis indicates the relative amounts of each type produced, and thus the degree of specialisation. This, in turn, gives insight into the aspirations of the architects of the day and the requirements of their builders.

Tileries are difficult to date because they seldom produce independently datable material other than the brick and tile and, in the recent past, reliance has been placed on archaeomagnetic dating of the last firing of the kiln, though the results can offer a wide range of possible dates. In the case of Little London we have complemented the dating evidence that the associated pottery provides (Ch. 4) with a series of both radiocarbon and archaeomagnetic dates (Chs 8–9). If the connection with Nero were to be confirmed, it would be important to determine whether production was confined to the short duration of Nero's reign, or whether the latter was but one brief episode in a much longer period of manufacture. The duration of production could give insight into the scale of supply to the town and to other settlements in southern England. If production proved to be short-lived and associated with Nero, the character of the assemblage could potentially inform us of the nature of the project or projects established in the emperor's name. That Little London supplied consumers other than those in Silchester itself is indicated by finds of relief-patterned flue-tiles identical to one found in the ploughsoil at Little London at locations as far afield as Cirencester (Glos.) to the north and Rockbourne (Hants.) to the south-west (Betts *et al.* 1997, die 39). The distribution of Little London products is pursued in

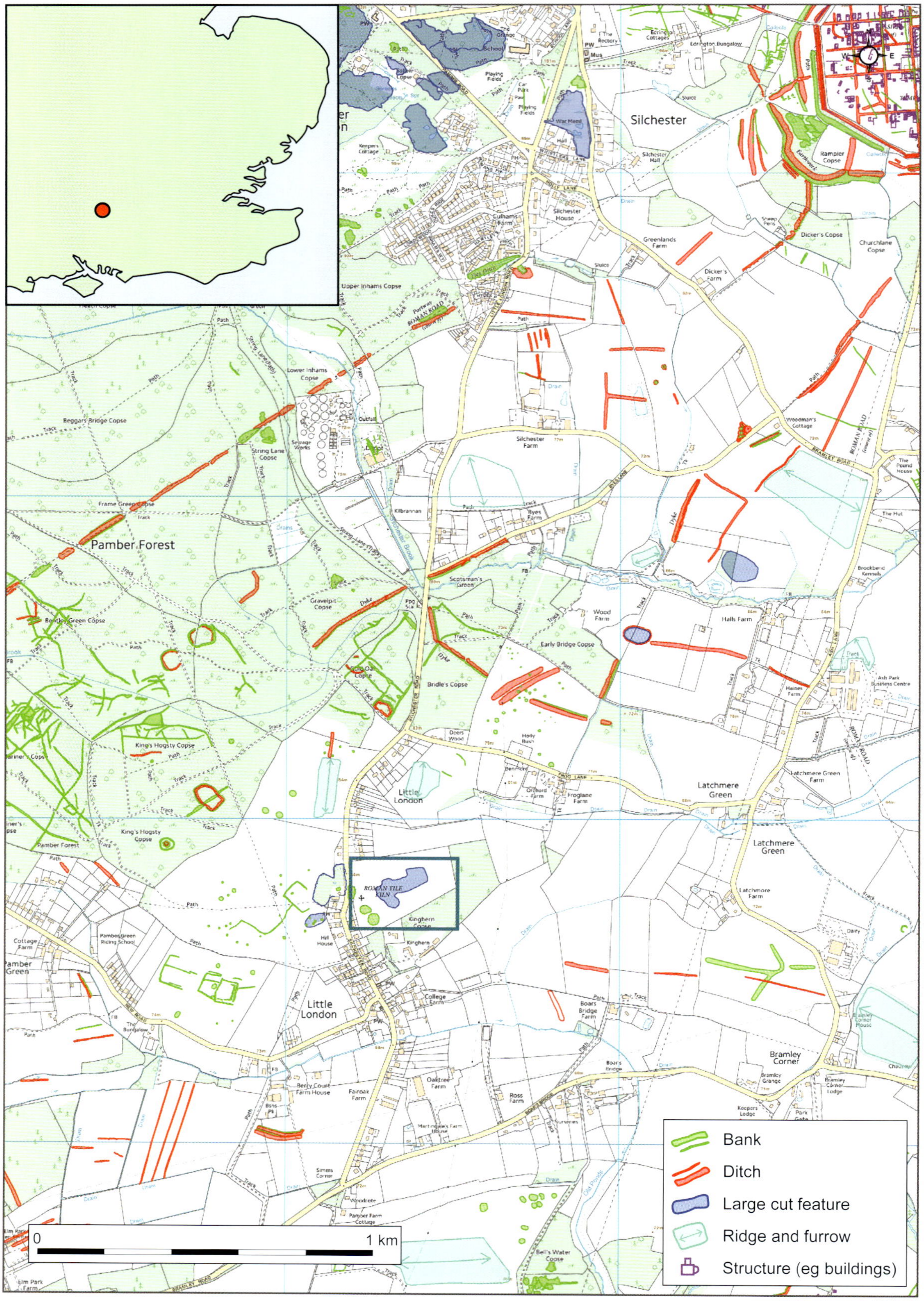

FIG. 1. Little London, Pamber, Hampshire. Location of the excavation in 2017 (*Crown Copyright and Database Right (2017) OS (Digimap Licence)*)

Chapter 5. Nero-stamped tile, however, has, to date, only been found at Silchester and Little London.

The background to the project takes us to 1925 when deep ploughing of the field to the east of the road running through the village of Little London (Pamber, Hants.) and opposite The Plough Inn revealed a spread of Roman brick and tile including highly fired pieces (FIG. 1). This prompted an excavation to explore the possibility that this was the site of a Roman brickworks (Karslake 1926). Although the precise location and extent of the excavation was not reported, it was claimed that Roman brick and tile were found to a depth of 8 ft 10 in (2.7 m). As no kiln structure was found, only large quantities of ceramic building material, it is possible that Karslake's trenches lay within a backfilled clay pit. Among the finds was a single tile, now in the British Museum, and the only surviving piece from the excavation, which was stamped with the abbreviated name and titles of the emperor Nero: NER[O] CL[AUDIUS] CAE[SAR] AUG[USTUS] GER[MANICUS] (Greenaway 1981). Its discovery followed the earlier find in 1903–4 by the Society of Antiquaries of London of a similar stamped tile in a cesspit adjacent to the latrines of the public baths of the Roman town at Silchester (Hope and Fox 1905, 366, fig. 13). Further finds of fragments of Nero-stamped tile were made during the excavations of the forum-basilica at Silchester (1980–6) and at Insula IX (1997–2014) (Fulford and Timby 2000, 118–19; Machin 2020, 423–5) (Warry, Appendix 1, pp. 176–8). All of these pieces are in a similar pale brown or yellowish-brown to pink fabric which Kevin Hayward found to be identical to that of tile collected from the surface of the field at Little London in 1957 and 1993 and retained in the Hampshire Cultural Trust's store at Chilcomb House, Winchester (Warry 2012, 50–1). No Nero-stamped tile has yet been found incorporated into a built structure.

As well as the finds of pieces of Nero-stamped tiles, the excavation at Insula IX also produced evidence of the re-use of monumental masonry in Bath stone in the foundations of an otherwise timber-framed town-house constructed towards the end of the first century A.D. (Fulford *et al.* forthcoming (a)). This pointed to the existence of an already demolished but earlier first-century monumental building or buildings at Silchester and raised the question whether the building project implied by the Nero tiles and the monumental masonry were connected (Fulford 2008). To pursue the question of the nature and extent of the Nero project at Silchester excavations were undertaken of a possible early building in Insula III (2013–16) (Fulford *et al.* 2013; 2014; 2015; 2016; forthcoming (b)), while re-examination of the public baths in Insula XXXIIIA to confirm whether or not the long-held belief that they were of Neronian date began in 2018 (Boon 1974, 121–37; Fulford *et al.* 2018b; 2019; forthcoming (b)). Further pieces of Nero-stamped tile were recovered from Insula III and also from the excavation of a newly discovered temple in the east of the town in Insula XXX (Fulford *et al.* 2017b; forthcoming (b)). Thus, every substantial modern excavation within the town, from Insula IX in the north-west to Insula XXX in the east, has produced examples of Nero tiles.

In contrast to the projects undertaken within the town walls to understand better the nature of the built Nero project at Silchester, the survey and excavation at Little London were designed, as we have seen, to confirm the existence or not of a Roman brick kiln or kilns and to undertake a systematic study of the recovered ceramic building materials, as well as of other finds, including associated environmental evidence, particularly the charcoal associated with the firing of the kiln (Ch. 6). Since there has been no other modern investigation of a Roman tilery in close proximity to, and demonstrably a supplier of, one of the major towns of Roman Britain, excavation at Little London has the potential to reveal some of its workings and working environment, as well as its full range of products.

Following geophysical survey by Historic England in 2015 (Ch. 2), which revealed indications of eight kiln-type structures as well as an extensive modern disturbance in the middle of the field, two areas (Trenches 1 and 2) with magnetic anomalies suggestive of at least three kiln structures were selected for open area excavation centred on SU 622 597 (FIG. 1). This took place over a period of four weeks in the summer of 2017. Following a summary of the results of the geophysical survey (Ch. 2), the excavations are described in Chapter 3. An unexpected discovery was that the kilns discovered in Trench 2 were, primarily at least, for the production of pottery. The large pottery assemblage is reported and its wider associations discussed in

Chapter 4, while the ceramic building material, mostly associated with the tile kiln found in Trench 1, is the subject of Chapter 5. Charcoal, evidence of the fuel used in the firing of the kilns, is reported and discussed in Chapter 6 and the radiocarbon dates analysed in Chapter 8. The enigmatic archaeomagnetic dating suggesting a medieval firing of the tile kiln is presented in Chapter 9. The results of the excavation are brought together and their wider significance discussed in the concluding Chapter 10.

CHAPTER 2

THE GEOPHYSICAL SURVEY

By Neil Linford, Paul Linford and Andrew Payne

Vehicle-towed caesium magnetometer and Ground Penetrating Radar (GPR) surveys were conducted over the suspected Roman tile production site prior to the excavation, with full details of the methodology and results provided in Linford *et al.* 2016. Results from both techniques

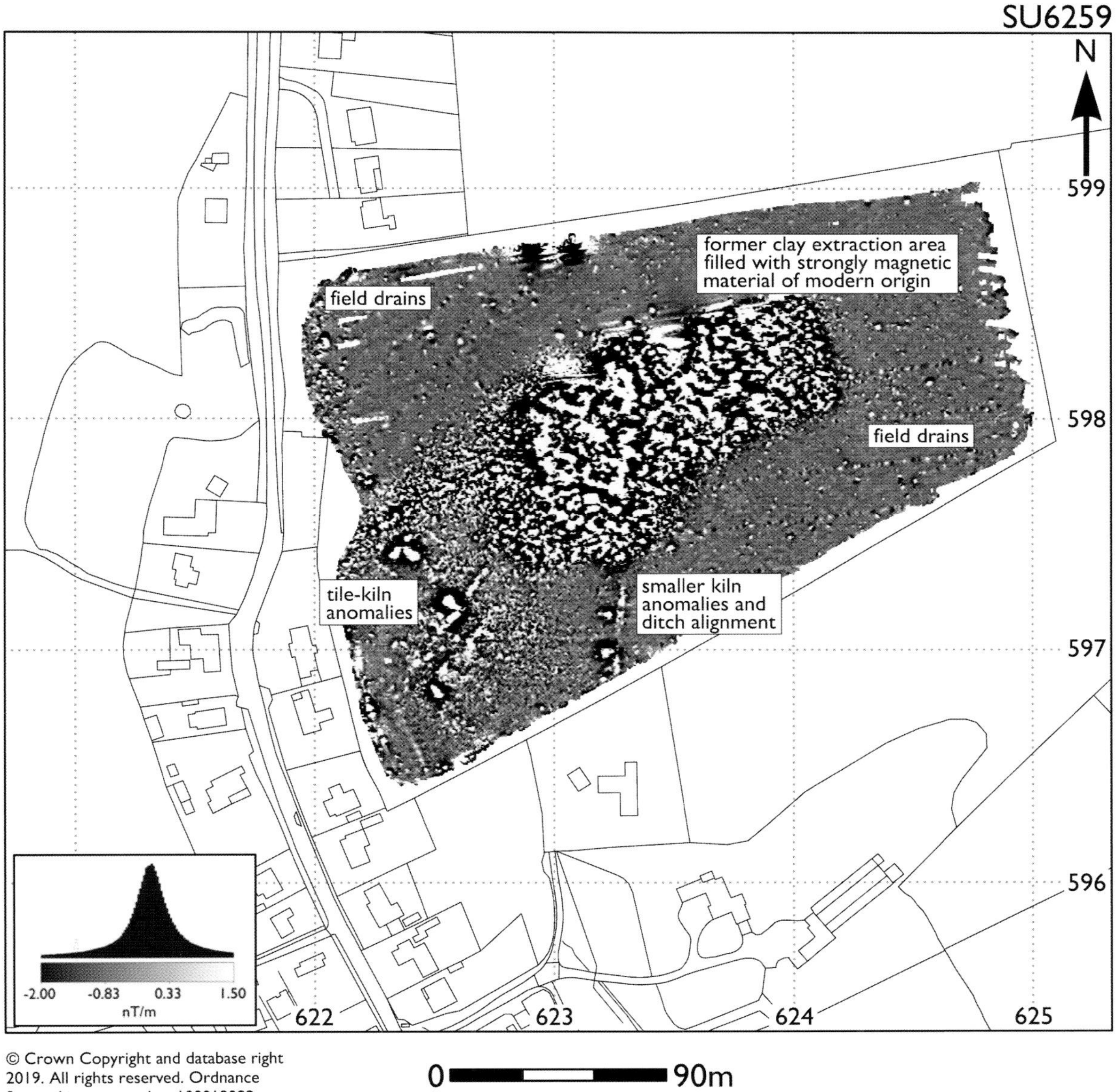

FIG. 2. Little London tilery. Linear greyscale image of the magnetic survey superimposed over the base OS mapping data showing the distinctive, high magnitude anomalies due to thermoremanent tile kilns

FIG. 3. Little London tilery. Greyscale image of the GPR amplitude time slice from between 7.2 and 9.6 ns (0.41 to 0.54 m) superimposed over the base OS mapping data, showing the response to field drains, the former trackway and geomorphology as high amplitude reflectors (white), together with low amplitude ditches (black). The inset figure shows the two possible kiln type anomalies shown at a depth of 0.27 to 0.41 m

were partially affected by known nineteenth-century clay pit workings associated with the brick-making industry in the area, although beyond this disturbance the plateau drift gravel deposits proved more responsive here than over the site of a prehistoric enclosure found approximately 100 m to the west (Linford *et al.* 2019). The caesium magnetometer survey covered an area of 5 ha using a 0.1 m x 0.5 m sample interval (Linford *et al.* 2018) and identified linear anomalies including a cluster of high magnitude, discrete thermoremanent responses characteristic of the remains of a group of approximately eight kiln-type structures, with some further less certain outliers. These kilns appear to be clustered in groups of two or three and the majority are located close to anomalies suggestive of probable linear boundaries and access trackways.

The GPR survey covered an area of 3.1 ha targeted over the kiln anomalies using a 0.075 m x 0.075 m samples density (Eide *et al.* 2018), with significant reflections recorded to an approximate depth of 2.3 m. The GPR results provided complementary detail of the anomalies mapped by the magnetometer survey and the historical land use of the area, including a network of field drains and a response to the geomorphology. Two discrete GPR anomalies, both with a diameter of 2 m and buried approximately 0.3 m from the surface, could possibly represent small kilns, although there is only a partial correlation with a corresponding high amplitude magnetic response.

CHAPTER 3

THE EXCAVATIONS

By Nicholas Pankhurst and Daniel Wheeler with Michael Fulford

INTRODUCTION

Two trenches, approximately 50 m apart, were hand-excavated after machine-stripping of the ploughsoil in the south-west corner of the field opposite The Plough Inn. To the west Trench 1, centred on SU 62258 59718, overlay one of a pair of strong magnetic anomalies identified by the geophysics, while Trench 2, centred on SU 62328 59713, overlay two similar anomalies adjacent to a north–south-aligned linear feature (FIGS 4–5). The total area excavated amounted to 850 m^2.

FIG. 4. The caesium magnetometry survey of the field with trench outlines

FIG. 5. Aerial view from the west of Trench 1 (bottom) and Trench 2 (upper) under excavation

TRENCH 1

Trench 1 (FIG. 6) was located above one of the clearest signals from the magnetometry survey, showing a pair of structures grouped close together with a potential linear feature running north-east towards the modern quarry pit to the north. A trench measuring 20 m by 20 m was opened with the removal by machine of the modern topsoil and a probable post-medieval ploughsoil on to a clear archaeological horizon which, despite having been scored by ploughing, already showed elements of the structures hinted at in the geophysics. Roman brick and tile were found in all the excavated features.

TRACKWAY DITCH 1 (FIGS 7–12)

Two parallel ditches running north-east/south-west and approximately 10 m apart were probably the earliest features within Trench 1. Interpreted as boundary ditches flanking a trackway, the absence of obvious post-conquest finds within the lower fills of both of these ditches hints at a pre-Roman date for their construction. The positioning of the kilns in relation to the western ditch seems deliberate with the firing chamber sunk into the remnant outer bank and the hollow of the ditch used for the stokehole and the second smaller kiln. Further analysis of the geophysics image shows that other potential brick kilns on the northern side of the trackway are similarly positioned to exploit the surviving earthwork; a pattern seen more clearly within Trench 2.

The most visible of the two ditches ran for approximately 25 m diagonally across the trench; it was generally V-shaped in profile with a flat base and measured a maximum of 2.65 m in width and 1.2 m in depth. The ditch was excavated at three points across the trench, most fully as [1181] in the north-east corner where it contained eight fills (FIGS 8–9). The primary fill was (1137): a friable, mid-reddish-grey, silty clay that had formed from the early erosion

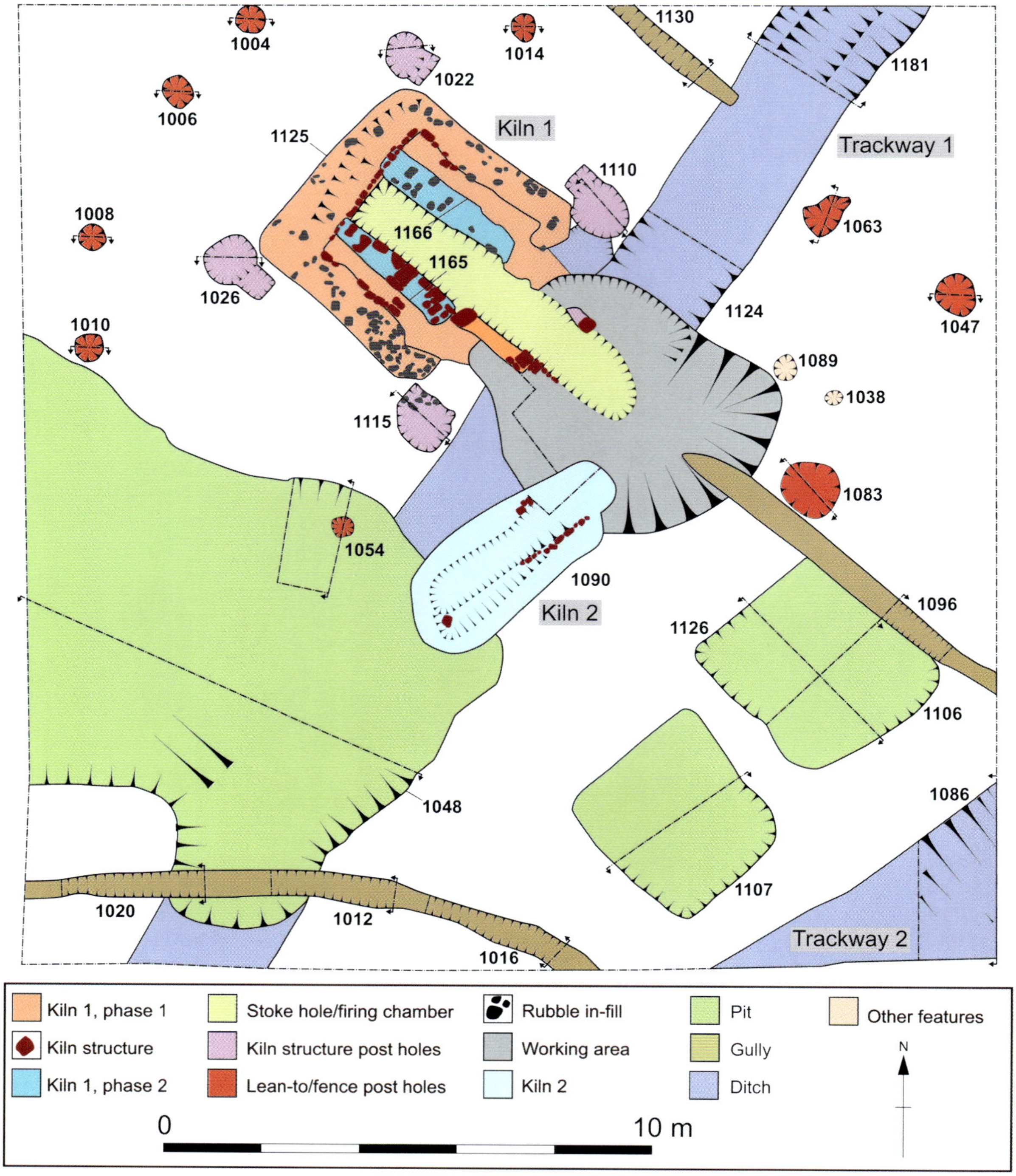

FIG. 6. Trench 1 showing cut features

of the sides and associated bank. (1137) measured 1 m wide and 0.2 m thick and produced 11 sherds of non-Little London kiln pottery of pre- or immediate post-conquest date which included the only imported Gallo-Belgic ware recovered from the site (Timby, below, p. 64). The subsequent four fills within the ditch were devoid of finds, perhaps suggesting a more rapid formation, possibly the result of deliberate backfilling to level the area. Overlying (1137) was (1134) which appeared to tip in from the south-eastern side. Measuring 1.58 m wide by 0.18 m thick, it was a friable, mid-bluish-grey, clay sand that was rich in redeposited London clay. Atop this was (1133): a firm, mid-reddish-brown, silty clay which measured 1.08 m wide by 0.22 m thick. There was then a substantial deposit (1136) which was 2.28 m wide and 0.44 m thick.

FIG. 7. Trackway ditches across Trench 1, looking west

Consisting of a friable, mid-reddish-grey, clay sand, this was probably the result of levelling the ditch hollow in preparation for the construction of the kiln to the south-west; the upcast natural clay from the cut of the kiln structure being used to consolidate the surrounding area. Overlying (1136) was a small deposit of thick clay (1135). Firm and light bluish-grey in colour, it measured 0.52 m wide and 0.12 m thick. The succeeding three deposits had all probably slumped into the top of the ditch during the use and subsequent abandonment of the nearby kilns and therefore gave an indication of what the ground surface was like in the local area — dirty and strewn with charcoal and waste material. Fill (1120) was a loose, dark blackish-brown, silty clay containing around 60 per cent charcoal and ash. Measuring 2.4 m wide and 0.16 m thick, this deposit was indicative of the general conditions surrounding the kiln during its use. Succeeding this dark layer was a firm, mid-reddish-brown, sandy silt (1037) which contained a significant amount of rubble-like brick and tile. Measuring 1.34 m by 0.62 m and 0.39 m thick, this was probably formed after abandonment of the kiln, possibly after the initial structure went out of use when the surrounding area was cleared of rubble in preparation for the installation of the two later, smaller kilns. The uppermost fill (1112) then formed in the remnant hollow of the ditch and measured 1.4 m wide and 0.22 m thick. Consisting of a loose, pinkish-grey, silty clay, (1112) contained both a significant amount of charcoal and waste ceramic building material (henceforth abbreviated CBM) suggesting it was formed during the later use of the kilns. Both horizons (1120) and (1112) produced small quantities of well-fragmented pottery comprising a mixture of local first-century coarse wares and Little London kiln wares (Timby, p. 64).

A south-west-facing section through the trackway ditch was also seen where the working area of the large kiln [1126] cut through it. Although not fully excavated to the base, it was recorded here as [1124] and measured 2.65 m wide and 0.54 m deep. Four fills were excavated in plan from the ditch at this point; the lowermost of which was (1142), probably the equivalent of

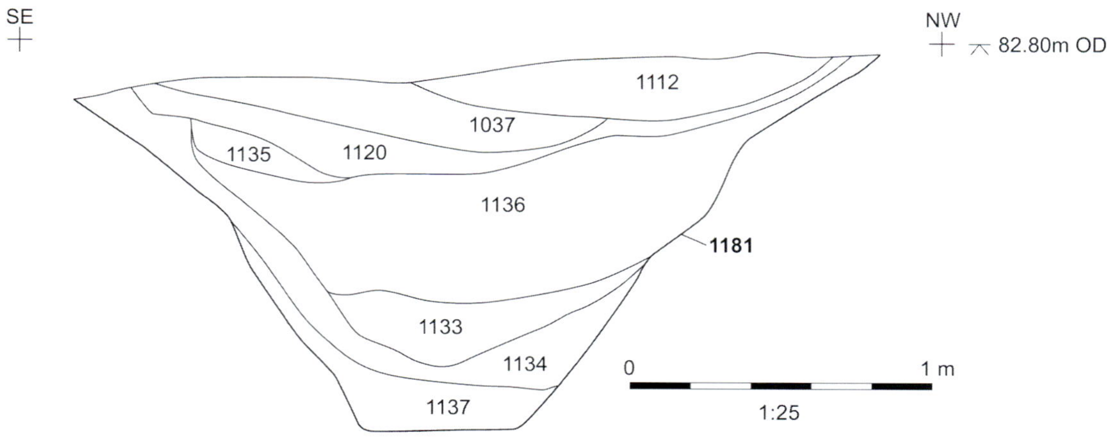

FIG. 8. Ditch [1181]

FIG. 9. Ditch [1181] looking south-west

(1136). (1142) was a firm, light reddish-brown, silty clay measuring 2.2 m wide and 0.25 m thick. Succeeding this was a firm, yellowish-grey, silty clay (1123) that was 0.6 m by 0.45 m and 0.1 m in thickness. Overlying this was a dark fill (1122) comprising around 80 per cent ash and charcoal; a very similar fill in look and feel to (1120). (1122) measured 0.8 m by 1.1 m and 0.09 m thick. The uppermost deposit – (1121) – was a firm, mid-greyish-brown, silty clay containing a good deal of waste CBM, ash and charcoal. Similar in composition to (1037), it measured 1.35 m by 1.8 m and 0.1 m in thickness. The upper three fills of ditch [1124] all contained waste brick and tile but no pottery.

The trackway ditch was also seen in the long cross-section dug through the large quarry pit [1048] on the western side of Trench 1 (FIGS 10 and 35). As the quarry pit sloped upwards on its eastern sides it cut through the upper extent of the ditch leaving just the base: cut [1078], measuring 0.88 m wide and 0.4 m deep. Like [1181] to the north, [1078] exhibited an almost-

FIG. 10. Base of ditch [1078] cut by quarry pit [1048], looking north-east

flat base turning sharply towards straight sides at a 45 degree angle. Only a single fill was seen within the cut: (1079) which was similar in make-up to (1137), the base fill of the ditch to the north. (1079) was a firm, light bluish-grey, silty clay of the same dimensions and was probably formed from redeposited natural clay mixed with early wash. (1079) contained 31 sherds of pottery most of which come from a Silchester ware lid and a copy of a Cam. 2 platter in grog-tempered ware (GR4). There were also five sherds of Little London kiln ware and a handful of pieces of CBM which may be contamination from the quarry fill (Timby, p. 64).

Further north, the upper fill of the ditch was also seen in the area between quarry pit [1048], Kiln 2, and the working area for the large kiln [1126]. Recorded as (1143) but not excavated, it was a friable, mid-bluish-black, sandy loam containing around 30 per cent charcoal. Similar to the dark fills seen in the upper areas of the ditch further along, (1143) measured 1.5 m by 0.9 m in plan.

TRACKWAY DITCH 2 (FIGS 11–12)

Located in the south-east corner of the trench was a small portion of a corresponding near-parallel ditch [1086] which was similar in size and form to [1181]. The upper deposits, probable slumps into the remnant hollow of ditch [1086], are similar to those seen at the top of [1181] also representing the appearance of the area surrounding the kilns during their use.

Excavated obliquely against the eastern side of the south-east corner of Trench 1, [1086] was 2.95 m wide and 1.43 m deep with straight, moderately sloping sides and a rounded base. Seven fills were contained within the ditch, the lowermost of which was a firm, orange-and-blue-mottled grey, clay sand (1094). The latter measured 1.18 m wide and 0.4 m thick and was made up of redeposited London clay that had eroded into the ditch during its initial stabilisation. Overlying was (1093), a firm, light brown, clay sand measuring 1.94 m wide and 0.4 m thick. Atop this was (1062): a firm, greyish-brown, clay sand which measured 2.28 m wide and 0.6 m thick. No finds were recovered from the lower two horizons but fill (1062) yielded 85 sherds of first-century A.D. pottery, none of which were Little London kiln wares but did include ten amphora sherds (Timby, p. 64). The overlying fill (1092), a loose, light brownish-grey, silty

FIG. 11. Oblique section through trackway ditch [1086], looking east

sand, appeared to have been tipped in from the north-western side, and was 1.62 m wide and 0.5 m in thickness. To this point, the initial four fills had no evidence of kiln wares, suggesting, like the parallel trackway ditch, that the lower deposits formed prior to the start of brick-and-tile-making in the area. The succeeding three layers, however, are obviously evidence of the functioning of the kilns and compare with the sequence seen in the corresponding trackway ditch across the trench. The next deposit, (1056), was rich in CBM and contained 26 sherds of Little London kiln ware (Timby, p. 64). Measuring 2.25 m wide and 0.28 m thick, it was a firm, mottled-orange/bluish-grey clay. Sealing across the top of the ditch was a dark burnt layer (1041) containing a substantial amount of ash and charcoal, 3.32 m wide and 0.12 m thick. It produced just five potsherds, three of which were oxidised Little London kiln wares (Timby, p. 64). The

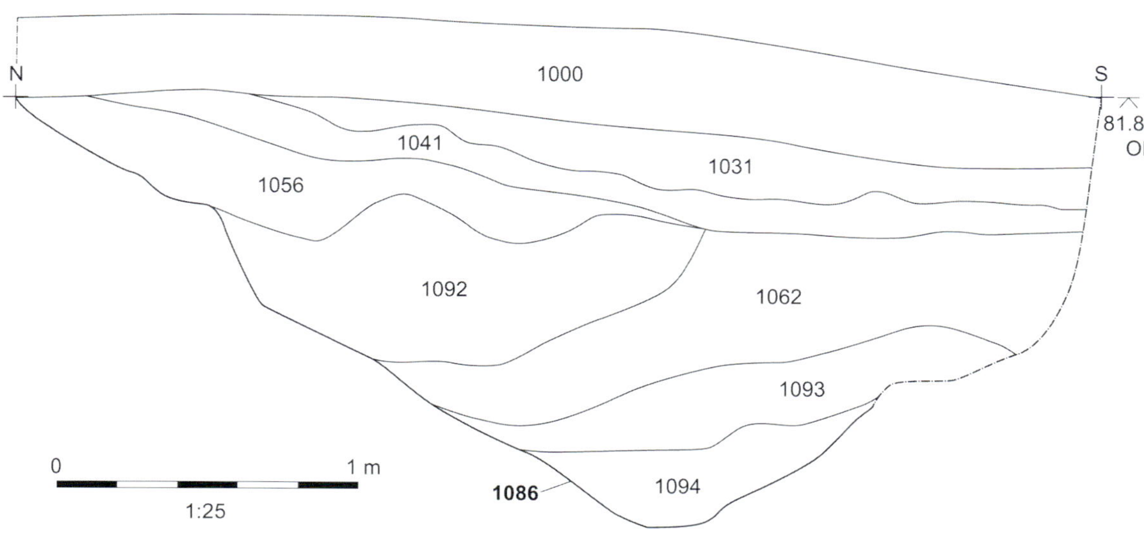

FIG. 12. Trackway ditch [1086]

final horizon, (1031), consisted of a substantial layer, 2.88 m wide and 0.2 m thick, of crushed and degraded brick and tile, perhaps discarded wasters or a demolition deposit resulting from the destruction or modification of one of the kilns.

KILN 1, PHASE 1 (FIGS 6, 13–20)

The brick-built structure of the main kiln measured 4.8 m by 7.2 m, comprising a roughly-rectangular firing chamber oriented north-west/south-east with a narrower, 2 m-long stokehole extending out from the south-east side. The firing chamber was cut 2.05 m deep below the base of the ploughsoil although it may have been slightly shallower initially. Each of the side walls was faced with thin, well-made bricks laid in uneven courses, as the facing of a brick rubble core. Emerging from the south-west side inside the structure were three short stubs of stacked bricks keyed into the main wall. These were the remnants of internal cross-walls that would have supported the surface on which the unfired bricks and tiles were placed. Where the stokehole met the entrance to the firing chamber a curving stack of four voussoir tiles on the south-west

FIG. 13. Kiln 1, with main structural elements highlighted

side probably formed the springer of an arched flue. It is likely that the cross-walls were similarly arched to allow the hot gases to circulate the full length of the firing chamber.

The construction cut [1125] for the kiln structure measured 4.8 m by 7.2 m and was 2.05 m deep to the base of the firing chamber. As none of the kiln walls were removed it was not possible to tell the exact method of construction, but it can be assumed that the foundation cut was packed with a dense rubble core of broken brick (1180) up to 1.2 m thick between it and the internal facing of brick. The back wall of the firing chamber **1161** was 1.2 m thick with a 0.36 m high façade of bricks surviving facing south-east. The bricks on all sides of the kiln were generally wide and thin, varying in size from 0.05 m in thickness and a width of 0.1 m to a thickness of 0.1 m and a width of 0.42 m. In the north-east corner, **1161** consisted of six courses of bricks arranged in a very rough stretcher bond. Although there was no recognised bonding material, the rubble core (1180) that backed the bricks acted as a binding matrix to aid stability. Central to the back wall and emanating from the firing chamber was a 1.5 m wide and 0.72 m high block of vitrified bricks, fused together and green and glassy in appearance (FIG. 14). The edges of this conglomerated lump were defined by the later narrowing of the firing chamber in its second phase (see below), suggesting it was the result of higher temperatures reached within the kiln once it was remodelled.

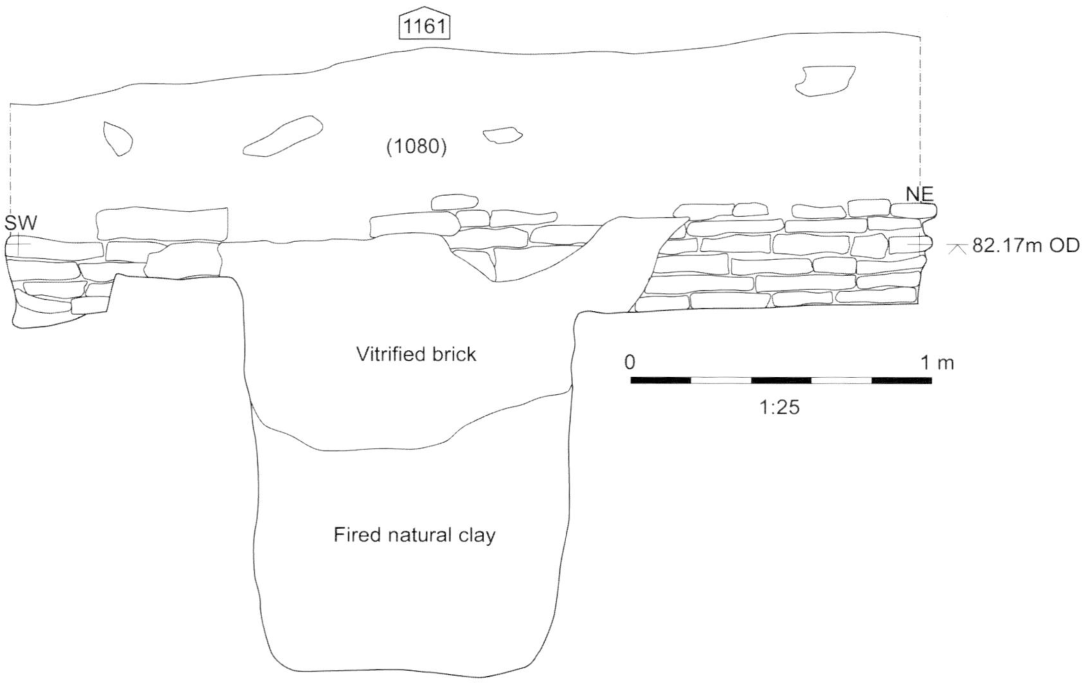

FIG. 14. **1161**: back wall of the firing chamber

The south-western wall of the kiln **1155** measured 4.6 m long by 0.88 m wide including the rubble core and was faced by a surviving brick frontage 2.6 m wide and 0.58 m high. Similarly roughly-coursed and with the same range of brick sizes as the back wall, **1155** included eight surviving courses, preserved particularly well because of the increased stability afforded by three cross-walls extending across the firing chamber. Likely to have originally been arched across the firing chamber, the cross-walls **1156**, **1157** and **1158** remained only as short stubs, each measuring 0.3 m wide with the best surviving – **1156** – being eight brick courses high (FIGS 15–16). The opposite kiln wall **1171** was much less well preserved with only a small element of brick-facing surviving in the northern corner. Overall the wall measured 4.8 m long and 0.72 m wide with the structural element three brick courses high and 1 m in length. A single cross-wall stub, **1170**, emerged from the north-east wall. Measuring 0.35 m wide and just 0.15 m long, it consisted of three courses of similar bricks and, although not entirely aligned with it, was probably the opposite match of **1158** across the firing chamber.

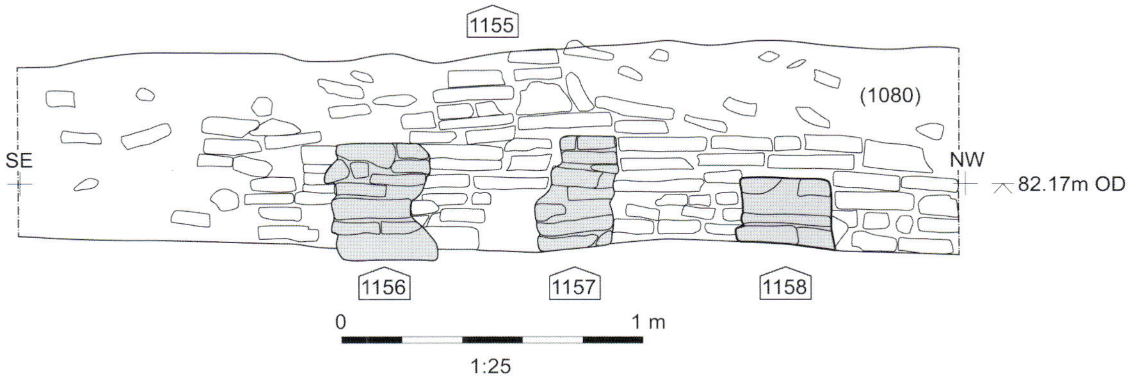

FIG. 15. Kiln wall **1155** with cross-walls **1156**, **1157** and **1158**

FIG. 16. Kiln wall **1155** looking south-west

The stokehole of the kiln ran for 2.4 m from the firing chamber towards the working area outside. Comprising two brick-built walls 1.12 m apart, the south-west side **1176** survived much more intact than the north-east side **1177**, which had almost entirely collapsed (FIG. 17). **1176** included up to six courses of bricks laid in a rough header/stretcher bond 0.38 m high. Centrally the bricks had once again vitrified, forming a conjoined mass 0.88 m wide. At the north-west end, closest to the kiln entrance, were four stacked voussoir tiles arranged as the springer for the arched entrance to the firing chamber (FIG. 18). The opposing wall **1177** was considerably poorer in preservation, with the structural element measuring just 0.6 m long and 0.2 m wide and consisting of one course of brick.

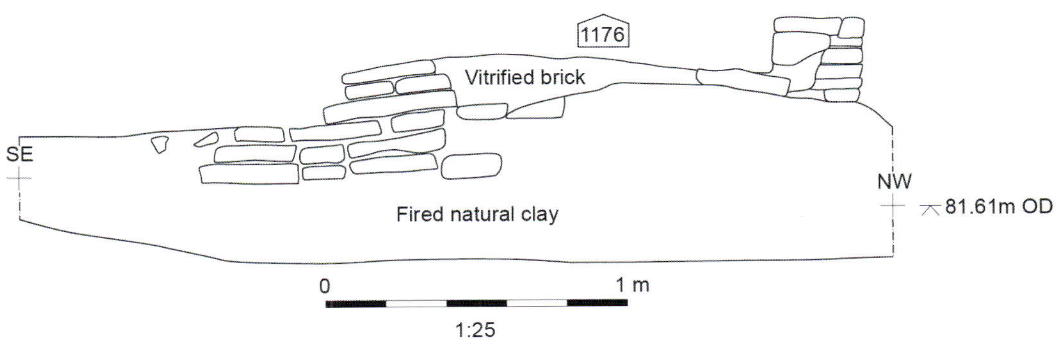

FIG. 17. North-east-facing side of stokehole, **1176**

FIG. 18. Springer for the stokehole arch at the entrance of the firing chamber, looking south-east

FIG. 19. Looking north-west from working area [1126] into Kiln 1

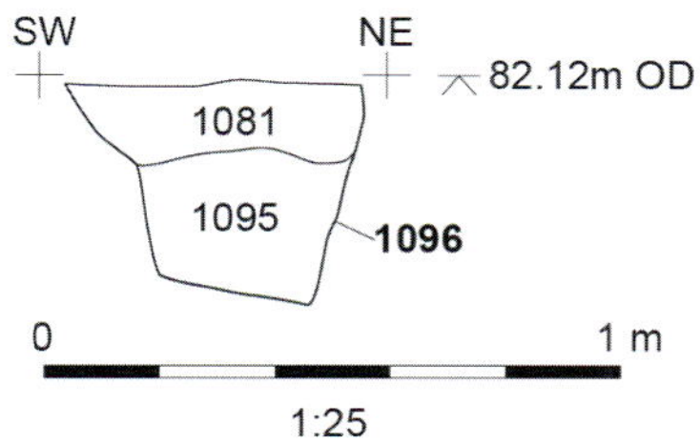

FIG. 20. Drainage gully [1096]

To the south-east of the flue-arch was a large open working area [1126]. This was sub-square in plan, measuring approximately 4 m by 5 m and sloping up from the flue-arch to around 0.8 m below the ploughsoil. It was sat within the hollow of the early ditch and appeared to serve — in their latest phases at least — both the main, larger kiln (Kiln 1) and the smaller example to the south-west (Kiln 2) (FIG. 19 and below, p. 27). The majority of the lower deposits within the working area were rich in burnt material as a result of the regular raking-out of the stokehole; however it is assumed that these deposits were associated with the later phase of the kiln and are thus described below. Running out from the working area on the same general alignment was a narrow, square-cut gully [1096], 0.47 m wide, 0.45 m deep and extending south-east for 6.8 m before reaching the eastern edge of the trench (FIG. 20). This straight-sided feature may have been dug as a drain, taking advantage of the natural slope down to the south-east and running into the hollow of the trackway ditch [1086]. The gully contained two fills, the lower of which was (1095): a compact, mid-yellowish-orange, silty clay, measuring 0.37 m wide and 0.34 m thick and containing no finds. Overlying was (1081) which was a compact, mid-greyish-brown, silty clay, 0.47 m wide and 0.18 m thick. Within was a high concentration of charcoal and some CBM, but no other dating evidence.

KILN 1 SUPERSTRUCTURE (FIGS 21–24)

Surrounding the kiln were a number of post-holes and other features aligned and associated with the structure. At each of the four corners of the firing chamber, just outside the rubble packing of the walls, was a substantial post-hole. Although varying in depth between 0.15 m and 0.6 m, each was over 0.6 m in diameter and [1110] had clear evidence of a central post-pipe, approximately 0.48 m in diameter. Associated with each post-hole was a shallow, rectangular, step-like cut, as illustrated in FIG. 21. Their function is unclear; perhaps they acted as the seating for buttressing or replacement posts. Although little can be inferred about the roofing of the structure, it seems almost certain that the posts inferred from these post-holes would have provided its support. No dating evidence was recovered from any of the four features.

FIG. 21. Post-holes around Kiln 1 with shallow steps highlighted. Looking south-east

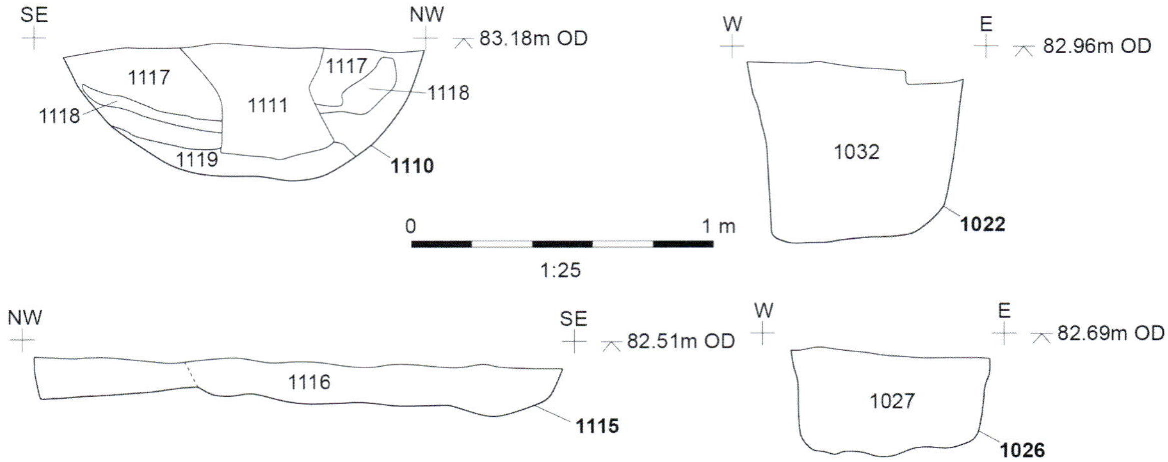

FIG. 22. Kiln 1 superstructure: profiles of post-holes

Of the post-holes at the front of the kiln, [1110], at the eastern corner, was the best preserved (FIGS 6, 22–23). It included three fills and an obvious central post-pipe. It was 1.2 m in diameter and 0.5 m deep, with the stepped extension to the north-west measuring 0.66 m by 0.3 m and 0.12 m deep. The lowermost fill (1119) was a soft, mid-orangish-yellow clay; probably natural clay disturbed during the cutting of the post-hole. It measured 0.8 m wide by 0.1 m thick and contained some CBM fragments. Overlying this was the larger post-packing fill (1117) measuring 1.2 m wide and 0.4 m thick. Consisting of a friable, light yellowish-brown sandy silt, this deposit had little of the typical packing material of brick and tile, otherwise seen in three of these four post-holes. Within (1117) was a darker lens of rubble-rich material probably scraped from the ground surface into the post-hole when it was backfilled. (1118) measured 1.02 m wide by 0.05 m thick and was a soft, mid-reddish-brown, sandy silt containing around 70 per cent

FIG. 23. Post-hole [1110] with central post-pipe

FIG. 24. Tile packing surrounding post-pipe within post-hole [1022]

brick rubble. The post-pipe was then defined by a significantly redder fill, indicative of infilling of kiln waste material once the post had been removed. This deposit (1111) was a soft, mid-brownish-red, sandy silt measuring 0.45 m wide and 0.35 m thick.

The corresponding post-hole at the front of the kiln was similar in shape to [1110] but considerably shallower (FIG. 22). Measuring 0.9 m by 0.7 m but only 0.15 m deep, [1115] also included a rectangular step extending to the north-west which was 0.52 m by 0.58 m and 0.15 m deep. Within the post-hole was a single fill, (1116), a friable, light yellowish-brown, clay sand of the same dimensions.

The two equivalent post-holes at the back of Kiln 1 each had straight sides and were smaller in diameter than the bowl-shaped examples seen at the front (FIGS 6 and 21). [1026] at the western corner of the kiln was the shallower of the two, measuring 0.65 m across and 0.33 m deep, with the extended step to the south-east 0.56 m by 0.62 m and 0.08 m deep (FIG. 22). The sides of the post-hole were straight and vertical, turning sharply into a flat base. Contained within was a single fill (1027), a friable, mid-yellowish-brown, sandy clay of the same dimensions as the cut. Like the two front post-holes, this fill contained little packing material.

[1022] on the northern corner of Kiln 1 measured 0.82 m in diameter and 0.6 m deep, with its step to the south-east 0.72 m by 0.38 m and 0.1 m deep (FIGS 22 and 24). Within was a single fill (1032) which included a large amount of packing of roof-tile. It was a firm, mid-yellowish-brown, sandy loam.

The absence of much packing in all but one of these post-holes suggests that they were part of the original structure of the kiln, excavated and filled before the kilns were fired. The one post-hole with much packing probably indicates a replacement post. Similar arrangements of large posts around the kiln have been noted at the later, rural tile kilns excavated at Crookhorn (Hants.) and Arbury, Cambridge. The similarity with the arrangement at Crookhorn is particularly striking (McWhirr 1979b, 175; Soffe *et al.* 1989, 101).

ANCILLARY STRUCTURES (FIGS 25–27)

Surrounding Kiln 1 were a number of post-holes and a beam-slot suggestive of secondary structures adjoining the main kiln (FIG. 25). After being formed and moulded, bricks and tiles would have been left to dry for a number of days before being fired. Storing these under-cover and close to the firing chamber may have utilised the residual heat from the kiln to aid this process. Likewise, firing the kiln would have required immense amounts of wood which would probably have been collected during the winter months. Storage structures would have allowed for the drying of the wood and, if built close to the kiln, could similarly have assisted drying. Alternatively, if the kiln was only employed seasonally, a surrounding fence or barrier might have proved useful for keeping out livestock or wildlife.

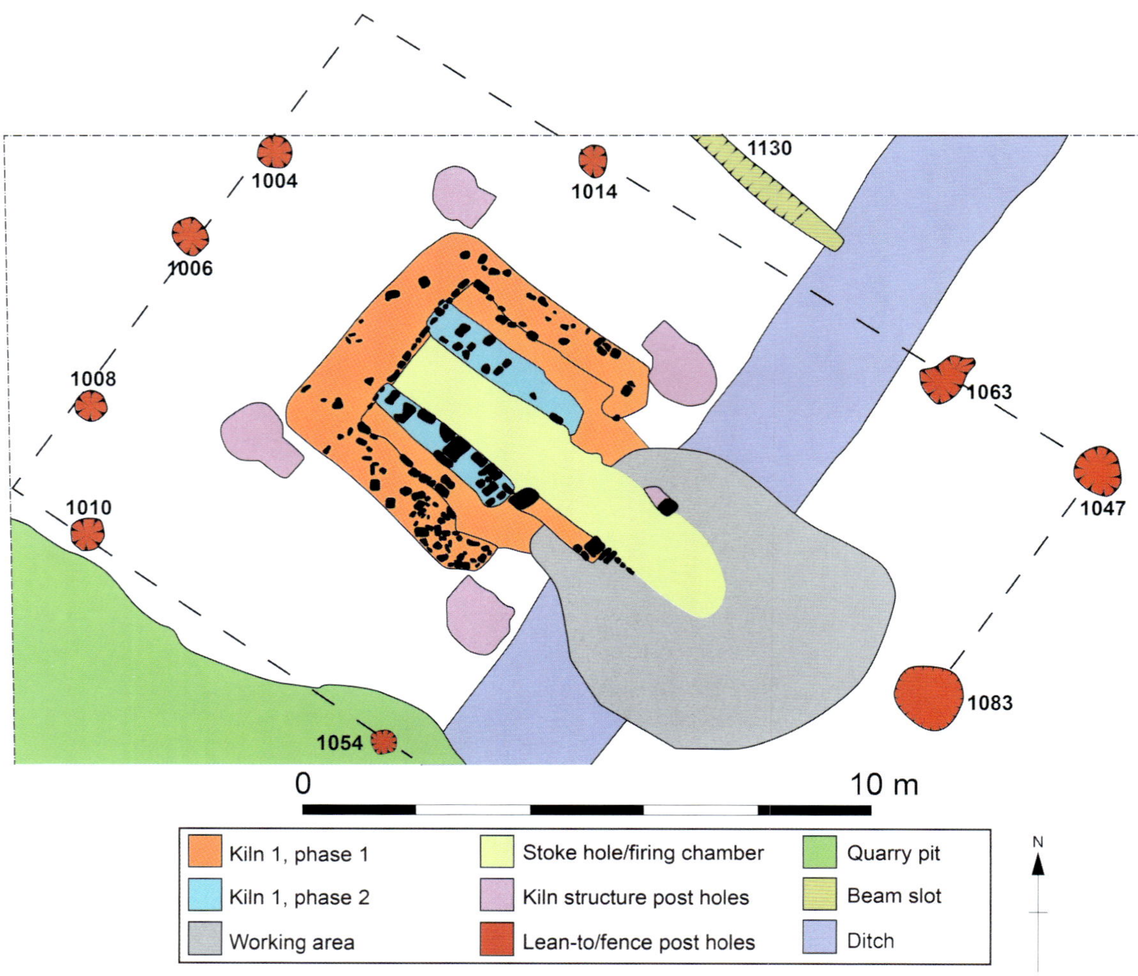

FIG. 25. Ancillary structures surrounding Kiln 1

A short stretch of beam-slot [1130] aligned with the wall of the firing chamber was located 3.5 m to the north-east of Kiln 1 (FIG. 26). Measuring 2.6 m long, 0.42 m wide and 0.2 m deep, the beam-slot may have supported some kind of lean-to shed which shared the north-east wall of the kiln. Within [1130] was a single fill, (1129): a firm, orangish-yellow clay of the same dimensions.

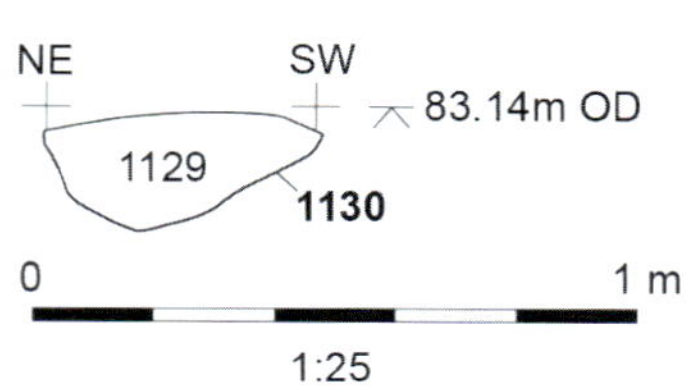

FIG. 26. Beam-slot [1130]

In the north-west corner of the trench was a line of three post-holes aligned with the back wall of the kiln: [1008], [1006] and [1004]. As with the beam-slot, these may have supported some kind of satellite building or a fence-line. A fourth post-hole [1010] slightly further south suggests that this alignment may have turned 90 degrees or curved sharply, but further examples in the direction leading towards [1054] were not located, perhaps because they were cut into the residual bank of the trackway and subsequently ploughed away. A similar arrangement is seen on the north-east side: three post-holes, [1014], [1063] and [1047], flank the kiln wall before turning south-westwards to a single example [1083] in line with the firing chamber of the kiln. Similarly, a gap is evident where the remnant of the trackway bank and surviving ditch would have been. The nine post-holes are summarised below (FIGS 25 and 27):

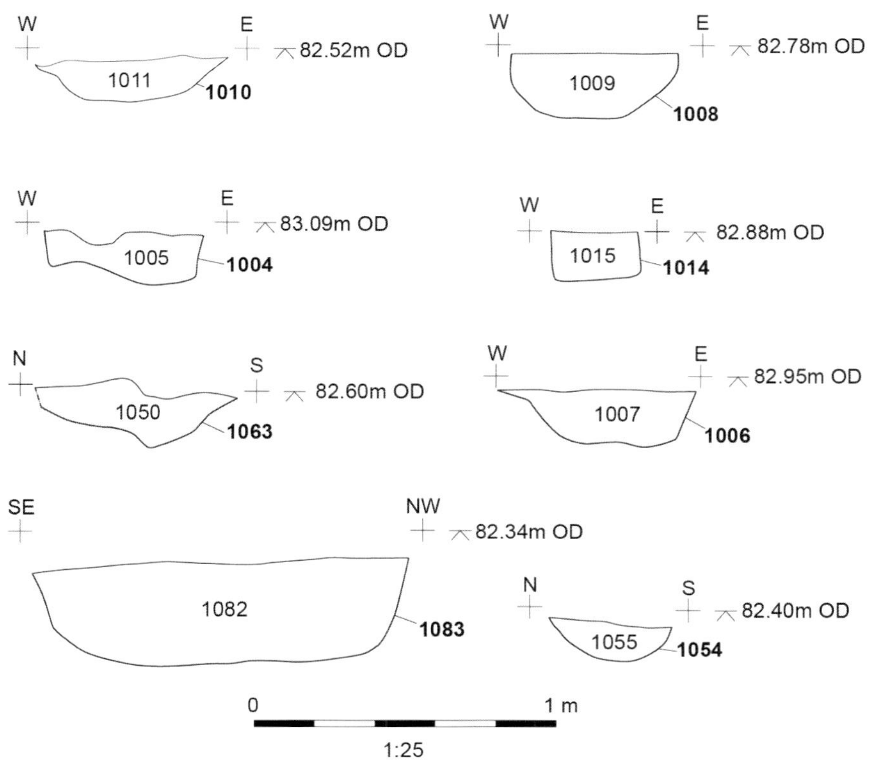

FIG. 27. Profiles of post-holes around Kiln 1

[1010] was circular in shape with a diameter of 0.64 m and a depth of 0.14 m. The sides were straight and moderately-sloping towards a flat base. Within was a single fill (1011) which was a firm, light brownish-grey clay including a large proportion of brick and tile.

[1008] was circular, measuring 0.55 m in diameter and 0.23 m deep. The sides sloped gradually to a rounded base. The single fill (1009) was a firm, light brownish-grey clay which consisted of around 40 per cent CBM packing. Two pieces of tile from (1009) were in the form of a skylight: a *tegula* with a central, circular hole (below, Machin, p. 100, FIG. 80).

[1006] was sub-rectangular in shape with moderately-sloping convex sides and a rounded base. Measuring 0.58 m by 0.31 m and 0.22 m deep, it contained a single fill. (1007) was a loose, light yellowish-grey clay containing CBM packing.

[1004] was circular in shape and measured 0.54 m in diameter by 0.24 m deep. The sides were straight and near-vertical with a sharp break of slope to a sloping base. Contained within was a single fill of the same dimensions as the cut. (1005) was a firm, mid-reddish-brown, silty clay consisting of around 50 per cent brick/tile and fired clay kiln furniture.

[1014] was ovoid in shape measuring 0.4 m by 0.44 m and 0.18 m deep. The sides were steep and straight leading to a flat base. Within was a single fill (1015): a soft, mid-brown clay containing four pieces of pottery and some degraded CBM packing.

[1063] was ovoid in shape, measuring 0.88 m by 0.77 m and 0.32 m deep. The base was undulating and irregular, turning gradually into gently-sloping convex sides. The northern side of the cut was heavily truncated by a plough-scar. Within was (1050): a friable, mid-brown, clay sand with around 40 per cent made up of brick and tile packing with a single sherd of Little London kiln ware.

[1047] was an irregular oval in shape, measuring 0.74 m by 0.65 m and 0.3 m deep. The sides were concave and moderately-sloping with a rounded base. Within was a single fill (1040): a soft, mid-yellowish-brown, sandy silt which included around 30 per cent CBM. 48 pieces of pottery from within (1040) included Little London kiln ware, Silchester ware, grog-tempered storage jar and a black sandy ware.

[1083] was the largest of the nine examples, measuring 1.3 m by 1.12 m and 0.35 m deep. Ovoid in shape with moderately-sloping, concave sides and a flat base, it included a single fill. (1082) was a soft, mid-greyish-brown, sandy silt with no finds and relatively few inclusions. The lack of brick and tile packing within [1083] may suggest that it was an unrelated pit rather than a post-hole.

[1054] was the smallest of the nine examples measuring 0.3 m in diameter and 0.15 m deep. It had shallow, concave sides leading to a flat base and contained a single fill. (1055) was a friable, greyish-black, sandy silt comprising over 50 per cent charcoal. The relatively shallow depth of this post-hole is probably because it had been cut into the remains of the since-ploughed-out trackway bank.

With the certain exception of the largest, [1083], all the above features contained CBM, a few also contained pottery including Little London kiln ware. This implies that, unlike the roof supports of the kiln, these post-holes were cut well into the life of the kiln and the associated pottery production located to the east (Trench 2).

KILN 1, PHASE 2 (FIGS 28–30)

A second phase of kiln use involved the reduction in width of the firing chamber. Although badly preserved, the surviving brick courses indicate a similar structure to that of the original with a number of brick arches supporting the floor of the firing chamber. The previous firing chamber was cut into and brick rubble was used to fill the gap between the primary and secondary structures. Evidence of the use of the kiln was indicated by the depth of 0.75 m to which the base of the firing chamber was worn or cut below the lowest course of the secondary brick lining. With this modification, the firing chamber almost became an extension of the stokehole, being approximately the same width (1.4 m), while continuing 3.15 m to the original back wall of the kiln. Much of the structural integrity of this second phase was seen to have been retained by the part-vitrification of the walls caused by the intense heat. This was particularly apparent at the back of the firing chamber (FIG. 28) where the entire wall had melded together into a green, glassy surface. This modification of the kiln would have resulted in the firing of smaller loads of brick. Whether this was caused by falling demand or by the difficulty of maintaining effective temperatures when firing the kiln in its original state is unclear.

The renovation of Kiln 1 largely consisted of cutting into the base of the existing firing chamber and installing rubble-founded supports on which to set a new series of cross-walls/arches. Recorded as [1165] and [1166], the cuts on the south-west and north-east sides respectively were effectively contemporaneous. A remodelling to clear out and increase the depth of the firing chamber may have taken place at this point, although, as its original depth was unknown, this cannot be assumed. On the south-west side a core of rubble (1168), measuring 2.9 m along the length of the firing chamber, 0.54 m wide and 0.28 m thick, was then inserted. On the opposite side a similar arrangement (1169) was installed: 3.15 m long by 0.68 m wide and 0.32 m thick.

Upon and within both (1168) and (1169) were set tile stacks as springers to support the cross-walls/arched supports. Similar to the arrangements in Phase 1, the remnant stubs survived significantly better on the south-west side than on the north-east, where none remained. Six

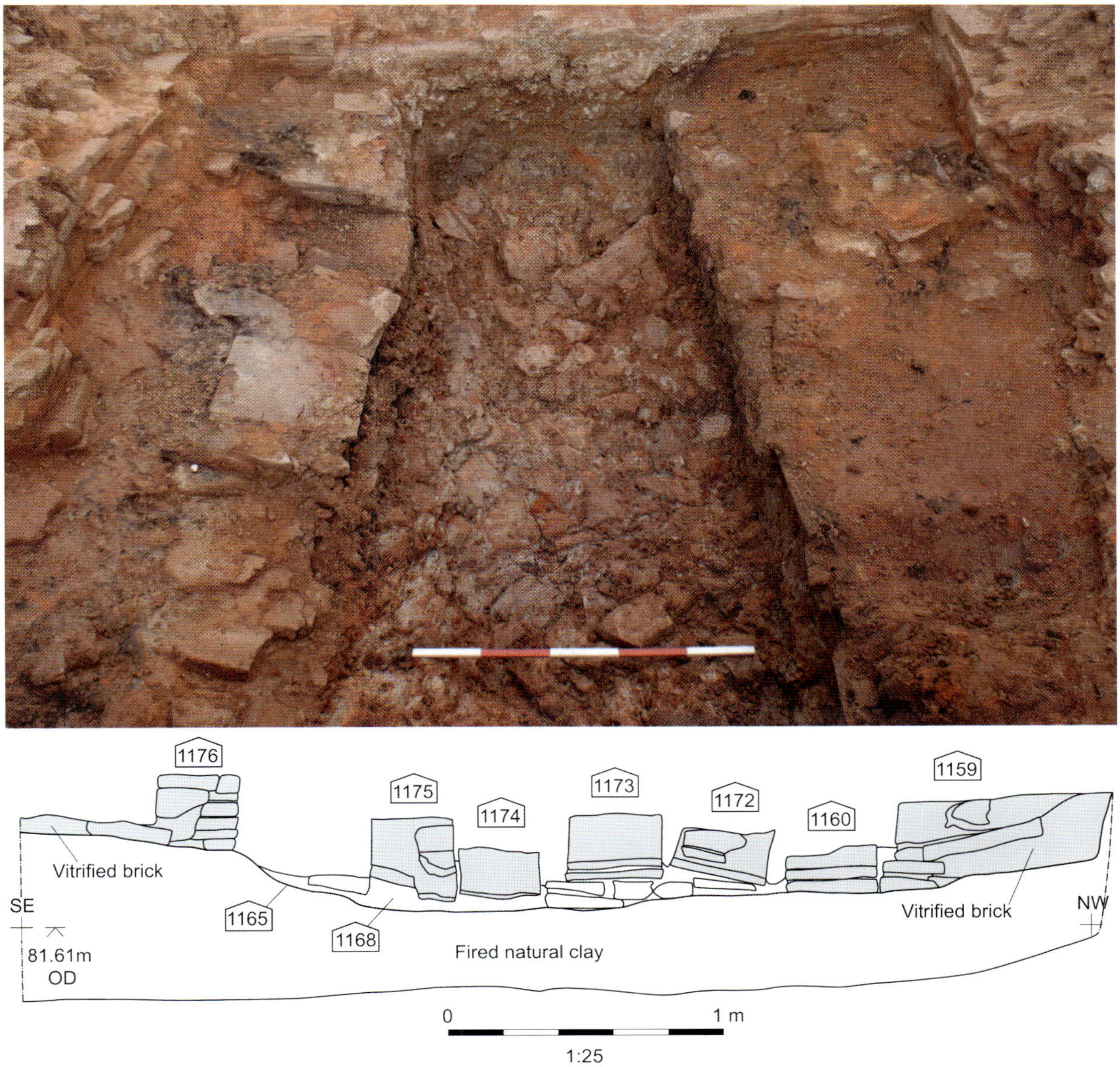

FIG. 28. (Top) Looking north-west into the reduced firing chamber of Kiln 1 with the new cross-walls/ arch springers (left). Post-abandonment collapse material sits at the base of the firing chamber against the vitrified back wall. (Bottom) North-east-facing wall of the remodelled firing chamber

distinct stacks were recorded upon (1168): **1159**, **1160**, **1172**, **1173**, **1174** and **1175** (FIG. 28). Although varying in their state of preservation, they were generally similar in size, with all but **1159** measuring around one tile width (approximately 0.3 m) and surviving up to four courses in height. In terms of length, **1173** extended the full distance of 0.52 m across (1168) whereas **1174** measured only 0.16 m. At the north-west end, **1159** had survived better due to its part-vitrification and fusing to the kiln back wall. **1159** measured 0.68 m by 0.42 m and consisted of three courses of tile.

Evidence of the final use of the kiln was visible at the base of the firing chamber in the form of a deposit of scorched clay measuring 5.62 m long by 1.38 m wide (FIG. 29). (1138), which was unexcavated, mostly consisted of the baked natural clay into which the firing chamber was cut, mixed with occasional ash and charcoal. The overlying deposits, rich in brick and tile wasters and degraded kiln furniture, represented the abandonment of the structure and its subsequent collapse. A substantial abandonment deposit lay across the entire base of the firing chamber measuring 4.4 m long, 1.4 m wide and up to 0.62 m thick. Excavated in four connected

FIG. 29. Scorched clay (1138) as the base of the firing chamber

segments so as to control spatially any finds, the deposit was recorded as (1087), (1097), (1098) and (1103). Consisting of a soft, light yellowish-blue clay, the layer was full of brick and tile, comprising around 75–90 per cent of the total bulk of the deposit. The last of the four areas to the south-east, (1103), included a piece of armchair voussoir with partial extrados (below, Machin, p. 118, FIG. 109). A radiocarbon sample taken from within (1098) returned a date range of 28–208 cal A.D. (juvenile *Betula sp.* charcoal 1903±24 BP, SUERC-90867).

On the south-west side of the kiln, overlying the six remnant cross-wall stubs, was a finer accumulation of burnt material from the later use of the kiln. Measuring 3.02 m by 0.68 m and 0.05 m thick, (1141) consisted entirely of residual ash and charcoal from the firing of the kiln. Sealing over the firing chamber to the level of the vitrified side wall **1176** (see above) was a thick post-abandonment layer, potentially a backfilling or levelling event. (1074) measured

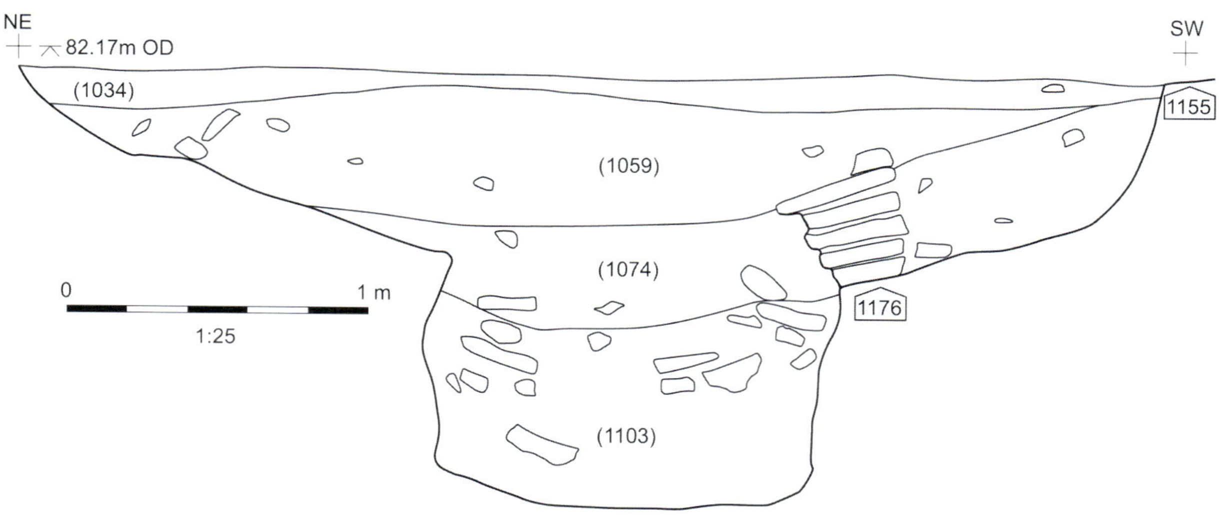

FIG. 30. Abandonment deposits within Kiln 1, looking into the stokehole from the firing chamber

3.1 m by 3.1 m and 0.4 m thick and was a friable, greenish-red, silty sand, which consisted of around 30 per cent waste CBM interleaved with a number of lenses of green sand (FIG. 30). The presence of five abraded sherds of pottery and an iron nail from within this layer also suggests it had formed not just from the collapse of the kiln superstructure. The overlying deposit (1059) was similarly mixed with the remains of the demolished kiln resulting from the silting up and potential levelling of the area long after the structure had gone out of use. Measuring 8 m by 4.6 m and 0.42 m thick, this compact, mid-reddish-brown, silty sand consisted of around 25 per cent brick and tile rubble including a piece of ceramic waterpipe.

KILN 2 (FIGS 6 and 31)

As predicted from the geophysics, a smaller second kiln was located central to the excavation trench. Measuring 4.5 m in length, 2.26 m in width and up to 0.8 m in depth, the kiln was set within a foundation cut [1090] dug into and on the same alignment as the early trackway ditch and exploiting its residual hollow. The structure itself was poorly constructed with walls up to 0.4 m thick made of packed rubble with only a very small amount of brick-facing surviving on the south-east side. The kiln was uniform in shape along its length with no obvious differentiation between the firing chamber and the stokehole. The internal space measured only 2.9 m in length by 0.8 m in width. Its shape and construction method were very similar to the secondary phase of Kiln 1 and, considering they both shared the same working area, it seems likely that they were contemporary. Kiln 2 was almost entirely devoid of pottery, unlike the smaller kilns seen in Trench 2 (below), suggesting it was used exclusively for tile production.

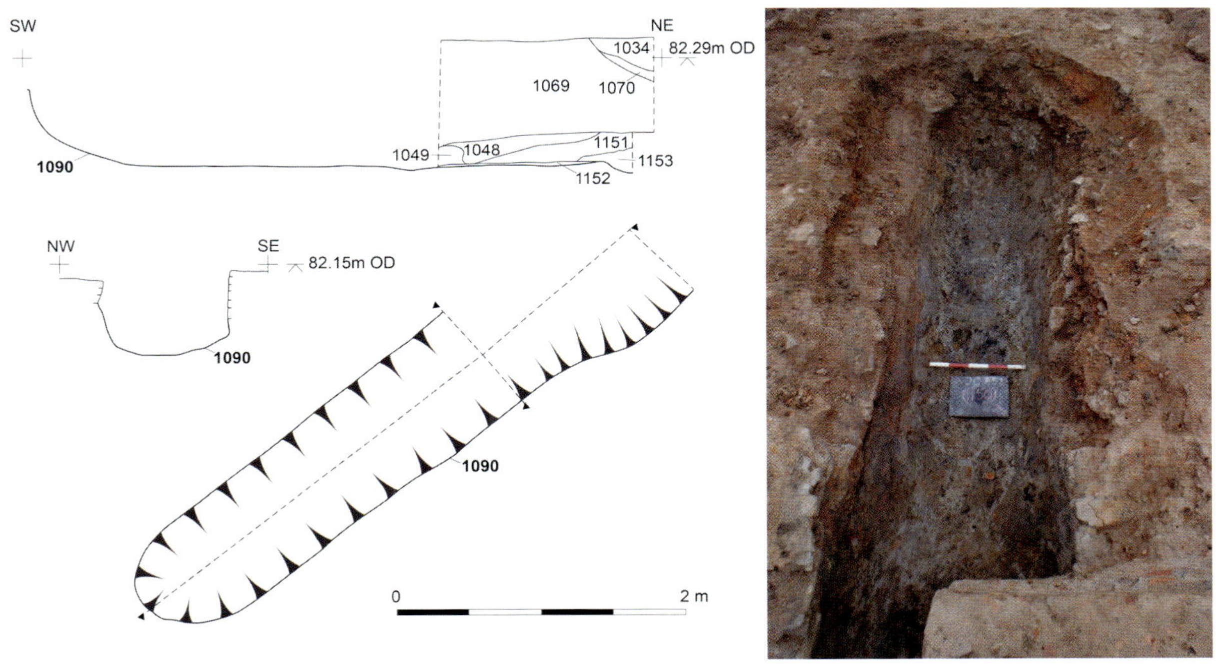

FIG. 31. Kiln 2: plan, profile and view of the kiln and its basal deposit (1150)

At the base of the kiln was a thin deposit of light bluish-grey clay with frequent inclusions of charcoal. Measuring 4 m by 0.78 m and 0.03 m thick, (1150) was probably material resulting from the firing of the kiln mixed with scorched natural clay disturbed during the raking-out process. Succeeding this layer was a looser, dark grey, silty sand (1149) that contained more charcoal and CBM as a result of the use of the kiln. This deposit had the same dimensions in plan as (1150) but was 0.05 m thick.

Overlying (1149) was the first evidence of the abandonment of the structure, (1147): a firm, bluish-grey, silty clay comprising around 50 per cent vitrified brick. Sloping against the back end of the kiln, this deposit measured 0.78 m by 0.4 m by 0.15 m thick and was probably formed through the collapse of the brick-lined edges of the kiln as it fell into disrepair. A rubble-like layer (1145) then formed above, similarly localised to the back of the kiln. It was a soft, blue clay measuring 0.75 m by 1.6 m and 0.4 m thick which was made up of around 40 per cent collapsed kiln structure. A thick tip of material (1146) at the south-west end of the structure was then deposited, perhaps representing more collapse of the back end of the kiln. Measuring 0.3 m by 0.4 m and 0.5 m thick, it was a loose, light reddish-yellow, silty sand. This was then overlain by (1144): a loose, blackish-grey, silty clay that measured 0.88 m by 0.3 m and 0.35 m thick. Comprising around 60 per cent waste brick and tile, this particular deposit was rich in comb-decorated tiles, perhaps suggesting that a large number of these had been produced here with the broken wasters subsequently backfilled into the kiln after its abandonment.

Within the entrance/stokehole of the kiln were several small localised deposits, indicative of the kiln's repeated use and maintenance. As a remnant of a kiln firing, (1152) was an ash-rich layer of loose, black, silty sand comprising around 80 per cent charcoal and measuring 1.1 m by 0.88 m and 0.04 m thick. Atop this was a similar deposit (1153) with more disturbed natural clay and less charcoal. Measuring 0.3 m by 0.28 m and 0.2 m thick, this layer was the result of cleaning out of the kiln and was approximately equal to (1085) in the working area (see below). Overlying it was another charcoal-dense deposit (1151), possibly evidence of a single firing episode of the kiln. Consisting of a loose, mid-greyish-black, silty sand with around 70 per cent inclusion of charcoal, it measured 0.6 m by 0.72 m and 0.1 m thick. Another, sandier, layer of rake-out was then deposited; (1148) was a loose, mid-brownish-yellow, silty sand measuring 1.13 m by 0.76 m and 0.13 m thick.

Across much of the kiln firing chamber and stokehole were then a series of substantial post-abandonment layers. (1091) sealed over both (1148) and (1144) and measured 4.5 m by 2.6 m and 0.46 m in thickness. Consisting of a firm, mid-reddish-brown clay silt, it was packed with brick and tile, perhaps suggesting a deliberate backfilling using nearby waste material. Within the fill were recovered another armchair voussoir and a Nero-stamped tile (Machin, p. 123, FIG. 115). The overlying layer (1060) was then interpreted as the abandonment of the local area: a slowly-accumulating deposit mixed with slumped-in rubble and other waste material including a single sherd of grog-tempered ware. It was a friable, light reddish-brown, sandy silt filling the remnant hollow of the kiln, measuring 2.8 m by 2.9 m and 0.32 m thick. (1060) was essentially the same as the overlying fill (1034) that covered Kiln 1 and the associated working area (below).

WORKING AREA (FIGS 6, 32–33)

With the — assumed to be contemporary — second-phase renovation of Kiln 1 and installation of Kiln 2 it seems likely that the associated working area may have been enlarged or at the very least cleaned out for its new dual purpose. Therefore it follows that all of the deposits contained within it would be contemporary with this later phase.

The lowermost layer within the working area was (1140): a remnant of material raked-out from one or both of the kilns. Measuring 2.82 m by 2.22 m and 0.18 m thick, the deposit consisted almost entirely of charcoal within a dark silty sand matrix. A radiocarbon sample taken from a hazelnut shell found within (1140) returned a date range of 29–130 cal A.D. (charred plant macrofossil 1918±21 BP, SUERC-90868). Above was a similar layer of raked-out charcoal, (1113), sat central within the working area. Consisting of a loose, dark grey, clay sand comprising around 70 per cent charcoal, the deposit measured 1.26 m by 2.12 m and 0.06 m in thickness. Overlying this was (1085) which was a substantial, friable, blackish-grey, clay silt layer spread across all of the working area and into the stokehole of Kiln 1. Measuring 5.96 m by 3.56 m and 0.06 m thick, it was probably a trampled layer: a mix of disturbed natural clay, charcoal and wasters formed through activity in the area during use of both kilns. The succeeding deposits were dumps around the edges of the working area indicating that maintenance of the area may have begun to wane even if the kilns had not gone entirely out of use. Layer (1102), tipped against the south-west side, consisted of a loose, light yellowish-brown, clay sand and measured 1.62 m by 0.7 m and 0.12 m thick. Across the working area was (1114) which was a combination

FIG. 32. Blue clay dump (1077) atop rubble (1071) within the working area

FIG. 33. Plough-scarred upper deposit (1034) across Kiln 1 and working area. Looking south-east

of various dumps sloping in from the north-east side. Overall, this was a firm, mottled-reddish-brown, silty clay measuring around 3.2 m by 1.6 m and 0.22 m thick.

Over both (1102) and (1114) was a larger deposit of rubble (1071) (FIG. 32), perhaps corresponding with the disuse of the kiln when the working area was used for dumping waste materials produced in the adjacent kiln(s) indicated by the geophysical survey (above, p. 5). Consisting of a mottled blue/reddish-brown clay, (1071) included 70–80 per cent tile wasters and measured 4 m by 3.24 m and 0.18 m thick. A thick layer of clay (1077) was then laid down, perhaps a deliberate levelling or surfacing indicative of the reuse of the working area. Alternatively, this may instead be backfilling with clay extracted from the quarry pit to the south-west that was unsuitable for brick-making and subsequently discarded. (1077) was a firm, light bluish-grey clay with very few inclusions; it measured 3 m by 2.5 m and was 0.4 m thick. There then followed a similar sequence: a large dump of waster-rich rubble (1069) overlaid by a thick deposit of blue clay (1070). (1069) consisted of a friable, mid-orangish-brown, clay silt which measured 3.26 m by 2.84 m and was 0.5 m thick. Found within the rubble was a second Nero-stamped tile (below, Machin, p. 123). (1070) was smaller in size, measuring 2.5 m by 1 m and 0.25 m thick, and was probably tipped into the working area from the north-east side. Consisting of a firm, light bluish-grey clay, it was also relatively lacking in inclusions of rubble and charcoal.

The succeeding deposits then illustrated the final abandonment of the kilns, with further backfilling of the working area followed by the gradual accumulation and erosion of nearby material into the hollow created by the redundant structures. Close to the stokehole of Kiln 1 was a small deposit of friable, light yellowish-brown, sandy silt: (1064). Measuring 1.5 m by 1.2 m and 0.15 m thick, it was relatively sterile with a small proportion of brick and tile waste. On the east side of the working area, overlying (1070), was another typical backfill dump of rubble. (1073) was a friable, mid-reddish-brown, sandy silt which measured 3.5 m by 1.5 m and was 0.2 m thick.

Uppermost and covering the entirety of the internal space of Kiln 1 and the working area was (1034) (FIG. 33): it is interpreted as the result of the slow weathering of the remaining kiln structures and the continuing silting-up of the residual depression. Consisting of a friable, mid-yellowish-brown, sandy silt, the deposit contained around 10 per cent brick and tile and had been further disturbed by later agricultural activity. Overall, (1034) measured 9.18 m by 3.4 m and was 0.3 m thick.

QUARRY PIT (FIGS 6, 34–37)

Two large circular hollows in the west and south of the field suggested the presence of quarrying associated with the tile and brick production (FIG. 34). The northern of these two potential extraction pits, [1048], measured approximately 35 m by 27 m and filled much of the west side of Trench 1 (FIG. 36). Excavation of approximately half the area of the pit as exposed in the trench revealed it to be relatively shallow with gradually sloping, concave sides and an uneven, undulating base sloping from east to west. From the surface, the fills of the pit could be seen to be hugely varied and difficult to follow but upon excavation a clearer picture of the sequence was established. Deposits in the excavated section measured 8.3 m by 4.7 m with a depth of 1.05 m. A smaller sondage (2.2 m by 1 m) was dug into the northern edge to compare the sequences but was stopped at 0.2 m below the surface. The proximity of this quarry pit to the kilns suggests contemporaneity and it is likely that quarrying for clay was spread over several years, perhaps corresponding with the life of the kilns. Subsequently, once enough clay had been removed it would have made the perfect place to dump waste material and thus, as expected, the lower fills within the pit consisted almost entirely of kiln rake-out and wasters (FIG. 35).

Lowermost within the quarry pit were two discrete deposits: (1049) and (1072). (1049) was a small patch of redeposited natural clay and gravel formed soon after the cutting of the pit. Measuring 1.05 m by 0.9 m and 0.05 m thick, it consisted of a friable, mid-bluish-grey, clay sand and yielded a small group of seven sherds of Little London kiln pottery along with a 10 mm diameter, possible, but completely illegible, copper-alloy coin. (1072) was a firm, mottled

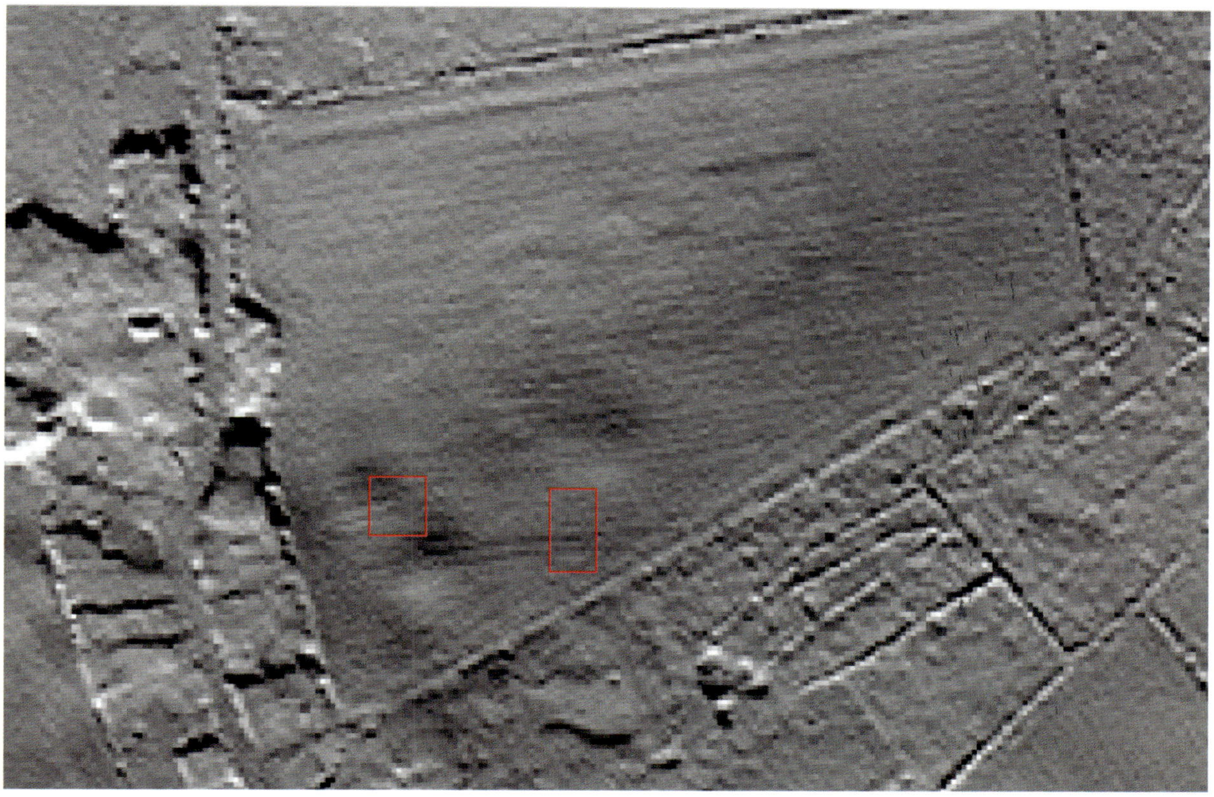

FIG. 34. Trench locations showing likely quarry pits within the field on hillshade model of Lidar DTM (© *Environment Agency/University of Reading*)

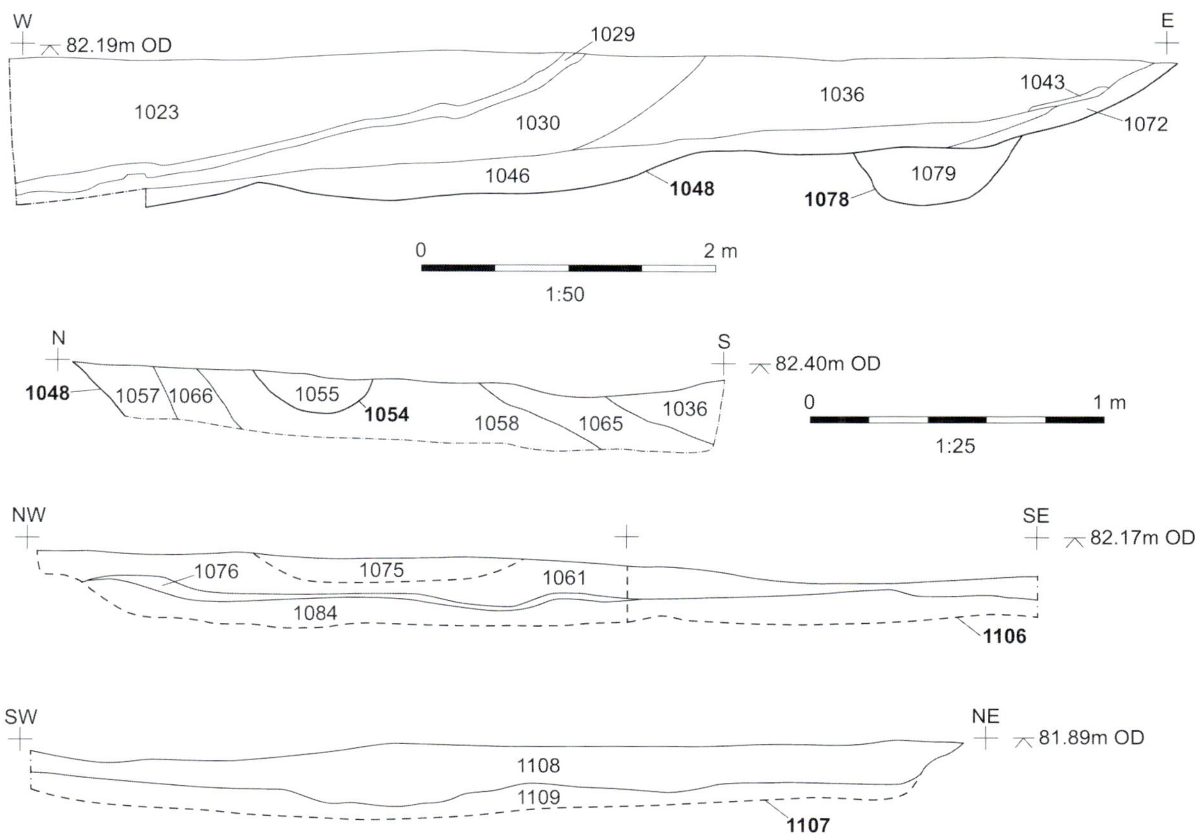

FIG. 35. Large section and section of smaller sondage through quarry pit [1048] and sections of possible puddling pits [1106] and [1107]

red and blackish-grey, sandy silt tipped in from the eastern edge of the pit. Measuring 3.2 m by 0.95 m and 0.15 m thick, it was a typical mixed dump of tile rubble merged with charcoal rake-out.

Both smaller deposits were then overlaid by a thick sandy layer (1046) that covered much of the base of the pit. Measuring 3.84 m by 2.2 m and 0.3 m thick, it consisted of a soft, light greenish-grey, silty sand. This deposit may be the result of the trampling of the sandy base of the pit by kiln workers entering the area to continue to extract better clay to the west. (1046) contained CBM with two antefixes, kiln furniture and a large assemblage of pottery, including Little London jars, flagons and the only example of a cheese press from the site (Machin, p. 102; Timby, p. 64). Another single-event dump was then deposited from the eastern side of the pit. (1043) was a loose, dark bluish-black, clay silt comprising around 80 per cent raked-out kiln-firing charcoal and measuring 1.44 m by 1.38 m and 0.02 m thick.

In the smaller section cut on the northern side of the pit the upper extent of a series of fills tipping into the pit could be seen (FIG. 35). A small part of each was excavated with finds recovered and recorded as follows.

(1057) was the earliest deposit and could be seen tipping in from the northern side of the pit. It measured 0.5 m by 1.9 m and was a friable, mid-purplish-red, silty clay containing a significant amount of scorched brick. Overlying (1057) was a charcoal-rich dump of kiln waste (1066). This measured 1.8 m by 0.18 m and consisted of a friable, mid-blackish-grey, silty clay. Sat above it was a thick layer of dumped brick and tile (1058) which was 1.1 m wide and could be seen arcing around the northern edge of the quarry pit for approximately 11 m. This was a firm, reddish-brown, silty clay and could have been formed either from the demolition and clearance of a structure, perhaps the first phase of Kiln 1, or from the waste from a kiln firing. Cut into this deposit was a small post-hole, [1054], which was probably part of a fence or lean-to associated with Kiln 1 (see above). Succeeding this was another heavy dump of charcoal, perhaps indicating the regeneration and reuse of one or more of the kilns; (1065) was a friable, blackish-grey, clay silt measuring 5.95 m by 0.2 m.

Common to both excavated sections was a substantial capping of rubble. (1036) measured

FIG. 36. Quarry pit [1048] looking north-west

8.5 m by 3.55 m and was 0.75 m thick. Consisting of a firm, mid-greyish-orange, clay silt, it was rich in brick and tile waste and, like (1058), may also have been the product of the demolition of a significant nearby structure or of waste from a kiln firing. Included within was a piece of thick-walled powdery oxidised ware: a probable saggar or kiln spacer (p. 77). Above it and similar in composition was (1030), dense with rubble and wasters, also suggestive of kiln waste or demolition of a nearby structure. Consisting of a firm, light orangish-brown, clay silt, it measured 4.8 m wide and 0.68 m thick and included a flat-rimmed hemispherical bowl with two grooves on the upper surface and a possibly deliberately-pierced base (Timby, p. 72). Sealing this was a thick layer of dumped burnt material, perhaps evidence of sustained use of the kilns again. Measuring 4.2 m by 3.3 m and 0.25 m thick, (1029) consisted of a friable, dark bluish-black, clay silt comprising 80–90 per cent raked-out charcoal (FIG. 37). A radiocarbon sample taken from within (1029) returned a date range of 52–130 cal A.D. (*Corylus avellana* charcoal 1915±19 BP, SUERC-90863). Uppermost within the large quarry-pit section was (1023), a 0.75 m thick, gradually accumulated layer including dumped CBM which measured 5.5 m by 4.05 m. Constituting a firm, light reddish-brown, clay silt, it was probably formed after the abandonment of the area and yielded a base sherd which had been trimmed into a disc shape (Timby, p. 77).

FIG. 37. (1029) Rake-out from kiln firing dumped into quarry pit [1048]. Looking south-east

POSSIBLE PUDDLING PITS (FIGS 6, 35)

Two large, square clay deposits in the south-east corner of the trench initially suggested the presence of clay-floored buildings. Both were oriented upon the more general north-west–south-east alignment of the kilns but were revealed to be shallow, steep-sided pits. Potentially these may have been puddling pits, used for mixing the raw clay with water to achieve the right consistency but also to remove impurities or add tempering to strengthen before firing.

The larger of the two pits, the north-easterly of the pair, was [1106] which measured 3.65 m by 3.75 m and 0.24 m deep; it was divided into roughly-equal quadrants with opposite quarters excavated. Square in shape with slightly-rounded corners, the pit boasted straight, vertical sides and a flat base. Contained within were four fills, two of which were dominant, clay-rich deposits.

The lowermost fill (1084) was a firm, dark yellowish-grey clay containing both charcoal and gravel and measured 3.4 m by 2.83 m and 0.1 m in thickness. Its relationship to the underlying natural clay was extremely diffuse and it was likely the remnant of quarried clay being mixed within the pit. The overlying fill (1076) was a thin deposit of loose, light greyish-white, sandy silt. This was only seen in the north-western quadrant and measured 1.85 m wide and 0.03 m thick and seemed to mark a brief period of change of use of the pit. Above it was another substantial deposit of heavy clay (1061) which spread across the full width of the pit; it measured 3.65 m by 3.75 m and was 0.15 m thick. Similar in composition to (1084), but containing a higher percentage of charcoal. A separate deposit of charcoal, (1075), was then recorded as the uppermost fill. This measured 0.65 m by 0.53 m and 0.02 m thick and was probably a remnant of the overlying dirty ground surface that surrounded the kilns and working areas.

The second pit [1107] was approximately 1 m to the south-west respecting the same alignment. It was slightly smaller, measuring 3.55 m by 3.2 m and 0.3 m in depth, and contained just two fills which were excavated in half-section. The lowermost fill, (1109), was a compact, mid-yellowish-grey, silty clay that contained some gravel. It measured 3.55 m wide by 0.08 m thick and, like the previous example, the boundary between this fill and the base of the pit was very diffuse. Above this was (1108), a similar deposit measuring 3.55 m wide and 0.22 m thick. It was composed of a firm, dark yellowish-grey, silty clay which was very similar to (1075) as described above.

SOUTHERN PALISADED ENCLOSURE (FIGS 6, 38–39)

Towards the south of Trench 1 was the shallow arc of a deep, straight-sided trench, 0.54 m wide and 0.67 m deep, which contained evidence of charred posts set to form a continuous palisade. It ran for approximately 15 m and, if extrapolated as a complete circle, would have had a diameter of roughly 35–45 m. The palisade trench cut through both the upper fills of the quarry pit and the trackway ditch [1024] and so is relatively late in the sequence. There was no evidence of structures within the — albeit very limited — internal space uncovered, but the palisade may have enclosed accommodation for the workforce of the pottery and tilery. Alternatively, with evidence of footprints in tiles left out to dry indicating that domesticated animals were being kept in the vicinity, the enclosure may have contained livestock.

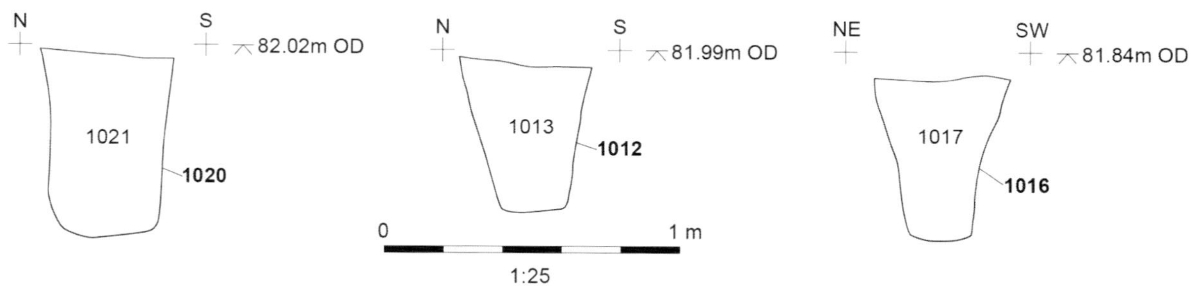

FIG. 38. Palisade trench: profiles

Three slots, [1020], [1012] and [1016], varying between 0.45 and 0.54 m wide and 0.59 and 0.67 m deep, were excavated across the palisade trench. Each was straight-sided with a flat base and contained fills (1021), (1013) and (1017) respectively. All fills consisted of a firm, mid-orangish-brown, silty clay containing some waste brick and tile and charcoal. Fill (1017) contained the remains of a charred post driven into the trench, the only post to be clearly identified in this trench (FIG. 39). Finds were limited to three sherds of pottery, including Little London kiln ware, and CBM.

FIG. 39. Charred post within palisade trench [1016]

SUMMARY

The relationship of Trackway Ditch 1 with Kiln 1 indicates that it was already in existence before the construction of the kiln. While there are some sherds of Little London ware among a larger pottery assemblage from the primary silts at the base of Ditch 1 in the truncated (and possibly disturbed) section revealed by the excavation of the quarry, Little London ware and CBM are absent from the otherwise late Iron Age/earliest Roman pottery assemblage from the primary silts of the completely excavated section of Ditch 1, as they are from the small section excavated of the primary silts of Ditch 2. This suggests that there was occupation in the immediate area which pre-dated the start of either pottery- or brick-and-tile-making.

There were altogether only four abraded pottery sherds from Kiln 1 and a single sherd from Kiln 2 and, although the total volume of the four post-holes supporting the cover over Kiln 1 is small, it is probably significant that they contained no sherds of Little London pottery, while other post-holes beyond the kiln did contain sherds of this ware. A single sherd of Neronian samian was recovered from isolated post-hole [1089] adjacent to, but not necessarily structurally related to Kiln 1. Altogether the evidence suggests that brick-and-tile-making began ahead of the production of pottery, but probably only by a short interval, as Little London wares were found in the primary fill of the adjacent quarry pit. Judging by the scarcity of pottery finds in its fill, it is just possible that Kilns 1 and 2 were abandoned either before pottery-making began, or continued after it had ceased, the latter more likely (see Ch. 8). Otherwise pottery- and brick-

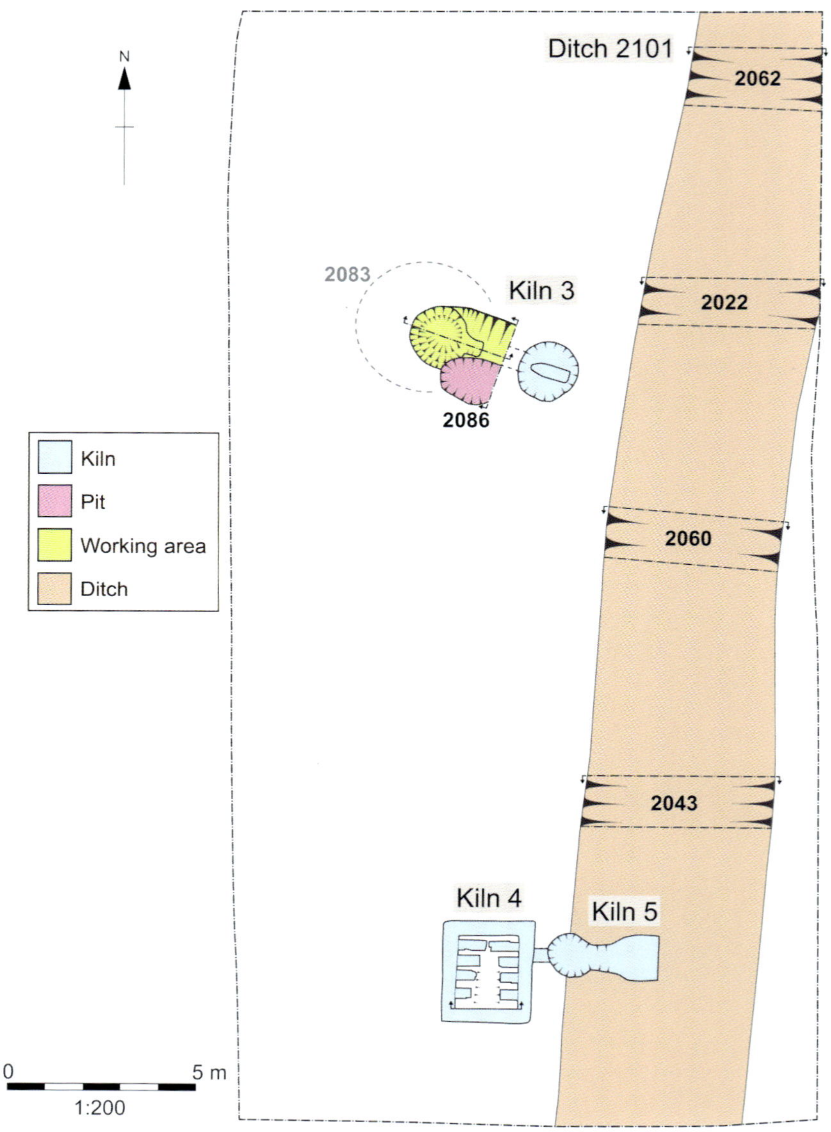

FIG. 40. Plan of Trench 2

and-tile-making, fired in different kilns, continued alongside each other. Even if early in the development of the production of both CBM and pottery at Little London, Kiln 1 was not necessarily the earliest, and we should recall the indications from the geophysics of the close proximity of adjacent kilns to the north and south (FIGS 2–3). Not only were the bricks which made up its structure fired elsewhere, discarded CBM was already available to be used to pack the post-holes which supported its superstructure. Equally production of brick and tile elsewhere across the site may not have ceased after the kiln was backfilled. Although the waste material which filled the kiln chamber could have derived from the levelling of an adjacent dump of kiln waste, it could equally well have been discard from the firing of one of the nearby kilns. The latest activity documented from Trench 1 was the creation of the palisaded enclosure revealed towards the southern limit of the excavation. It was cut into the upper deposits of the backfilled quarry pit and so could post-date brick-and-tile- and pottery-making, at least in this area of Little London.

TRENCH 2

Trench 2 was located approximately 50 m to the east of Trench 1 and measured 15 m by 30 m. Like Trench 1, it was focused on two strong geophysics signals and a linear anomaly running north–south towards the large quarry pit at the top of the field (FIGS 40–41). Below the topsoil, the older ploughsoil had mixed with a gradually-formed deposit of hill-wash making the underlying horizon of natural geology difficult to determine. Obvious concentrations of brick and tile were apparent at the location of both potential structures but edges of other features were difficult to determine.

FIG. 41. Trench 2, looking south-west

CIRCULAR POTTERY KILN (KILN 3) (FIGS 42–46)

Identified from the surface as a clear scorched, red circle, Kiln 3 (cut [2040]) was a circular, updraught structure which measured 1.66 m in diameter and was 0.88 m deep at its lowest point (FIGS 42–43). The edge of the firing area of the kiln had no architectural construction but was instead cut directly into the natural clay with a narrow flue/stokehole (1.92 m in width) entering into the western side and giving the appearance that it had been tunnelled through. There was no trace of a constructed arch. Through firing, the outer edges had baked solid thus stabilising the integrity of the kiln and the stokehole. Built into the chamber was a central tongue pedestal/plinth emerging from the eastern side and running for 0.98 m towards the stokehole; the latter was not excavated where it entered the kiln at which point it was 0.4 m wide. Constructed of seven courses of mixed box-flue tile and brick, the plinth, **2087**, measured 0.42 m high and 0.24 m wide and similarly had been scorched *in situ* under intense heat. The bricks and tiles were laid in semi-stretcher coursing held by a white mortar bond that had turned pink

FIG. 42. Kiln 3 looking north-west after the removal of *tegulae* **2050** from the central plinth

with firing. Around the edge of the circular chamber ran a small shelf approximately 0.22 m wide into which had been moulded a number of small recesses that probably held horizontal supports. Originally, prefabricated clay fire-bars may have been laid from the central plinth to the outer shelf to support the ceramics being fired, thus allowing the hot air to circulate freely below. However, it seems in the latest use of the kiln these supports had been replaced with reused *tegulae* roof tiles, **2050**, three of which remained fixed to the top of the plinth. The broken remains of several more were found at the base of the chamber mixed within a thin layer of pottery wasters.

The lowermost deposit within the kiln was (2051): a loose, blue sand measuring 1.22 m by 0.6 m and 0.04 m thick. This may have been a deliberate sand inclusion used as an insulator to protect the sides and base of the central plinth from the furnace heat which was evidenced by the high concentration of charcoal within the deposit. Overlying this was (2037) which consisted of a firm, mid-yellowish-blue, sandy clay measuring 1.2 m by 1.3 m and 0.22 m thick. Within this were a number of broken *tegulae*, once part of the upper firing floor **2050** which had collapsed into the base of the kiln. This marks the end of the use of the kiln, with the succeeding deposits

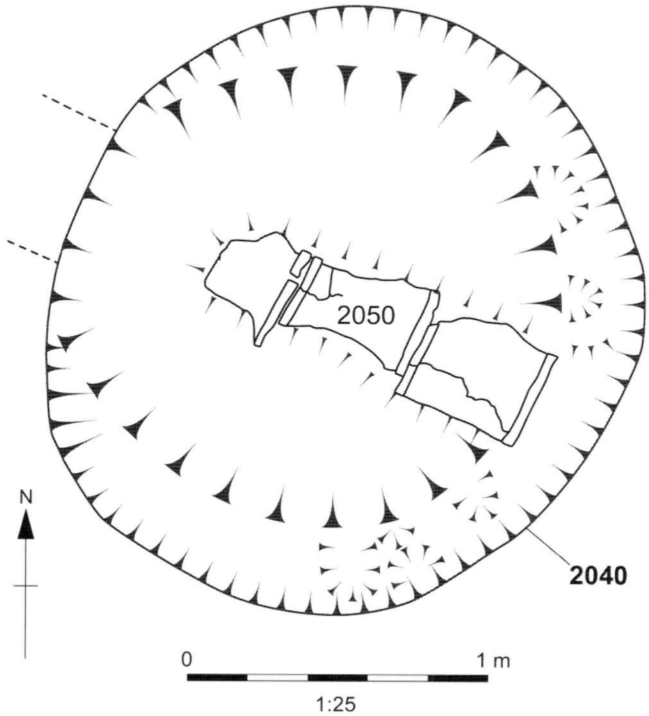

FIG. 43. Plan of Kiln 3

formed from a mixture of the collapse of the structure and backfill. (2051) and (2037) yielded a high number of white or pale pink/orange oxidised wares with examples of flat-rimmed bowls, jars, one flagon handle and a lid: very probably the type of pottery being fired in the kiln (Timby, p. 65). A radiocarbon sample taken of juvenile oak charcoal from within (2037) returned a date range of 27–208 cal A.D. (juvenile *quercus sp.* charcoal 1904±24 BP, SUERC-90860).

(2038) was a small lump of collapsed kiln structure that sat upon the remnant kiln floor, **2050**, surviving upon the central plinth. Consisting of a friable, mid-red, clay sand, it measured 0.32 m by 1.18 m and was 0.12 m thick and included a large percentage of the material that probably made up the original dome structure of the kiln: thin tiles and a scorched clay bond. Overlying this was (2018): a thick, light-grey clay measuring 1.7 m by 1.5 m and 0.35 m thick. This was one of the main deposits within the disused kiln and seems to represent a backfilling event, extraneous clay from elsewhere dumped here out of convenience. It contained one iron nail. The succeeding two fills, (2007) and (2006), were both later accumulations of slumped material filling the remnant hollow of the abandoned kiln. (2007) was a firm, mid-brownish-yellow, sandy clay which measured 1.8 m by 1.6 m and was 0.2 m thick. (2006) was similar in composition and size, the result of the accumulation of ploughsoil within the surviving depression. It contained a small fragment of colourless vessel glass.

Following the line of the flue running westwards from the kiln, a slot was dug revealing a sizeable working area that was not readily apparent from the surface (FIGS 44–46). Although not excavated to its full length, the flue ran from the kiln into a 3.5 m by 3 m area which sloped downwards towards the shaft of the flue (1.92 m wide) at a depth of over 1.1 m. The depth and bowl-shaped nature of the wider working area suggest it may have been set into an already existent hollow such as a clay-extraction pit, which may also have served as a well.

Cut number [2083] was assigned to the wider feature into which the flue and working area were set. Its full extent could not be established in plan due to the masking nature of the combined natural clay and ploughsoil but it seems likely that it was once a considerable open feature like that of the quarry pit seen in Trench 1. Within this cut, which was not bottomed, was a substantial fill of redeposited clay that was seen on all sides of the working area and stokehole: (2082). This was a firm, mid-orangish-brown clay which contained occasional inclusions of charcoal and waste tiles. It seems likely that this may have been the result of the upcast of surplus clay, deposited here from the construction of one or more earlier semi-subterranean kilns or structures in the area. Another, darker fill was also seen within the larger feature, pre-dating the construction of the kiln. (2080), a friable, mid-bluish-grey, clay sand, was at the base of the working area cut and measured 0.92 m across with an unknown depth.

The relationship between the cuts for the working area [2079] and the 'stokehole' [2084] is a little obscure at this point. Although it seems possible that they are both contemporary and dug at the same time, the shape of the rake-out deposits (2061), (2076) and (2077) leading along the stokehole is considerably wider than the flue opening that can be seen internally within the kiln. This perhaps hints at two phases of the kiln: first, a slim, circular working area [2079] firing heat through a longer, narrow, arched flue into the kiln which was then replaced by a more

FIG. 44. Working area and collapsed flue leading to circular pottery kiln (Kiln 3). Looking south-east

open working space [2084] almost adjacent to the firing chamber requiring virtually no flue.

The narrow working area [2079] was circular in shape with straight, vertical sides and a small shelf on one side projecting towards the kiln. It measured 1.68 m by 1.92 m and was excavated to a depth of 1.05 m with the earliest excavated context tipping towards the flue. Its dimensions suggest that it was a pit pre-dating Kiln 3. Depending on how much they subsided during the life of the kiln, some of the wasters from the lower fills could have originated from another kiln close by. Lowermost within the cut was (2078), a friable, dark grey, silty clay containing around 30 per cent charcoal. This measured 0.86 m wide by 0.4 m thick and was a typical mixed deposit representing a solid early period of activity. Negligible pottery was recovered from (2078) suggesting it was formed before there was much kiln waste lying around. The overlying deposit (2073) then represents a sequence of single firings, a grouped layer of thin layers of rake-out laminated between deposits of clay. This deposit represents continued clearing of the working area after each firing and contained a mixture of different soils which overall measured 1.46 m by 1.12 m and 0.22 m thick. A dark layer of burnt rake-out (2071) then tips into the working area. Measuring 1.28 m by 0.98 m and 0.14 m thick, it was a firm, dark grey, clay and probably represented a single firing episode that was then left *in situ*.

The cut of the stokehole, [2084], leading from [2079] towards the kiln, was seen to be

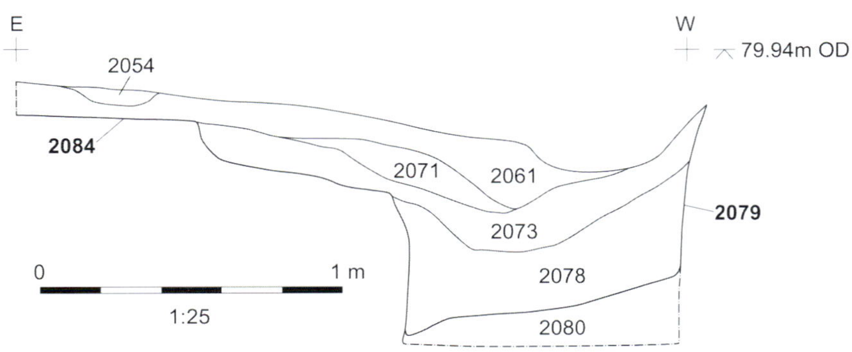

FIG. 45. North-facing section through the working area and stokehole leading to Kiln 3

generally linear, running east to west, with moderate concave sides and a flat base. Within it were a number of lenses of charcoal divided by clay resurfacings, each perhaps equating with a single firing and subsequent reuse. Although some effort was made to excavate each individual lens, a number of contexts in this area demonstrate several events, with layers (2077), (2076) and (2061) representing a number of firings, maintenance and reuse. (2077), (2076) and (2061) were each a friable, dark grey, sandy clay measuring up to 1.2 m wide and 0.1 m thick. (2061) ran 2.35 m to the west and overlay (2071). The upper lenses within (2061) represent the final use of the kiln, with the succeeding deposits formed during the abandonment of the structure. (2076) contained a small assemblage of 26 sherds of whiteware including one collared-flagon rim, whereas (2061) yielded a particularly large assemblage of nearly 800 sherds of pottery nearly all of which comprise kiln products (Timby, p. 65). Curved-wall platters were particularly prominent with a minimum of 43 vessels. Of note from this group of material is the only stamped mortarium (SF208) (Timby, p. 59, FIG. 56; Tomlin, p. 60). A radiocarbon sample taken from juvenile oak charcoal found within (2076) returned a date range of 5–125 cal A.D. (juvenile *quercus sp.* charcoal 1941±24 BP, SUERC-90862). This context also contained one iron nail.

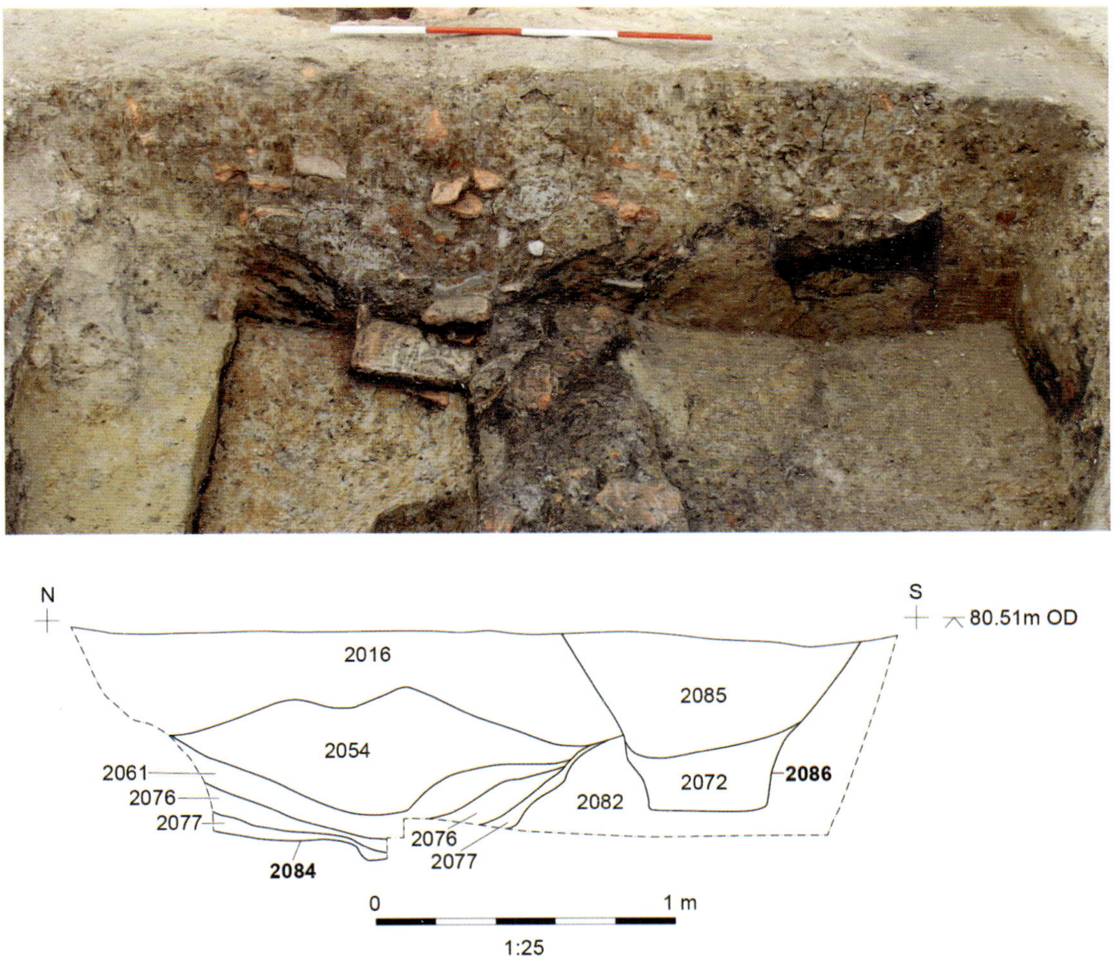

FIG. 46. West-facing section through the collapsed flue

The overlying deposit (2054) was formed through the collapse of the flue combined with the backfilling of clay into the area. Consisting of a firm, mid-grey clay measuring 4 m by 2.2 m and 0.44 m thick, it included lenses of redeposited London clay and tile wasters from nearby. Uppermost above the flue was (2016), a mixed backfill layer consisting of a friable, mid-brownish-grey, sandy clay. Seen as 1.82 m wide and 0.35 m thick, it was probably more extensive and the same event as the backfill within the kiln firing chamber. (2016) produced a further 109 sherds, including a sherd of Flavian South Gaulish samian and some pieces of probable kiln furniture in the form of saggars (Timby, p. 62), and a small fragment of a square bottle of colourless glass.

Slightly to the south was cut [2086], which was elliptical in shape and measured 1.4 m by 1.2 m and 0.6 m deep. [2086] appeared to post-date the backfilling of the kiln and working area, although its lower fill (2072) suggested it was related to kiln activity nearby, perhaps a rubbish pit for discarding rake-out and wasters as it contained 138 sherds of pottery and CBM (Timby, p. 65) (FIGS 40, 46). The pottery is unusual in composition with at least ten platters, including three stamped examples, and two dolia. The presence of platters from within (2072) suggests the backfill of pit [2086] came from the same source as that used to backfill the kiln. (2072) was a friable, black, sandy clay containing around 95 per cent dumped charcoal and measuring 1.4 m by 1.25 m and 0.26 m thick. Overlying this was a backfill deposit, (2085), which was similar in make-up to the uppermost layer seen within the kiln, flue and working areas. (2085) measured 1.4 m by 1.2 m and was 0.42 m thick.

SOUTHERN KILN SEQUENCE — KILNS 4 AND 5 (FIGS 47–53)

Two small kilns in the south of Trench 2 illustrated three distinct phases of pottery production in this area. The earliest structure was a well-built rectangular kiln (4) with a stokehole and working area to the south, which eventually went out of use and fell into disrepair. A smaller, circular-chambered kiln (5) was then constructed approximately 1 m to the east, using the hollow of the collapsed Kiln 4 as the working area for firing the stokehole. This circular kiln was then redeveloped in a secondary phase with the stokehole turned to the opposite side utilising the slope into the north–south ditch as the working area.

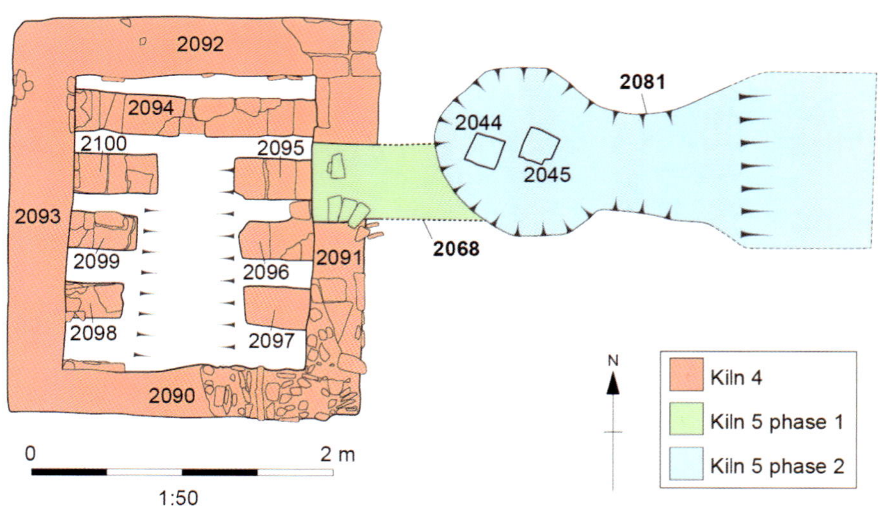

FIG. 47. Plan of pottery Kilns 4 and 5 in the south of Trench 2

RECTANGULAR POTTERY KILN 4 (FIGS 47–51)

The earliest kiln (4) was a single-flued, updraught kiln, rectangular in shape and constructed of well-made coursed bricks and reused *tegulae*. The outer walls were up to 0.4 m thick, giving maximum dimensions of the structure of 2.38 m by 2.74 m. It was cut into the natural clay to a depth of 1.2 m. Around one third of the stokehole arch survived on the southern wall and four pairs of internal cross-walls formed arches to support the floor over the firing chamber. Within a shallow hollow dug into the base of the kiln was a deposit of charcoal and ash mixed with a scattering of broken pottery, an assemblage once again dominated by flagons and other pale wares (Timby, p. 67). As the kiln fell into disrepair or was demolished, the chamber was almost entirely filled with the remains of the collapsed walls and superstructure.

The four walls of the kiln, **2090–2093**, were all integrated as one structure, laid in a stretcher

FIG. 48. The southern pottery kilns, Kiln 4 (left) and Kiln 5 (right), looking north

course with a sandy lime-mortar bond. The bricks were generally around 0.38 m by 0.28 m with a thickness of 0.04 m, but with some having been cut down to fit the dimensions of the structure. The largest of the *tegulae* measured up to 0.44 m by 0.35 m with a thickness of 0.07 m. The back wall of the kiln, **2092**, survived to a height of fourteen courses (1.2 m) of brick with increased robbing towards the south nearer the stokehole leaving just seven.

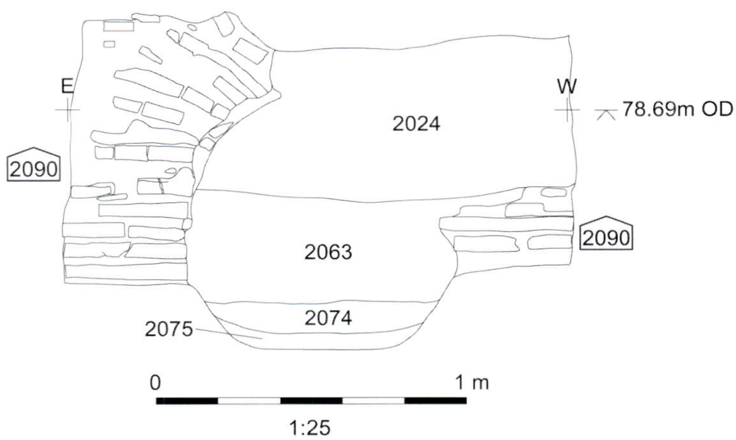

FIG. 49. Surviving stokehole arch in Kiln 4

Approximately a third of the stokehole archway survived within southern wall, **2090**, standing to a height of 0.9 m (FIG. 49). The construction method was more haphazard than that of the adjoining lower walls with a less co-ordinated arrangement of lower-quality bricks and a higher structural emphasis on the mortar bond.

Within the firing chamber survived the springers for four cross-walls which would have originally supported the floor that held the pottery vessels. Three of the cross-walls remained as six small stubs, **2095–2100**, emanating from the side walls, whereas the fourth, **2094** at the back of the kiln, stretched almost fully across the chamber, and demonstrated how the corbelling of the bricks would have supported the firing surface. Although the cross-walls were not keyed into the outer kiln walls, they were constructed with bricks similar to those used in the outer walls and were clearly of the same construction phase. **2094** at the back of the kiln survived to a height of ten courses; robbing and collapse caused the general increase in structural decay towards the south. **2098** in the south-west corner survived to a height of only four courses and, along with **2099**, displayed evidence of the bricks fusing together under the heat of firing.

FIG. 50. Ashy deposit (2075) at the base of the firing chamber of Kiln 4. Looking south towards the stokehole

FIG. 51. Looking north-east into Kiln 4, showing corbelling of the brickwork on cross-wall **2094**. The Phase 1 flue of Kiln 5 can be seen above the east wall **2091** of Kiln 4

At the base of the kiln was a small hollow running from the stokehole arch to the back of the firing chamber which contained a deposit of blue sand (2075). Measuring 1.6 m by 0.64 m with a thickness of 0.06 m, the layer was rich in charcoal and contained numerous large pieces of charred wood from the kiln firings. A radiocarbon sample taken from a portion of oak charcoal returned a date range of 39 cal B.C.–82 cal A.D. (juvenile *quercus sp.* charcoal 1964±24 BP, SUERC-90861). The lack of pottery from this layer suggests that it represented a period when the kiln was regularly maintained, with any broken wasters removed after each firing. Above this was (2074): a soft, light bluish-grey, silty sand which measured 0.6 m by 0.76 m and 0.12 m thick. It produced 162 sherds of pottery which were a mixture of white, grey and under-fired whiteware sherds with examples of flagons, jars and lids in a variety of firing colours (Timby, p. 67). This layer shows that the kiln was still being used but without being cleared out of wasters. The inclusion of degraded brick suggests the superstructure was beginning to disintegrate when this context was forming. The overlying deposit (2063) then marks a shift towards the complete abandonment of the structure. This was a firm, light-red, sandy clay measuring 2.4 m by 1.58 m with a thickness of 0.35 m. Among collapsed kiln material, a large cache of 268 pottery sherds, all from jars (Timby, p. 67), from this layer does hint at some continued firing of the kiln. Subsequently a 0.64 m thick layer of collapsed kiln structure, including possible superstructure (2024), completely sealed the remains of the kiln.

An exploratory slot was dug into the suspected working area to the south of pottery Kiln 4. Measuring 1.4 m long and 0.8 m wide, the slot reached an arbitrary depth of 0.96 m and revealed three distinct deposits. The lowermost, (2066), was a typical deposit of rake-out, 0.32 m thick and consisting of a charcoal-rich, firm, greyish-black clay. Above this sat (2065) which was up to 0.55 m thick. This was a compact, mid-orange, sandy clay which had formed mostly from the collapsed masonry that made up the stokehole arch. Uppermost was (2064), a mixed deposit combining further kiln collapse, deliberate backfill and disturbance by later agriculture. (2064) was a compact, yellowish-brown, silty clay up to 0.38 m thick (Timby, p. 67).

FIG. 52. The Phase 1 flue from Kiln 5 linking with the working area in Kiln 4 to the west

CIRCULAR POTTERY KILN 5, PHASE 1 (FIG. 52)

Before the complete abandonment of the firing chamber of Kiln 4, the space was used as the working area for a newly-built kiln (Kiln 5) to the east. The exact form of this new kiln is unknown, but it seems most likely that it was very similar to the circular structure of the second phase of Kiln 5. All that survived of Phase 1 was a short stretch of the flue [2068] which ran east to west from the remains of the circular firing chamber to the working area in the abandoned hollow of Kiln 4. The flue measured 1.1 m long by 0.64 m and 0.15 m deep and can be seen in profile in the side of the firing chamber.

A 0.03 m-thick layer of rake-out (2069) sat at the base of the flue, comprising 90 per cent ash and charcoal within a loose, silty clay matrix. It produced one tiny colourless glass bead (Crummy, p. 179). This deposit spread into the working area within the hollow of abandoned Kiln 4 as (2017). Formed from trampled rake-out, this layer measured 1.58 m by 1.26 m and was up to 0.1 m thick. The flue was then covered by collapsed structural material (2070), a firm, mid-orangish-grey clay layer containing a number of tiles that supported the stokehole. This measured 1.1 m by 0.64 m and 0.2 m thick and was similar in make-up to the later abandonment layers in Kiln 4.

FIG. 53. Kiln 5 Phase 2. Looking east from the firing chamber down the stokehole towards the ditch

CIRCULAR POTTERY KILN 5, PHASE 2 (FIG. 53)

The second phase of Kiln 5 involved the switching of the orientation of the flue so that it ran eastwards, sloping into the hollow of the north–south ditch that flanked the eastern edge of Trench 2. The chamber of the kiln was also redeveloped with a new lining, and presumably therefore a new dome. Unlike the other nearby examples, Kiln 5 produced very little pottery with just 11 sherds one of which was post-medieval in date (Timby, p. 69). Overall, the kiln chamber was 1.16 m in diameter and 0.52 m deep, with the flue extending approximately 1.7 m to the east before sloping away into the ditch. A rudimentary lining of clay mortar (2052) up to 0.1 m thick was applied to the chamber and stokehole and had hardened and darkened through the firing of the kiln.

Within the centre were two stacks of *pilae*, **2044** and **2045**, presumably used in a similar fashion as the tongue plinth in pottery Kiln 3, to support a surface for the vessels during firing. Each stack consisted of a series of *bessales* tiles measuring 0.2 m square and 0.05 m thick fixed together with a clay-based mortar. **2044** and **2045** consisted of eight courses and seven courses of *bessales* respectively, with the basal courses fused together due to the heat of the firings. The top of stack **2044** was scorched black suggesting it was at the level of the firing floor and exposed to the heat of the chamber.

Lowermost within the kiln was a small layer of rake-out material (2058) within the stokehole. Consisting of a hard, bright orangish-red, silty clay, it measured 0.38 m by 0.39 m and 0.02 m thick and probably represented the early uses of the kiln when it was well maintained. Above it and central to the chamber was a hard burnt layer (2053) which was spread around the supporting stacks. Potentially an attempt at re-lining the kiln after a series of uses, it consisted of a hard, dark grey clay, scorched and vitrified in many places and rich in charcoal. This layer measured 1.12 m by 1.96 m and was 0.1 m thick. Above this was (2035): a friable, mid-orange, silty clay which represented the last uses of the kiln before it fell into disrepair. Measuring 1.14 m by 1.05 m and 0.21 m thick, it contained a great deal of collapsed kiln structure, including a series of thin curved tiles (Machin, p. 96). Once the firing process was complete, the roof could be broken down to this level to retrieve the finished vessels and then built up again for the next use. Overlying (2035) was a thick layer of rubble derived from the collapse of the kiln superstructure and the continued dereliction of the area as a whole. Filling the firing chamber and 1.58 m by 1.18 m and 0.25 m thick, it included a large number of broken tiles possibly resulting from the dumping of waste from other kilns nearby.

A disturbed layer of rubble (2005) then covered the whole area across both kilns and working areas. Formed of a mixed, mid-orangish brown, silty clay it was strewn with brick and tile waste that had been further disturbed by later ploughing. (2005) was 4.96 m by 2.82 m and 0.28 m thick.

Towards the east were two ditch fills that sat within the mouth of the stokehole as it opened into the ditch. The shape of the stokehole shows that the ditch had already silted up or been backfilled quite substantially at this point but still offered enough of a hollow to act as a working area for the kiln. Both deposits were typical of the later ditch fills (see below) and appear to post-date the abandonment of the kiln. The lower of these two deposits, (2056), was a hard, mid-greyish-brown, silty clay that was 0.20 m thick, whereas the upper layer, (2055), was a friable, light yellowish-grey, sandy clay measuring 0.26 m in depth.

NORTH–SOUTH DITCH 2101 (FIGS 54–55)

The substantial north–south ditch 2101 revealed along the eastern edge of Trench 2 appeared much less obvious on the surface than had been indicated on the geophysics scan. The edges were extremely diffuse and masked by ploughing and colluvial wash. Only a scattering of CBM in the upper deposit indicated any kind of feature, initially thought to be a shallow pathway. Four slots each 2 m wide were placed along the length of this faint impression revealing a ditch averaging over 4.5 m wide and 1.4 m deep. Generally V-shaped in profile with a narrow, flat base, the ditch contained few finds near the base, suggesting that it was constructed before intense tile- and pottery-making activity began in the vicinity. As in Trench 1, it seems the pottery kilns had been deliberately located to exploit a boundary and used the partly-filled ditch to deposit waster material. The positioning of the kilns therefore seems to preclude a bank on the west side of the ditch. Thus, although there was no trace of the accompanying bank within the excavated area, it presumably flanked the ditch on its eastern side. During the use of the nearby kilns, the ditch was filled with large amounts of waste pottery with nearly 3,000 sherds found within the four slots dug into it (Timby, p. 69).

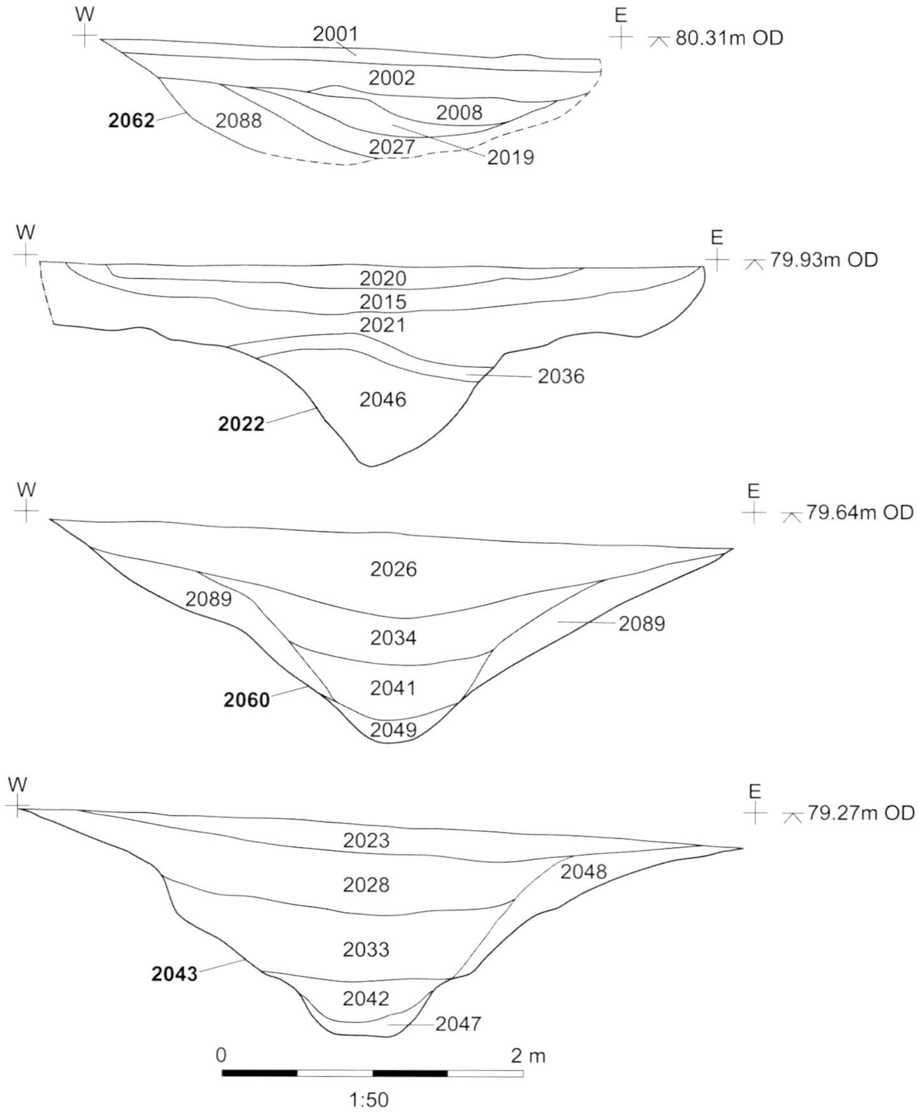

FIG. 54. North–south Ditch 2101, profiles

[2062]

The northernmost slot through the ditch was the most fruitful in terms of finds with over 2,000 pottery sherds retrieved (Timby, p. 70). Clearly a dumping ground for pottery that did not survive firing, it seems likely that much of this material came from nearby Kiln 3, but the ditch may also have been a midden for more general waste. The presence of household ceramics in fabrics other than those made at Little London, as well as samian ware, glass and a piece of tazza, also hints at nearby occupation. The volume of finds recovered from this area of the ditch meant that time did not allow it to be fully excavated and it was abandoned at around a depth of 0.8 m and a width of 3.3 m.

Seen lowermost within the ditch slot was (2088) against the western edge. This was a firm, light yellowish-grey clay that measured 1.4 m wide and 0.32 m thick. Formed of redeposited natural clay which had eroded from the sides of the ditch, it yielded no finds. Overlying this was (2027) which was a firm, mid-whitish grey clay, potentially from a demolished structure. This deposit measured 2.4 m wide and 0.18 m deep and may have been the result of sustained dumping from a nearby kiln mixed with the discarded remains of the kiln itself after renovation. The pottery from (2027) is exceptional in that it consisted almost entirely of kiln products with multiple examples of flagons, mortaria and lids with a few flat-rimmed bowls, a chimney

FIG. 55. Slot [2060] looking north-west

piece and the only tazza from the site (Timby, p. 70). It also produced one iron nail. Sat above was (2019): a firm, dark grey, sandy clay which was similarly dominated by kiln wares. (2019) measured 1.85 m wide by 0.24 m thick and was rich in charcoal rake-out as well as containing CBM and iron nails. Sat above this was (2008): a firm, mid-greyish-brown, sandy clay which measured 1.62 m wide and 0.18 m thick. This was the most abundant fill in terms of pottery with 801 sherds which included a high proportion of Alice Holt wares, and a few sherds of samian of which the latest sherds were an early-to-mid Flavian Drag. 37 and a Drag. 29, dated *c.* A.D. 60–85, of South Gaulish ware and a sherd of Les Martres de Veyre ware, probably of Trajanic date (Bird, p. 63). This group also contained small fragments of colourless glass, including a square bottle, and one iron nail. The tenor of the group from (2008) is slightly later than the other ditch assemblages and it may represent a slightly later re-cut into the top of the ditch or simply later backfilling. Overlying (2008) was a layer of intrusive ploughsoil (2002) and a cleaning layer (2001).

[2022]

Ditch cut [2022] was approximately 5 m further to the south and measured 4.62 m wide and 1.42 m deep. In this instance the sides of the ditch were more convex in shape, sloping down to a pointed base. Just 62 pottery sherds were recovered from within the slot, surprisingly few relative to [2062] and given its proximity to Kiln 3 (Timby, p. 69).

The lowermost fill, (2046), was a friable, light brownish-grey, sandy clay which measured 1.42 m wide and 0.6 m thick. This was sealed by (2036), a friable, mid-purple-grey, clay sand which measured 1.78 m wide and 0.12 m thick. Both of these basal fills contained no artefacts and the slightly heaped nature of their deposition suggests they may have been the result of deliberate backfilling rather than a gradual natural accumulation. Stratified above was (2021): a friable, light brownish-grey, sandy clay measuring 3.62 m wide and 0.32 m thick. This covered much of the upper extent of the ditch and contained the first finds, a few sherds of kiln wares.

Overlying was (2015) which measured 4.2 m wide and 0.18 m thick and yielded the bulk of the pottery, further kiln wares including a collared-rim flagon and lid knobs (Timby, p. 69). (2015) was a friable, mid-blackish-grey, sandy clay containing one iron nail which was then overlaid by a mixed layer of accumulated sandy clay. (2020) measured 3.1 m wide and 0.15 m thick and was formed by the silting-up of the hollow of the ditch and disturbed by ploughing.

[2060]

Slot [2060], which was a further 5–6 m to the south, contained just four fills with some edge collapse. The sides of the ditch here were slightly convex and sloped gently into a rounded base. Attached to either side was (2089): a firm, mid-brownish-yellow layer of eroded clay measuring 1.5 m wide and 0.25 m thick. Probably contemporary with this was fill (2049) which sat at the base of the ditch and measured 0.86 m wide and 0.18 m thick. It contained just 15 sherds of local handmade coarse wares including the knob from a Silchester ware lid and one tiny opaque black glass bead (Crummy, p. 179). Stratified above was (2041) which was a firm, mid-grey clay measuring 1.36 m wide and 0.36 m thick. This horizon yielded a large deposit of 254 sherds of pottery, including kiln waste, amongst which were two sherds of South Gaulish samian dated respectively to the Neronian-Flavian and Neronian-early Flavian periods (Bird, p. 63). Further finds came from level (2034), a firm, mid-brown-yellow clay which measured 2.6 m wide and 0.3 m thick and contained a further 146 sherds of pottery, CBM and a fragment of whetstone. The uppermost fill was (2026), a mid-brown-grey, sandy clay measuring 4.54 m wide and 0.6 m thick. This was a general silting layer that still yielded a smaller quantity of pottery and additional CBM.

[2043]

Furthest south in Trench 2, cut [2043] was 4.8 m wide and 1.46 m deep and boasted slightly irregular, convex sides and a flat base. Significantly, flint-tempered Silchester ware accounted for nearly 70 per cent of pottery from this slot with kiln products contributing just 10 per cent. As with the previous examples, there was a layer of redeposited natural clay eroded from the sides, (2048). This consisted of a firm, dark orangish-grey, sandy clay upon the eastern side of the ditch and measured 1.9 m wide and 0.3 m thick. Basal fill (2047) was similar in its formation, a typical primary deposit produced from redeposited natural clay during the initial construction of the ditch. It consisted of a friable, mottled greyish-orange, sandy clay and measured 0.9 m wide and 0.16 m thick. Overlying was (2042): a friable, mid-grey, sandy clay which measured 1.3 m wide and 0.3 m thick. This contained the first artefacts within this slot, a number of pottery sherds dominated by Silchester ware but also including a single piece of kiln ware (Timby, p. 70). The succeeding fill (2033) was a friable, light-grey, sandy clay measuring 2.35 m wide and 0.46 m thick. This yielded some relief-patterned tile, iron nails and the largest pottery assemblage from the slot: 216 sherds, of which only 11 per cent were products from the kilns. Overlying this was (2028): a firm, dark grey, sandy clay which measured 3.7 m wide and 0.42 m thick and contained a smaller, yet similar array of finds including an iron nail and part of an iron knife (Crummy, p. 179). The uppermost horizon (2023) was consistent with that seen in the preceding slots: a later silting layer mixed with ploughed-in subsoil. Measuring 4.1 m wide and 0.18 m thick, it consisted of a firm, mid-yellowish-grey, silty clay with a few inclusions of pottery and CBM.

SUMMARY

Although the north–south ditch and the kilns are discrete features, it is possible to propose a chronological development of activity in Trench 2 from a combination of the relationships local to each feature or group of features and the associated dating evidence. The earliest kiln is likely to be Kiln 4 whose design mirrors that of the larger brick Kiln 1 and it is stratigraphically earlier than the circular Kiln 5. Its construction was predicated on the availability of bricks to make it and this adds further weight to the evidence from Trench 1 that brick and tile production preceded, if only by a short interval, the making of pottery. Like Kiln 5, Kiln 3 is circular and could, therefore, be contemporary with it. It is certainly later than the deep feature [2079] which, partly-filled, was used as its stokehole. Other than the radiocarbon dates, the waster pottery and CBM, the only independent dating evidence from the kilns is a single sherd of a Flavian South Gaulish Drag. 35 giving a *terminus post quem* for the filling of the stokehole of Kiln 3.

The earliest feature of all in Trench 2 is likely to be the north–south ditch 2101 whose basal fills either lacked any datable finds at all, except the probable post-conquest, tiny black glass bead, or included small quantities of local, non-kiln wares. This, and the absence of the types of pottery present in the primary fills of the trackway ditches in Trench 1, would suggest it is a post-conquest feature. The geophysics gives no indication of kiln structures to the east of the ditch and so it is likely that it had been created as a boundary before any pottery kiln was established.

Other than kiln wares the earliest datable material from the ditch are two sherds of South Gaulish samian of Neronian-Flavian and Neronian-to-early Flavian date from (2041), which appears to be the primary fill of a localised re-cut of the ditch in slot [2060]. Otherwise dumps of both waste pottery and other non-kiln wares are confined to the uppermost deposits of the ditch, most notably in the northernmost slot [2062], where the latest samian from (2008) included a Drag. 29, *c.* A.D. 60–85, a Drag. 37 of early-to-mid-Flavian date and a Les Martres de Veyre Drag. 36 of probable Trajanic date.

The probable Trajanic sherd is the latest closely datable pottery from the entire excavation and, along with three sherds of a second-century Dorset BB1 flat-rimmed dish from the initial cleaning of Trench 2, indicates some continuing occupation to the north of Trench 2 into the early second century. The abundance of wasters as well as of other, non-kiln, domestic pottery in the northernmost slot of the north–south ditch reinforces the possibility of both nearby settlement and a further kiln or kilns to the north of Trench 2. Given the tendency for rubbish to accumulate in ditch terminals, it is also possible that the northernmost slot is close to an entrance-way. The absence of Flavian-Trajanic forms among the waste pottery suggests that pottery production, like that of brick and tile, was confined to the Neronian to early Flavian period.

CHAPTER 4

THE POTTERY

By Jane Timby
with a report on the samian by Joanna Bird and on the mortarium stamp by Roger Tomlin

INTRODUCTION AND METHODOLOGY

The excavation resulted in the recovery of 6,118 sherds of pottery weighing 86.2 kg and with 76.39 estimated vessel equivalents (EVE). Of this, some 635 sherds, 8.9 kg, came from Trench 1 and 5,497 sherds, 77.45 kg, from Trench 2. Most of the pottery dates to the early Roman period accompanied by a few intrusive sherds of post-medieval date. As this is a pottery production site, unsurprisingly a significant proportion of the pottery (73.5 per cent count, 69.4 per cent weight) comprises kiln waste. The assemblage was recorded using recommendations outlined in Barclay *et al.* 2016. To this end it was examined macroscopically and sorted into fabrics based on the inclusions present, the frequency and grade of the inclusions and the firing colour. Wares already documented at Silchester follow the same coding (cf. Timby 2018) or, where relevant, follow the codes used in the National Roman Fabric Reference Collection (Tomber and Dore 1998). The kiln products were divided broadly according to firing colour, texture and/or surface finish. Very small, shattered fragments were not classified and are excluded from the percentages. The sorted fabrics were quantified by sherd count and weight by recorded context. Rims were additionally coded to form and measured for the diameter and percentage present for the estimation of rim equivalence (EVE) (cf. Orton *et al.* 1993). A type series has been created specifically for the kiln products. The resulting data were entered onto an MS Excel spreadsheet a copy of which is deposited with the archive.

The condition of the material is variable with a mixture of good, relatively unabraded, sherds and more fragmented wares giving an overall average sherd weight of 14 g. There is no perceptible compositional difference between the assemblages recovered from the two trenches, although a greater amount came from Trench 2. Surface preservation is mixed and, as much of this is kiln waste, some sherds were too burnt to classify.

DESCRIPTION OF KILN FABRICS AND ASSOCIATED FORMS (Table 1)

The kiln wares have been divided up into nine fabric groups (K1–K9) on the basis of firing colour and surface finish. In many cases this is not necessarily the intended colour as many sherds are under- or over-fired. The fabric used is essentially the same composition throughout, although with two variations in terms of the grade of the quartz-sand inclusions present producing finer and slightly sandier variants. In some sherds iron inclusions form a more prominent component in the clay used. Whilst most sherds are plain with no surface treatment others have been slipped. The sherds were sorted macroscopically and examined under a binocular microscope (x20).

K1: White-fired wares. A moderately hard fired ware with a sandy texture. The core can vary from white through to pink overlapping with fabric K7. The matrix contains a common frequency of well-sorted, fine-sub-angular quartz < 0.3 mm. Some quartz grains are iron-stained pink; others are white or clear opaque. A sparse frequency of rounded, iron-rich orange-red grains up to 1 mm are also scattered through the fabric. All the mortaria, with one exception, have angular, black, grey and white flint trituration grits, generally ranging from 2 to 5 mm in

TABLE I. QUANTIFIED SUMMARY OF ALL THE ROMAN POTTERY FROM LITTLE LONDON

	Code	Description	No.	No. %	Wt	Wt %	Eve	Eve%
IMPORTS	LGF SA	South Gaulish samian	12	0.2	163	0.2	0.28	0.4
	CNG TN	Central Gaulish *terra nigra*	2	0.0	56	0.1	0.3	0.4
	GAB TN	Gallo-Belgic *terra nigra*	1	0.0	10	0.0	0	0.0
	GAB TR1A	Gallo-Belgic *terra rubra*	8	0.1	9	0.0	0	0.0
	GYFMIC	fine grey micaceous ware	3	0.0	38	0.0	0.1	0.1
Amphora	BAT AM	Baetican amphora	14	0.2	1290	1.5	0	0.0
	GAL AM	Gallic amphora Dr 2-4	6	0.1	137	0.2	0	0.0
REGIONAL	DOR BB1	Dorset black burnished ware	3	0.0	31	0.0	0.12	0.2
LOCAL	ALH RE	Alice Holt-type reduced wares	684	11.2	6033	7.0	7.83	10.3
	SIL F1	Silchester flint-tempered ware	555	9.1	12790	14.8	4.97	6.5
	FL2FE	finer flint-tempered, iron-rich	1	0.0	77	0.1	0	0.0
	GR1-4	grog-tempered	52	0.9	418	0.5	0.4	0.5
	GRSJ	grog-tempered storage jar	172	2.8	4342	5.0	0.41	0.5
	GRSA	sandy with grog	3	0.0	11	0.0	0	0.0
	GRSAOR	sandy with grog and organic	2	0.0	58	0.1	0.2	0.3
	SAFEFL	sandy with iron and flint	39	0.6	442	0.5	0.44	0.6
UNKNOWN	BWSY	black sandy ware	36	0.6	246	0.3	0.28	0.4
	CA	calcareous temper	1	0.0	10	0.0	0	0.0
	GYSY	misc. grey sandy wares	25	0.4	176	0.2	0	0.0
	MISC	miscellaneous sandy	5	0.1	46	0.1	0.03	0.0
Kiln wares	K1	white-fired	1884	30.8	25145	29.2	25.63	33.6
	K2	grey slightly sandy	157	2.6	2134	2.5	1.88	2.5
	K3	fine oxidised ware	52	0.9	968	1.1	1.59	2.1
	K4	fine grey ware, iron-rich	29	0.5	333	0.4	1.84	2.4
	K5	grey-slipped	85	1.4	1244	1.4	3.08	4.0
	K6	fine grey ware	48	0.8	699	0.8	1.94	2.5
	K7	pink-orange (under-fired K1)	1558	25.5	14191	16.5	13.72	18.0
	K8	oxidised	581	9.5	8075	9.4	8	10.5
	K9	white ware with colour-coat	22	0.4	874	1.0	0.67	0.9
	K00	burnt sherds	31	0.5	293	0.3	0.61	0.8
	MORT1	white ware mortaria	41	0.7	4982	5.8	1.61	2.1
	MORT2	white ware mortaria	2	0.0	505	0.6	0.15	0.2
	MORT3	as K7	3	0.0	342	0.4	0.31	0.4
TOTAL			6117	100.0	86167	100.0	76.39	100.0

size. One vessel, the only stamped example (FIG. 59.22), appears to have internal surface slurry but no grits. Fabric K1 accounts for 42.8 per cent by count and 51.2 per cent by weight of the kiln wares. It was used primarily for flagons (types FL1a–c, FL3 and FL5); bowls (BL1, BL2); jars (J2, J3, J5); lids (L1) and mortaria (M1–5). There is also a single beaker (BK2).

Superficially and texturally the fabric is very similar to Verulamium white ware and indeed would have been classified as Verulamium-type ware when encountered in previous assemblages from Silchester. At x20 magnification wasters from the Brockley Hill kilns show marginally coarser sand particles which appear to be composed of two grades, a finer and a slightly coarser;

the latter with rounded grains up to 0.5 mm in size. In general terms the quartz in the Brockley Hill sherds appears less iron-stained from the samples examined.

K2: Grey sandy ware. Texturally as K1 but fired grey. A moderately uncommon variant accounting for 3.5–3.6 per cent (by count and weight) of the kiln wares. Vessels include one flagon (FL2), a beaker (BK3), jars (J3, J6), several platters (PL1) and lids (L1).

K3: A fine oxidised ware, mid to dark orange in colour. The matrix contains a sparse to moderate scatter of mainly rounded, orange-brown iron up to 1 mm across and very rare (accidental?) flint. The quartz sand is very fine and not visible at x20 magnification. This ware contributes a very minor amount, 1.2/1.3 per cent by count/weight to the overall assemblage. Vessels mainly comprise platters (PL1), with single examples of a flanged bowl (BL1) and a two-handled flagon (FL4).

K4: A fine, grey ware with frequent iron specks representing a reduced version of K3. Black iron streaking is more prominent on the vessels surfaces. The matrix contains a moderate scatter of angular to rounded, black and red-brown iron mainly 0.5–1 mm in size and finer. As with K3 there is no quartz sand visible at x20 magnification. K4 is a minor fabric accounting for just 0.6 per cent (by count and weight) overall. Forms are almost exclusively restricted to curved wall platters (PL1) with a single shallow bowl (BL6).

K5: Grey-slipped, sandy ware. As K3/K4 but with a pale grey, semi-matt slip on the vessel surfaces, generally poorly adhered. This ware contributes 1.9 per cent by count, 2.1 per cent by weight, with most of the examples coming from working area [2079] below Kiln 3 [2040]. Vessels are almost exclusively restricted to curved-wall platters (PL1, PL3).

K6: Hard fired, very fine, blue-grey ware. This appears to be an over-fired version of K4. The fabric has a slightly crystalline, cindery texture with inclusions of angular to sub-angular black iron. It features in similar proportion to the other grey wares at 1.1 per cent (count) and 1.2 per cent (weight) and only occurs as curved-wall platters (PL1).

K7: A softer, oxidised/pink ware which is most likely an under-fired version of K1. The more friable nature is reflected in the figures as it makes up 35.7 per cent count of the kiln wares but only 24.3 per cent by weight. Vessels are dominated by flagons (FL1a, FL3, FL5) and jars (J3, J6) accompanied by bowls (BL1, BL5), beakers (BK3), lids (L1) and single examples of a dish/saggar (D1) and platter (PL1).

K8: An oxidised, sandy version of K1/K2. This ware contributes 12.9 per cent of the assemblage by count, 13.5 per cent by weight. It appears in a range of forms including flagons (FL1a–b, FL5), jars (J3, J6), lids (L1, L2) and single examples of a platter (PL1), dish/saggar (D1), a possible strainer (S1) (FIG. 61.71) and a cheese press (CP1). The lids feature several knobs.

K9: Orange-slipped, white ware. A small number of white ware sherds (K1) have a matt orange-red or brownish-red surface which seems to be from a surface slip. It forms a very minor amount, 0.5 per cent count, 1.5 per cent weight, of the overall assemblage. There is only a single rim present, from a flagon (FL3).

FORM TYPE SERIES (Table 2)

A total of 41 types have been defined from the discarded kiln products many of which are represented by single examples. Complete profiles were extremely rare, so the typology is largely based on rim fragments. The competency of the potters is variable, reflected in bases that are either extremely thick and heavy or so thin that they have split. Overall flagons make up over half the discarded assemblage (51.8 per cent) by EVE followed by almost equal quantities (11–14 per cent) of bowls, platters and jars. All other forms account for 4 per cent or less.

TABLE 2. INCIDENCE OF FORMS PRODUCED AT LITTLE LONDON BY ESTIMATED (RIM) EQUIVALENCE (EVE)

Forms	Type (Kiln wares)	Type No.	EVE	EVE %	Fig. No.
Flagon	collared rim	FL1a	19.91	32.7	11, 13–14, 52–4
	rectangular collared rim	FLb	4.44	7.3	2
	square collared rim *	FLc	1.00	1.6	50
	expanded squared rim *	FL2	0.22	0.4	38
	disc-mouthed	FL3	3.52	5.8	4–5, 39, 56
	double-handled, triangular rim*	FL4	0.53	0.9	12
	ring-necked	FL5	1.33	2.2	57–8
	flared with beaded rim*	FL6	0.27	0.4	55
	funnel-mouthed*	FL7	0.00	0.0	51
	miscellaneous other	FL	0.27	0.4	
Bowl	flanged rim deep bowl	BL1	6.06	10.0	15–16, 59
	flat beaded rim hemispherical*	BL2	0.15	0.2	7
	grooved flat rim hemispherical*	BL3	0.10	0.2	60
	short flat rim straight-walled	BL4	0.11	0.2	61
	shallow flat rim*	BL5	0.08	0.1	17
	flanged beaded rim*	BL6	0.03	0.0	18
	flanged bowl*	BL7	0.15	0.2	10
	tripod bowl*	BL8	0.00	0.0	35
	miscellaneous other	BLmisc	0.15	0.2	
Dish	curved wall dish	D1	0.53	0.9	84
Platter	curved wall with foot-ring	PL1	8.00	13.2	3, 27–8, 41
	curved with lid-seating*	PL2	0.07	0.1	62
	beaded rim curved wall*	PL3	0.29	0.5	29
Beaker	short everted rim	BK1	0.27	0.4	40
	sharply everted with offset*	BK2	0.15	0.2	19
	sharply everted globular	BK3	0.16	0.3	20–1, 63
Jar	everted, hooked rim*	J1	0.35	0.6	8
	dolium-type flat rim	J2	0.24	0.4	30–1
	expanded rim neckless jar	J3	5.19	8.5	42–4, 46–7, 72
	necked jar/bowl with rolled rim	J4	0.15	0.2	73–4
	triangular cordoned rim*	J5	0.12	0.2	32
	necked, cordoned jar	J6	1.18	1.9	75
	necked with carinated shoulder	J7	0.30	0.5	33–4
	grooved outer rim face *	J8	0.35	0.6	45
Lid	plain rim	L1	2.16	3.6	26, 48–9, 68, 70
	flat, perforated*	L2	0.05	0.1	69
Mortarium	hooked flange, low bead	M1	0.81	1.3	9, 22–3
	hooked flange, low bead	M2	1.00	1.6	24, 65–6
	hooked flange, level bead*	M3	0.12	0.2	64
	double-beaded, flat flange*	M4	0.25	0.4	67
	double-beaded, rolled tip flange*	M5	0.23	0.4	25
	miscellaneous – incomplete	M	0.05	0.1	
Cheese press		CP1	0.45	0.7	6
Tazza	tazza*	TZ1	0.03	0.0	76
TOTAL			60.82	100.0	
	* = single example only				

Flagons

FL1a: Collared-rim flagon (Hofheim type) (FIGS 58.11, 13–14; 60.52–54). As *Camulodunum* (Cam.) 140. Single-handled flagon with a cylindrical neck and out-curved triangular lip undercut on the exterior. Rim diameters range between 50 mm and 80 mm. The form can be traced back to the later Augustan military sites in the Rhineland. In Britain the form is common in the Claudio-Neronian period and is the main flagon type found on many of the early military sites, for example, Colchester, Usk, Kingsholm, Longthorpe and Wroxeter. Production of the form ceased in the early Flavian period. It is also associated with presumed civilian kilns at Duxford (Anderson and Woolhouse 2016), Eccles (Detsicas 1977) and Canterbury (Jenkins 1956; 1960).

FL1b: Collared-rim flagon with a more rectangular rim with a slightly concave inner face and undercut on the exterior (FIG. 58.2). A similar variant is also found at Bricket Wood (Saunders and Havercroft 1977, fig. 5.8–12).

FL1c: Square-collared rim (FIG. 60.50). A single example in fabric K1 was recovered from Ditch 2101 slot [2060].

FL2: Heavy mouthed flagon with a squared rim expanded on the interior (FIG. 60.38). A single example in fabric K2 from Kiln 4 (2031).

FL3: Disc-mouthed flagon (FIGS 58.4–5; 60.39, 56). Single-handled flagon ranging in diameter from 26 to 56 mm. The form falls within Cam. types 149–151 and was made at a number of other centres including Bricket Wood and Brockley Hill (Davies *et al.* 1994, fig. 35.162–3; Marsh and Tyers 1978, type ID), although never seems to have been particularly popular. The flagon has continental origins and was found at Novaesium (Filtzinger 1972, form 16) and Hofheim (Ritterling 1913, form 55).

FL4: Double-handled flagon with a short triangular rim and a conical neck as Cam. type 167 (FIG. 58.12). Only a single example is present. A similar form was made at Bricket Wood (Saunders and Havercroft 1977, fig. 5.30; Marsh and Tyers 1978, type IE).

FL5: Ring-necked flagon (FIG. 60.57–58). A single-handled flagon with a ringed neck, limited to six examples, all from Ditch 2101 slot [2062]. The form can be traced back to Augustan-Tiberian sites on the Continent and is one of the main types to be found in the South-West from the Neronian period with examples documented from Exeter (Bidwell 2021), Lake Farm (Darling 1986), Tiverton (Maxfield 1991) and the Corfe Mullen kiln (Calkin 1935) amongst others. The South-West examples often have a more cupped profile with four or more rings. In the South-East the form becomes well documented from the early Flavian period onwards, essentially replacing the collared-rim form. Examples were found in the immediately pre-Boudican levels at Verulamium dated A.D. 55–60 (Saunders and Havercroft 1977, 125). The earlier forms have several evenly shaped rings which generally decrease in number with time whilst the upper ring expands. This form of flagon can be widely paralleled and was made at Brockley Hill and Bricket Wood (ibid., fig. 5.34–54), as well as at the early Roman establishments at Gloucester and Colchester (kiln 23) (Hull 1963, fig. 84).

FL6: Slightly beaded, flared rim. A single example was recovered from Ditch 2101 slot [2062] (FIG. 60.55). Possibly related to Southwark form IH2, a Verulamium area product (Marsh 1983, fig. 233).

FL7: A double-handled, large flagon missing the upper rim (FIG. 60.51). A carination at the handle attachment suggests it may be a funnel-mouth flagon allied to Cam. type 169/170, another type with continental parallels. The form was made at Bricket Wood (Saunders and Havercroft 1977, 122; fig. 5.25–27) and Eccles (Detsicas 1977, fig. 3.4).

Handles: In total 92 detached handle fragments were recovered. Apart from a single round-sectioned example, these are all strap handles from flagons with two-, three- and four-ribbed forms. Of the classifiable pieces 70.5 per cent are three-ribbed followed by two-ribbed at 18.2 per cent and just four examples of four-ribbed.

Bases: Most of the flagons appear to have foot-ring bases although a few are flat.

Bowls

BL1: Deep, flanged rim, hemispherical bowl (FIGS 58.15–16; 60.59). The flat down-turned rim generally has two grooves on the inner and outer margins. The angle can vary from almost horizontal to well inclined; there is also some variability in the width of the rim. Vessels are mainly produced in fabrics K1 and K8. As with the flagons, the form has continental military origins and in Britain appears on early military sites such as Usk (Greene 1973, fig. 1.10), Longthorpe (Dannell and Wild 1987, fig. 41. 58b) and Kingsholm (Darling 1985, fig. 25.41–42). The form was made at Colchester (Hull 1963, kiln 23), Brockley Hill and Bricket Wood (Saunders and Havercroft 1977, fig. 8).

BL2: Deep, hemispherical bowl with a flat flange and small bead rim (FIG. 58.7). A single example in fabric K7.

BL3: Flat-rim, deep, hemispherical bowl. The rim has a single groove on the upper surface. A single example from Ditch 2101 slot [2060] in fabric K1 (FIG. 61.60).

BL4: Short, flat-rim bowl probably with one or two grooves. Two poorly preserved examples both in oxidised ware (FIG. 61.61).

BL5: Shallow bowl with a hemispherical body and a flat, double-grooved rim. A single example fired orange (fabric K8) (FIG. 58.17).

BL6: Shallow, hemispherical bowl displaying a beaded, flanged rim. A single example in fine oxidised ware was recovered from working area [2079] (FIG. 58.18).

BL7: Fragment of a double-grooved, flanged-rim bowl. Represented by a single example made in fine grey ware (K4) (FIG. 58.10).

BL8: Tripod bowl. A single pod recovered from the flue area of Kiln 3 [2040] suggests that tripod bowls were possibly made unless this piece performed some other function (FIG. 59.35).

Dish?

D1: Simple curved-wall vessel with a flat top to the rim and a flat base. There are just five examples, three of which are heavily burnt. The slightly crude form might suggest these vessels were made to be used as kiln furniture (FIG. 62.84).

Beakers

BK1: Short everted rim beaker. The rim is slightly bevelled on the interior. A single example fired white (FIG. 60.40).

BK2: Sharply everted, thickened rim beaker with a small offset below the rim (FIG. 59.19).

BK3: Sharply everted rim, globular beaker (FIGS 59.20, 21; 61.63). Broadly similar forms were made at Colchester (Hull 1963, fig. 84.11) but with roughcast decoration.

Mortaria

In total 13 rims of mortaria are present all of which comprise the flanged type as opposed to the earlier wall-sided vessels. There is diversity in form perhaps pointing to a phase of experimentation at this time in mortaria production also seen at other contemporary kiln sites such as Eccles (Hartley 1977a, 28).

M1: Dropped hooked flange with a low bead (FIGS 58.9; 59.22–23). This group includes the only stamped mortarium from the site (FIG. 59.22) (see below). Unlike all the other vessels grouped here, this one does not appear to have any specific trituration grits but has a finely sorted cream slurry containing well-sorted quartz, fine pellets of clay or grog and iron. Whether further grits were intended to be added is not known. The vessel has concentric grooving on the flange and interior. The other vessels have fine flint-trituration grits composed of white, grey and black angular fragments. The bead on one example (FIG. 58.9) is quite high, approximating Cam. type 195A (Hawkes and Hull 1947, 256) noted as appearing in the Neronian period. This bears close comparison with some of the Northern Gaulish examples, notably Gillam (1970) type 238 (cf. Hartley 1977b, fig. 2.1).

M2: Dropped hooked flange with a low bead and hemispherical body (FIGS 59.24; 61.65–66). Fabric: K7.

M3: Dropped hooked flange with a small bead level with the top of the flange (FIG. 61.64). A broadly similar form is illustrated from Colchester (Hull 1963, fig. 68.19).

M4: Double-beaded with a short, almost flat flange (FIG. 61.67).

M5: Double-beaded with a short flange with a rolled tip (FIG. 59.25). Flint trituration grits.

Lids

L1: Simple lids with plain rims with domed or flatter profiles ranging in diameter from 120 mm through to 360 mm (FIGS 59.26; 60.48–49; 61.68, 70). Most were probably designed to go with the flanged-rim bowls type BL1. One example has a single perforation. Most lids are in white or oxidised fabrics with a few grey ware examples. Six detached lid knobs are present and are all of solid construction. These all feature in oxidised fabrics. Lids of similar simple form were made at the Verulamium and Eccles kilns amongst others.

L2: One example of a small, flat lid with at least two surface grooves and a single perforation (FIG. 61.69).

Strainer

S1: A single example of a possible strainer represented by a flat base-sherd with multiple perforations (FIG. 61.71). The other possibility is that this is a detached lid knob with multiple perforations.

Platters

PL1: Curved-wall platter copying Cam. type 16. The vessels are furnished with a shallow foot-ring with a distinctive finger groove outside the foot, a trademark of the potter. At least seven, possibly eight, vessels carry a central, poorly impressed, potter's name stamp (see below). The diameters range from 140 mm through to 300 mm, with the highest frequency in the 180–200 mm range. The vessels occur in fine grey fired ware (K2, K4), oxidised ware (K8) and grey-slipped ware (K5) (FIGS 58.3; 59.27–28; 60.41). The form appears to be a direct copy of the Gallo-Belgic form usually found in *terra nigra* and dating to the latest phase of the industry in the period *c.* A.D. 40–70/75. In addition to the rims a large number of base-sherds with foot-rings were recovered.

PL2: Curved-wall platter with an internal off-set/lid-seating in grey sandy ware K2 (FIG. 61.62).

PL3: Curved-wall platter with a beaded rim and a shallow foot-ring. The base has a compass-incised, double-line circle in the centre surrounding a potter's stamp (see below). This form is represented by a single example in oxidised ware (FIG. 59.29).

Cheese press

CP: A single example of a perforated cheese press came from quarry pit [1048] (FIG. 58.6). The form is one with military origins which occurs in the late Augustan-Claudian levels at Novaesium (Filtzinger 1972, taf. 47.7). Similar vessels were made at Eccles (Detsicas 1977, fig. 3.4.97); less commonly at Brockley Hill (Seeley and Thorogood 1994) and at the military sites at Usk (Greene 1993, type 28) and Longthorpe (Dannell and Wild 1987, 151).

Jars

J1: Everted, slightly hooked rim jar with a slight shoulder carination. A single example recovered from Trench 1 (FIG. 58.8).

J2: Flat rim dolium-type jar. An unusual form with just two examples in fabric K1 (FIG. 59.30–31). For discussion see below.

J3: Neckless, globular-bodied jar with an expanded rolled, or slightly squared, rim (FIGS 60.42–44, 46–47; 61.72).

J4: Necked jar/bowl with a rounded, slightly beaded rim (FIG. 61.73–74).

J5: Triangular-rimmed jar with a narrow external cordon. Another white-fired singleton recovered from Kiln 3 [2040] (FIG. 59.32).

J6: Necked, cordoned jar (FIG. 61.75).

J7: Necked jar with a high, angular carinated shoulder and a small beaded rim (FIG. 59.33–34). This form can be directly paralleled with similar vessels from the kiln site in Field 410, Brockley Hill (Castle 1973a, fig. 2.4–5). Tyers (1998, 296) considers that these distinctive jars might be related to a similar style of jar made in the area of Lyon and to its east.

J8: Jar with a grooved outer rim (FIG. 60.45).

Bases: The jars generally have flat bases many of which show concentric marks on the underside where the vessel has been removed from the wheel using a wire.

Tazza

TZ1: A single example of an oxidised tazza with a carinated profile decorated with finger frilling on the lip and carination (FIG. 61.76). Tazze feature amongst the products of the Verulamium kilns at Bricket Wood (Saunders and Havercroft 1977, fig. 11.203) and Brockley Hill (Tyers 1983, 11).

POTTERS' STAMPS

1. FIGS 56; 59.22. Mortarium type M1. Deposit (2061), [2084/2079]. Fabric K1 variant. Impressed stamp to right of spout; other side missing. The stamp is set within an ansate-shaped frame with the first and last letters located within the ansates. Reading slightly faint over the flange making some letters difficult to decipher (Tomlin, below). The vessel has scoring on the flange and lower interior but not immediately adjacent to the spout. The interior appears to have a thin wash of slurry but no very clear trituration grits. The fabric is slightly coarser than the other mortaria but falls into the expected spectrum of wares from the kilns.

Other occurrences of ansate-shaped stamps have been noted at Colchester as part of the overall frame and with a rectangular surround. This includes the Verulamium potter Secundus dated A.D. 60–90 (Hartley 1999, S17; S19) and the Sexti Valerii group of potters thought to be working at Colchester in the same period (ibid., 201, fig. 4.26.84 and 105–9). Finds from this group elsewhere seem to imply production before the Boudican destruction. Hartley (ibid., 201) suggests that this group of potters, linked by the same *praenomen* and *nomen*, were freedmen who customarily took the *praenomen* and *nomen* of their former owner. The potter A. Terentius Ripanus, probably based in Gloucester, also used an ansate panel for his stamps (Birley 1949,

FIG. 56. The mortarium stamp

fig. 2.3), in this case with a herringbone border on the top and bottom. An example of this stamp came from the College of Art pottery kilns, Gloucester (Rawes 1972, fig. 8. M10). The mortaria produced by this potter have a bead lower than the flange thus resembling the Little London M1 type. Hartley (1972, 50) suggests a date of A.D. 60–90 would fit the work of A. Terentius Ripanus whose products have been documented at Alcester, Castleford, Caerleon and Wroxeter. Other examples of ansate-framed stamps include a mortarium from the Apple Tree Farm military kiln site, Heworth, York, in Eboracum oxidised ware which is dated to the early second century (Wilson and Price 2002, fig. 7.82). None of the examples of ansate stamps cited have a letter placed within the ends of the frame which currently seems unique to the Little London die.

The only direct parallel for the Little London vessel at present comes from a find made in excavations at Thames Valley Park to the east of Reading (Smith and Barnes 1997). The vessel, thought at the time to be a product from the Verulamium region, came from an enclosure ditch (Mepham 1997, fig. 37.20). It shows one surviving, poorly impressed stamp to the right of the spout interpreted as RICAII which appears to be from the same die as the Little London stamp. In total 34 sherds of Verulamium mortaria are noted as present from this site (ibid., table 13) which may well be further examples of Little London vessels.

The mortarium stamp *By R.S.O. Tomlin*

Ansate stamp, 51 by 13 mm, impressed across the flange at right-angles to it. Only four letters have registered well: the small capitals in the two *ansae*, A (left) and O (right); the first letter within the rectangular panel, which is R; and mid-way, the letter A. Between R and A, there are two letters, both quite faint: I (or possibly a narrow E) and C (or possibly G). A is followed by two verticals, both even more faint: H, II and EI are possibilities, but it rather looks as if the first 'I' extends right at the foot, suggesting LI. With these reservations, the following reading is proposed: A RICALI O

As Timby has already noted, ansate mortarium stamps are uncommon; and the only previous instance of this stamp is Mepham 1997, 62, no. 20 (said to be 'stamped RICAII on rim'), which can be read from fig. 37.20 as [.] RICAII O. There is no other ansate stamp with a letter in each *ansa*. Such a design-element was rare, to judge by legionary 'centurial' stones in Britain: these are quite often ansate, but only two have letters in the *ansae*, *RIB* 1389 and 2137, presumably the initials of centurions.

The meaning of the Little London stamp may only be conjectured. Hartley (1999, 201) has rightly suggested that the Sextus Valerius group of stamps at Colchester record different freedmen of the same master, who all took their patron's *praenomen* and *nomen* but retained their own (slave) name as a *cognomen*. By analogy with this group, the Little London stamp would be that of an A(ulus) O(...) Ricalus, who used the form *A(uli) Ricali O(...)*: his *praenomen*, *cognomen*, *nomen* in the genitive case. His most likely *nomen* would then be *O(ctavius)* or *O(ppius)*.

His *cognomen* is more difficult. *Ricalus* is unattested, but the unique name *Uricalus* is found at Bath (*Tab. Sulis* 94.1, where it is compared with *Calus*, which is attested). It is possible, though, that the potter's name was really *Regalis*. As already noted, E and G are just possible, although I and C look much more likely; but confusion may occur between unstressed <*e*> and <*i*> and between <*c*> and <*g*>. *Regalis*, although a Latin *cognomen*, was popular in Celtic-speaking provinces because it 'embodied' the Celtic name-element found in, for example, the titles of Mars Riga (*RIB* 711) and Mars Rigonemetis (*RIB* III, 3180). *Regalis* is indeed the name of a Colchester mortarium potter (Hartley 1999, S70), but although the end of the Little London name can be read as LI (genitive), there is no S: –LIS or even –IS cannot be read.

Addendum

There is a hint of a rightward stroke at the top and bottom of 'I'; and perhaps even at the middle; and likewise a short vertical stroke making 'C' into 'G'. (But the two latter traces are very slight, and may only be over-interpretation of the low, granular surface.) Nonetheless, A REGALI O, *Regali(s)* between *A* and *O*, seems a likely reading.

2. FIGS 57; 59.29. Platter forms PL1, PL3. At least seven, possibly eight, platters are stamped with what appears to be the same die. In two cases just the edge of the impression is visible. The stamps are in all cases extremely poorly defined and partly clogged with clay. In two vessels only the edge of the cartouche is visible and one is too worn to detect any letters, showing just the rectangular surround. It is difficult to tell if the letters are legible or illiterate as some appear to be, and the surrounding rectangular frame is poorly defined. In all cases the stamps are centrally placed on platter bases and in at least one case surrounded by an incised circle. Both forms PL1 and PL3 were stamped, with three or four examples occurring in grey-slipped ware (fabric K5), two in fine oxidised ware (K3) and two in fine grey ware (K2). Five vessels came from working area [2079], two from the backfill of Kiln 3 [2040] and one from Ditch 2101 slot [2060]. No other examples of this potter's work have been identified from Silchester or the surrounding area to date.

GRAFFITI

Two examples of pre-firing graffiti and three examples of post-firing graffiti were identified. The base of a mortarium from Kiln 4 (2031) had a cross on the underside made before firing (FIG. 62.85). A body sherd from Ditch 2101 slot [2062] showed the edge of a graffito at the break similarly made before firing (FIG. 62.87).

Of the three examples with post-firing graffiti, two are body sherds of kiln ware (FIG. 62.88–89) and one is a grey sandy ware with the graffito on the underside of the base (FIG. 62.86), all from Ditch 2101 slots [2060/2062].

FIG. 57. Potters' stamps on platter forms PL1 and PL3

KILN FURNITURE

At least six, very thick walled, curved sherds in kiln ware may come from saggars or some other form of kiln furniture. Only one of these, recovered from quarry pit [1048], has a rim (FIG. 62.83). The five other sherds came from the backfills of Kiln 3 [2040], mainly in fabric K7, but with one totally burnt piece. Other sherds/vessels which perhaps should be seen as potential kiln furniture are the dishes (D1) (FIG. 62.84) which are quite crudely made. There are six examples of these, three completely burnt, two in fabric K7 and one in fabric K8. Five were recovered from the upper fill of Ditch 2101 slot [2062] and one from Kiln 3 [2040].

NON-KILN WARES

THE SAMIAN *By Joanna Bird*

Trench 1

Post-hole [1089] (1088)
Plain bowl, probably Ritt. 12 rather than Curle 11, La Graufesenque, Neronian.

Trench 2

Ditch section [2060] (2041)
Drag. 29 or 37 probably, La Graufesenque. There are faint traces of what is probably moulded decoration, but nothing identifiable. Neronian to Flavian.
Drag. 27, La Graufesenque, Neronian to early Flavian.

Ditch section [2062] (2008)
Drag. 29 rim, La Graufesenque. Only fragments of the upper zone decoration survive. *c.* A.D. 60–85.
Drag. 29, La Graufesenque; probably a different vessel from the rim sherd. Traces of a possible mould signature are present below the decoration, of which only a fragment survives. *c.* A.D. 55–75.
Drag. 37 base (two sherds), La Graufesenque, early to mid-Flavian.
Drag. 27, La Graufesenque, Neronian to early Flavian.
Drag. 15/17 or 18, La Graufesenque, Neronian to Flavian.
Foot-ring, La Graufesenque, second half of first century.
Drag. 36, Les Martres-de-Veyre, probably Trajanic.

Kiln 3 [2040] stokehole (2016)
Drag. 35, La Graufesenque, Flavian.

OTHER WARES (Table 1)

Non-kiln wares make up 26.5 per cent of the assemblage by count, 30.6 per cent by weight. These comprise a mixture of imported wares and local first-century A.D. coarse wares with three second-century sherds from a Dorset black burnished ware flat-rim dish from cleaning over Trench 2. A significant proportion of the non-kiln wares, 71 per cent, were recovered from the large Ditch 2101 slots [2022/2043/2060/2062] with a further 15 per cent distributed across other Trench 2 contexts and 14 per cent from Trench 1. Imported wares include a Cam. 2 platter and Cam. type 52 dish both in Central Gaulish *terra nigra* (CNG TN) (FIG. 59.36), a carinated beaker Cam. 120 in Gallo-Belgic *terra nigra* (GAB TN) and nine sherds from a pedestal beaker in *terra rubra* (GAB TR1 A). A decorated bowl in micaceous grey ware (FIG. 61.79) from the upper fill of Ditch 2101 slot [2062], may also be a continental import. Amphorae include 14 sherds of Baetican type and a much worn handle from a Dressel 2-4, probably in a Lyon/Rhône Valley fabric.

The remaining non-kiln assemblage comprises coarse wares overwhelmingly dominated by products of the Alice Holt kilns which contribute 11.2 per cent to the overall assemblage. These include everted, bevelled and beaded rim jars, neckless jars, necked, cordoned jars/bowls (FIG. 61.80), 'Atrebatic'-type bowls and dishes (FIGS 59.37; 61.81–82), a lid, a beaker and a flask. Coarse flint-tempered Silchester wares account for a further 9.1 per cent (count) of the total assemblage and mainly comprise large jars and lids, including a fine example with a solid knob (FIG. 61.77). The remaining coarse ware assemblage consists of a range of grog-tempered wares, including a storage jar and a necked, cordoned jar (FIG. 61.78), and an iron-rich sandy ware with flint (SAFEFL). This ware is not one instantly recognisable from the Silchester assemblages but has been found on sites in the hinterland. Featured sherds include beaded rim jars and a lid. Most of the sherds come from Ditches [1181] and 2101 slots [2022/2062] and working area

[2079]. Six sherds from one handmade vessel were in the primary fill (2029) of Ditch 2101 slots [2022/2062].

MODIFIED SHERDS

A few of the bases of the kiln products had been holed and in most cases this could be accidental due to poor throwing where the bases had become too thin, or may have been a deliberate act by the potter when discarding failures. Vessels which appear to be deliberately holed include a flagon base with a foot-ring from Ditch 2101 slot [2062], a bowl (BL1) from quarry pit [1048] and possibly a vessel with four holes also from Ditch 2101 slot [2062].

A sherd from an oxidised, grog-tempered storage jar from Ditch 2101 slot [2062] (2008) appears to have an iron object piercing the wall. The item is extremely corroded but could possibly be the remains of an iron strap or repair rivet. Two base-sherds from quarry pit [1048] and Ditch 2101 slot [2060] may have been trimmed to form two circular disks or stoppers (FIG. 62.90–91). The one from quarry pit [1048] is quite abraded.

DISTRIBUTION OF POTTERY

TRENCH 1

Trackway ditch [1086] produced a total of 164 sherds weighing 2100 g and with 0.95 EVEs. No pottery was recovered from the lower fills with the first group of material coming from deposit (1062) with 85 sherds. None of these wares are kiln products, with sherds of Silchester ware, Alice Holt ware (FIG. 58.1), one calcareous-tempered ware and ten sherds of amphorae comprising Baetican and Gallic sherds. The latter features a very worn and abraded Dressel 2-4 type handle and is probably in a Lyon fabric. A further group of 26 sherds of pottery came from layer (1056), all of which are kiln fabrics including a collared-rim flagon (FIG. 58.2) suggesting that the trackway ditch had been dug and partially backfilled before the kilns were in operation. Sealing horizon (1041) with just five sherds included a mixture of kiln ware amongst which is a platter (FIG. 58.3), Baetican amphora and Alice Holt ware, whilst layer (1040) produced 48 sherds also of mixed type with kiln ware, Silchester ware, grog-tempered storage jar and a black sandy ware.

Ditch [1024] produced pottery from three levels including the primary fill (1137). In total 82 sherds weighing 678 g and with 0.44 EVEs were present. Primary fill (1137) produced 11 sherds comprising a Gallo-Belgic *terra nigra* beaker Cam. type 120 and nine fragmentary sherds from a *terra rubra* (TR1A) pedestal beaker and a grog-tempered ware jar. This group could be immediately pre- or post-conquest in date. Layers (1134/1133/1136) forming the main ditch fills were aceramic with the remaining pottery coming from the uppermost layers. Deposit (1120) contained just seven sherds, which feature kiln ware and Silchester ware, whilst fill (1112) yielded a larger assemblage of 61 sherds consisting of kiln ware, Silchester ware, Alice Holt wares and a beaded-rim jar in an iron-rich sandy fabric.

The section through quarry pit [1048] encountered a further section of ditch (1025) (ditch [1078]) with a single fill (1079) containing 31 sherds of pottery most of which come from a Silchester ware lid and a copy of a Cam. type 2 platter in grog-tempered ware (GR4). There are also five sherds of kiln ware which may be contamination from the quarry fill.

Quarry pit [1048] contained a moderately large assemblage of 274 sherds weighing 4805 g and with 4.43 EVEs. The bulk of the material is kiln waste, 75 per cent by count, with the remaining sherds mainly of Silchester ware and Alice Holt reduced ware. The kiln wares include two examples of disc-mouthed flagons (FL3) (FIG. 58.4–5), the only cheese press from the site (FIG. 58.6), a jar (type J1) (FIG. 58.8), at least two mortaria (FIG. 58.9) and four flat-rimmed bowls (BL1–2) (FIG. 58.7). One of the mortaria is worn from use and one base appears to have been deliberately holed. The group also includes a possible saggar (FIG. 62.83).

No pottery was recovered from the square pits [1106] and [1107] but very small groups of pottery came from the various other features on the site including post-holes [1014], [1045],

[1089], [1038], [1063]; gullies [1016], [1020]; and drain [1024]. With the exception of post-holes [1038] and [1089], all these features produced sherds of kiln ware indicating contemporaneity with the production period. Post-hole [1089] produced a single sherd of Neronian samian whilst post-hole [1038] had one sherd of Silchester ware.

Aside from drain [1024], the tile kiln produced very little pottery with just four abraded sherds of kiln ware from the upper fills. Kiln 2 was similarly devoid of pottery with a single sherd of grog-tempered ware from rubble (1060).

TRENCH 2

Kiln 3 [2040] and associated features (Tables 3 and 5)

Pottery from the various deposits associated with Kiln 3 [2040] amounted to some 1,799 sherds weighing just under 24 kg (Table 3). A further 138 sherds, 1.9 kg, came from later pit [2086]. The assemblage has been split into four groups: pottery from the rake-out in the stokehole area mixed with material from the upper levels of working area [2079]; pottery from within the kiln structure; material from the upper levels and demolition deposits; and finally pottery from cut [2086].

None of the pottery recovered from Kiln 3 [2040] could directly be related to the use of the kiln but was recovered from abandonment deposits within and above the kiln structure. Layers (2006), (2037–8), (2051) and (2076) collectively yielded a modest group of 201 sherds weighing 1.9 kg and with 1.21 EVEs. Forms include flagon, flat-rimmed bowls, jars and lids but no platters. A larger amount of pottery, some 1,013 sherds weighing 14.0 kg and with 14.07 EVEs, was recovered from layers overlying the kiln (2007, 2016, 2018, 2054, 2061). This contained the greatest number of non-kiln wares, although still only 8 per cent of the total. Of note amongst these is a single sherd of South Gaulish samian dish Drag. 35 dated to the Flavian period, a sherd of Baetican amphora and two Central Gaulish micaceous *terra nigra* vessels (Cam. 2 platter and Cam. 52 bowl (FIG. 59.36)), potentially of pre-conquest date. The remaining wares comprise grog-tempered ware, Silchester ware, Alice Holt reduced wares, including a 'Surrey-type' bowl (FIG. 59.37), and various reduced sandy wares. The kiln wares from these upper fills are dominated by white-fired ware (K1) and under-fired ware (K7) which together account for 73.9 per cent by sherd count followed by oxidised wares (K8) at 7.6 per cent. Each of the other wares accounts for less than 3 per cent of the assemblage. Forms include flagons (FIG. 58.11–12); bowls, including a single pod or leg (FIGS 58.15; 59.35); beakers (FIGS 58.10–18; 59.19–21); mortaria (FIG. 59.22–25); lids; platters and jars (FIG. 59.32). In terms of forms, collared-rim flagons (FL1) dominate (28.8 per cent EVE) followed by curved-wall platters (28.7 per cent), flat-rimmed bowls (17.8 per cent) and mortaria (8.7 per cent).

Working area [2079] produced a very small assemblage of three sherds of kiln ware weighing 128 g from fill (2078). The rake-out from the stokehole mixed with the upper pit levels (2071) produced a further 163 sherds of pottery, 2709 g and with 4.57 EVEs. Apart from one sherd of Silchester ware and six of Alice Holt reduced ware, the sherds are all kiln products and are particularly dominated by white wares (fabric K1) at 43 per cent count, followed by oxidised/pink wares (fabric K7) at 29.45 per cent. Just over half the rims, 50.7 per cent EVEs, comprise collared-rim flagons (FL1) (FIG. 58.13–14) followed by 36.4 per cent curved-wall platters (PL1) and a smaller number of bowls (FIG. 58.16, 18), thus mirroring the repertoire from [2079].

Pit [2086], thought to cut the kiln deposits, produced a sizeable assemblage of 138 sherds weighing 1932 g and with 3.33 EVEs. With two exceptions, the sherds are all Little London kiln wares, and are dominated by grey-slipped wares (fabric K5) followed by fine oxidised wares (fabric K3). Most of the fabric K5 sherds are curved-wall platters (types PL1, PL3) (FIG. 59.27–29) which effectively account for 58.7 per cent EVE, followed by collared-rim flagons (type FL1a) at 28 per cent EVE. Of particular note is the presence of the only two examples of dolia-type jars (Type J2) (FIG. 59.30–31); two jars with carinated shoulders (FIG. 59.33–34); a bowl (FIG. 58.17); and a lid (FIG. 59.26). The similarity of this material with that from within the kiln itself suggests the fills were derived from a similar source material. This is the largest dump of

TABLE 3. QUANTIFIED SUMMARY OF FABRICS FROM DEPOSITS ASSOCIATED WITH KILN 3 [2040]

		Kiln structure fills [2040]						Upper fills Kiln 3 [2040]						Rake-out /Working area [2079]					
Fabric	**Description**	**No.**	**No. %**	**Wt**	**Wt %**	**EVE**	**EVE %**	**No.**	**No. %**	**Wt**	**Wt %**	**EVE**	**EVE %**	**No.**	**No. %**	**Wt**	**Wt %**	**EVE**	**EVE %**
K1	white ware	151	75.5	1539	79.4	0.64	52.9	438	43.2	5702	40.5	2.95	21.0	70	42.9	1308	48.3	2.31	50.5
K2	grey sandy	0	0.0	0	0.0	0	0.0	14	1.4	144	1.0	0.35	2.5	0	0.0	0	0.0	0.00	0.0
K3	fine oxidised	0	0.0	0	0.0	0	0.0	15	1.5	347	2.5	0.73	5.2	19	11.7	384	14.2	0.43	9.4
K4	fine grey with iron specks	0	0.0	0	0.0	0	0.0	9	0.9	122	0.9	0.78	5.5	8	4.9	129	4.8	0.78	17.1
K5	grey-slipped	0	0.0	0	0.0	0	0.0	12	1.2	151	1.1	0.27	1.9	0	0.0	0	0.0	0.00	0.0
K6	hard fired grey ware	4	2.0	22	1.1	0.07	5.8	29	2.9	438	3.1	1.25	8.9	11	6.7	198	7.3	0.41	9.0
K7	oxidised pink	41	20.5	332	17.1	0.32	26.4	311	30.7	2691	19.1	4.21	29.9	48	29.4	561	20.7	0.52	11.4
K8	oxidised sandy	2	1.0	24	1.2	0.18	14.9	77	7.6	1119	8.0	1.15	8.2	0	0.0	0	0.0	0.00	0.0
K9	colour-coated whiteware	0	0.0	0	0.0	0	0.0	6	0.6	43	0.3	0	0.0	0	0.0	0	0.0	0.00	0.0
K0	burnt black	0	0.0	0	0.0	0	0.0	3	0.3	89	0.6	0	0.0	0	0.0	0	0.0	0.00	0.0
M1	whiteware mortaria	0	0.0	0	0.0	0	0.0	16	1.6	1855	13.2	0.96	6.8	0	0.0	0	0.0	0.00	0.0
M2	whiteware mortaria	0	0.0	0	0.0	0	0.0	2	0.2	505	3.6	0.15	1.1	0	0.0	0	0.0	0.00	0.0
BAT AM	Baetican amphora	0	0.0	0	0.0	0	0.0	1	0.1	16	0.1	0	0.0	0	0.0	0	0.0	0.00	0.0
CNG TN	Central Gaulish TN	0	0.0	0	0.0	0	0.0	2	0.2	56	0.4	0.3	2.1	0	0.0	0	0.0	0.00	0.0
LGF SA	South Gaulish samian	0	0.0	0	0.0	0	0.0	1	0.1	5	0.0	0.17	1.2	0	0.0	0	0.0	0.00	0.0
ALH RE	Alice Holt reduced ware	0	0.0	0	0.0	0	0.0	28	2.8	237	1.7	0.51	3.6	6	3.7	121	4.5	0.12	2.6
SIL F1	Silchester ware	1	0.5	14	0.7	0	0.0	14	1.4	210	1.5	0.21	1.5	0	0.0	0	0.0	0.00	0.0
GR	grog-tempered	0	0.0	0	0.0	0	0.0	2	0.2	21	0.1	0	0.0	1	0.6	8	0.3	0.00	0.0
GR4	grog-tempered	0	0.0	0	0.0	0	0.0	13	1.3	127	0.9	0.08	0.6	0	0.0	0	0.0	0.00	0.0
GRSA	grog-and-sand-tempered	1	0.5	8	0.4	0	0.0	0	0.0	0	0.0	0	0.0	0	0.0	0	0.0	0.00	0.0
SAFLFE	sand, flint & iron	0	0.0	0	0.0	0	0.0	0	0.0	0	0.0	0	0.0	0	0.0	0	0.0	0.00	0.0
GYFSY	fine grey sandy	0	0.0	0	0.0	0	0.0	2	0.2	19	0.1	0	0.0	0	0.0	0	0.0	0.00	0.0
GYSY	grey sandy	0	0.0	0	0.0	0	0.0	13	1.3	104	0.7	0	0.0	0	0.0	0	0.0	0.00	0.0
BWSY	black sandy	0	0.0	0	0.0	0	0.0	4	0.4	55	0.4	0	0.0	0	0.0	0	0.0	0.00	0.0
BWNF	fine brown sandy	0	0.0	0	0.0	0	0.0	1	0.1	11	0.1	0	0.0	0	0.0	0	0.0	0.00	0.0
TOTAL		**200**	**100.0**	**1939**	**100.0**	**1.21**	**100.0**	**1013**	**100.0**	**14067**	**100.0**	**14.07**	**100.0**	**163**	**100.0**	**2709**	**100.0**	**4.57**	**100.0**

grey-slipped sherds from the site with the remainder associated with the upper levels of Kiln 3 [2040].

Kiln 4 (2031) (Tables 4–5)

The primary deposit (2075) within the firing chamber was aceramic, but a moderately large group of 162 sherds, 1892 g and with 1.58 EVEs, came from layer (2074). These are all derived from kiln products with a mixture of broken oxidised and reduced sherds, the former dominating, and with examples of flagons (FL1a, FL2) (FIG. 60.38), jars (J3) (FIG. 60.47) and lids (FIG. 60.49). Backfill deposit (2063) yielded a larger group of 2,687 sherds, weighing 140 kg and with 3.93 EVEs. Apart from three sherds of Silchester ware, all the sherds are from kiln products, mostly in oxidised fabrics, some of which are over-fired, and almost exclusively comprise sherds from jars, particularly form J3 (FIG. 60.42–45), suggesting these resulted from a single failed firing, and one lid (FIG. 60.48). Upper level (2024) yielded a further 66 sherds, eight of which are Silchester ware, the remainder kiln wares with just two rims from a jar and platter and a flagon handle.

The sondage into the stoke-pit of Kiln 4 (2031) produced a further 325 sherds of pottery weighing 4373 g and with 212 EVEs from layers (2064–2066). Again, the sherds are all kiln products with the range of forms represented by just one or two vessels, including mortaria,

TABLE 4. QUANTIFIED SUMMARY OF FABRICS FROM KILN 4 (2031)

		Kiln 4 (2031)					
Fabric	**Description**	**No.**	**No. %**	**Wt**	**Wt %**	**EVE**	**EVE %**
K1	white ware	503	50.0	5310	52.8	4.85	53.9
K2	grey sandy	64	6.4	963	9.6	0.76	8.5
K3	fine oxidised	0	0.0	0	0.0	0	0.0
K4	fine grey with iron specks	0	0.0	0	0.0	0	0.0
K5	grey-slipped	0	0.0	0	0.0	0	0.0
K6	hard fired grey ware	0	0.0	0	0.0	0	0.0
K7	oxidised pink	317	31.5	2221	22.1	2.88	32.0
K8	oxidised sandy	77	7.6	663	6.6	0.33	3.7
K9	colour-coated whiteware	3	0.3	22	0.2	0	0.0
K0	burnt black	0	0.0	0	0.0	0	0.0
M1	whiteware mortaria	1	0.1	406	4.0	0	0.0
M2	whiteware mortaria	0	0.0	0	0.0	0	0.0
BAT AM	Baetican amphora	0	0.0	0	0.0	0	0.0
CNG TN	Central Gaulish TN	0	0.0	0	0.0	0	0.0
LGF SA	South Gaulish samian	0	0.0	0	0.0	0	0.0
ALH RE	Alice Holt reduced ware	5	0.5	16	0.2	0	0.0
SIL F1	Silchester ware	32	3.2	450	4.5	0.17	1.9
GR	grog-tempered	3	0.3	6	0.1	0	0.0
GR4	grog-tempered	0	0.0	0	0.0	0	0.0
GRSA	grog-and-sand-tempered	2	0.2	3	0.0	0	0.0
SAFLFE	sand, flint & iron	0	0.0	0	0.0	0	0.0
GYFSY	fine grey sandy	0	0.0	0	0.0	0	0.0
GYSY	grey sandy	0	0.0	0	0.0	0	0.0
BWSY	black sandy	0	0.0	0	0.0	0	0.0
BWNF	fine brown sandy	0	0.0	0	0.0	0	0.0
TOTAL		**1007**	**100**	**10060**	**100.0**	**8.99**	**100**

TABLE 5. DISTRIBUTION OF VESSEL TYPES ASSOCIATED WITH KILNS 3 [2040] AND 4 (2031)

			Kiln 3 [2040]		Upper fills [2040]		Rake-out		Working area [2079]		Kiln 4 (2031)	
Forms	**Type**	**Type No.**	**EVE**	**EVE %**	**EVE**	**EVE %**	**EVE**	**EVE %**	**EVE**	**EVE %**	**EVE**	**EVE %**
Kiln wares												
Flagon	collared rim	FL1	0.35	40.7	3.69	43.6	2.26	103.2	1.00	40.7	0.87	38.8
	squared rim, wide mouthed	FL2	0.00	0.0	0.00	0.0	0.00	0.0	0.00	0.0	0.15	6.7
	disc-mouthed flagon	FL3	0.00	0.0	0.00	0.0	0.00	0.0	0.00	0.0	1.00	44.6
	double-handled, triangular rim	FL4	0.00	0.0	0.53	6.3	0.00	0.0	0.00	0.0	0.00	0.0
	ring-necked	FL5	0.00	0.0	0.12	0.0	0.00	0.0	0.00	0.0	0.00	0.0
Bowl	flat rim deep bowl	BL1	0.22	25.6	2.28	27.0	0.37	16.9	0.00	0.0	0.05	2.2
	other bowls	B	0.00	0.0	0.10	1.2	0.20	9.1	0.00	0.0	0.00	0.0
Dish	curved-wall dish/kiln furniture	D1	0.00	0.0	0.07	0.8	0.00	0.0	0.00	0.0	0.00	0.0
Platter	curved-wall copy Cam. 16	PL1	0.07	8.1	3.67	43.4	1.62	74.0	2.09	85.0	0.27	12.1
Beaker	short everted rim	BK1	0.00	0.0	0.40	4.7	0.00	0.0	0.03	1.2	0.27	12.1
Jar	dolium	J2	0.00	0.0	0.32	3.8	0.00	0.0	0.10	4.1	0.35	15.6
	expanded rim neckless jar	J3	0.42	0.0	0.24	2.8	0.00	0.0	0.00	0.0	0.35	15.6
	necked jar	J4	0.00	0.0	0.00	0.0	0.00	0.0	0.24	9.8	0.00	0.0
Lid	simple domed with a plain rim	L1	0.15	17.4	0.27	3.2	0.00	0.0	0.00	0.0	0.95	42.4
Mortarium	mortarium	M1	0.00	0.0	1.11	13.1	0.00	0.0	0.00	0.0	0.00	0.0
sub-total			**0.86**	**100.0**	**8.46**	**100.0**	**2.19**	**100.0**	**2.46**	**100.0**	**2.24**	**100.0**
Non-kiln wares												
Jar	beaded rim jar		0.00	0.0	0.11	8.7	0.12	100.0	0.00	0.0	0.00	0.0
	necked jar		0.00	0.0	0.26	20.5	0.00	0.0	0.10	100.0	0.00	0.0
Bowl	'Surrey'-type bowl		0.00	0.0	0.25	19.7	0.00	0.0	0.00	0.0	0.00	0.0
	beaded rim bowl		0.00	0.0	0.08	6.3	0.00	0.0	0.00	0.0	0.00	0.0
	Cam. 52		0.00	0.0	0.24	18.9	0.00	0.0	0.00	0.0	0.00	0.0
Dish	fine ware dish		0.00	0.0	0.17	13.4	0.00	0.0	0.00	0.0	0.00	0.0
Platter	Cam. type 2		0.00	0.0	0.06	4.7	0.00	0.0	0.00	0.0	0.00	0.0
Lid			0.00	0.0	0.10	7.9	0.00	0.0	0.00	0.0	0.00	0.0
sub-total			**0.00**	**0.0**	**1.27**	**100.0**	**0.12**	**100.0**	**0.10**	**100.0**	**0.00**	**0.0**

platter (FIG. 60.41), lid, bowl, flagon (FIG. 60.39), jar (FIG. 60.46) and beaker (FIG. 60.40). One mortarium base-sherd had a pre-firing graffito in the form of a cross (FIG. 62.85).

Kiln 5 (2052)

Kiln 5 produced very little pottery. Two sherds of kiln ware, including a flagon handle, were recovered from deposit (2069) with a further 75 sherds from rubble layer (2005). The latter comprises mainly kiln wares, but also includes 20 sherds of Silchester ware and sandy grog-tempered ware. There is a single rim from a collared flagon (type FL1a).

Ditch 2101

The large linear ditch running through Trench 2 yielded a particularly large assemblage of some 2,862 sherds weighing 44.5 kg and with 34.87 EVEs (Table 6). The distribution of material across the four slots excavated is slightly uneven with the greatest amount of material by far, some 2,095 sherds, 73 per cent, coming from slot [2062] at the northern end. The lowest incidence of sherds is that from slot [2022] located nearest to the excavated Kiln 3 [2040]; with 400 and 301 sherds respectively from slots [2060] and [2043].

Slot [2022] produced some 62 sherds of which just under half are kiln wares from fills (2015) and (2021). The only featured sherds are a collared-rim flagon and lid knobs. Primary fill (2029) produced 11 sherds of non-kiln wares including Silchester ware and an iron-rich sandy

TABLE 6. QUANTIFIED SUMMARY OF FABRICS FROM DITCH 2101

		Trench 2 Ditch 2101					
Fabric	**Description**	**No.**	**No. %**	**Wt**	**Wt %**	**EVE**	**EVE %**
K1	white ware	507	17.7	7565.5	17.0	11.51	33.0
K2	grey sandy	65	2.3	895	2.0	0.77	2.2
K3	fine oxidised	2	0.1	41	0.1	0.05	0.1
K4	fine grey with iron specks	5	0.2	34	0.1	0.1	0.3
K5	grey-slipped	0	0.0	0	0.0	0	0.0
K6	hard fired grey ware	2	0.1	17	0.0	0.06	0.2
K7	oxidised/ pink	712	24.9	6510	14.6	3.89	11.2
K8	oxidised sandy	379	13.2	4943	11.1	5.38	15.4
K9	colour-coated whiteware	5	0.2	766	1.7	0.67	1.9
K0	burnt black	8	0.3	230	0.5	0.51	1.5
M1	whiteware mortaria	22	0.8	2152	4.8	0.66	1.9
BAT AM	Baetican amphora	6	0.2	880	2.0	0	0.0
LGF SA	South Gaulish samian	10	0.3	138	0.3	0.11	0.3
ALH RE	Alice Holt reduced ware	499	17.4	4950	11.1	6.35	18.2
SIL F1	Silchester ware	444	15.5	10745	24.1	3.71	10.6
GR	grog-tempered	3	0.1	22	0.0	0.03	0.1
GR4	grog-tempered	7	0.2	66	0.1	0	0.0
GRSA	grog-and-sand-tempered	3	0.1	64	0.1	0.2	0.6
OXGR	grog-tempered storage jar	155	5.4	4092	9.2	0.41	1.2
SAFLFE	sand, flint & iron	9	0.3	247	0.6	0.1	0.3
GYFSY	fine grey sandy	3	0.1	38	0.1	0.1	0.3
GYSY	grey sandy	10	0.3	75	0.2	0.03	0.1
BWSY	black sandy	6	0.2	58	0.1	0.23	0.7
TOTAL		**2862**	**100**	**44528.5**	**100**	**34.87**	**100**

and flint-tempered ware. Slot [2043] to the south produced some 299 sherds weighing 5,038 g. A significant amount of this, 69 per cent by count, comprises sherds of flint-tempered Silchester ware. Kiln products contribute just 10 per cent by count, 16 per cent by weight, with examples of collared flagon, mortaria and flat-rimmed, hemispherical bowls. Slot [2060] produced some 400 sherds of which 68 per cent are kiln products with quite a diverse range of forms, including lids, curved-wall platters, collared flagons, flat-rim bowls and a single pod. Two sherds of South Gaulish samian from (2041) are attributed a Neronian–early Flavian date (see Bird above). Silchester ware is again well-represented along with a small quantity of Alice Holt ware and other early or pre-Roman local wares. The primary fill (2049) contained just 15 sherds of local handmade coarse wares including the knob from a Silchester ware lid. Kiln wares start showing up in abundance from (2041) alongside a variety of other wares.

The northernmost slot, [2062], was ceramically the most prolific with some 2,095 sherds weighing 44.5 kg, but also the most fragmented of the ditch groups. Some 65.6 per cent of the assemblage by count comprises kiln products which might strongly suggest further kiln structures to the north beyond the trench. The lowest fill (2088) produced eight sherds of kiln waste followed by a further 788 sherds from layer (2027). This group is exceptional in that 94.3 per cent is composed of kiln products with multiple examples of flagon, mortaria and lids with a few flat-rimmed bowls and the only tazza from the site (FIG. 61.76). The flagons are dominated by collared-rim types with a minimum number of 17 vessels accompanied by four ring-necked forms and single examples of types FL3 and FL6 (FIG. 60.50–58). Horizon (2019) with 393 sherds is similarly dominated by kiln waste, 88.7 per cent. Over half the sherds from this slot came from upper fill (2008) with some 801 sherds. This group has a high proportion of Alice Holt grey wares (39 per cent count) along with 12 per cent Silchester ware and 14 per cent oxidised grog-tempered storage jar. The Alice Holt ware includes at least three 'Surrey' or 'Atrebatic'-type bowls. Also present are eight sherds of South Gaulish samian, with one base of early–mid-Flavian date and one sherd possibly Trajanic. Kiln wares contribute 33 per cent and include examples of ring-necked flagon, mortaria, curved-wall dishes and a perforated lid knob. The tenor of the group from (2008) is slightly later than the other ditch assemblages and it may represent a slightly later re-cut into the top of the ditch or simply later backfilling.

Looking at the assemblage from Ditch 2101 overall (Table 6), kiln wares make up just under 60 per cent by count, 52 per cent by weight of the assemblage, with a diverse range of products. All the identified fabrics are present apart from the grey-slipped variant (fabric K5). The under-fired fabric K7 accounts for nearly 25 per cent by sherd count but just 14.6 per cent by weight, reflecting its softer nature. White-fired wares account for 17 per cent by count and 17.7 per cent by weight. Overall, collared-rim flagons (Type FL1) dominate, accounting for 65 per cent EVE, followed by flat-rim bowls (Type B1/2) (FIG. 60.59) at 10.2 per cent EVE, ring-necked flagons at 5.6 per cent EVE and mortaria at 3.9 per cent EVE. Other forms include bowls (FIG. 61.60–61); platters (FIG. 61.62); beakers (FIG. 61.63); mortaria (FIG. 61.64–67); lids (FIG. 61.68–71) and jars (FIG. 61.72–75). The non-kiln wares (FIG. 61.77–80, 82) are dominated by Silchester ware, which makes up nearly 25 per cent by weight, but also include Baetican amphora, Alice Holt grey ware, South Gaulish samian and local, indigenous coarse wares. Jars dominate the form range with several larger storage vessels. Four examples of simple graffiti feature amongst the ditch assemblage, three on kiln products and one on a local coarse ware (FIG. 62.86–89).

CATALOGUE OF ILLUSTRATED SHERDS

Trench 1: Trackway ditch [1086]

1. Narrow-mouthed jar or beaker with a small, slightly concave lip. Black sandy ware with a dark red-brown core. Probably an Alice Holt product. (1062).
2. Collared-rim flagon type FL1b. Fabric: K1. (1056).
3. Curved-wall platter type PL1. Fabric: K8. (1041).

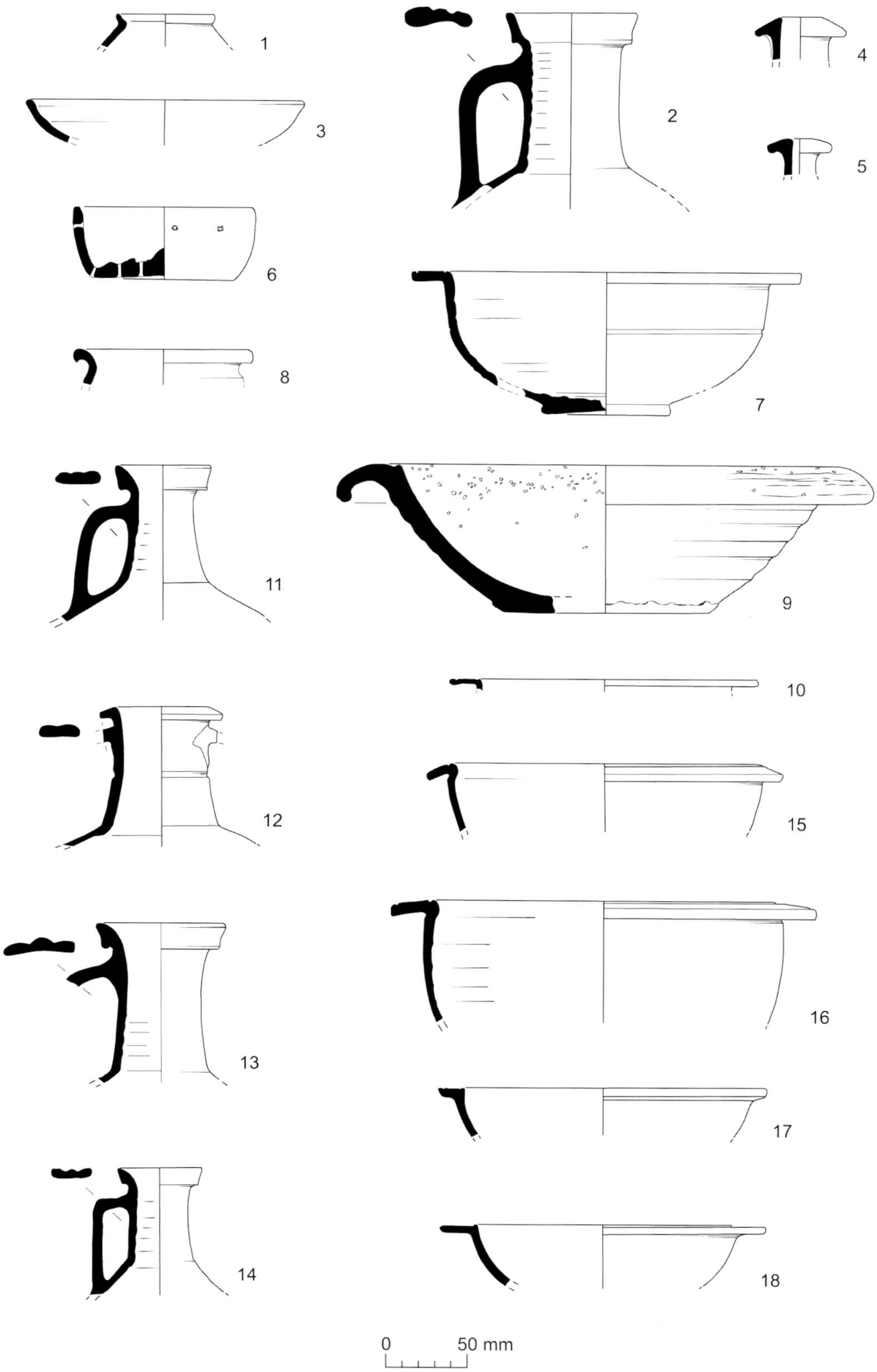

FIG. 58. Pottery from Trench 1 trackway ditch [1086] (1–3), quarry pit [1048] (4–9), Kiln 2 (1145) (10), and Trench 2 Kiln 3 [2040] (11–18) (Scale 1:4)

Trench 1: quarry pit [1048]

4. Disc-mouthed flagon type FL3. Fabric: K1. (1046).
5. Small version of flagon type FL3. Fabric: K7. (1046).
6. Small cheese press with a perforated floor and wall. The holes were made before firing but have spalled on the outside of the base. Fabric: K8. (1046).
7. Flat-rim hemispherical bowl with two grooves on the upper surface, variant of type BL1. The centre of the base is holed, possibly deliberately. Fabric: K7. (1030).
8. Small jar with a slightly hooked rim and slight shoulder carination, type J1. Fabric: K1. (1046).
9. Mortarium type M1. The lower interior is worn smooth from use. Fabric: K1. (1043).

Trench 1: Kiln 2

10. Flanged rim bowl, BL7. Small fragment. Fabric: K4. (1145).

Trench 2: Kiln 3 [2040]

11. Collared-rim flagon type FL1a. Fabric: K1. (2061).
12. Double-handled flagon type FL4. Fabric: K1. (2061).
13. Collared-rim flagon type FL1a. Fabric: K1. (2071).
14. Collared-rim flagon type FL1a. Fabric: K7. (2071).
15. Flat-rim bowl, type BL1 variant with a single groove. Fabric: K1. (2054).
16. Flat-rim bowl, type BL1 variant with two grooves. Fabric: K7. (2071).
17. Flanged-rim bowl, type BL5. Fabric: K8. (2037).
18. Shallow, hemispherical bowl with a flat flange and a small beaded rim, type BL6. Fabric: K7. (2071).
19. Beaker type BK2. Fabric: K3. (2061).
20. Beaker type BK3. Fabric: K3. (2061).
21. Beaker type BK3. Fabric: K2. (2054).
22. Mortarium type M1. K1 variant. The vessel has scoring on the flange and lower interior but not immediately adjacent to the spout. The interior appears to have a thin wash of slurry but no very clear trituration grits. Impressed stamp to right of spout. Stamp set within an ansate-shaped frame. Reading slightly faint over the flange; possible reading: A REGALI O. (2061) (p. 59).
23. Mortarium type M1 with a simple spout. (2054).
24. Mortarium type M2. (2054).
25. Mortarium with a double-beaded rim, type M5. Upper fill of [2084].
26. Simple lid type L1. Fabric: K1. (2037).
27. Curved-wall platter type PL1. Fabric: K4. (2072).
28. Curved-wall platter with a shallow foot-ring, type PL1. Outline of a central abraded stamp with no letters visible. Fabric: K4. (2073), SF 212.
29. Curved-wall platter with a slightly beaded rim, type PL3. Central illegible stamp set within a double incised circle. Fabric: K5. (2072), SF 209 (p. 61).
30. Flat rim dolium-type jar J2. Fabric: K1. (2072).
31. Flat rim dolium-type jar J2. Fabric: K1. (2072).
32. Wide-mouthed jar with a short everted rim, type J5. Fabric: K1. (2054).
33. Jar type J7 with a high carinated shoulder. Fabric: K7. (2037).
34. Jar type J7 with a high carinated shoulder. Fabric: K4. (2072).
35. Single vessel leg (pod) with a slight depression at the base. Round cross-section. Form BL8. Fabric: K7. (2054).
36. Flared bowl Cam. type 52. Fabric: CNG TN. Surfaces abraded. (2061).
37. Wheel-made 'Surrey-type' bowl. Fabric: ALH RE (black variant). (2054).

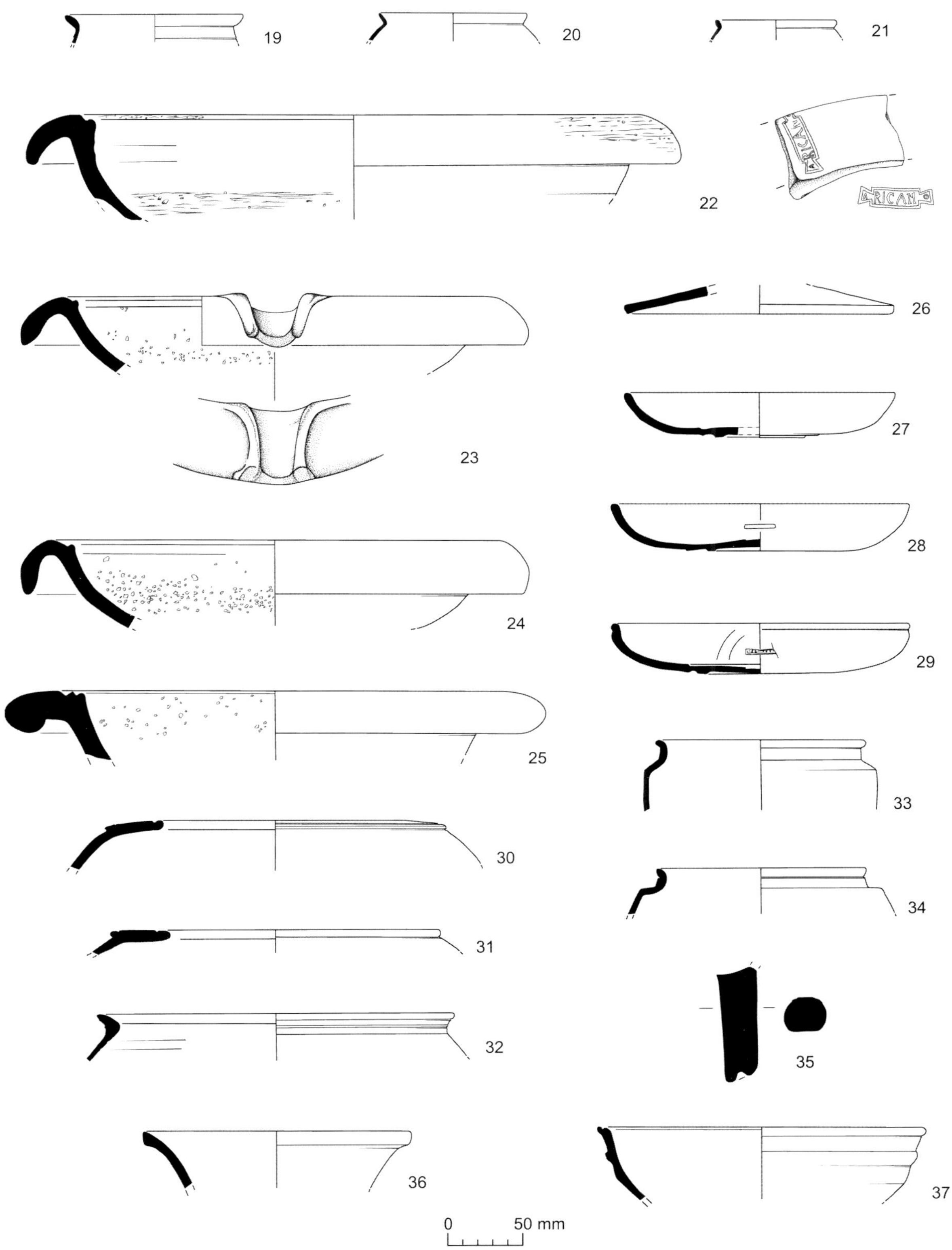

FIG. 59. Pottery from Trench 2 Kiln 3 [2040] (19–37) (Scale 1:4)

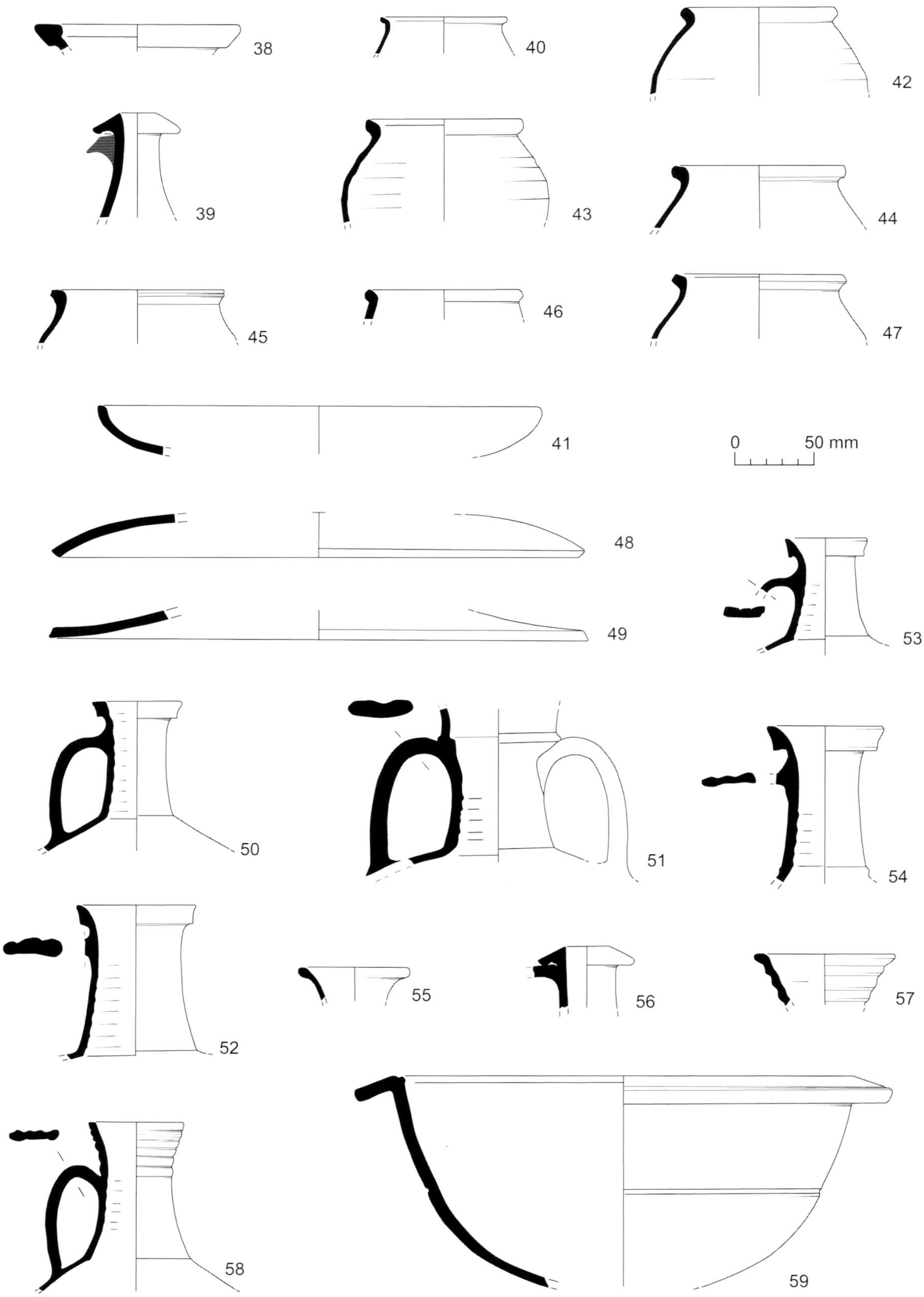

FIG. 60. Pottery from Kiln 4 (2031) (38–49) and Trench 2 Ditch 2101 (50–59) (Scale 1:4)

Trench 2: Rectangular Kiln 4 (2031)

38. Collared-rim flagon thickened on the interior. Type FL2. Fabric: K2. Kiln chamber backfill (2074).
39. Single-handled, disc-mouthed flagon FL3. Fabric: K7. Stoke-pit backfill (2066).
40. Beaker type BK1. Fabric: K1. Stoke-pit backfill (2066).
41. Curved-wall platter type PL1. Fabric: K8. Stoke-pit backfill (2066)
42. Jar type J3 with a slightly facetted body. Fabric: K1. Deposit (2063).
43. Jar type J3 with a slightly facetted body. Fabric: K1. Deposit (2063).
44. Jar type J3. Fabric: K1. Deposit (2063).
45. Jar type J8 with an externally grooved rim. Fabric: K7. Deposit (2063).
46. Jar type J3. Fabric: K1. Stoke-pit backfill (2066).
47. Jar type J3. Fabric: K1. Chamber backfill (2074).
48. Large lid, type L1. Fabric: K2. Deposit (2063).
49. Large lid type L1. Fabric: K2. Chamber backfill (2074).

Trench 2: Ditch 2101

50. Collared-rim flagon, type FL1c. Fabric: K1. Ditch slot [2060] (2041).
51. Funnel-mouthed, double-handled flagon, type FL7. Fabric: K1. Ditch slot [2060] (2041).
52. Single-handled, collared-rim flagon, type FL1a. Fabric: K1. Ditch slot [2062] (2019).
53. Single-handled, collared-rim flagon, type FL1a. Fabric: K1. Ditch slot [2062] (2019).
54. Single-handled, collared-rim flagon, type FL1a. Fabric: K1 (over-fired). Ditch slot [2062] (2027).
55. Flared-rim flagon type FL6. Fabric: K1. Ditch slot [2062] (2027).
56. Disc-mouthed flagon type FL3. Fabric: K9. Ditch slot [2062] (2027).
57. Ring-necked flagon type FL5. Fabric: K1 (over-fired). Ditch slot [2062] (2027).
58. Ring-necked flagon type FL5. Fabric: K1 (over-fired). Ditch slot [2062] (2008).
59. Large hemispherical bowl, type BL1. Fabric: K1 with a grey inner core and pale orange margins. Ditch slot [2062] (2019).
60. Bowl type BL3. Fabric: K1. Ditch slot [2062] (2019).
61. Short flat-rim bowl, probably grooved, type BL4. Ditch slot [2060] (2034).
62. Curved-wall platter type PL2. Fabric: K2. Ditch slot [2062] (2019).
63. Beaker type BK3. Fabric: K7. Ditch slot [2062] (2013).
64. Abraded rim of a mortarium type M3. Fabric: K1. Ditch slot [2043] (2028).
65. Mortarium type M2 with sparse flint trituration grits. Fabric: K7. Ditch slot [2060] (2041).
66. Mortarium type M2. Fabric: K7. Ditch slot [2062] (2027).
67. Mortarium type M4. Fabric: K1 with a blackened interior and flange. Ditch slot [2062] (2019).
68. Small, simple, concave lid with a single perforation made before firing (L1). Fabric: K1. Ditch slot [2062] (2019).
69. Small, simple, flat lid with a single perforation made before firing (L2). Fabric: K8. Ditch slot [2062] (2027).
70. Simple lid type L1. Fabric: K1. Ditch slot [2062] (2019).
71. Perforated base from a possible strainer. Holes made before firing. Fabric: K8. Ditch slot [2062] (2008).
72. Expanded rim, wide-mouthed jar (J3). Fabric: K2. Ditch slot [2062] (2027).
73. Necked jar/bowl J4. Fabric: K2. Ditch slot [2062] (2019).
74. Necked jar/bowl J4. Fabric: K2. Ditch slot [2062] (2019).
75. Cordon-necked jar, form J6. Fabric: K2. Ditch slot [2062] (2019).
76. Tazza. Fabric: ?K8 burnt. Ditch slot [2062] (2027).
77. Handmade lid with a solid knob. Fabric: Silchester ware. Ditch slot [2060] (2049).
78. Handmade, cordon-necked jar. Fabric: GRSA. Ditch slot [2060] (2049).

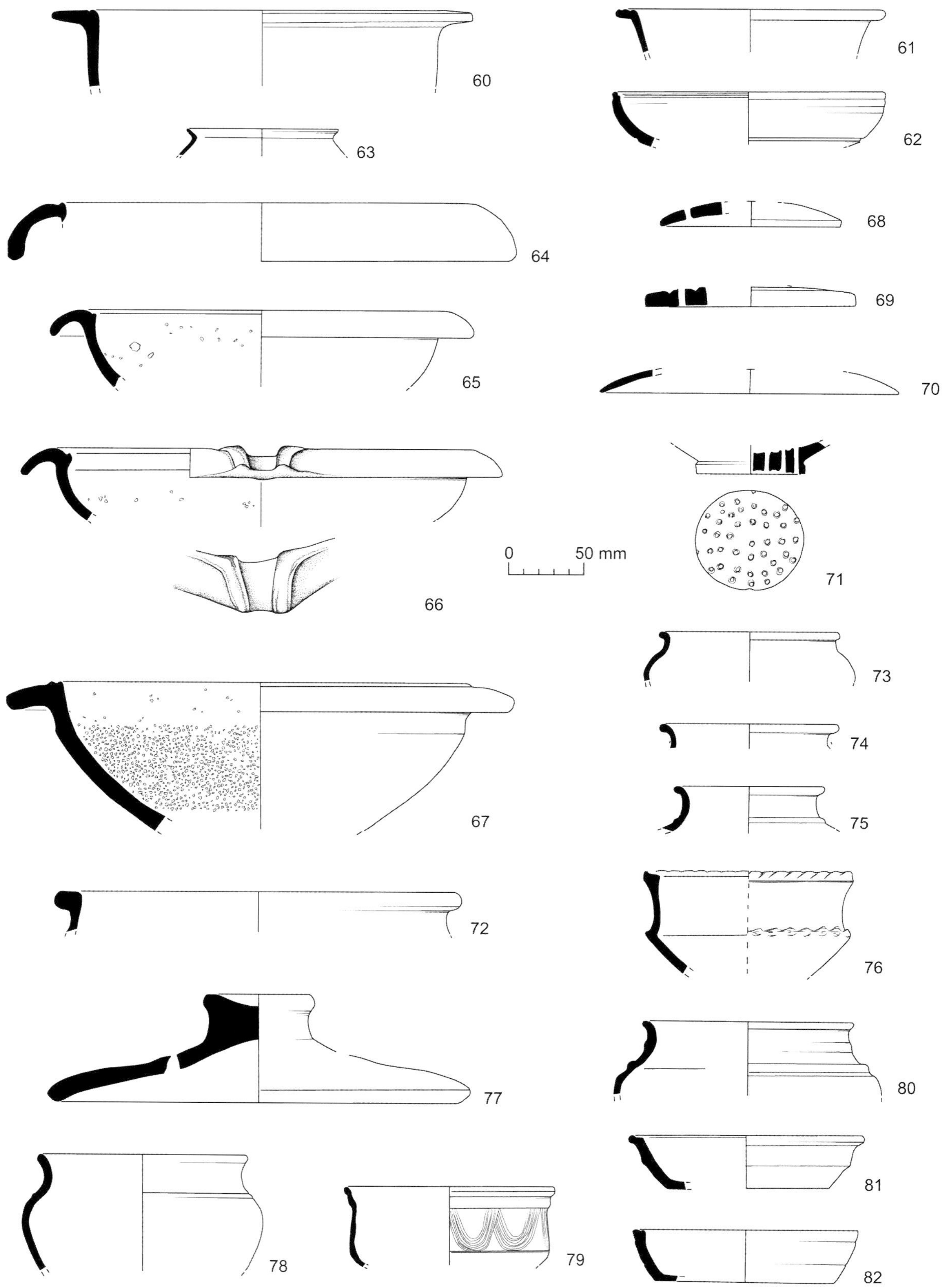

FIG. 61. Pottery from Trench 2 Ditch 2101 (60–82) (Scale 1:4)

79. Small bowl loosely copying a samian bowl with lightly combed decoration. Fabric: GYFMIC. Ditch slot [2062] (2008).
80. Wide cordon-necked jar. Fabric: ALH RE. Ditch slot [2062] (2008).
81. Shallow variant of an Atrebatic bowl (Lyne and Jefferies 1979, Class 5). Fabric: ALH RE (black variant). Burnt. Ditch slot [2062] (2008).
82. Dish with a single groove on top of the rim. Fabric: ALH RE (black variant). Ditch slot [2062] (2008).

Kiln furniture

83. Probable saggar or kiln spacer. Thick-walled powdery oxidised ware as fabric K8. Quarry pit [1048] (1036).
84. Dish or kiln furniture, D1. Fabric: K8. Ditch slot [2062] (2008).

Graffiti

85. Base of a mortarium with flint trituration grits. A cross was inscribed on the base before firing. Fabric: K1. Fill of Kiln 4 (2031) stokehole (2066).
86. Base from a closed form with a post-firing graffito incised onto the underside. Fabric: GYSY. Ditch slot [2060] (2041), SF 205.
87. Body sherd with edge of graffito incised before firing. Fabric: K7. Ditch slot [2062] (2027).
88. Body sherd with part of a simple graffito made after firing. Fabric: K7. Ditch slot [2062] (2027).
89. Body sherd with graffito incised after firing. Fabric: K7. Ditch slot [2062] (2027).

Modified sherds

90. Flat base-sherd with an abraded break possibly suggesting re-use. Fabric: K1. Quarry pit [1048] (1023), SF 5.
91. Trimmed base-sherd. Fabric: K7. Ditch slot [2060] (2026). SF 203.

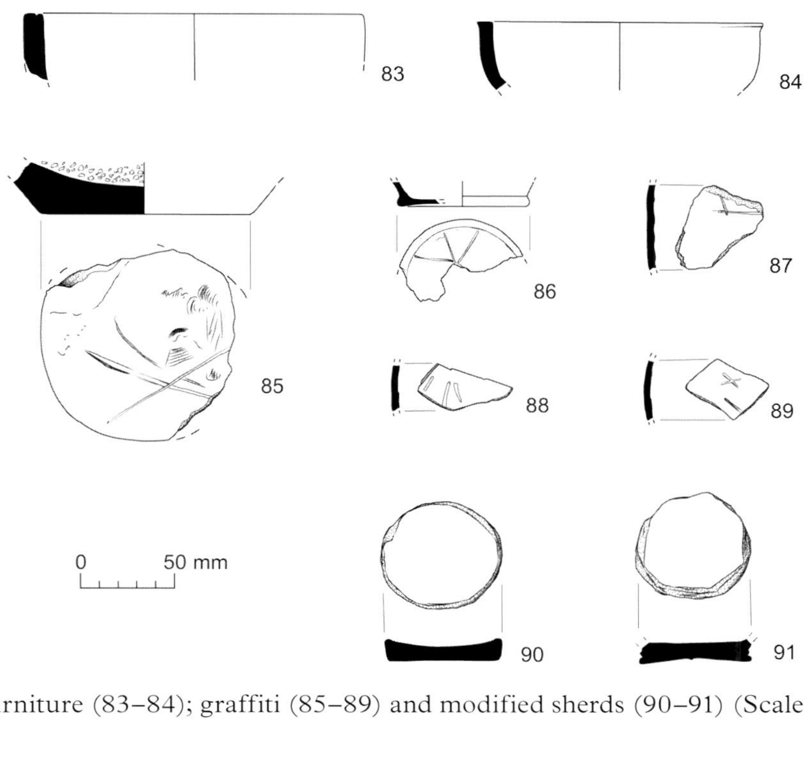

FIG. 62. Kiln furniture (83–84); graffiti (85–89) and modified sherds (90–91) (Scale 1:4)

DISCUSSION

FORMS

The pottery assemblage recovered from Little London can be dated to the Neronian–early Flavian period on typological grounds; from the association with a nearby tile kiln producing Neronian stamped tiles and from the dating of the small quantity of associated samian. As with all kiln excavations, unless the final load of pottery had been abandoned *in situ* in the chamber, it is uncertain whether pottery recovered from the kiln structures represents waste from the use of that particular kiln or from an adjacent kiln(s). The only kiln on the site to contain much pottery was Kiln 3 [2040] and the very mixed nature of the debris from the fills, with both reduced and oxidised wares present, strongly suggests this was not the debris from a single last firing of this kiln, but waste which had accumulated from the general area after its abandonment. A kiln assemblage also represents the failures and may not necessarily reflect the complete range of output. In the case of Little London it is not possible to directly link the production of a specific vessel form to any particular structure and there are undoubtedly further kilns at the location. The paucity of associated finds from the other kilns and a general similarity of material make it impossible to sequence the operation of the kilns or link them with the firing of a specific product.

The range of vessels produced at Little London is distinctly Roman in character, with flagons, mortaria and tableware amongst other types. Whilst quite a wide range of types has been defined, many are present as single examples. On the basis of the recovered pottery, collared-rim flagons, flat-rim bowls and curved-wall platters are the most frequent types found, suggesting that these were the main forms produced. This would reflect the prevalence of these particular forms elsewhere at this time. However, whilst it is possible to individually parallel many of the types made with those made at other broadly contemporary production sites in Britain, both military and civilian, it is difficult at present to find a direct parallel which embraces all, or a significant number of the individual types, most notably the platters, alongside the other wares. Some key contemporary production sites, for example, Eccles, Kent, have not been published in detail, whilst other sites such as Oaksey, Minety, Wilts., have been subjected to extremely limited excavation and publication. More useful comparison can be made with production sites in the Verulamium area, specifically Bricket Wood and Brockley Hill.

As noted above flagons are a particular feature of the Little London kilns and account for 52 per cent EVE of the complete assemblage. The most ubiquitous type, and perhaps the most difficult to make, is the collared-rim flagon (FL1) accounting for 32.7 per cent overall (Table 2). This was made at many sites in the Claudian–early Flavian period and can be shown to have an Augustan military pedigree on the Continent (Greene 1993, 17). The general form was made at military, or assumed military, kilns at the legionary fortresses at Usk, Longthorpe and Kingsholm amongst others, and at civilian or presumed civilian kilns, for example, those in the Verulamium area, Eccles, Minety, Duxford, Hoo (Blumstein 1956), Canterbury (Jenkins 1956), possibly Sugar Loaf Court, London (Chadburn and Tyers 1984) and Colchester (see Table 7). There are minor variations in the rim shape, perhaps most notably at Longthorpe and Duxford, where the external face is slightly concave and undercut, presumably reflecting the quirks or background of individual potters. At Little London significant concentrations of the form were recovered from the Trench 2 boundary ditch and Kilns 3 [2040] and 4 (2031). Although the fabric was not known when the bulk of the Silchester Insula IX and Forum Basilica assemblages were recorded and, if present, would have probably been recorded as Verulamium-type ware, there have been negligible examples of collared-rim flagons in the Silchester assemblages. In Britain, although not necessarily on the Continent (Tyers, pers. comm.), the trend is for collared-rim flagons to be succeeded by the ring-necked form from the early Flavian period. The ring-necked flagon (FL5), also made at many of the production sites cited above, with the exception of Duxford, is generally quite rare in Silchester as a whole. The low incidence of this form at Little London could suggest that the kilns had been abandoned before the form became popular, supported by the fact that all the examples documented came from the upper fills of

Ditch 2101. The disc-necked flagon (FL3), another form with a strong continental pedigree, was also quite widely produced, although never common. Examples have been found at the Verulamium kilns, Eccles and Colchester. A similar picture is presented by the *Camulodumum* type 169/170 (FL7), although only one example of this type was recognised at Little London. Types FL2, FL4 and FL6 are also rare occurrences at Little London and seemingly not popular types elsewhere.

An analogous pattern is shown with the bowls in that the most common forms at Little London, namely those with horizontal or dropped flanges (BL1, BL3), were extensively made at the Verulamium kilns and feature at Colchester and Usk. Other bowl forms are rarer, although examples of BL3–5 feature in the Bricket Wood assemblage. Beakers are not particularly common in any of the assemblages, although it can be observed that butt beakers were made at Verulamium and probably at Eccles but do not feature at Little London.

In terms of tableware, the curved-wall platters (PL1) with functional foot-rings, in oxidised, reduced and grey-slipped wares are a particular feature at Little London, contributing 13.15 per cent EVE to the assemblage. Some vessels bear an illiterate potter's stamp (see above). These forms can be directly linked back to the Gallo-Belgic form Cam. type 16 and were widely made on the Continent. This style of platter was particularly common at the Roman fort at Hofheim where Ritterling (1913) suggests it dated from at least A.D. 40. This was one of the latest forms to feature in the Gallo-Belgic potters' repertoire and is one of the few Gallo-Belgic products, along with cups Cam. type 58 and bowls Cam. type 46, to be associated with early military sites in Britain although by no means exclusively. The main import period falls between *c.* A.D. 40 and 70. Although in general terms the form was widely copied in Britain, the only close parallels for the production of similar fine ware platter imitations so close to the originals in Britain come from Eccles, where there are also copies of Cam. types 8, 12–14 as well as stamped 16s, and Colchester, where examples with imitation stamps came from a grave in Colchester West cemetery (May 1930, 290–1) dated to the Neronian period. Examples were also recovered in association with collared flagons in Colchester kilns 34 and 35 (Niblett 1985, 51) and from Wherstead, Suffolk (Rigby 2001). Curved-wall platters were made at Usk, but show an external base angle and the foot-ring is not always functional (Greene 1993, 41, type 29.2). Most of the military vessels appear to be copying the flat-based Pompeian red ware form which presumably functioned more as a cooking vessel. Wares with imitation stamps were also made at a few other production, or presumed production, sites in Britain, but are either slightly later in date, for example, Wiggonholt, Sussex (Evans 1974) and West Stow, Suffolk (Rigby 1990) or not on Cam. type 16 platters, as at Keston, Kent (Philp 1999) or Rushden, Northants. (Woods and Hastings 1984).

The cheese press is another rare form in early contexts but appears at Eccles, Usk and amongst early pottery groups at Brockley Hill (Seeley and Thorogood 1994). The type was particularly popular with the military potters at Longthorpe fort (Dannell and Wild 1987, 151), but this seems to be exceptional.

Jars are less easy to directly compare and most production sites manufactured vessels showing a diversity of rim and body shape. Two particular types, however, can be highlighted: first, Little London type J2 with the flat dolia-type rim which is quite rare. Dolia-type vessels do feature among the Usk fortress coarse wares (Greene 1993, type 17) but these vessels, which Greene (ibid., 34) traces back to forms found in Republican Italy, differ considerably in the rim detail. Typologically closer examples of dolia were made by the XXth Legion at the Novaesium kilns (Filtzinger 1972, taf. 69, abb. 9, 11–13). Another close parallel for the form comes from two examples from a kiln site excavated in Gloucester (Rawes 1972, fig. 5.51–2), which would also have probably developed from the military kilns set up at Gloucester. Interestingly the XXth Legion was also stationed there for a period of time. The form also features at Camulodunum (Cam. type 275) in Roman and native ware but with just three examples in Roman 'buff' ware.

The other jar form found at Little London which appears to have a direct continental antecedence is type J7 with the high carinated shoulder. Identical jars were produced at Brockley Hill (Castle 1973a, fig. 2.4–5), with similar vessels with high shoulders from Eccles (Detsicas 1977, fig. 3.4.83) and Usk (Greene 1993, type 13). Tyers (1998, 226) considers the type to originate from the Lyon area whilst Greene (1993, fig. 12) shows the distribution to be focused in a zone extending eastwards from central France across Switzerland with a scatter of examples along the Rhine.

The mortaria found at Little London account for 4.04 per cent of the kiln assemblage and show great diversity of form, although all fall within the flange and beaded category as opposed to the wall-sided forms more common in pre- and early Roman contexts in Britain. Both types were made at Novaesium (Filtzinger 1972) and the flanged form, including stamped examples, was made at Lyon in the second half of the first century A.D. (Saison-Guichon 2001, fig. 4). In general terms, examples with a bead lower than the flange can be paralleled at the Verulamium and Eccles kiln sites and are found in many Neronian and early Flavian assemblages. A single stamped mortarium was recovered from the flue of Kiln 3 [2040] (FIGS 56; 59.22) (see above). It is presumed that this vessel was made on site, although the absence of trituration grits stands it apart from the other mortaria. The stamp set within the ansate-shaped frame is unusual and the die currently unique; it is a style more often associated with legionary stamped tile. One aspect to be addressed, but impossible to determine, is whether the mortaria production should be seen as separate from the other wares, and whether any of the kilns were designated specifically for the firing of these considerably heavier vessels, which may have required higher firing temperatures. The association of mortaria and other stamped vessels alongside tile production has been attested at some of the Italian brickyards in the Tiber Valley and Campania (Hartley 1973). Here, where there was a regular practice of stamping tile, it has been observed that the same names occur on both the tile and mortaria (ibid.). There are several instances of mortaria being made at certain tileries, for example, Holt, Eccles, Minety and perhaps the Verulamium region, but not stamped with the same die stamp. In Britain there have only been eight recorded examples of mortaria and tile being impressed with procuratorial stamps using the same die stamp, all from London (Betts 1995; Hartley 1996). This strongly suggests they were being made in the same workshop(s) although using different clays. At least three of the six mortaria with procuratorial stamps from London examined by Hartley (1996, 148) are identified as typical of the Verulamium kilns and the other three examples, although not totally typical, fall into the same broad group. They are attributed a date range of A.D. 80/90–120. There is little evidence the tiles from the Watling Street tileries were stamped, although Suggett (1953, 186) found two fragments both showing the letter N retrograde (Betts 1995, die type 8). Unfortunately, both fragments are now lost and cannot be verified. Clearly such instances are a rarity but the presence of the ansate-shaped stamp with clearly defined letters strengthens an official link between the production of the mortaria and the tile at Little London. However, as Hartley (1996) points out, the method used to make tiles is quite different to that used to make mortaria, so it is possible the potter making mortaria was also making other vessels.

The double-beaded mortaria (types M4, M5) by contrast appear to be a particularly rare variety and do not feature amongst the types made at the Verulamium potteries. A broadly similar example is published from Exeter (Hartley 1991, 194, type TC4) from the late military levels (*c.* A.D. 50–*c.* 85). This vessel, made in a non-local fabric, was regarded as a potential import and recently western France, specifically Brittany, has been suggested as a possible source (Hartley and Tomber 2006, 26; Bidwell 2021). Typologically, the Exeter vessel differs slightly in that the bead nearest the flange is slightly smaller than the inner bead whereas in the Little London examples the beads are of similar size. A mortarium stamped by the potter Lesbius from Colchester, dated A.D. 50–80, may also come from the same workshop as the Exeter vessel; the only other parallel is from Nanstallon, Cornwall (Hartley 1999, 198) although the rim profile differs. The Nanstallon assemblage also features an unstamped double-beaded mortarium (Fox and Ravenhill 1972, fig. 22.6). Another close parallel, particularly for type M5, comes from a vessel published from Richborough, described as being made of hard, pinkish white clay with grit in the interior surface (Bushe Fox 1932, 185 and pl. 41.355). The vessel came from the late first-century filling of the Claudian ditch. Although the sample is small, if the mortaria are related to types made in western Gaul, not only do they show a distribution strongly biased towards the South-West (cf. Bidwell 2021, fig. 12.6), but the unusual profiles may have some ramifications for the cultural origins of the potter who was making the Little London vessels.

Products which do not feature amongst the output from the Little London kilns, but which were made at the Verulamium region kilns, include butt beakers, honey pots and open lamps. Lamps also feature in pottery made at the military kilns at Usk, Kingsholm and Longthorpe and at potentially non-military kilns such as Sugar Loaf Court and Brockley Hill. In addition, a number of sites, for example, Eccles, Sugar Loaf Court and Colchester, were also producing fine cups and roughcast beakers comparable to wares being produced in Central and Southern Gaul. In the light of the recent discovery of an early fort at London (Dunwoodie *et al.* 2015), the Sugar Loaf Court kilns may in fact have a military link (see below). Of the various production sites discussed above, at least four — Brockley Hill, Eccles, Oaksey and Canterbury — had tileries (see discussion below).

POTTERY PRODUCTION AT LITTLE LONDON

The vessels produced at Little London are the products of specialist potters familiar with Roman forms, kiln construction and the use of white-firing clays. These are not indigenous potters experimenting with new forms, but potters familiar with continental types and the most likely candidates are either those individuals brought across the Channel with the Roman army at the conquest or craftsmen following in its wake. Initially, many of the Claudio-Neronian military establishments appear to have been producing pottery for their own consumption, supplementing any available local pottery. Many forms regularly used in Roman cooking and dining practices did not exist in pre-Roman Britain other than as imports. It would seem likely that, in the first instance, before the necessary supply systems could be established, the army would have been self-sufficient bringing essential stock and equipment as part of the baggage train. It has been noted that the earliest military levels excavated in the legionary fortress at Colchester show an overall paucity of imported fine wares, with the exception perhaps of samian, and no imported mortaria (Timby 2004). There was, however, evidence of locally made military products from the earliest layers (A.D. 44–49), with examples of Colchester mortaria, colour-coated ware, fine black and grey wares, oxidised cream and orange tablewares and coarser, oxidised and reduced grey wares. This would suggest the necessary expertise was immediately available to start 'on-site' production of pottery and probably other items of essential equipment. Hartley (1985, 92) also observed that it was very likely that mortaria would have been made at Colchester soon after A.D. 43.

A similar situation prevailed at other early military sites, for example, Kingsholm/Gloucester, Usk, Wroxeter and Longthorpe. The assemblages from these sites all share a very characteristic profile of forms, featuring flagons, mortaria, honey pots, face pots, bowls, cups, cheese presses and open lamps, most, or all, of which are reflected in the assemblages from the military forts along the Rhine. Comparison with the Claudio-Neronian military kilns at Longthorpe (Dannell and Wild 1987) demonstrates that, whilst the same broad complement of types feature — namely, flagons, bowls, beakers, platters, mortaria, dishes, jars, lids and cheese presses — there are considerable differences in the typological detail. The flagons do not have the simple collared-rim profile, but are more moulded externally and there are no ring-necked examples. The few mortaria comprise wall-sided forms and an unusual flanged type (Hartley 1987, fig. 35); the beakers are predominantly cornice-rim types and the platters mainly copy samian types. Additional forms include small hemispherical cups imitating Central Gaulish forms, lamp filler or feeding bottles and open lamps. At Usk there is again considerable overlap in forms in terms of flagons, flanged-rim bowls and some jars, but less so in terms of the mortaria, which equate to Cam. type 192, while the platters generally have non-functional or no foot-rings. Distinctive types made at Usk but not found at Little London include face pots (Greene 1973, type 18), handled bowls (ibid., types 20, 22), copies of samian forms (ibid., type 21), cups (ibid., types 23–5) and open lamps (type 27).

From the Neronian period there seems to be an expansion of ceramic production in southern Britain exemplified by the kilns seen along Watling Street near Verulamium; the Alice Holt kilns, Surrey; at urban settlements developed out of Roman fortresses such as Colchester and, later, Gloucester; and from individual, short-lived kilns such as at Duxford, Cambs. (Anderson and Woolhouse 2016), Eccles, Kent (Detsicas 1977), Hoo St Werburgh, Kent (Blumstein 1956; Davies *et al.* 1994, 38) and Sugar Loaf Court, London (Chadburn and Tyers 1984). This is followed by a second phase of more extensive ceramic production from the Flavian-Trajanic period with the establishment, or expansion, of many of the large regional industries and a greater standardisation of output.

TABLE 7. COMPARISON OF FORMS FROM CONTEMPORARY KILN SITES

Typology	Little London	Usk	Brockley Hill/Ver	Bricket Wood	Eccles	Oaksey, Minety	Colchester Kiln 23	Colchester Kiln 26	Gloucester College of Art
FL1									
FL2									
FL3									
FL4									
FL5									
FL6									
FL7									
BL1									
BL2									
BL3									
BL4									
BL5									
BL8									
D1									
BK1									
BK2									
BK3									
PL1									
PL2									
CP									
J1									
J2									
J3									
J4									
J5									
J6									
J7									
J8									
L1									
M1									
M2									
M3								? Not made here	
M4									
M5									
TZ									
butt beaker									
honey pot									
lamp									
tiles									

Table 7 compares the output of selected contemporary kilns in Britain against the Little London typology. Whilst most of the kilns were producing broadly the same classes of vessels there is much variability in terms of which types were present at each site. On present evidence none of the kilns appears to be replicating the exact range of types seen at Little London. The earliest kilns in the Verulamium complex, namely those at Brockley Hill (Field 410) (Castle 1973a), show one of the closest overlaps in many of the types produced. This industry was producing Roman forms before the Boudican revolt and appears to have been a civilian enterprise supplying the newly established markets at Verulamium, Colchester and London. In its early phases the potters were making mainly collared flagons, bowls, funnels, lamps, tazze, jars, mortaria, plain dishes with flat bases, lids and wine amphorae of Dressel 2-4 form (Tyers 1998). Of the two kilns excavated at Brockley Hill (Castle 1973b), one is rectangular in form whilst the other is a normal updraught type with a pear-shaped furnace and projecting tongue pedestal. These particular structures are of early second-century date and not associated with the earliest pottery but could reflect earlier antecedents.

The potter or potters at Little Munden Farm, Bricket Wood (Saunders and Havercroft 1977), located some 7 km away from Brockley Hill, appear to have been active in the period A.D. 55–75 and show a similar overlap, particularly in terms of flagons, bowls and lids. The kiln at Little Munden is an updraught type with a rectangular-shaped firing chamber featuring a central tongue pedestal and tile-built piers. Unfortunately, there is no evidence that the stamped mortaria made at the site were specifically fired in this kiln or whether it fired mixed consignments. Hartley (1976, 152) observed that in the early second century the Verulamium mortarium potters often had workshops at more than one location. There is also evidence of extensive brick and tile production in the Verulamium region from the first and second centuries with kilns documented at Blackboy pits, Netherwylde Farm, Park Street, Old Parkbury and Elstree (Saunders and Havercroft 1977, fig. 1). Over this period it has been estimated that the Watling Street tileries provided around 90 per cent of the tile used in London (Crowley and Betts 1992, 221).

A large number of kilns have been excavated at Colchester but four in particular can be identified as early in date, although it is not certain whether these were operated by the military or civilians. Kiln 23 at Colchester (Hawkes and Hull 1948, 106; Hull 1963, fig. 83) was rectangular in plan with clay walls (see further discussion below). The structure was badly burnt and the interior contained burnt clay and the remains of buff flagons and jugs interpreted by the excavator as the last load from the kiln itself. The reconstructed forms include disc-mouthed flagons (Cam. 149–50), ring-necked flagons (Cam. 154) and reeded-lip flagons (Cam. 171). Other vessels found in, or in association with the kiln included hemispherical colour-coated bowls/cups (Cam. 62), ovoid colour-coated roughcast beakers (Cam. 94b), one hemispherical bowl with a flat rim (Cam. 244), some platters (Cam. 17) and a few lid fragments (Hawkes and Hull 1948, fig. 58). The kiln is dated to the period immediately before the Boudican revolt of A.D. 61. Hawkes and Hull also note an unfinished kiln nearby (1947, 106; 281ff.). A further three kilns have also been identified at Colchester dating to the Claudio-Neronian period: kiln 26 (Hull 1963, 157–61) and kilns 34–5 (Swan 1984, mf 287), two of which (26 and 34) were also rectangular in form. Kiln 26 produced a number of buff flagons (Cam. 140, 143, 149, 154), honey pots and bowls. Other wares were associated with the structure but not definitely made there. To the north of Colchester two pre- or early Flavian kilns were excavated at Wherstead (Gill *et al.* 2001) producing a mixture of 'Belgic' and Roman forms presumably destined for the nearest urban centre at Colchester.

At Eccles there is evidence for pottery and tile production from the Neronian period which had apparently ceased by A.D. 65 (Detsicas 1977, 29). The pottery includes platters, jugs, beakers, including vessels with roughcast decoration, lids, cheese presses, flagons (collared, disc-mouthed and ring-necked) and various mortaria, including wall-sided, flanged with an upright rim and hammer-head types (cf. Davies *et al.* 1994, fig. 28.126–9). Some platter forms, in particular Cam. types 8 and 14, in Eccles-type fabrics were stamped (Rigby pers. comm.) and at least one can be paralleled at the Arcadia Buildings site in Southwark. The reason for locating a pottery and tile industry at Eccles is not clear. At least some of the products appear to have achieved a non-local distribution with pottery, roofing tile, flue tile and mortaria ascribed to an Eccles source reaching London (Davies *et al.* 1994, 36; Chadburn and Tyers 1984, 22). A small amount of ceramic building material in the Eccles fabric has been identified at Silchester (Machin 2018, 121–3). Greene (1979, 85) and Pollard (1988, 188–9) suggest the Eccles production represents an estate interest and that the unusual range of forms may be connected with the authority that commissioned the building of the subsequent villa at the same location.

The evidence from Oaksey is more enigmatic. Minety is well-known as the location of an extensive tile industry with at least ten tile kilns known along with probable stone structures and clay pits (McWhirr 1984). One of these was partly excavated in 1974 (Scammell nd). Although negligible dating evidence was recovered the excavator dated the use of the kiln to *c.* A.D. 80–90. Further subsequent investigations in 1984 in an area away from the initial excavation revealed pottery wasters mixed with tile and fired clay. Although again a date of *c.* A.D. 80 is given, the illustrated pieces would suggest a late Neronian–early Flavian date is perhaps more likely. The assemblage includes several flagons with collared-rim, ring-necked examples and disc-mouthed forms, and flanged-rim mortaria with the beads level with the top of the flange but lacking any internal trituration grits and jars. The pottery appears to have been oxidised or reduced but as this is waster material this is not necessarily certain. Due to its proximity, Cirencester was undoubtedly one of the main markets for the Minety kilns although tile products have been found further afield, for example at Silchester (Machin 2018; 2020).

At Gloucester the picture with regards local pottery supply is quite complicated and not fully understood. A number of kilns are now known, or suspected, which may in essence be documenting the transition from military production to a civilian pottery industry supplying the new *colonia* founded at some point in the late first century A.D. The earliest Roman pottery is that from the short-lived legionary fortress located at Kingsholm dating to the Neronian period. Further kilns dating to the Flavian-Trajanic period have been excavated at Berkeley Street (Hurst 1972; Timby 1991), Kingsholm Rugby Ground and the College of Art site (Rawes 1972). The fabrics of the Kingsholm fort and the other sites are completely different in character and there is a different suite of vessels associated with the later kilns. These later kilns located both within and outside the defences were presumably initially supplying the occupants of the second fortress and *vicus* and then, from the later first and second centuries, the *colonia*. More recently, another kiln site has been excavated just outside Gloucester at Longford also dating to the later first and early second century (P. Booth, pers. comm.) and further kilns have been found on the College of Art site (CA 2016) suggesting substantial local demand.

From the above it can be seen that the various components of the range of vessels found at Little London can be paralleled with the products from several other kilns in Britain, both military and civilian in the pre- and early Flavian periods. These assemblages can be distinguished from other contemporary kilns such as those at Rushden (Woods and Hastings 1984), Chichester (Down 1978) and Keston (Philp 1999), where the products are very much influenced by copies of Gallo-Belgic forms, particularly platters, butt and girth beakers and jars, suggesting that either potters, perhaps of Gallo-Belgic origin, were arriving in the pre-conquest period or enterprising indigenous potters were adopting new forms copying the imported wares. The potters at Little London were clearly familiar with continental forms, specifically ones that have a strong connection with the military repertoire, and they are thus likely to be immigrants. Various mechanisms could explain their presence at Little London. They could be potters still officially under the aegis of the Roman military, particularly as the tilery appears to have been under imperial control on the basis of the stamped tiles (see below, Ch. 10, for further discussion). Alternatively, as has been suggested by Swan (1984, 8), military establishments attracted civilian potters to work in their immediate vicinity so the existence of the tilery may have attracted potters already in Britain and who were originally in the employ of the army but subsequently setting up independently. A third possibility is that these were civilian potters with no military connection but with continental backgrounds who saw an entrepreneurial opportunity in the newly conquered territory and were part of a flood of non-military, economic immigrants. The Roman army undoubtedly acted as a catalyst in stimulating trade and manufacturing activity and evidence is accruing to suggest that many of the early legionary camps on the Rhine were occupied by military personnel alongside civilians and officials (Willems and van Enckevort 2009). At Nijmegen there was an extensive *canabae* outside the legionary fortress with strip buildings occupied by potters, glass-blowers, butchers and bakers catering for the troops (ibid., 26).

If it is accepted that the potters are migrants, then one might expect to identify a specific region or regions for the likely origins of the individuals based on the individual styles of pottery made as has been attempted for the Usk assemblage (Greene 1993). This becomes problematic with the Little London assemblage as it appears to show rather a mixture of influences. At Brockley Hill, Tyers (1998, 290) highlights two vessels in terms of searching out a possible area of origin for the potters there: one based on the angular shouldered jar (Little London type J7), the other on the Dressel 2-4 type amphorae. The former may have developed from a similar style of jar found in the area around Lyon and seen in Britain at Usk (Greene 1993, type 13) and Sugar Loaf Court, London (Davies *et al.* 1994, fig. 68). It is suggested that the potter making the amphorae at Brockley Hill may have originated from the Upper Rhine or eastern-central Gaul where similar forms are known to have been made (Tyers 1998, 296). Of the other forms at Little London, the curved-wall platters copying the Cam. 16s would seem to originate from Gallia Belgica with kilns producing the forms known at Trier, Courmelois, Reims and Tours-sur-Marne. Although the form is well-known in Britain, both as imports and generic copies, there are probably only three other locations — Colchester, Wherstead and Eccles — where stamped copies were made closely adhering to the original forms. The mortaria from Little London are quite diverse in form but none approximate the Cam. form type 192 which appears to be the standard type made at Usk, Gloucester and Colchester. Type M1 is similar to Cam. 195/Gillam 238 for which a source in the Oise valley, northern France is now likely. This was among the most common types of mortarium imported into Britain in the first century. There may also be a link with western Gaul with mortaria types found largely in south-west Britain.

In conclusion, we are perhaps seeing in Britain in the Neronian-early Flavian period a new era of pottery production composed of at least five strands which by the later Flavian-Trajanic period had coalesced to create a more widespread, standardised industry. At one end of the spectrum are the potters producing vessels following the later Iron Age traditions where the repertoire is dominated by jars, seen for example with Silchester ware, Savernake ware, the Durotrigan-early Roman potters at Poole Harbour and perhaps the earliest phases of the Alice Holt potteries. These are industries with, or potentially with, pre-conquest origins which continued to function in the early Roman period. At the other end of the spectrum are the kilns which can be identified as directly linked with the legionary forts and fortresses to which a military label can be attached, such as Usk, Kingsholm, Wroxeter and Longthorpe. A third group can be identified where the potters are diversifying their repertoire to produce an array of forms, many with a Gallo-Belgic antecedence such as copies of platters, girth and butt beakers alongside jars and bowls, but not the flagons, mortaria and other forms found in the military assemblages. The kilns at Chichester and those inferred at Keston and in the Dorchester-Abingdon axis (Timby *et al.* 1997) may fall into this group. This could reflect an initial wave of craftsmen crossing the Channel and establishing themselves in new territory, or enterprising potters attempting to copy the new fashions, reflecting the adoption of new social, cooking and dining practices. The fourth group are those assemblages which appear to be a mixture of 'Belgic' style vessels and copies of Gallo-Roman forms alongside more Roman types such as flagons and beakers as seen at Wherstead, Suffolk, and Canterbury and developing at the Alice Holt potteries. These may be catering for both a military and local market; perhaps local potters working alongside, or apprenticed to immigrant potters.

The fifth strand, and the more enigmatic, is that currently encompassing Little London and sites like Eccles, Little Munden, Brockley Hill and Minety, which have a more military signature but are not ostensibly linked to a military establishment, for which a ready consumer market was available. In some cases, as may have happened with the Sugar Loaf Court kiln, the subsequent discovery of a military fort (Dunwoodie *et al.* 2015) or other installation may change the interpretation. It is suggested that the potters working at these locations were either trained by the army, or were following in its wake and were familiar with the 'Roman' repertoire. In some respects the output at these kilns differs very little from that seen at the known military forts but it is very difficult to create a template specific for each of the categories as there is no standardised repertoire which can be seen replicated at the various sites. Each location displays considerable variability. Given all the economic and social turbulence at this time, it is more than likely that there is no one model but a variety of strands which came together to mark a new era of pottery production in southern Britain and it is at centres such as Colchester and Gloucester where the industry can be seen transitioning from military to civilian and catering for both markets.

CHAPTER 5

THE CERAMIC BUILDING MATERIAL

By Sara Machin with Michael Fulford

INTRODUCTION

This chapter analyses the corpus of ceramic building material (CBM) in terms of both fabric and form. The catalogue includes all bricks and tiles recorded, from the typical Roman roofing and brick forms to more unusual types, all manufactured at Little London. Since we know the source of the material, the summary fabric descriptions serve to demonstrate the variety that can be seen within the output of a single production centre in the context of its local geology. The confirmation of Little London as the production centre of the Nero-stamped tiles found at Silchester (*Calleva Atrebatum*) raises questions about the purpose or purposes for which the tilery was established. For what building or buildings was this material, which includes some very specialist forms, produced? Was it solely for consumption in *Calleva*?

METHOD

All CBM recovered during the excavation was separated by context into its constituent forms and recorded on site by weight and count. A total of 17,036 items was recorded from the two trenches with a total weight of just over 4.5 tonnes (4584 kg). Trench 1 accounted for 3406.56 kg with a total of 11,245 fragments while Trench 2 produced 1177.38 kg, a total of 5,791 items. The average fragment weight was 269.07 g.

All forms were catalogued according to Brodribb's (1987) typology along with detailed descriptions of more specialised forms. The dimensions of all complete bricks and tiles were recorded. Flat pieces greater than 30 mm thick and without further distinguishing features have been classified as bricks. The presence of complete dimensions meant that some bricks were able to be assigned to specific form types, e.g. *lydion, bessalis*. Flat pieces measuring less than 30 mm thickness and thus likely to be of *tegulae*, *imbrices* and other forms, but without further diagnostic features, were recorded simply as tile. Flue-tile was recorded noting the occurrence of distinctive scoring, combing, relief-patterning and vents. *Tegulae* were identified where a flange was present, or where there was clear evidence of a flange having been removed, or where a lower or upper cutaway could be identified. Any surface features including signatures, scoring and footprints were also recorded. Lower cutaways and signatures were recorded by type according to Warry's typology (2006, 4, 149).

Small fragments which could not be assigned to a particular form were recorded as unidentified. Such pieces accounted for 6,368 items (430.32 kg). A small number of these were retained as fabric samples: 58 fragments weighing a total of 4.6 kg. Throughout the catalogue, references are made to examples of similar forms recorded during excavations at Silchester, including material held in the Reading Museum archive, most of which was retained by the Society of Antiquaries during their 20-year programme of excavations across the town (1890–1909). For the great majority of this collection there is no further information about provenance other than it derives from within the Roman town.

The ceramic building material which was retained after on-site recording includes examples of the complete range of forms and fabrics characteristic of the output of the site, as well as all examples of unusual forms, stamped material and complete pieces. It was not possible to assign all the material processed on site to a fabric series prior to discard owing to the volume of material recovered. The retained material amounts to 938 items with a total weight of 516.55 kg. All retained material was inspected using a 10x binocular microscope and macroscopic descriptions of the fabrics were based on PCRG (2010) by examination of a fresh break where possible. The colours of the exterior, interior and core of each fabric are described with reference to the Munsell Color Soil Chart. The material was assigned to the fabric groups established by Machin (2018). Petrographic thin sections were prepared of a number of fabric samples to enable detailed characterisation of the fabric range. Petrographic fabric summaries include reference to the raw material resources available on site.

SITE LOCATION AND GEOLOGY

The field in which the tilery is located straddles two distinct geological formations. To the north is the *Windlesham Formation*, which is part of the Bracklesham Group, and to the south is the *London Clay Formation* (Clay, Sand & Silt) (FIG. 63).

The **Thames Group** includes the *Harwich* and *London Clay* formations (Mathers and Smith 2000, 11). The *London Clay Formation* comprises mottled, non-calcareous fine sandy and silty clays (Jarvis 1968, 6) with subordinate, thin glauconitic sands and pebble beds. It is a fossiliferous unit, of shallow-marine origin, with extensive outcrop, especially in the east of Berkshire. The formation varies in thickness from less than 60 m to *c.* 90 m at Wokingham (Allen 2017, 76). At its outcrop there is generally a brown-weathered zone several feet thick, probably coloured as a result of the oxidisation of iron pyrites in the original deposit. Locally, there are sandy seams, with the lower sandier beds preferred for exploitation in the nineteenth century, with production focusing on bricks, and to a lesser extent tiles (idem).

Above the *London Clay Formation* lie the early to middle Eocene sediments of the predominantly sandy **Bracklesham Group**, which incorporates the *Bagshot Formation*, *Windlesham Formation* and *Camberley Sand Formation* (Jarvis 1968, 12; Mathers and Smith 2000). The *Windlesham Formation* outcrops on the high ground between Wokingham and Finchampstead,

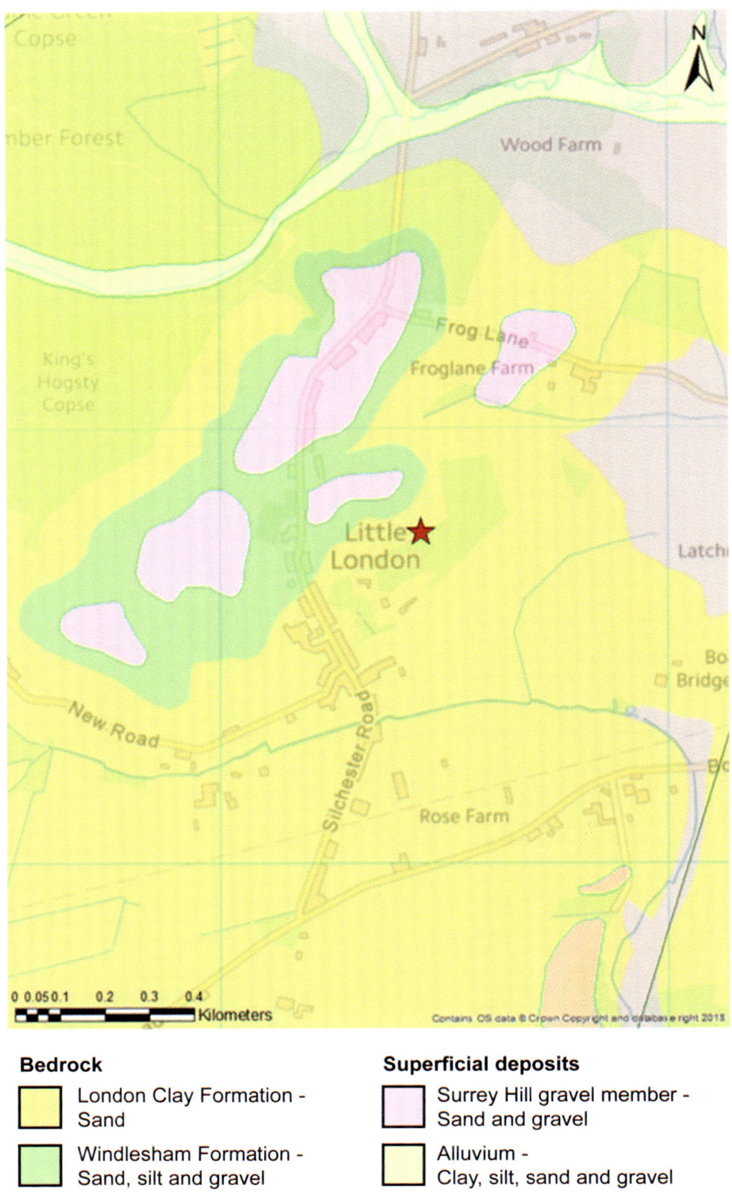

FIG. 63. Little London geological formations

with restricted outcrops to the south-east of Silchester at Hazeley Heath, and to the south-west at Little London. It comprises up to 20 m of dark green to brown, highly glauconitic, bioturbated sand and clay (Mathers and Smith 2000, 13). The *Windlesham Formation* is overlaid in places by the Surrey Hill Gravel Member (formerly *Plateau Gravels*) which is characterised by clasts of abundant angular flints, common rounded flints, sporadic Lower Greensand and very sparse quartz and quartzite (Osborne White 1909, 87).

FABRICS

While all the retained Little London CBM was examined in hand specimen, a selection of material was examined in petrographic thin section to establish the mineralogy and composition of the different fabrics present. Three fabrics from the Silchester CBM fabrics series could be identified within the material (Machin 2018) and these are described below.

As described above, there were two clay sources available in the immediate vicinity of the kilns: *London Clay Formation* dominates the local geology with an outcrop of *Windlesham Formation* to the north-west. This has therefore resulted in a variety of fabrics which comprise a combination of the clay sources in varying proportions presenting a range of degrees of heterogeneity.

Amongst the material were also many examples where the clay had been under-fired, resulting in a soft fabric which became malleable when water was applied. There was also a large proportion of material that was over-fired, showing signs of sintering and vitrification, resulting in a smooth glass-like fabric with melted moulding sand on surfaces giving a green glass-like finish.

FABRIC GROUP 1 (SILCBM1) (Machin 2018, 74–83) (FIGS 64–65)

This is a hard, moderately micaceous, homogeneous fabric, with sandy texture and irregular fracture. It is iron-rich and typically oxidised throughout with red (2.5YR 5/8) surfaces, margins, and core. The matrix has very common, fine quartz sand throughout with varying proportions of coarse to very coarse quartz sand (1–4 per cent). There are sparse red iron-oxide grains visible along with sparse large flint inclusions, up to 2 cm. Rare examples of heat-altered glauconite have also been identified in thin section. Inclusions are weakly bi-modal, double spaced, exhibiting weak to moderate alignment.

Fabric variant SILCBM1B is distinguished by a much higher proportion (*c.* 30 per cent) of fine quartz sand present. There are typically few voids evident making it a dense, hard fabric. The occasional reduction in optical activity is the result of a high firing temperature.

This fabric group has been shown to have derived from *London Clay Formation* sources (Machin 2018, 76). The *London Clay Formation* has variability in terms of its lithology and

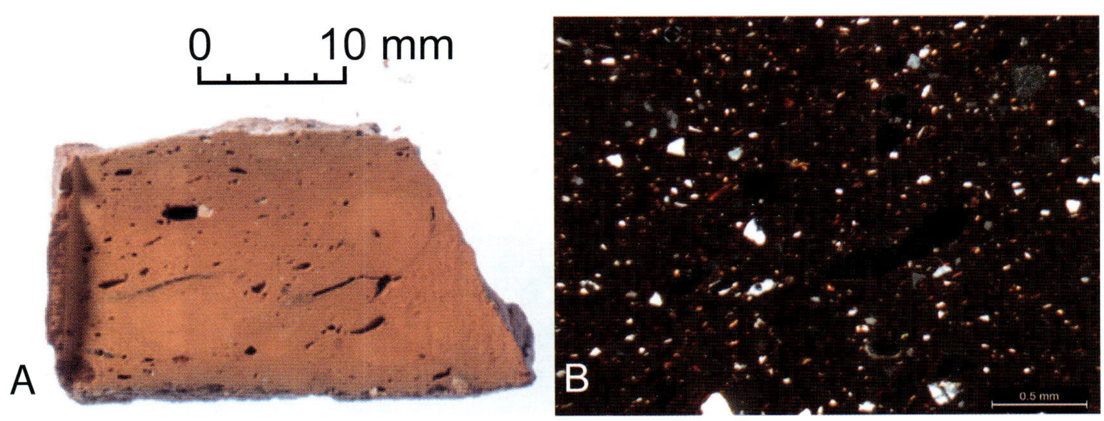

FIG. 64. SILCBM1A: (A) Hand specimen; (B) Photomicrograph of thin section (XP (Crossed-polars); x40 magnification)

FIG. 65. SILCBM1B: (A) Hand specimen; (B) Photomicrograph of thin section (XP; x40 magnification)

quartz sand components, with the upper beds comprising mottled, non-calcareous fine sandy or silty clays (Jarvis 1968, 6) with localised sandy seams (Allen 2017, 75). This could account for the variability between fabrics SILCBM1A and SILCBM1B, although there is also the potential for the variation to be due to the anthropogenic addition of quartz sand during processing.

FABRIC GROUP 3/4 (SILCBM3 and SILCBM4) (Machin 2018, 89–102) (FIGS 66–67)

SILCBM3 is a typically heterogeneous fabric with ferruginous bands and clay streaks visible. Surface colours vary from very pale brown (10YR 7/3) to pink (7.5YR 7/4 pink) and yellowish-brown (10YR 5/4). This fabric is generally oxidised throughout but with some examples of reduced cores (2.5Y 5/1 grey) and rare examples of reduction to surfaces, resulting in a greyish-brown colour (10YR 5/2). Most examples show evidence of being poorly worked with folds and voids visible within the fabric. This fabric is an example of the imperfect mixing of a naturally variegated clay defined by the zones of iron-rich and pure crystalline clay, rather than anthropogenic heterogeneity introduced as a result of the mixing of two different raw materials (Quinn 2013, 42). The raw clay has only been partially processed, insufficient to produce a homogeneous fabric. Quartz is present in the form of moderate, fine silt-sized grains (15 per cent) within the matrix and sparse, larger coarse-sand grains visible throughout. Rare red iron oxides can also be identified along with rare flint/chert inclusions. Argillaceous inclusions take the form of clay pellets, pale yellow-brown in colour, of a fine-grained, purely-crystalline clay. The pellets have diffuse-to-merging boundaries and are distorted, indicating they were plastic at the time of processing. There are also rare examples of grog, angular inclusions of previously fired clay, exhibiting clear boundaries, probably derived from crushed kiln material. There are a small number of examples of darker reddish-brown pellets indicating a higher iron content. Inclusions are moderately bi-modal, single-to-double spaced, exhibiting weak orientation. This highly heterogeneous fabric exhibits a wide range of inclusions, all within a common mixed base clay.

Fabric variant SILCBM3B is typically a more homogeneous variant of the fabric, though containing the same suite of inclusions. It is evident through the variety within this fabric group that the raw material was subjected to different amounts of processing before forming and firing, with some examples showing a higher degree of heterogeneity with highly ptygmatic regions visible. Geo-chemical and petrographic analysis has confirmed that the *Windlesham Formation* is the raw material clay source for this fabric.

SILCBM4 is an iron-poor fabric with occasional fine pale cream clay lenses throughout. It is a hard-sandy fabric with irregular fracture. The surface colours vary from a very pale brown (10YR 7/4) to pink (7.5YR 7/4). The fabric is generally oxidised throughout, though reduced examples are consistently mid-grey on all surfaces and throughout the body of the samples.

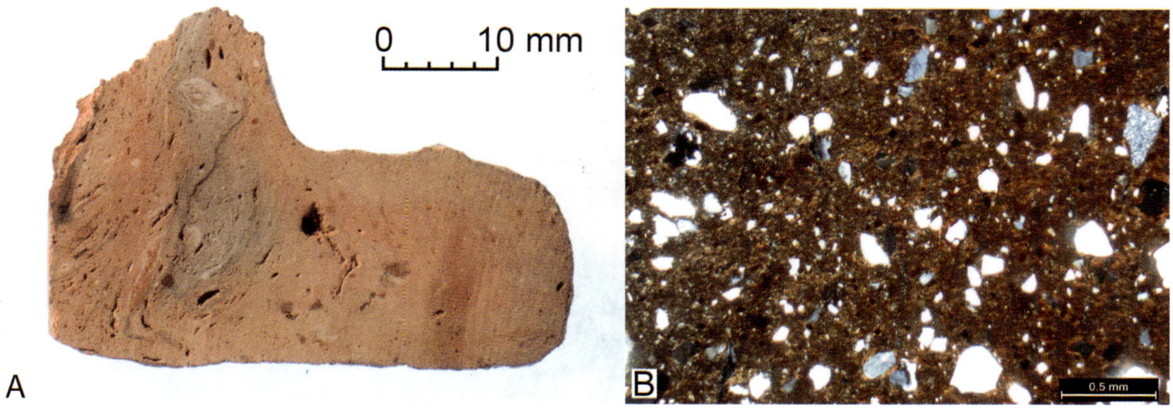

FIG. 66. SILCBM3: (A) Hand specimen; (B) Photomicrograph of thin section (XP; x40 magnification)

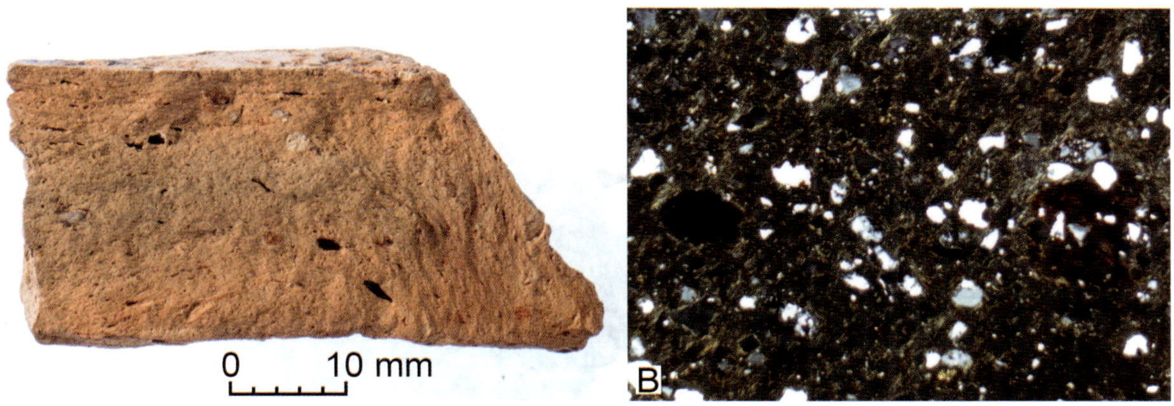

FIG. 67. SILCBM4: (A) Hand specimen; (B) Photomicrograph of thin section (XP; x40 magnification)

The SILCBM4A samples are generally homogeneous whereas the SILCBM4B variant exhibits a large number of pale cream clay pellets resulting in a higher degree of heterogeneity. This is probably a result of a lesser degree of weathering and processing of a naturally variegated clay, rather than the anthropogenic mixing of two different source clays. These clay phenomena have clear to merging boundaries, taking the form of equant, typically rounded pellets, with some evidence of distortion, indicating they were plastic at the time of processing and firing. This fabric has common fine quartz-sand throughout resulting in a sandy texture. There are sparse small iron-rich grains present, with some samples of SILCBM4A having a higher proportion of iron-rich inclusions (10 per cent). Mineral inclusions identified comprise heat-altered glauconite grains, hornblende and plagioclase feldspar. Inclusions are unimodal, single spaced, exhibiting moderate orientation. Geo-chemical and petrographic analysis results show that SILCBM4 also correlates with the *Windlesham Formation* clay source. This would therefore show that the SILCBM3 and SILCBM4 are all variants of the same fabric group.

FABRIC 5 (SILCBM5) (Machin 2018, 103–9) (FIG. 68)

SILCBM5 is an iron-rich, non-calcareous, homogeneous fabric, typically oxidised throughout with some reduced examples. Surface colours vary between red (2.5YR 5/6) and light red (2.5YR 6/6). The fabric comprises a very fine-grained matrix, with sparse quartz-silt present. It is slightly micaceous, typically mid-brown-orange in colour in XP and PPL. There is a moderate proportion (10–15 per cent) of well-rounded fine quartz-sand, which may be an anthropogenic addition. It also features sparse angular-to-subangular flint fragments, probably added along

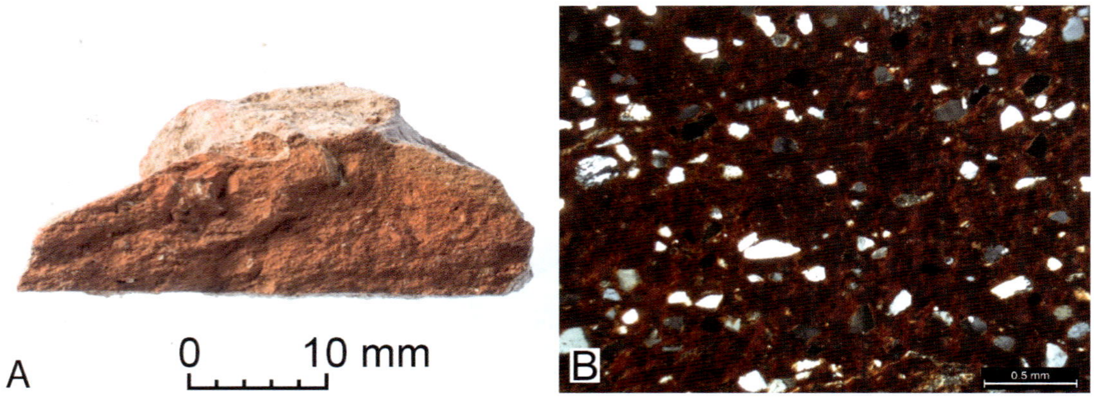

FIG. 68. SILCBM5: (A) Hand specimen; (B) Photomicrograph of thin section (XP; x40 magnification)

with the coarser quartz component. The fabric exhibits very pale brown (10YR 7/3) clay pellets and streaks. These argillaceous inclusions are rounded, equant pellets of a highly birefringent clay, with sharp-to-merging boundaries. The fabric has moderate optical activity, with reduced activity due to a higher firing temperature noted in the SILCBM5B sub-group. The other mineral inclusions comprise heat-altered glauconite grains and plagioclase feldspar. Inclusions are unimodal, single-to-double spaced, exhibiting weak orientation. A source of this fabric was not previously identified; however, it is most likely a result of a combination of the two raw material sources available at Little London. There are no inclusions present in the SILCBM5 fabric that are not identified in either Fabric Group 1 or Fabric Group 3/4. Some examples show evidence of laminating throughout, a potential indicator of the incomplete mixing of two different clays.

ASSEMBLAGE COMPOSITION

Excluding unidentified fragments, the composition of the Little London assemblage is dominated by bricks whose weight accounts for 45 per cent of the material, followed by tile (28 per cent by weight) and roofing tile (25 per cent by weight). However, when measured by number of fragments, the material is dominated by roofing tile (40 per cent), with 28 per cent brick and 26 per cent tile.

TABLE 8. THE COMPOSITION OF THE LITTLE LONDON CBM ASSEMBLAGE

Form	**Weight (g)**	**Count**
Brick	1867465	3047
Roofing	1035350	4237
Flooring (*opus spicatum*)	590	4
Hypocaust (flue-tile)	89525	634
Tile	1147837	2730
Tile-stamped	630	3
Vaulting (voussoirs)	9455	5
Waterpipe	615	8
Unidentified	430324	6368
TOTAL	**4581791**	**17036**

FORMS CATALOGUE

The material has been divided into seven key form groups: brick, tile, roofing, flooring, hypocaust, vaulting, waterpipes. Within these groups, where it has been possible, material has been further divided into particular form categories based on dimensions, distinctive features or other diagnostic characteristics.

Brick

Flat pieces greater than 30 mm thickness are assigned to the brick category. These amounted to 3,047 items with a total weight of 1867.47 kg accounting for 45 per cent of the recorded material by weight (28 per cent by count). As very few complete examples were recovered, the absence of *bipedales* may be more apparent than real.

Bessalis

There were four examples of bricks that could be identified as *bessalis*. These are small square bricks, measuring approximately 200 mm^2, the equivalent of ⅔ Roman foot. They are typically used to create *pilae*, to support the *suspensura*, the floor suspended above a hypocaust (Brodribb 1987, 36). The complete *bessales* recorded had an average weight of 2.74 kg each. One example, measuring 200 mm^2, has an unusual signature on the surface in the form of a quadrant around one corner (FIG. 69). There is an example of a *bessalis* with the same signature in the Reading Museum archives (Accession: 1995.98.82). Another complete example from Little London is slightly smaller, measuring only 187 mm^2.

Three examples were recovered from Trench 1 – (1029)x2 and (1032) – and a single example from Trench 2 – (2028). *Pilae* of this type have been recorded on a number of occasions during excavations at Silchester. The Society of Antiquaries described numerous hypocausts uncovered during their 20-year programme of excavations, 28 of which are described as pillared (Machin 2018, 54), constructed with *pilae* beneath the *suspensura*. *Pilae* were also utilised in 'composite' hypocausts where a system of channels between earthen or rubble baulks led to a central chamber filled with *pilae* (FIG. 70).

At Little London, *bessales* were found to have been used to construct the *pilae* which supported the floor of the circular pottery kiln (Kiln 5) (above, p. 46).

Lydion

Five bricks could be categorised as *lydions*, where surviving dimensions were sufficient to make a positive identification. A *lydion* is a flat brick measuring approximately one Roman foot by one-and-a-half Roman feet (295.7 mm by 443.5 mm). One complete example recorded had a total weight of 11.3 kg. The four *lydions* found at Little London all had a 'spacer' of clay added centrally to the surface of the brick (below, p. 97, for a discussion regarding 'spacers'). *Lydions* were used for a range of purposes, including being considered most suitable for bonding courses in walls. Bonding courses are considered to have emerged as a device to provide a firm and level base for walls, developing to be used at regular intervals through the height to aid construction of tall, slender walls by ensuring their trueness (DeLaine 1997,

FIG. 69. *Bessalis* with quadrant signature (1029)

145). There are very few examples of bonding courses reported at Silchester, those recorded predominantly occur in the public buildings, including the temples and temenos wall of Insula XXX, the west gate (Machin 2018, 48), the Hadrianic-Antonine forum-basilica, as revealed at the north end of the basilica (Fulford and Timby 2000, 59), and the *mansio* baths as illustrated

FIG. 70. Composite hypocaust below *tepidarium* at Silchester bath-house (Insula XXXIII)

FIG. 71. *Pilae* supports within Kiln 5 (2052)

FIG. 72. *Lydion* used as a liner of Kiln 5 (2052)

by the Society of Antiquaries in the baths structure in Insula VIII (Hilton Price 1887, pl. XIX). *Lydions* were also observed within the structure of the bath-house at Silchester during the recent excavations. *Lydions*, however, could also have been used as large flooring bricks, both for internal and external pavements, with examples recorded in the timber forum-basilica (Period 5, *c.* A.D. 85–125) contexts and further examples identified in tile settings flanking either side of the entrance to the forum from the basilica (Fulford and Timby 2000, 51).

One particularly distorted *lydion* was found to have been used as a lining of Kiln 5 – (2052) (FIG. 72).

Chamfered bricks

Nine examples of bricks were recorded where one end had been cut at an angle, i.e. chamfered. This was typically along the shorter edge of the brick and at an angle of between 45 and 70 degrees (FIG. 73). Eight of the bricks were cut to remove clay from the top of the brick, while a single example was 'undercut' removing clay from the underside. This chamfering is understood to have facilitated the overlap of the bricks when used in bonding courses, thus creating a superior join between two bricks (Brodribb 1987, 40). If the brick was to be used in this way, then it means that alternate bricks would have been laid 'upside-down' to facilitate the overlap. This was seen to be the case during the recent re-excavation of part of the Silchester public bath-house (Insula XXXIII) (Fulford *et al.* 2018b; 2019). There is a single example of a *lydion* with a chamfered end in the Reading Museum Silchester archive. Examples of chamfered brick were recovered from Period 2B levels at the legionary bath-house in Exeter; these were 75 mm thick, 260 mm wide and at least 250 mm in length (Bidwell 1979, 153).

Scored brick

Eight fragments of brick, each in excess of 30 mm thickness, were recorded where the surface

FIG. 73. Chamfered brick (1098)

had been scored. This scoring could have been to assist keying into a mortar bed or to provide a key for plastering, as is more typically found on box-flue tiles and wall-jacketing *parietalis*. The scoring on these bricks, however, was of a more rectilinear design rather than the typical diamond-shaped lattice found on flue-tiles (FIG. 74). There are two examples with signatures visible on the surface, and one example with a 'spacer' scar present. There is a possibility that these bricks had been scored to be broken into tesserae after firing.

Brick – column

Three examples of 'segmented' brick were recorded with a total weight of 6.68 kg. The bricks ranged in thickness from 58 to 68 mm. None of the examples was complete. All examples included one curved edge and at least one straight edge (FIG. 75). Moulding sand present on the surviving edges evidences their production in a mould. These bricks would probably have been used to create columns which were then plastered and decorated with stucco. All three have curved edges which would have produced a column with a diameter of approximately 560 mm. One example had been made with two straight edges creating an angle of 135 degrees (1000). Two of these bricks together could have been used around a right-angled corner or square post to form a column. In Roman Britain examples of column bricks are rare and, where bricks are used to form columns, these are typically found to be semi-circular or formed into quadrants.

Brick – narrow

There were 16 examples of unusually narrow bricks, with an average width of 137.2 mm. These bricks have a total weight of 30.1 kg and average 41.2 mm in thickness (FIG. 76). There were no examples complete in length. Bricks of similar dimensions with a width of 6 in (*c.* 150 mm) were reported from the military tileworks at Holt. These bricks were found *in situ*, used as kiln bars to traverse the flues and create the firing floor within a pottery kiln (Grimes 1930, 40, 136;

FIG. 74. Scored brick: possible tessera production (1098)

fig. 30). Other examples were recorded in the CBM assemblage from Princesshay, Exeter, where the site included brick-making debris, probably associated with the construction of the forum-basilica and town baths (Pearce and Steinmetzer forthcoming, 82). An example is also held in the archive of the material retained during the excavation of the tile and pottery production site at Oaksey Park, Minety (Scammell n.d.). These unusually narrow bricks have therefore typically been interpreted as fire-bars or kiln furniture. Seven of the examples from Little London were recovered from the fill of Kiln 4 (2031). A single example was recorded during the 2019 excavation season at the Silchester bath-house.

Spacers

As mentioned above, a large number of the bricks in the assemblage have 'lumps' of clay added to the upper surface of the brick. These have often been described as *mammatae*, clay additions designed to create a cavity when used in heating systems. All the

FIG. 75. Column fragments: (A) (1000); (B) (1074); (C) (1074)

FIG. 76. Narrow brick (2035)

FIG. 77. Hoofprint underneath spacer (1046)

examples recorded on the Little London material were very insubstantial, typically <2 cm in height, and were therefore clearly not for this function. These lumps of clay would have been added to the surface of bricks to act as spacers, to create a gap between the bricks when they were stacked for drying and within the kiln during firing (Wheeler and Wheeler 1936, 141; Cunliffe 1971, 43). Depending on the intended final use of the brick, the 'spacer' was sometimes retained and examples are found at sites such as Silchester and Fishbourne (Brodribb 1987, 40). It is likely that the spacers were added just before firing, or at least after the brick had partially dried, evidenced by an example where the spacer has been added on top of a hoofprint (FIG. 77).

It has also been suggested that these bricks were used sanded-side up as paving, the nibs anchoring the tile into the mortar bed below (Betts 2006, 81).

Roofing

Roofing material incorporates the typical *tegulae* and *imbrices*, along with more specialist roof furniture in the form of antefixes, chimneys and skylights. A total of 4,237 items of roofing material was recorded with a weight of 1035.35 kg. Roofing material accounts for 25 per cent of the corpus by weight (40 per cent by count).

Tegulae and imbrices

Tegulae represented 2,521 items, with a weight of 792.83 kg, whilst *imbrices* accounted for 1,699 items, 237.89 kg in weight.

A single complete *tegula* was recorded, with a length of 488 mm and weight of 10.65 kg. The

FIG. 78. *Tegula colliciaris* (2037)

average length of the *tegulae* was 472.83 mm, whilst *tegulae* beds varied in thickness between 17 and 32 mm. All signatures recorded on *tegulae* were Warry Type S1 (Warry 2006, 149), taking the form of a single semi-circle to the bottom surface of the *tegula* bed (see below for other signatures recorded on the Little London material). There is a single example of a *tegula* with a pre-formed nail-hole, which was located 62 mm from the top of the *tegula* bed and 124 mm from the surviving flange.

All lower cutaways recorded were of Warry Type C5 (Warry 2006, 4), with 28 complete cutaways recorded. This type of cutaway was formed using a mould insert that ran the full height of the flange, and the diagonal cut was made after moulding using a knife (ibid., 24). All Little London examples confirm this method of production having moulding sand from the insert present on the vertical edges of the cutaway, with the diagonal cut made with a knife after moulding. With a *terminus ante quem* of A.D. 68, the confirmation of Little London as the producer of the Nero-stamped *tegulae* contradicts Warry's dating of his cutaway type C5 (A.D. 160–260) (2006, 72–3).

Tegula colliciaris

Within the *tegulae*, there is one unusual example. This *tegula* has all the typical features of a *tegula*, including a lower cutaway Warry Type C5, but the bed of the *tegula* has been cut obliquely, at an angle of 120 degrees. The cut starts at 47 mm from the left-hand flange thus allowing space to accommodate the *imbrex*. This example was found within the fill of Pottery Kiln 3 [2040]. This *tegula* was fired in a reducing atmosphere resulting in a uniform grey colour (FIG. 78).

Roofing tiles cut in this way are known as *tegulae colliciares*, derived from *collicia* meaning a gutter or gulley. They were used at the intersection of two sloping roofs forming a valley. The overlapping joints of such gutter segments could either be fitted dry or sealed with lead or watertight mortar (Gerding 2013, 180) (FIG. 79). Excavations at Silchester have shown a

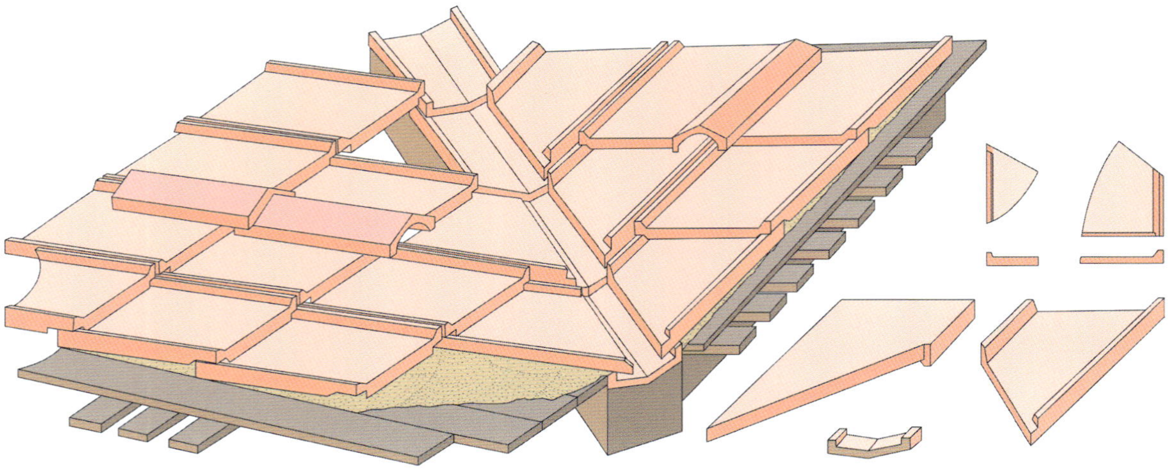

FIG. 79. Example of roof covering of *tegulae colliciares* (after Gerding 2013, A9.21)

number of buildings whose layout would have included roof valleys, notably the forum-basilica in Insula IV and the public bath-house in Insula XXXIII. The *tegula colliciaris* is an example of a type of building material probably produced to order for a specific building. An example of such a cut *tegula* is known from Roman Southwark, London. This example had the top right corner removed, approximately 180 mm from the bottom of the tile, and is thought to have been specially made for a 45-degree roof junction (Pringle 2002, 153). Flat tiles, not *tegulae*, cut at an angle to fit a junction between two roofs are also known from the Courage's Brewery site in northern Southwark (Betts 2003, 113).

Skylight

The roofing material also included five fragments of two *tegulae* which were manufactured with a central hole surrounded by a raised border. The holes measure between 130 mm and 140 mm in diameter, the circumference around the outer edge of the raised border measures approximately 300 mm. The central hole was cut after the forming of the *tegulae* and the edge of the hole was indented to act as a key for the addition of the border. The Little London *tegulae* are examples of Wikander Type 1, with a plain opening surrounded by a raised border, with estimated diameters varying between 16 cm and 31 cm (FIG. 80). It is the simplest and probably the oldest type (Wikander 1983, 91–3). Both the Little London examples were found within a post-hole in Trench 1 [1008] located approximately 3.5 m from the eastern corner of Tile Kiln 1 [1125].

The function of these tiles has been debated, typically being considered to have been either to let in light and air, or to let out smoke. Research has shown that their use was not restricted to a particular type of building and Wikander (1983) concludes that the use of skylight tiles was varied and they could be used to fulfil whatever need existed. The dating of the use of this type of tile is difficult due to extensive re-use and recycling of material, but its origin is believed to have been on the Greek mainland in the sixth century B.C. (ibid., 94). Ludowici reports the discovery of some interesting brick fragments, namely roofing with smoke openings and with dormers in different sizes, with one example bearing the stamp of *legio I*, from Rheinzabern (1912, 191–2) (FIG. 81).

Brodribb (1987, 19) cites only two examples of these from Roman Britain, one from the tile and pottery production centre at Holt, which was described by Grimes as an outlet for smoke (1930, 135) and featured a perforation of approximately 210 mm diameter, and the other from Colchester (Crummy 1992b, 256, fig. 7.2). More recently, an example was found at Paternoster Square, London, where the hole is described as possibly a ventilation hole or smoke vent and therefore it may have been linked in some way to a chimney (Betts 2006).

FIG. 80. Skylights (1009)

FIG. 81. Example of a skylight, opening 15 cm (after Ludowici 1912, 192, fig. 142)

Outside of Roman Britain, examples have been found at Conimbriga, Portugal, which are very similar in form to the Little London examples. Roofing at Conimbriga was made of typical *tegulae* and *imbrices*, and these special forms were described as being used to allow smoke from the fireplace to escape. Here they have been dated to the Augustan period (27 B.C.–A.D. 14) (Alarcáo 2000, 33, 99). They are also known from Pompeii, where one example was discovered *in situ* on the roof of a house from Regio V. The example from Pompeii shows that these *tegulae* were used in conjunction with traditional *tegulae* on the roof slopes (FIG. 82). If used with a chimney, one would expect the *tegulae* to be laid flat, along the ridge of the roof but there is no evidence to suggest that the bases of chimneys were angled to fit on a sloping roof.

Measurements of the internal circumference of the possible lamp-chimneys from Little London (below, p. 105) and the external circumference of the raised border around the central holes in these *tegulae* also do not support their use in conjunction with lamp-chimneys. It is most probable that they served as vents or skylights with the raised border deflecting the majority of any rainfall around the opening.

FIG. 82. Example of a skylight *in situ* at Regio V, Pompeii (© *Massimo_Osanna (Instagram)*)

Antefix

Two fragments have been identified as parts of antefixes, ceramic ornaments attached to the end of the lower course of *imbrices* at the edge of roofs. One example takes the form of the lower portion of a face, including the lips and chin (FIG. 84). Vines are visible below the chin and the right-hand edge is raised up to form the border, as is seen on the Silchester antefix examples held in the Reading Museum collections (below).

The other example takes the form of part of the plaque/surround of the antefix (FIG. 83). This differs somewhat in fabric, being a paler cream colour, possibly the result of different firing conditions. The surface is quite abraded, but it is possible to make out the frame of the plaque and part of the vine scroll, which show it to be the bottom right-hand corner of the antefix.

Neither of the examples has any sign of moulding sand on the surface. Antefix moulds would have been made from fired clay which retains some porosity after firing. When wet clay was then applied to it, the mould would absorb moisture from the surface, thus drying it. This allowed for the mould to be removed, leaving a clear rendition of the antefix without the need for any separating agent (G. Taylor, pers. comm.)

There are four fragments of antefix, seemingly from the same mould, held in the Reading Museum Silchester collection, two on display in the museum and two held in the archive. One example is described in the report of the investigations into the environs of the forum-basilica, in Insula IV, as 'part of an antefix with a crudely executed face, which evidently belonged to a building of some importance' (Hope 1893, 561) (FIG. 85). Another fragment is described by

FIG. 83. Antefix (1046)

FIG. 84. Antefix (1046)

Cotton in the report of her excavations of the town rampart between the north gate and the amphitheatre. It was found in an occupation layer, dated to *c.* A.D. 100–120, and is described as having been made in a local mould since it is identical to the three other examples previously recorded (Cotton 1947, 127). The two examples on display are more complete, but are not referenced in any of the published excavation reports.

Boon saw the images as representations of a local deity, noting that 'the face is male, beardless, and has hair *en brosse* surmounted by wings or horns' (Boon 1974, 169). He considered that

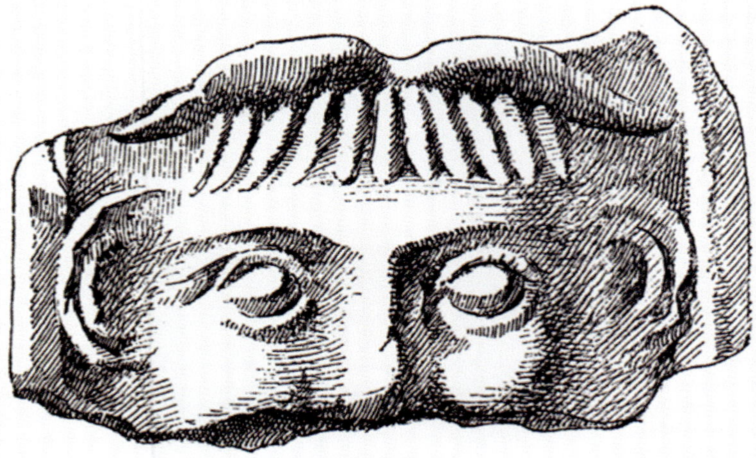

FIG. 85. Fragment of antefix found by the Society of Antiquaries (after Hope 1893, fig. 3)

they might all depict wind gods designed to protect the dwelling against storms and evil spirits (ibid., 170) (FIG. 86). Previously the Silchester examples had been interpreted by Toynbee as displaying an outlandish version of Medusa, the features below the chin representing knotted snakes, and had been compared with an antefix recovered at Dorchester, Dorset where the face, though similar in other respects, was bearded and so seen as a male Medusa (Toynbee 1964, 430–1, pl. XCIXc). Antefixes with a Medusa head have also been found in Colchester (Crummy 1992b, 252–3, fig. 7.1). None is from a closely dated context but they are probably to be associated with the legionary fortress. We can also add the four examples with human (?female) faces recovered from Period 1A contexts from the legionary bath-house at Exeter and dated *c.* A.D. 55/60–75 (Bidwell 1979, 56–7, 149, pl. XVIII, 1–2). Many more fragments were recovered from later levels associated with the legionary bath-house, with other finds recorded from across the town after 1979 (P. Bidwell, pers. comm.).

Boon, observing that most antefixes have been found on military sites, typically bearing inscriptions of the occupying legion, suggested they were placed along the eaves to close the open ends of the *imbrices*, and this is supported by the antefixes from Exeter which show scars where they were detached from their *imbrices* (Bidwell 1979, 149). By contrast, Boon saw the scarcity on civilian sites as evidence of a different function, to serve as finials to finish the gable-ends of private houses or public buildings (Boon 1957, 148).

That there was a long ancestry of stylistically similar facial depictions on

FIG. 86. Almost complete antefix (after Boon 1957, 148, fig. 28)

antefixes is indicated by the mid-fourth-century B.C. representations of Artemis Bendis from Taranto (BM Collection 1849,0724.2; 1856,1226.434; 1884,1011.6) (cf. Blagg 1979, 277–80). Fragments of antefix were also described by Ludowici, at the same site, Rheinzabern, which produced the skylights (see above) (Ludowici 1912).

Chimney

Ten small fragments of possible lamp-chimney were recovered with a total weight of 780 g. Five fragments join together to make a large portion of a tiered-vessel (FIG. 87). This has pie-crust decoration and the fractures provide evidence that the chimney was constructed in a number of separate sections and subsequently joined together. The ribbing to the interior surfaces suggests that this chimney was coil built with the exterior surfaces smoothed. Its interior diameter is estimated at 200 mm. There are two other fragments of this chimney which do not join with the rest.

Three fragments of possible lamp-chimney, also with pie-crust decoration, evidence arched-window vents. They are of a finer version of Fabric 5 than the other pieces and are very similar to the wheel-thrown chimney fragments recovered from second-century contexts at Silchester Insula IX, which have triangular window-vents (Timby 2011).

Ceramic roof accessories of this type have been described as decorative finials as well as functional chimneys. Based on comparable examples from the Continent, Lowther (1934) changed his interpretation from chimneys or ventilation cowls, to votive or religious artefacts. He argued that, if they were chimneys, they would be found in far greater numbers, and in association with box-flue tiles of hypocaust systems. They typically take the shape of a tiered, tapering cylinder with triangular, window-like vents. Examples have been found at numerous sites in Britain with a corpus collated in a posthumous paper by Lowther (1976) where he again discussed their possible function. Brodribb suggested that the fumes from vertical box-flues could have emerged into a roof space sealed from the rooms below, and from there escaped through a chimney (1987, 32).

The fragments of possible lamp-chimney at Little London and Silchester compare stylistically with the examples from Ashtead, Surrey (Lowther 1934), also a brick and tile production centre, and Verulamium (Wheeler and Wheeler 1936). At both sites fragments feature window-vents and pinched pie-crust decoration. There are rare examples of lamp-chimneys from Roman London; they have been found at Billingsgate Buildings, Plantation Place, and at the pottery production centre located in the Walbrook Valley (Betts 2015, 175, fig. 158; Seeley and Drummond-Murray 2005, 56).

It has been suggested that the form of these chimneys would be more suited to the production skills of a potter rather than a tile-maker, with some examples shown to have been wheel-thrown in sections. The Roman tile and pottery kiln site at Berkeley Street, Gloucester, included chimneys in their repertoire. The reconstructed form is shown to have similarities to the Ashtead and Verulamium examples and the evidence of their having been wheel-thrown supports, at least in part, the association of lamp-chimneys with pottery production (Timby 1991, 25). Indeed, two of our three examples were found among waste from the pottery kilns, only one from near the tile kiln, from the ditch of Trackway 2, but also associated with pottery wasters.

Previously, Lowther had suggested a third-to-fourth-century date for these objects. Noting the similarity between them and stone finials and the lack of smoke-staining, he favoured their interpretation as decorative finials, rather than chimneys (Lowther 1976, 41). With the exception of two examples, which are actually integrated into curved ridge tiles, there is no evidence of how they were set on the roof.

Bearing in mind the fact that the above items were wheel-thrown, it is also possible that fragments of finer fabric are not of lamp-chimneys but of terracotta ovens or *tannur* and part of the pottery, rather than CBM, repertoire at Little London. Few examples are known from Roman Britain though this may be the result of mis-identification (Darling 2012, 355). There is an example from the legionary tile and pottery production centre at Holt (Grimes 1930, 184, fig. 60.9) (FIG. 88). This is described as an oven of red ware with a thickened rim decorated with

FIG. 87. Fragments of chimney: (A) (1031); (B) (2027); (C) (2014)

thumb impressions. An example of a similar form, described as a portable brazier which could would have been fuelled by charcoal or wood, has been found at Pompeii (Roberts 2019, 164, fig. 180) (FIG. 89).

Flooring

Opus spicatum

Although any type of brick could have been used for flooring, *opus spicatum* was specifically designed for this purpose. Four examples were recorded at Little London, with a total weight of 590 g. There were no complete examples, the fragments measuring on average 86.5 mm wide and 18.5 mm thick. *Opus spicatum* bricks were typically laid on edge in a herringbone pattern and were recommended by Vitruvius for use on floors open to the elements (*De architectura* 7.1.3). While the examples from Little London clearly have no signs of wear, as they never left the kiln site, the majority of the examples identified in the Reading Museum Silchester collection, 113 in total, are worn smooth on one side. The Society of Antiquaries recorded the

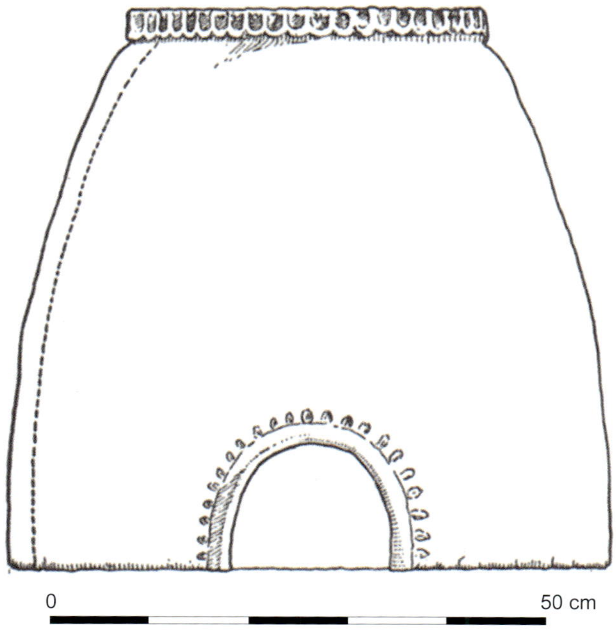

FIG. 88. Example of ceramic oven from Holt (after Grimes 1930, 184, fig. 60.9)

FIG. 89. Portable brazier from Pompeii (after Roberts 2019, fig. 180)

use of *opus spicatum* in the *frigidarium* of the public baths, describing its floor as paved with herringbone bricks measuring 6"x 3"x 2" laid on the side (Hope and Fox 1905, 343). A few of these were observed *in situ* on the floor of the *frigidarium* during the 2019 re-excavation of the bath-house (FIG. 90). It is likely that the great majority of the *opus spicatum* bricks in the Reading Museum collections were found in the public baths.

Hypocaust

Flue-tile

Box-flue tiles take the form of a pipe, typically thin-walled and square or rectangular in cross-section. They could be easily mortared and fixed to the wall to enable hot air to rise from the under-floor voids up the inside of the walls and so help heat the space above. Box-flue tiles were made in a number of sizes and forms. No complete example was found at Little London and it is possible that some are fragments of specialist forms of box-tile, including hollow voussoirs, half-box flues and double-box flues. The material from Little London has therefore been categorised by the method of keying, whether by combing, scoring or roller-stamping. A total of 634 fragments of flue-tile has been identified with a total weight of 89.53 kg (Table 9).

TABLE 9. THE QUANTITIES OF EACH TYPE OF BOX-FLUE TILE RECORDED IN THE LITTLE LONDON ASSEMBLAGE

Types of box-flue tile	**Weight (g)**	**Count**
Flue-tile – no keying	31406	265
Flue-tile – combed	1700	16
Flue-tile – scored	32745	190
Flue-tile – relief-patterned	18084	136
Parietalis	4830	24
Parietalis – relief-patterned	760	3
TOTAL	**89525**	**634**

FIG. 90. *Opus spicatum* flooring *in situ* (top) and as impressions after removal (below) at Silchester bath-house in 2019

There was a single example of a box with a complete height of 122 mm and two examples with a complete depth measurement of, respectively, 76 mm and 92 mm. There were 12 examples of complete widths, ranging from 112 to 224 mm (mean = 172.45 mm), which illustrate the variation in the dimensions of the flue-tiles manufactured at Little London. Vents through the sides of the box-flue were recorded on 55 examples. Both circular and rectangular shapes were identified with some examples having two vents on each side (FIGS 91–92). There is no correlation between the form of keying and the shape of the vent.

Flue-tile – combed

There were 34 fragments of combed flue-tile with a total weight of 4890 g. The material was very fragmentary and most of the examples were in a reduced fabric, over-fired with evidence of vitrification in places (FIG. 93). The combed flue-tile was typically thin-walled with an average thickness of 16.9 mm. 20 fragments were recovered from context (1144), fill of Kiln 2 in Trench 1.

Flue-tile – scored

There were 190 fragments of scored flue-tile with a total weight of 32.745 kg. The scored flue-tile typically featured a lattice design and had an average thickness of 18.7 mm (FIG. 94).

Parietalis

A total of 27 pieces of flue-tile were identified as *parietales*. These weighed 5590 g and were typically thicker than box-flue tiles averaging 26.38 mm. *Parietales* or facing-tiles were used to form a cavity for warm air when complete box-flue tiles were not utilised. These were vertically

FIG. 91. (above) Example of box-flue tile with circular vent

FIG. 92. (right) Example of box-flue tile with rectangular vent

FIG. 93. Combed flue-tile (1144)

FIG. 94. Example of scored flue-tile (1040)

attached to walls using iron T-cramps and spacers. The majority were scored to provide a key, either with a grid or lattice design, while three were keyed with a relief-patterned design (see below). There were six examples with a notch to the edge to accommodate the T-cramp for mounting to the wall (FIG. 95). Three examples were identified in the Insula IX archive (Machin 2018), all of which were in fabrics originating from the Little London tilery.

Relief-patterned flue-tiles

There were 139 examples of relief-patterned keyed flue-tiles at Little London, with a total weight of 18.84 kg, accounting for 20 per cent of the flue-tile recorded at Little London. Relief-patterned tiles differ from others in that, instead of having been combed or scored, the surface has been keyed with an impressed design applied using a roller. The patterns vary from relatively simple, geometric diamond-and-lattice designs to complex motifs and often elaborate decorative schemes, albeit solely to provide a key for wall-plaster rather than for decoration. Whilst relief-pattern keying is primarily found on box-flue tiles, a number of other types have been found to have been keyed in this way, including voussoir, *parietalis*, and flat wall-tile (Betts *et al.* 1997, 8–12). Once the requisite roller had been made, no greater effort would be involved than that necessary to comb or score the surface and the resultant product could be readily identified as the work of an individual craftsman or workshop, which, it was thought, would facilitate payment according to output (Lowther 1948, 6).

There are examples of four of the published relief-patterned designs in the assemblage from Little London (FIG. 96). Three of the dies, 38, 39, and 68, belong to the diamond-and-lattice group while Die 54 is included in the miscellaneous group in the corpus of relief-patterned tile (Betts *et al.* 1997). The breakdown of dies by weight and count is shown in Table 10. Of these four dies, three are known to have been found at Silchester, but there are no known examples of Die 54 from within the Roman town.

FIG. 95. Scored *parietalis* with notch for T-cramp: (A) (1046); (B) (1101)

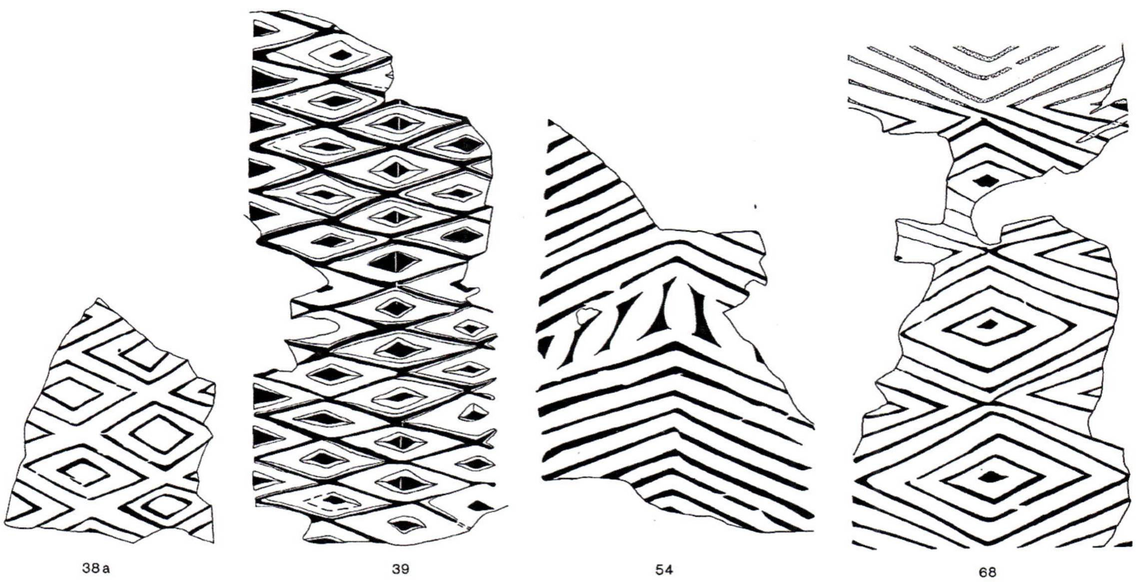

FIG. 96. Relief-patterned dies found at Little London (after Betts *et al.* 1997, figs 27b, d, e and f)

TABLE 10. QUANTITIES OF THE VARIOUS RELIEF-PATTERNED DIES FOUND AT LITTLE LONDON

Relief-patterned die no.	**Weight (g)**	**Count**
38	8644	77
39	8000	43
54	1530	15
68	670	4
TOTAL	**18844**	**139**

Three examples of Die 39 have been applied to wall-facing bricks (*parietalis*), rather than box-flue tiles. All of these examples are thicker than the box-flue tile, averaging 26 mm, and one example has a notch to one edge to accommodate the iron T-cramp used to fix it to the wall.

The identification of tiles with matching dies informs the study of the mechanisms behind their distribution and of roller-stamped tiles more generally. Lowther noted examples of the same die made in different fabrics suggesting the movement of the tiler, or at least the roller, between different production centres (1948, 6). This led to the suggestion of the movement of itinerant, specialist tile-makers between production centres where demand for these specialist products had arisen, rather than the movement of the somewhat fragile, final products. The movement of tilers, rather than tiles, was to some extent based on the long-held assumption that CBM was a high-bulk, low-value commodity and therefore would not have been transported over long distances.

Die 38

Die 38 has a small number of known examples with a relatively widespread distribution (Betts *et al.* 1997, 108–9) (FIG. 97). Single examples are recorded from Winchester, Hants., and Canterbury, Kent, but, since both are now apparently lost, their fabrics could not be examined. Eighteen examples have so far been recorded from Silchester; six in the Reading Museum Silchester collection, one in the Lowther collection held at the British Museum and recorded as from Silchester, and another 11 examples have so far been recorded during the re-excavation of the Silchester public bath-house. Recently, a single example has also been reported from a site in Sonning, Berks. (Williams forthcoming).

The only other example is held in the collection at the Ashmolean Museum. It is a single tile donated to the museum by a resident of Oxford. The tile is recorded as being from Alchester. A label on the reverse of the tile reads 'Roman Brick Tile from Aichester' (FIG. 98). The first two letters are certainly open to interpretation, but it has generally been accepted to refer to the Roman settlement at Alchester, Oxon. This example shows elements of overlapping roller, as does one example from Little London (FIG. 99). All examples of Die 38 examined were found to be made of Little London SILCBM3/4 fabrics.

Die 39

Die 39 is another diamond-and-lattice design, albeit with smaller design elements (Betts *et al.* 1997, 109) (FIG. 100). There is also one example from Little London with overlapping roller patterns (FIG. 101). Another example of Die 39, found during field-walking, was recorded from Little London prior to the 2017 excavation (Greenaway 1981, 291). This item has since been lost. Examples of Die 39 have been recorded to the south-west and north-west of Little London (FIG. 102).

There are now 14 examples known from Silchester; five are held in the Silchester collection at Reading Museum and another four were recovered from the excavations of Insula IX (Warry 2011, 226–8). A further five examples have been recorded from the re-excavation of the Silchester bath-house. Other examples of Die 39 are known from Cirencester, Glos., where three have been examined by Machin, along with two examples found in the archive from the villa excavation at Littlecote Park, Wilts. (Walters and Phillips 1979, 7). The CBM assemblage from the roadside villa at Lower Wanborough, Wilts. included another two examples (Mepham 2001, 313) and a single example is known from Rockbourne Villa, Hants. (RCHM 1983, 132), all three examined by Machin. Four specimens of tile keyed with Die 39 were also recovered during the 1988 Brooks excavation in Winchester where they had been made into tesserae and incorporated into a mosaic pavement of late Roman date, A.D. 240–400 (Betts *et al.* 1997, 109). This fragment of mosaic floor could not be located in the archive and has been recorded as lost. However, the fabric of these has been described as resembling the fabric of the Little London example (Foot 1974).

Macroscopic and petrographic inspection of the Die 39 flue-tiles shows the majority are of fabrics within the range found at Little London. The Littlecote villa and Rockbourne examples are all of Fabric Group 3/4. One of the Lower Wanborough examples is of Fabric Group 4, while the other is a coarse, iron-rich fabric corresponding to Little London Fabric Group 1.

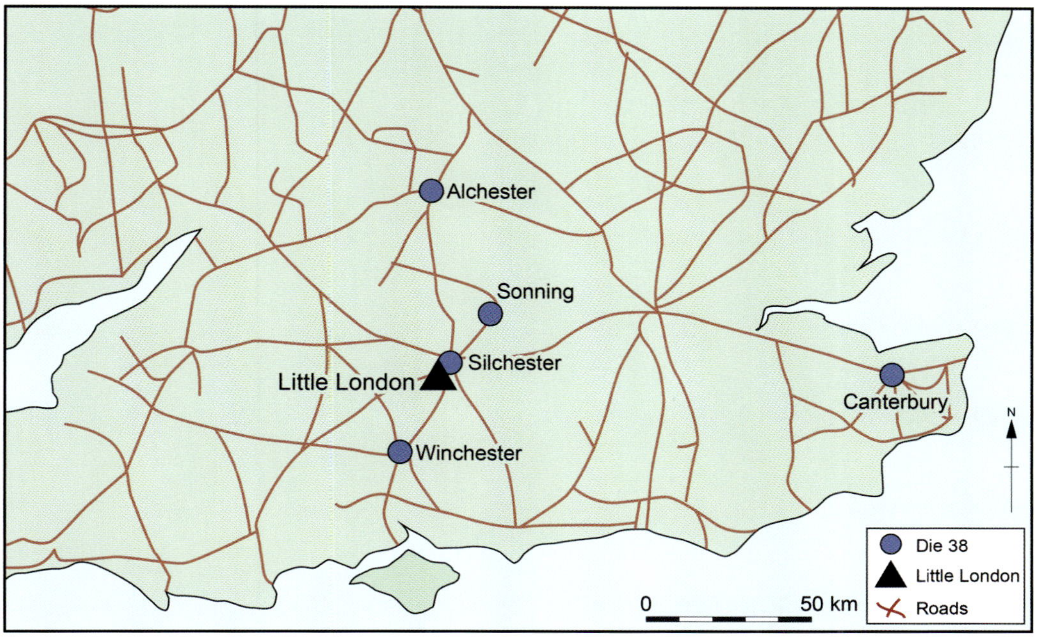

FIG. 97. Distribution of examples of Die 38

FIG. 98. (A) Example of Die 38 from Alchester; (B) Label on the reverse side (*Copyright Ashmolean Museum. Accession number: 1967.609*)

One of the Cirencester examples is of a fabric not represented in the Little London fabric range. Comparison with material from other production centres shows a match with tiles from the tilery at Minety, Wilts. (Scammell n.d.). Minety is known to have produced relief-patterned tiles, supplying both Lower Wanborough and Cirencester, as well as other sites, although only examples of Die 56 have been found at Minety itself. Analysis of all the examples of Die 39 therefore shows that Little London material was transported to nearby Silchester, south-west to Winchester and Rockbourne, as well as north-west to Cirencester, Lower Wanborough and Littlecote villa. Flue-tile with Die 39, potentially produced at Minety, appears to have been transported to Cirencester.

FIG. 99. Die 38 with overlapping prints (2008)

FIG. 100. Example of Die 39 (2008)

FIG. 101. Example of Die 39 with overlapping roller (1098)

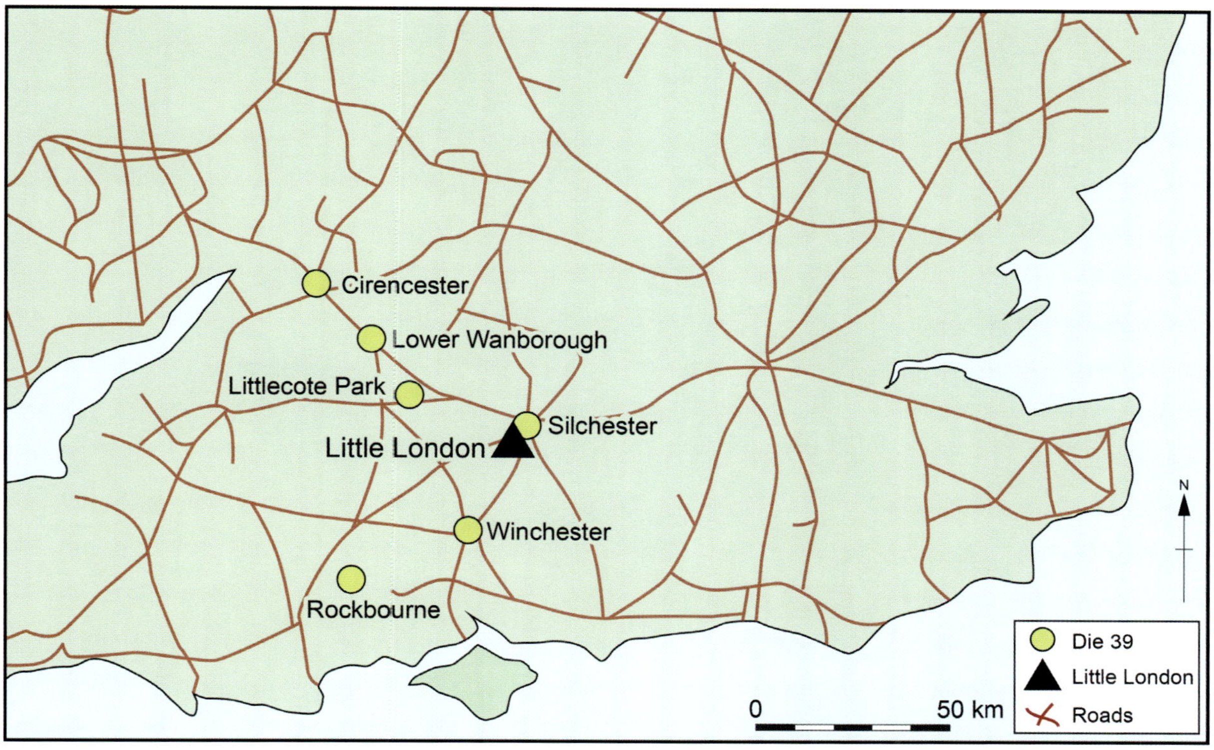

FIG. 102. Distribution of examples of Die 39

FIG. 103. Example of Die 54 (2008)

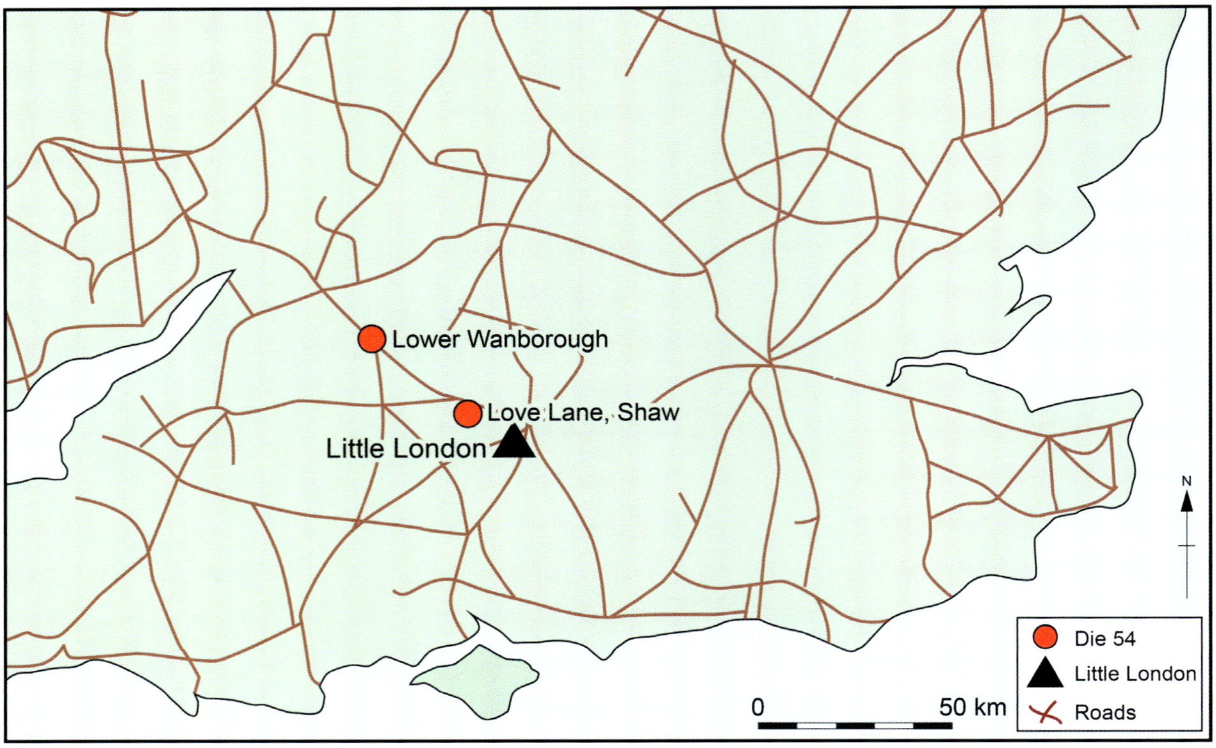

FIG. 104. Distribution of examples of Die 54

Die 54

Die 54 is categorised among the group of miscellaneous designs in the corpus of relief-patterned tile (Betts *et al.* 1997, figs 27b–c, 118) (FIG. 103). The corpus only includes two examples, one unstratified from Lower Wanborough (Mepham 2001) and one from the pottery production centre at Love Lane, Shaw, near Newbury, Berks. (FIG. 104), where two circular kilns were excavated along with a large quantity of Roman brickwork showing evidence of being subjected to extreme heat (Wilson 1974, 457; Ford 1974). The shape and size of these kilns are more indicative of pottery production than the manufacture of brick and tile. The Little London examples are of Fabric Group 4, a coarse sandy and moderately heterogeneous fabric, buff-cream in colour. The Shaw and Lower Wanborough examples are of an iron-rich coarse fabric, matching the Lower Wanborough example of Die 39 (described above) and indicative of a *London Clay Formation* source, potentially Little London Fabric Group 1.

Die 68

The final type of diamond-and-lattice design in the Little London corpus is of Die 68 (Betts *et al.* 1997, 126), of which four examples were recorded from the excavation. This has larger design elements than both Dies 38 and 39 (FIG. 105).

Tiles keyed with this design are known from four of the sites where Die 39 was also found. They demonstrate a linear distribution along Ermin Street from Silchester, Hants., north-west to Cirencester, Glos. (Machin 2018, 244) (FIG. 106). Two examples are known from Silchester, one from a tile-setting in the entrance of the Flavian timber basilica dating to *c.* A.D. 85 (Fulford and Timby 2000, 45), the other recovered from a make-up associated with the construction of the successor, masonry forum-basilica *c.* A.D. 125/150 (ibid., 68). Six examples of Die 68 were found in the archive from the 1964–66 investigations at Cirencester abbey and Saxon church (Wacher 1965; Brown and McWhirr 1966; 1967). A number of examples were recovered from Littlecote villa, Wilts., but there is no published reference to specific dies, although the first interim report

FIG. 105. Example of Die 68 (2013)

of the excavations mentions a large number of roller-stamped box-flue tile fragments recovered during the 1978 season (Walters and Phillips 1979, 7). At Lower Wanborough, Wilts., one specimen of Die 68 from context (WAN1766) is incorrectly identified as an example of Die 13 (Mepham 2001, 313, fig. 109.8). Another very small fragment was also identified by Machin in the assemblage (Context: (WAN67A IX (1)).

All but one of the examples examined are of Little London Fabric Group 3/4, being heterogeneous with varying proportions of quartz, iron oxides and clay pellets. One example from Cirencester differs in that it is an homogeneous iron-rich fabric with a high proportion of fine quartz-silt throughout the matrix and thus showing similarities in composition to the material from the tilery at Minety, Wilts.

Tile

As per the methodology, fragments <30 mm thick with no features to allow them to be assigned to a specific form category were recorded as tile. They accounted for 2,730 items with a total weight of 1147.84 kg representing 28 per cent of the material by weight (26 per cent by count). As discussed above (p. 87), it is probable that many of these fragments belong to *tegulae*, box-flue tile etc.

Vaulting

Voussoir – solid

While it is possible to make curved arches with any size of flat bricks by adjusting the amount of mortar to induce a curve, there are some bricks specifically designed for the purpose. These solid voussoirs, or *cuneatus*/*cuneati*, could be used radially, taking advantage of the tapering thickness, or vertically where the width tapers (Lancaster 2015a, 40). No complete solid voussoirs were recovered from Little London, but two fragmentary examples were identified. One, weighing 2680 g, has a complete width at the thicker end of the voussoir, with the thickness tapering from 48 to 38 mm (FIG. 107). The other is from the thinner end of a voussoir, weighing 2470 g, the thickness increasing from 20 to 38 mm. Both examples have moulding sand applied to all sides. Using *cuneati* radially minimised the mortar between the bricks, regularising the thickness of the mortar joints, thus reducing the time required for the mortar to dry (DeLaine 1997, 164) and enabling a more even transfer of forces from one brick to the next (Lancaster 2015a).

Voussoir – armchair

Three fragments of armchair or rib-vaulting voussoirs have been identified, with a total weight of 6150 g. None of the examples was complete. All three were recovered from Trench 1. One (1032) includes the tenon (*intrados*) found at the bottom of the voussoir with a rebate of 52 mm

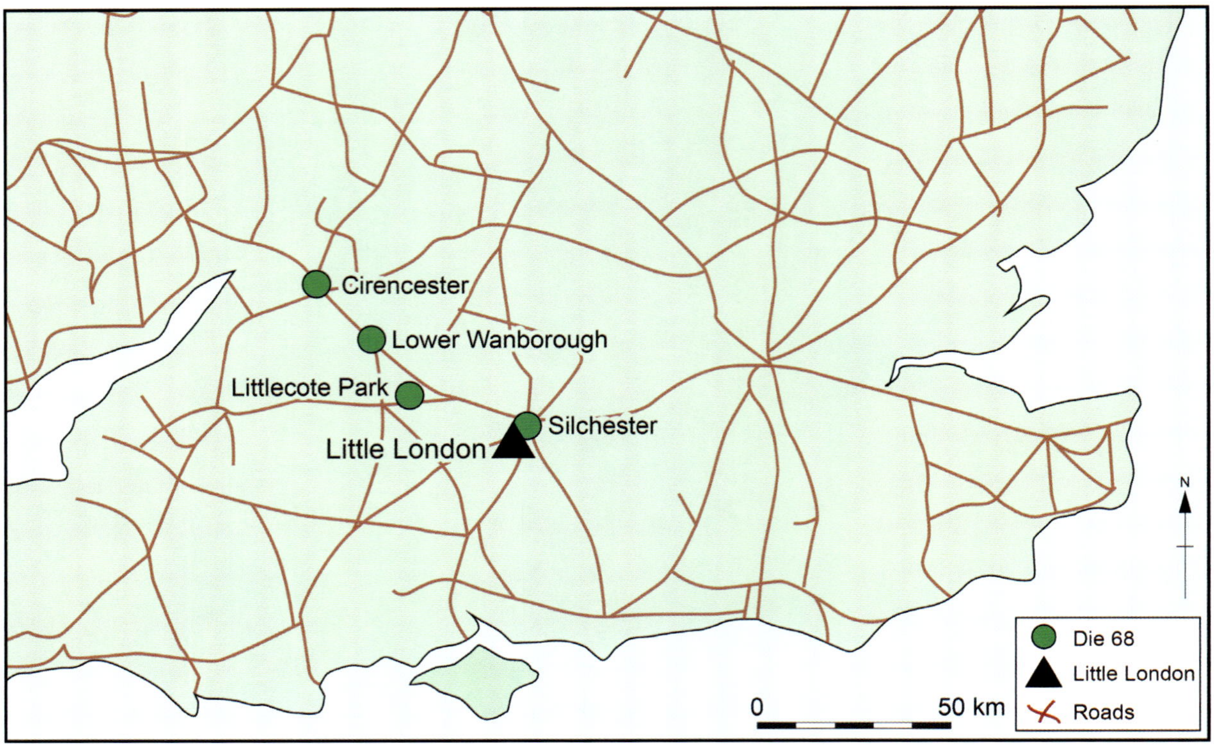

FIG. 106. Distribution of examples of Die 68

and height of 40 mm. There is a partial signature (Warry type-S2) in the form of a double semi-circle applied to the surface (Warry 2006, 149) (FIG. 108). The second (1091) includes the mortice (*extrados*) found at the top on both sides. Although the third piece has no complete dimensions (1103) (FIG. 109), it includes a portion of one *extrados* confirming its identification as an armchair voussoir.

FIG. 107. Solid voussoir showing tapering width and thickness (1121)

All three examples have moulding sand applied to all sides. Assuming that all armchair voussoirs made on site were of the same form, the presence of both *intrados* and *extrados* and the lack of a central perforation mean that these are examples of Bouet Type 3 (Bouet 1999, 94). Despite the lack of complete dimensions, it is also evident that at least two of the examples taper in width from the top to the bottom and are therefore of Bouet Type 3b, with a slight tapering of thickness also evident. This type of voussoir would have been used with two slabs to create a conduit or hollow arch (Bouet 1999).

FIG. 108. Armchair voussoir (1032)

FIG. 109. Armchair voussoir (1103)

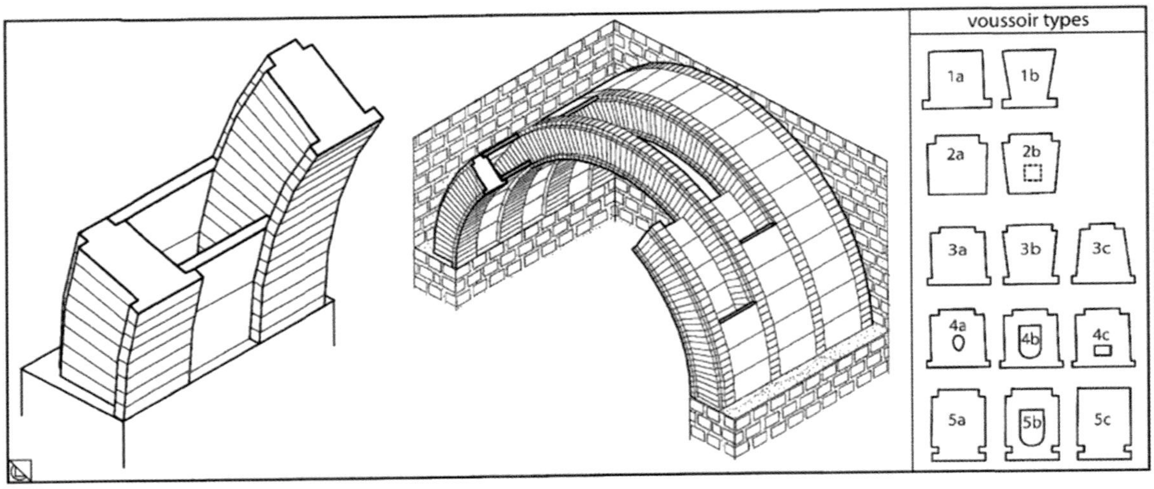

FIG. 110. Diagram of the use of armchair voussoirs in vault construction (after Lancaster 2015a, 153, fig. 101)

It is the most common system of vaulting recorded, accounting for 79 per cent of identifiable components (Lancaster 2015a).

A number of advantages have been attributed to the use of the armchair voussoirs for ribbing. It is a lightweight construction method compared to a solid arch and easier to build without the need for centering, thus facilitating quicker construction without the need for complex wooden supports (FIG. 110). The hollow vault would also protect any wooden roof structure from moisture generated in the bath (Fincker 1986, 148). While the hollow channel could have been connected to vertical flues to provide heating for the vault (Bouet 1999), the system could have offered sufficient structural, constructional and thermal insulation benefits to justify its use without being directly connected to a wall heating system (Lancaster 2015a). These voussoirs were typically used to span quite small vaults, of 3–5 m span, and the technique provided a way to build them quickly and economically.

The armchair voussoir ribbing is almost exclusively used for the vaults in baths (Lancaster 2015a) and its distribution is limited to the western Mediterranean with the greatest concentration found in France, followed by the Iberian peninsula, Britain and Morocco (Lancaster 2015a, 169). The absence of these forms in Roman Italy has been seen as the reason why they are not mentioned in the classical literature on architecture (Fincker 1986, 144). The early examples in both France and Iberia appear in small public baths during the first century A.D., whereas later they are found concentrated mainly in private bath-houses with the technique becoming popular as part of the urbanisation process (Lancaster 2015b, 243).

In Britain Lancaster has identified 24 sites with armchair voussoirs, of which 13 can be associated with the military and two with villa sites, the remaining nine being unattributed (Lancaster 2015a, 170). Stamped evidence on examples from Roman Britain shows that the military were producing armchair voussoirs by the early second century. Military production seems to have been a major agent of diffusion within Britain with patterns of adoption relating to military expansion via the soldiers recruited from areas where armchair voussoirs had been used (Lancaster 2015a, 170–1). Examples have been found at a number of sites in Roman London, including at the Winchester Palace site (Spall 2004), Southwark (Betts 2003, 116) and the Guildhall amphitheatre (Betts 2008, 165). All these sites also produced tiles bearing procuratorial stamps. Armchair voussoirs were also used in the construction of the vaulted roof of the baths at Chester, albeit made of tufa rather than clay (Fincker 1986, 146).

FIG. 111. Curved brick (2035)

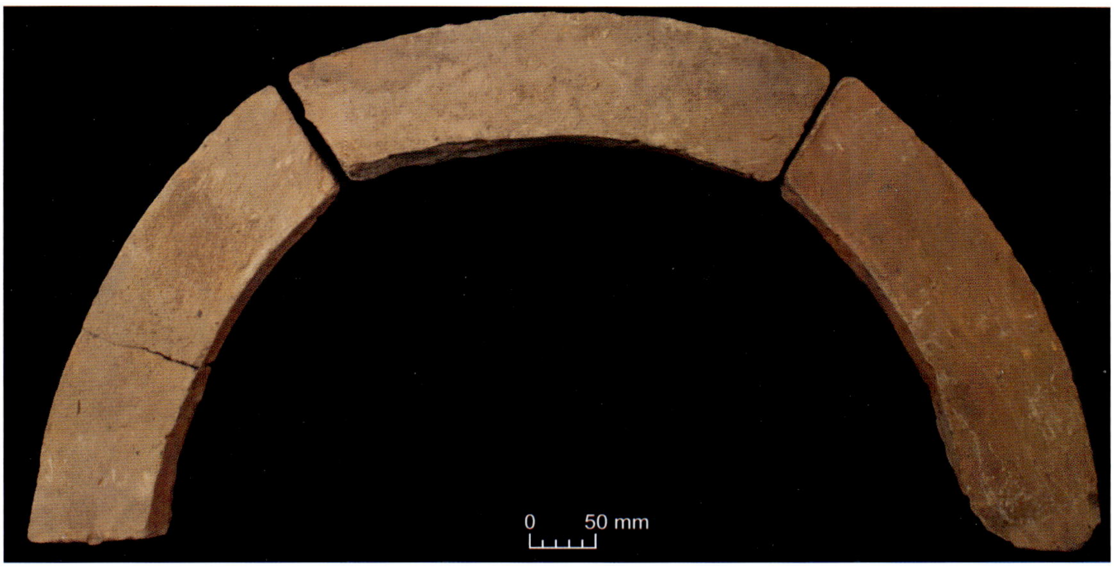

FIG. 112. Three curved bricks arranged in an arch

Brick – curved

There were 39 fragments of curved bricks recorded, with a total weight of 46.18 kg. These averaged 96 mm in width and their total length is approximately 400 mm (FIG. 111). Thirty of the examples were recovered from (2035), the fill of Kiln 5.

Set vertically these bricks could have been used to produce a 3-brick barrel-vault. This form of arch construction was used to span small spaces, typically of 60 cm width and, like armchair-voussoirs discussed above, eliminated the need for wooden centering during construction, thus providing a quick and economical method of vaulting narrow spaces. The 3-brick method meant that the two side bricks could be mortared to the preceding ring and then the top brick inserted to act as a keystone. This technique also facilitated the use of lime mortar, without the need for quick drying alternatives (Lancaster 2015a, 45). If arranged in this way, the Little London examples would form an arch with a span of approximately 60 cm (FIG. 112).

The earliest examples of 3-brick barrel-vaults are found in the aqueduct in Athens, built by Hadrian and dedicated by Antoninus Pius in A.D. 140. Here the vaults covering sections of the aqueduct channel were built of specially-made, curved bricks so that three of them together created a semi-circular arch (Lancaster 2015a, 50–7; 2009, 377). The distribution of this type of 3-brick arch is limited to Greece and Asia Minor (Lancaster 2015a, 40). That these items typically relate to

FIG. 113. Waterpipe fragments (1036)

urban aqueducts and drainage infrastructure puts them into a special category where the military is known to have expertise. This, along with the suggested development of the construction technique, that it originated in the region of Parthia, means that the most likely agent of the spread of this technological advancement would have been military personnel just returned from Trajan's Parthian war (Lancaster 2015a, 65–7). However, the find of this type of brick at Little London makes it clear that the innovation had occurred by the A.D. 50s or 60s, though this by no means negates a possible origin in the East. Aqueducts and other water management projects were very expensive and so were often imperially sponsored, as in the case of the Hadrianic aqueduct at Athens (Lancaster 2010, 466). Such projects required specialist knowledge that was not typically available in the local pool of builders, so the necessary expertise was drawn from the military. The same type of bricks was also used to construct the vertical air vents (*putei*) typical of Roman aqueducts, using six bricks to create a circular shaft (Lancaster 2015a, 52).

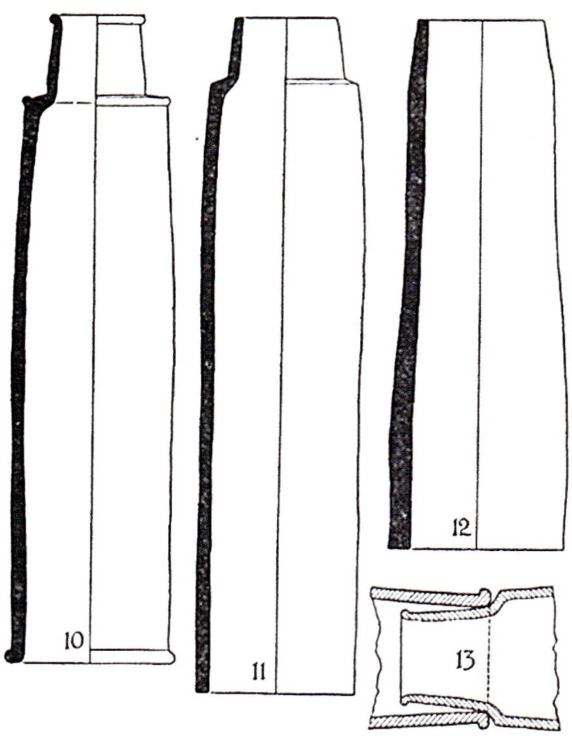

FIG. 114. Waterpipes from the legionary tileworks at Holt (after Grimes 1930)

Waterpipe

Six small fragments of ceramic waterpipe have been identified in the Little London assemblage, with a total weight of only 725 g and the diameter of the pipes measuring *c.* 18–20 cm (FIG. 113). Two of the fragments have the remains of a collar or socket to facilitate the joining of the pipes. It would appear that the pipes had been wheel-thrown, evidenced by the rilling present on the internal surfaces. This was also noted on the socketed waterpipes found at the legionary tileworks at Holt (Grimes 1930, 134, fig. 60.10–13) (FIG. 114).

Pipes had a number of uses in Roman buildings including bringing water to or from buildings or gardens, internal piping within a bath-house, or drainage (Spall 2004). There appear to be no standard shapes or sizes. The earliest dated occurrence in Britain appears to be a dump containing a significant quantity of ceramic waterpipe fragments from the Winchester Palace site on the Southwark waterfront which was deposited in the A.D. 50s and early 60s (Open Area 4, Yule 2005, 6, 23–5). Pipes of similar internal diameter to those at Little London were found at the Flavian palace at Fishbourne where they were used to supply water to the fountains and basins in the garden (Cunliffe 1971, 47). However, smaller pipes with an internal bore of 2 cm were found in Claudio-Neronian contexts at Fishbourne (idem). The larger form of waterpipe was also present at Conimbriga, Portugal. They had a cylindrical body slightly widening at the extremities, one of which presents a mortise-shaped *cyma* collar of smaller diameter (Alarcáo 2000). We should also note the pipes with rim and base of similar diameter, and so with no obvious means of linkage, from a dump dated *c.* A.D. 60–70 at Winchester Palace, Southwark. Pringle suggested they might have been used as *pilae* (2007, 207–8).

MARKINGS ON BRICK AND TILE

STAMPED BRICK AND TILE

A key objective of this excavation was to confirm whether the site at Little London did indeed produce the tiles stamped with the name and title of the emperor Nero (A.D. 54–68). The material recovered during the 2017 excavation included two examples which can be added to the existing 17 known Nero-stamped tiles. One, a partial impression, includes the letters **NE** (SF12 (1091)) (FIG. 115A). The other has clear lettering: **N[ERCLCAEAV]G·GER**. The E and R are ligatured (SF8 (1069)) (FIG. 115B). Another tile has a partial circular impression with no letters visible, but whose dimensions match that of the stamped tiles (FIG. 116). All three stamped tiles are *tegulae*.

SIGNATURES

A total of 44 examples of signature was recorded on the retained brick and tile and categorised according to Warry (Warry 2006, 149). Forty of the examples were Warry type S1, taking the form of a single semi-circle. Of these, 19 were recorded on *tegulae*, 20 on bricks and one on a tile. There is one example of a quadrant signature around the corner of a *bessalis* (see above, FIG. 69). One of the armchair voussoirs from (1032) had a Warry type S2 signature, featuring two semi-circles (see above, FIG. 108), while a second of this type was recorded on a brick from (2026). Finally, a single brick featured a Warry type C1 signature from (1046).

FOOTPRINTS

Animal, bird and human footprints are often found on tile, the impressions having been made after the tiles were laid out to dry before firing. Animal footprints provide evidence of the composition of animal communities (Bar-Oz and Tepper 2010), the nature of the infrastructure, and activities surrounding the tilery. Historically, it has not been possible to provenance foot-impressed tiles recovered from settlement sites, so their value as environmental indicators is necessarily limited. However, a coherent assemblage recovered from a tilery, as here at Little London, has very considerable value in this regard (cf. Cram and Fulford 1979, 202), the more so as no identifiable skeletal remains of animals were found in the excavations.

Footprint recording

The details recorded of the footprints identified on bricks and tiles included the metrics of the print, images and identifications. It is acknowledged that all print measurements are approximately 10 per cent smaller than when first impressed as a result of shrinkage during the drying process and firing (Brodribb 1987, 4). The prints have been divided into three categories:

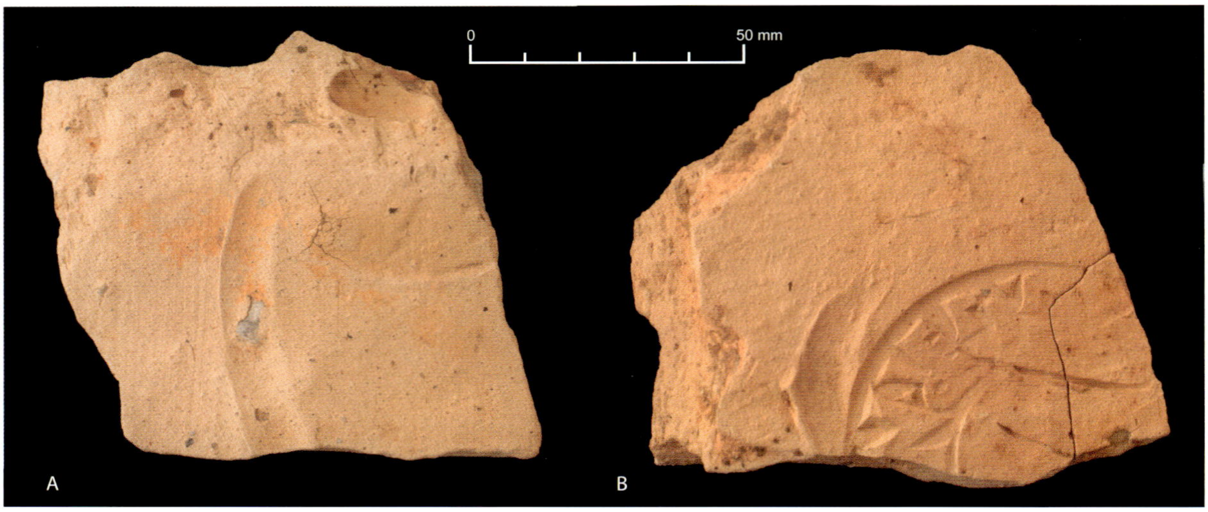

FIG. 115. Nero-stamped tiles: (A) SF12 (1091); (B) SF8 (1069)

FIG. 116. Potential Nero-stamped tile (SF4 (1031))

(a) those made by ungulates — animals with hoofs, cloven or otherwise, including domesticated species such as cattle, pigs and sheep/goat along with wild species; (b) other mammals including cats and dogs, other wild species and humans; (c) impressions made by birds, both domesticated and wild bird species. This section concludes with a discussion of the environments surrounding the tilery and the activities taking place alongside brick and tile production.

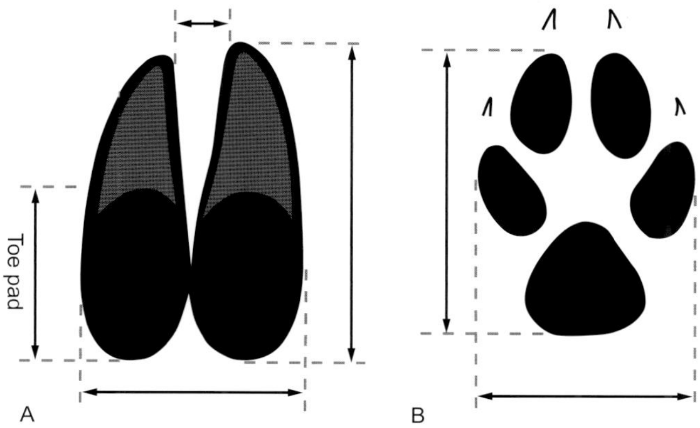

FIG. 117. Locations for measurements of: (A) hoofprints; (B) pawprints (after Bang and Dahlstrom 1974)

Ungulates

The length and width of the hoofprints were recorded, along with a measurement of the gap between the toes (FIG. 117A). A note was made as to whether the print was symmetrical, along with details of any other diagnostic characteristics displayed in the print. In addition, ages of the sheep and cattle who made the footprints have been estimated following Barr and Bell (2017).

Other mammals

The length and width measurements of the pawprints were recorded (FIG. 117B), also noting the presence/absence of claw impressions and the number of toe-pads present. Brief descriptions of morphological features were also recorded.

Birds

The bird footprints have been measured according to Brown *et al.* (2003) and assigned to the relevant size category according to their length (enormous >140 mm; large 100–140 mm; medium 75–99 mm; small 31–74 mm; minute <30 mm). The lengths of the first and third toes were recorded. Notes were made as to whether the print was symmetrical, and the toes segmented. The angle between the second and fourth toes was measured to assist with the identification of the species which was done using the criteria defined by Bang and Dahlstrom (1974).

Footprint assemblage

A total of 47 footprints has been recorded on the bricks and tiles recovered from Little London. Of these, there are 24 identified as of ungulates, 22 of other mammals, and a single bird print. Foot-impressed tiles are not common, representing 0.003 per cent of the total CBM assemblage of over 17,000 pieces, but, for example, this figure is very comparable to the proportion of foot-impressed tile (0.004 per cent) recorded on over 23,000 items of CBM of all periods and fabrics from the Silchester forum-basilica excavation (Timby 2000, 116; Cram 2000; Machin 2018, 263).

Ungulate prints

Ungulate footprints have been identified on a total of 24 bricks and tiles. Of these, nine are incomplete or distorted prints with indeterminate morphology, where it has not been possible to identify the species. The remaining 15 examples comprise red and roe deer, cattle and sheep/goat.

FIG. 118. Sheep hoofprints on a brick (1032)

Sheep/goat

Impressions from the hooves of sheep/goat account for 4 of the 15 confirmed ungulate prints. Experimental work by Cram (2000, 123) showed that it is not possible to distinguish the prints made by a sheep from those of a goat. The hoofprints are typically asymmetrical and the size, dependent on the age and breed, is usually about 50–60 mm long and 40–50 mm wide (Bang and Dahlstrom 1974, 73). Using the method described by Barr and Bell (2017), one example has been identified as being made by a sheep aged between three and five months old, indicating that these tiles were laid out to dry during the lambing season, usually in the spring months of March and April. Another example has been estimated to have been made by a sheep aged around nine months old with two examples made by fully-grown adult specimens, estimated to be aged approximately 20+ months (FIG. 118). Three hoofprints on a tile in Fabric 3 in Reading Museum are also of young animals, two newborn and one of three to four months (Machin 2018, 281). A single hoof-print on Fabric 4 from Silchester is of an older sheep of about 29 months (ibid., 285).

Cattle

There are three cattle-hoof impressions; they are rounded prints, often broad in relation to their length. All of these were made by newborn cattle, less than one month old. Both cattle prints in Fabric 3 from Silchester itself are also of newborn animals (Machin 2018, 281). The absence of hoofprints made by older cattle does not negate their presence near the tileworks. For there to be young cattle, there must be older individuals, too, but it is likely that any brick or tile trampled by fully grown cattle would be destroyed and not make it to the kiln for firing.

Red deer

There are five examples of hoofprints made by red deer (FIG. 119). Red deer prints exhibit a roughly parallel, broad track, with the outer edges of the hooves curving symmetrically towards

FIG. 119. Red deer hoofprint (1097)

the tip (Bang and Dahlstrom 1974, 66).

The examples recorded range in length from 44 to 71 mm and in width from 44 to 53 mm. All these examples are indicative of a young or female animal, being smaller than would be expected for a fully grown red deer stag (K. Barr., pers. comm.), which typically measures 80–90 mm in length and 60–70 mm in breadth. One example clearly shows the rear pad of the hoof, which accounts for approximately one third of the whole impression (FIG. 119). There is a single hoofprint of a young or female red deer from Silchester itself in Fabric 4 (Machin 2018, 285).

Red deer are indigenous to Britain and are typically found in wooded environments and on farmland fringes, actively selecting broadleaved woodland and areas with cover over upland heath and conifer forest (Staines *et al.* 2008, 579). Red deer hinds usually calve between mid-May and late July.

Roe deer

There are three examples of roe deer hoofprints, characterised by smaller, pointed tracks, typically 45 mm long and 30 mm wide. When walking, the hind foot registers in the fore-hoof track (Bang and Dahlstrom 1974, 69). One example measures 23 mm in length and is indicative of young deer (FIG. 120). There is also a single print of a young roe deer in Fabric 3 from Silchester itself (Machin 2018, 281).

The birth of roe deer kids peaks from May to mid-June (Hewison and Staines 2008, 608), thus indicating tiles laid out to dry in the summer. The two larger prints measure 36 mm and 45 mm and exhibit blunter tips suggestive of adult roe deer. Roe deer are found in a variety of habitats with open mixed coniferous and deciduous woodland, but where sufficient cover is provided (Hewison and Staines 2008, 606), can also use agricultural fields in these areas too. It is therefore not surprising to find a mix of roe and red deer alongside sheep and cattle.

Other mammal prints

There are 23 bricks and tiles which include other mammal footprints, of which ten are partial

FIG. 120. Roe deer hoofprint

pawprints with insufficient characteristics to make a positive identification and so have been categorised as unidentified. The remaining 13 prints have been identified as made by either cat or dog. No wild mammal prints were identified on the material. However, in addition to examples of dog and cat prints on Fabrics 3 and 4 from Silchester itself, there is also a single footprint of a hare or rabbit (Machin 2018, 286).

Dog

A total of ten pawprints have been identified as dog prints, with breadth measurements ranging from 26 mm to 61 mm (FIG. 121). In the Roman period, the size of dogs becomes more variable than in preceding periods, with shoulder heights ranging from 23 to 72 cm compared to heights of 29–58 cm in the Iron Age (Yalden 1999, 99). There are no examples of larger footprints indicative of wolf, typically up to 100 mm broad for the fore-foot and 70 mm for the hind-foot

FIG. 121. Dog pawprint (1103)

FIG. 122. Cat pawprint (1102) (left)

FIG. 123. Hobnail boot-print (above)

(Bang and Dahlstrom 1974, 56). The range of sizes may represent a variety of different ages of dog as well as perhaps reflecting a variety of dog breeds present at the kiln site. Dog prints are also well represented in Fabrics 3 and 4 in the Silchester assemblage where Machin noted that their print sizes indicate a more restricted range of dog sizes than later (2018, 282, 286, 288).

Cat

There are three cat prints identified on the kiln products. Cat footprints are distinguished from those made by dogs by their overall size and the lack of claw impressions, as, unlike dogs, cats retract their claws. The overall pad is almost circular in shape with the toe pads well defined and separated from the three-lobed intermediate pad (Bang and Dahlstrom 1974, 42). Two of the cat prints have complete breadth measurements, 40 mm and 42 mm, with the other example having an incomplete width measurement of at least 32 mm (FIG. 122). A medium-sized cat would leave a pawprint about 30–35 mm long and 30 mm wide (ibid., 43). Cat prints are also represented in the Silchester assemblage in Fabrics 3 and 4, including of two kittens and one large cat (Machin 2018, 282, 286).

Identifying domestic cats can be somewhat uncertain from the archaeological record (O'Connor 1992, 112) not least because of the difficulties in distinguishing their bones from those of the wild cat *Felis silvestris*. Some of the tracks of cats are large enough to have been made by wild cats whose prints are typically 40 mm long and 35 mm broad.

It seems quite unusual that there are only 'domestic' animals evidenced in the mammal footprints recorded. However, while there are no examples of wild mammal prints in the Little London assemblage, there is the single print of a hare or rabbit in Fabric 4 noted above from Silchester.

Bird prints

A single, partial bird footprint impression was recorded. This exhibited two segments of a single toe and therefore has insufficient characteristics for the species to be identified. Four chicken footprints have been identified on Fabrics 3 and 4 from Silchester itself as well as single examples of a possible tern, a bird found in Britain between April and October, and a raven (Machin 2018, 283, 286–7).

Human

There is a single example of an imprint made by the sole of a hobnail boot in the kiln material. The impressions show a pattern of large studs covering much of the sole. It is a basic pattern found widely in the western provinces (FIG. 123). Often, basic utilitarian shoes have fewer studs with larger heads, presumably to spare the expense of iron (Greene 2014, 33). Prints of hobnail boots have been found on three tiles in Little London fabrics at Silchester itself (Machin 2018, 282, 286).

Footprints: Discussion

By considering the footprint assemblages, we can establish a picture, or at least a partial picture, of the working environment as well as insight into some of the infrastructure at Little London, including access to raw materials and seasonality of the production cycle. It is traditionally assumed that tile-making in Britain was restricted to the summer months, to facilitate the laying out of tiles to dry during the least inclement weather. Indeed, Boon's study of all tiles marked with dates before firing argued for a seasonal activity which would call for other occupations such as farming to support the tile-makers (Boon 1974, 279, 365). With the evidence of the prints of lamb and of red and roe deer hinds suggesting that making and firing was under way by May, Little London adds to this picture of seasonal activity. The practice of more recent traditional industries in north-west Europe also suggests that brick-making was a summer occupation. This however relates only to the forming and firing of the tiles, the other related activities of clay preparation, weathering, and timber felling for fuel would most likely be autumn and winter tasks. Tile-makers were thought to be engaged in farming activities for some of their remaining time (Soffe *et al.* 1989, 83), suggesting that the tile industry was complementary to agriculture and stock-rearing. Domesticated livestock prints would not be expected where tile-making was a full-time, year-round occupation, leaving no opportunity for farming or stock-keeping (Cram and Fulford 1979, 201).

The footprints of cattle and sheep are almost evenly represented on the bricks and tile in the Little London and Silchester (Little London) material. This mirrors quite well the evidence of the faunal assemblages at Silchester itself in the Claudio-Neronian period, particularly at Insula IX (Ingrem 2020), but also at the forum-basilica, though cattle are a little more numerous there (Grant 2000). However, the Little London prints are dominated by those made by young animals, including neonates, which indicate animal breeding (Grant 2004, 380). While the Little London animals were alive when they made their marks on the tiles, their age profile is markedly different to that of the faunal remains found in contemporary urban assemblages, as is the case at Silchester, which typically show a broader age range (cf. Ingrem 2012, 190–1). However, there is likely to be an inherent bias here as tiles impressed by heavier, mature animals were unlikely to have made it from the drying-shed to the kiln.

While red and roe deer are the commonest of the wild animals represented by their prints at Little London, accounting for 29 per cent of all the identifiable footprints, there are only two examples in Fabrics 3 and 4 at Silchester itself. Nevertheless, taking the two assemblages together, deer still account for 15 per cent of the identifiable prints. This is considerably greater than their representation among the faunal remains of Claudio-Neronian Silchester where, like dog, the two species together account for less than one per cent of assemblages (Grant 2000, 426, table 62; Ingrem 2020, table 46).

Domestic mammals, cat and dog, were kept alongside the domestic livestock. Dog are the most abundant of all the identifiable prints at Little London, accounting for about one third of the assemblage. This compares with their representation on Little London fabrics at Silchester itself where they account for even more, almost half of the identifiable prints (Machin 2018,

280, 285). By contrast the skeletal remains of dog in Claudio-Neronian Silchester account for less than one per cent of the faunal assemblage (Grant 2000, 426, table 62; Clark 2020; Ingrem 2020, table 46). Compared with the wide range of footprint sizes recorded on Roman CBM, the range of sizes at Little London is somewhat restricted with the lowest complete measurement at 26 mm and the highest at 61 mm (cf. Machin 2018, 282, fig. 10.30). Nevertheless the variation in size is consistent with the range of estimated dog shoulder heights (Clark 2011, 277) and reflects the variability in the sizes of dog breeds in Roman Britain.

Cat remains are relatively rare from Roman Britain and are present in far fewer assemblages than dogs (Allen 2018, 97–8). Here, at Little London, the prints of dogs outnumber those of cats about three to one, though in Silchester the ratio in favour of dog prints on Little London products is greater, about six to one. To date, as there are no skeletal records of cats so far from late Iron Age and Claudio-Neronian Silchester, the Little London prints represent the earliest records of cat from Silchester and its environs.

Of the birds represented in the combined Little London and Silchester Fabrics 3 and 4 assemblages of identifiable prints, those of chicken are only slightly more numerous than those of wild birds, accounting for 6 per cent of the total assemblage. This is slightly higher than the representation of galliforms in Claudio-Neronian faunal assemblages (2–4 per cent) (Grant 2000, 426, table 62; Ingrem 2020, table 46).

What concluding remarks might we make about the assemblage of footprints at Little London and on Little London fabrics at Silchester itself? First, the incidence of these prints is very low, significantly less than one per cent of assemblages in Silchester and at Little London. This suggests that access to the sheds where the brick and tile were dried before firing was not easy, but perhaps easier for birds and small or young animals than for adults. However, we should consider whether the survival of the prints of the small and the young is merely a reflection of a situation where the weight of an adult completely destroys the impressed tile which is then discarded before firing and does not survive in the archaeological record. We cannot therefore exclude bias in the composition of the assemblage.

On the other hand, the rarity of the prints and the preponderance of those of young or neonate animals might suggest a degree of deliberate selection, where sick or vulnerable animals were given shelter and cared for in the spaces where the brick and tile were drying. Is it chance that we find the prints of young red and roe deer, or were they also found or hunted in the wild and then given protection and cared for — and eventually consumed — like the domestic animals?

We have observed that the representation of species and their age profiles in the combined Little London and Silchester Fabrics 3 and 4 assemblages is markedly different from what has been found among the Claudio-Neronian faunal assemblages from the town. Most striking is the complete absence of the prints of pig on Little London products, though it accounts for up to one third of the skeletal remains of the three major domesticates in the town (Grant 2000, 426, table 62; Ingrem 2020, table 46). Even from the much larger sample (152) of identifiable footprints in the London Clay Formation Silchester CBM Fabric 1 recovered from the town, there is only one example of the print of a pig (Machin 2018, 265, fig. 10.3). Surprising, too, is the incidence of wild animals, particularly deer, compared with their representation in the skeletal record from the town. Among the prints of ungulates represented in finds from the town in the Silchester CBM Fabric 1, roe deer (mostly young) (13) are only just second to sheep/goat (14), with cattle (4) a distant third (idem). It does look as if there is a degree of preferential selection of (mostly) young deer at Little London and in those locations where Silchester CBM Fabric 1 was made.

If there remains uncertainty as to whether the deer were accidental intruders in the drying-shed or whether they played a role in the animal husbandry practised at Little London, there can be little doubt that the raising of cattle and sheep/goat and the keeping of chickens formed part of the working life of the brick- and tile-makers. Estimating the relative importance of stock-raising at Little London is more difficult because we do not know the circumstances which led to the impressions being made on the drying tiles. On the face of it, however, the numbers are small, suggesting perhaps that animal husbandry was very much subordinate to the production of the brick and tile.

Finally, what can be inferred about the nature of the shed(s) in which the brick and tile were laid out to dry before firing? It is unlikely to have been completely open, otherwise we might expect there to have been more animals infiltrating the building and leaving their footprints. On the other hand, it is unlikely to have been completely enclosed because the circulation of air would have helped the tile to dry. While it might have been deliberate choice to devote some of the space to the stabling of (mostly) young sheep/goat, cattle and deer, the presence of dogs (especially), cats, chicken and other birds and small mammals may best be explained by their taking advantage of doors or gates casually left open as the brick and tile were brought in and laid out to dry.

CONCLUSIONS

With its association both with the production of pottery of pre- to early Flavian typology and the Nero-stamped tile, the Little London tile kiln described in Chapter 3 is among the earliest of its kind so far to be discovered in Britain. As we have seen with Kiln 4, rectangular kilns were also used for firing pottery and this may have been the case with the earliest kilns found at Colchester (cf. Swan 1984, 83–5). This tile kiln is among a very small number from Roman Britain where the associated assemblage of waster brick and tile has been reported. The latter is of considerable importance because it provides a snapshot of the not inconsiderable range of types of ceramic building material which was current in the 50s and 60s of the first century A.D. and deemed necessary to meet the architectural requirements of the time. This includes types which have rarely been found elsewhere in Britain.

It is clear that, while most of the Little London material is of the standard forms of brick, tile and roofing tile found across Roman Britain and beyond, there is a small proportion (6 per cent by count; 2 per cent by weight) of more specialised products, the most abundant of which is the hypocaust flue-tile. Together, these are indicative of specific types of building project or projects for which such specialised materials were required. However, if there is a close correlation between the numbers of the different types of waste material and the quantities successfully required, then output was overwhelmingly dominated by the production of brick, tile and roofing material. We should remind ourselves of the fragmentary nature of the material and the rarity of complete examples, such that the absence of *bipedales*, hollow voussoirs and half-box or double-box flue-tile is probably more apparent than real.

These specialised forms were clearly made to order to fit architectural designs, down to the details of types and sizes of bricks needed to complete construction. Judging by their scarcity, the *tegulae colliciares*, armchair voussoirs, and bricks for the 3-brick barrel vaults are not typical products of a Romano-British tilery and were not utilised in the construction of domestic dwellings or other small structures. They were not part of the repertoire produced at Holt later in the first century (Grimes 1930). Armchair voussoirs can provide a particular insight into the type of building for which the material was being produced, Fincker (1986, 144) noted their association with public and private bath-houses; he therefore assumed that these specialist forms were designed for a specific function linked to the construction of baths built between the end of the second and beginning of the fourth century. The presence of this type of voussoir at Little London demonstrates that the form was already being used before *c.* A.D. 70. Likely destinations for material of this kind were bath-houses, including the Neronian public bath-house at Silchester which was built with material from Little London (Fulford *et al.* 2018b; 2019). It is also useful to compare the Little London assemblage with that recovered from the legionary bath-house at Exeter dated A.D. 55/60–75 and so contemporary with production at Little London (Bidwell 1979). There, *bipedales* and small numbers of both full-box and half-box flue-tile were recovered, but none *in situ* and mostly residual in Period 2 and later contexts (ibid., 148–51). The absence of voussoir tile at Exeter is perhaps explained by the estimated size of the vaults which required concrete in order to span a room width of almost 10 m.

A very similar range of materials to that found at Little London was produced by the workshop of *legio XX* at Holt, Denbighshire, which was established in the later first century and not before *c.* A.D. 75, to provide for the building of its fortress at Chester (Grimes 1930). We have noted above types which were not produced at Holt and, by the same token, we can observe that the bridge tiles and ridge tiles evident at Holt have not so far been found at Little London. The antefixes at Holt are not ornamented with representations of the human face, but with the boar, the emblem of *legio XX*. The report does not mention any finds of relief-patterned flue-tile.

By contrast the range of types produced at the late first-/early second-century rural tilery at Great Cansiron Farm, Hartfield, E Sussex, was limited to brick, roofing tile, flue-tile and voussoirs (Rudling 1986, 208–9). Archaeomagnetic dating of the last firing of the kiln gives a date of *c*. A.D. 120 at 68 per cent confidence level (ibid., 198). While there is no quantification of the different types produced at Holt, at Great Cansiron Farm we see that 49 per cent (by weight) of wasters were of *imbrex* and *tegula*, and 33 per cent of flat bricks, including the *bessalis*, *pedalis* and *lydion* types (idem). As our definition of brick, based on thickness, is more restrictive than that used at Great Cansiron Farm, which embraced any tile which could not be classified as a *tegula* or box-flue, comparisons between the two sites are not exactly like-for-like. Nevertheless, brick at Little London amounts to more, at 45 per cent (by weight), and roofing tile considerably less, at 22.5 per cent than the proportions at Great Cansiron Farm. There is also a difference in the proportions of flue-tile between the two sites: 7.4 per cent at Great Cansiron and 2 per cent at Little London. Several factors may account for these differences, such as chronology and variation in wastage rates of the various types produced at the two sites, but the greater representation of the more strictly defined brick category at Little London may be linked to a greater demand for its use as string or levelling courses in masonry buildings as, for example, in the public bath-house at Silchester compared with the demand for such brick in the rural context of the Weald. By the same token, the greater proportion of roofing tile at Great Cansiron may reflect a greater emphasis in its use on timber-framed buildings.

Where differences may reflect change over time is with the treatment of the flue-tile. While, by weight, scored (20.1 per cent) and relief-patterned (36.5 per cent) examples account for over half of the flue-tile recorded at Little London, scored flue-tile is absent and relief-decorated amounts to only 0.04 per cent by weight of the flue-tile assemblage at Great Cansiron. On the other hand, while combing accounts for over 90 per cent by weight of the flue-tile at Great Cansiron, at Little London, with only 16 combed fragments, the figure is considerably less, at 0.2 per cent. The evidence from Little London makes it clear that relief-patterned and scored flue-tile were made side-by-side in the pre-Flavian period bringing forward the date for the start of their production from *c*. A.D. 75 (Black 1985) by between 15 years (production from *c*. A.D. 60) and 25 years (production from *c*. A.D. 50), a time when tile production is first evidenced in London (Betts 2017, 368). Although scored flue-tile has been noted from pre-Flavian contexts in London, so far there has been no report of relief-patterned tile, despite the relative abundance with which it is found there (cf. Pringle 2007). The slight representation at Great Cansiron suggests that production had ceased there by the late first/early second century. Little London is unlikely to have been the first workshop to make relief-patterned tile in Britain and a fuller discussion of the dating of relief-patterned tile and its implications can be found in Fulford and Machin (2021).

Among the more distinctive products of Little London are these relief-patterned flue-tiles, which have now been found, not only nearby at Silchester, but at a variety of quite distant locations including the major towns of Cirencester and Winchester and, also, possibly, Canterbury. With the discovery by Machin that the diamond-and-lattice die 81, which has been found at Fishbourne and Chichester, is also of Little London fabric, but not represented in this excavated sample, another major town can now be added to this list. The Chichester examples were recovered from contexts pre-dating the Flavian phase of the bath-house at Tower Street (Down 1978, 142–4). A Little London flue-tile has also apparently been found at distance at the small town of Alchester, Oxon.

Although the presence of flue-tile does not necessarily imply the construction of bath-houses, this is very likely to have been the case in this very early, Claudio-Neronian phase in the occupation of Britain. At the very least, they signify the building of houses with heated rooms and thus indicate a Little London contribution to the building of hypocausts and/or bath-houses in about a dozen different locations. These tiles have been noted and kept in museum archives because of their distinctive decoration, while the great majority of CBM has been discarded without further record. Given that relief-decorated flue-tile is but one of the many types of CBM produced at Little London, we can perhaps regard it as a proxy for a greater volume and diversity of Little London CBM at the various locations where it has been found.

If the proportion of tile from the Claudio-Neronian/early Flavian phase of Silchester Insula IX attributed to the workshop at Oaksey Park, Minety, Wilts., can be regarded as a guide, then we might suppose that, correspondingly, Little London may have supplied about 10 per cent of the CBM consumed at places as far away as Cirencester at this time (Machin 2020, 414). Indeed, the sharing of the relief-patterned die 39 between Little London and Minety and the similarities in their pottery assemblages (Timby, above, p. 84) suggests that the two workshops were operating in tandem. The evidence from first- and early second-century London also indicates that between 5 and 15 per cent of the CBM supplied to it came from quite distant tileries such as Eccles and a second north Kent source (London fabric 3226). An as yet unlocated tilery in West Sussex, probably close to Stane Street, also supplied London at this time (Betts 2017, 371–6).

To date Silchester is the only place where we have some indication of the scale of consumption of CBM from Little London. Although there has been no systematic study of fabric and form of recently excavated CBM from the town, the incidence of either Nero-stamped tile or relief-decorated tile shows the occurrence of Little London material at all sites within the walls excavated since 1980: public baths (Insula XXXIII), forum-basilica (Insula IV), temple (Insula XXX), Insula III and Insula IX. The greatest variety of forms has been noted at the bath-house, including flue-tile, *opus spicatum* and voussoir. Given that building in timber remained the norm through the first century A.D., especially for domestic and commercial buildings, about 25 per cent of the Little London production consumed at Silchester would have been used for roofing. Of the relatively small number of pieces of CBM retained from Claudio-Neronian (Period 1) contexts at Insula IX, half by count, 28 per cent by weight, is in Fabric Groups 3 and 4 (Machin 2020). Representation of retained Little London fabric groups in Insula IX decreases in the following period, *c.* A.D. 85–125/50, to 36 per cent by count (Machin 2018, 203) and, if not already residual by the end of the first century, its occurrence is certainly residual thereafter.

CHAPTER 6

WOOD CHARCOAL ANALYSIS: EVIDENCE FOR SITE ECONOMY AND ENVIRONMENT

By Catherine Barnett

INTRODUCTION

Contexts sampled during the excavation were assessed for their ability to provide samples suitable for radiocarbon dating and for wood charcoal analysis. The charcoal comes from six bulk sediment samples of 15–40L taken from discrete contexts and processed by flotation. As at most sites, some of the assemblages come from secondary contexts, the charcoal having been removed from the point of burning and dumped elsewhere, but primary/*in-situ* kiln deposits were also considered. The scale of, and close physical relationship of, the dumps of charcoal in the working areas and quarry pit mean it is relatively safe to assume the assemblages all directly relate to spent fuel from the excavated kilns, with a simple taphonomic path. Of the six contexts available for analysis, two primary contexts contained only sparse charcoal, and, while identifications were made for radiocarbon dating, the assemblages were too small to warrant analysis. Four contexts were subject to full charcoal analysis, all being of early Roman age and with a total fragment number of 390. Analysis has therefore been small-scale but related to one specific group of activities, i.e. industrial-scale pottery-, tile- and brick-making, and within the wider local context provided by analysis of the substantial early Roman assemblages analysed and dated for Silchester Insula IX (Period 1) (Barnett 2020a and b) and late Iron Age–early Roman contexts analysed for the Silchester Environs project (Barnett 2019; Barnett and Fulford in prep.).

METHODS

A small number of individual charcoal assemblages were selected to address specific questions at the tilery concerning economy, resource acquisition and activities represented by burning. Together these contemporaneous assemblages also provide data on vegetation and landscape in the local area. An evaluation was made of stratigraphic integrity, relationship to archaeological events in the on-site record (e.g. rake-out from kiln, primary deposition in the stokehole), volume/fragment number, and capacity to support other archaeological or palaeoenvironmental analyses and dating.

Wood charcoal >2 mm was separated from the processed flots and the residue scanned or sorted. A random grab subsample was taken from large assemblages, normally *c.* 100 fragments. Those assemblages of <100 fragments >2 mm were identified in their entirety and were prepared for identification according to standard methodology (Leney and Casteel 1975; Gale and Cutler 2000). Each was fractured with a razor blade to show three planes: transverse section (TS), radial longitudinal section (RLS) and tangential longitudinal section (TLS), and examined under bi-focal epi-illuminated microscopy at magnifications up to x400 using an Olympus BHM microscope.

Identification followed the anatomical characteristics described by Richter *et al.* (2004), Schweingruber (1990) and Butterfield and Meylan (1980). Access to modern reference material was limited. Identification was to the lowest taxonomic level possible, usually genus, but sometimes species, where anatomical or external morphological features were highly diagnostic. Juvenile twigwood and roundwood were separated from mature where the whole radius was visible, or where maturity was apparent from ring curvature and ray divergence.

Reflectance analysis of charcoal can provide evidence of original burn temperature (Ascough *et al.* 2010; McParland *et al.* 2009; 2010) but is time-consuming. Instead a rough estimate of the proportion of any assemblages noticeably more reflective by eye was noted during analysis.

Quantification is by fragment number of each taxon per sample (Table 11) and species ubiquity across the site (i.e. number of single-sample contexts in which each species appears). Concentration on ubiquity, a qualitative measure, arguably overcomes issues of differential fragmentation (due to taphonomic process, post-depositional process, sampling and processing), and over-representation of targeted types for particular activities at the site, so allowing consideration of woodland structure. Studies on quantitative measures indicate that the fragmentation rate is similar for all taxa (Chabal 1992) and that recording volume, fragment number or weight as indices leads to similar results in terms of relative taxonomic representation, suggesting fragment counts and the resultant percentage data are meaningful (cf. Chabal 1997; Keepax 1988, 70–9). It provides a non-homogenised dataset, allowing patterns of relative input/differential exploitation to be considered (Asouti and Austen 2005), both indices are used here to maximise the findings. Interpretation of individual taxon preference and habitat is with reference to modern plant ecology (Ellenberg 1988; Peterken 1993; Stace 2010). Latin binomials are given once at first appearance, common names throughout, nomenclature is according to Stace (2010).

RESULTS

Four contexts were fully analysed and while the minor differences between those are outlined in this report, it is also appropriate to consider the site assemblage as one entity, as below. The assemblages are known to be coherent and of early Roman age, with only well-stratified and well-dated contexts selected for analysis. While the contexts relate to different individual events and phases of site use and are unlikely to be truly contemporary, the radiocarbon dates returned and the excavated artefactual evidence indicate that they are broadly so, at least on a decadal scale. The limited number of contexts available and scale of analysis mean that taxa less frequently selected or those less common in the landscape are most likely absent from the identifications but useful information has been gained on economy and activity.

The taxa identified in the wood charcoal assemblage and their relative proportions are shown in Table 11 and FIG. 124, and their taxonomic grouping given in Table 12. Only five taxa were represented among the total assemblage of 390 fragments identified. Oak (*Quercus* sp.) was ubiquitous (6 of 6 contexts), heavily dominating all samples and making up 94 per cent of the total site assemblage. A minimum of 16 per cent of the total assemblage (21 per cent of the oak) was juvenile, mainly roundwood cut at 4–8 years. The fragmentary nature of the samples means that there was likely to be a greater percentage still in the original assemblage, with age only discernible on the better-preserved pieces. Small quantities of hazel (*Corylus avellana*), birch (*Betula* sp.), ash (*Fraxinus excelsior*) and a member of the Maloideae were also identified and present in 1–2 of 6 contexts (FIG. 125). The charcoal pieces in the samples analysed were in relatively good condition but those from the rest of the contexts sampled and assessed were highly fragmentary and the charcoal relatively sparse. Impregnation with iron oxides was common, markedly so for context 2075, the basal deposit in Kiln 4 (2031).

Kiln 1

A sparse and fragmentary assemblage was recovered from the primary collapse layer (1098), an abandonment deposit spread across the base of the firing chamber **1161** of Kiln 1, the large brick

TABLE 11. WOOD CHARCOAL IDENTIFICATIONS

Feature	Context	Context description	Sample	Sample type	Comments	Phase/ period	*Betula pendula/ pubescens*	*Corylus avellana*	*Fraxinus excelsior*	*Maloideae*	*Quercus* sp.	*Quercus* juvenile	Unidentifiable	Unidentifiable twigwood	Total identified	Other
Kiln 1, firing chamber **1161**	1098	Primary collapse of Phase 2 main brick kiln, abandonment deposit across base of the firing chamber **1161**	114	Wood charcoal from 40L bulk sample	Poor condition, small friable fragments, assume remnants left after clean-out. 14C date but analysis not warranted	Early Roman	1	0	0	0	0	0	0	0	1	
Quarry pit [1048] with dumps of spent fuel from Kiln 1	1029	First dump of charcoal in quarry pit [1048], 4.2 m by 3.3 m in size	102	Wood charcoal from 40L bulk sample	Clean and fresh but flaky fragments. 11 young *Quercus* sp. pieces – roundwood, too fragmented to see if rod-like	Early Roman	0	1	0	0	88	11	0	0	100	
Kiln 2, [1090]	1140	Rake-out from smaller later tile kiln, Kiln 2 [1090]	127	Wood charcoal from 25L bulk sample	Excellent condition, large assemblage, dominated by mature frags. Occ highly reflective	Early Roman	0	0	12	0	87	0	0	1	100	
Kiln 3, [2040]	2037	Second deposit overlying sand in the small circular pottery/flagon kiln, Kiln 3 [2040], with broken *tegulae*, part of the upper firing floor **2050** collapsed into the base of the kiln along with fuel remnants	206	Wood charcoal from 40L bulk sample	Small frags and assemblage, assume remnants left after clean-out/from collapse. 14C date but analysis not warranted (presence of oak noted)	Early Roman	0	0	0	0	0	1	0	0	1	
Associated with Kiln 3, [2040]	2076	Rake-out from Kiln 3 [2040] (small circular pottery kiln) into the working area	220	Wood charcoal from 15L bulk sample	Good condition, variety of frag. sizes small up to 12mm. Numerous roundwood pieces recorded (several with whole radius or diameter preserved), but, due to fragmentation, undiff./mature *Quercus* sp. frags may also be rwd. Rwd 4–8 yrs: 8x 16 mm 5 yrs, 3x 20 mm 6 yrs, 2x 4–6 yrs, 2x 10 mm 8 yrs (narrow rings), 3x 12 mm 3 yrs, 2x 20 mm 7–8 yrs	Early Roman	0	0	0	1	74	45	0	0	120	
Kiln 4, (2031)	2075	Ashy basal deposit in firing chamber of earliest, square pottery/flagon kiln, Kiln 4 (2031) (*in-situ* fuel remnants)	219	Wood charcoal from 20L bulk sample	Assemblage size good, but pieces dirty and with mineral impregnation. Several vitrified iron-rich non-charcoal lumps	Late Iron Age to Early Roman	2	3	0	0	54	6	3	0	68	Fe-rich vitrified non-charcoal lumps
Total							3	4	12	1	303	63	3	1	390	
Spp Ubiquity (presence in X of 6 contexts)							2	2	1	1	6	5	1	1		

TABLE 12. TREE AND SHRUB TAXA REPRESENTED AT LITTLE LONDON TILERY

Family	Sub-Family	Genus/Species	Common name
FAGACEAE		*Quercus* sp. (*robur/petrea*)	Oak
BETULACEAE		*Betula pendula/pubescens*	Silver/downy birch
		Corylus avellana	Hazel
ROSACEAE	Maloideae (formerly Pomoideae)	(Maloideae)	Pomaceous fruits, e.g. apple, pear, whitebeam, hawthorn
		e.g. *Crataegus* type	Hawthorn
		e.g. *Sorbus* type	Whitebeams, e.g. rowan, service-tree
OLEACEAE		*Fraxinus excelsior*	Ash

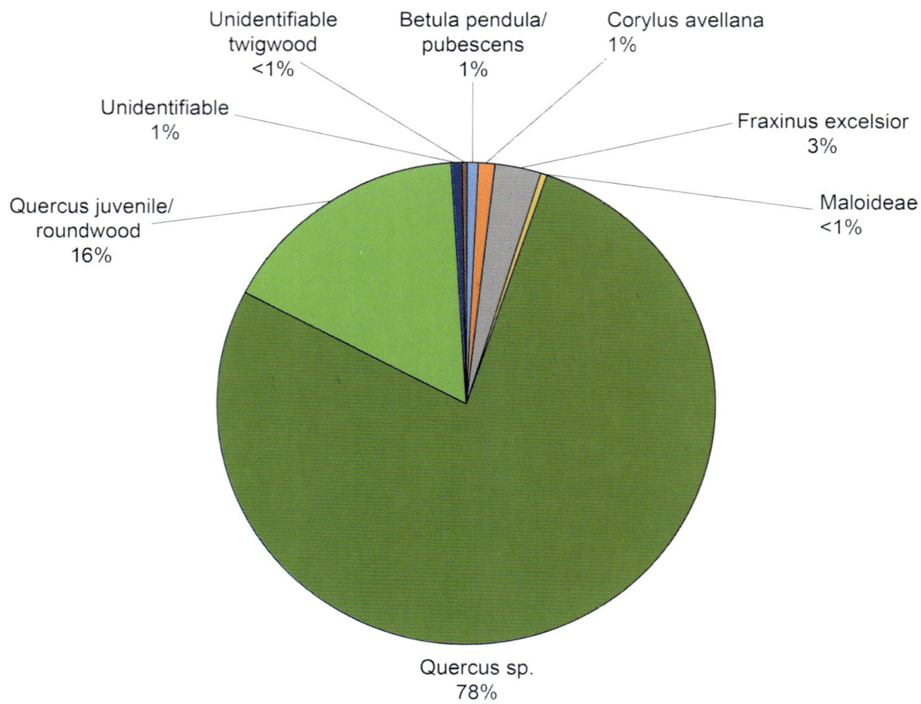

FIG. 124. Pie chart to show proportions of taxa represented, all contexts

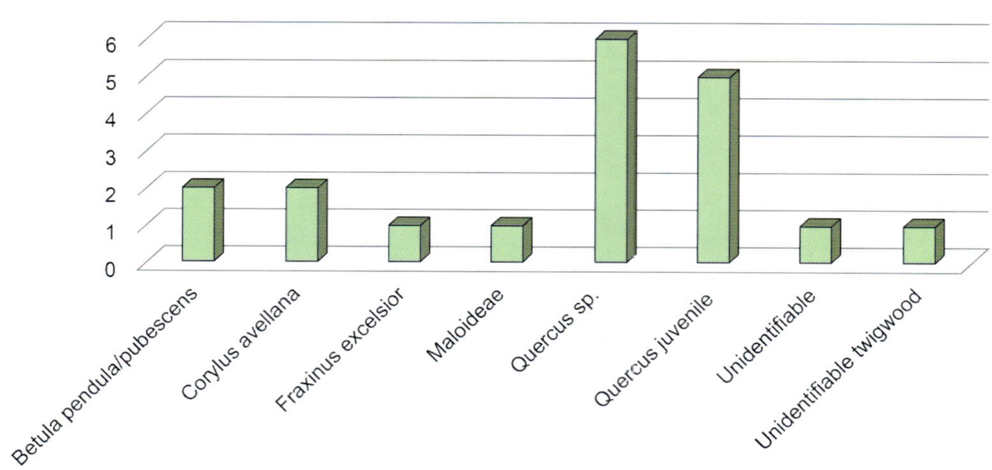

FIG. 125. Bar graph to show species ubiquity

TABLE 13. RADIOCARBON DATES FROM LITTLE LONDON

Feature	Context	Context description	Sample	Material dated	Species ID	Lab. code	14C date	±	δ13	cal date		Unmodelled cal range rounded out to 10 yrs	Period
										from	to		
Kiln 3, [2040]	2037	Second deposit overlying sand in the small circular pottery/flagon kiln, Kiln 3 [2040], with broken *tegulae*, part of the upper firing floor **2050** collapsed into the base of the kiln along with fuel remnants	206	Wood charcoal	<10 yrs juvenile *Quercus* sp.	SUERC-90860	1904	24	-25.9	20	210	27 cal AD (1.5%) 40AD 48AD (91.7%) 140AD 155AD (1.0%) 168AD 195AD (1.1%) 208 cal AD	Early Roman
Kiln 4, (2031)	2075	Ashy basal deposit in firing chamber of earliest, square pottery/flagon kiln, Kiln 4 (2031) (*in-situ* fuel remnants)	219	Wood charcoal	<10 yrs juvenile *Quercus* sp.	SUERC-90861	1964	24	-24.3	-40	90	40cal BC–90 cal AD	Late Iron Age to early Roman
Associated with Kiln 3, [2040]	2076	Rake-out from Kiln 3 [2040] (small circular pottery kiln) into the working area.	220	Wood charcoal	5 yr juvenile *Quercus* sp.	SUERC-90862	1941	24	-25.3	1	130	1–130 cal AD	Early Roman
Quarry pit [1048] with dumps of spent fuel from Kiln 1	1029	First dump of charcoal in quarry pit [1048], 4.2 m by 3.3 m in size	102	Wood charcoal	*Corylus avellana* charcoal	SUERC-90863	1915	19	-25.9	50	130	50–130 cal AD	Early Roman
Kiln 1, firing chamber **1161**	1098	Primary collapse of Phase 2 main brick kiln, abandonment deposit across base of the firing chamber **1161**	114	Wood charcoal	<10 yrs juvenile *Betula* sp.	SUERC-90867	1903	24	-27.7	20	210	28AD (1.3%) 39AD 50AD (91.8%) 140AD 155AD (1.1%) 168AD 195AD (1.2%) 208AD	Early Roman
Kiln 2, [1090]	1140	Rake-out from smaller later tile kiln [1090]	127	Charred plant macrofossil	1 frag. hazelnut shell	SUERC-90868	1918	21	-24.0	20	130	28AD (3.1%) 38AD 50AD (92.3%) 130AD	Early Roman

kiln used over two phases. Oak was present, along with birch (*Betula* sp.). As shown in Table 13, a fragment of the latter was dated to 50–140 cal A.D. (1903±24 BP, SUERC-90867) but there was insufficient material for meaningful charcoal analysis. Fuel from the working life of this kiln is better represented by the nearby first charcoal dump (1029) excavated from quarry pit [1048] over an area of 4.2 m by 3.3 m. 99 per cent of the charcoal within the dump was of oak with just one fragment of hazel identified. 11 per cent of the oak was of roundwood but the pieces were too fragmented to gauge the age of cutting. The hazel fragment was dated to 50–130 cal A.D. (1915±19 BP, SUERC-90863).

Kiln 2

The charcoal assemblage in the rake-out (1140) from the smaller, later tile Kiln 2 [1090] was dominated by large, mature fragments of oak but with 12 per cent mature ash. A few fragments were markedly reflective, indicating a high temperature of burning, and others vitrified and glassy. A fragment of charred hazelnut shell from the sample was dated to 30–130 cal A.D. (1918±21 BP, SUERC-90868).

Kiln 3

A charcoal-rich deposit (2037) immediately overlying a base of clean sand in the small circular pottery Kiln 3 [2040] also contained broken *tegulae* and has been interpreted as part of the firing floor collapsed into the base of the kiln. The charcoal proved highly fragmented and relatively sparse, one fragment of juvenile oak was removed for dating (50–140 cal A.D. 1904±24 BP, SUERC-90860) but no further analysis attempted. However, the associated rake-out (2076) which had been spread into the working area, and which contained 26 sherds of white ware including one collared flagon rim, provides insights into fuel use during active use. The large well-preserved assemblage contained at least 38 per cent oak roundwood pieces, several with the whole radius or diameter preserved, enabling the age at cutting to be recorded. These young branches or poles were all between 4 and 8 years old when cut, with 5 years dominant (see Table 11). Due to fragmentation, other pieces identified as undifferentiated/mature oak may also have been roundwood. The assemblage of >99 per cent oak also contained a single fragment of Maloideae, a taxonomic group which contains taxa such as hawthorn and apple. Juvenile oak from the sample was dated to 1–130 cal A.D. (1941±24 BP, SUERC-90862).

Kiln 4

The ashy basal deposit (2075) in the firing chamber of the earliest, square pottery Kiln 4 (2031) is thought to contain *in-situ* fuel remnants. A smaller total count was achieved than for the other samples, with 68 fragments >2 mm. Of these, 88 per cent were oak, including 8 per cent roundwood pieces, with 4 per cent hazel, 3 per cent birch and 4 per cent unidentifiable. Several vitrified, iron-rich, non-charcoal lumps were present in the sample and much of the charcoal had suffered mineral impregnation (including iron oxides). This kiln is believed on the basis of the excavated sequence to be the earliest of the pottery kilns, and indeed juvenile oak from (2075) yielded a slightly earlier radiocarbon date than the other features, late Iron Age to early Roman 40 cal. B.C.–90 cal A.D. (1964±24 BP, SUERC-90861).

DISCUSSION

The dates returned indicate activity involving the four kilns took place within a relatively short timespan. All dates correspond closely and are clearly early Roman, with the exception of SUERC-90861 from Kiln 4 which may be a little earlier (late Iron Age–early Roman) (see Table 13, and Hamilton, Ch. 8).

The ability of on-site charcoal analysis to answer the archaeological and palaeo-environmental questions has been reviewed by Barnett (2019) for the wider Silchester Environs project. To summarise, it has been argued (e.g. Théry-Parisot *et al.* 2010; Asouti and Austen 2005; Chabal 1997) that, while wood gathered for fuel tends to be of low species diversity, collection takes place repeatedly and randomly around and close to its point of use, using the least effort required (Shackleton and Prins 1992). It follows therefore that the relative proportions of individual taxa in long-term accumulations of material and in the total site assemblage are a reflection of abundance in the local environment, despite some over-representation of types that create more deadwood. However, there are also functional and socio-cultural factors or filters to be considered (Théry-Parisot *et al.* 2010; Smart and Hoffman 1988). Taxa are sometimes targeted for particular purposes and their presence may hint at the activities represented. For instance, woods used for construction are dominated by the strong and durable (e.g. oak and alder). Their over-representation in certain contexts is likely, but across whole sites, types common in the local woodlands will also occur. Given the nature of this site, a bias in selection towards wood of taxa capable of providing high or sustained burning temperatures, and therefore giving a less clear picture of the wider woodland structure, may reasonably be expected.

The substantial body of evidence provided by the analysis of 1,788 fragments in 26 samples from 21 contexts representing the contemporary, *c.* 40-year Claudio-Neronian/early Flavian (Period 1) phase of activity at nearby Silchester Insula IX, coupled with the results from the preceding Period 0 (Late Iron Age), provide a comparative context for these findings from Little London (Barnett 2018b; 2020a). There, multiple feature types and the activities they represent were examined. Findings by context varied according to those activities, but the total site assemblage provides a good picture of landscape and domestic exploitation of the local tree and shrub resource for both Periods 0 and 1, covering the period from *c.* 20/10 B.C. to *c.* A.D. 85. In contrast, the samples from the Little London tilery represent one restricted group of activities, and are presumed to be solely the fuel from large-scale pottery, brick and tile production. The assemblage from Insula IX included a minimum of 20 woody taxa, Little London only five. There, too, oak was dominant overall, both in terms of percentage of the total assemblage and in species ubiquity, with oak appearing in every context and sample, and forming 75 per cent of the total analysed site charcoal assemblage, 63 per cent being mature or of undifferentiated age, 10 per cent roundwood and 2 per cent twigwood. There is apparently even greater dominance in the tilery fuel remains, with oak (*Quercus* sp.) making up 94 per cent of the total site assemblage, with a minimum of 16 per cent (21 per cent of the oak) being juvenile. As argued by Barnett (2020a), although oak is today (and probably was then) the most common British broadleaf tree type (with oak-dominant forest forming 23 per cent of non-conifer areas (Forestry Commission 2003, table 3)), the percentage of oak described here far exceeds the oak component of typical mixed woodland today (also at *c.* 23 per cent, ibid.). Not only is targeted exploitation indicated, but direct encouragement and management of this taxon.

Absent types at Little London include heathland taxa (rare but present at Insula IX) and, more notably, wetland taxa (relatively common at Insula IX at >3 per cent, alder, willow/poplar). Only taxa of open and closed dry deciduous woodland are represented at the tilery and seemingly a limited range of habitats were exploited. Clearly, with only five taxa represented among the total assemblage of 390 fragments identified and the overwhelming dominance of oak, there was highly targeted exploitation of key taxa to fuel the kilns. Were analysis carried out on a larger scale, the range might prove greater, with rarer/less exploited taxa found in small numbers, but the picture of highly focused resource selection and use is apparent. A contrast is demonstrated between these two geographically close and broadly contemporary sites. Whether the greater species diversity at Silchester Insula IX (Periods 0 and 1) indicates use of a less extensive or regularly cropped woodland management system, or a relative lack of industrial contexts reliant on pre-charred fuel or specifically dense, high calorific types (oak, beech, elm, ash) requiring high temperature burn, is debatable.

The high (minimum) proportion of roundwood at Little London is of note. At Insula IX, the annual growth ring count for the roundwood where the whole radius was visible varied from cut at 3–15 years, but with 5–10 years dominant, whereas at Little London roundwood cut at 4–8 years dominates. The assemblages analysed were fragmentary and it was not possible to get a full age profile or to see whether pieces were long and rod-like, as might be expected from a managed source (Edlin 1949, 70–1), but the prevalence of roundwood pieces cut at 4–8 years with a peak in those cut at 5 years is at least suggestive of use of woodland stands managed by coppicing or pollarding on a short rotation (Rackham 2001, 8–9; Edlin 1949, 155–7).

Recent work conducted as part of the Silchester Environs project provides clearer evidence of rotation cropping and of oak stand management for the late Iron Age to mid-Roman periods in the immediate area of the tilery. Pollen analysis of enclosure ditch sequences at Pamber Forest and the linear monument at Wood Farm shows periods of abnormally high oak flowering that suggest coppiced or pollarded oak stands were established during the Iron Age to early Roman period (Dark in prep.). Mid–late Roman Pit 3020 (located within the footprint of middle Iron Age Enclosure 3) at Pamber Forest (Fulford *et al.* 2017a; Barnett and Fulford in prep.) has been interpreted as a possible charcoal preparation structure. The volume of charcoal recovered was high, with four substantial and distinct layers of charred oak. The base of the feature was formed of a large plank-like piece >30 years when cut, but the three overlying layers contained pieces cut at 15–20 years (Barnett 2019). The preservation of the single-taxon layers by charring without ashing, despite the large quantity of dense highly calorific wood, indicates moderate, controlled temperatures. This, coupled with the form of the feature and the presence of rubified soil and associated encircling post-holes, suggests the presence of a charcoal preparation stack (Barnett 2019). It compares well with the form of the nineteenth- to twentieth-century woodland charcoal-making features described by Edlin (1949, 160–5). A managed source of oak for this charcoal preparation has been interpreted from the presence of the same-age oak pieces.

While highly reflective pieces were not dominant in the Little London assemblage, the charcoal in the rake-out (1140) from the smaller, later tile kiln 2 [1090] of large, mature fragments of oak and mature ash did contain some markedly reflective fragments, and others that were vitrified and glassy. The work of McParland *et al.* (2009; 2010) indicates the reflective pieces were subject to fierce burning temperatures (>850–1000°C) and may have been pre-prepared as fuel charcoal to help achieve those high temperatures for firing the tiles associated with this particular feature.

Of particular relevance in interpreting the results for the Little London kilns is the charcoal analysis of ten samples from kilns, working areas and associated tip lines in colluvium of spent fuel downslope from the kilns undertaken for a late Roman site at Frith End (Barnett 2011), and for two chambers of a substantial contemporary kiln nearby in Alice Holt Forest (Chisham 2008), both sites used for Alice Holt pottery production. Of the 1,550 charcoal fragments identified across the Frith End site, only 29 pieces were of taxa other than oak (hornbeam (*Carpinus betulus*), willow/aspen (*Salix/Populus*), Maloideae, holly (*Ilex aquifolium*), ash (*Fraxinus excelsior*) and possible beech (*Fagus sylvatica*)). It was noted that the Frith End kiln structures yielded small, scrappy assemblages, as at Little London, presumably due to regular cleaning out of the fuel waste. The richest, from clamped kiln/oven F116, was dominated by oak at 90 per cent, with lesser (mature) hazel plus a few pieces of Maloideae charcoal, representing possible kindling.

Large quantities of charcoal were deposited beyond the kilns in scoops, hollows and as tip lines of oak-dominated charcoal. The tip lines were interleaved with thick bodies of fast-accumulated (late Roman) colluvium with no apparent stasis horizons developed between and in the context of a series of substantial downslope erosional features dissecting the hill. Barnett (2011) suggested this slope instability indicated substantial local disturbance during the Romano-British period due to local deforestation during the lifetime of the kilns, related to clearance for their construction and/or tree felling for fuel use. However, the preservation of large areas of managed woodland would have been required in the wider area for the long-term operation of the industry. Hollows/scoops 5179 and 5183 were particularly rich in charcoal yet contained only two taxa (oak and hazel) and were dominated by roundwood. 5179 contained 97 per cent oak roundwood while 5183 contained both oak (40 per cent) and hazel (45 per cent) roundwood, the remainder being mature pieces of the two taxa. The volume of roundwood in these two scoops enabled consideration of the age profile. The oak pieces from 5179 were harvested at between 3 and *c.* 32 years of age but dominantly at 5–15 years (*c.* 63 per cent) and 21–26 years (*c.* 22 per cent), while both the oak and hazel from 5183 were cut at 5–25 years (Barnett 2011). Plotting of the age of the roundwood when cut for the site as a whole demonstrated a clear propensity for cutting hazel and oak rods at 5–10 years (see Barnett 2011, table 3, reproduced as Appendix 3, Table 22), though pieces of oak roundwood, up to 25 years old when cut, were common and mature oak timbers were used as well.

A larger assemblage and greater range of taxa were found within the Alice Holt Forest kiln structure, with fuel waste from the last firings apparently not cleaned out. Notably, there was a substantial difference in assemblages between the remains from the north and south flues. Mature oak was common in the north flue, with alder (*Alnus glutinosa*) and hazel roundwood and less common oak roundwood, field maple (*Acer campestre*, mature and roundwood), birch (*Betula* sp.), ash (*Fraxinus excelsior*), willow/poplar (*Salix/Populus*) and Maloideae. Oak also dominated the south flue, but at least half of it was young, rod-like pieces of roundwood up to 15 mm in diameter, cut at 2–5 years growth, with most cut at 3 years. Many of the fragments were fissured, reflective and partly vitrified, indicating high temperatures of burn and possibly the use of damp wood in this flue. The south flue also contained willow/aspen and birch, with lesser quantities of hazel, ash, holly and Maloideae. A contrast in the temperatures required/attained, boosted by the use of smaller tinder, including grass and weed stems, is indicated. The findings from both analyses were found to be comparable to a smaller assemblage previously described for nearby waste dump AH5 (Pratt 1979), where roundwood dominated, mostly of oak but with hazel and possible willow also described. An experimental firing of the type of kiln found at Alice Holt found that long, straight (coppiced) poles 20 mm in diameter and 0.6 m long worked best for the main firing in the constricted flues, with finer brushwood being used for producing higher temperatures (Lyne and Jefferies 1979, 13), the diameter consistent with the site findings (Barnett 2011; Chisham 2008).

A pattern of regular management of both oak stands and oak-hazel coppice rotation to produce vigorous straight shoots as a fast-growing crop (e.g. Edlin 1949, 82–4; Buckley 1992) is apparent for the two Alice Holt kiln sites, indicating woodland management employed on a large scale in order to provide a predictable and substantial fuel source for the Alice Holt pottery industry. Different techniques, temperatures and activities are also indicated, with different taxa and maturity of pieces selected accordingly. Due to the poorer preservation of the Little London assemblage, in particular the fragmented nature of the charcoal, such detailed examination of intra-site and intra-kiln activities and techniques has not been possible. The underlying pattern of short rotation cropping (here oak rather than oak-hazel) to fuel the tile, brick and pottery industry is, however, perhaps supported, as is the deliberate encouragement of oak-dominated woodland stands around Little London. This is likely to reflect reuse of the already established local woodland management patterns (see Barnett 2019). The scale of fuel dumping is far less than observed at Alice Holt and with no evidence for major deforestation or new soil instability, it is tentatively suggested that activity at Little London was more restricted and perhaps of shorter duration and/or more rapidly established in response to an immediate need.

CONCLUSIONS

Charcoal analysis coupled with radiocarbon dating of a limited number of contexts within, and associated with, a short phase of use of tile and pottery kilns at Little London has provided data on woodland management and use of woody resources to fuel the industry. All dates correspond closely and are early Roman, with the possible exception of SUERC-90861 from Kiln 4 (late Iron Age–early Roman), and the tight relative dating provided by the presence of Nero-stamped tiles from this site is notable (see Hamilton, Ch. 8).

Samples from primary kiln contexts proved sparse, presumably due to repeated rake out of spent fuel (fragmented charcoal and ash) before each firing. More substantial assemblages were found in the individual kiln working areas and the dumps into the adjacent quarry pit representing the rake-out.

Only five taxa were found overall, with an overwhelming 94 per cent of the total site assemblage being oak, with small quantities of hazel, birch, ash and a member of the Maloideae. It is suggested that oak was both deliberately encouraged in the local area and targeted for use, as supported by pollen and charcoal data generated by the Silchester Environs project for nearby sites (Wood Farm, Pamber Forest). A single habitat (managed dry woodland) source has been suggested with heathland and wetland taxa entirely absent in the samples analysed for the tilery, in contrast to Silchester Insula IX which exhibited far greater species diversity, though in part due to the scale of analysis with rare or uncommonly selected taxa well represented there.

The assemblages associated with the five kilns excavated at Little London have been described individually, with differences between them presented. Of note is that the large well-preserved assemblage from deposit (2037) in small circular pottery Kiln 3 [2040] with broken *tegulae*, thought to represent the collapsed firing floor, contained a minimum 38 per cent oak roundwood pieces 4–8 years old when cut, with 5 years dominant. A minimum of 16 per cent (21 per cent of the oak) of the total site assemblage was found to be juvenile, with roundwood cut at 4–8 years dominant and a peak at 5 years, but this figure is likely to be an under-representation due to high levels of fragmentation, with the lack of full diameter visibility preventing assessment of age when cut for the majority of pieces. It was not possible to see whether the pieces were originally long and rod-like, as might be expected from a managed source, but the prevalence of young roundwood pieces is suggestive of the use of woodland stands managed by coppicing or pollarding on a short rotation.

The context for this site and analysis is provided by more substantial charcoal and dating analyses as well as pollen work undertaken on early Roman contexts (*c*. A.D. 44–85) for Insula IX (Barnett 2020a; 2020b) and late Iron Age–early Roman contexts at Pamber Forest, Wood Farm and the Little London Linear analysed for the Silchester Environs project (Barnett 2019; Barnett and Fulford in prep.; Dark in prep.), with clearer evidence of rotation cropping, oak stand management and charcoal preparation for fuel use for the late Iron Age to mid-Roman periods in the immediate environs of Little London. It is suggested that the managed woodland and pattern of cropping had already been established during the late Iron Age around Silchester and Little London and was continued or re-established by the Roman tile- and brick-makers.

Comparison has also been made with the detailed evidence from two late Roman Alice Holt kiln sites (Barnett 2011; Chisham 2008), with well-preserved charcoal for which a profile of age when cut could be established, with the archaeobotanical and geoarchaeological findings indicating that woodland management was employed on a large scale in order to provide a predictable and substantial fuel source for the Alice Holt pottery industry. The findings for the Little London tilery are in keeping in terms of targeted exploitation and likelihood of short rotation cropping, but the scale of management and environmental impact is seemingly smaller and the different techniques and temperatures indicated within those Alice Holt sites, with different taxa and maturity of pieces selected for different kiln-related activities, not discernible at Little London.

CHAPTER 7

THE CHARRED PLANT REMAINS

By Lisa Lodwick

INTRODUCTION

There are few reports on plant macrofossils from tile kilns in Roman Britain. Samples were processed in a modified 'Siraf' flotation tank. Flots were retained on a 0.25 mm mesh and residues were retained on a 0.5 mm mesh and sorted by eye. All plant remains were sorted and identified using a binocular microscope at x10–x40 magnification. Nomenclature follows Stace (2010).

RESULTS

Charred plant macrofossils were very sparse, especially in contrast to abundant charcoal (Barnett, Ch. 6). Flots contained high proportions of roots, indicating bioturbation and the potential for contamination of the samples from later activity. 29 samples were assessed, and only 15 items were identified, with an average density of 0.03 items/L. The taxa identified are *Hordeum* sp. (barley) grains, a single *Triticum spelta* (spelt) glume base, two *Triticum spelta/dicoccum* (spelt/emmer) grains and one possible *Triticum* free-threshing (wheat) grain. A handful of wild taxa were identified: *Stellaria media* (common chickweed), *Rumex* sp. (docks), *Persicaria lapathifolia/maculosa* (pale persicaria/redshank). These taxa are all common occurrences in the Late Iron Age–Roman phases at Insula IX (Lodwick 2020), other than the possible free-threshing wheat grain.

TABLE 14. THE CHARRED PLANT REMAINS

Context		**2017**	**2046**	**1112**	**1074**	**1046**	**1061**
Sample		**204**	**203**	**115**	**111**	**105**	**107**
Feature		Kiln rake-out/ burning	ditch	ditch	kiln	pit	pit
Sample volume/L		35	40	NA	43	30	4
cf. *Hordeum* sp.	grain		2				
Triticum cf. *spelta/dicoccum*	grain			2			
Triticum spelta	glume base					1	
Triticum cf. free-threshing	grain				1		
cf. Cereal indet.	grain					1	
Chenopodiaceae	seed				1		
cf. S*tellaria media* gp. (L.) Vill.	seed	1					
Persicaria lapathifolia/maculosa	seed	1					
Rumex sp.	seed						1

indet.	stem	1					1
indet.	seed	2					1
indet.	bud			2			

DISCUSSION

The scant archaeobotanical data provide no evidence for the diet of the kiln operators or the agricultural system provisioning them. However, it can be said that there is no evidence for the significant use of crop-processing by-products as fuel in the kilns. This stands in contrast to evidence from pottery kilns where straw and chaff were used as fuels, for example at a first-century kiln at Stowmarket in Suffolk (Plouviez 1989) and Claudio-Neronian kilns at Greenhouse Farm, Cambridge (Gibson and Lucas 2002). Archaeobotanical studies of tile kilns are rare as opposed to charcoal studies, and the only example known to the author is a tile kiln at Coberley villa, Glos., where hawthorn shrub was identified as a fuel in a tile kiln on the basis of fruits and thorns (Wessex Archaeology 2008). At other tileries, such as Great Cansiron Farm, Hartfield, E Sussex, fuel use has been identified on the basis of charcoal, showing the use of birch and oak (Cartwright 1986).

CHAPTER 8

LITTLE LONDON AND SILCHESTER INSULA IX: RADIOCARBON DATING AND CHRONOLOGICAL MODELLING

By Derek Hamilton

Chronological models were constructed using radiocarbon dates from the Little London site and Silchester, Insula IX. The dated material from Little London all comes from the fills of kiln features (e.g. kilns and waster dumps) that are directly related to ceramics and bricks specifically associated with the emperor Nero (A.D. 54–68). Furthermore, the archaeological evidence suggests the site was relatively short-lived, perhaps in use for no more than 15–20 years. The dating evidence from Insula IX focuses particularly on the Period 0 (pre-Roman Iron Age) and Period 1 (Romano-British) remains (Fulford *et al.* 2018a; 2020).

Twenty-four samples were submitted to the Scottish Universities Environmental Research Centre (SUERC) where they were pretreated and measured by accelerator mass spectrometry (AMS) following the methods described in Dunbar *et al.* (2016). There are six results from Little London and 19 results from the two periods at Insula IX. The lab. maintains rigorous internal quality assurance procedures, and participation in international inter-comparisons (Scott 2003; Scott *et al.* 2010) indicates no laboratory offsets, thus validating the measurement precision quoted for the radiocarbon ages.

The results are presented (Tables 13 and 15) as conventional radiocarbon ages (Stuiver and Polach 1977). They have been calibrated using the internationally agreed terrestrial calibration curve (IntCal20) of Reimer *et al.* (2020) and the OxCal v4.4 computer program (Bronk Ramsey 2009). Simple calibrated results are presented at 95% confidence intervals (unless otherwise noted) in plain text and rounded outward to ten years. The italicised dates presented in the text below are posterior density estimates derived from mathematical modelling of archaeological problems and have been rounded outward to five years. These dates can change with the addition of new data or when the modelling choices are varied.

METHODOLOGICAL APPROACH

A Bayesian approach (Buck *et al.* 1996) has been applied to the interpretation of the chronology of archaeological activity at Little London and Insula IX. Although simple calibrated dates are accurate estimates of the radiocarbon age of samples, this is not, usually, what archaeologists really wish to know. It is the dates of the archaeological events represented by those samples that are of interest. For example, the start and end of activity associated with the pottery production at Little London is of particular interest. The chronology of this activity can be estimated not only by using the absolute dating derived from the radiocarbon measurements, but also by using stratigraphic relationships between samples and the relative dating information provided by the archaeological phasing.

The methodology used here allows the combination of these different types of information explicitly, to produce realistic estimates of the dates of archaeological interest. The posterior density estimates produced by this modelling are not absolute, rather they are interpretative estimates, which can and will change as further data become available and as other researchers choose to model the existing data from different perspectives. The technique used is a form of Markov Chain Monte Carlo sampling and has been applied using the program OxCal v4.4 (http://c14.arch.ox.ac.uk/). Details of the algorithms employed by this program are available in Bronk Ramsey (1995; 1998; 2001; 2009) or from the online manual. The algorithm used in the models can be derived from the OxCal keywords and bracket structure shown in FIGS 126, 128 and 130.

SAMPLES AND MODELS

The six radiocarbon results from Little London were made on short-life samples of wood charcoal and a single charred nutshell (Ch. 6, Tables 13 and 15). They are considered here within

TABLE 15. RADIOCARBON DATES FROM LITTLE LONDON AND INSULA IX THAT ARE PRESENTED IN THE CHRONOLOGICAL MODELLING

Lab ID	**Context**	**Material dated**	**δ¹³C (‰)**	**δ¹⁵N (‰)**	**C:N**	**Radiocarbon age (BP)**
Little London						
SUERC-90860	2037	charcoal: *Quercus* sp.; <10 years	−25.9			1904 ±24
SUERC-90861	2075	charcoal: *Quercus* sp.; <10 years	−24.3			1964 ±24
SUERC-90862	2076	charcoal: *Quercus* sp.; <10 years	−25.3			1941 ±24
SUERC-90863	1029	charcoal: *Corylus avellana*	−25.9			1915 ±19
SUERC-90867	1098	charcoal: *Betula* sp.	−27.7			1903 ±24
SUERC-90868	1140	charred hazelnut shell	−24.0			1918 ±21
Insula IX						
SUERC-65370	10441	charcoal: *Alnus glutinosa*; juvenile	−25.4			2020 ±29
SUERC-65371	10442	charred seed: *Olea europaea* stone	−23.6			2014 ±29
SUERC-65372	10442	charcoal: *Corylus avellana*; twigwood	−27.0			2038 ±26
SUERC-65374	12751	animal bone: Canis; miniature	−20.2	9.9	3.2	2024 ±30
SUERC-65375	15685	charcoal: *Quercus* sp.; vitrified sapwood	−25.1			3943 ±29
SUERC-65376	12714	charcoal: *Corylus avellana*	−25.3			2017 ±29
SUERC-65380	11117	charcoal: *Betula* sp.	−26.6			2020 ±29
SUERC-65381	14653	charred seed: *Pisum sativum*	−25.4			2034 ±29
SUERC-65382	11602	charcoal: *Corylus avellana*; knotwood	−26.6			2038 ±26
SUERC-65383	11603	charred grain: *Hordeum* sp.	−24.9			1992 ±29
SUERC-66262	12117	charcoal: *Quercus*	−23.9			2015 ±26

		sp.; twigwood				
SUERC-84812	15968	charcoal: Maloideae; twigwood	−24.6			1962 ±26
SUERC-84813	9520	charcoal: *Quercus* sp.; twigwood	−24.4			1900 ±26
SUERC-84814	16790	charred grain: cereal indet.	−22.5			1996 ±26
SUERC-84815	16924	charcoal: *Quercus* sp.; roundwood	−25.4			1989 ±26
SUERC-84819	14616	charcoal: *Quercus* sp.; twigwood	−24.5			1988 ±26
SUERC-84820	15328	charcoal: *Calluna* sp.	−25.9			1931 ±26
SUERC-84821	15366	charred grain: *Triticum spelta*	−22.9			1960 ±26
SUERC-93672	11193	human bone: femur	−21.5	7.1	3.3	1945 ±32

a simple Bayesian chronological model of the 'bounded phase-type' described in Hamilton and Kenney (2015). This model follows the assumption that the material dated comes from a potential set of samples that represent a relatively uniform deposition process. As such, these results provide an estimated start and end date for the represented activity, with the difference between the two used to calculate the overall span of the activity.

From Insula IX, there are 17 radiocarbon results on macrobotanical remains (short-lived wood charcoal and charred seeds or nutshell) and further results from an animal bone and a human bone sample. Sixteen results were originally modelled and reported in Barnett (2020b).

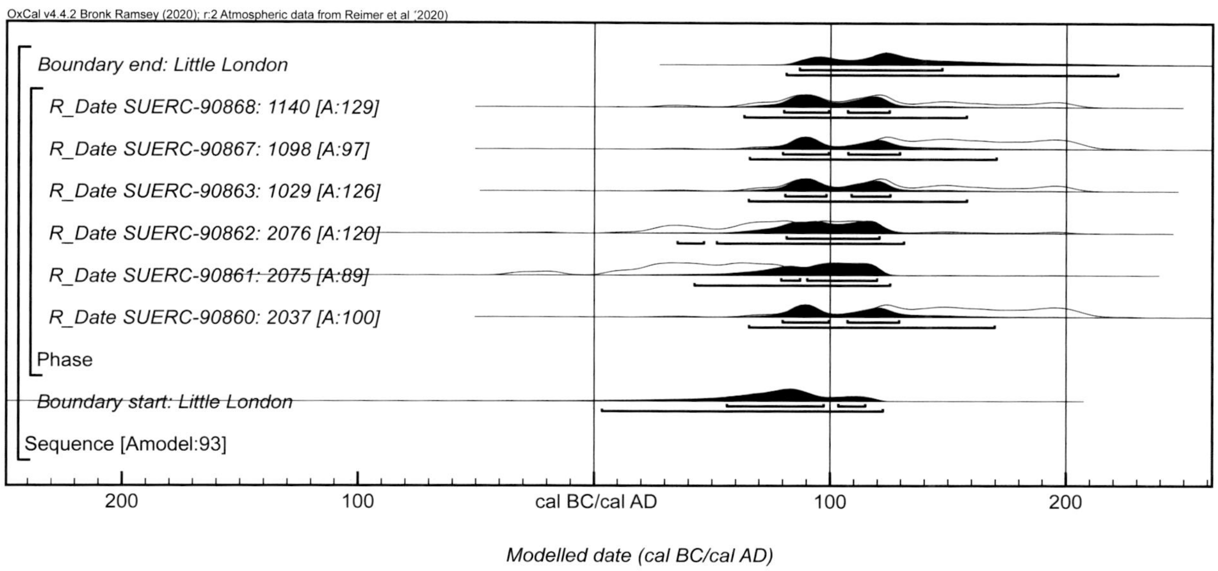

FIG. 126. Chronological model for Little London. Each distribution represents the relative probability that an event occurred at some particular time. For each of the radiocarbon measurements two distributions have been plotted, one in outline, which is the result of simple radiocarbon calibration, and a solid one, which is based on the chronological model used. The other distributions correspond to aspects of the model. For example, '*start: Little London*' is the estimated date that activity began, based on the radiocarbon dating results. The large square 'brackets' along with the OxCal keywords define the overall model exactly

One result from Period 0 (SUERC-65375) was excluded as it is Bronze Age and likely reworked material. The remaining radiocarbon results are placed into two sequential periods of activity, with Period 0 prior to Period 1. The chronological model has then been used to provide a chronology for the overall activity of the two periods, with the transition between the two being equal to the end of Period 0 and start of Period 1 for the purposes of calculating the span of each period. The model follows the same format as the preferred Model 2 of Barnett (2020b), though is updated to account for the release of a new internationally-agreed calibration curve (IntCal20).

RESULTS

Little London

The model has good agreement between the radiocarbon dates and the assumption that they are all from a single period of activity (Amodel=93). The model estimates this activity began in *cal AD 1–125 (95% probability*; FIG. 126; *start: Little London*), and probably in *cal AD 55–120 (68% probability*). The activity ended in *cal AD 80–225 (95% probability*; FIG. 126; *end: Little London*), and probably in *cal AD 85–150 (68% probability*). The total span of the activity is estimated at *1–200 years (95% probability*; FIG. 127; *span: Little London*), and probably *1–80 years (68% probability*).

The radiocarbon dating and modelling are coarse when compared to the dating framework provided by the typology-derived chronology. However, a primary question was whether the radiocarbon dating might be considered to support the material culture-derived dating. To investigate this, a model was produced that simulated a series of six radiocarbon results from organic material that died in the 15 years between A.D. 54 and 68, to compare the results of that model with the actual radiocarbon-dated results. The simulated results were given an error of ±24 years, to maintain parity with the majority of the originally modelled ^{14}C results.

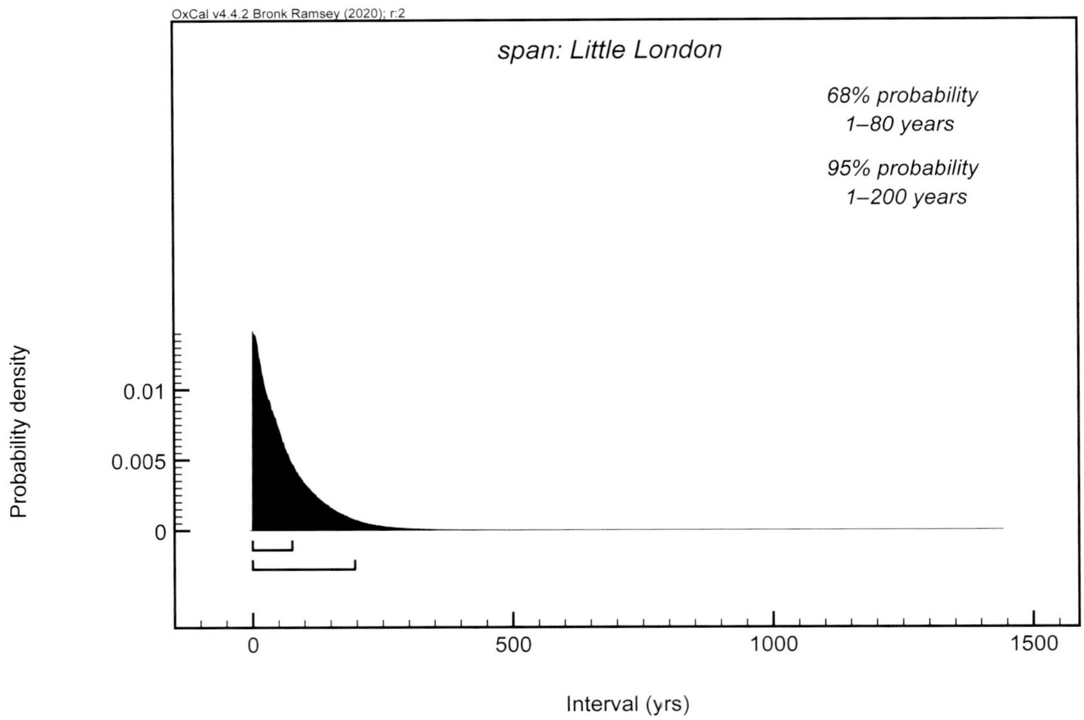

FIG. 127. Span of dated activity as derived from the chronological model shown in FIG. 126

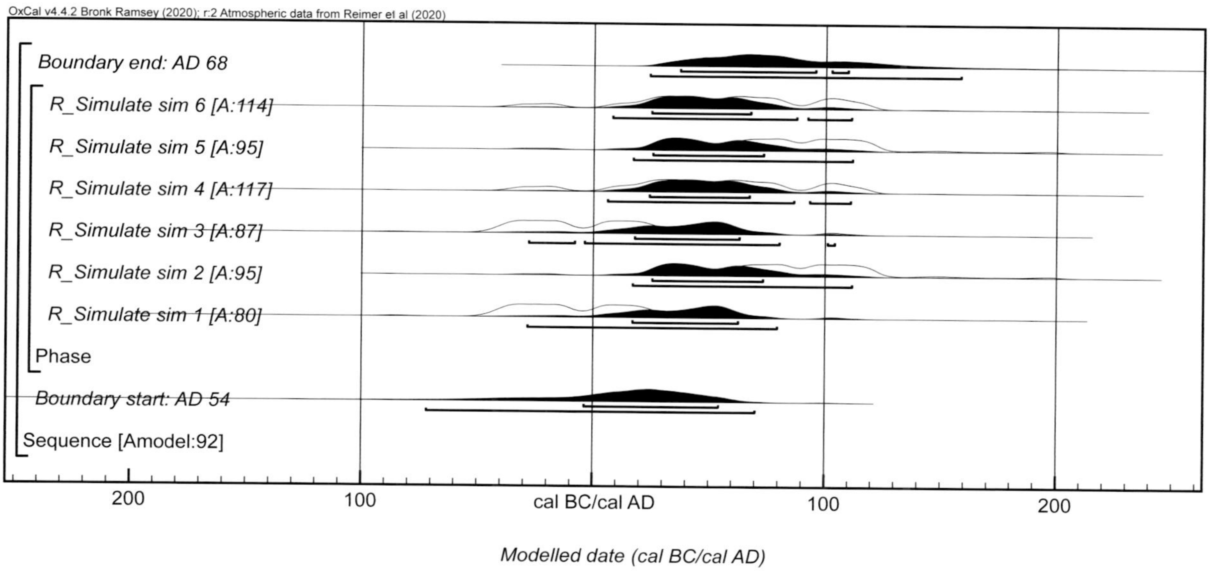

FIG. 128. Chronological model based on simulated dates for the period A.D. 54–68. The model follows the same parameters as in FIG. 126

The simulation model was run 20 times and the results were very similar each time, suggesting that with this number of dates and in this area of the calibration curve robust results can be expected. The final model run is shown in FIG. 128. This version of the model estimates the activity began in *75 cal BC–cal AD 55* (*95% probability*; FIG. 128; *start: AD 54*), and probably in *5 cal BC–cal AD 55* (*68% probability*). The activity ended in *cal AD 25–160* (*95% probability*; FIG. 128; *end: AD 68*), and probably in *cal AD 35–110* (*68% probability*). The overall span of activity, which from the typo-chronological evidence is thought to be 15 years, is estimated at *1–200 years* (*95% probability*; FIG. 129; *span*), and probably *1–90 years* (*68% probability*).

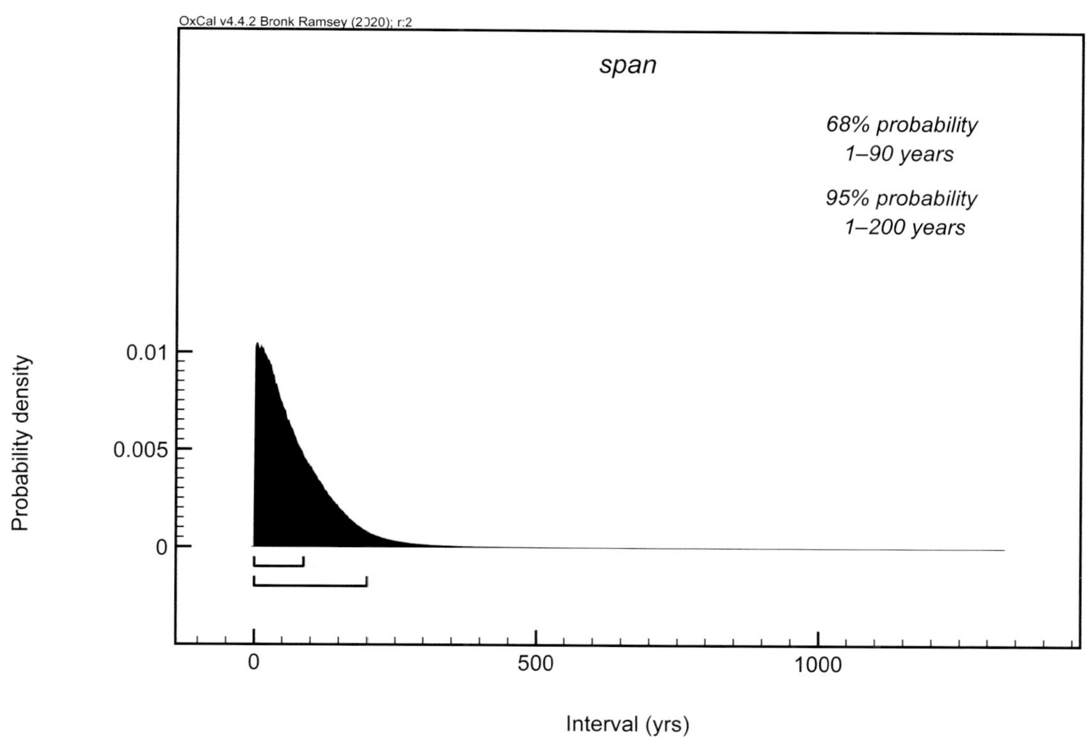

FIG. 129. Span of activity represented in the simulated model in FIG. 128

In simply comparing the start and end probabilities for the two models and the ranges, it would appear that the actual radiocarbon chronology derived from samples of unknown age is slightly later than might otherwise be expected. When comparing the probabilities for the radiocarbon chronology against the calendar dates of the generally accepted typo-chronology, there is only a 23% probability *start: Little London* occurred prior to A.D. 54 and 33% probability it began prior to A.D. 68. Furthermore, the radiocarbon chronology provides a 100% probability *end: Little London* occurred after A.D. 68. This suggests the material remains that were dated by their typo-chronology may have been residual in the contexts from which they were recovered.

Silchester Insula IX

The model has good agreement between the radiocarbon dates and the phasing (Amodel=159). The model estimates activity in Insula IX began in *60 cal BC–cal AD 10 (95% probability*; FIG. 130; *start: Insula IX Period 0*), and probably in *50–1 cal BC (68% probability)*. The transition to the Period 1 activity occurred in *35 cal BC–cal AD 45 (95% probability*; FIG. 130; *start: Insula IX Period 1*), and probably in *cal AD 1–30 (68% probability)*. The dated Period 1 activity in Insula IX ended in *cal AD 25–175 (95% probability*; FIG. 130; *end: Insula IX Period 1*), and probably in either *cal AD 35–50 (10% probability)* or *cal AD 65–130 (58% probability)*. The modelling estimates the Period 0 activity spanned *1–85 years (95% probability*; FIG. 131; *span: Insula IX Period 0*), and probably *1–50 years (68% probability)*. The Period 1 activity spanned *1–175 years (95% probability*; FIG. 131; *span: Insula IX Period 1*), and probably *25–125 years (68% probability)*.

Despite the new calibration curve, the chronological framework for Insula IX is very robust. The slight differences that can be noted between the model results presented here and those in Barnett (2020b) can likely be the result of the modelling process, with slight variations between model runs almost always being observed.

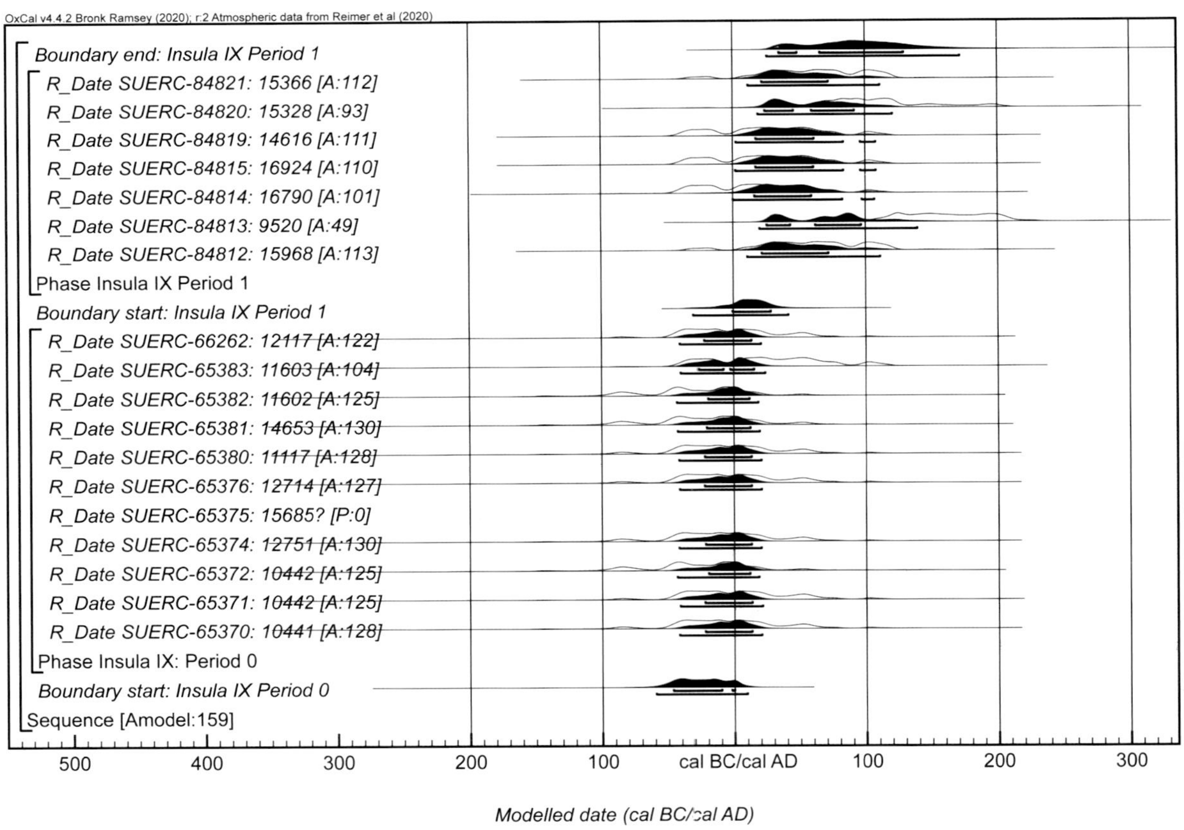

FIG. 130. Chronological model for the activity at Insula IX. The model follows the same parameters as in FIG. 126

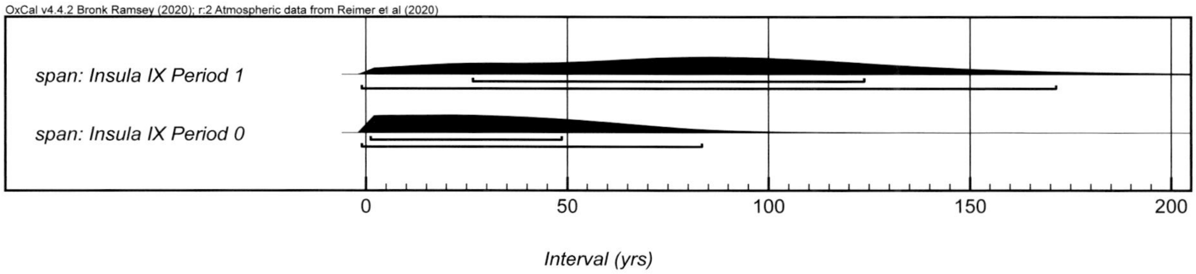

FIG. 131. Spans of activity for Periods 0 and 1 at Insula IX. The spans are derived from the model shown in FIG. 130

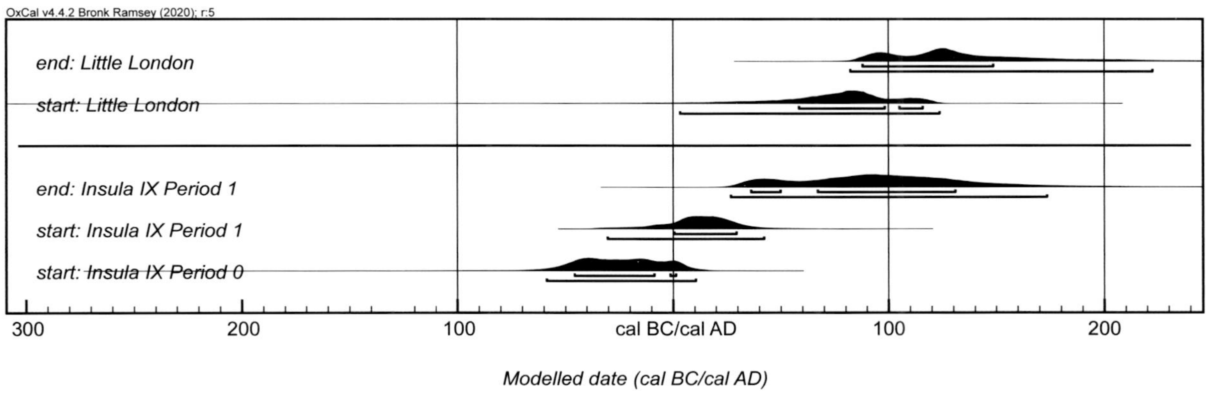

FIG. 132. Comparison of the start and end dates for the modelled activity at Little London and Insula IX. The probabilities are derived from the models shown in FIGS 126 and 130

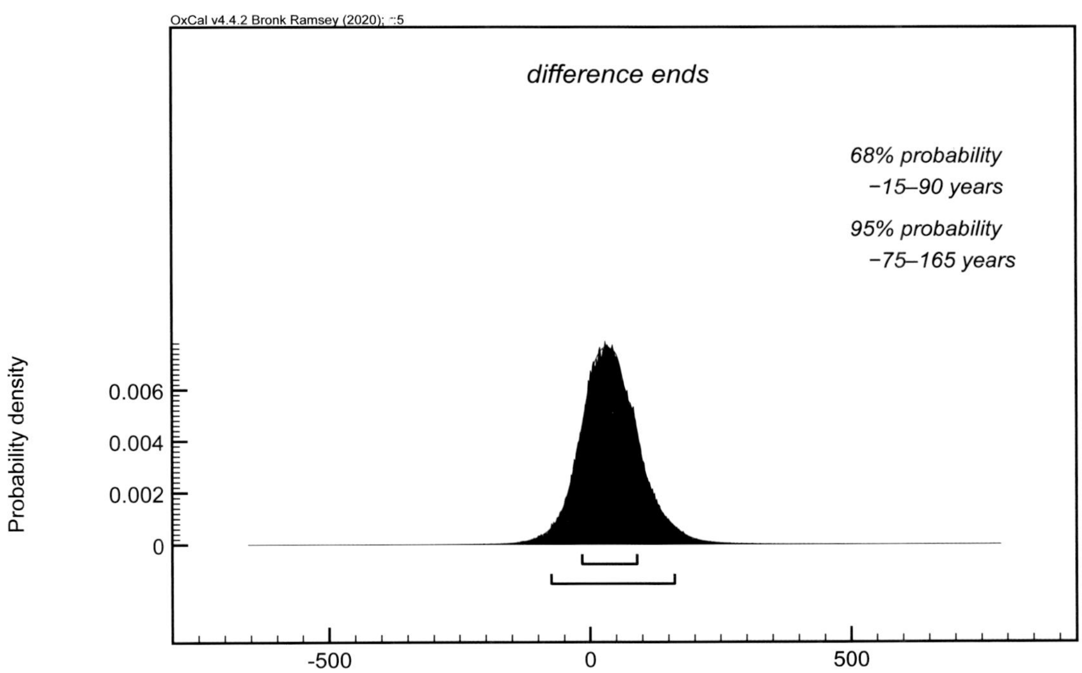

FIG. 133. Difference between the probabilities *end: Insula IX Period 1* and *end: Little London*, shown in FIG. 132

Little London vs. Silchester Insula IX

A further level of analysis was undertaken, whereby the probabilities from Little London and Insula IX were compared (see FIG. 132 for a graphical visualisation). This comparison results in there being a 94% probability that *start: Insula IX Period 1* occurred prior to *start: Little London*, but only a 33% probability that *end: Insula IX Period 1* occurred prior to *start: Little London*. Furthermore, there is a 77% probability that *end: Insula IX Period 1* took place prior to *end: Little London*. Therefore, the dating supports a narrative whereby Period 1 activity at Insula IX began prior to Little London, but that Little London may have continued on in activity for as many as *165 years* (*95% probability*; FIG. 133; *difference ends*), but probably no more than *90 years* (*68% probability*). Similarly, the modelling does not exclude activity at the two sites from ending at the same time.

CHAPTER 9

ARCHAEOMAGNETIC INVESTIGATION OF TWO FIRED FEATURES AT LITTLE LONDON

By David P. Greenwood, Sam E. Harris and Catherine M. Batt

SUMMARY

This report describes the archaeomagnetic investigations of two fired features, interpreted as a small pottery kiln and a brick kiln, recorded during the excavations at Little London, Silchester. A total of 74 specimens were collected from the two features: one sample set of 20 specimens from the small pottery kiln (University of Bradford Sample Register no. 217, Lab Code AM278–LL1); and three sample sets from the brick kiln: one of 20 specimens (Sample Register no. 124, Lab Code AM276–LL2); one of 25 specimens (Sample Register no. 125, Lab Code AM277–LL3); and one of nine specimens (Sample Register no. 126, Lab Code AM279–LL4). All of the specimens had a measurable remanence, indicating that the material sampled contained sufficient magnetic minerals to record a stable magnetic direction.

The magnetic directions obtained from the small pottery kiln (Lab Code AM278–LL1) were too scattered to obtain a date. Analysis of the samples suggested that this was due to either movement within the feature or insufficient heating of the material sampled.

The magnetic directions recorded by the three sample sets from the brick kiln were well grouped and appeared to record the geomagnetic field when last cooled. When calibrated against the current UK archaeomagnetic reference curve (Batt *et al.* 2017) at 95% confidence levels, AM276–LL2 and AM277–LL3 gave single age ranges, AD 882–AD 1065 and AD 835–AD 1023 respectively. AM279-LL4 gave a number of possible age ranges, including AD 469–AD 556, AD 806–AD 886 and AD 933–AD 1111. Combining the archaeomagnetic directions from all three sample sets for the brick kiln gave a single age range of AD 882–AD 1043.

The archaeomagnetic data from the brick kiln show a clear indication of a stable magnetic direction, obtained at the last time of heating. However, the date obtained does not match with the expected archaeological age. Further discussion of the exact contexts sampled is required to ascertain whether there is any possibility of later reheating having affected the structure or whether there has been undetected post-firing disturbance.

An introduction to archaeomagnetic dating can be found in Appendix 5. Detailed magnetic measurements are available in electronic form on request from the Archaeomagnetic Dating Laboratory, University of Bradford.

SUMMARY OF ARCHAEOMAGNETIC INFORMATION

Lab Code:	**AM278-LL1**
Feature:	Small pottery kiln (Kiln 5)
Site – latitude:	51.333° N
Site – longitude:	1.107° E
Magnetic deviation:	2.810° E
No. of samples (taken/used in mean):	20/19
AF demagnetisation applied:	20mT
Distortion correction applied:	n/a
Declination (at site):	355.5°
Inclination (at site):	65.1°
Alpha-95 (α_{95}):	8.8°
Precision parameter (k):	15.5
Date range (95% confidence):	undated due to high α_{95} (>5°)
Archaeological date range:	Cuts into earlier Romano-British square pottery Kiln 4, *c.* A.D. 50–100

Lab Code:	**AM276-LL2**
Feature:	Brick kiln (Kiln 1) (Base) – different from AM277 in colour
Site – latitude:	51.333° N
Site – longitude:	1.107° E
Magnetic deviation:	2.810° E
No. of samples (taken/used in mean):	20/18
AF demagnetisation applied:	20mT
Distortion correction applied:	n/a
Declination (at site):	15.4°
Inclination (at site):	64.3°
Alpha-95 (α_{95}):	1.9°
Precision parameter (k):	329.0
Date range (95% confidence):	AD 882–1065
Archaeological date range:	*c.* A.D. 50–100

Lab Code:	**AM277-LL3**
Feature:	Brick kiln (Kiln 1) (base) – different from AM276 in colour
Site – latitude:	51.333° N
Site – longitude:	1.107° E
Magnetic deviation:	2.810° E
No. of samples (taken/used in mean):	25/23
AF demagnetisation applied:	20mT
Distortion correction applied:	n/a
Declination (at site):	15.8°
Inclination (at site):	65.3°
Alpha-95 (α_{95}):	1.7°
Precision parameter (k):	310.7

Date range (95% confidence):	AD 835–1023
Archaeological date range:	*c*. A.D. 50–100

Lab Code:	**AM279-LL4**
Feature:	Brick kiln (Kiln 1) (walls)
Site – latitude:	51.333° N
Site – longitude:	1.107° E
Magnetic deviation:	2.810° E
No. of samples (taken/used in mean):	17/16 (sub-specimens produced from blocks)
AF demagnetisation applied:	20mT
Distortion correction applied:	n/a
Declination (at site):	9.1°
Inclination (at site):	64.1°
Alpha-95 (α_{95}):	2.0°
Precision parameter (k):	325.2
Date range (95% confidence):	AD 469–556, AD 806–886, AD 933–1111, AD 1484–1615
Archaeological date range:	*c*. AD 50–100

Lab Code:	**AM276-LL2, AM277-LL3 & AM279-LL4 combined**
Feature:	Brick kiln (Kiln 1)
Site – latitude:	51.333° N
Site – longitude:	1.107° E
Magnetic deviation:	2.810° E
No. of samples (taken/used in mean):	54/59
AF demagnetisation applied:	20mT
Distortion correction applied:	n/a
Declination (at site):	13.5°
Inclination (at site):	64.8°
Alpha-95 (α_{95}):	1.2°
Precision parameter (k):	231.9
Date range (95% confidence):	AD 855–1043
Archaeological date range:	*c*. A.D. 50–100

SITE AND CONTEXT DETAILS

Samuel Harris, from the University of Bradford, collected archaeomagnetic specimens in four sample sets from two fired features at the site of Little London, Silchester, on 7 September 2017. This study investigates the sample sets from the two fired features: a small pottery kiln (AM278-LL1, sample register no. 217) and a brick kiln (AM276-LL2, sample register no. 124; AM277-LL3, sample register no. 125; AM279-LL4, sample register no. 126) to determine whether the date of last heating can be ascertained.

POTTERY KILN 5 (AM278-LL1)

This feature was believed to be a small pottery kiln to the south end of the trench (FIG. 134). This small feature cut into an earlier square, brick-built pottery kiln. 20 oriented button specimens were taken from the circumference of the feature, with the most orange-coloured

FIG. 134. Archaeomagnetic sampling of LL1. Specimens numbered from 1 to 20 in clockwise direction starting north-west. Specimens 18, 19 and 20 came from the raised material in south which was either the remaining clay lining or a dump of clay lining. Image taken facing north, 0.50 m scales (Photo: Harris 2017)

FIG. 135. Archaeomagnetic sampling of LL2 (Context 1138) in the centre of the brick kiln. Specimens numbered 1 to 20 consecutively, from left to right, starting at the top of the image. Image taken facing north-west, 0.50 m scale (Photo: Harris 2017)

material targeted. There were a few areas which had cracked and therefore material could not be obtained. The only remaining clay lining for this feature was at the southern end and it was not possible to say whether this was *in situ*.

BASE OF BRICK KILN (KILN 1) (AM276-LL2)

LL2 comprises 20 oriented tube specimens (FIG. 135) taken from the base of the large brick kiln from a small area of orangey brown silty sand (Context 1138). Markedly different in colour from LL3 (FIGS 135 and 136), this area may represent different firings of the kiln after its initial use.

BASE OF BRICK KILN (AM277-LL3)

LL3 comprises 25 oriented tube specimens, also from the base of the brick kiln, from a bright red sandy silt (Context 1139); it may therefore represent a different burning event (see FIGS 135 and 136).

FIG. 136. Archaeomagnetic sampling of LL3 (Context 1139). Specimens numbered 1 to 25 consecutively, from left to right, starting at the top of the image. Specimen number 25 sits between specimens numbered 22 and 24. Image taken facing north-west, 0.50 m scale (Photo: Harris 2017)

FIG. 137. Archaeomagnetic sampling of LL4. Specimens were taken from around the rim of the kiln (white arrows mark its corners). Image taken facing west (Photo: Harris 2017)

WALL OF BRICK KILN (AM279-LL4)

In order to obtain a representative set of material from the large brick kiln, nine oriented blocks were taken from around the inside of the kiln using the button method (FIG. 137). Specimens numbered LL4/6 and LL4/7 were from vitrified material at the back of the kiln and may represent some of the highest temperatures from the kiln.

ANALYSIS

The four sample sets (AM276 to AM279) were consolidated with sodium silicate solution at the Archaeomagnetic Dating Laboratory, University of Bradford. After allowing the specimens time to dry and consolidate, those specimens taken using the button method (AM276-LL1 and AM279-LL4) were cut in order to fit into the magnetometers. A number of buttons had become detached from specimens during transport and trimming. Therefore, sub-samples were created from the larger specimens in order to ensure that there were enough samples to produce meaningful mean measurements (see Tables 16 and 19). Each sample set was then measured using a Molspin fluxgate large sample spinner magnetometer to investigate the natural remanent magnetisation (NRM) recorded in each specimen. The stability of the specimens was investigated through a pilot study of a subset, using step-wise alternating field (a.f.) demagnetisation (progressively in steps from 2.5mT to 100mT). The results of the pilot studies showed a single stable component after 20mT through to the origin. Secondary components (often laboratory viscous overprints) of the magnetisation were removed from the remaining specimens by demagnetisation, leaving the archaeologically significant characteristic remanent magnetisation (ChRM). The mean declination values obtained for each sample set were corrected for local magnetic variation; necessary as the orientation was carried out using a magnetic compass. The magnetic measurements for the NRM, the ChRM and the a.f. field used to remove the secondary components of the magnetisation have been summarised in Tables 16 to 19.

RESULTS FOR POTTERY KILN 5 (AM278-LL1)

The initial intensity values were low but high enough to be measurable. However, the scatter of NRM magnetic directions was high with an initial α_{95} value of 8.0°, indicating that the specimens may not have been *in situ* when collected, or that they had not all recorded the same magnetic field, or that the scatter may have been caused by viscous magnetic overprints which arise from post-heating changes to the specimens. A stereographic projection of the NRM directions is presented as FIG. 138.

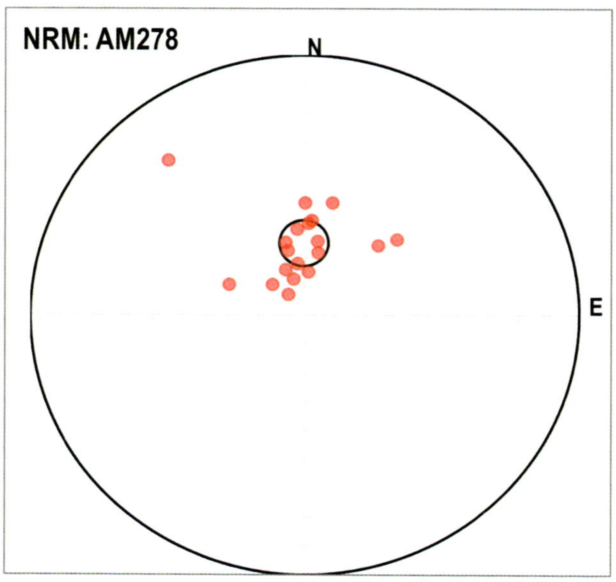

FIG. 138. Stereographic projection of the NRM directions of AM278-LL1. The small black circle represents the a95 angle around the mean direction

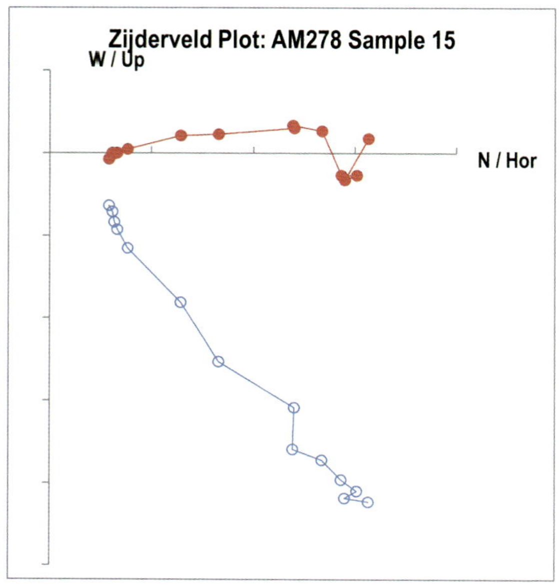

FIG. 139. Representative Zijderveld plot from AM278-LL1 showing the removal of the viscous overprint at 20mT

Three specimens with higher intensity values (LL1/4, LL1/6 and LL1/15) were selected for step-wise alternating field demagnetisation to investigate possible viscous overprint and magnetic stability of the specimens. This reveals the characteristic remanent magnetisation (ChRM), which is the archaeologically relevant magnetisation, shown as straight lines of Zijderveld plots (FIG. 139).

The pilot demagnetisation study showed a viscous overprint, removed at 20mT, and then single component magnetisation. The remaining 17 specimens were demagnetised at 20mT to determine the ChRM directions, however, the scatter of directions increased to an α_{95} value of 8.8°, which strongly suggested that the material was not *in situ* when sampled, or that the specimens had not been heated sufficiently. A stereographic projection of the ChRM directions is shown in FIG. 140.

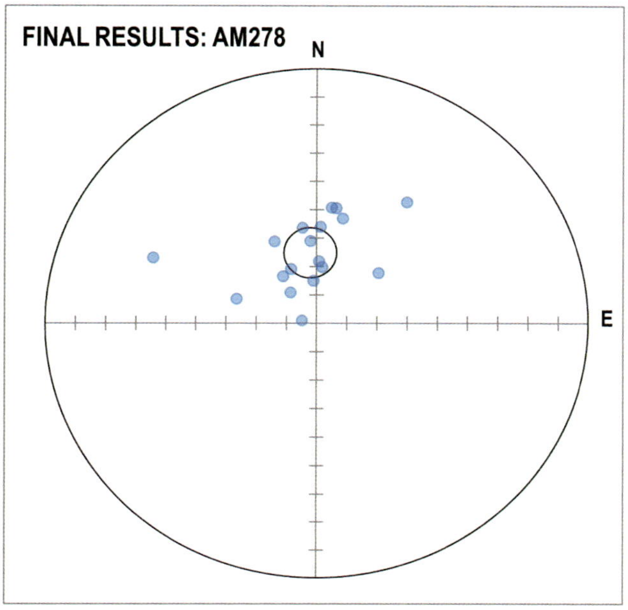

FIG. 140. Stereographic projection of ChRM directions from AM278-LL1. The small black circle represents the a95 angle around the mean direction

The scatter of directions about the mean is too great to use the mean direction and associated α_{95} value (8.8°) to calibrate a meaningful age determination using the current UK archaeomagnetic calibration curve (see Appendix 4).

TABLE 16. Details of the archaeomagnetic analysis of the nrm and ChRM for AM278-LL1 (mean declination values are corrected for local magnetic variation)

	NRM				ChRM			
Specimen	**DEC** °	**INC** °	**Intensity arb.**	**a.f. field**	**DEC** °	**INC** °	**Intensity arb.**	**Comments**
LL1/1	343.8	77.3	2.513	20mT	356.9	75.7	1.011	
LL1/2	346.0	67.8	0.839	20mT	293.3	31.6	0.289	
LL1/3	11.4	68.6	17.214	20mT	2.9	68.9	8.355	
LL1/5	4.9	75.5	55.132	20mT	5.9	70.8	33.300	Pilot
LL1/7	323.6	81.4	0.391	20mT	334.8	58.6	0.245	
LL1/10	352.9	72.0	29.293	20mT	336.6	69.7	6.863	Pilot
LL1/10A	49.8	50.3	1.190	20mT	35.8	38.8	0.411	
LL1/11	293.4	63.9	6.012	20mT	288.3	62.0	1.287	
LL1/12	315.2	75.4	9.593	20mT	326.0	70.3	1.856	
LL1/12A	346.5	64.7	1.804	20mT	321.8	76.5	0.516	
LL1/13	45.7	56.3	8.105	20mT	49.6	63.7	6.150	
LL1/14	320.2	20.7	1.424	N/A	N/A	N/A	N/A	Button detached
LL1/14A	9.1	64.5	1.277	20mT	13.8	52.7	0.703	
LL1/15	338.2	73.9	0.624	20mT	282.5	85.3	0.255	
LL1/16	4.8	57.6	102.288	20mT	352.1	56.5	60.666	
LL1/17	355.4	60.7	80.803	20mT	2.8	56.3	47.472	Pilot
LL1/18	13.1	50.1	37.400	20mT	9.6	49.0	25.364	
LL1/19	0.9	51.5	49.105	20mT	7.4	49.4	33.164	
LL1/20	2.3	58.4	27.938	20mT	356.2	61.5	15.938	
MEANS	**359.4**	**65.8**	**α_{95}=8.0**		**355.5**	**65.1**	**α_{95}=8.8**	

RESULTS FOR BRICK KILN (KILN 1) (AM276-LL2, AM277-LL3 and AM279-LL4)

The three sample sets (AM276-LL2, AM277-LL3 and AM279-LL4) produced very similar results. The initial intensities of the samples from the base (AM276-LL2 and AM277-LL3) were considerably higher than those for wall samples (AM279-LL4) (see Table 17), suggesting that the base of the kiln had been subjected to higher temperatures in the past than the area around the inside of the kiln sampled in 2017. However, the intensity values were higher overall than those recorded for the small pottery kiln and the scatter of NRM directions was very small (see Table 17). These initial results suggested that the specimens were *in situ* when collected and that they all recorded the same magnetic field. Stereographic projections of the NRM directions are presented in FIG. 141.

Three specimens from each sample set were chosen for step-wise alternating field (a.f.) demagnetisation in order to reveal the characteristic remanent magnetisation (ChRM), which is the archaeologically relevant magnetisation, shown as straight lines on Zijderveld plots (FIG. 142). All nine specimens showed very similar behaviour with a viscous overprint, and so the remaining specimens were demagnetised at 20mT. A statistical test (McFadden 1982) identified statistical outliers to be removed from the final ChRM results (FIG. 143).

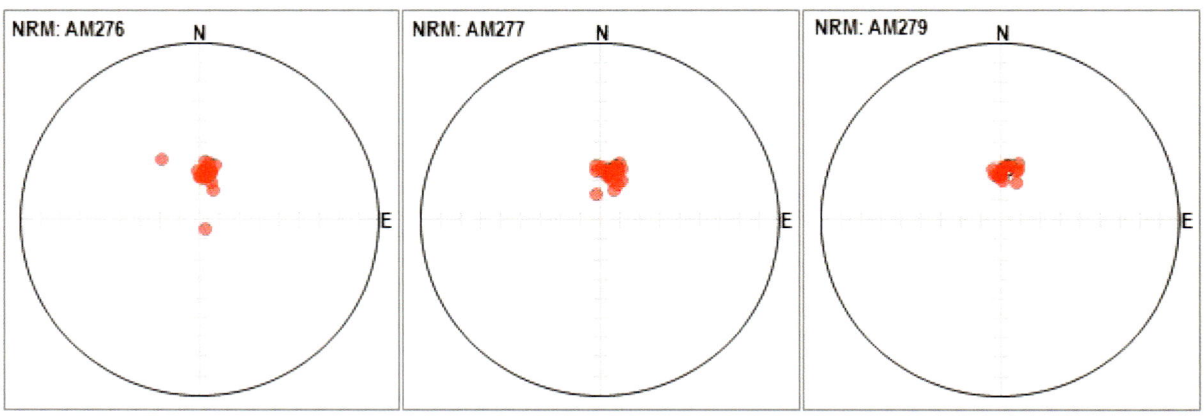

FIG. 141. Stereographic projections of the NRM directions of the three sample sets from the brick kiln

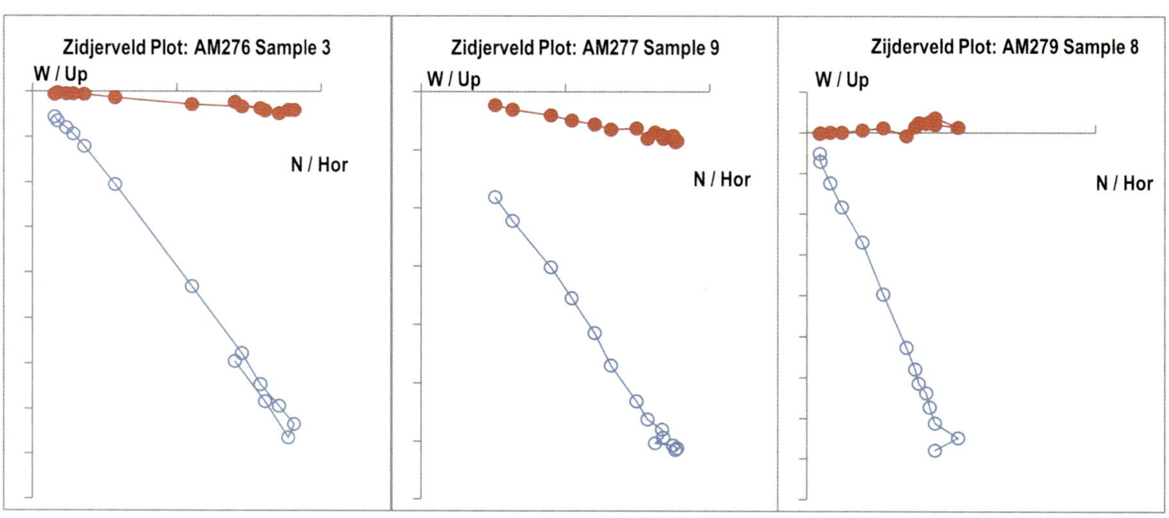

FIG. 142. Representative Zijderveld plots of the three sample sets from the brick kiln

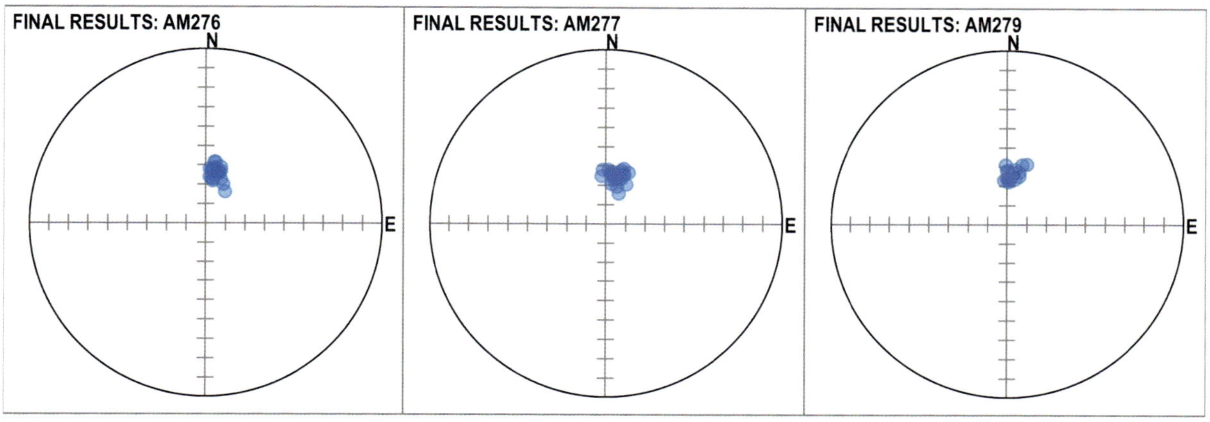

FIG. 143. Stereographic projections of ChRM directions of the three sample sets from the brick kiln

TABLE 17. Details of the archaeomagnetic analysis of the nrm and ChRM for AM276-LL2 (mean declination values are corrected for local magnetic variation)

	NRM				ChRM			
Specimen	DEC °	INC °	Intensity	a.f. field	DEC	INC	Intensity	Comments
LL2/1	6.5	60.9	978.335	20mT	9.8	58.6	671.372	
LL2/2	9.6	66.6	1320.774	20mT	10.0	65.0	831.836	
LL2/3	5.0	65.5	412.974	20mT	7.3	62.7	485.659	Pilot
LL2/4	5.5	65.5	1405.179	20mT	7.8	63.6	806.495	
LL2/5	329.2	54.0	582.578	20mT	N/A	N/A	N/A	Outlier
LL2/6	16.8	61.6	1260.162	20mT	15.2	60.1	658.055	
LL2/7	359.2	65.2	1010.529	20mT	4.7	62.7	697.589	
LL2/8	9.7	63.6	848.080	20mT	9.8	61.5	548.627	
LL2/9	13.3	65.7	1031.764	20mT	16.9	62.4	653.429	
LL2/10	9.0	65.2	865.869	20mT	14.6	63.5	394.736	
LL2/11	3.8	68.7	576.807	20mT	9.7	67.3	296.780	
LL2/12	13.7	64.7	1423.537	20mT	14.6	63.1	952.014	Pilot
LL2/13	144.8	84.5	398.858	20mT	N/A	N/A	N/A	Outlier
LL2/14	0.7	68.1	670.044	20mT	5.5	66.3	451.541	
LL2/15	11.1	68.5	761.506	20mT	19.9	66.5	525.096	
LL2/16	10.6	61.6	366.317	20mT	8.7	58.9	216.404	
LL2/17	26.6	73.0	1183.182	20mT	31.8	71.7	995.502	Pilot
LL2/18	18.8	70.6	738.794	20mT	24.4	68.6	443.204	
LL2/19	6.7	69.4	750.799	20mT	9.1	68.5	453.048	
LL2/20	12.6	66.0	1677.170	20mT	15.0	63.6	1090.049	
MEANS	**10.2**	**67.3**	α_{95}**=3.6**		**15.4**	**64.3**	α_{95}**=1.9**	

TABLE 18. Details of the archaeomagnetic analysis of the NRM and ChRM for AM277-LL3 (mean declination values are corrected for local magnetic variation)

	NRM				ChRM			
Specimen	**DEC** °	**INC** °	**Intensity**	**a.f. field**	**DEC**	**INC**	**Intensity**	**Comments**
LL3/1	21.6	65.1	455.370	20mT	19.1	65.3	360.216	
LL3/2	20.3	62.6	791.299	20mT	16.8	62.6	465.827	
LL3/3	24.3	62.9	660.523	20mT	24.1	61.6	355.551	
LL3/4	357.6	62.4	500.637	20mT	357.7	62.3	294.158	
LL3/5	28.1	67.6	639.595	20mT	27.4	67.7	498.160	
LL3/6	2.8	63.3	1038.477	20mT	3.8	62.8	588.980	
LL3/7	25.7	73.3	369.892	20mT	N/A	N/A	N/A	Outlier
LL3/8	3.2	65.2	706.535	20mT	5.1	64.2	377.250	
LL3/9	26.5	70.5	322.557	20mT	23.1	73.0	277.782	Pilot
LL3/10	12.2	68.0	703.559	20mT	10.8	67.1	533.609	
LL3/11	356.8	65.2	449.169	20mT	355.8	65.9	394.753	
LL3/12	20.7	62.2	570.374	20mT	20.5	63.2	468.794	
LL3/13	16.0	69.2	472.383	20mT	16.1	70.6	349.011	
LL3/14	11.2	67.6	1275.384	20mT	8.0	69.4	845.913	Pilot
LL3/15	14.1	65.9	586.742	20mT	12.1	66.4	438.576	
LL3/16	12.0	65.9	393.399	20mT	11.1	66.2	313.277	
LL3/17	20.2	63.9	650.438	20mT	20.4	63.5	571.025	
LL3/18	15.3	63.3	728.477	20mT	13.1	64.4	579.428	Pilot
LL3/19	9.8	64.0	616.169	20mT	7.7	64.7	482.608	
LL3/20	350.9	77.3	359.328	20mT	N/A	N/A	N/A	Outlier
LL3/21	15.1	66.5	491.778	20mT	16.1	66.5	414.929	
LL3/22	15.9	62.4	931.183	20mT	8.8	63.2	747.109	
LL3/23	8.7	65.6	538.055	20mT	8.6	64.5	434.335	
LL3/24	17.9	61.4	620.612	20mT	16.8	61.0	479.652	
LL3/25	19.6	60.0	756.574	20mT	18.4	60.1	661.913	
MEANS	**16.9**	**65.9**	α_{95}**=1.9**		**15.8**	**65.3**	α_{95}**=1.7**	

TABLE 19. Details of the archaeomagnetic analysis of the NRM and ChRM for AM279-LL4 (mean declination values are corrected for local magnetic variation)

	NRM				ChRM			
Specimen	**DEC** °	**INC** °	**Intensity**	**a.f. field**	**DEC**	**INC**	**Intensity**	**Comments**
LL4/1	7.9	62.3	52.183	20mT	359.9	59.8	44.413	
LL4/2	11.7	62.9	28.023	20mT	13.0	62.4	22.651	
LL4/2A	19.6	60.4	55.316	20mT	18.8	57.6	46.007	Pilot
LL4/2B	18.0	64.0	27.437	20mT	14.3	64.1	22.258	
LL4/3	4.3	64.0	20.354	20mT	8.6	61.3	15.112	
LL4/3	6.9	62.4	26.906	20mT	N/A	N/A	N/A	Outlier
LL4/5	2.2	63.5	34.815	20mT	0.8	62.1	31.119	
LL4/6	353.7	64.4	42.701	20mT	1.7	62.4	29.734	Pilot
LL4/8	359.0	67.0	16.278	20mT	1.4	66.0	12.712	
LL4/8A	20.7	63.3	10.577	20mT	14.6	58.8	9.396	
LL4/9	3.1	70.1	48.795	20mT	10.4	66.4	38.323	Pilot
LL4/9A	2.2	68.4	16.865	20mT	4.5	66.6	14.101	
LL4/9B	0.4	66.6	29.412	20mT	3.6	66.0	25.123	
LL4/9C	359.7	68.8	12.787	20mT	3.3	67.3	10.646	
LL4/9D	358.9	66.0	14.093	20mT	0.3	66.9	12.158	
LL4/9E	24.1	69.4	7.865	20mT	2.1	68.7	6.340	
LL4/9F	353.9	67.6	10.074	20mT	356.7	67.2	8.210	
MEANS	**9.4**	**65.6**	**α_{95}=2.1**		**9.1**	**64.1**	**α_{95}=2.0**	

ARCHAEOMAGNETIC DATING

The mean ChRM direction for the small pottery kiln was not datable as the α_{95} value of 8.8° exceeded the 5° normally considered the maximum α_{95} value for dating purposes (Tarling 1983). The mean ChRM directions for the brick kiln all had α_{95} values less than 5° and were therefore dated with the UK archaeomagnetic calibration curve (Batt *et al.* 2017) using a Matlab tool developed by Pavón-Carassco *et al.* (2011), and using the reference location of Meriden (latitude = 52.43° N, longitude = 1.62° W). The date ranges were constrained between 1000 B.C. and present. These ranges (Table 20), calculated at the 95% confidence level, are shown in FIGS 146–149 in Appendix 4.

TABLE 20. Summary of ChRM directions, corrected for magnetic variation, and the calibrated date ranges

	DEC	**INC**	**α_{95}**	**Date ranges at 95% confidence level**
AM276 (LL2)	15.4	64.3	1.9	AD 882–1065
AM277 (LL3)	15.8	65.3	1.7	AD 835–1023
AM279 (LL4)	9.1	64.1	2.0	AD 469–556, AD 806–886, AD 933–1111, AD 1484–1615
AM276-LL2, AM277-LL3 & AM279-LL4 combined	13.5°	64.8°	1.2°	AD 855–1043

DISCUSSION AND CONCLUSION

The sample set (AM278-LL1) from the small pottery kiln at Little London resulted in a scatter of magnetic directions that gave a α_{95} value >5°, and was therefore not datable. The intensity values for this sample set were also very low for a fired feature, which suggests that a sufficiently high temperature had not been reached in the areas sampled.

The brick kiln, on the other hand, had a high and stable magnetisation, which appeared to record the geomagnetic field in the past. The magnetic directions obtained for the floor samples were very similar and yielded similar date ranges. The magnetic directions for the wall samples had a slightly more westerly direction and yielded some overlapping dates but also other possibilities. The intensity values for the wall samples were significantly lower than for the floor samples which might suggest a lower heating temperature. The magnetic directions from all three areas can be combined to give a single date for the feature.

The archaeomagnetic dating results suggest that the brick kiln last cooled at some time between AD 850 and 1050. The date range is larger than would be hoped for with the small associated α_{95} values, and this may be a reflection of the paucity of archaeomagnetic data for this period. It would be possible to improve on these date ranges by combining them with other dating evidence in a Bayesian model. It is also possible that further refinements to the British archaeomagnetic dataset may allow the precision of the date to be improved in the future. The suggested date range is not in good accordance with the archaeological evidence suggesting a Romano-British date. Whilst the inclination of the samples is consistent with this earlier date, the declination rules out that possibility. Further discussion is required to understand whether the discrepancy is due to post-firing disturbance, not visible at the time of sampling, or to a later episode of reheating.

CHAPTER 10

CONCLUDING DISCUSSION

By Michael Fulford

INTRODUCTION

With the excavation of one of, potentially, three adjacent brick kiln clusters, the production of Roman ceramic building material at Little London has been confirmed. In addition, the unexpected discovery of three small kilns close by has added pottery to the range of products from the site. Although the manufacture of ceramic building material may have commenced a little ahead of the pottery, it would seem that the two facets of the industry so far identified at Little London continued side-by-side. What is harder to assess is what proportion of the activities carried out at Little London have survived ancient and modern interventions. It is evident from the LiDAR that there are further backfilled clay pits in the south-west corner of the field (FIG. 34). These are similar in size and character to the clay pit partly investigated in Trench 1 and we assume they are probably Roman, but the much larger area in the middle of the field shown as disturbed on the geophysics (FIG. 2) is a more recent intervention and is marked on the 1872 OS map (Truscoe 2017, 96–8, fig. 75). How much structural evidence of early Roman date any of this quarrying may have destroyed cannot be determined, but we should remain open to the possibility that there were more brick kilns and associated workshops than currently survive. For example, there are clay pits similar in size to those in the south-west corner of our field on the west side of the present day Silchester to Little London road (ibid., fig. 76). Even with a sample of over 17,000 pieces we cannot be certain how well it captures the full range of products. For example, Machin has identified tile with relief-patterning of type die 81 as a Little London product (p. 133) but it is not so far represented in the Little London CBM assemblage. In the case of the pottery, it looks from the concentration of waster pottery at the northern end of the ditch in Trench 2, that there was probably at least one further pottery kiln outside the excavated area, notwithstanding the lack of indicative signals from the geophysics.

Pottery from the primary fills of the trackway ditches in Trench 1 points to nearby settlement around the time of the Roman conquest and the imported pottery suggests the inhabitants enjoyed relatively high status. Perhaps the occupants were already engaged in pottery making and this attracted interest in the site and the decision to locate the Roman brick-and-tile- and pottery-making industries here. The earliest definite post-conquest activity is represented by the construction of Kiln 1, including the digging of the post-holes for its roofing structure, and the excavation of the north–south ditch in Trench 2 and construction of the presumed, associated bank. The find of a Nero-stamped tile in the fill of Kiln 1 provides a *terminus ante quem* of A.D. 54–68 for the start of brick and tile production (and a *terminus post quem* for the abandonment of Kiln 1), but we should be open to the possibility that the imperial stamping represented the appropriation of an already existing industry. Pottery-making began shortly after the tile kiln (or kilns) were established and then, intermingled with dumps of brick waste in Trench 1, continued alongside the production of brick and tile.

THE KILNS

The characteristic rectangular form of Kiln 1 compares well with other tile kilns recorded from Roman Britain, the design of tile kilns remaining essentially unchanged throughout the Roman period (McWhirr 1979b). Indeed, the closest parallel for the roof structure at Little London is that which covered the tile kiln at Crookhorn, Hants., operating in the later third and early fourth century (Soffe *et al.* 1989, fig. 14). The internal dimensions of the tile kiln (Kiln 1) in its first phase (3 by 3.2 m) compare reasonably well with many of those listed by McWhirr (1979b, 104–7, table 6.1), but the majority are not well dated. It is not as large as second-century Eccles (4.9 by 4.7 m), but is closer in size to the larger of the later first-/early second-century military kilns, Brampton 1 and 2, in Cumbria. Of the seven single-flue kilns at the late first-century legionary tilery at Holt all but kilns 2 and 7, which are described as pottery kilns, are considerably larger than Kiln 1 at Little London. The average internal area of the five larger kilns at Holt, at 18.6 m^2, is almost exactly twice the size of Little London Kiln 1 (9.6 m^2), but Brampton 1 and 2 are only a little larger, averaging 10.98 m^2. In its second phase Little London Kiln 1 was reduced by about one fifth (20.6 per cent) to an internal area of 7.62 m^2. We can only speculate as to the reasons for the alteration: perhaps a reduction in demand, or a more effective use of fuel to reduce wastage? Kiln 2 was poorly preserved and it is difficult to distinguish where the firing chamber ends and the flue begins but, on the basis of the internal width of 2.26 m, it would seem to be close in size to Kiln 1 in its second phase.

Even smaller is the rectangular Kiln 4 in Trench 2, which was certainly devoted to firing pottery but may have been used occasionally for making brick and tile, perhaps some of the more specialist pieces only required in small quantities. Its internal dimensions of 2 by 1.6 m give it an area of 3.2 m^2, almost exactly one third of the internal surface area of Kiln 1. There are parallels, also thought to be for firing pottery, for this size of rectangular kiln from Colchester (Hull 1963, kilns 7, 17 and 31). It is possible that other tile kilns of similar, small dimensions listed by McWhirr (1979b) in table 6.1 were also used in this way. However, even the smaller of the two single-flue kilns at Holt, described as pottery kilns, had a greater internal surface area of 5.04 m^2, the other being very considerably larger at 13.52 m^2.

THE KILN PRODUCTS

The range of ceramic building material embraces both the common types, such as the brick used for the string courses, a requisite for building in masonry at this time, and the roofing tile for buildings of both masonry and timber construction, and, more specifically, the specialist range, such as the vaulting tile, flue-tile and *pilae* necessary for the construction of bath-houses and heated rooms. While the commoner types produced find parallels among a range of urban, roadside and rural sites, especially villas, in south-east Britain, there are comparatively few examples of the less common types stratified among such settlements in pre- and early Flavian contexts. An important contribution of Little London is, therefore, the insight that it gives into the range of types of ceramic building material thought necessary for building in masonry, especially bath-houses, in the third quarter of the first century A.D. It is, to date, the earliest brick kiln assemblage to be published from Roman Britain.

The three pottery kilns are all different and we have already commented above on the rectangular Kiln 4. The circular, single-flue Kilns 3 and 5 are well paralleled by the Claudio-Neronian–early Flavian kilns at Duxford, Cambs., with examples of both free-standing (as in our Kiln 5) and projecting 'tongue support' pedestals (as in our Kiln 3) (Anderson and Woolhouse 2016). A kiln with a free-standing support was also found at the earlier, Claudio-Neronian military pottery at Longthorpe, but the great majority of the 28 or 29 kilns recorded there were surface-built and no traces of such structures have so far been identified at Little London (Dannell and Wild 1987).

The range of pottery products finds multiple parallels in Neronian and early Flavian Britain associated both with assemblages from kilns and with site, especially military (fortress), assemblages. More specifically, Timby (Ch. 4) sees Little London belonging to a group of kilns which includes those at Eccles, Little Munden, Brockley Hill and Minety. They produced Roman forms not previously part of the repertoire of potters in the immediate pre-conquest period. In the case of Little London, the commonest forms are collared-rim flagons and curved-wall platters and there are also types with no close parallels from Britain. Timby concludes that the potters were migrants, though some who worked at Little London may have worked previously elsewhere in Britain, rather than coming direct from the Continent. The mortaria, for example, suggest a link with the South-West.

In the case of the brick and tile, while some of the commoner forms, such as flat bricks and roofing tile, see little change over time, there are some characteristics of the assemblage, such as the thinness and scoring of the flue-tile, which are closely paralleled elsewhere in Britain in pre-Flavian contexts (Ch. 5). This means that, while there can be no doubt of Claudian/Neronian–early Flavian production, there remains the possibility that the production of the commoner forms, which account for two thirds of the wasters, could have continued for longer.

CHRONOLOGY

To help us determine the length of production at Little London we have four sources of evidence to consider: the typology of the pottery produced; other datable pottery; a suite of radiocarbon dates; and archaeomagnetic dating. There is also the evidence to be reviewed from *Calleva* itself where most of the Little London production was probably consumed. The date range of the pottery produced at Little London fits within a Neronian–early Flavian span; the absence of ring-necked flagons suggests that pottery-making ceased no later than the early Flavian period. Of the other types of datable pottery, the small assemblage of samian, mostly from the uppermost fill of the north–south ditch in Trench 2, is predominantly of Neronian–early Flavian or of Neronian–Flavian date. There are, however, two later sherds: one of early-to-mid-Flavian date from the fill of the stokehole of Kiln 3, the other probably Trajanic from the top of the ditch in Trench 2. Two sherds of second-century Dorset BB1 were also recovered from the base of the ploughsoil in Trench 2.

There is also the archaeomagnetic dating to consider (Ch. 9), which suggests an early medieval date (A.D. 850–1050) for the last firing of Kiln 1. This is completely at odds with the dates derived from the material culture and the radiocarbon dating, including from Kiln 1, and should be set aside. However, is it just possible that the kiln was accidentally discovered between the ninth and the eleventh century — the floor of the combustion chamber perhaps collapsing and drawing attention to the kiln's existence — and a fire lit within it?

Derek Hamilton's modelling of the radiocarbon dates (Ch. 8), the samples taken from a representative range of contexts from across both trenches (p. 148, Table 15), supports a period of production of 1–200 radiocarbon years at 95 per cent probability or 1–90 radiocarbon years at 68 per cent probability. This is quite similar to what he has calculated for Silchester Insula IX Period 1 (*c.* A.D. 44–85): 1–140 years at 95 per cent probability, or 15–110 at 68 per cent probability. This would suggest that the period of production at Little London was of similar duration to the Period 1 occupation of Insula IX, approximately 40 calendar years. While it is to be expected that the radiocarbon start date of Little London would be later than that for Insula IX Period 1, it is surprising that its end date is later. This would imply that production of both ceramic building material and pottery continued later, towards the end of the first century, longer than has been estimated on the basis of the samian and the typology of the pottery produced at Little London. One possible explanation for the difference is that, with only one certainly late sample, the Insula IX radiocarbon samples largely comprised charcoal fragments from early or mid-range contexts in the Period 1 sequence (Barnett 2020b, 533), while all but one of the Little London samples derive from the latest firings of the kilns. And, as Hamilton concludes 'the modelling does not exclude activity at the two sites from ending at the same time' (p. 154).

From *Calleva* itself we find evidence from the samples retained from the excavations of the forum-basilica and of Insula IX that the Little London CBM fabrics (SILCBM3 and 4) are most abundant in the pre- and early Flavian phases of both sites, their representation residual thereafter and declining over time as a proportion of the assemblage (Machin 2018, 222–5). Recent and continuing excavation of *Calleva*'s bath-house, long thought to be early in the development of the town on the basis of its skewed orientation with the Roman street grid and the proxy evidence of a Nero tile from a nearby pit, has confirmed that bricks in the Little London fabric were used exclusively in the façade of the pre-Flavian structure (Fulford *et al.* 2018b; 2019). Timby has identified pottery in Little London fabrics from Insula IX from its Period 1, Claudio-Neronian and early Flavian phase. Classified as oxidised or cream sandy wares, they belong to her 'miscellaneous sandy wares', and account for less than 1 per cent of the group, the small quantity perhaps an indication of a short-lived production (Timby 2020, 325–6; 372–3). To conclude, pottery and brick and tile production at Little London appears to have been limited to a short span of some 30 or 40 years, *c.* A.D. 50/60–*c.* A.D. 80/90.

THE CONTEXT OF PRODUCTION

We need now to consider what might have prompted the establishment of the industry and the possible context of the imperial appropriation. One of the distinctive products of Little London are the 'diamond and lattice' relief-patterned flue-tiles (FIG. 96). Examples in the Little London fabrics have been found not only at Silchester, but also at a range of locations from Cirencester to the north-west to Chichester and Winchester to the south. Because, historically, only unusual brick and tile, such as relief-patterned fragments, was retained from excavations for permanent archiving, it is not possible to assess the overall contribution of Little London building materials to those places and potential projects where examples of its relief-patterned tile have been found. It is reasonable, however, to assume that the loads delivered included a significant proportion of the types in greatest demand such as bricks and roofing tile, as well as the more specialised types such as flue-tile and *pilae* for bath-house and heated room construction. Similarly patterned flue-tile to that produced at Little London has been found in quantity in London, but also in smaller amounts at a number of locations across southern Britain, for the most part south of the Fosse Way. Its production is attested at Minety, Wilts., also alongside the production of pottery, and Minety brick was also found associated with Little London material in pre- and early Flavian contexts in Silchester Insula IX (Machin 2020).

A possible context for the quite widespread production of the materials necessary to construct bath-houses and heated rooms was the need to provide accommodation, usually described as *mansiones* and *mutationes*, along the major roads of the province. There is a parallel from Thrace, a Roman province since A.D. 46, for the construction of such road stations (there termed *tabernas et praetoria*) in Nero's reign, from an inscription dated A.D. 61–2 (*CIL* III.2.6123; Fulford and Machin 2021). The location of the Little London brickworks is close to Latchmere Green, where the road leading south from *Calleva* divides, with one route leading to Chichester, the other to Winchester. We can only speculate that its positioning was determined so that it could more easily serve demand to the south as well as *Calleva* itself, although, as we have seen, its products are also found at a distance to the north-west as far as Cirencester.

The above pattern of distribution can be compared with those of other industries operating in the pre-Flavian period. Betts has mapped the findspots of products which he attributes to a workshop at Eccles, Kent. They are distributed along or close to Watling Street from Canterbury west to London and then north-east from London through Chelmsford to Colchester (2017, 371, fig. 17.3). There is a similar linear distribution of a north Kent red-tile fabric, whose place of manufacture has yet to be identified. In this case it is limited to a scatter along or close to Watling Street between Canterbury and London with one outlying findspot at Gosbecks, Colchester (ibid., 372, fig. 17.4). Finally, there is a later first-century fabric, another instance where the location of the workshop has yet to be discovered but is thought to be in West Sussex, probably near Chichester and Stane Street, whose distribution extends from Chichester to London with a further findspot beyond at Barking on the Colchester road (ibid., 373, fig. 17.5). The reach of the above industries, supplying locations up to about 100 km from their presumed places of manufacture, is very reminiscent of that of Little London (and Minety). We should also note the distribution of relief-patterned box-flue tiles in MOLA fabric 3069 along Watling Street between London and Verulamium and to rural settlements in the countryside west of the Roman road. Although not securely dated, this production is likely to be broadly contemporary with Little London and Minety (ibid., 375–6, fig. 17.8).

The one road along or beside which we have, as yet, little clue as to the possible early sources of brick and tile is the Devil's Highway between London and Silchester; and the former is the one major town within potential striking distance of Little London where material attributable to this workshop has not yet been found nor, for that matter, systematically searched for. If we consider the relief-patterned tile, there are examples of die 66 from Isleworth, close to the road in west London and of die 104 at the crossing of the Thames at Staines (*Pontes*). The only other site in east Berkshire with a record of relief-patterned tile is Old Windsor, also not far from the road, with an example of die 46. While die 66 has been found in London and Verulamium, but mainly on sites in Surrey, die 104 has only otherwise been recorded on multiple examples from Verulamium. Die 46 has so far been found only in Essex at Chelmsford, Colchester and the villa at Great Tey (Betts *et al.* 1997). Although we do not know whether or not examples of the same die were being produced in the same workshop and where these were located, including whether there were tileries close to London on the west side, as a working hypothesis we suggest these tiles came from workshops either close to London or via London from sources to the north, east or south, but not from the west, not from the direction of Silchester.

When did the manufacture of brick and tile begin in Roman Britain? It is certainly documented during the lifetime of the legionary fortress at Colchester and was well established to serve the development of the *colonia* established on the site of the fortress in A.D. 49 (Crummy 1992b). Pre-Boudican consumption of brick and tile is also attested in *Londinium*, which was founded by A.D. 50 (Betts 2017, 368; Pringle 2007). At Verulamium, a *municipium* by A.D. 60 according to Tacitus, the picture is less clear: Frere found a tiled floor in the Period 1 buildings in Insula XIV destroyed A.D. 60 (1972, 15), while pre-Flavian thin-walled tiles were noted at the Insula XIX baths (Niblett and Thompson 2005, 85). Pre-Flavian production is attested in the Neronian–early Flavian proto-palace period at Fishbourne, W Sussex (Cunliffe 1971, 43), as it is at Silchester, both by virtue of the Nero tiles, and by the presence of ceramic building material in pre-Flavian deposits, as in the forum-basilica and Insula IX (Timby 2000; Machin 2020). Nero gives a certain *terminus post quem* of A.D. 54–68 for production at Little London, but does not exclude the possibility of production as early as (late) Claudian times. Until there is evidence for brick and tile production at or near Silchester before A.D. 54, it would seem very probable that it started there a few years later than it did in and around London and Colchester. This would explain why Little London products did not spread east to London because demand there was already being satisfied.

One puzzle over dating remains: why, if, in almost every aspect, the types of brick and tile present in the Little London assemblage can be paralleled in pre-Flavian contexts elsewhere, relief-patterned tile is not so far similarly represented in such dated assemblages, especially in *Londinium*, where very many examples have been found. Perhaps it is only a matter of time, or is there an element of circularity here? As it has been widely accepted as starting only from *c.* A.D. 70, since Black's paper on dating (1985), has any deposit excavated since the mid-1980s containing relief-patterned tile automatically been regarded as post A.D. 70?

Returning to the context of the establishment of Little London and Minety, if it was part of a project to set up road stations west of London in Nero's reign, it is odd that no Nero-stamped tile has yet been found at any location other than Silchester and Little London. If other stamped or otherwise marked tile was routinely being looked for among the excavated assemblages of ceramic building material and then kept, particularly since the publication of Lowther's corpus of 1948 drew attention to relief-patterned tile, it might be expected that Nero-stamped tile would also have been spotted had it been there in the first place, for example during the large-scale excavations which took place in the 1960s and 70s in Chichester, Cirencester and Winchester. Its absence may, of course, simply reflect its scarcity; only one clearly stamped piece has been found among the large assemblage of brick and tile reported here, but that rarity might be because stamping in this manner was short-lived and only aimed at material supplying projects at *Calleva* itself. Certainly, Nero-stamped tile has now been recognised in every major excavation within the town since the conclusion of the Society of Antiquaries work in 1909. From the time when major excavations began again in 1980, examples have been found from across the town, in Insulae III, IV, IX and XXX as well as from the baths in Insula XXXIII.

The Silchester Nero tiles (*RIB* 2.2482; Appendix 1) have no obvious predecessor or parallel in Roman Britain. They are the earliest official tile stamps from Britain and the circular form recalls the brick stamps of Rome and the Tiber valley. There are instances of circular stamps from later in the first or second century, for example on a *stilus* tablet from London (*RIB* 2443.2) and on *Classis Britannica* tiles (*RIB* 2481.89–99), but procuratorial and legionary stamps on tile of later first- and second-century date were contained exclusively within a rectangular, ansate or oblong frame (*RIB* 2459–63; 2485). Twentieth-century commentators simply referred to the Nero tiles, if at all, as evidence of early urban development supported by an imperial-owned tilery (e.g. Richmond 1963, 168; Frere 1967, 288). More recently Frere has re-interpreted the tiles as evidence of the take-over by the emperor of an estate belonging to a *princeps* of the Atrebates, perhaps as a result of the forcible recall of loans under Decianus Catus, the procurator of Britain at the time of the Boudican rebellion, or earlier, when the supporters of Caratacus were eliminated and Cogi-/Togidubnus' principality was established (1999, 283).

While there is no other evidence at this time of this practice of stamping in the north-western provinces, there are Nero-stamped tiles from north-eastern Italy and Dalmatia (e.g. Pellicioni 2012). They were produced on estates formerly belonging to C. Vibius Pansa, which were probably confiscated by the triumvirate after his death in 43 B.C., though imperial-marked tile only appears certainly to begin with Tiberius, then continuing through his successors to Vespasian. Unlike the circular Little London/Silchester stamps, these are in a rectangular frame and expressed as, for example, NER. CAES. PANS; NERONIS CLA. PAN. Compared with the widely distributed Italian stamps, Little London stamped tiles have only been found in Silchester.

An alternative interpretation to that suggested by Frere (above) presents itself: according to Tacitus, Nero despatched his trusted freedman, Polyclitus, to hold an inquiry in the aftermath of the Boudican rebellion (*Annals* 14, 38–9). With Colchester, London and Verulamium destroyed, *Calleva*, a communications hub with roads leading to significant destinations in all directions, only 40 miles west of London, but distant from the heartland of the rebellion, would have been a suitable place to set up his headquarters and a base for the vast retinue (*ingenti agmine*) which Tacitus, almost certainly exaggerating, tells us Polyclitus brought with him. *Calleva* would also have been a good temporary base for Classicianus, the newly appointed procurator of the province. Polyclitus would have found *Calleva* little changed from how it was before the conquest and one could easily conceive of a reason for him to divert existing production at Little London to provide the materials to initiate or develop an existing building programme in *Calleva*, the provision, or completion, of a bath-house probably being the highest priority. Acting on the emperor's behalf, one can see a context for him to use the stamp of imperial authority. Indeed, given the parallel for circular stamps from Rome, it is possible he brought a tile-maker with him. We do not know when Polyclitus arrived in Britain, nor how long he stayed, but he may well have spent several months, including the winter of A.D. 60/61, on the island. While it is unlikely that all the projects initiated by him were completed during his time in the province, they were evidence of a continued commitment to Britain. An intervention in A.D. 60/61 of a relatively short duration might well account for the small number of stamps recovered and their concentration only in *Calleva* (cf. Fulford *et al.* 2020, 3–9, 596–7; Fulford 2021, 58–61). Perhaps the listing of *Calleva* as the starting or end point of three itineraries in the later *Antonine Itinerary* enshrines a distant memory of the role played by the town in the aftermath of the Boudican rebellion (Rivet and Smith 1979, 166–7).

Timby has remarked on the scarcity of flagons and mortaria in the Claudio-Neronian and early Flavian pottery assemblage from Silchester Insula IX and the production of these forms at Little London would have served to remedy this deficiency (if that was how it was perceived) (Timby 2020). It seems strange that, given *Calleva* was being well supplied with a range of wheel-thrown pottery from Alice Holt, that industry did not also make flagons and mortaria in the pre-Flavian period. Was the pottery-making at Little London a very short-lived affair established to meet the sudden demands of an imperial-sponsored retinue arrived from Rome and/or a garrison of reinforcements from Germany? In this regard it is important to note that the pottery kilns are located next to a substantial V-profiled ditch whose original excavation seems to be only just ahead of the start of brick and tile and pottery production. This feature was not further investigated in 2017 but it remains a high priority to see if more of its course can be located and to determine the nature of what it contained — if, indeed, it was, as seems likely, part of an enclosure. It is, of course, tempting to see this as a section of a fort or fortress defence, but the closer parallel is provided by the enclosure ditches (Yards 1 and 2) 400–500 m distant from the Longthorpe fortress, where the great majority of the Claudio-Neronian kilns were distributed along and respected the northern edges of the ditches, a situation very reminiscent of the arrangement of the three pottery kilns at Little London (Dannell and Wild 1987, figs 2 and 4). The pre- and early Flavian Duxford kilns were, for the most part, also located outside a succession of contemporary substantial ditched enclosures (Anderson and Woolhouse 2016, fig. 3). Neither Longthorpe nor Duxford has produced evidence of brick production, but it is important to note the separation of activities at Little London. The brick kiln and the two adjacent kiln clusters, likely also to be brick kilns, are set some 60 m west of the pottery kilns.

The Nero tiles make it clear that there definitely was an official input into the development of Little London and a unit of the army would have been the most likely agency to deliver the project. While Timby's analysis reveals some of the complexities in finding an origin or origins for the types of pottery made there, there is at least one element, the antefix, in the brick and tile assemblage, which has a very strong military association, while the assemblage as a whole, but not the kilns and their dispositions, is best paralleled at the late first-century legionary pottery and tilery at Holt. The character and distribution of the kilns at Little London recalls the patterns at Duxford and Longthorpe, a far cry from the organisation of kilns, workshops, baths and barracks at Holt.

While the typology of the pottery made at Little London indicates a short period of production, beginning no earlier than *c.* A.D. 50 (and, possibly, as late as A.D. 60/61) and ending in the 70s, and probably no later than *c.* A.D. 80, the radiocarbon modelling hints that some production, more likely ceramic building material than pottery, may have continued until towards the end of the first century. Why did production stop? If the tilery's brief was to provide materials for the building of road stations between (and including) *Calleva* and its nearest equivalent neighbours, places which were to become the *civitas* capitals of Cirencester, Chichester and Winchester, this was a task of limited scope: once all the necessary building was completed, the production of ceramic building material and pottery could stop. We can only speculate whether, had there been a continuing private demand for these materials, production might have been allowed to continue to meet it, but the evidence from *Calleva* itself suggests that it was not until the mid-80s and the establishment of the *civitas Atrebatum* that demand picked up again and a new tilery, now exploiting the London Clay rather than the Windlesham Formation and its location not known, was established to meet it (Machin 2018; Fulford *et al.* forthcoming a).

ENVIRONMENTAL IMPACT

It is important to return to a consideration of the impact of the industry at Little London on the local environment. A very striking outcome of Barnett's analysis of the charcoal (Ch. 6) is the extraordinarily high representation of oak — over 90 per cent of the assemblage, a percentage which far exceeds the oak component (about 23 per cent) of typical mixed woodland today. There is also a relatively high incidence of 4–8-year-old oak roundwood. Although at 75 per cent oak is the dominant taxon within the town from the late Iron Age through to the early Flavian period, other species of wood are present and the proportion of roundwood less. While the character of the urban assemblage argues for management by coppicing of the local woodlands, Little London indicates even more clearly both targeted exploitation and direct management by pollarding and coppicing on a short rotation of the woodland.

A similar situation in terms of a very high, also over 90 per cent, representation of oak seems to have been the case at the legionary tilery at Holt, Denbighs., but the sample analysed was small (Hyde 1930). Barnett also notes a similar privileging of oak at kilns associated with the Alice Holt pottery industry, some 15 miles south-east of Little London. On the other hand, that a very high representation of oak was not necessarily always the case is indicated at the late first-/early second-century rural tilery at Great Cansiron Farm in the Weald of East Sussex where oak was second to birch and supplemented by hazel (Cartwright 1986).

SUBSISTENCE

While the presence of tiles impressed with animal footprints has been taken as evidence of tile-making going hand-in-hand with agricultural activities (e.g. Cram and Fulford 1979, 208; cf. Peacock 1979, 6), all we can say with confidence is that it provides only limited evidence for a modest degree of animal husbandry and this is consistent with the almost total lack of crop-processing debris from across the excavated area (Ch. 7). The Little London tile assemblage shows that the incidence of animal-foot impressions is very low and that the range of animals whose presence is captured on the tile does not correlate closely with the range of skeletal evidence from *Calleva* itself, most notably in the absence of the prints of pig, one of the commoner sources of meat in the town. It is also skewed towards younger animals generally whose weight would not completely destroy a tile. On the other hand, there is over-representation of young red and roe deer compared with the assemblages from the town. Together the number of deer prints slightly exceeds those of cattle and sheep or goat. It may be that the workforce could take advantage of the woodland environments from which they sourced their fuel to supplement their diet with wild game. Only a few tiny fragments, none identifiable to species, of animal bone were found at Little London to compare with the evidence of the footprints. There are also very few finds other than waste pottery and ceramic building material to help us characterise life in the pottery- and tile-works. In contrast with contemporary pottery production in the east of England where crop-processing waste was used as fuel (p. 146), the lack of such material in the carbonised assemblages, combined with the negative faunal evidence, suggests that agricultural activity played little part in the life of the workforce at Little London, the scale of production of both tile and pottery allowing no time for it.

WORKFORCE

Two tiny glass beads, one from a kiln, the other from Ditch 2101 in Trench 2 hint at the possibility of a female presence in the workforce (Appendix 2).

CONCLUDING REMARKS

To conclude, we might consider how we might characterise the Little London industries and how they relate to the modes of brick and tile production first proposed by Peacock in 1979 and then further developed in his *Pottery in the Roman World: an Ethnoarchaeological Approach* (1982). For brick and tile he proposed five modes: household production, the small rural brickyard, the nucleated brickyard complex, the estate brickworks and, fifth, municipal production, a category which included procuratorial and imperial ownership, as here at Little London. This last category was subsequently developed to include military production (ibid., 11, 136–51). Except where there were opportunities to exploit transport by water, a broad assumption, reinforced by ethnographic parallels from eighteenth- and nineteenth-century Britain, was that bricks rarely travelled more than 5–10 miles from source (Peacock 1979, 6). Peacock noted exceptional examples of the long-distance movement of military-produced brick in Germany along the Rhine and in Britain of brick produced for the *Classis Britannica* in the Weald transported across the Channel to the fleet-base at Boulogne (1982, 145–6).

Peacock also noted that the great majority of tile kilns reported from Roman Britain were more than 20 km distant from any town and favoured an interpretation that they were essentially estate kilns (1982, 8). He was puzzled by the scarcity of kilns close to towns but did note the official RPG-stamped tile produced next to the *colonia* at Gloucester (ibid., 9). The distribution of these tiles is largely local to the city and sites close by, but with an exceptional presence at the defended roadside settlement at Kenchester, 45 km to the north-west of Gloucester (*RIB* 2486–8). Little London clearly fits into the category of production by an official organisation, but it challenges the assumption that brick did not travel far by road. If the 10 per cent presence of Minety tile at Silchester (p. 134), some 100 km distant from the kilns, can be used as a proxy, Little London tile may well account for a similar proportion in the reverse direction at Cirencester, where so far its presence is only evidenced by a few retained finds of distinctive, relief-patterned tile. While Little London products certainly account for the great proportion of pre-Flavian brick and tile consumed at Silchester, it is reasonable to suppose that their presence at towns like Chichester, Cirencester and Winchester was more than a token one. We just need a greater focus on the characterisation and quantification of assemblages of ceramic building material from these and the other places where relief-patterned tile in Little London fabrics has been found to get a better grasp of the range and scale of consumption. It is also clear from the work done in *Londinium* that the pattern of extended distribution from Little London is not unusual in the first century A.D. (above, p. 170). We have already noted pre- and early Flavian Minety tile at Silchester and the overall distribution of the stamped tile attributed to Minety in the second century may well reflect the overall situation in the first (cf. Warry 2017). In *Londinium* small quantities of tile provenanced from Eccles, Kent, and from, as yet, unlocated tileries in north Kent and near Chichester in West Sussex also demonstrate that the long distance movement of ceramic building material by road was far from exceptional at this time (Betts 2017, 368–75). Tile from Eccles has also been noted from as far away as Silchester but not necessarily in the first century (Machin 2018, 121–2). One of the drivers for the establishment of the tilery at Little London may have been to contribute to the construction of public buildings, especially road stations, and the additional cost of transporting cart loads of brick and tile long distance may have been absorbed by the procurator or managed through the imposition of local levies on transport.

Little London is also not unusual as an industry in the pre- and early Flavian period in its conjunction of pottery and brick and tile production. As we have seen, this has also been found at Eccles, Kent and at Minety, Wilts., and it is a reasonable hypothesis that the two went together at pre- and early Flavian Colchester, Brockley Hill and the workshops along Watling Street supplying pre-Flavian London and Verulamium. With the only very recent recognition of pottery production at Little London, it is not surprising that it has not been widely identified elsewhere. *Calleva* was probably its major market, but the stamped mortarium has matches from a site on the Thames near Reading (p. 60) and Timby has, since 2017, identified further sherds, including of a disc-mouthed flagon and a drop-flanged bowl, of Little London ware from a site at Hartshill Copse, Thatcham, W Berks. (Timby forthcoming). Whether the pottery was distributed as far as the brick and tile remains to be seen.

FUTURE WORK

Even though much of the Little London complex has been destroyed by historic quarrying, much remains to be investigated. Our trenches investigated a total of 850 m^2, approximately 10 per cent of the area in the south-west of the field where the geophysics has indicated good survival of extensive below-ground archaeology. All of the kiln structures excavated in 2017 were backfilled intact. Long may they and all the surviving archaeology at Little London be preserved!

APPENDIX 1

THE NERO TILE-STAMPS FROM LITTLE LONDON AND SILCHESTER

By Peter Warry

The Roman Inscriptions of Britain II.5 (*RIB*) published in 1993 lists five tiles with circular stamps of the emperor Nero, four were found at Silchester and the fifth at Little London. Since then a further sixteen stamped tiles have been found (three at Little London and thirteen at Silchester) and these, together with the original five, are listed in Table 21. *RIB* suggested that all five of the original tiles were probably stamped with different dies; however the additional stamped tiles allow these dies to be reappraised and it is now proposed that dies 2481.3 and 2481.5 are probably the same as 2481.1 and 2481.2 is probably the same as 2481.4. Now, two further dies can be identified from the new stamped tiles.

The detail of the drawing of die 2481.1 in *RIB* differs from the actual tile (Greenaway 1981); in particular the G of Germanicus is wrongly positioned and the N of Nero is wrongly shaped. If these points are adjusted then die 2481.3 can be seen to be a part of 2481.1. Die 2481.5 neatly, and pretty much exactly, fills in the missing CAE of Caesar and also includes part of the central rosette. Small find no. 41 (see FIG. 144) confirms parts of this reconstruction and adds a ligatured E to the R of GER[MANICUS]. Die 2482.4 is probably the same as 2482.2 because the diameters of the dies match as does the spacing of the letters, however the letters themselves have been drawn 25 per cent larger. Small find no. 796 confirms the accuracy of the 2482.2 lettering.

Two new dies (3 and 4) have been identified as illustrated below. Neither of these dies has been found with the stippled texture that is normal for dies 1 and 2 which is attributed to the end grain of the wood into which the dies have been cut showing through. Although some of the impressions are too poor to rule out the possibility that they may have been made by other dies, it is probable that only the four dies illustrated in FIG. 144 have been used for all of the stamped tiles.

Most of the recent finds have been on probable *tegulae* with the stamp positioned typically 2 cm from the base of the tile and the die orientated to place Nero's name either at the bottom or the top of the stamp (FIGS 144–145).

TABLE 21. TABLE OF ALL KNOWN NERO TILE STAMP DIES

***RIB* no.**	**Site no.**	**Context**	**Type**	**Position (cm from base), Nero orientation**	**Die**
2482.1	Little London	topsoil	tile	n/a	Die 1, possible stippling
2482.2	Silchester	baths	brick	n/a	Die 2, stippled
2482.3	Silchester	basilica	brick	n/a	Die 1, possible stippling
2482.4	Silchester	basilica	brick	n/a	Die 2?, stippled
2482.5	Silchester	basilica	brick	n/a	Die 1, not stippled?

SF no.					
7912	A2000.20	2478	*tegula*?	2, bottom	Die 1, stippled
5688	A2006.50	7054	*tegula*?	2.5, n/a	Die 1?, stippled
5678	A2009.20	10607	*tegula*?	4, n/a	Die 2?, stippled
543	A2014.41	30324	*tegula*?	1.5, left	Die 2?, stippled
609	A2014.41	30050	*tegula*?	1, bottom L	Die 4, not stippled
796	A2014.41	30410	*tegula*	2, bottom	Die 2, stippled
904	A2014.41	30411	*tegula*?	n/a	indecipherable
1430	A2016.70	34003	brick?	n/a	Die 3, not stippled
4	A2017.51	1031	brick?	n/a	indecipherable
8	A2017.51	1069	brick?	n/a	Die 3, not stippled
12	A2017.51	1091	*tegula*?	3, bottom	Die 1?, not stippled?
40	A2017.50	5087	*tegula*?	3, top R	Die 1, too poor for stippling
41	A2017.50	5087	*tegula*?	2, bottom	Die 1, stippled
42	A2017.50	5087	*tegula*?	3, top	Die 4, not stippled
44	A2017.50	5087	*tegula*?	n/a	Die 4, not stippled
458	A2017.51	2025	*tegula*?	n/a	indecipherable

FIG. 144. Nero stamp dies full size

FIG. 145. Photographs of the better Nero tile stamps (approximately actual size)

APPENDIX 2

OTHER FINDS

INTRODUCTION *By Michael Fulford*

Finds other than pottery and ceramic building material were very rare. As with the non-kiln pottery, the great majority of artefacts were recovered from the north–south ditch 2101 in Trench 2. Apart from one very corroded possible coin from Trench 1, there were no other objects of copper alloy from the entire excavation. Iron is represented by part of an iron knife (below) and a few corroded nails. The great majority of these were found in the upper fills (five contexts) of the north–south ditch in Trench 2, with one in a lower fill. Two nails were associated with Kiln 3 in Trench 2 and two were found in Trench 1. A small fragment of colourless vessel glass was found associated with Kiln 3 and further small fragments including of a square bottle in the upper fill of Ditch 2101. There were a very few fragments of unidentifiable animal bone. Whether the rarity of animal bone is a reflection of soil conditions or represents the actual situation is not known.

CATALOGUE *By Nina Crummy*

There are only three objects requiring further comment. One, part of an iron knife, appears to be of Manning's Type 9 (1985, 113, fig. 28), with a back that angles downwards to the point and to the end of the rod handle (SF 202). Examples from London are probably from early post-conquest deposits in the Walbrook (ibid.). An early context also suits a tiny colourless glass spacer bead from kiln rake-out (SF 214), and one of opaque black glass from the fill of slot [2060] (SF 218). Spacer beads of this size are rarely recovered, and consequently are missing from Guido's classification for Roman Britain (1978) and from Cosyns' classification of black glass beads, where the term spacer bead is used for much larger forms than SF 218 and the smallest beads do not include any of hexagonal section (2011, 106–7). Nevertheless, SF 214 may be set in the context of first-century colourless vessel glass (Cool and Price 1995, 36–8, 42–3; Cool 2020, 315), and SF 218 in that of black glass game counters found in the first-century legionary fortresses at Usk and York, and in Claudian-Neronian contexts at Colchester (Cool and Price 1995, 129–30; Cool *et al.* 1995, 1650, nos 5839–42, fig. 764; Crummy 1983, 92; 1992a, 220).

SF 202. (2028), fill of slot [2043]. Iron knife blade fragment with a curved back at its highest just before the junction with the handle. The line of the edge is obscured. Part of an integral handle remains, square in section and curving downwards to continue the line of the back. Total length 85 mm, surviving width approximately 30 mm.

SF 214, Sample 226. (2069), flue rake-out. Tiny clear glass spacer bead with rounded sides. Length 1 mm, diameter 2 mm.

SF 218, Sample 216. (2049), fill of slot [2060]. Tiny hexagonal opaque black glass spacer bead. Length 1 mm, width 2 mm.

APPENDIX 3

AGE OF ROUNDWOOD WHEN CUT ALICE HOLT KILNS, FRITH END

By Catherine Barnett

TABLE 22. AGE OF ROUNDWOOD WHEN CUT (WHERE DISCERNIBLE), FRITH END ROMANO-BRITISH AND LATE ROMANO-BRITISH CONTEXTS (Barnett 2011, table 3)

Sample	Species	Age when cut	Total no. pieces
59790 Colluvium (F081) <2>	*Quercus* sp.	16	4
W3481 Pot fill 1004 sf 2002 (1084) <3006>	*Corylus avellana*	5–10	55
	Ilex aquifolium	5	1
59790 Colluvium F082 (F083) <3>	*Quercus* sp.	5–6	6
W3481 Pot fill 1007 sf 2001 (1009) <3002>	*Quercus* sp.	20–22	5
59790 Colluvium F086 (F085) <5>	*Quercus* sp.	>6–10 12	4 2
59793 Pot production feature 5179 (5174) <3203>	*Quercus* sp.	3 5–10 11–15 16–20 21–26 *c.*32	1 19 18 7 13 1
59793 Scoop rel. to pot production 5183 (5184) <3204>	*Quercus* sp.	5–10 15 16–20 25	3 2 3 1
	Corylus avellana	5–10 11–15 16–20 21–25	3 0 7 2

APPENDIX 4

CALIBRATED AGE RANGES USING THE UK ARCHAEOMAGNETIC CALIBRATION CURVE

By David P. Greenwood, Sam E. Harris and Catherine M. Batt

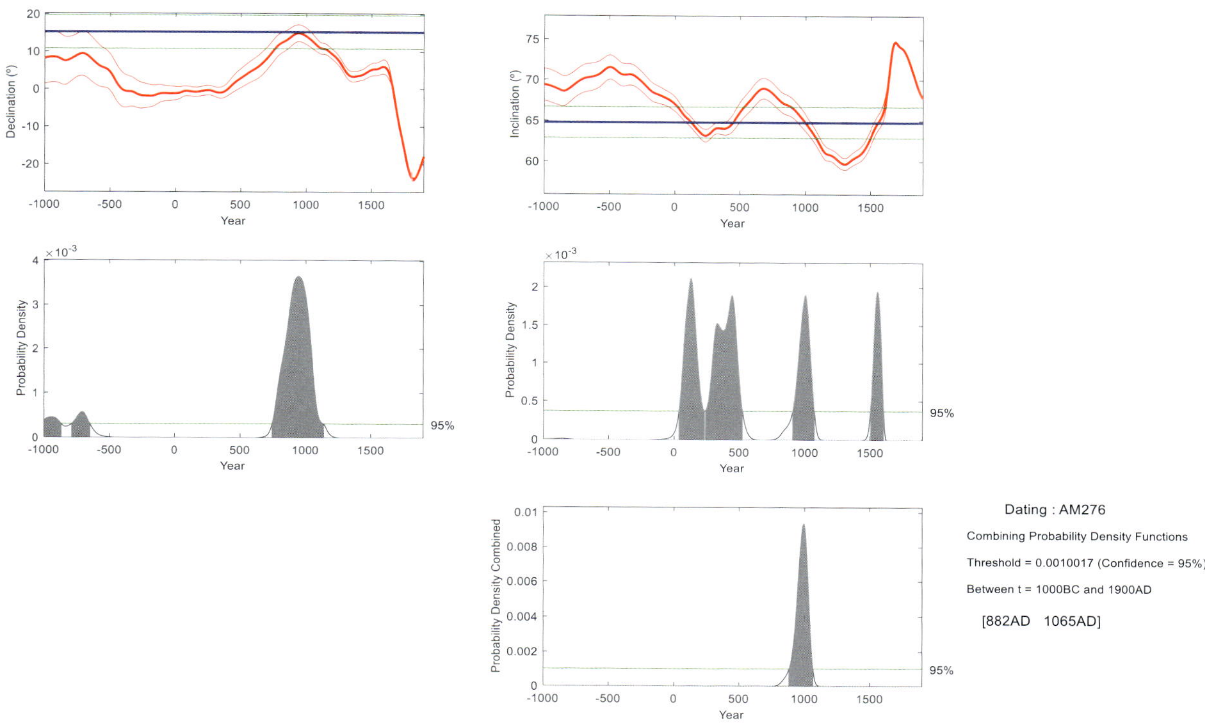

FIG. 146. Constrained and calibrated date ranges for AM276 (LL2) using UK geomagnetic field model ARCH-UK.1. Top row shows master secular variation curves for the observation site (red bold curves with red error bands) of the declination and inclination with the archaeomagnetic directions (blue line) and associated scatter (green lines). Middle row shows the individual probability density functions for the declination and inclination – the green line indicates the 95% probability threshold. Bottom row shows the combined probability density marked with the green line of 95% probability, and the archaeomagnetic age range

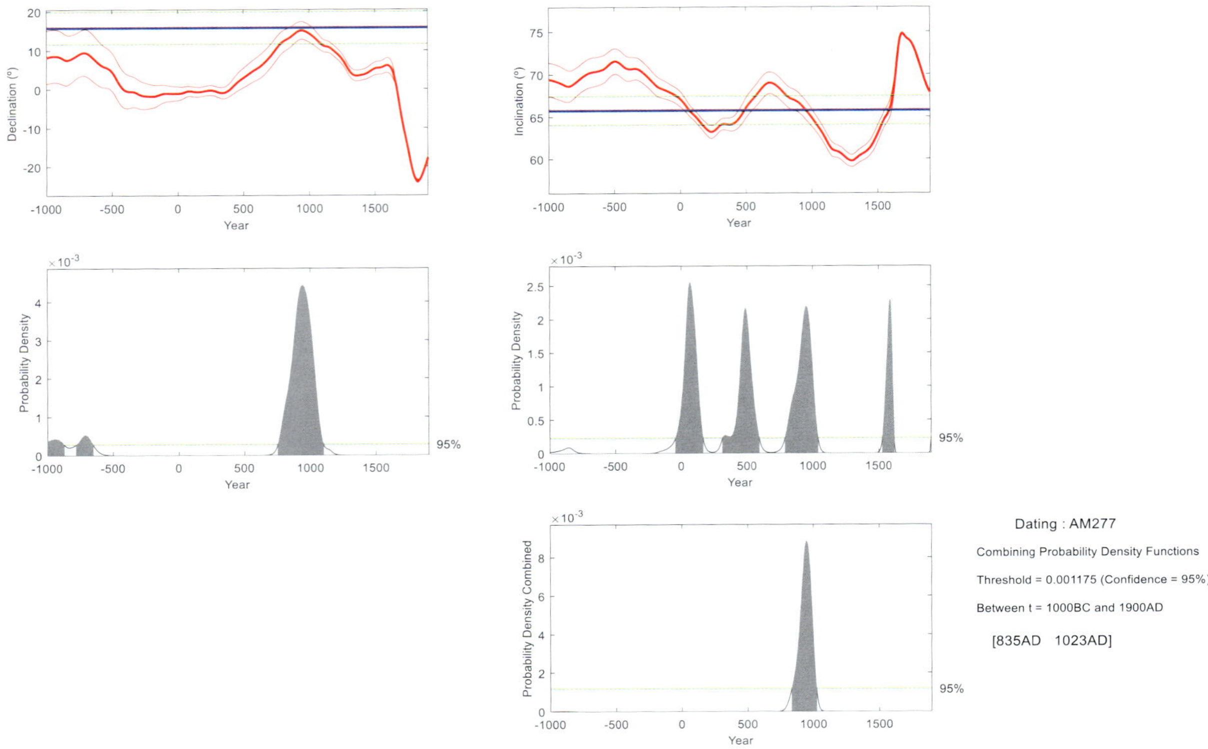

FIG. 147. Constrained and calibrated date ranges for AM277 (LL3) using UK geomagnetic field model ARCH-UK.1. Top row shows master secular variation curves for the observation site (red bold curves with red error bands) of the declination and inclination with the archaeomagnetic directions (blue line) and associated scatter (green lines). Middle row shows the individual probability density functions for the declination and inclination – the green line indicates the 95% probability threshold. Bottom row shows the combined probability density marked with the green line of 95% probability, and the archaeomagnetic age range

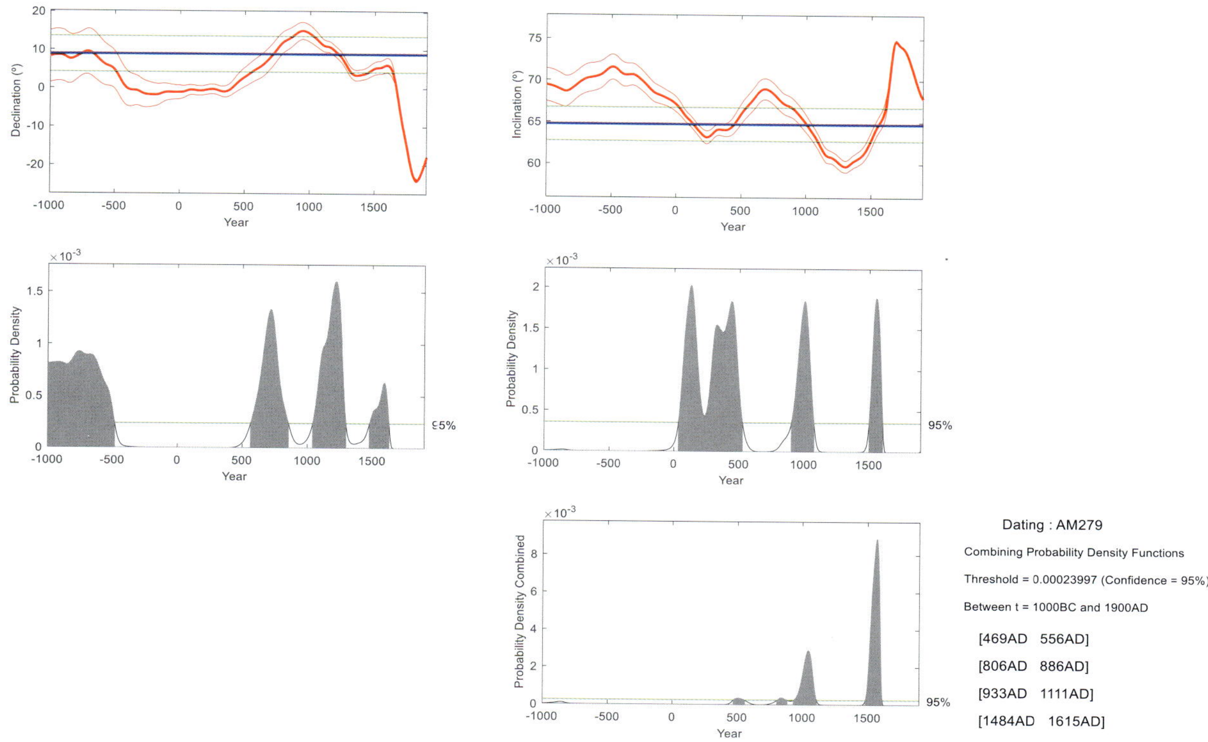

FIG. 148. Constrained and calibrated date ranges for AM279 (LL4) using UK geomagnetic field model ARCH-UK.1. Top row shows master secular variation curves for the observation site (red bold curves with red error bands) of the declination and inclination with the archaeomagnetic directions (blue line) and associated scatter (green lines). Middle row shows the individual probability density functions for the declination and inclination – the green line indicates the 95% probability threshold. Bottom row shows the combined probability density marked with the green line of 95% probability, and the archaeomagnetic age ranges

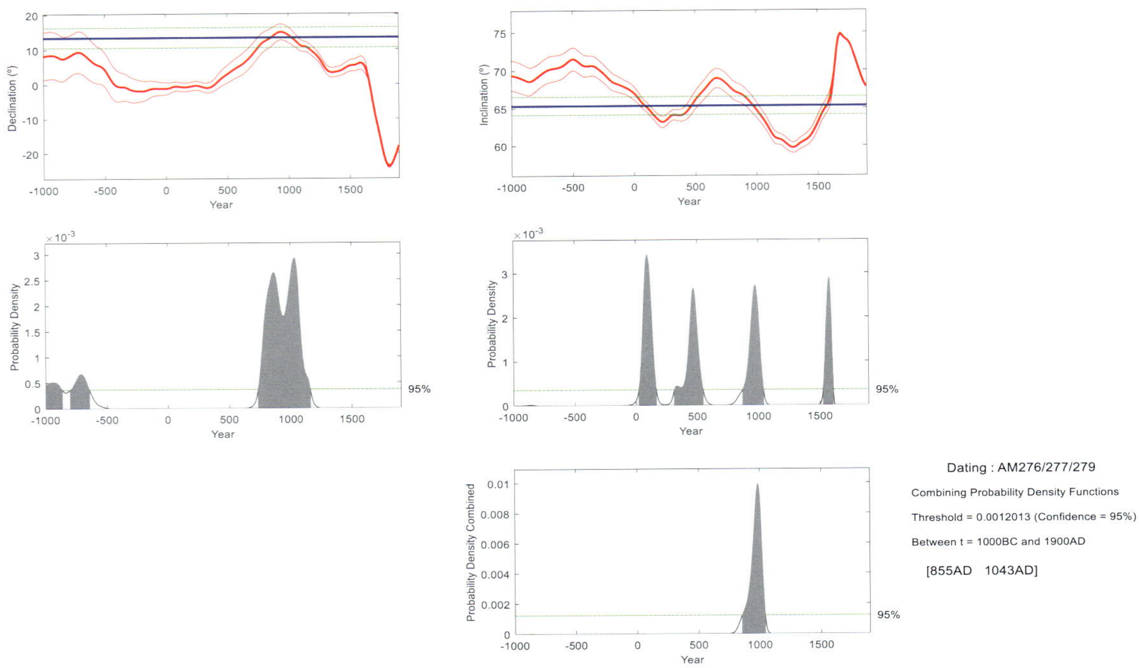

FIG. 149. Constrained and calibrated date ranges for AM276, 277 and 279 combined using UK geomagnetic field model ARCH-UK.1. Top row shows master secular variation curves for the observation site (red bold curves with red error bands) of the declination and inclination with the archaeomagnetic directions (blue line) and associated scatter (green lines). Middle row shows the individual probability density functions for the declination and inclination – the green line indicates the 95% probability threshold. Bottom row shows the combined probability density marked with the green line of 95% probability, and the archaeomagnetic age ranges

APPENDIX 5

AN INTRODUCTION TO ARCHAEOMAGNETIC DATING

By David P. Greenwood, Sam E. Harris and Catherine M. Batt

PRINCIPLES

Archaeomagnetic dating is a derivative dating method, based on a comparison of the ancient geomagnetic field, as recorded by archaeological materials, with a dated record of changes in the Earth's field over time in a particular geographical area. The geomagnetic field changes both in direction (declination and inclination) and in strength (intensity) and archaeomagnetic dating can be based on either changes in direction or intensity or a combination of the two. Dating by direction requires the exact position of the archaeological material in relation to the present geomagnetic field to be recorded, and so the material must be undisturbed and sampled *in situ*. Dating by intensity does not require *in-situ* samples but is less precise and experimentally more difficult. The laboratory at Bradford uses archaeomagnetic dating by direction.

SUITABLE MATERIALS FOR DATING

For archaeological material to be suitable for dating using magnetic direction it must contain sufficient magnetised particles and an event must have caused these particles to record the Earth's magnetic field. Many geologically derived materials, e.g. soils, sediments, clays, contain sufficient magnetic minerals. There are primarily two types of archaeological events which may result in the Earth's magnetic field at a particular moment being recorded by archaeological material: heating and deposition in air or water.

If materials have been heated to a sufficiently high temperature (>400°C) they may retain a thermoremanent magnetisation (TRM), which reflects the Earth's magnetic field at the time of last cooling. Suitable archaeological features would include hearths, kilns and other fired structures.

Sediments may acquire a datable detrital remanent magnetisation (DRM) from the alignment of their magnetic grains by the ambient field during deposition. Such an effect allows deposits in wells, ditches and streams to be dated. However, this aspect of archaeomagnetic dating is still under development, as factors such as bioturbation and diagenesis, can cause post-depositional disturbance of the magnetisation.

Archaeomagnetic dating can be applied to features expected to date from 5000 B.C. to the present day, as this is the period covered by the calibration curve. However, as discussed below, the precision of the date obtained will vary according to the period being dated.

SAMPLING

Samples of robust fired materials are taken by attaching a 25 mm flanged plastic reference button to a cleaned stable area of the feature using a fast-setting epoxy resin (Clark *et al.* 1988).

The button is levelled, using a spirit level, and held in place with a small bead of plasticine while the resin sets. The direction of north is then marked on the button using a magnetic compass, sun compass or gyrotheodolite, and the button removed with a small part of the feature attached to it. Samples are trimmed and consolidated in the laboratory with a solution of 10% polyvinylacetate in acetone, or sodium silicate solution. Sediments and friable fired materials are sampled by insertion of a 2 cm diameter plastic cylinder, onto which the direction of north is marked. Magnetometers used are sufficiently sensitive for only small samples (*c.* 1 cm^3) to be required; approximately 15 samples are needed from each feature and it may be possible to select the sampling location to minimise the visual impact if the feature is to be preserved.

LABORATORY MEASUREMENTS

In the laboratory a spinner magnetometer is used to measure the remanent magnetisation of each sample (Molyneux 1971). The measurement indicates the relative strength and direction of the magnetic field of the sample. The stability of this magnetisation is then examined by placing the sample in alternating magnetic fields of increasing strength (2.5 to 100mT) and removing the magnetisation step-by-step. The demagnetisation measurements allow removal of any less stable magnetisations acquired after the firing or depositional event, leaving the magnetisation of archaeological interest. It can also be used to indicate the magnetic mineralogy of the samples using information relating to the field required to reduce the intensity to half its original value, known as the median destructive field (MDF); higher values are indicative of harder magnetic minerals such as haematite (Sternberg *et al.* 1999). The results of measurements of the direction of magnetisation of a group of samples are represented on a stereographic plot, which shows declination as an angle measured clockwise from north and inclination as a distance from the perimeter.

STATISTICAL ANALYSIS

The magnetic directions from a number of samples expected to have the same date are combined to find a mean direction, the precision of which is defined using Fisherian statistics (Fisher 1953). The alpha-95 (α_{95}) represents a 95% probability that the true mean direction lies within a cone of confidence around the observed mean direction, and would be expected to be less than 5° for dating purposes. A value larger than this indicates that the magnetic directions of the samples are scattered and therefore do not all record the same magnetic field.

Samples observed to be discordant from the mean directional value are assessed using a statistical test defined by McFadden (1982) which shows that given the observed grouping of the N concordant observations, with resultant vector of length R, there is a probability P that an outlier from the same distribution will exceed an angle $\gamma_{(1-P)}$ from the mean of the concordant group, where

$$cos\gamma_{(1-P)} = 1 - \frac{(R+1)(N-R)}{R}\left[\left(\frac{1}{1-(1-P)^{1/(N+1)}}\right)^{1/(N-1)} - 1\right]$$

Thus, with $P = 0.05$, if the outlier lies further than $\gamma 0.95$ from the mean of the other N observations then it may be concluded with 95% confidence that the outlier is discordant with the other observations and therefore can be removed from the analysis.

CALIBRATION OF DATES

Once the mean ChRM direction has been obtained this is dated by comparing it with a calibration curve showing changes in the Earth's field over time. As the variation of the Earth's magnetic field is not predictable (Batt 1997), the pattern of change has to be established by independent dating, typically historical records, radiocarbon or dendrochronology. The UK calibration curve is compiled from direct measurements of the field which extend back to

A.D. 1576 in Britain, and from archaeomagnetic measurements from features dated by other methods. As the geomagnetic field changes spatially, data for the calibration curve can only be drawn from within an area approximately 1000 km across and all magnetic directions must be corrected mathematically to a central location (Noel and Batt 1990). There is a single calibration curve for England, Scotland and Wales and directions are corrected to Meriden (latitude = 52.43° N, longitude = 1.62° W).

British archaeological dates are calibrated using the secular variation curve developed by Batt *et al.* (2017), using a Matlab tool developed by Pavón-Carassco *et al.* (2011). Additional global secular variation curves can also be used, such as ARCH3k.1 and CALS3k.3 datasets (Korte *et al.* 2009). The secular variation curves differ in terms of the datasets that have been used to construct them, for example: the ARCH3k.1 curve is a global database of archaeomagnetic data only, while the CALS3k.3 curve is also a global database of archaeomagnetic data but incorporates lake sediment magnetic data. This results in subtly different calibrated age ranges being produced for the same magnetic directions.

PRECISION OF DATES

There are a number of factors that will influence the error margins of the dates obtained:

- Differential recording of the field by different parts of the feature.
- Disturbance of the material after firing/deposition.
- Uncertainties in sampling and laboratory measurements.
- Error margins in the calibration curve itself.
- Uncertainties in the comparison of the magnetic direction with the calibration curve.
- Spatial variation of the geomagnetic field.

The precision of the calibration curve varies according to the archaeological period and so the precision of the date obtained will depend on the archaeological dates. As the geomagnetic field has occasionally had the same direction at different times, it is also possible to have two or more alternative dates for a single feature. In most cases the archaeological evidence can be used to select the most likely of these.

Given the number of different factors it is not possible to give a general feature for the precision of archaeomagnetic dates but there will be an error margin of at least ±50 years. It is important to note that since the method relies on the reliability of previously dated sites the calibration curve can be improved as more measurements become available. Features that cannot be dated or given broad age ranges now, may be datable in the future.

BIBLIOGRAPHY

Alarcáo, A.M. 2000: *Museu Monográfico de Conimbriga*, Lisbon

Allen, J.R.L. 2017: 'Geological resources and their exploitation in the Berkshire chalklands of the later nineteenth century: a first survey', *Landscape History* 38(1), 67–80

Allen, M. 2018: 'The social context of animals and exploitation of wild resources', in Smith *et al.* 2018, 98–118

Anderson, K. and Woolhouse, T. 2016: 'Continental potters? First-century Roman flagon production at Duxford, Cambridgeshire', *Britannia* 47, 43–69

Ascough, P.L., Bird, M.I., Scott, A.C., Collinson, M.E., Cohen-Ofri, I., Snape, C.E. and Le Manquais, K. 2010: 'Charcoal reflectance measurements: implications for structural characterization and assessment of diagenetic alteration', *Journal of Archaeological Science* 37(7), 1590–9

Ashmore, P.J. 1999: 'Radiocarbon dating: avoiding errors by avoiding mixed samples', *Antiquity* 73, 124–30

Asouti, E. and Austin, P. 2005: 'Reconstructing woodland vegetation and its relation to human societies, based on the analysis and interpretation of archaeological wood charcoal macro-remains', *Environmental Archaeology* 10, 1–18

Bang, P. and Dahlstrom, P. 1974: *Animal Tracks and Signs*, London

Barclay, A., Knight, D., Booth, P., Evans, H., Brown, D. and Wood, I. 2016: *A Standard for Pottery Studies in Archaeology: Prehistoric Ceramics Research Group, the Study Group for Roman Pottery and the Medieval Pottery Research Group*, http://romanpotterystudy.org/new/wp-content/uploads/2016/06/Standard_for_Pottery_Studies_in_Archaeology.pdf

Barnett, C. 2011: 'Frith End Wood charcoal analysis', unpub. Wessex Archaeology report, project ref. 59794

Barnett, C. 2018a: 'Radiocarbon dating', in Fulford *et al.* 2018a, 346–8

Barnett, C. 2018b: 'The wood charcoal and waterlogged wood', in Fulford *et al.* 2018a, 314–26

Barnett, C. 2019: 'Fuelling the fires: the contribution of wood charcoal analysis to a landscape scale project at and around pre-conquest Iron Age Silchester and a reflection on its wider implications', in *Environmental Archaeology* 25(2), 227–45

Barnett, C. 2020a: 'The wood charcoal', in Fulford *et al.* 2020, 515–29

Barnett, C. 2020b: 'Radiocarbon dating', in Fulford *et al.* 2020, 530–5

Barnett, C. and Fulford, M.G. (eds) in prep.: *Silchester Environs: The Landscape Context of Iron Age Calleva*, Oxford

Bar-Oz, G. and Tepper, Y. 2010: 'Out on the tiles: animal footprints from the Roman site of Kefar 'Othnay (Legio), Israel', *Near Eastern Archaeology* 73(4), 244–7

Barr, K. and Bell, M. 2017: 'Neolithic and Bronze Age ungulate footprint-tracks of the Severn Estuary: species, age, identification and the interpretation of husbandry practices', *Environmental Archaeology* 22(1), 1–14

Batt, C.M. 1997: 'The British archaeomagnetic calibration curve: an objective treatment', *Archaeometry* 39(1), 153–68

Batt, C.M., Brown, M.C., Clelland, S.-J., Korte, M., Linford, P. and Outram, Z. 2017: 'Advances in archaeomagnetic dating in Britain: new data, new approaches and a new calibration curve', *Journal of Archaeological Science* 85, 66–82

Betts, I.M. 1995: 'Procuratorial tile stamps from London', *Britannia* 26, 207–29

Betts, I.M. 2003: 'Stone and ceramic building materials', in C. Cowan, *Urban Development in North-West Southwark*, MoLAS Monograph 16, London, 105–19

Betts, I.M. 2006: 'The building material', in S. Watson, *Development on Roman London's Western Hill: Excavations at Paternoster Square, City of London*, MoLAS Monograph 32, London, 79–81

Betts, I.M. 2008: 'The building materials', in N. Bateman, C. Cowan and R. Wroe-Brown, *London's Roman Amphitheatre: Guildhall Yard, City of London*, MoLAS Monograph 35, London, 164–8

Betts, I.M. 2015: 'Ceramic tile and brick', in Dunwoodie *et al.* 2015, 174–9

Betts, I.M. 2017: 'The supply of tile to Roman London', in D. Bird (ed.), *Agriculture and Industry in South-Eastern Roman Britain*, Oxford, 368–83

Betts, I.M., Black, E.W. and Gower, J. 1997: *A Corpus of Relief-patterned Tiles in Roman Britain*, *Journal of Roman Pottery Studies* 7 (for 1994)

Bidwell, P.T. 1979: *The Legionary Bath-house and Basilica and Forum at Exeter*, Exeter Archaeological Report 1, Exeter

Bidwell, P. 2021: 'Pottery supply in Roman Exeter and the South-West', in S. Rippon and N. Holbrook (eds), *Studies in the Roman and Medieval Archaeology of Exeter*, Exeter Archaeological Report 8, Oxford, 309–25

Bird, D. 1996: 'Reflections on the choice of Brockley Hill as a pottery production site', *Journal of Roman Pottery Studies* 12, 22–5

Bird, J., Hassall, M.W.C. and Sheldon, H. (eds) 1996: *Interpreting Roman London. Papers in Memory of Hugh Chapman*, Oxford

Birley, E. 1949: 'Mortarium stamps in Gloucester museum', *Transactions of the Bristol and Gloucestershire Archaeological Society* 67 (for 1946–48), 374–80

Black, E. 1985: 'The dating of relief-patterned flue-tiles', *Oxford Journal of Archaeology* 4, 353–76

Blagg, T. 1979: 'The use of terra-cotta for architectural ornament in Italy and the western provinces', in McWhirr 1979a, 267–84

Blumstein, M. 1956: 'Roman pottery from Hoo', *Archaeologia Cantiana* 70, 273–7

Boon, G.C. 1957: *Roman Silchester*, London

Boon, G.C. 1974: *Silchester: The Roman Town of Calleva*, Newton Abbott

Bouet, A. 1999: *Les matériaux de construction en terre cuite dans les thermes de la Gaule Narbonnaise*, Paris

Brock, F., Higham, T., Ditchfield, P. and Bronk Ramsey, C. 2010: 'Current pretreatment methods for AMS radiocarbon dating at the Oxford Radiocarbon Accelerator Unit (ORAU)', *Radiocarbon* 52, 103–12

Brodribb, G. 1987: *Roman Brick and Tile*, Gloucester

Bronk Ramsey, C. 1995: 'Radiocarbon calibration and analysis of stratigraphy: the OxCal program', *Radiocarbon* 37, 425–30

Bronk Ramsey, C. 1998: 'Probability and dating', *Radiocarbon* 40, 461–74

Bronk Ramsey, C. 2001: 'Development of the radiocarbon calibration program', *Radiocarbon* 43, 355–63

Bronk Ramsey, C. 2009: 'Bayesian analysis of radiocarbon dates', *Radiocarbon* 51, 337–60

Brooks, H. 2004: *Archaeological Excavation at 29–39 Head Street. Colchester, Essex. May–Sept 2000*, Colchester Archaeological Report 0268 (cat.essex.ac.uk/reports/CAT-report-0268.pdf)

Brown, P.D.C. and McWhirr, A. 1966: 'Cirencester 1965', *The Antiquaries Journal* 46(2), 240–54

Brown, P.D.C. and McWhirr, A. 1967: 'Cirencester 1966', *The Antiquaries Journal* 47(2), 185–97

Brown, R., Quinn, D., Shields, C. and Lawrence, M. 2003: *Tracks and Signs of the Birds of Britain and Europe* (2nd edn), London

Buck, C.E., Cavanagh, W.G. and Litton, C.D. 1996: *Bayesian Approach to Interpreting Archaeological Data*, Chichester

Buckley, G.P. 1992: *Ecology and Management of Coppice Woodlands*, London

Bushe-Fox, J.P. 1932: *Third Report on the Excavations of the Roman Fort at Richborough, Kent*, Reports of the Research Committee of the Society of Antiquaries of London 10, Oxford

Butterfield, B.G. and Meylan, B.A. 1980: *Three-Dimensional Structure of Wood. An Ultrastructural Approach*, London/New York

CA 2016: *Gloscat Redevelopment Project, Media Studies Site, Brunswick Road, Gloucester, Archaeological Excavation Report 15620*, unpub. Cotswold Archaeology report

Calkin, J.B. 1935: 'An early Romano-British kiln at Corfe Mullen, Dorset', *Antiquaries Journal* 15 no. 1, 42–55

Camulodunum = Hawkes and Hull 1947

Cartwright, C. 1986: 'Charcoal', in Rudling 1986, 220–2

Castle, S. 1973a: 'Trial excavations in Field 410, Brockley Hill, part 1', *The London Archaeologist* 2 (2), 36–9

Castle, S. 1973b: 'Trial excavations in Field 410, Brockley Hill, part 2', *The London Archaeologist* 2 (4), 78–83

Chabal, L. 1992: 'La représentativité paléoécologique des charbons de bois archéologiques issus du bois de feu', in J.L. Vernet (ed.), *Les charbons de bois, les anciens écosystèmes et le rôle de l'homme, Bulletin de la Société Botanique de France* 139(2–4), 213–36

Chabal, L. 1997: *Forêts et sociétés en Languedoc (néolithique final, antiquité tardive). L'anthracologie, méthode et paleoécologie*, Documents d'archéologie française 63, Paris

Chadburn, A. and Tyers, P.A. 1984: *Early Roman Pottery from Fenchurch Street, Early Roman Pottery from the City of London* 5, unpub. DUA Archive Report, Museum of London

Chisham, C. 2008: 'The charcoal', in V. Eirbeck, G. Jones, A.B. Powell and R.H. Seager Smith, 'A Roman pottery kiln, kiln furniture and new vessel forms from Alice Holt Forest, Hampshire', *Hampshire Studies* 63, 110–28

Clark, A.J., Tarling, D.H. and Noel, M. 1988: 'Developments in archaeomagnetic dating in Britain', *Journal of Archaeological Science* 15(6), 645–67

Clark, K. 2011: 'The dog assemblage', in Fulford and Clarke 2011, 271–9

Clark, K. 2020: 'The dog remains', in Fulford *et al.* 2020, 467–9

Cool, H.E.M. 2020: 'The vessel glass', in Fulford *et al.* 2020, 302–19

Cool, H.E.M. and Price, J. 1995: *Roman Vessel Glass from Excavations in Colchester, 1971–85*, Colchester Archaeological Report 8, Colchester

Cool, H.E.M., Lloyd-Morgan, G. and Hooley, A.D. 1995: *Finds from the Fortress*, The Archaeology of York 17/10, York

Cosyns, P. 2011: *The Production, Distribution and Consumption of Black Glass in the Roman Empire during the 1st–5th Century AD. An Archaeological, Archaeometric and Historical Approach*, unpub. PhD thesis, Free University of Brussels, Belgium; www.academia.edu/2046608/Roman_black_glass

Cotton, M.A. 1947: 'Excavations at Silchester 1938–39', *Archaeologia*, 92, 121–67

Cram, L. 2000: 'Foot-impressed tiles', in Fulford and Timby 2000, 123–6

Cram, L. and Fulford, M. 1979: 'Silchester tile making – the faunal evidence', in McWhirr 1979a, 201–9

Crowley, N. and Betts, I.M. 1992: 'Three *Classis Britannica* stamps from London', *Britannia* 23, 218–22

Crummy, N. 1983: *The Roman Small Finds from Excavations in Colchester 1971–9*, Colchester Archaeological Report 2, Colchester

Crummy, N. 1992a: 'Roman small finds from the Gilberd School site', in P. Crummy, *Excavations at Culver Street, Gilberd School, and Other Sites in Colchester 1971–85*, Colchester Archaeological Report 6, Colchester, 206–50
Crummy, N. 1992b: 'Roman and post-Roman tile and daub', in P. Crummy, *Excavations at Culver Street, the Gilberd School, and Other Sites in Colchester 1971–85*, Colchester Archaeological Report 6, Colchester, 251–9
Cunliffe, B. 1971: *Excavations at Fishbourne 1961–1969. Vol. II: The Finds*, Reports of the Research Committee of the Society of Antiquaries of London 27, London
Dannell, G.B. and Wild, J.P. 1987: *Longthorpe II. The Military Works-Depot: An Episode in Landscape History*, Britannia Monograph 8, London
Dark, S.P. in prep.: 'The pollen evidence', in Barnett and Fulford in prep.
Darling, M.J. 1985: 'Roman pottery', in H.R. Hurst, *Kingsholm*, Gloucester Archaeological Report 1, Cambridge, 55–93
Darling, M.J. 1986: 'Lake (pottery)', unpub. ms
Darling, M. 2012: 'Stuffed dormice or tandoori chicken in Roman Britain?', in D. Bird (ed.), *Dating and Interpreting the Past in the Western Roman Empire: Essays in Honour of Brenda Dickinson*, Oxford, 346–57
Davies, B., Richardson, B. and Tomber, R. 1994: *A Dated Corpus of Early Roman Pottery from the City of London*, CBA Research Report 98, London
DeLaine, J. 1997: *The Baths of Caracalla: A Study in the Design, Construction and Economics of Large-scale Building Projects in Imperial Rome*, JRA Supplementary Series 25, Portsmouth, RI
Deru, X. 1996: *La céramique belge dans le nord de la Gaul. Caractérisation, chronologie, phénomènes culturels et économiques*, Louvain-la-Neuve
Detsicas, A.P. (ed.) 1973: *Current Research in Romano-British Pottery*, CBA Research Report 10, London
Detsicas, A.P. 1977: 'First-century pottery manufacture at Eccles, Kent', in Dore and Greene 1977, 19–36
Dore, J. and Greene, K. (eds) 1977: *Roman Pottery Studies in Britain and Beyond*, BAR International Series S30, Oxford
Down, A. 1978: *Chichester Excavations 3*, Chichester
Dunbar, E., Cook, G.T., Naysmith, P., Tripney, B.G. and Xu, S. 2016: 'AMS ^{14}C dating at the Scottish Universities Environmental Research Centre (SUERC) Radiocarbon Dating Laboratory', *Radiocarbon* 58, 9–23
Dunwoodie, L., Harward, C. and Pitt, K. 2015: *An Early Roman Fort and Urban Development on Londinium's Eastern Hill: Excavations at Plantation Place, City of London, 1997–2003*, MOLA Monograph 65, London
Edlin, H.L. 1949: *Woodland Crafts in Britain*, London
Eide, E., Linford, N., Persico, R. and Sala, J. 2018: 'Advanced SFCW GPR systems', in R. Persico, S. Piro and N. Linford (eds), *Innovation in Near-Surface Geophysics Instrumentation, Application, and Data Processing Methods*, Amsterdam, 253–85
Ellenberg, H. 1988: *Vegetation Ecology of Central Europe* (4th edn), Cambridge
Evans, K.J. 1974: 'Excavations on a Romano-British site, Wiggonholt, 1964', *Sussex Archaeological Collections* 112, 97–151
Filtzinger, P. 1972: *Novaesium V: Die römische Keramik aus dem Militärbereich von Novaesium*, Limesforschungen 11, Berlin
Fincker, M. 1986: 'Les briques claveaux: un materiau de construction spécifique des thermes romains', *Revue Aquitania* 4, 143–50
Fisher, R.A. 1953: 'Dispersion on a sphere', *Proceedings of the Royal Society London A* 217, 295–305
Foot, R. 1974: *Report on the Brick and Tile from The Brooks Excavation*, Winchester Museum Service unpub. report
Ford, S.D. 1974: 'Love Lane, Shaw', *CBA Group 9 Newsletter* 4, 9–10
Forestry Commission 2003: *National Inventory of Woodland and Trees – Great Britain*, Edinburgh
Fox, A. and Ravenhill, W. 1972: 'The Roman fort at Nanstallon, Cornwall', *Britannia* 3, 56–111
Frere, S. 1967: *Britannia. A History of Roman Britain* (1st edn), London
Frere, S. 1972: *Verulamium Excavations Vol. 1*, Reports of the Research Committee of the Society of Antiquaries of London 28, Oxford
Frere, S. 1999: *Britannia. A History of Roman Britain* (4th edn), London
Fulford, M. 2008: 'Nero and Britain: the palace of the client king at *Calleva* and imperial policy towards the province after Boudicca', *Britannia* 39, 1–13
Fulford, M. (ed.) 2012: *Silchester and the Study of Romano-British Urbanism*, JRA Supplementary Series 90, Portsmouth, RI
Fulford, M. 2021: *Silchester Revealed: The Iron Age and Roman Town of Calleva*, Oxford
Fulford, M. and Clarke, A. 2011: *Silchester: City in Transition*, Britannia Monograph 25, London
Fulford, M. and Machin, S. 2021: 'Building Britannia: pre-Flavian private and public construction across southern Britain', *Britannia* 52, 207–25
Fulford, M.G. and Timby, J.R. 2000: *Late Iron Age and Roman Silchester. Excavations on the Site of the Forum-Basilica 1977, 1980–86*, Britannia Monograph 15, London
Fulford, M., Barnett, C. and Clarke, A. 2015: *Silchester and its Environs. Excavation and Survey 2015*, University of Reading
Fulford, M., Barnett, C. and Clarke, A. 2016: *Silchester and its Environs. Excavation and Survey 2016*, University of Reading
Fulford, M., Clarke, A. and Pankhurst, N. forthcoming (a): *Silchester Insula IX.* Oppidum *to Roman City. Final Report on the Excavations 1997–2014*, Britannia Monograph

Fulford, M., Clarke, A. and Pankhurst, N. forthcoming (b): *Living, Bathing and Worshipping in Silchester. Excavations in Insulas III, XXX and XXXIII 2013–21*, Britannia Monograph

Fulford, M., Barnett, C., Pankhurst, N. and Wheeler, D. 2017a: *The Silchester Environs Project. Excavation and Survey 2017*, University of Reading

Fulford, M., Clarke, A., Durham, E. and Pankhurst, N. 2018a: *Late Iron Age Calleva. The Pre-Conquest Occupation at Silchester Insula IX*, Britannia Monograph 32, London

Fulford, M., Clarke, A., Durham, E. and Pankhurst, N. 2020: *Silchester Insula IX: The Claudio-Neronian Occupation of the Iron Age* Oppidum, Britannia Monograph 33, London

Fulford, M., Clarke, A., Pankhurst, N. and Lucas, S. 2013: *Silchester. The 'Town Life' Project 2013*, University of Reading

Fulford, M., Clarke, A., Pankhurst, N. and Lambert-Gates, S. 2014: *Silchester. The 'Town Life' Project 2014*, University of Reading

Fulford, M., Clarke, A., Lambert-Gates, S., Eaton, J. and Durham, E. 2017b: *Silchester Insula XXX. Temple Excavation 2017*, University of Reading

Fulford, M., Clarke, A., Durham, E., Fry, R., Machin, S., Pankhurst, N. and Wheeler, D. 2018b: *Silchester Roman Town. The Baths 2018*, University of Reading

Fulford, M., Clarke, A., Durham, E., Fry, R., Machin, S., Pankhurst, N. and Wheeler, D. 2019: *Silchester Roman Town. The Baths 2019*, University of Reading

Gale, R. and Cutler, D. 2000: *Plants in Archaeology*, Kew

Gerding, H. 2013: 'Roofs and superstructures', in D. Blackman, B. Rankov, K. Baika, H. Gerding and J. Pakkanen, *Shipsheds of the Ancient Mediterranean*, New York, 141–84

Gibson, D. and Lucas, G. 2002: 'Pre-Flavian kilns at Greenhouse Farm and the social context of early Roman pottery production in Cambridgeshire', *Britannia* 33, 95–127

Gill, D., Plouviez, J., Symonds, R.P. and Tester, C. 2001: *Roman Pottery Manufacture at Bourne Hill, Wherstead*, EAA Occasional Paper 9, Ipswich

Gillam, J.P. 1970: *Types of Roman Coarse Vessels in Northern Britain* (3rd edn), Newcastle-upon-Tyne

Grant, A. 2000: 'Diet, economy and ritual: evidence from faunal remains', in Fulford and Timby 2000, 425–82

Grant, A. 2004: 'Domestic animals and their uses', in M. Todd (ed.), *A Companion to Roman Britain*, Oxford, 371–92

Greenaway, J. 1981: 'The Neronian stamped tile from Little London, near Silchester', *Britannia* 12, 290–1

Greene, E.M. 2014: 'If the shoe fits: style and status in the assemblage of children's shoes from Vindolanda', in R. Collins and F. McIntosh (eds), *Life in the Limes: Studies of the People and Objects of the Roman Frontiers*, Oxford, 29–37

Greene, K. 1973: 'The pottery from Usk', in Detsicas 1973, 25–37

Greene, K. 1979: *Report on the Excavations at Usk 1965–1976. The Pre-Flavian Fine Wares*, Cardiff

Greene, K. 1993: 'The fortress coarseware', in W.H. Manning, *Report on the Excavations at Usk 1965–1976, The Roman Pottery*, Cardiff, 3–124

Grimes, W.F. 1930: *Holt, Denbighshire: the Works-Depot of the Twentieth Legion at Castle Lyons*, London

Guido, M. 1978: *The Glass Beads of the Prehistoric and Roman Periods in Britain and Ireland*, Society of Antiquaries of London Research Report 35, London

Hamilton, D. and Kenney, J. 2015: 'Multiple Bayesian modelling approaches to a suite of radiocarbon dates from ovens excavated at Ysgol yr Hendre, Caernarfon, North Wales', *Quaternary Geochronology* 25, 72–82

Hartley, K.F. 1972: 'Mortaria', in Rawes 1972, 48–50

Hartley, K.F. 1973: 'La diffusion des mortiers, tuiles et autres produits en provenence des fabriques italiannes', *Cahiers d'Archéologie Subaquatique* 2, 49–60

Hartley, K.F. 1976: 'The stamped mortaria', in S. Castle, 'Roman pottery from Radlett, 1959', *Hertfordshire Archaeology* 4 (1974–76), 151–2

Hartley, K.F. 1977a: 'Mortaria', in Detsicas 1977, 26–8

Hartley, K.F. 1977b: 'Two major potteries producing mortaria in the first century A.D.', in Dore and Greene 1977, 5–17

Hartley, K.F. 1985: 'The mortaria', in Niblett 1985, 92–3, microfiche 2: E7–G5

Hartley, K.F. 1987: 'The mortaria', in Dannell and Wild 1987, 127–8

Hartley, K.F. 1991, 'Mortaria', in Holbrook and Bidwell 1991, 189–215

Hartley, K.F. 1996: 'Procuratorial mortarium stamps', in Bird *et al.* 1996, 147–51

Hartley, K.F. 1999: 'The stamped mortaria', in Symonds and Wade 1999, 195–211

Hartley, K.F. and Tomber, R. 2006: *A Mortarium Bibliography for Roman Britain*, Journal of Roman Pottery Studies 13, Oxford

Hawkes, C.F.C. and Hull, M.R. 1947: *Camulodunum. First Report on the Excavations at Colchester 1930–39*, Reports of the Research Committee of the Society of Antiquaries of London 14, Oxford

Hewison, A.J.M. and Staines, B.W. 2008: 'Genus capreolus', in S. Harris and D. Yalden (eds), *The Mammals of the British Isles*, Southampton, 605–17

Hilton Price, F.G. 1887: 'Further notes upon excavations at Silchester', *Archaeologia* 50(2), 263–80

Holbrook, N. and Bidwell, P. 1991: *Roman Finds from Exeter*, Exeter Archaeological Report 4, Exeter

Hope, W.H.St J. 1893: 'The surroundings of the basilica and forum', in G.E. Fox and W.H. St John Hope, 'Excavations on the site of the Roman city of Silchester, Hants, in 1892', *Archaeologia* 53, 560–71

Hope, W.H.St J. and Fox, G.E. 1905: 'Excavations on the site of the Roman city of Silchester, Hants, in 1903 and 1904', *Archaeologia* 59(2), 333–70

Hull, M.R. 1963: *The Roman Potters' Kilns of Colchester*, Reports of the Research Committee of the Society of Antiquaries of London 21, Oxford

Hurst, H.R. 1972: 'Excavations at Gloucester 1968–71. First interim report', *Antiquaries Journal* 52, 24–69

Hyde, H.A. 1930: 'Report on plant material', in Grimes 1930, 185–6

Ingrem, C. 2012: 'Animals in the economy and culture of Roman Britain', in Fulford 2012, 184–212

Ingrem, C. 2020: 'The animal remains', in Fulford *et al.* 2020, 443–67

Jarvis, R.A. 1968: *Memoirs of the Soil Survey of Great Britain – Soils of the Reading District*, Harpenden

Jenkins, F. 1956: 'A Roman tilery and two pottery kilns at Durovernum (Canterbury)', *Antiquaries Journal* 36, 40–56

Jenkins, F. 1960: 'Two pottery kilns and a tilery of the Roman period at Canterbury', *Archaeologia Cantiana* 74, 151–61

Karslake, J.B.P. 1926: 'Discovery of a Roman brickfield near Silchester', *Antiquaries Journal* 6, 75–6

Keepax, C.A. 1988: *Charcoal Analysis, with Special Reference to Archaeological Sites*, unpub. PhD thesis, University of London

Korte, M., Donadini, F. and Constable, C.G. 2009: 'Geomagnetic field for 0-3ka: a new series of time-varying global models', *Geochemistry, Geophysics, Geosystems* 10(6), DOI: 10.1029/2008GC002295

Lancaster, L. 2009: 'Early examples of so-called pitched brick barrel vaulting in Roman Greece and Asia Minor: a question of origin and intention', in M. Bachmann (ed.), *Bautechnik im antiken und vorantiken Kleinasien: International Konferenz 13–16 Juni 2007*, Istanbul, 371–92

Lancaster, L. 2010: 'Parthian influence of vaulting in Roman Greece? An inquiry into technological exchange under Hadrian', *American Journal of Archaeology* 114(3), 447–72

Lancaster, L. 2015a: *Innovative Vaulting in the Architecture of the Roman Empire: 1st to 4th Century CE*, Cambridge

Lancaster, L. 2015b: 'Bricks and tile, innovations and the transmission of technical knowledge', in E. Bukowiecki, R. Volpe and U. Wulf-Rheidt (eds), *Il laterizio nei cantieri imperiali. Rome e il Mediterraneo. Atti del I workshop "Laterizio" (Roma 27–28 novembre 2014), Archaeologia dell'Architettura 20*, Rome, 28–245

Leney, L. and Casteel, R.W. 1975: 'Simplified procedure for examining charcoal specimens for identification', *Journal of Archaeological Science* 2, 153–9

Linford, N., Linford, P. and Payne, A. 2016: *Silchester Environs Project, Little London Roman Tilery, Pamber, Hampshire, Report on Geophysical Survey, July 2015*, Historic England Research Reports Series 41/2016

Linford, N., Linford, P. and Payne, A. 2018: 'Advanced magnetic prospecting for archaeology with a vehicle-towed array of caesium magnetometers', in R. Persico, S. Piro and N. Linford (eds), *Innovation in Near-Surface Geophysics Instrumentation, Application, and Data Processing Methods*, Amsterdam, 121–49

Linford, N., Linford, P. and Payne, A. 2019: *Silchester Environs Project, King's Hogsty, Pamber, Hampshire, Report on Geophysical Survey, July 2016*, Historic England Research Reports Series 18/2019

Lodwick, L. 2020: 'The charred, mineralised and waterlogged plant remains', in Fulford *et al.* 2020, 485–514

Lowther, A.W.G. 1934: 'The Roman "chimney-pots" from Ashtead, and parallel examples from other sites', *Surrey Archaeological Collections* 42, 61–7

Lowther, A.W.G. 1948: *A Study of the Patterns on Roman Flue-Tiles and their Distribution*, Research Papers of the Surrey Archaeological Society 1, Guildford

Lowther, A.W.G. 1976: 'Romano-British chimney-pots and finials', *The Antiquaries Journal* 61, 35–48

Ludowici, W. 1912: *Römische Ziegel-Gräber. Katalog IV. Meiner Ausgrabungen in Rheinzabern 1908–1912. Stempel-namen, Stempel-bilder, Vrnen-gräber*, Munich

Lyne, M.A.B. and Jefferies, R.S. 1979: *The Alice Holt-Farnham Roman Pottery Industry*, CBA Research Report 30, London

Machin, S.L. 2018: *Constructing Calleva: A Multidisciplinary Study of the Production, Distribution, and Consumption of Ceramic Building Materials at the Roman Town of Silchester, Hampshire*, unpub. PhD thesis, University of Reading

Machin, S. 2020: 'The ceramic building material', in Fulford *et al.* 2020, 412–27

Manning, W.H. 1985: *Catalogue of the Romano-British Iron Tools, Fittings and Weapons in the British Museum*, London

Marsh, G. and Tyers, P. 1978: 'The Roman pottery from Southwark', in *Southwark Excavations 1972–74 Vol. II*, London and Middlesex Archaeological Society/Surrey Archaeological Society Joint Publication 1, London, 533–82

Mathers, S.J. and Smith, N.J.P. 2000: *Geology of the Reading District – a Brief Explanation of the Geological Map (Sheet explanation of the British Geological Survey. 1: 50 000 Sheet 268 Reading)*, Nottingham

Maxfield, V.A. 1991: 'Tiverton Roman fort (Bolham): excavations 1981–1986', *Devon Archaeological Society* 49, 25–98

May, T. 1930: *Catalogue of the Roman Pottery in the Colchester and Essex Museum*, Cambridge

McFadden, P.L. 1982: 'Rejection of palaeomagnetic observations', *Earth and Planetary Science Letters* 61, 392–5

McParland, L., Collinson, M., Scott, A. and Campbell, G. 2009: 'The use of reflectance for the interpretation of natural and anthropogenic charcoal assemblages', *Archaeological and Anthropological Sciences* 1(4), 249–61

McParland, L.C., Collinson, M.E., Scott, A.C., Campbell, G. and Veal, R. 2010: 'Is vitrification in charcoal a result of high temperature burning of wood?', *Journal of Archaeological Science* 37, 2679–87

McWhirr, A. (ed.) 1979a: *Roman Brick and Tile: Studies in Manufacture, Distribution and Use in the Western Empire*, BAR International Series 68, Oxford

McWhirr, A. 1979b: 'Roman tile-kilns in Britain', in McWhirr 1979a, 97–189

McWhirr, A. 1984: *The Production of Roman Brick and Tile in Roman Britain*, unpub. PhD thesis, University of Leicester

Mepham, L. 1997: 'Iron Age and Roman pottery', in Smith and Barnes 1997, 48–66

Mepham, L. 2001: 'The marked tiles', in A.S. Anderson, J.S. Wacher and A.P. Fitzpatrick, *The Romano-British 'Small Town' at Wanborough, Wiltshire: Excavations, 1966–1976*, Britannia Monograph 19, London, 313–16

Molyneux, L. 1971: 'A complete results magnetometer for measuring the remanent magnetisation of rocks', *Geophysical Journal of the Royal Astronomical Society* 24, 429–33

Niblett, R. 1985: *Sheepen: An Early Roman Industrial Site at Camulodunum*, CBA Research Report 57, London

Niblett, R. and Thompson, I. 2005: *Alban's Buried Towns. An Assessment of St Albans' Archaeology up to AD 1600*, Oxford

Noel, M. and Batt, C.M. 1990: 'A method for correcting geographically separated remanence directions for the purpose of archaeomagnetic dating', *Geophysical Journal International* 102, 753–6

O'Connor, T.P. 1992: 'Pets and pests in Roman and medieval Britain', *Mammal Review* 22(2), 107–13

Orton, C., Tyers, P. and Vince, A. 1993: *Pottery in Archaeology*, Cambridge

Osborne White, H.J. 1909: *The Geology of the Country around Basingstoke – Memoirs of the Geological Survey Sheet 284*, London

Pavón-Carassco, F.J., Rodríguez-González, J., Osete, M.L. and Torta, J.M. 2011: 'A Matlab tool for archaeomagnetic dating', *Journal of Archaeological Science* 38, 408–19

PCRG 2011: *The Study of Prehistoric Pottery: General Policies and Guidelines for Analysis and Publication* (3rd edn), PCRG Occasional Papers 1 and 2

Peacock, D. 1979: 'An ethnoarchaeological approach to the study of Roman bricks and tiles', in McWhirr 1979a, 5–10

Peacock, D. 1982: *Pottery in the Roman World: An Ethnoarchaeological Approach*, London

Pearce, P. and Steinmetzer, M. forthcoming: 'Excavation of the Roman deposits at Princesshay, Exeter, 2005–6', *Proceedings of the Devon Archaeological Society*

Pellicioni, M.T. 2012: *La Pansiana in Adriatico. Tegole romane per navigare tra le sponde*, Ferrara

Peterken, G. 1993: *Woodland Conservation and Management* (2nd edn), London

Philp, B. 1999: *The Roman Villa Site at Keston, Kent. Second Report (Excavations 1967 and 1979–90)*, Kent Archaeological Report 8, Dover

Plouviez, J. 1989: 'A Romano-British pottery kiln at Stowmarket', *Proceedings of the Suffolk Institute of Archaeology* 37, 1–12

Pollard, R. 1988: *The Roman Pottery of Kent*, Kent Archaeological Society Monograph 5, Maidstone

Pratt, J.E. 1979: 'Charcoal samples from Dump AH 5, Pit B. 1', in Lyne and Jefferies 1979, 62

Pringle, S. 2002: 'Specialist appendices: the building materials', in J. Drummond-Murray and P. Thompson (eds), *Settlement in Roman Southwark*, MoLAS Monograph 12, London, 151–61

Pringle, S. 2007: 'London's earliest Roman bath-houses?' *London Archaeologist* 11.8, 205–9

Quinn, P. 2013: *Ceramic Petrography: The Interpretation of Archaeological Pottery and Related Artefacts in Thin Section*, Oxford

Rackham, O. 2001: *Trees and Woodland in the British Landscape* (rev. edn), London

Rawes, B. 1972: 'Roman pottery kilns at Gloucester', *Transactions of the Bristol and Gloucestershire Archaeological Society* 91, 18–59

RCHM 1983: 'West Park Roman villa, Hampshire', *Archaeological Journal* 140(1), 129–50

Reimer, P.J., Bard, E., Bayliss, A., Beck, J.W., Blackwell, P.G., Bronk Ramsey, C., Buck, C.E., Cheng, H., Edwards, R.L., Friedrich, M., Grootes, P.M., Guilderson, T.P., Haflidason, H., Hajdas, I., Hatté, C., Heaton, T.J., Hoffmann, D.L., Hogg, A.G., Hughen, K.A., Kaiser, K.F., Kromer, B., Manning, S.W., Niu, M., Reimer, R.W., Richards, D.A., Scott, E.M., Southon, J.R., Staff, R.A., Turney, C.S.M. and van der Plicht, J. 2013: 'IntCal13 and Marine13 radiocarbon age calibration curves 0–50,000 years cal BP', *Radiocarbon* 55, 1869–87

Reimer, P.J., Austin, W.E.N., Bard, E., Bayliss, A., Blackwell, P.G., Ramsey, C.B., Butzin, M., Cheng, H., Edwards, R.L., Friedrich, M., Grootes, P.M., Guilderson, T.P., Hajdas, I., Heaton, T.J., Hogg, A.G., Hughen, K.A., Kromer, B., Manning, S.W., Muscheler, R., Palmer, J.G., Pearson, C., Plicht, J.v.d., Reimer, R.W., Richards, D.A., Scott, E.M., Southon, J.R., Turney, C.S.M., Wacker, L., Adolphi, F., Büntgen, U., Capano, M., Fahrni, S.M., Fogtmann-Schulz, A., Friedrich, R., Köhler, P., Kudsk, S., Miyake, F., Olsen, J., Reinig, F., Sakamoto, M., Sookdeo, A. and Talamo, S. 2020: 'The IntCal20 Northern Hemisphere Radiocarbon Age Calibration Curve (0–55 cal kBP)', *Radiocarbon* 62, 725–57

Richmond, I.A. 1963: *Roman Britain* (2nd edn), Harmondsworth

Richter, H.G., Grosser, D., Heinz, I. and Gasson, P.E. (eds) 2004: 'IAWA list of microscopic features for softwood identification reprint', *International Association of Wood Anatomists Journal* 25, 1–70

Rigby, V. 1990: 'The potters' stamps', in West 1990, 86–9

Rigby, V. 2001: 'The potters' stamps', in Gill *et al.* 2001, 23–4

Ritterling, E. 1913: *Das frührömische Lager bei Hofheim im Taunus*, Annalen des Vereins für nassauische Altertumskunde und Geschichtsforschung 40, Wiesbaden

Rivet, A.L.F. and Smith, C. 1979: *The Place-Names of Roman Britain*, London

Roberts, P. 2019: *Last Supper in Pompeii*, Oxford

Rudling, D. 1986: 'The excavation of a Roman tilery on Great Cansiron Farm, Hartfield, East Sussex', *Britannia* 17, 191–230

Saison-Guichon, A. 2001: 'Les mortiers de cuisine en céramique commune claire à Lyon', *SFECAG, Actes du Congrès de Lille-Bavay*, 465–78

Saunders, C. and Havercroft, A.B. 1977: 'A kiln of the potter Oastrivs and related excavations at Little Munden Farm, Bricket Wood', *Hertfordshire Archaeology* 5, 109–56

Scammell, A.J. nd: *A Report on the Excavation of a First Century Tile and Pottery Complex at Park Farm, Oaksey, Wilts 1973–4,* unpub. report Devizes Museum

Schweingruber, F.H. 1990: *Microscopic Wood Anatomy* (3rd edn), Birmensdorf

Scott, E.M. 2003: 'The Third International Radiocarbon Intercomparison (TIRI) and the Fourth International Radiocarbon Intercomparison (FIRI) 1990–2002: results, analysis, and conclusions', *Radiocarbon* 45, 135–408

Scott, E.M., Cook, G.T. and Naysmith, P. 2010: 'A report on phase 2 of the Fifth International Radiocarbon Intercomparison (VIRI)', *Radiocarbon* 52, 846–58

Seeley, F. and Drummond-Murray, J. 2005: *Roman Pottery Production in the Walbrook Valley: Excavations at 20–28 Moorgate, City of London, 1998–2000,* MoLAS Monograph 25, London

Seeley, F. and Thorogood, C. 1994: 'Back to Brockley Hill', *London Archaeologist* 7 (9), 223–9

Shackleton, C. and Prins, F. 1992: 'Charcoal analysis and the "principle of least effort": a conceptual model', *Journal of Archaeological Science* 19, 631–7

Smart, T.L. and Hoffman, E.S. 1988: 'Environmental interpretation of archaeological charcoal', in C.A. Hastorf and V.S. Popper (eds), *Current Paleoethnobotany*, Chicago/London, 165–205

Smith, A., Allen, M., Brindle, T., Fulford, M., Lodwick, L. and Rohnbogner, A. 2018: *Life and Death in the Countryside of Roman Britain*, Britannia Monograph 31, London

Smith, L. and Barnes, I. 1997: 'Terrace area excavations (W64), 1987', in I. Barnes, C.V.A. Butterworth, J.W. Hawkes and L. Smith, *Excavations at Thames Valley Park, Reading, 1986–88. Prehistoric and Romano-British Occupation of the Floodplain and a Terrace of the River Thames*, Wessex Archaeology Report 14, Salisbury, 9–77

Soffe, G., Nicholls, J. and Moore, G. 1989: 'The Roman tilery and aisled building at Crookhorn, Hants, excavations, 1974–75', *Proceedings of the Hampshire Field Club* 45, 43–112

Spall, C. 2004: 'Ceramic building material', http://www.archaeologicalplanningconsultancy.co.uk/mono/001/pdf/cbm.pdf [Accessed 14 July 2015]

Stace, C. 2010: *New Flora of the British Isles* (3rd edn), Cambridge

Staines, B.W., Langbein, J. and Burkitt, T.D. 2008: 'Genus cervus', in S. Harris and D. Yalden (eds), *The Mammals of the British Isles*, Southampton, 573–87

Sternberg, R.S., Lass, E., Marion, E., Katari, K. and Holbrook, M. 1999: 'Anomalous archaeomagnetic directions and site formation processes at archaeological sites in Israel', *Geoarchaeology* 14(5), 415–39

Stuiver, M. and Polach, H.A. 1977: 'Reporting of ^{14}C data', *Radiocarbon* 19, 355–63

Suggett, P.G. 1953: 'Report on the excavations at Brockley Hill, Middlesex, August and September 1951', *Transactions London and Middlesex Archaeology Society* 11(2), 173–88

Symonds, R.P. and Wade, S. 1999: *Roman Pottery from Excavations in Colchester, 1971–86*, Colchester Archaeological Report 10, Colchester

Swan, V.G. 1984: *The Pottery Kilns of Roman Britain*, RCHM(E) Supplementary Series 5, London

Tarling, D.H. 1983: *Palaeomagnetism. Principles and Applications in Geology, Geophysics and Archaeology*, London/New York

Taylor, M. 1981: *Wood in Archaeology*, Princes Risborough

Théry-Parisot, I., Chabal, L. and Chrzavzez, J. 2010: 'Anthracology and taphonomy, from wood gathering to charcoal analysis: a review of the taphonomic processes modifying charcoal assemblages in archaeological contexts', *Palaeogeography, Palaeoclimatology, Palaeoecology* 291, 142–53

Timby, J. 1991: 'The Berkeley Street pottery kiln, Gloucester', *Journal of Roman Pottery Studies* 4, 19–31

Timby, J. 2000: 'The ceramic tile', in Fulford and Timby 2000, 116–22

Timby, J. 2004: 'The prehistoric and Roman pottery', in Brooks 2004, 50–88

Timby, J. 2011: 'The ventilators or finials', in Fulford and Clarke 2011, 229–31

Timby, J.R. 2018: 'The pottery', in Fulford *et al.* 2018a, 151–213

Timby, J. 2020: 'The pottery', in Fulford *et al.* 2020, 320–77

Timby, J. forthcoming: 'Late Iron Age and Roman pottery', in S. Preston, *Later Bronze Age to Middle Iron Age Occupation, Late Iron Age to Early Roman Enclosures and Cremations, and Medieval Occupation at Hartshill Copse, Thatcham, West Berkshire*, Reading, 48–52

Timby, J.R., Booth, P. and Allen, T.G. 1997: 'A new early Roman fineware in the Upper Thames Valley', unpub. ms Oxford Archaeology

Tomber, R. and Dore, J. 1998: *The National Roman Fabric Reference Collection: A Handbook*, http://www.romanpotterystudy.org/

Toynbee, J.M.C. 1964: *Art in Britain under the Romans*, Oxford

Toynbee, J.M.C. 1973: *Animals in Roman Life and Art*, London

Truscoe, K. 2017: *Silchester Iron Age Environs Project: Aerial Photograph and Lidar Survey Results*, Historic England Research Report Series 77, London

Tyers, P.A. 1983: *Verulamium Region Type White-ware Fabrics from London*, Early Roman Pottery from the City of London 4, MoL archive report

Tyers, P.A. 1998: 'Amphoras and the origins of the Brockley Hill Roman pottery industry', *London Archaeologist* 8(11), 292–7

Wacher, J. 1965: 'Cirencester 1964: fifth interim report', *The Antiquaries Journal* 45(1), 97–110

Walters, B. and Phillips, B. 1979: *Archaeological Excavations in Littlecote Park, Wiltshire 1978 – First Interim Report*, Littlecote Park

Warry, P. 2006: *Tegulae: Manufacture, Typology and Use in Roman Britain*, BAR British Series 417, Oxford
Warry, P. 2011: 'The ceramic building material', in Fulford and Clarke 2011, 220–31
Warry, P. 2012: 'The Silchester tile industry', in Fulford 2012, 49–75
Warry, P. 2017: 'Production, distribution, use and curation: a study of stamped tile from Gloucestershire', *Britannia* 48, 77–115
Wessex Archaeology 2008: *Coberley Villa Coberley, Gloucestershire. Archaeological Evaluation and Assessment of Results*, Salisbury: Wessex Archaeology. Report reference: 65311.01
West, S.E. 1990: *West Stow, Suffolk: The Prehistoric and Romano-British Occupations*, East Anglian Archaeology Report 48, Bury St Edmunds
Wheeler, R.E.M. and Wheeler, T.V. 1936: *Verulamium*, Reports of the Research Committee of the Society of Antiquaries of London 11, Oxford
Wikander, O. 1983: 'Skylight-tiles in the ancient world', *Opuscula Romana* 14, 81–99
Willems, W.J.H. and van Enckevort, H. 2009: *Ulpia Noviomagus: Roman Nijmegen, the Batavian Capital at the Imperial Frontier*, Journal of Roman Archaeology Supplementary Series 73, Portsmouth
Williams, J. forthcoming: *Land at Caversham Quarry, Sonning Eye*, Thames Valley Archaeological Services, Reading
Wilson, D. 1974: 'Sites explored', *Britannia* 5, 396–460
Wilson, P. and Price, J. (eds) 2002: *Aspects of Industry in Roman Yorkshire and the North*, Oxford
Woods, P.J. and Hastings, B.C. 1984: *Rushden: The Early Fine Wares*, Northampton
Yalden, D. 1999: *The History of British Mammals*, London
Yule, B. 2005: *A Prestigious Roman Building Complex on the Southwark Waterfront*, MoLAS Monograph 23, London

INDEX

THE PREHISTORIC SOCIETY

The Drowning of a Cornish Prehistoric Landscape

THE PREHISTORIC SOCIETY

The Drowning of a Cornish Prehistoric Landscape

Tradition, deposition and social responses to sea level rise

by
Andy M. Jones & Michael J. Allen

Prehistoric Society Research Paper No. 14
2023

THE PREHISTORIC SOCIETY
Series Editor: Michael J. Allen
Managing Editor: Julie Gardiner

OXBOW | books
Oxford & Philadelphia

Published in the United Kingdom in 2023 by
The Prehistoric Society

and

OXBOW BOOKS
The Old Music Hall, 106–108 Cowley Road, Oxford, OX4 1JE

and in the United States by
OXBOW BOOKS
1950 Lawrence Road, Havertown, PA 19083

Hardcover Edition: ISBN 978-1-78925-923-0
Digital Edition: ISBN 978-1-78925-924-7 (epub)

A CIP record for this book is available from the British Library

Library of Congress Control Number: 2023932529

Printed in Malta by Melita Press

For a complete list of Oxbow titles, please contact:

UNITED KINGDOM
Oxbow Books
Telephone (0)1226 734350
Email: oxbow@oxbowbooks.com
www.oxbowbooks.com

UNITED STATES OF AMERICA
Oxbow Books
Telephone (610) 853-9131, Fax (610) 853-9146
Email: queries@casemateacademic.com
www.casemateacademic.com/oxbow

Oxbow Books is part of the Casemate Group

Front cover: Marizion Marsh viewed from the east, looking towards Penzance, image: David Wootton (rspb-images.com) © RSPB

Rear cover

Upper: The Mount's Bay submerged forest at low tide with St Michael's Mount in the background/distance, image: Greg Martin/Cornwall Live

Middle: The Dando terrier rig perched on a raft against the southern edge of Marazion Marsh, image: M.J. Allen

Lower: Penzance Heliport barrow excavation viewed from the air

CORMAC PZE PENZANCE HELIPORT European Union European Regional Development Fund

THE PREHISTORIC SOCIETY RESEARCH PAPERS

The Prehistoric Society Research Papers publish collections of edited papers covering aspects of Prehistory. These may be derived from conferences, or research projects; they specifically *exclude* the publication of single excavation reports. The Research Papers present the fruits of the best of prehistoric research, complementing the Society's respected *Proceedings* by allowing broader treatment of key research areas.

The Research Papers is a peer-reviewed series whose production is managed by the Society.

Further information can be found on the Society's website (www.prehistoricsociety.org)

THE PREHISTORIC SOCIETY

The Prehistoric Society's interests are world wide and extend from the earliest human origins to the emergence of written records. Membership is open to all, and includes professional, amateur, student and retired members.

An active programme of events – lectures, study tours, day- and weekend conferences, and research weekends – allows members to participate fully in the Society and to meet other members and interested parties. The study excursions cater for all preferences from the relatively luxurious to the more economical, including highly popular student study tours. Day visits to sites are arranged whenever possible.

The Society produces two publications that are included with most categories of membership: the annual journal, *Proceedings of the Prehistoric Society* and the topical newsletter, *PAST*, which is published in April, July and November. In addition the *Prehistoric Society Research Papers* are published occasionally on which members may have discount.

Further information can be found on the Society's website (www.prehistoricsociety.org), or via the Prehistoric Society's registered address: ℅ Institute of Archaeology, University College London, 31–34 Gordon Square, London, WC1H 0PY.

The Society is a registered charity (no. 1000567)

THE PREHISTORIC SOCIETY RESEARCH PAPERS

Other volumes in this series, available from Oxbow Books

No. 1. *From Bann Flakes to Bushmills – papers in honour of Professor Peter Woodman*
eds N. Finlay, S. McCartan, N. Milner & C. Wickham-Jones (2009)

No. 2. *Land and People – papers in memory of John G. Evans*
eds M.J. Allen, N. Sharples & T. O'Connor (2009)

No. 3. *Materialitas: working stone, carving identity*
eds B. O'Connor, G. Cooney & J. Chapman (2010)

No. 4. *Is there a British Chalcolithic? People, place and polity in the later 3rd millennium*
eds M.J. Allen, J. Gardiner, A. Sheridan & D. McOmish (2012)

No. 5. *Image, Memory and Monumentality: archaeological engagements with the material world*
eds A.M. Jones, J. Pollard, M.J. Allen and J. Gardiner (2012)

No. 6. *Settlement in the Irish Neolithic: new discoveries at the edge of Europe*
by Jessica Smyth (2014)

No. 7. *The Beaker People: isotopes, mobility and diet in prehistoric Britain*
eds M. Parker Pearson, A. Sheridan, M. Jay, A. Chamberlain, M. Richards & J. Evans (2019)

No. 8. *First Farmers of the Carpathian Basin: changing patterns in subsistence, ritual and monumental figurines*
by Eszter Bánffy (2019)

No. 9. *Bell Beaker Settlement of Europe: the Bell Beaker phenomenon from a domestic perspective*
ed. Alex M. Gibson (2019)

No. 10. *Re-peopling La Manche: new perspectives on Neanderthals archaeology and landscapes from La Cotte de St Brelade*
eds Beccy Scott, Andrew Shaw, Katharine Scott & Matt Pope (2023)

No. 11. *The Social Context of Technology: non-ferrous metalworking in later prehistory*
by Leo Webley, Sophia Adams & Joanna Brück (2020)

No. 12. *Neolithic Stone Extraction of Britain and Europe; an ethnoarchaeological perspective*
by Peter Topping (2021)

No. 13. *Fragments of the Bronze Age: the destruction and deposition of Bronze Age metal work in south-west Britain and its wider context*
by Matthew G. Knight (2022)

No. 14. *The Drowning of a Cornish Prehistoric Landscape: tradition, deposition and social responses to sea level rise*
by Andy M. Jones & Michael J. Allen (2023)

CONTENTS

LIST OF FIGURES AND TABLES

List of Figures

List of Tables

AUTHORS

ANDY M. JONES
Cornwall Archaeological Unit
Cornwall Council
Room 4G
Pydar House
Pydar Street
Truro, Cornwall
TR1 1XU
Email: Andy.Jones@cau.org.uk

Andy Jones is Projects Manager with the Cornwall Archaeological Unit. His research interests include the Neolithic and Bronze Age periods, particularly the uplands and coastal areas of western Britain. He has published extensively on the prehistory of the south-west peninsula, especially in relation to ceremonial monuments and the deposition of artefacts.

MICHAEL J. ALLEN
Allen Environmental Archeology
Redroof, Green Road
Codford
Wiltshire
BA12 0NW
Email: aea.escargots@gmail.com

Mike Allen is an environmental archaeologist and geoarchaeologist running a small environmental archaeology company (Allen Environmental Archaeology). His research interests are primarily in prehistory and reconstructing patterns of land-use and landscape resources. His own expertise analysis is snails, sediments and soils. He has published widely enviromnetal archaeology and prehistory, and is the Series Editor of the Prehistoric Society Research Papers, and editor for Oxbow's Studying Scientific Archaeology.

CONTRIBUTORS

Jens Andersen
Camborne School of Mines
University of Exeter
Penryn Campus
Penryn
Cornwall, TR10 9FE
Email: J.C.Andersen@exeter.ac.uk

Nigel Cameron
Environmental Change Research Centre
Department of Geography
University College London
Gower Street
London, WC1E 6BT
Email: n.cameron@ucl.ac.uk

A.J. Clapham
Email: a.j.clapham@hotmail.co.uk

Matthew G. Knight
National Museums Scotland
Chambers Street
Edinburgh, EH1 1JF
Email: M.Knight@nms.ac.uk

C.T. Langdon
School of Geography and Environmental Science
University of Southampton
Southampton, SO17 1BJ
Email: c.t.langdon@soton.ac.uk

Anna Lawson-Jones
Email: annaljones@talktalk.net

Henrietta Quinnell
39D, Polsloe Road
Exeter, EX1 2DN
Email: H.Quinnell@exeter.ac.uk

R.G. Scaife
School of Geography and Environmental Science
University of Southampton
Southampton, SO17 1BJ
Email: r.scaife@soton.ac.uk

Emma Smith
Wysing Arts Centre
Fox Road
Cambridge, CB23 2TX
Email: info@emma-smith.com

Laura Ratcliffe-Warren
1 Trewardreva Cross
Constantine
Falmouth
Cornwall, TR11 5QB
Email: lrconservation@btinternet.com

Roger Taylor
Independent researcher

Christina Tsoraki
School of Archaeology and Ancient History
University of Leicester
University Road
Leicester, LE1 7RH
Email: ct293@leicester.ac.uk

Anna Tyacke
Email: annatyacke@btinternet.com

ABSTRACT

Between 2018 and 2019, Cornwall Archaeological Unit undertook two projects at Mount's Bay, Penwith. The first involved the excavation of a Bronze Age barrow and the second, environmental auger core sampling in Marazion Marsh. Both sites lie within an area of coastal hinterland, which has been subject to incursions by rising sea levels. Since the Mesolithic, an area of approximately 1 kilometre in extent between the current shoreline and St Michael's Mount has been lost to gradually rising sea levels. With current climate change, this process is likely to occur at an increasing rate. Given their proximity, the opportunity was taken to draw the results from the two projects together along with all available existing environmental data from the area.

For the first time, the results from all previous palaeo-environmental projects in the Mount's Bay area have been brought together. Evidence for coastal change and sea level rise is discussed and a model for the drowning landscape presented. In addition to modelling the loss of land and describing the environment over time, there is a broader discussion of changing worlds and social responses including the wider context of the Bronze Age barrow and later Bronze Age metalwork deposition in the Mount's Bay environs are considered. The effects of the gradual loss of land are discussed in terms of how change is perceived, its effects on community resilience, and the construction of social memory and narratives of place. These arguments have relevance beyond this project and also to many drowned or submerged settlements. Importantly, these show that it is the loss of land that accompanies settlements and arenas of the dead that have a profound social and economic effect.

The volume demonstrates how the environmental data that survive for this part of south-west England have an importance that extends well beyond that region in showing the long-term effects of climate change and rising sea levels, and people's responses to these over time.

RÉSUMÉ

Entre 2018 et 2019, la Cornwall Archaeological Unit a entrepris deux projets autour de la Mount's Bay, Penwith. Le premier a consisté en la fouille d'un tumulus de l'âge du Bronze et le second, en un échantillonnage environnemental par carottage à la tarière dans le marais de Marazion. Les deux sites se trouvent dans une zone d'arrière-pays côtier, qui a subi des incursions dues à l'élévation du niveau de la mer. Depuis le Mésolithique, une zone d'environ 1 kilomètre d'étendue entre le littoral actuel et St Michael's Mount a été perdue en raison de la montée progressive du niveau de la mer. Avec le changement climatique actuel, ce processus est susceptible de se produire à un rythme croissant. Compte tenu de leur proximité, l'occasion a été saisie de rassembler les résultats des deux projets ainsi que toutes les données environnementales disponibles dans la région.

Pour la première fois, les résultats de tous les projets paléo-environnementaux précédents dans la région de Mount's Bay ont été rassemblés. Les témoins des changements littoraux et de l'élévation du niveau de la mer sont discutés et un modèle pour la submersion du paysage est présenté. En plus de la modélisation de la perte de terres et de la description de l'environnement au fil du temps, une discussion plus large est menée sur l'évolution des milieux et des réponses sociales, y compris le contexte plus large du tumulus de l'âge du Bronze et des dépôts métalliques de l'âge du Bronze final dans les environs de la Mount's Bay. Les effets de la perte progressive de terres sont discutés en termes de perception du changement, de ses effets sur la résilience de la communauté, et de la construction de la mémoire sociale et des récits des lieux. Ces arguments sont pertinents au-delà de ce projet et également pour de nombreux établissements ennoyés ou submergés. Ils montrent surtout que c'est la perte de terres touchant les habitats et les espaces des morts qui a un effet social et économique profond.

Le volume démontre que les données environnementales qui subsistent pour cette partie du Sud-Ouest de l'Angleterre ont une importance qui s'étend bien au-delà de cette région en montrant les effets à long terme du changement climatique et de l'élévation du niveau de la mer, ainsi que les réponses des sociétés à ces phénomènes au fil du temps.

ZUSAMMENFASSUNG

Die Cornwall Archaeological Unit führte in den Jahren 2018-2019 zwei Projekte in Mount's Bay, Penwith, durch. Das erste umfasste die Ausgrabung eines bronzezeitlichen Grabhügels und das zweite Bohrbeprobungen mit einem Erdbohrer in Marazion Marsh. Beide Fundorte liegen in einem Gebiet des Küstenhinterlands, das Verwässerungen durch steigende Meeresspiegel ausgesetzt war. Seit dem Mesolithikum ging ein Gebiet von ungefähr einem km Ausdehnung zwischen der heutigen Küstenlinie und St. Michael's Mount durch den allmählich steigenden Meeresspiegel verloren. Durch den derzeitigen Klimawandel wird sich dieser Prozess sehr wahrscheinlich fortsetzen oder sogar beschleunigen. Aufgrund ihrer Nähe wurde die Gelegenheit genutzt, die Ergebnisse der beiden Projekte zusammen mit allen verfügbaren Umweltdaten aus diesem Gebiet zusammenzuführen.

Zum ersten Mal sind die Ergebnisse aller bisherigen paläoökologischen Projekte im Mount's Bay-Gebiet zusammengetragen worden. Die Daten zu Veränderungen der Küstenlinie und zum Anstieg des Meeresspiegels werden diskutiert und ein Modell für die versinkende Landschaft vorgelegt. Neben der Modellierung des Landverlustes und der Beschreibung der Umwelt im Verlauf der Zeit werden auch die sich verändernden Lebenswelten und die sozialen Reaktionen erörtert, einschließlich des weiteren Kontextes des bronzezeitlichen Grabhügels und der jüngeren bronzezeitlichen Metalldeponierungen im Umfeld von Mount's Bay. Die Folgen des allmählichen Landverlusts werden in Hinblick darauf diskutiert, wie Wandel wahrgenommen wurde, wie er sich auf die Resilienz der Gemeinschaft auswirkte und wie soziales Gedächtnis und Ortsnarrative konstruiert wurden. Diese Argumente sind über dieses Projekt hinaus und für viele andere versunkene oder überflutete Siedlungen und Landschaften von Bedeutung. Vor allem zeigen sie, dass der Verlust von Land Siedlungen und Orte der Toten betrifft und tiefgreifende soziale und ökonomische Auswirkungen hat.

Dieser Band zeigt, dass die Umweltdaten, die für diesen Teil Südwestenglands überliefert sind, eine Bedeutung haben, die weit über diese Region hinausgeht, da sie die langfristigen Auswirkungen von Klimawandel und steigendem Meeresspiegel und die Antworten der Menschen hierauf im Laufe der Zeit zeigen.

ACKNOWLEDGEMENTS

Excavations at the Heliport barrow were carried out by CAU and funded by Penzance Heliport Limited funded the work. Ryan Smith undertook drone photography during the course of the excavation also produced the line drawings for this report. The site staff were Anna Lawson-Jones, Megan Val-Baker and Ryan Smith together with a number of volunteers: Richard Hoskins and Sara Rogers; plus Truro College students Chris Chappell, Joel Smith, Ben Moore, Lilly Roberts and Oscar Lawson-Jones. Thanks are due in particular to Andy Jones and Sean Taylor of the Cornwall Archaeological Unit for their assistance and discussion in the field relating to geoarchaeological coring undertake prior to the excavation. The coring Marazion Marsh was set up through the auspices of Andy Jones, with project aims defined by Adam Sharp. Fieldwork and analysis was funded by Cormac Consulting and the fieldwork was supported by members of the Cormac team; in particular Emma Blakesley, Ben Beattie, the coring crew, and Ryan Smith (CAU), and overseen by Mike Allen.

We thank Lorraine Mepham of Wessex Archaeology for making comments on the Victorian ink well.

The microwear analysis was carried out as part of the Leverhulme funded *Beyond the Three Age System* project (RPG-2017-375) at the School of Archaeology and Ancient History, University of Leicester which explores changing material histories from the Neolithic to the Iron Age through microwear analysis. Anna Tyacke would like to thank Dr Peter Northover for his comments on the copper alloy ingot.

Much of the environmental interpretation was discussed with the analyst (see chapters 6 & 9) and we thank, in particular, Alan Clapham, Rob Scaife and Cath Langdon for discussion of the environment and sea-level. Cath Langdon thanks Rob Scaife for use of his pollen review of Cornwall and commenting on the pollen text, and Nigel Cameron thanks Mike Allen for providing the samples for diatom assessment and analysis, and the palaeo-environmental assessment report and for background information about the geoarchaeological investigation and earlier research at the site.

We would like to thank Francis Shepherd for producing Figure 1.2, and Fiona Fleming for producing the Lidar image, Figure 1.3 (and reading the draft chapter). We also thank Jim Parry, National Trust Archaeologist for supplying Figure 1.6 (and permission for its reproduction here), George Scott for redrawing the barrow plans and sections and environmental Figures 2.2, 2.3, 2.4, 2.5, 2.6, 2.7 & 2.8, and Gary Young for producing Figure 3.2. Greg Martin kindly provided photos of the submerged forest (Figures 14.8 & 14.9).

We appreciate the numerous people with whom we have discussed our overall conclusions; these include Matt Knight for information on the metal hoards in the vicinity, Ralph Fyfe for provision of undergraduate work (Mount's Bay sea-level) and permission to cite. Previous drafts benefitted on comments and encouragement from colleagues: Andy Jones would like to thank Fiona Fleming who read Chapter 1, and Henrietta Quinnell for reading an early draft of Chapter 13). The authors (Andy & Mike) would like to thank Richard Bradley reading earlier drafts of in particular Chapter 14. We thank Alison Sheridan for her detailed comments and assistance in getting the text into better shape and allowing us, hopefully, to provide a clearer image of our thoughts and interpretation. Finally we thank Ben Andrews (picture researcher RSPB) and the RSPB for permission to reproduce David Wotton's image on the cover.

Andy M. Jones and Michael J. Allen
December 2022

The Prehistoric Society would like to add thanks to thank Alison Sheridan who took on much of the refereeing of the volume as the Series Editor (Mike Allen) could not do this for his own volume; we thank our referees and members of our Editorial Advisory Committee, and our reviewers for their expert advice and opinions. The Society thanks the Cornwall Archaeological Society for a financial contribution to this publication. In particular, I would like to offer my thanks to Julie Gardiner (Prehistoric Society, managing editor & Oxbow Books, publisher), for her advice, assistance and especially assisting in copy editing, and also once again to Julie Blackmore of Frabjous Books for typesetting yet another of our volumes with skill, proficiency, design and dexterity.

Michael J. Allen
January 2023

SECTION 1:

BACKGROUND

1

Dealing with a drowned landscape

Andy M. Jones

In 2018 and 2019 Cornwall Archaeological Unit undertook two significant archaeological projects in the Mount's Bay area of West Penwith, on the low-lying strip of land between Marazion in the east and Penzance at the western end of the bay, which forms the interface between the sea and the rising ground behind to the north (Figs 1.1 & 1.2). The

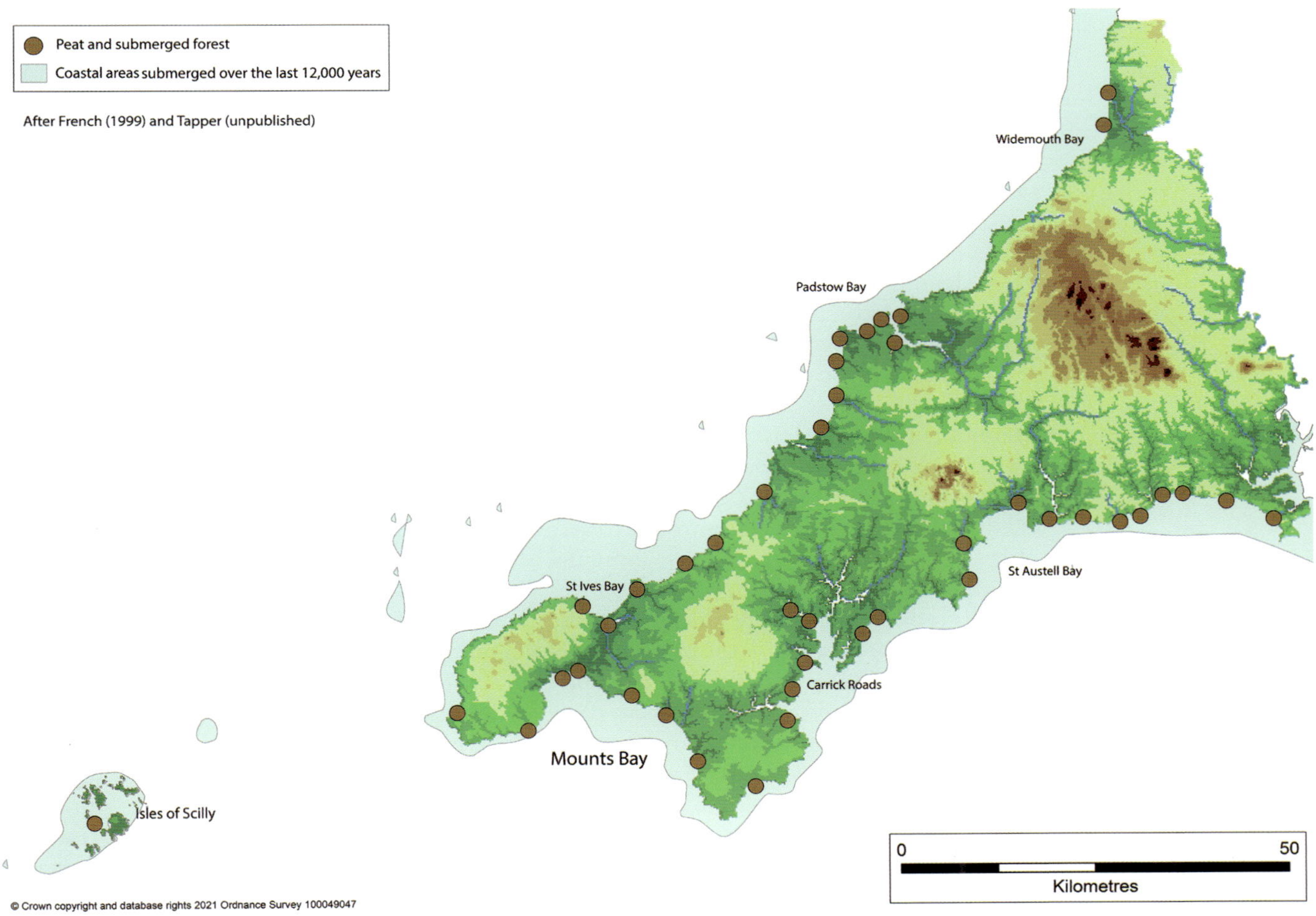

Figure 1.1: Map showing land lost from around Cornwall and Isles of since c. *12,000 BP and areas of submerged forest*

first, at the Heliport site, was what appeared initially to be a small and fairly 'scrappy' barrow on the edge of the former wetlands, but which has subsequently been shown to be an intriguing monument with an unexpectedly long history of use, adjacent to an area with a well-preserved peat sequence, which was also investigated as part of the project.

The second site differed in that there was no monument to excavate and, aside from a small-scale watching brief, the project was instead largely an environmental recording exercise within Marazion Marsh, an important wetland reserve for breeding and over-wintering birds at the eastern end of Mount's Bay. Its special, perhaps in the past 'magically' perceived character, is potentially indicated by the very large number of Roman coins which had been deposited into it (Penhallurick 2009, 150). It too proved to contain a 'treasure trove' of information relating to long-term changes to the environment over several millennia, something that is, in an age of global warming, just as important a concern to modern communities as to those who inhabited the area in prehistory.

The results from two significant projects located in close proximity provided the opportunity to include all the analyses undertaken on the materials from the barrow and the auger sampling from Marazion Marsh and draw them together with the previous work undertaken in West Cornwall, so that they have a much wider significance than a typical site report. Extended works on the archaeology of south-west Britain and elsewhere tend to follow two trends. The first type of work is often focused on the more remote upland areas such as Dartmoor, Bodmin Moor, Exmoor or West Penwith, where a combination of extensive areas of upstanding archaeological monuments and dramatic topographical features can often, with the aid of the palaeo-environmental record, be linked together to form narratives of long-term human engagement with the landscape (eg, Johnson & Rose 1994; Riley & Wilson-North 2001; Newman 2011; Herring *et al.* 2016). Often projects which take place in these remote landscapes are focused on monuments or 'palimpsest' settlement patterns and are for the most part quantitative and typo-chronological in scope; although some scholars have attempted to move beyond sites and embed social relations into their narratives (eg, Strong 1997; Bender *et al.* 2007; Jones 2016a; Tilley 2017).

The second, and most frequent, form of extended archaeological reporting is that which results from larger-scale development of buried archaeological sites. Often it is the case that little is known about these sites prior to excavation and the resulting publication is typically a form of mitigation, with the focus being the production of an accurate record of what has been removed (eg, Fitzpatrick *et al.* 1999; Mudd & Joyce 2014). This type of technical reporting is the most frequent for archaeological sites, of which there are incredibly large numbers. Ben Roberts (2013, 531), for example, has noted that in the period between 1990 and 2007 there had been 19,000 fieldwork evaluations in Britain and Ireland, 20 per cent of which had produced evidence for prehistoric activity. It can be the case that the remit of these types of project precludes the possibility of extended lengthy syntheses which consider the wider context of the project. Increasingly, supporting technical additional data are uploaded on to online repositories such as ADS, so that they can be accessed later for inclusion within research-focused projects. Indeed, several 'big picture' projects and publications have drawn on and made good use of the data that are now more widely accessible (eg, Bradley 2007; Bradley *et al.* 2016a; Brück 2019; Bland *et al.* 2020; Webley *et al.* 2020; Booth *et al.* 2021; Cooper *et al.* 2021). A danger remains, however, that detailed localised narratives associated with place, areas or kinship connections (cf. Johnston 2020) can be lost in individual technical site reports, or only appear as a findspot in a bigger grand narrative (eg, Barclay & Brophy 2021), with what have been termed by Cipolla *et al.* (2021) 'Royal Science Ambitions'.

To a certain extent this trend can be seen in our study area, where previous archaeological recording and sampling has tended to go into 'grey literature' or conversely appear as individual site reports in more specialist focus journals (eg, Healy 1996a; Camidge & Randall 2009; Timpany 2009; Fyfe *et al.* 2017; Sharpe 2017; Southwest Archaeology, forthcoming). Given that this volume developed as a result of two separate archaeological investigations, which are not in the first instance obviously associated with an extensive upstanding archaeological landscape, and were undertaken as 'developer-led' projects, they too could well have ended up within the second category of archaeological reporting, that is to say as a 'preservation by record' account.

Arguably, however, this volume marks something of a departure as it moves beyond the individual sites and is instead concerned with placing the results into the context of their *longue durée* landscape setting, a topographically defined strip of land approximately 4.5 km long between the settlements of Penzance and Marazion, which is for the most part under 1 km wide and up to just 10 m Ordnance Datum above sea-level. Consideration, however, is also given to the 'lost land' which in the Mesolithic extended for a further kilometre to the south and connected St Michael's Mount to the mainland. Likewise, the relationships with the higher ground to the north and West Penwith are also discussed as the lowland strip is recognised as being part of a wider landscape and indeed seascape. Today, the southern extent of the project area is demarcated by the ever-encroaching sea and the northern side by the start of a notable rise in the topography. Aside from the eastern and western ends which are marked by distinctive topographical features (see below), the area appears to be more or less 'featureless'. Consequently, despite the acknowledgement of the significance of certain aspects of the archaeology it has never been considered in its wider context, that is to say, either as an important, potentially ambiguous, transitional zone between and linking the high ground with the open sea, or a place which prior to submergence, was a diverse landscape containing myriad resources.

Perhaps very surprisingly, the long palaeo-environmental record for this area has never been synthesised before and the prehistoric sites and findspots within the area have tended to be dealt with as separate entities, yet consideration of both aspects is essential for understanding changes and impacts on the occupation of the area. Changes to patterns of inhabitancy caused by rising sea-levels will have occurred before and during the Bronze Age (and continue to do so), especially in coastal areas of the south-west region (eg, Bell 2013, 319; Fig. 1.1); although to date only the Isles of Scilly have had very detailed analytical work undertaken; that work showed that large areas were becoming submerged during the Neolithic and Bronze Age periods (Charman *et al.* 2016, 206–211; Barnett *et al.* 2020). Those archaeological discussions of the effects of loss of land on human communities that have been written have tended to be of an androcentric, economic nature, with changing patterns of wetland occupation and land management being focused on.

The loss of land, however, does not only have detrimental economic outcomes. Changes also affect the nature of social relations, not only between humans but also between human and non-human inhabitants (eg, Kohn 2013; Cipolla *et al.* 2021; van den Berg 2021). As Neil Price (2020, 31–32) has pointed out in relation to the Viking world, people believed that they shared their world with 'others' who were not human and who did not have to be seen to be considered real. Comparable beliefs are likely to have existed in later prehistory too and we should not expect our definitions of where boundaries between the animate and the inanimate and the human and non-human lay to be the same as those in the past. The slow death of trees and the incremental submergence of substantial tracts of land would not only have impacted on many of those who lived in the area by changing access to resources but would also have altered human relationships, and the often overlooked non-human relationships (as discussed, for example, by Shaw 2016), by severing connections with place and the communities of plants and animals that occupied them. The sea is often a source for stories and myths of lost lands and settlements (eg, Marsden 2019) and the dark skeletal branches and stumps of the trees in submerged forests would have fed stories and social remembrances of lost places (eg, Leary 2015).

The social memory of rising waters and preserved tree stumps around Cornwall and the Isles of Scilly could even have given rise to the well-known legends about lost lands such as Lyonesse (Reid 1913, 100; Crawford 1927; Hencken 1932, 34). This publication therefore draws several elements together to consider the drowning landscape of Mount's Bay in prehistory from both social and economic perspectives. Indeed, the title of the volume takes its inspiration from Charles Thomas's (1985) much admired work, *Exploration of a drowned landscape: Archaeology and History of the Isles of Scilly*. That work, too, was both a serious and reflective volume concerned with telling

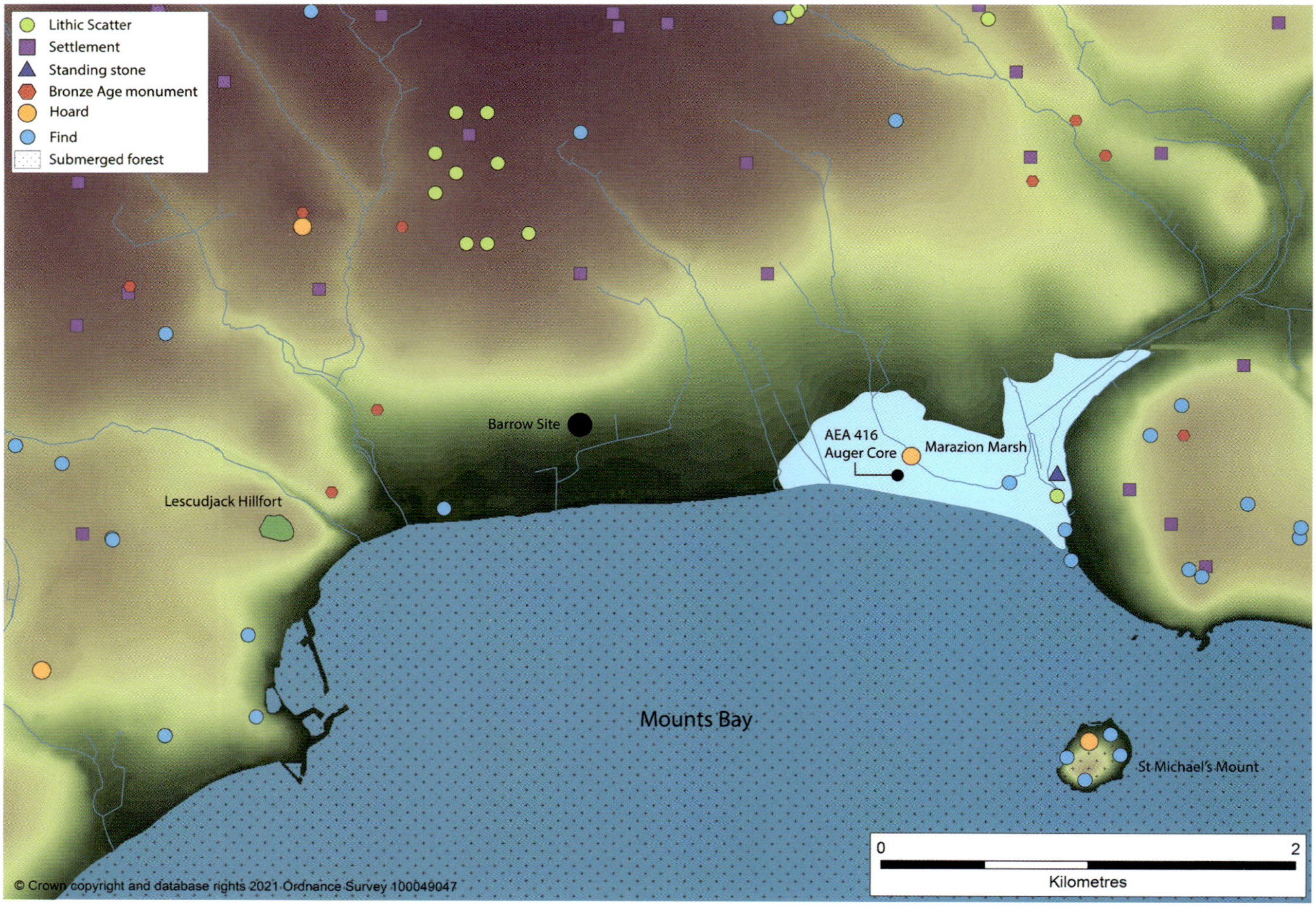

Figure 1.2: Location map showing the project area and the investigated sites with prehistoric and Roman period sites as identified in the Cornwall and Isles of Scilly Historic Environment Record

the long-term story of another submerged landscape.

Location, archaeological setting and research questions: the Mount's Bay area

The Mount's Bay area lies at the western end of Cornwall (Figs 1.2 & 1.3). The eastern end of the bay is dominated by the St Michael's Mount, an iconic topographical feature, situated approximately 0.5 km beyond the current limit of dryland. Despite rising to a height of only 95 m OD, the low-lying land to the north means that it is visible both from the sea and from the land and its distinctive profile has caught the attention of artists (see Satchell *et al.* 2015, 422–439) and writers, with Harris Stone describing it as a '*weirdly pyramidical, and uneven in outline… a steep mass of rock which rises straight up from the sea*' (Harris Stone 1912, 222). As such it can be regarded as a 'persistent place' used by people who were navigating across the sea and over the land from prehistory onwards (eg, O'Brien 2021).

For most of the time the Mount is an island surrounded by water, apart from around eight hours each day at low tide when it is approachable from land by walking along the causeway (Herring 1993, 26). Journeys on foot to the Mount from dryland are not, today at least, part of the awe inspiring, or personhood-changing travels such as those made in prehistory may have been (eg, Helms 1988; Needham 2000). Nor indeed, partly thanks to the causeway, are they as exciting or revelatory as those to remote coastal places can still sometimes be (eg, Macfarlane 2019). The physical separation and potential for getting 'cut off' or at least getting one's feet wet can still, however, sometimes engender a distinct feeling of wariness. This is especially true out of season on a stormy day visit to or from the

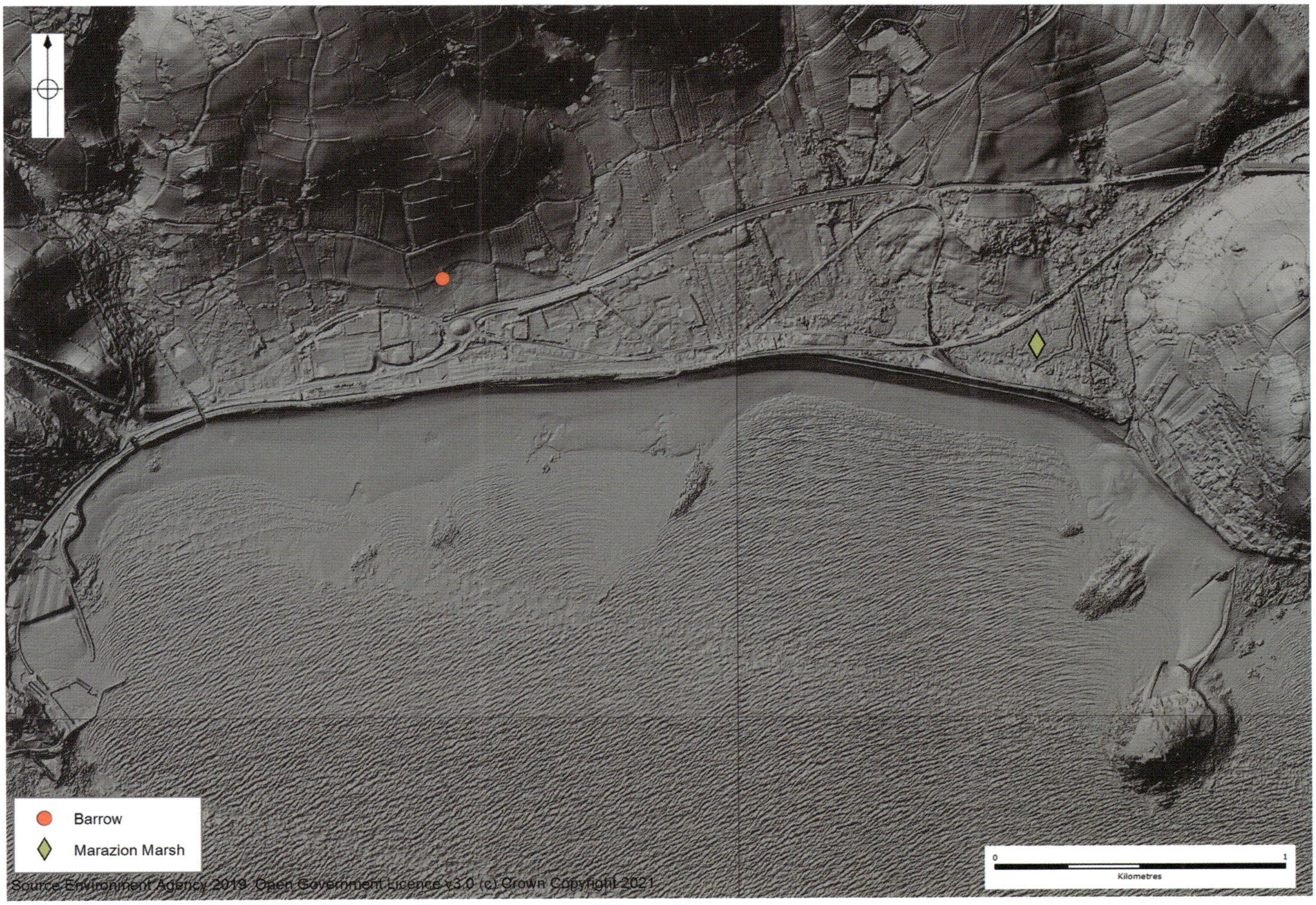

Figure 1.3: Lidar image showing the investigated sites and the low strip of land forming the coastal hinterland. Note how the modern transport system, roads and rail bisect the low ground

Mount (without the aid of a tide timetable) on foot when the tide is rising.

By contrast, the western end of Mount's Bay is now largely covered by the urban settlements of Penzance and Newlyn, although in later prehistory the western end of the Bay would have been dominated by the ramparts associated with the hillfort at Lescudjack (Kirkham, forthcoming) which, despite being surrounded by more recent urban development, still retains extensive views over the bay and St Michael's Mount (Fig. 1.4). The mature Monterey pines emerging from its summit ensure that the hillfort site still forms a prominent landmark on the skyline.

The land between St Michael's Mount and Lescudjack is largely composed of a long sandy shore behind which is lower-lying ground under 10 m OD. Much of the area – and beyond to the south – would, for much of prehistory, have been a mosaic of wet woodland and open spaces, a marshy liminal zone before sea-level rise led to the increasing submergence of areas, in what is now Mount's Bay, and the establishment of a beach and harder seashore during the later prehistoric period. A great deal of the land behind the beach became enclosed farmland, including the site of the excavated barrow (see Chapter 2). Today, however, most of this low expanse has been built over, and there have been significant alterations to the character of the coastal strip since the earlier 19th century, let alone since prehistory. In the 19th century a railway was built upon a causeway which runs parallel with the coast and there is widespread evidence for former extractive industries for brick clay, as well as mining. In the 20th century landfill, housing, supermarkets, industrial units, roads, carparks and tourism-related infrastructure, have covered much of the low-lying ground, leaving few unaltered 'natural' spaces. To these pressures we must of course also remember the effects of climate change (cf. Phillips 2007) and continuing sea-level change – the two being partly related – and the resulting coastal erosion and submergence.

Most people pass quickly through this area on a dual carriageway or on board a train, probably without giving what lies beneath their feet much thought. The area is, as the naturalist Roger Deakin noted, a gateway zone (2000, 140), and if archaeology is thought about at all, it will almost certainly be the iconic sites such as Lanyon Quoit, Men-an-Tol or the Merry Maidens stone circle to the west that come to mind. Marazion Marsh itself, however, towards the eastern end of the bay, still retains a flavour of the natural wetland environment which would have been more widespread in prehistory. Indeed, even today, walking amongst the towering reeds interspersed by pools of water can still give a sense of separateness from both the higher ground to the north and sea that lies to the south.

The archaeological background

Despite this 'coastal squeeze' and a lack of upstanding prehistoric monuments found in other parts of West Penwith or the along the Cornish coastline (eg, Herring 2016a; Nowakowski 2016a; Jones 2009–10), the littoral around Mount's Bay does nonetheless contain a number of significant archaeological findspots, most notably of Bronze Age metalwork (Knight 2022; Chapter 12) (Fig. 1.1). The zone also possesses an exceptionally rich palaeo-environmental record, with peat deposits stretching back into the Mesolithic and preserved trees from submerged prehistoric forests beneath the sands, the stumps of which sometimes emerge after storms and survive as proxies for land and wet, alder-dominated woodlands which included birch, oak, hazel and willow, lost to the gradual rising sea-levels in prehistory (Harkness & Wilson 1979; Reid 1913, 100–102; de Beer 1960; French 1999) (Fig. 1.5). This exceptional environmental record from the area will form the background for much of the synthesis given in the succeeding chapters (Chapters 6, 9, 10, 11 and 14).

West Penwith (and probably also Mount's Bay) are, of course, also thought to be amongst the few places in Britain to be identifiable from pre–Roman Conquest classical sources, with the Mount sometimes being suggested by several scholars to be *Ictis*, a place of pre-Conquest exchange (eg, Oldfather 1933; de Beer 1960; Cunliffe 2001, 305), thereby offering a tantalising glimpse of otherwise undocumented communities in the far west of Britain. Indeed, this brief record has inspired archaeological writers to include Mount's Bay on maps and diagrams of prehistoric trade routes (eg, Hencken 1932; Fox 1938; Bowen 1972), long before the first properly recorded prehistoric metalwork finds were made in the 1990s and 2000s (Herring 2000; Jones & Quinnell 2011a).

However, despite the long-held association with prehistoric trade routes, prior to the archaeological recording in 2018 and 2019 as part of the projects described here, comparatively few archaeological interventions had been undertaken within the coastal strip. As a consequence findspots, other than those of metalwork (Chapter 12) and prehistoric sites remain scarce. A spotted slate axe-hammer was recorded from Eastern Green (Stone & Wallis 1951) and a standing stone has been suggested to have existed on the eastern side of Marazion Marsh as the Tithe Award records the location as 'Longstone Meadows Tenement'. No actual standing stone, however, has been recorded and the suggested location of the stone on the eastern side of the marsh (Fig. 1.2) is perhaps unlikely. It is also unfortunate that much of the development within this zone had taken place in an era which predated requirements for archaeological monitoring, and the records from the project area consist of reports of antiquarian finds made over a century ago (eg, Borlase 1769; Edmonds 1849; Evans 1881), or else have been derived from palaeo-environmental research that was not specifically designed to answer archaeological questions (eg, Healy 1996a).

The land adjacent to the coastal strip has, however, fared rather better. In particular, archaeological recording in the 1990s on St Michael's Mount has shed more light on its prehistoric character, confirming it as a significant place since at least the 1st millennium BC (eg, Herring 2000). Moreover, metal detecting and chance discoveries have led to major artefactual discoveries being made in the area, most notably by the recovery of an important Late Bronze Age metalwork hoard on St Michael's Mount (Knight 2022; Knight *et al.* 2015) (Fig. 1.6). These finds have very significantly altered our understanding of later prehistoric activity and long-distance contacts, and as such they will be discussed in subsequent chapters (Chapters 12 and 14). These more recent discoveries remind us that the people who inhabited the area during the later Bronze Age did not dwell in isolation from the wider world and were, in fact, well connected with communities in Continental Europe, and linked to extensive networks by the sea (eg, Lehoërff & Talon 2017). At least intermittent connections and social relations between West Penwith and far-flung communities may well have run deep, as evidenced by successive shared cultural features, including Early Neolithic portal dolmens, with their Irish Sea comparanda (Kytmannow 2008; Jones 2020a); Early Bronze Age entrance graves, with their connections both to south-east Ireland and to the Channel Islands (Kirkham 2011; Jones 2016a); and Atlantic rock art in the form of cupmarks (Jones & Kirkham 2013; Valdez-Tullett 2019; Bradley 2020, 18–27). There are marked concentrations of all three cultural features in West Penwith.

Artefacts and materials in particular have also had a long history of being circulated from west Cornwall, including the distinctive axeheads made from the hard and distinctively coloured metagabbros or 'greenstones' in the Neolithic, followed by tin and later copper, and also the gold that was exported to Ireland and used to make Early Bronze Age lunulae and other objects (eg, Clough & Cummins 1988; Mattingly *et al.* 2009; Ehser *et al.* 2011; Standish *et al.* 2015; Jones *et al.* 2017; Carey *et al.* 2022; Krause *et al.* 2021; Berger *et al.* 2022). The exchange of these items may have drawn visitors to special or visually striking places such as Mount's Bay and led to the creation of long-term social relations (eg, Bradley *et al.* 2016a; Jones, forthcoming a). These relations were also sometimes linked to shared practices, notably the hoarding and selective deposition of metalwork which is widely found in the western European Bronze Age (eg, Bradley 1990; Bradley *et al.* 2018; Fontijn 2019; Webley *et al.* 2020). During the later Bronze Age West Penwith was part of an extensive western European network of contacts – the 'Atlantic Late Bronze Age – with shared traditions, including architectural forms such as roundhouses and circular enclosures (Bradley *et al.* 2016a, 213–266), and it is noteworthy that West Penwith has a significant concentration of later Bronze Age metalwork hoards, with one of the notable foci for metalwork deposition being the Mount's Bay area (eg, Pearce 1983). Given its significance, the character of depositional practices in the Mount's Bay area will form the subject for Chapter 12. Indeed, the area was already part of a cross-Channel 'maritory' during the Early Bronze Age (Needham 2009; Sheridan & Shortland 2004; Nicolas 2016). Kinship and social relations in the Mount's Bay area may therefore have been vibrant, outward looking and maritime, as much as land based, and the nature of connections, local and distant, human and non-human will be explored in subsequent chapters.

The objectives and questions

The recovery of very significant amounts of new palaeo-environmental information together with the excavation of an unusual later Bronze Age monument, itself associated with Late Bronze Age metalwork, constitutes a great advancement in knowledge of the later prehistoric activity and change in Mount's Bay and the wider West Penwith landscape. The results also, however, have raised a several key questions about the nature of inhabiting a landscape in a time of change, which included the following:

- What was the effect of climate change, how much sea-level and coastal change was there in prehistory and how quickly did the change occur?
- How did changes to the land and sea-level rise influence human activity and inhabitation of the landscape; and how did people in a changing world respond to those changes?
- Can the loss of land, and the changing character of the local topography, be associated with the increase of metalwork/hoard deposition which is evident in the later Bronze Age?
- What was the narrative behind the barrow? Why was it constructed where it was? And why was it reused in the Late Bronze Age, at a time when barrow construction was a rare event?
- What evidence is there for the social and economic effect of the landscape drowning

Figure 1.4: (above) View through the trees from Lescudjack hillfort across Mount's Bay towards St Michael's Mount

Figure 1.5: (below) A prehistoric tree stump, part of the submerged forest at Chyandour, (re)emerging from beneath the sands after the storms of 2014

Figure 1.6: The St Michael's Mount hoard site being recorded. (Photograph: Jim Parry)

in the Bronze Age, how might social relations have been affected by shifting landscapes and patterns of contact?

- How did the loss of landscape shape subsequent generations' perceptions of their past? Did the loss of land lead to the creations of myths and stories?

These questions will be addressed in the following chapters to build a narrative that uses archaeological and environmental data to consider how people lived and adapted to change as the sensory world around them altered, and how the landscape gradually shifted from being a diverse mosaic of wet woodland and open areas, to the one we know today featuring marsh, sand and open sea. The narrative also considers how these changes might have affected both local and more distant social relations.

The results of the project also have much wider significance, given the current sea-level rise which involves more regular tidal surges, storm damage and which threatens and destroys coastal archaeological sites. Indeed, in Cornwall excavations have already been carried out after storm damage has occurred to such sites (Jones 2009–10; Jones & Mikulski 2015); this work echoes that of the CHERISH Project in Wales and Ireland (http://cherishproject.eu/en/), and the SCAPE project in Scotland (https://scapetrust.org/), which have been monitoring and documenting changes to eroding archaeological sites. In Wales and Scotland there are now historic environment climate change subgroups (Barker 2020; https://www.historicenvironment.scot/about-us/what-we-do/climate-change/). These interventions are likely to become much more frequent and widespread, and archaeological and heritage sites across Britain, Europe and beyond are already suffering damage, with many more under threat (eg, van Heeringen & Theunissen 2007; Wickham-Jones 2015; 2018; Vousdoukas *et al.* 2022).

Volume structure

This, the resulting monograph, is divided into four parts with specialist appendices at the end. The chapters have been arranged by theme, so that they can be read sequentially, with the fourth interpretative section picking up and expanding upon on the key findings of the volume given at the end of the monograph. This section, the first, outlines the background to the archaeological projects at the Penzance barrow and Marazion Marsh and their context, and sets the out the scope of the succeeding chapters, and conventions used.

The second section is concerned with the excavations at the Penzance Heliport barrow. The opening chapter describes the methods and results from the 2018 excavations and the environmental coring at the barrow site (Chapter 2). This is followed by specialist reporting on the analysis of the artefactual assemblage, including the ceramics, worked stone, flint and the copper alloy ingot (Chapters 3, 4, and 5). The artefactual chapters are followed by the environmental analysis of the samples taken on and beyond the barrow, including pollen, diatoms, waterlogged plant remains, and charred plant remains (Chapter 6). The section concludes with the radiocarbon determinations from the barrow (Chapter 7).

The third section presents the results from the augur core sampling at Marazion Marsh in 2019. A brief background to the project and sampling methodology is given (Chapter 8) and this is followed by the specialist analyses of the environmental samples, including pollen, plant macrofossils and marine shells from the core and the radiocarbon dating obtained on the samples (Chapter 9). The section concludes with a geoarchaeological overview of the Marazion Marsh area (Chapter 10).

The fourth, synthetic, section draws together the results from the analyses and places them within a much wider context than would be the case with a standard excavation report of a developer-funded project. This section has six principal areas of focus, which are linked to the original questions raised by the projects. The first (Chapter 11) places the results from both the Heliport and Marazion Marsh projects within their wider context by providing a model of the drowning Mount's Bay landscape from the Upper Palaeolithic through to the Late Neolithic. The second chapter in this section (Chapter 12) considers the significant evidence for the selective deposition of metalwork from the Middle Bronze Age to the Roman period in the Mount's Bay area. A particular focus lies in the Late Bronze Age when there was a significant increase in the number of sites associated with metalwork, especially at the eastern end of the bay. The third (Chapter 13), is concerned with the interpretation of the nature and character of activity in the area of the Penzance Heliport barrow and its wider significance. This chapter is focused upon later prehistoric occupation but is especially concerned with the Bronze Age and the excavated round barrow when significant changes to the surrounding landscape were occurring. It places the results from the excavation into their broader regional context.

The fifth part of this section (Chapter 14) provides an overview of the major themes that have arisen from the preceding chapters, including the changing nature of the environment and how this could have affected communities over time, and the opportunity is taken to synthesise the results into the wider west Cornish setting and beyond. It reviews the results from both the current projects and previous research to consider the effects of sea-level and landscape change over several millennia, especially during the later Bronze Age, where there are two broadly contemporary trends, a considerable increase in obvious human activity in the area and the formation of a hard shoreline. Shifting patterns of dwelling, settlement, kinship connections, distant connections, community resilience, ceremonial activity, and the effects of gradual loss of land in the area of Mount's Bay over time to stimulate myth and story are considered. Suggestions for avenues for further research and consideration of lives lived at a time of change and rising, numinous waters are also made. This latter reflection is important for considering how people in the past may have perceived and reacted to the loss of their land. It is also a timely reminder that in the 21st century this is an ongoing and increasing experience for coastal communities around the globe who are threatened and being displaced by the rising waves of what has been termed the Anthropocene era (cf. Braje 2016; Macfarlane 2019, 74–75).

This section ends with a short concluding 'last word' that looks beyond archaeological interpretations of change. Artists have of course played an important part in documenting the coastline of Britain (eg, Satchell *et al.* 2015), in terms of creating a record of what has been lost archaeologically and of the communities who have lived by the sea. It is therefore fitting that the last part of this section, Chapter 15, presents a contribution from the EXPERIENCE project, an arts project which has been making installations, involving different communities and gathering their perceptions of the submerged forest. This section brings the lived experiences of Mount's Bay into the present, and is an important reminder that archaeology represents one narrative amongst many in any perception of landscapes, and these will differ according to social group, dwelling perspective, gender and individual experience (cf. Bender & Winer 2001; Edmonds 2004, 29–30; Koskinen-Koivisto & Seitsonen 2019; Seitsonen 2021). Places, landscapes and our perceptions of them are anything but static; they are multifaceted and myths are constantly in the making.

Finally, at the end of the volume, there are two specialist appendices: the first relates to the conservation of the copper alloy ingot and the second comprises the borehole logs and accompanying photographs from the sample cores.

SECTION 2:

EXCAVATIONS AT THE PENZANCE HELIPORT BARROW

2

Penzance Heliport barrow: auger survey and excavation 2018

Andy M. Jones and Anna Lawson-Jones with Michael J. Allen

In 2018 the Cornwall Archaeological Unit was commissioned by Penzance Heliport Limited to undertake a programme of archaeological recording of what appeared to be a ring ditch associated with a relatively small barrow, which was just about discernible as a low rise in a field on the eastern side of Penzance (Fig. 2.1). The 2018 archaeological investigations followed two previous stages of recording. A geophysical survey (AOC 2017) had identified the barrow site and in 2017 an evaluation opened up the area of the barrow and 14 further trenches across the field (Southwest Archaeology 2018) (Fig. 2.2). The evaluation trenching, which involved stripping of the site and the almost total excavation of features in quadrant 4 (the eastern quadrant), confirmed that the site was Bronze Age in date and comprised an oval ring ditch measuring approximately 12 m by 15 m, the north-east portion of which had been subject a great deal of later disturbance by large pits and post-medieval field boundaries. Aside from a few abraded sherds of pottery no prehistoric artefacts or features were identified beyond the barrow area, although deposits of peat were found beneath layers of 'Made Ground' (*ibid.*).

In 2018 the full programme of archaeological mitigation commenced with the excavation of the barrow and environmental sampling. The environmental recording involved coring to investigate the geoarchaeological potential beyond the barrow and the excavation of the barrow itself. In total 19 profiles were recorded, enabling the deposits within the site to be modelled and profiled. A humose layer was recorded in three locations, and palaeo-environmental subsamples obtained from three. The humose layer seemed better preserved than previously recorded. Consequently, the potential existed for pollen (land-use and vegetation data) and diatoms (reflecting the nature of the local watery environment – for example, depth, flow, salinity) to be preserved, and to define local land-use history in which to set the barrow. As the upper portion of the dated and analysed sediment profile is contemporary with the Bronze Age barrow in the same field, then these data and interpretations significantly enhance our understating of that monument, the activities associated with it, and the land-use and landscape in which it resided. The 2018 excavations involved the re-stripping of the site and the excavation of those parts of the barrow which had not already been opened during the evaluations in 2017. The soil stripping revealed that the evaluations had inadvertently been focused on the most disturbed part of the barrow. The aim of the excavation project was, therefore, to understand better the chronology of the barrow sequence, and the character of activities associated with it. On completion of the excavations an archive level report was produced (Lawson-Jones 2019) which, along with the evaluation report, provides much of the stratigraphical information given below.

The remainder of this chapter provides the background to the project, a description of the barrow excavation and the coring. It commences with a description and results from the environmental coring and is followed by the stratigraphy associated with the barrow site. The results from the analysis of the charred plant macrofossils and charcoal, the radiocarbon dating and specialist examination of artefacts from the barrow are presented in Chapters 3–7. An interpretative discussion of the results from the barrow excavations is given in the subsequent synthetic section at the end of this volume (Chapter 13).

Location

The Penzance Heliport barrow site is located on low-lying ground just 8 m OD above sea-level, on the eastern edge of Penzance and west of Longrock (SW 48974 31522), not far from the main A30 approach and Jelbert Way. The site was situated within what appeared to an unremarkable pasture field, opposite recent commercial developments which currently include Halfords, B&M and KFC (Fig. 2.1). The barrow was sited below the bottom of a slope to the north on the upper edge of ground that sloped very gently down towards the south and Mount's Bay and St Michael's Mount (Fig. 2.9). In the past the site is likely to have been set on a more appreciable knoll, above an area which was prone to flooding and marshiness. The first edition historic OS mapping from 1809, for example, depicts the very wet and low-lying environment in which the barrow is set, and shows a long east to west-lying pool to the south of the barrow.

Today the barrow site lies within the parish of Ludgvan; however, historically it the lay within the parish of Gulval, in land classified by Historic Landscape Classification (HLC) as Anciently Enclosed Land (Cornwall County Council 1996), and the sinuous pattern of fields established during the medieval period can be seen on the historic 1880 and 1908 OS mapping, and on the Tithe Map. The 1843 Gulval Tithe Map and apportionments shows that the barrow lay within an arable field named 'Hay Moor', while many of the surrounding field names allude to frequent waterlogging in the past (eg, Long Moor Marsh, Eastern Moor, Withey Moor, Hay Moor, Forwebban Moor and Marsh Moor). Today many of the field boundaries depicted on the historic mapping have been removed, including two that ran along the immediate eastern and southern edges of the barrow (Southwest Archaeology 2018, fig. 23).

As outlined in Chapter 1, no archaeological sites of prehistoric date were hitherto known in the immediate vicinity of the project area. The Cornwall and Scilly Historic Environment Record shows possible medieval drainage or ridge and furrow just to the south of the barrow (MCO 51201). However, the nearest documented prehistoric sites lie to the south-west. Approximately 700 m away, a stone axe-hammerhead was found (MCO576) and on the shore beyond is a submarine forest (MCO55163) and Holocene peat layers (Chapter 6). Aside from the prehistoric settlements at Lescudjack and St Michael's Mount there are no upstanding prehistoric settlements or monuments within the immediate area of the coastal strip. Prehistoric settlements and ceremonial sites including lithic scatters, enclosures and barrows are located on the higher ground to the north over 800 m away (see Chapters 1 & 14). The majority of the adjacent farms and settlements of medieval origin such as Kenegie, Gulval and Ludgvan are also located in this less marginal zone. In addition to prehistoric deposits and medieval field patterns, much later features are known in the wider vicinity. These sites include post-medieval clay extraction pits and brickworks, located to the east, which made use of the underlying alluvial clays. Some of the large pits reported on in this chapter may in fact relate to this later extractive activity.

1. Geoarchaeological fieldwork; putting the Penzance Heliport barrow into its (pre-)historic landscape context

Michael J. Allen

An archaeological desk-based assessment (WYG Group Ltd 2017a) and a geoarchaeological and palaeo-environmental desk-based assessment (WYG Group Ltd 2017b) had outlined the archaeological and geoarchaeological significance of the site. In particular the combination of the presence of a previously unknown barrow, and stratified deposits of possible geoarchaeological and palaeo-environmental interest which may relate to this, indicated a potential that was explored. A review of geotechnical logs

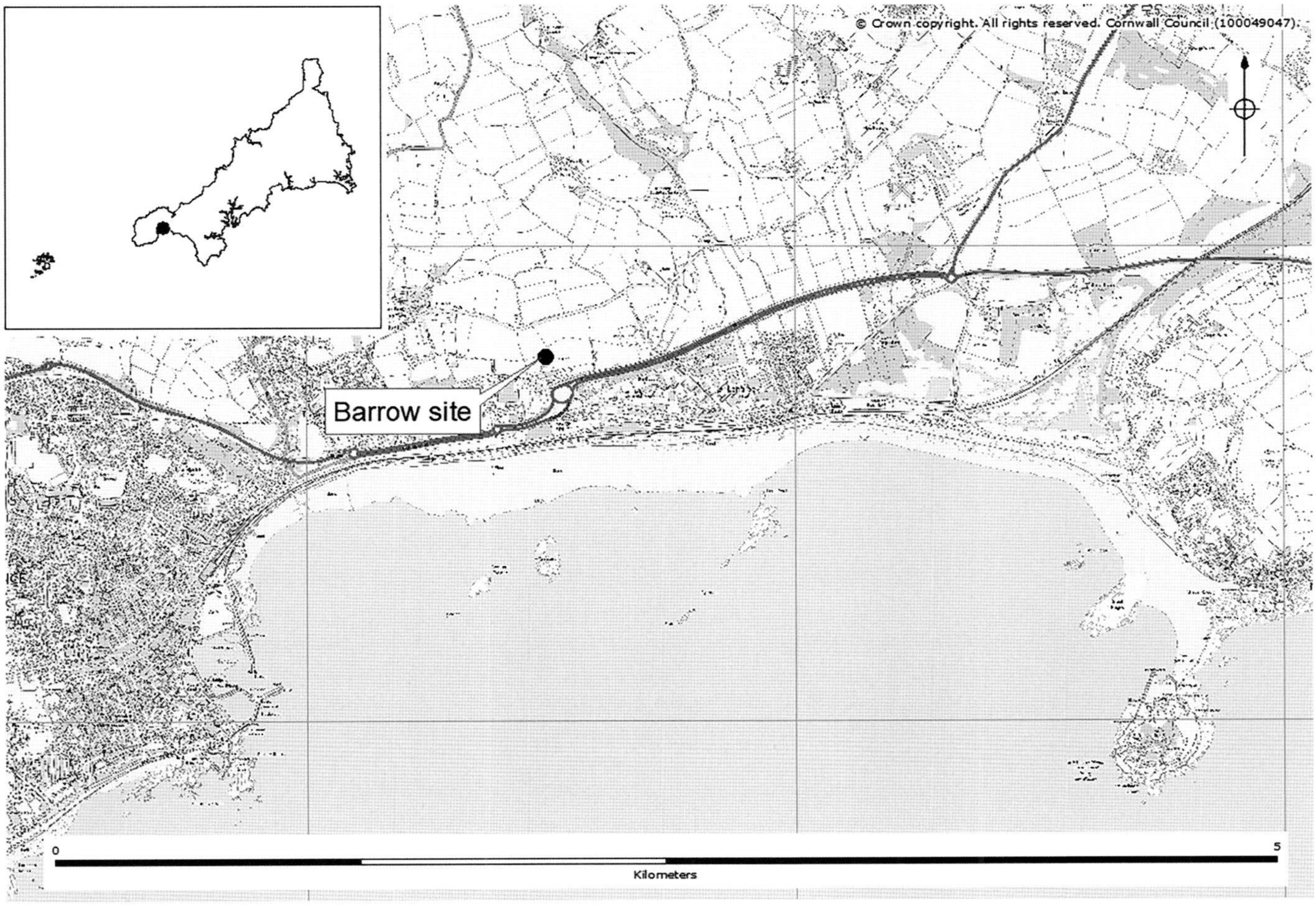

Figure 2.1: Map showing the location of the barrow

from trial pits and boreholes that had been undertaken across the site (Fig. 2.2) showed the presence of high level non-coastal humose or organic deposits over alluvium across the site. The stratigraphy was highly variable and initial suggestions were that the sequences 'have low value for understanding environmental changes in the area' and that palaeo-environmental assessment or analysis was not recommended (Southwest Archaeology 2018, 2.2.1, 9). Despite this recommendation, the combination of geotechnical interventions (WYG Group Ltd 2017a; 2017b) and archaeological evaluation (Southwest Archaeology 2018) made it clear that the data obtained from previous coring did in fact indicate the potential for deposit modelling, radiocarbon dating and possibly also detailed palaeo-environmental analyses. Consequently, a new coring programme with specific geoarchaeological (rather than geotechnical) aims was undertaken, and the results of the deposit recording and modelling are given below as a way of setting the scene for the results of the excavation of the Bronze Age barrow. The accompanying palaeo-environmental and radiocarbon data from the geoarchaeological cores are presented in Chapters 6 and 7 respectively.

As a result of previous investigations (as detailed below), geoarchaeological fieldwork was concentrated to the west of the site in an area already defined as containing deposits 'of potential geoarchaeological and palaeo-environmental significance' (Southwest Archeology 2018; Fig. 2.2). In addition, it was felt that any data recovered from this exercise might assist in determining the landscape, land-use and environmental history associated with a Bronze Age round barrow (as discussed below).

Geology, topography and soils

The site embraces two irregularly shaped fields, which were in pasture at the time of survey

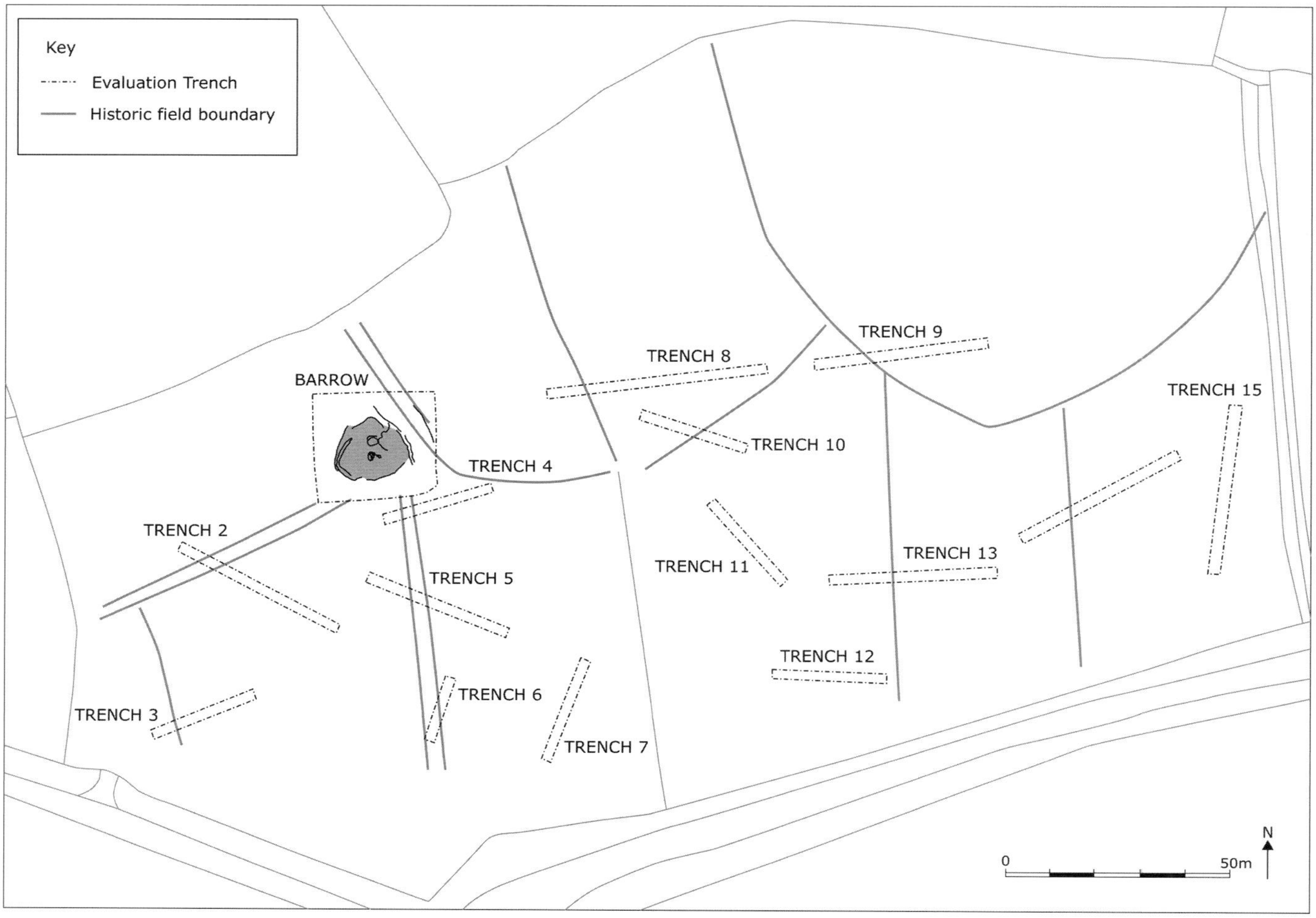

Figure 2.2: Map showing the barrow excavation area and the positions of the evaluation trenches

and coring. The geology is recorded as slate and siltstone of the Mylor Slate Formation including Hornfelsed Slate and Hornfelsed Siltstone (Goode & Taylor 1988; Shail 1989), overlain locally by alluvium. The soils are mapped as typical brown earths of the Denbigh 2 Association (Findlay *et al.* 1984). The area lies on a gentle slope, below the high Moor, falling to the south from an altitude of around 10 m OD to 5 m OD. The lowest land lies along its southern boundary, and in particular the south-east corner of the site (Fig. 2.1). This topographical location seems significant. It is at the base of the steep slope to the Moor, and its most southerly point has views not only southwards to the coast, but also eastwards over the Red River and Marazion Marsh which, as we will see later, may be significant. At a landscape scale, the site is not directly related to, or effected by, changing sea-level (Healy 1993; 1999a) and consequent coastline changes (despite previous assertions by, for example, Southwest Archaeology 2018), but afforded views of the former major Pleistocene and early Holocene (Mesolithic) rivers that exist today in the form of offshore palaeovalleys (Camm & Dominy 1998; Camm 1999), and which may well have been significant drainage courses and communication routeways during the early Holocene, as discussed later (Chapters 11 and 14).

Geoarchaeological background

Geotechnical investigations were undertaken across the site by Ian Farmer Associates in September 2016 and December 2016 to January 2017 (Ian Farmer Associates 2017; WYG Group Ltd 2017b). This included 23 trial pits dug to between 1.6 and 4.1 m depth, three boreholes, and 20 cable percussion boreholes cored to 7.45 m depth. Made ground was recorded in every hole to depths of 0.3 to 1.0 m overlying what is reported to be alluvial material. No peat or organic remains were recorded in the first set of 12 trial pits, but the coring recorded 'pockets of peat' at between 1.2 m and 2.2 m. The deposits generally overlay sandy silts to great depths. Borehole logs at lower altitudes to the south of the site at Eastern Green (see Fig. 2.8, below) recorded 'soft odorous unbedded dark brown amorphous peat' at between 1.6 m and 2.6 m depth (2.11 m to 1.11 m OD) (WYG Group Ltd 2017b; Southwest Archaeology 2018). Further investigation of the peat at this site by Ralph Fyfe (University of Plymouth) reported that the peat seemed to be a humose sediment rather than true peat (that is, humified peat deposits), arising from the desiccation and degradation of the peat (WYG Group Ltd 2018a; Fyfe 2018). Recent investigations to the south-west of the site (ECO3980) between 5 m and 10 m OD revealed late prehistoric and early medieval peat and alluvial layers, up to *c.* 1 m thick and becoming thinner towards the site (WYG Group Ltd 2017b).

Other major coastal-related peat sequences at Marazion Marsh (see Chapter 10, and Healy 1995; 1999b) and Chyandour (James & Guttman 1992) show both the importance of peat (as discussed below) and of changing sea-level around the coast of west Cornwall (Healy 1993; 1999a, fig. 2.14; see Chapter 11). Further south in Mount's Bay an extensive submerged Mesolithic/Neolithic forest (MCO55163) exists, along with Holocene peat layers. The peat at the Heliport site, however, falls altitudinally much higher than others in the area, and is not affected by sea-level changes, but is a result of local conditions, and probably increased groundwater at the base of the Moors. Nevertheless, because of the presence of long reported peat sequences in west Cornwall (eg, Marazion Marsh, Chyandour and the Mount's Bay submerged forest: Scourse & Furze 1999) and the occurrence of humose and humified peat on site it was concluded that: 'Overall, the site investigation results suggested some potential for deposits of palaeo-environmental significance within the south-east and eastern parts of the site. The stratigraphy is highly variable, and this could reflect the range of historic land regimes as well and truncation of deposits caused by the removal of field boundaries and hedgerows in the past.' (WYG Group Ltd, 2017b, 6).

Aims

The geoarchaeological aims were specified (WYG Group Ltd 2018b) as follows:

To undertake a programme of geoarchaeological analysis across the development site, to include:

- A geoarchaeological auger survey, associated sampling;
- palaeo-environmental/geoarchaeological analysis; and
- the production of a detailed deposit model

in order to provide information on the episodes and conditions of peat formation within the area and the relationship to deposits in the local landscape, such as Marazion Marsh; and to provide information on the environment during the construction and use of the barrow monument, in order to place the excavated remains within a wider landscape and palaeo-environmental context.

Objectives

- To provide a sediment record, deposit model and transect through the deposits.
- To enable detailed recording, and sub-sampling for palaeo-environmental remains (pollen, diatoms) from the sediments.
- To core and recover a sequence of Holocene sediments and peat deposits, from which a long geoarchaeological and palaeo-environmental record can be obtained.

The overall project design and methodology was designed to assist in meeting a series of defined research aims in the SWARF research agenda (Webster 2008), and in particular:

Research Aim 17: Improve the quality and quantity of environmental data and our understanding of what it represents.

Research Aim 23: Improve our understanding of past climate and sea-level changes together with their effects on people's relationships with landscapes and the sea.

The emphasis on submerged forests and peat bed resources is of particular relevance to the site.

Approach and methods

The proposed method was to undertake a two transects of staggered core points at *c.* 20 m apart which together could create a single profile as well as providing some spatial

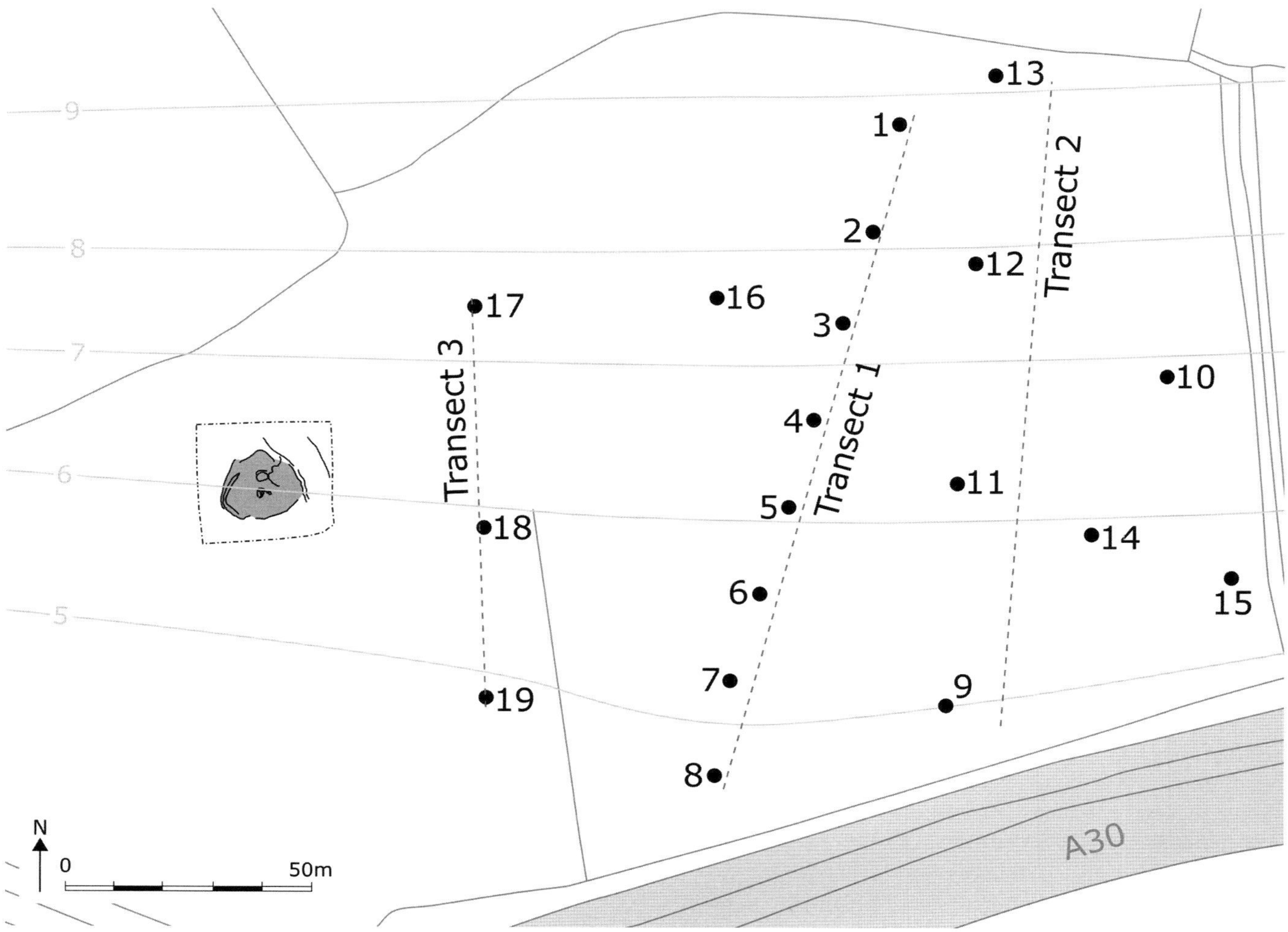

Figure 2.3: The locations of boreholes and transects

variability (Allen 2018a). This comprised an estimated 10–14 boreholes staggered across two parallel transects. In reality, once on site, the two transects were augmented by three additional boreholes in the south-eastern portion of the site, and a transect of three holes in the western field to the east of the excavated barrow (Fig. 2.3).

Field methods

Mechanical coring was undertaken by a sub-contracted company using a Dando dynamic terrier tracked window sampling rig operating a diesel-driven drop (percussion) hammer driving window samples of 117 mm (stepping down to 102 mm and 87 mm) diameter, under the geoarchaeological supervision of Michael J. Allen. The recovered window sample cores were logged and photographed in the field (Appendix 2.1 & 2.2). Decisions were made on site for recovery and retention of undisturbed samples in sleeved cores for removal to AEA (Allen Environmental Archaeology) laboratory facilities for detailed geoarchaeological recording and subsampling (Appendix 2.1 & 2.3). All boreholes were backfilled, heeled-in and reinstated as far as possible, and the location and OD heights were recorded for all cored points. Provision had been made to augment the proposed 10–14 cores with hand-augering using a combination of dutch augers of 5–7 cm diameter and a gouge auger of 2.5 cm diameter. In the event, however, it proved to be not necessary to undertake any hand augering.

Survey and recording

The location and OD height of each borehole were initially recorded on site using a hand held GPS (archive) and more precise survey data were recorded by the Cornwall Archaeological Unit and are used in this report (Table 2.1). The borehole locations are indicated in Figure 2.3. Undisturbed 1 m-long window samples were photographed in the field (Appendix 2.2), and the selected and retained cores recorded at the AEA laboratory facilities were photographed with a scale. The deposits were recorded on site and at the AEA laboratory facilities using standard pedological terminology following Hodgson (1997), and soil colours recorded moist with a Munsell soil colour chart in daylight conditions. The field and laboratory logs are provided in Appendix 2.1.

Laboratory methods: geoarchaeological record and subsampling

Cores from three boreholes (comprising seven 1-metre cores) were retained and removed to AEA laboratory facilities. Each was cut open, and not extruded to ensure no compression or distortion of the sediments. Following careful and judicious cleaning of the exposed cut surfaces, full descriptions were made of the sediments in each core (following terminology outlined by Hodgson 1997), and texture, structure inclusions and boundaries/ contacts were recorded. Particular attention was paid to the presence of any potential stasis (*in situ* pedogenesis), erosion faces and of anthropogenic activity and artefacts. The logs were transcribed into tabulated records (Appendix 2.1). A photographic record was made of each core examined (Appendix 2.3). All undisturbed deposits of the peaty or humose horizons were carefully examined under illuminated magnification for the presence of ecofacts and identifiable and suitable datable (radiocarbon) organic material. After description, subsampling (see Chapter 6), and destructive examination for the recovery of artefacts, the remaining core material was discarded.

Results

Coring

The programme of geoarchaeological coring was undertaken between 26th and 29th November 2018. Originally a series of two transects of boreholes totalling *c.* 10–14 cores was proposed to examine, in particular, the 'humose' layer and alluvium. Fieldwork, however, completed a series of 19 cores of generally to 3 m, but up to 4 m, deep from across the entire site of the defined area (Figs 2.2 & 2.3). A total of 55 m of core stratigraphy was logged in the field, and 7 m of undisturbed core removed for more detailed description, subsampling, and assessment. A series of three transects perpendicular to the slope (generally north–south) were cored to the west and south of the barrow, and augmented by four additional spot locations (Fig. 2.3).

The coring was original proposed at 10 m staggered intervals divided between two north–south transects; that is to say, *c.* 7 or 8 along each transect at 20 m making a composite transect of *c.* 14–16 profiles at 10 m intervals. Transect 1 was completed at the proposed 20 m intervals with 8 cores recorded (T1/1-8). It became clear that the uniformity of deposits and the scale of the operation that 20 m intervals was sufficient along one transect. What was deemed beneficial was a wider spatial coverage. Consequently coring was conducted along a second transect and four cores recorded at *c.* 50 m intervals (T2/9, and T2/11–13). A third transect of just 3 profiles was recorded *c.* 45 m east of the Bronze Age barrow comprising boreholes T3/17–19. Three additional cores were placed the east and especially south east where deposits are likely to be deepest and humose deposits best expressed (based on existing records and topography); boreholes 10, 14, and 15 (Fig. 2.3). This array provided much greater spatial coverage for mapping and deposit modelling and an additional perpendicular transect nearer the barrow.

Geoarchaeology and deposit modelling; deposit extent and significance

Stratigraphy

Mechanical coring continued to a maximum of 4 m, and in most cases a consistent deposit, albeit not the natural geology/bedrock (Mylor Slate Formation of slate and siltstone), was recorded as the base. The three north–south sediment profiles are recorded in Figure 2.4. Sequences between 2 m and 4 m were recorded; all reached a broadly consistent yellowish brown silt loam, generally encountered at between 1.9 m and 2.3 m depth. This yellowish brown (10YR 5/8 – 6/8) silt varied occasionally being a brownish yellow (10YR 6/8), a strong brown (7.5YR 5/6) and even and reddish

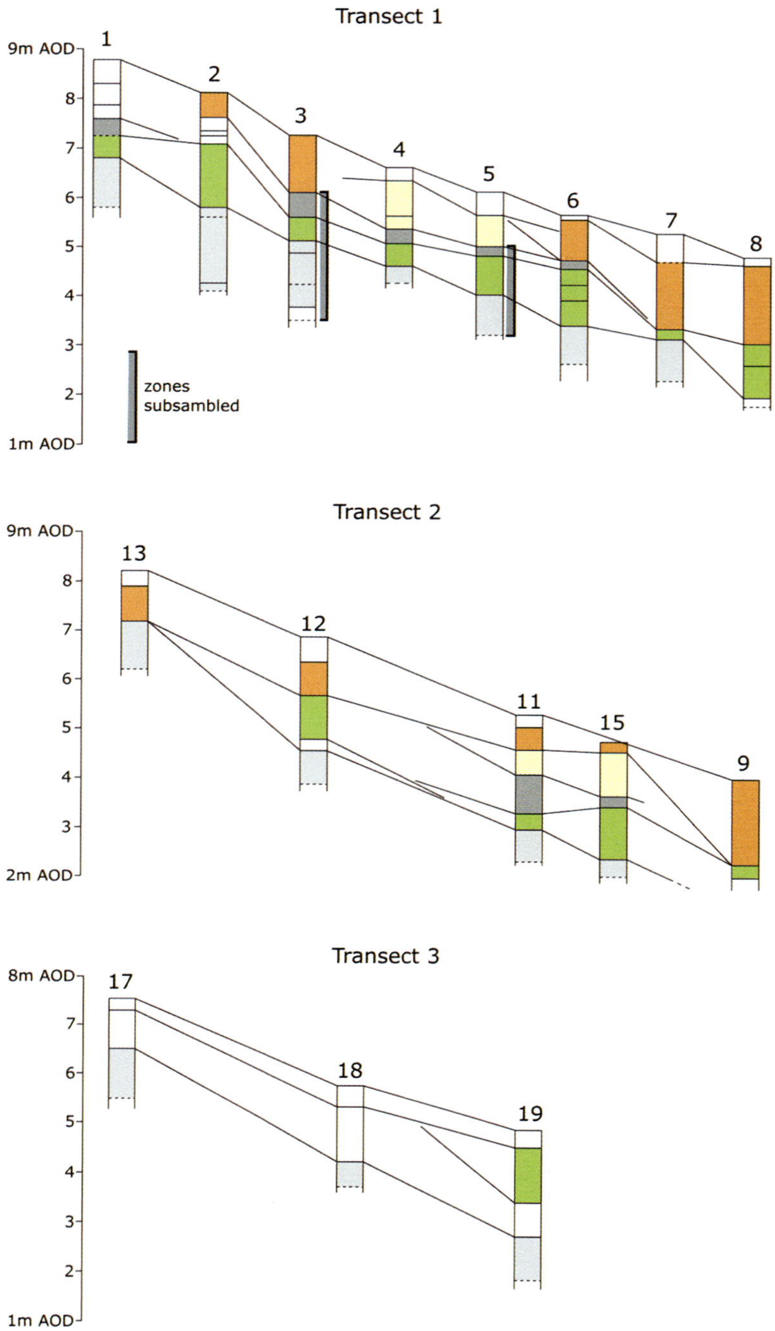

Figure 2.4: Profiles of transects 1 and 2 (top) and profile of transect 3 (note the lack of humose layer) (bottom)

brown (5YR 5/8) silt loam and sandy silt loam. This silt loam was considered an early Holocene or Pleistocene Head, and is taken as the base for this study, being consistent below any humose or peat deposits (see Fig. 2.4), and below the probable construction impact. In two cases (T1/2 and T1/3; Fig. 2.5) sand was recovered beneath this.

In general terms five main sedimentary units can be defined across the site. In some cases the definition of made ground was difficult with such a small window on the sediments recovered in the core, and deposits have only been allocated to this unit where there was clear recent material (pottery, cloth, or alien sediments). Consequently the records in the logs (Appendix 2.1) and recorded in Figures 2.4 and 2.5 should be considered as conservative. Previous studies (WYG Group Ltd 2018b; Southwest Archaeology 2018) have indicated widespread occurrence of made ground across the site, presumably in part a result of construction of the retail park to the south.

The sediment units have been defined as:

1. Holocene colluvium
2. Humose layer (sometimes peaty/humified peat)
3. 'Alluvium'
4. Basal colluvium
5. Sand

Although there are some local complications and additional horizons the four main stratigraphic units are recorded more-or-less consistently across the site. The upper horizons in boreholes T1/4, T1/5, T1/6, T2/11 and T2/15 for instance are more complex and may be made ground (redeposited soil and sediment material), see below.

Made ground (Fig. 2.5)

Up to 1.6/1.8 m of made ground has been confidently identified over a large area of the eastern field including its northern edge. Previously made ground has been reported as being more widespread, but the conservative ascription of made ground here may account for that. It was not always obvious, with only the relatively small window of the core to view, whether the sediments were redeposited and constituted made ground, or were *in situ* sediments. Due to this potential uncertainty, the made ground mapped in Figure 2.5 is that which clearly comprises recent deposits by virtue of the artefacts it contained (modern and Victorian pottery, modern cloth, etc.), or the clearly recent or alien deposits. Plastic and woollen clothing have been found to depths of 1.6 m and a complete, late 19th/early 20th century (Victorian), ink bottle (see Lawson-Jones 2019) at 1.65 m depth. It is assumed that much of the

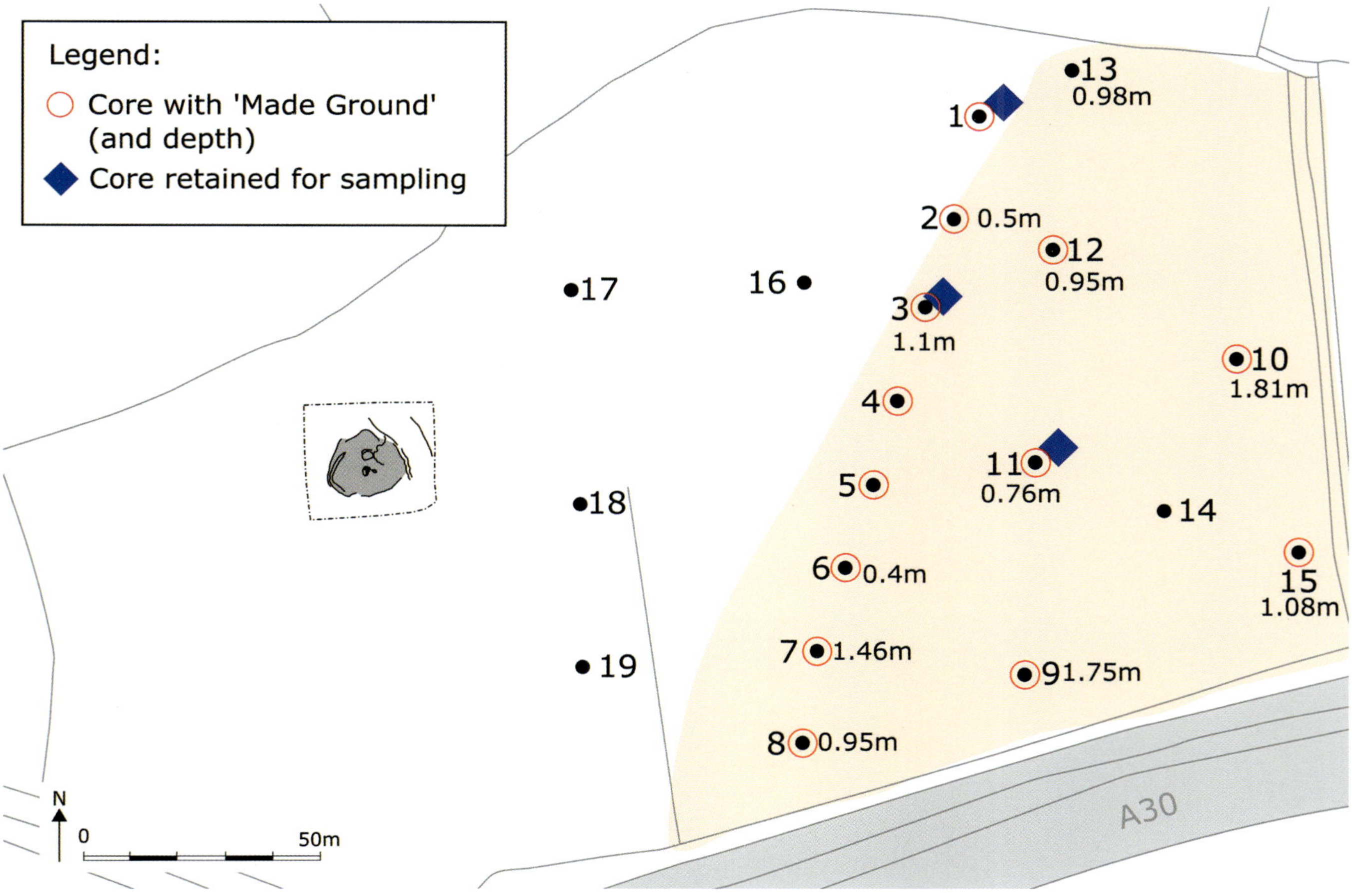

Figure 2.5: Occurrence of definite made ground (this is a conservative record as some deposits could not clearly be seen as made ground, as opposed to colluvial deposits) in relation to the sample cores

made ground relates to the decommissioning of the former heliport and construction of the retail park to the south of Jelbert Way.

Holocene colluvium (Unit 1)

The upper deposits, where obviously recognisable made ground did not exist, consisted of an upper colluvial deposit. This is present especially in cores T1/4, and T2/11 and T2/15 (Fig. 2.4). In general, it comprises a stony yellowish brown (10YR 5/3) to greyish brown silt loam, and represents colluvium probably resulting from human activity (clearance, tillage) upslope (cf. Bell 1983; Allen 1991) from the adjacent steep side of the Moor, or in one or two instances this may be unconfirmed recent deposits of soil material (made ground). This is post-2580–2460 cal BC in date, and it is tempting to ascribe the colluviation to activity associated with the barrow's construction and use. However, changes in the pollen spectra from the humose deposits above may also be linked with the barrow-related activity (see Chapter 6).

Table 2.1: Location of the 19 borehole / core points

Core	E	N	OD
T1/1	149098.818	31592.481	8.81
T1/2	149093.297	31569.827	8.084
T1/3	149086.997	31550.763	7.228
T1/4	149081.336	31530.116	6.617
T1/5	149076.149	31511.999	6.097
T1/6	149070.349	31493.891	5.658
T1/7	149064.496	31475.583	5.257
T/18	149061.075	31455.952	4.758
T2/13	149118.358	31602.675	9.225
T/212	149114.264	31563.289	7.874
T2/11	149110.618	31517.082	6.358
T2/9	149108.604	31470.654	5.014
10	149153.422	31539.589	6.747
14	149137.813	31506.465	6.129
15	149166.5	31497.303	5.735
16	149061.719	31556.168	7.268
17	149012.36	31554.186	7.523
18	149014.117	31507.648	5.708
19	149014.751	31471.924	4.837

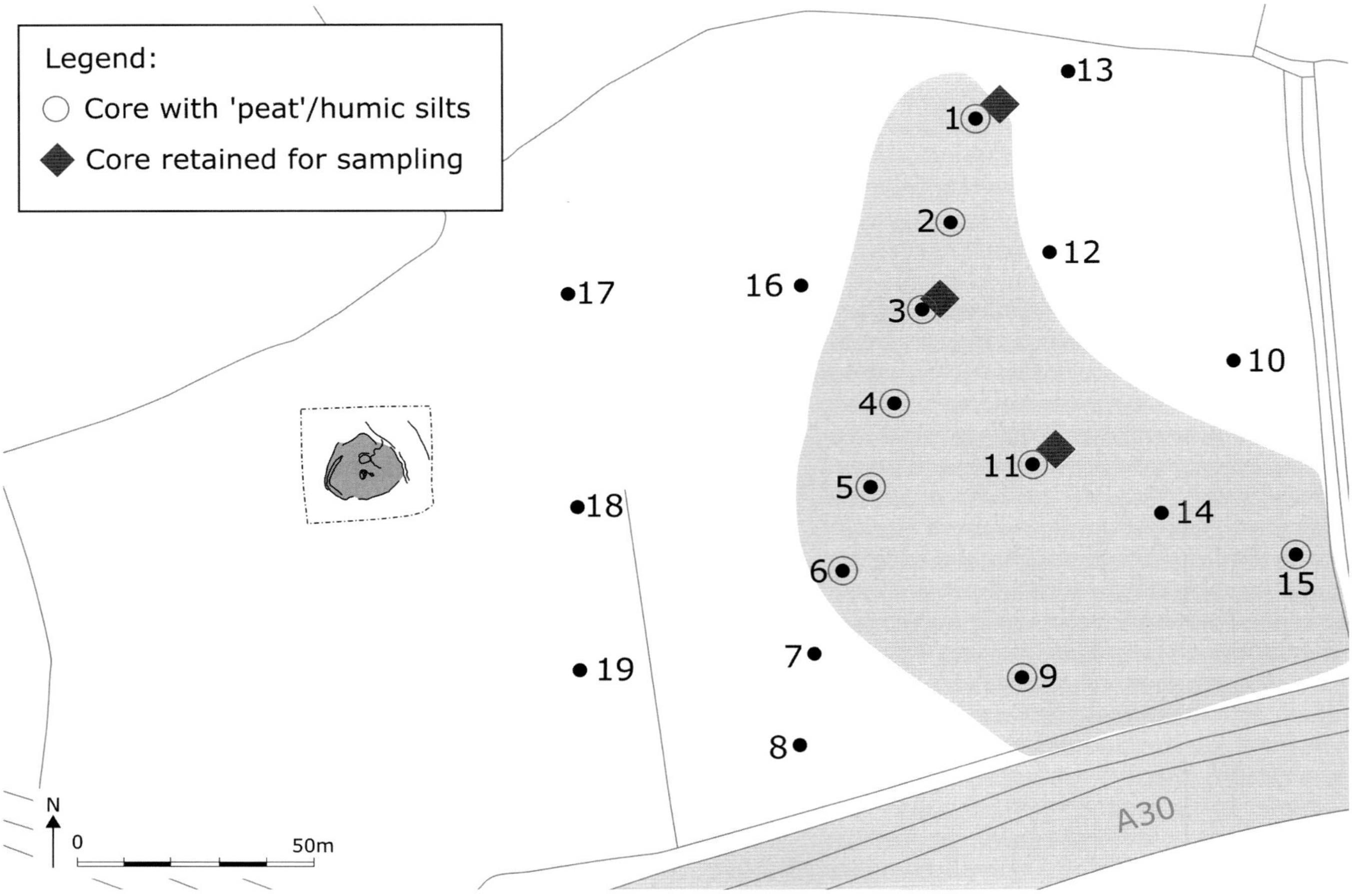

Figure 2.6: Occurrence and extent of the humose deposit in relation to the sample cores

Humose deposit/s (Unit 2.1 and 2.2; Fig. 2.6)
The most significant deposit in terms of geoarchaeological and palaeo-environmental potential is clearly the humose deposits (labelled 'peat' in Appendix 1). In transect 1 this layer occurs at an altitude of between 7.61 and 5.15 m OD (0.95 m to 1.25 m depth), and in transect 2 and elsewhere between 5.15 m and 4.16 m OD (1.18 m and 1.22 m depth), see Table 2.2. It was generally 0.25 to 0.30 m thick but locally up to 0.45–0.83 m.

The humose layer varied from a very dark brown humic silt and humified silty peat (T1/3), to dark brown or very dark grey (minroegenic) silt (T1/4 and T1/5). Towards the eastern end of the site it is thicker and a humified peat (T1/11), with occasional *Phragmities* reed stem cases (T15). As Fyfe has indicated (2018), in many cases this seems to be minerogenic and desiccated peat (humose deposit); however, in transects 1 and 2 (Fig. 2.4; Appendix 2.1), more humic humified peats seem to occur. In some locations the humose layer could be divided into two visually distinct portions, namely an upper humose layer being a very dark brown to dark brown humic, almost stone-free, silt loam; possibly a highly humified peat (Unit 2.1), above a very dark grey humified stone-free silty peat (Unit 2.2). In one location (T1/6) two separate humose layers seem to occur. Both are humic silts and are separated by a fine-grained grey minerogenic 'alluvium'. A Chalcolithic date of 2580–2460 cal BC (4006±23 BP, SUERC-95372) within this deposit offers the possibility of the upper part of this deposit being coeval with barrow-associated activity, where significant changes in the pollen are recorded (Chapter 6).

Seven monoliths of humose deposits examined previously by Fyfe from the Southwest Archaeology field evaluation show considerable variability (Fyfe 2018). Moreover, the presence of a single and uniform humose deposit is now questioned as a result of the geoarchaeological coring here (see Fig. 2.3; Appendix 2.1 & 2.2). Furthermore, in some cases deposits with

Core	*1*	*3*	*3*	*4*	*5*	*6*	*11*	*15*
Altitude top (m OD)	*7.61*	*6.20*	*6.13*	*5.37*	*5.15*	*4.71*	*5.14*	*4.16*
Top	120	120	110	125	110	95	122	108
Base	145	150	155	148	130	113	205	130
Top	–	–	–	–	–	148	–	–
Base	–	–	–	–	–	156	–	–

Table 2.2: Occurrence and depth (cm) of the humose layer

better preservation and limited plant matter survival (that is, those which are more peaty than humose) were present. Consequently, many of the mainly minerogenic, desiccated humose deposits may have low potential and even low value for palaeo-environmental analysis. However, those which are better sealed and better preserved, and associated with long sediment histories, have a higher palaeo-environmental potential.

This deposit may represent a stasis, and soil formation in local wet conditions. It could, indicate water ponding at the base of the slope, in a former (now largely buried) minor valley running south to south-eastwards at base of the steep slope to the upland Moor to the north. The deposit accumulation at location at the base of the slope may have been on a former spring line which ran just to the north of the barrow. This would account for its minerogenic and humic/humose character, rather than being a more plant-rich peat. The deposit is laterally variable, and in some places more organic matter and preserved wood and plant remains were present. It provided greater potential for pollen survival and analysis than Fyfe had indicated (2018), and so three cores were retained for palaeo-environmental and radiocarbon sampling (see Chapters 6 & 7).

'Alluvium' (Unit 3; Fig. 2.7)
A grey to greyish brown silt, generally with few stones, occurred over the basal colluvium and beneath the humose layer. It is fine-grained and well-sorted, suggesting fluvial, slow water, or overbank flood deposits. It does, however, occur just at the footslope, but relatively high up the incline at the base of the slope – which may question its alluvial/fluvial origin. Nevertheless, this minerogenic deposit has the potential to preserve pollen, and thus add to the potential land-use history record.

Basal colluvium (Unit 4)
A lower yellowish brown to reddish brown silt loam with rare medium-sized stones, becoming dark yellowish brown and sandier with depth, was considered to be colluvium and largely a result of mass movement. It may even be Pleistocene Head, and is discussed above. It overlies sand deposits (Unit 5).

Sand (Unit 5)
Sand was encountered in two locations, T1/2 and T2/3, higher on the footslope. These were dark, manganese-stained sand, and a greenish yellow wet sand, probably representing local sand blow and dunes against the footslope, or Pleistocene sand deposits (cf. Brean Down; ApSimon *et al.* 1961; Bell 1990) and more locally on the Lizard Peninsula (Antoine *et al.* 2003; Catt & Staines 1982; Bell & Brown 2008).

Unallocated deposits
These are present especially in T1/2, T1/4, T1/5 and T3/18 (Figs 2.6 & 2.7). Some of these may relate to made ground, especially in T1/1 and T1/2.

Palaeo-environmental evidence

Apart from the geoarchaeological record obtained in the field and enhanced by the more detailed logging of core T1/3, T15 and T211, the undisturbed samples also provided the opportunity to subsample for palaeo-environmental proxies such as pollen and diatoms, from which local land-use histories can be obtained (see Chapter 6).

Radiocarbon

In order for the geoarchaeological sequences and any palaeo-environmental sequence to complement usefully the archaeological record, it is essential to provide a chronology against which to compare with the archaeological narrative. Consequently, samples of water-logged plant remains, and where these were not available, small sediment samples for

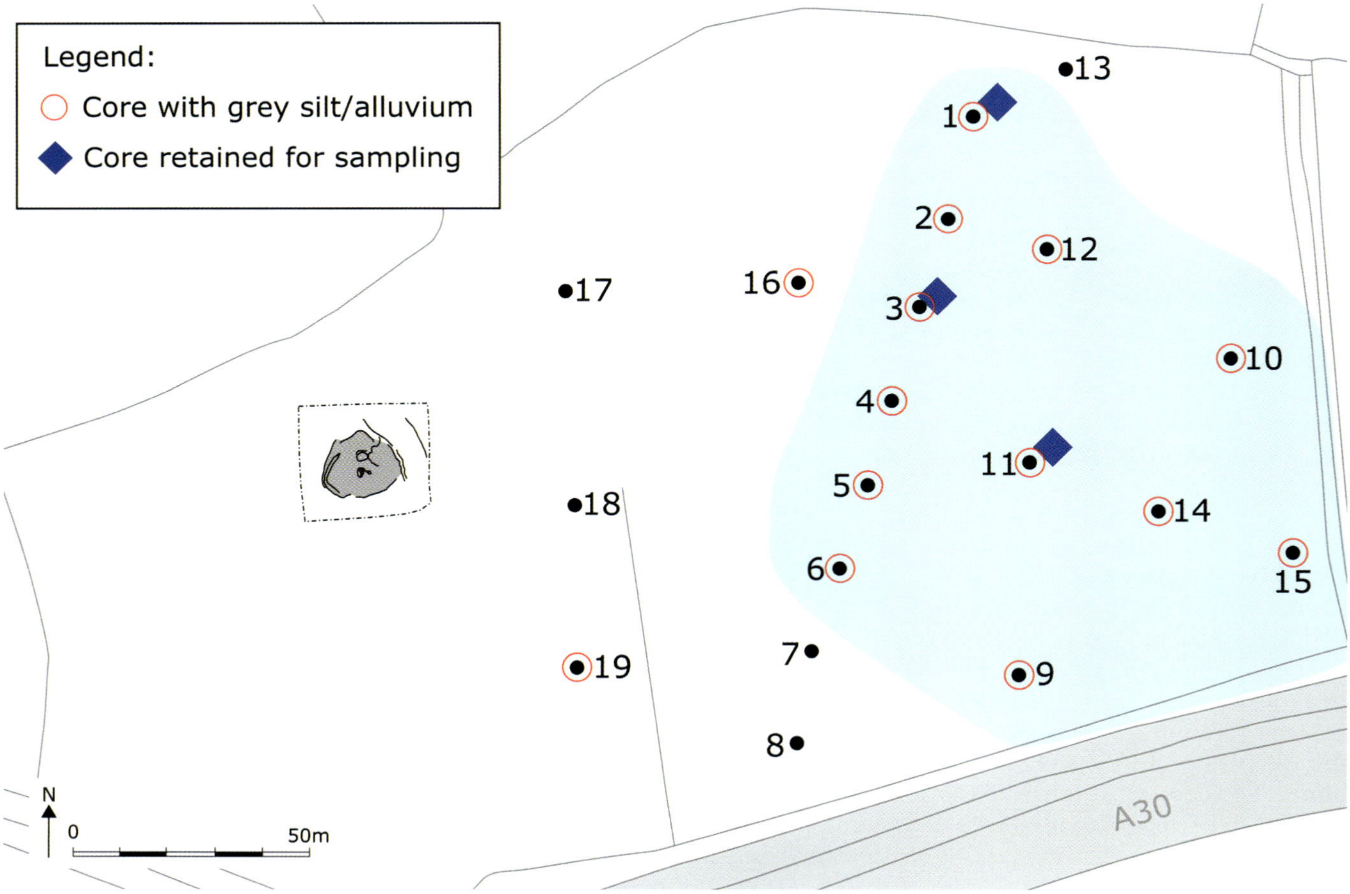

Figure 2.7: Occurrence and extent of the 'alluvium' in relation to the sample cores

humin acid were taken. Nine samples were taken. From core T1/3 these comprised a small roundwood twig at the top of deposits (@ 114 cm), a humin acid sample from the contact/boundary *within* the thick humose layer (@ 131 cm), and a basal humic acid sample (@ 155 cm). These were complemented by small bulk samples for humin acid dates from the top and bottom of the humose layer in T1/5 at 102 cm and 110 cm respectively. From the longer, but root intruded, sequences in T2/11 two samples of plant matter (@178 cm × 2) and two for humin acids (@180 cm and 196 cm) were taken. These results are reported in Chapter 6; see also Table 6.2.

Core	*Depth cm*	*Unit*	*Find description*
T1/3	11	Topsoil	White glazed pottery
T1/3	68	0 Made Ground	Glass (bottle)
T1/7	130	0 Made ground	Willow pattern pottery
T1/7	130	0 Made ground	Glass vessel
T2/9	161	0 Made ground	Glass (bottle)
T2/9	165	0 Made ground	19th/20th century ink pot
T2/11	95	0 Made ground	Slate cut 44 × 70 mm
15	98	0 Made ground	Willow pattern pottery × 2
T1/4	180	3 Alluvium	White glazed porcelain

Table 2.3: Finds recovered from cores

Artefacts from the cores

During the fieldwork, the surface of the cores was carefully cleaned to facilitate descriptions (before they were returned to the borehole). During the preparation and description of the cores a number of artefacts were noticed (see logs; Appendix 2.1), and seven of these were retained (Table 2.3). Unsurprisingly, they mostly came from made ground, and in one case (T1/4), the upper portion of the alluvium immediately beneath recognisable made ground. The artefacts were predominantly of late 19th to 21st century date and included willow pattern pottery, white porcelain, bottle and fine vessel glass, cut slate, and a complete small stoneware 19th/20th century ink pot, probably of Victorian or later date (as these artefacts disappear around about the time of the First World War; Lorraine Mepham, pers. comm. 30/11/18).

The three radiocarbon dates (Chapter 7) provide an outline chronological framework for the sediments and deposit model. Although undated, we assume the basal colluvium (Unit 4) is Pleistocene or very early Holocene in date. There is no obvious early Holocene event to cause colluviation, and these deposits may be very broadly allied with some of the lower slope deposits at, for instance, Brean Down (Bell 1990).

The grey silts (aka 'alluvium') seem to be water-sorted, and their character suggests flowing water in the shallow valley dating to the early Holocene – that is, the Mesolithic period, and pre-dating the basal humose deposit 2.1 at 155 m which produced a radiocarbon date

Figure 2.8: Geoarchaeology of the site; profile through the site showing the stratigraphy as observed in the Southwest Archaeology evaluation. Trenches and test pits, relative to the height of the profiles from Eastern Green (Southwest Archaeology forthcoming); Chyandour (James & Guttman 1992) and Marazion Marsh (Healy 1995;1999a) (vertical scale exaggerated for clarity). (From Southwest Archaeology 2018, fig. 3)

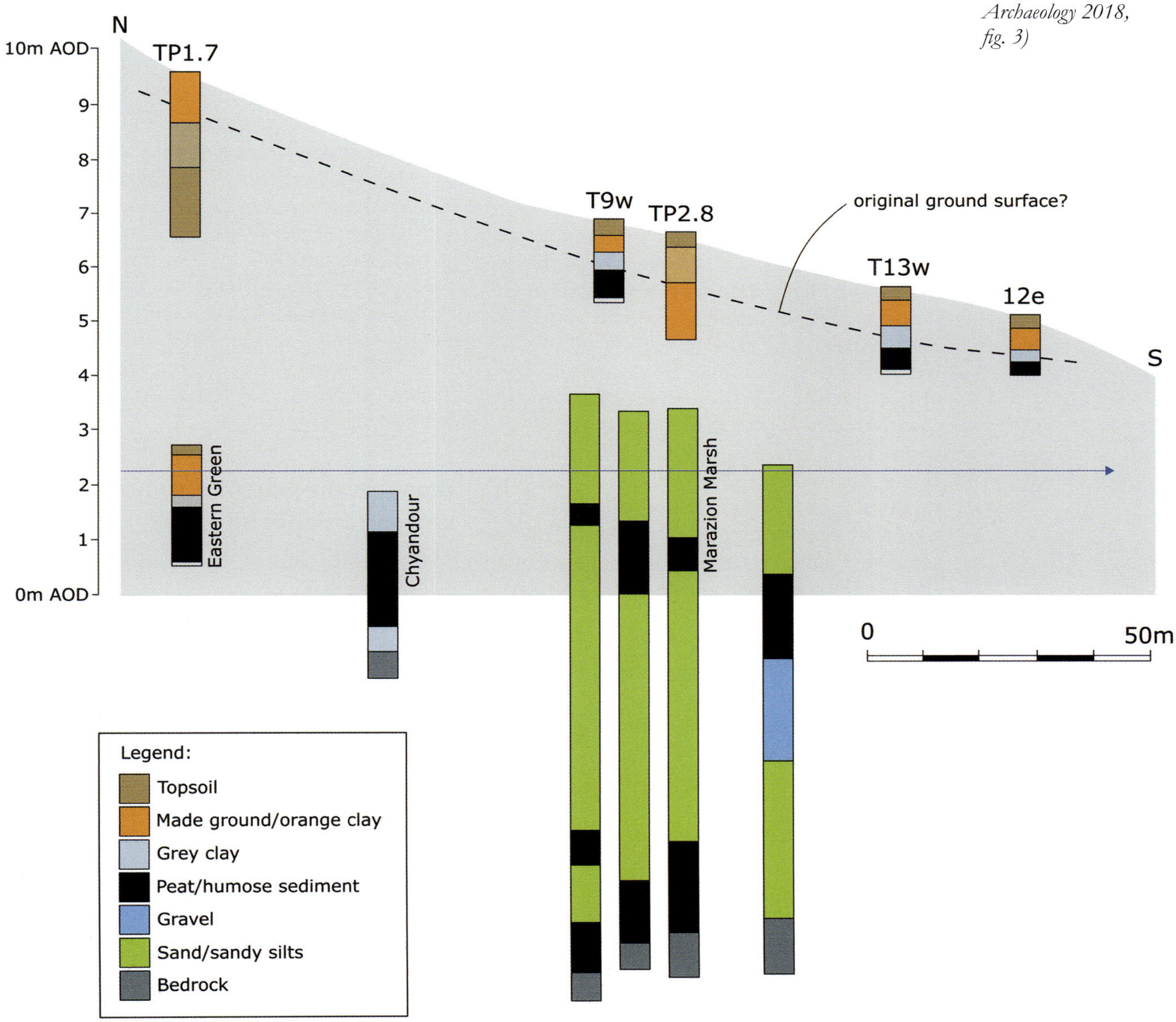

Figure 2.9: The barrow site prior to excavation. Note the position of the barrow at the base of the slope which rises to the north

of result 4230–4060 cal BC (SUERC-87224, 5321±23 BP; see Chapter 7). These deposits suggest a low-energy spring issuing from the base of the slope of the Moor. A phase of drying and reduction in the water flow is indicated by the humose deposits. This suggests a move from wet environments to damp terrestrial ones with stands of reeds (*Phragmites*). They were accumulating through the Chalcolithic period (sediments dated at 1.31 m dated to 2580–2460 cal BC; 4006±27 BP, SUERC-96372) and Bronze Age. The upper portion of these may possibly be equated to activity associated with the barrow's construction and use (see pollen, Chapter 6). This in turn was sealed by Holocene colluvium suggesting later clearance and tillage on the adjacent drier slopes towards the Moor, either associated with the Early Bronze Age barrow and Late Bronze Age activity associated with it, or with post-barrow activity.

It is clear that, contrary to previous suggestions (Southwest Archaeology 2018), that the humose deposits here are not related to relative sea-level as those at Marazion Marsh, Chyandour and Mount's Bay area are; they occur at too high an altitude and are a result of the local topographical conditions (see Fig. 2.8). Humose deposits have formed in a shallow spring valley in the foot of the steep Moor. Changing groundwater conditions, and the build-up of sediment, filled the shallow valley with colluvium and led to the creation of an essentially dry and terrestrial landscape. Colluviation occurred, we suggest, in the Late Bronze Age, probably after the barrow use. It is, therefore, appealing to relate the later period of humose sediment deposition to the period when the barrow was constructed, as deposit represents sparkling fresh spring water trickling as small seasonal stream issuing from the base of the slope. Form here the area looked over both the coast and the area of Marazion Marsh with brackish (and only later fresh) water. This is discussed in Chapters 9 and 10.

2. Results from the barrow excavation

Andy M. Jones and Anna Lawson-Jones

The results from the excavation of the Penzance Heliport barrow are presented here by feature and in stratigraphic sequence. The barrow was excavated by quadrant (Figs 2.10 & 2.11) with a numerically linked block of numbers for each quadrant. For the purposes of this publication the numbering system from the excavation is used but has been simplified and one context number has been retained. For example, the alluvial deposit, which was numbered separately in each quadrant as 103, 206, 304 and 415, is solely referred to as 103 in the following text. Full descriptions of the excavation methodology and site contexts are given in the project archive report (Lawson-Jones 2019). The following section will provide the results in stratigraphical order from bottom to top.

Beneath the barrow: alluvial silt and sand deposits

The oval-shaped barrow appears to have been deliberately positioned on a low-lying rise of natural alluvium 103, which had been laid down over sand blow/possible dune deposits of dark orange sand and small gravel (Fig. 2.12). Environmental recording beyond the barrow (as described above and in Chapter 6) identified similar deposits at two locations and suggested the presence of dunes and blown sand deposits. Deposits of sand 410 were also recorded below the barrow in the eastern quadrant 4. This layer was found beneath pit 412 under a 0.09 m surviving depth of alluvium 103. Given that the pit reached a depth of 0.68 m, this means that the overall thickness of the alluvium above the deposits of sand 410, at least at this point, was 0.77 m.

Figure 2.10: Plan of the barrow showing the location of the quadrants and the position of the drawn sections

The alluvium in the immediate area of the barrow was off-white to very pale grey with some orange and yellow patches. The pale alluvium beneath the barrow would have stood out clearly against the wider expanse of darker, heavy, overlying clay (Fig. 2.12). The notably light colour of the alluvial 'natural' beneath the mound may have been intensified by heating, as suggested by the presence of near black charcoal-rich inner mound material 200, which contained small heat fractured stones (see below; Fig. 2.13).

Beyond the confines of the barrow and mound, to the north, west and east, was a deposit of darker and denser clay. Results from the geoarchaeological auguring results (Chapter 6) suggest that this clay equates with the Holocene colluvium resulting from earlier human activity, for example as a consequence of land clearance and tillage further upslope.

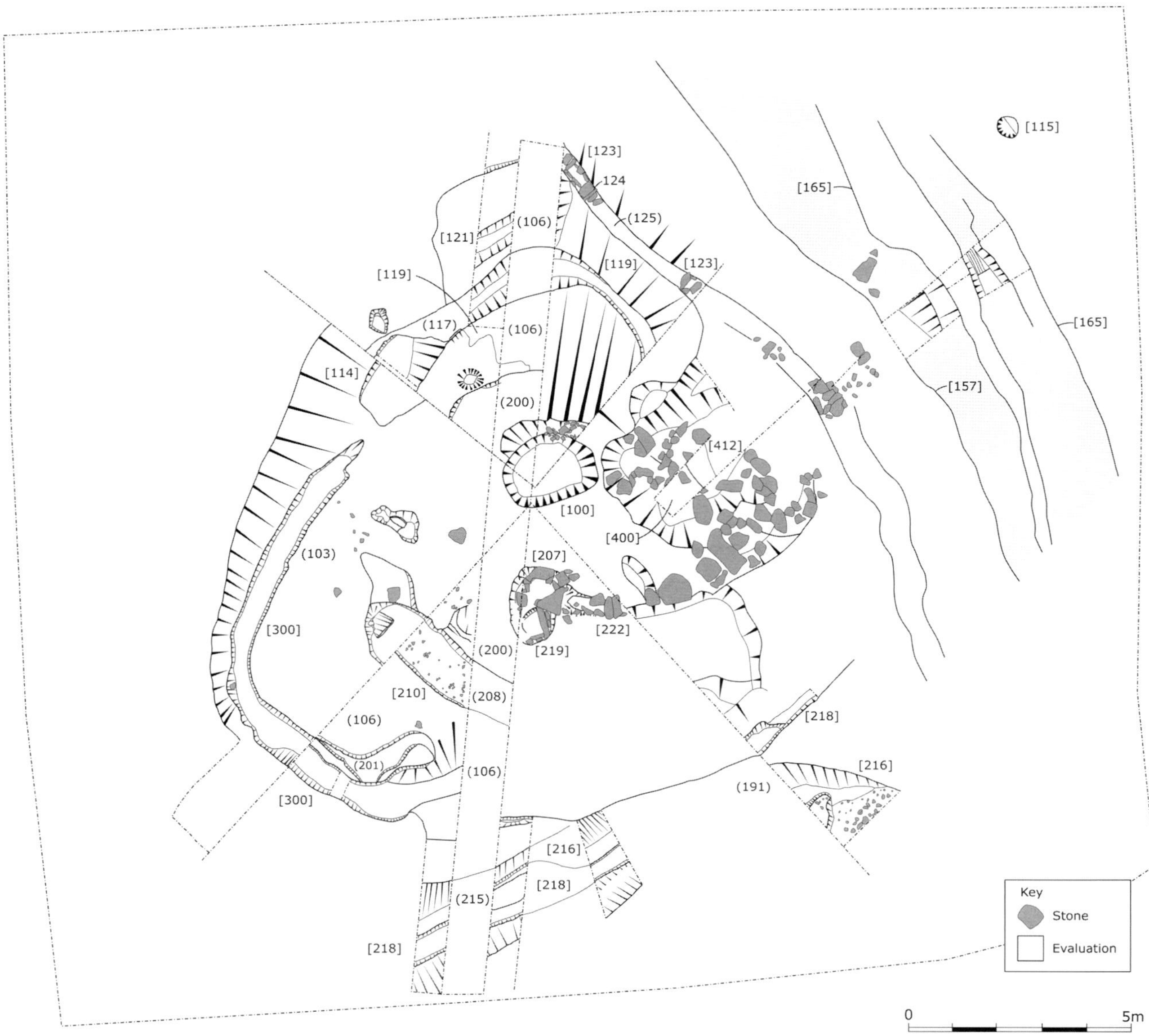

Figure 2.11: Plan of the barrow showing the excavated features and contexts

The topsoil certainly deepened towards the south, and particularly the south-eastern corner of the site. This indicates that the barrow stood at a junction just below the 10 m OD contour, at the foot of a slope which rose up to the north and was situated above the lower lying ground to the south.

Encircling the barrow: barrow ditch 300 and bank 201

The barrow ditch which encircled the mound was first revealed by the geophysical survey and was partially excavated during the evaluation stage (AOC 2017; Southwest Archaeology 2018). During excavations in 2019 it also became apparent that there was an internal bank and the barrow site is likely to have been an unmounded enclosure barrow in its primary phase.

The barrow ditch

Ditch 300 was found to have a variable 0.55 m to 0.9 m width and a depth of 0.22 m (Figs 2.10, 2.11, 2.13 & 2.22). As it swung north and east its base rose and the sides splayed. A single fill 301 was recorded in the most north-westerly slot as a dark grey to off-white plastic clay. The

Figure 2.12: The barrow viewed from the air and from the south. Note the pale colour of the underlying alluvium 103 contrasted with the dark overlying mound 200

two remaining slots in the western quadrant 3 produced upper fill 303, which was mid-greyish white plastic silty clay with frequent angular stones, and a less stony lower fill 302. A sample of *Corylus* charcoal taken from ditch 300 during the evaluation produced a later Early Bronze Age radiocarbon determination, SUERC-78029, 3391±29 BP, 1750–1630 cal BC (Southwest Archaeology 2018, 26).

In the southern quadrant 2 the upper fill 213 was mid-dark brown compact silty clay. The lower fill 214 was patchy mid-grey clay with frequent small angular stones and charcoal flecking. Fill 214 also contained 2 waterworn smoothed pebbles SF 1 of flint/chert and SF 2 of quartz, which were recorded as lying on the base of the ditch cut. These were the only pebbles noted from the ditch fill and as such their similar positioning may be significant (Chapter 13). The barrow ditch in both quadrants 2 and 3 was well defined with steep sides and a near flat to slightly concave base. It formed the western side of an apparently irregular oval ditch. The southern quadrant 2 terminal did not appear to have any continuation on into the eastern part of the barrow, quadrant 4.

The northern quadrant, ditch 3 300 terminal may, however, have continued on as ditch 119 in quadrant 1 (Fig. 2.22), although it was not immediately recognised as such in the field because of intervening shallow post-barrow feature 114. Ditch 119 had gentle straight sloping sides with a near flat base, but poor edge definition. It had a variable width, extending up to 1.2 m wide and up to 0.25 m deep. Fill 117 was mid-greyish brown compact silty clay, with frequent subangular small stones and charcoal, which merged with both fill 104, the fill of pit 114 and the

Figure 2.13: (above) Barrow ditch 300 fully excavated in excavated ditch in quadrant 3 looking north. Note in situ *mound material 200 on the right-hand side of the picture*

Figure 2.14: (right) Cist complex 228 looking west along linear arrangement 222. Note the two large distinctive terminal stones in the foreground. The upper rounded SF 12 may have been deliberately split

outer mound material 106. The fill contained a single flint SF 8, a flake (Chapter 4). The eastern part of ditch 119 became rapidly narrower and more gully-like in character, and appeared increasingly disturbed or altered by the large pits excavated in 2017 (Southwest Archaeology 2018).

The inner bank 201

Running around the internal edge of the ditch in the southern part of the barrow, quadrant 2 was a remnant bank 201 (Figs 2.10, 2.11, 2.20 & 2.23). It was visible as a pale, mixed redeposited clayey deposit of variable width ranging from 0.6 m to 1 m in width. It averaged 0.09 m high and was visible projecting up through the plough-truncated mound material 106. The bank was recorded as a rather lumpy-looking deposit, which appeared to consist of fist-sized handfuls or possibly spadefuls of upcast clay from the inner ditch 300. It is considered likely that this rather ephemeral remnant bank originally ran around the entire inner edge of the ditch. However, any original extension

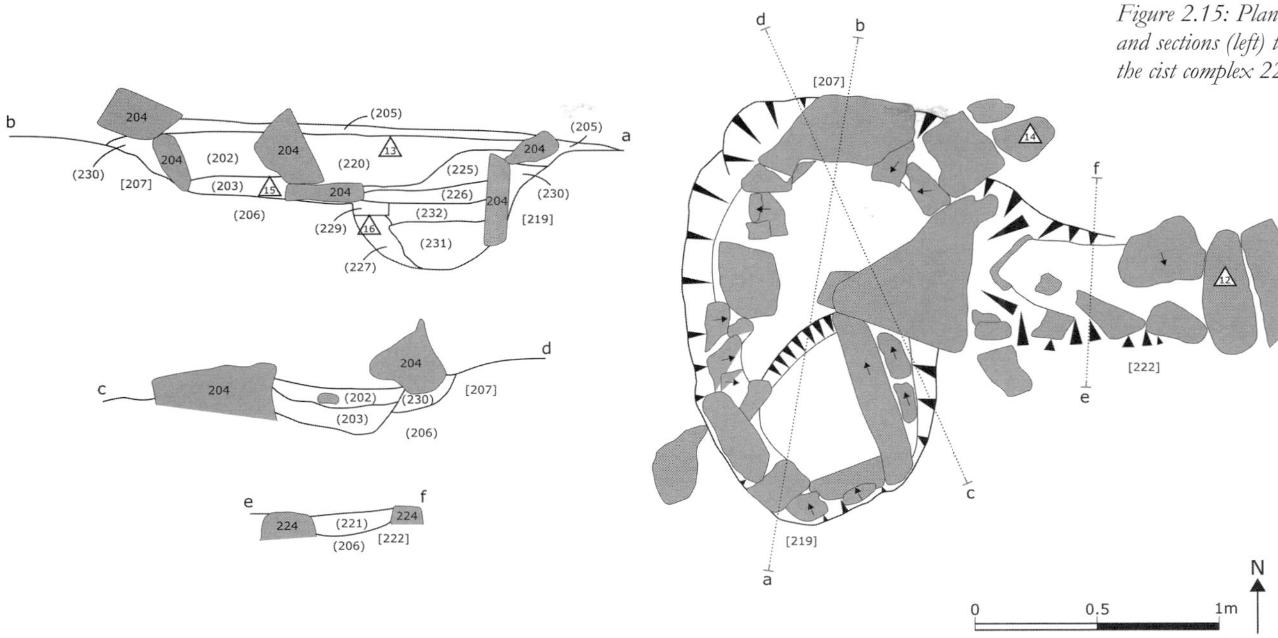

Figure 2.15: Plan (right) and sections (left) through the cist complex 228

of the ditch and bank to form a complete oval circuit will have been destroyed through subsequent activities and natural processes on the site, including pit-related digging, episodic ploughing, and the slumping of barrow contexts due to periodic waterlogging. Despite the disturbance to much of the circuit of the bank 201, it is probable that the bank had originally contained and defined the barrow site, and likely that it predated the construction of the inner mound by several centuries and was contemporary with, and derived from, the digging of the ditch 300.

Figure 2.16: Post excavation view of cist 207 viewed from the east

Below the barrow mound: cist complex 228, stony patches, depression 210 and ?central pit 100

Several features were uncovered beneath the mound, including two small cists of Late Bronze Age date, stony patches and a depression. A large pit 100 was also recorded close to the centre of the site. This pit is of uncertain origin and is likely to have been heavily disturbed or to post-date the barrow. In addition to archaeological features, two undiagnostic flint waste flakes were found below the barrow mound during the evaluation stage (Chapter 4).

Cist complex 228

Cist complex 228 consisted of three main elements: a northern cist 207, an attached southern cist 219, and a short linear extension 222 running east from the junction of the two cists. Stones 204 defined and formed parts of all three and linked the group together in the centre of the barrow. Filling the gap between the mostly tight-fitting stones and the edges of the cut features was deposit 230, a grey brown slightly loamy silty clay. A potentially split stone

Figure 2.17: Cists 207 and 219 after excavation, viewed from the north

SF 12 (Figs 2.10, 2.11, 2.14 & 2.15) was found on the eastern edge of cist 207, along with a few other stones on the western edge of cist 219 and southern edge of 222, which were originally a part of the arrangement of stones 204 (Fig. 2.15) and were subsequently dislodged. It is not, however, certain whether these features were contemporary with one another.

Northern cist 207

Cist 207 (Figs 2.16 & 2.17) was defined by a steep-sided, near-square cut which was lined by selected and carefully positioned/ upright stones 204. Loose brown clay silt 205 was recorded between the highest projecting stones, and is likely to have been a post-cist deposit associated with cist fill settling (or possibly redeposition following the 2017 evaluation). It did, however, contain three pebbles. Of these, one was of quartz and two of flint, which may have been redeposited from prehistoric contexts (Chapter 4). The upright stones beneath appeared largely undisturbed (Fig. 2.17).

Internally the cist measured 0.5 m by 0.4 m in plan and was 0.3 m deep with a flat base. It was cut into alluvial clayey silt 103 and contained two distinct fills. The upper fill 202 was uneven mid greyish brown plastic clayey silt and ash with occasional small stones and charcoal flecks. It had a maximum depth of 0.22 m. The lower fill 203 was dark brownish black, soft, loose and silty, and contained charcoal, which was derived from species which grow on disturbed ground. In common with the mound 200 it also contained oak charcoal and some indeterminate cereal fragments. It is possible that this assemblage derived from a pyre (Chapter 6). The layer was 0.08 m deep and became progressively gritty with depth. A Late Bronze Age copper alloy ingot fragment, SF 15 (Chapter 5, Figs 5.1, 5.2, 5.3, & 5.4; Appendix 1), which appeared to have been wrapped in an organic material, was found at its base, just above the flat alluvial clayey silt base. A sherd of Beaker pottery, the surface of which has been charred, was also recovered from fill 203 (Chapter 3). The date of the copper alloy ingot is supported by a Late Bronze Age radiocarbon determination SUERC-47292, 2734±27 BP, 930–810 cal BC, which was obtained on *Ulex* charcoal from the fill (Chapter 7).

Separating cist 207 from southern cist 219 was an upright dividing stone set above a flat stone slab, which lay on the base of cist 207. These two stones were excavated as was a potentially shaped stone SF 14, which was originally positioned on the north-eastern upper edge of 207.

Southern cist 219

Cist 219 (Figs 2.10, 2.11, 2.14 & 2.18) was defined by a steep-sided, near-square cut which again was lined by selected and carefully positioned stones 204. As with cist 207 there was a thin uppermost spread probably relating to late disturbance 205. The cist measured 0.9 m by 0.8 m internally and was 0.57 m deep. It had a flat base and concave sides cut into the underlying alluvial clayey silt 206. The cist contained eight fills (see Fig. 2.15).

Running parallel with the most obviously positioned upright stone slab forming the eastern edge of 219 was the distinctive wedge of mid-brownish yellow clay 224, which overlay 220 on this side of the cist. It was 0.05 m to 0.1 m thick and may have formed part of a clay capping for the cist. It is possible that an equivalent western spread of context 224 was removed in 2017, but equally, had it been present, it could have been removed in antiquity or during past onsite activity (see below).

Beneath 224 was fill 220, a dark greyish black friable clay silt with small stones, frequent charcoal flecks and one larger burnt piece of root. It was uncertain in the field whether the root was *in situ* or intrusive. Underlying 220 was fill 225 which had a stepped profile, rising up from 0.16 m deep on the south-west to 0.05 m in the north-east. It was dark brown-grey compact but soft, slightly gritty silty clay.

Beneath was black, soft ashy (possibly organic), stone-free silt 226. This ran across the entirety of the cist with a uniform depth of 0.08 m. It overlay light yellowish cream, compact clay 229 and dark brownish grey silty clay 232. Fill 226 contained six quartzite pebbles SF 38 (Chapter 4), which are likely to have been deliberately introduced into the cist. Clay 229 formed a wedge in the northern part of the cist, level with the step separating cist 219 from higher northern cist 207. Its abrupt southern edge suggested either a removed stone or a cut edge possibly equating with the southern edge of lower 227. Silty clay 232 was identical to 227. Both fills were dark brownish grey silty clay with occasional charcoal flecks. Context 232 ran beneath 226 and was 0.08 m deep, while 227 ran up the southern, eastern and western sides of the cist from the base. It was 0.15 m wide and extended upwards for approximately 0.22 m. It contained small, smooth dark pebble SF 16, which noticeably becomes blood red in colour when wet (Chapter 4). Contained on three sides by 227 was steep-sided deposit 231. This appeared in section to form an intriguing steep-sided basket or pot-like profile, the fill of which was very dark grey to black, fine soft loose silt of possible organic or ashy origin.

Linear component 222

An east to west-running linear feature 222 was attached to cists 207 and 219. It was 1.6 m long, 0.33 m wide and 0.1 m deep. It was partially lined with shallowly inclined stones (Figs 2.14 & 2.15). The eastern end was marked by two larger north to south-aligned stones (part of 204), including the split cobble SF 12. This was a very distinctive piece of stone, with two near flat faces caused by having had both sides split away.

Stony patches below mound 200

Between the inner charcoal-rich mound 200 (see below) and the underlying pale alluvium 103 in the northern quadrant 1 and the southern quadrant 2 were patches of stones that had been pushed down into the underlying alluvium. A number of these stones were found to have been affected by heat, showing signs of discolouration and limited fracturing. Nothing artefactual was found in association with the stones. However, given the charcoal-rich overlying mound material 200, it was considered likely that the stones were connected with the formation of the mound, which may have formed through either a single period of burning (for example, as a pyre), or perhaps episodic fires on the barrow site.

Figure 2.18: Cist 219 half excavated, viewed from the west

Depression 210

On the western side of the southern part of the barrow in quadrant 2 was a shallow depression or a possible, poorly-defined, ditch-like feature 210. This appeared to be infilled by the charcoal-rich mound material 200 located above it, and the ground beneath it was stony (Fig. 2.19). The upper deposit within the

Figure 2.19: The excavated slot through depression 210. Note similarity of fill with mound material and the stoniness beneath the depression

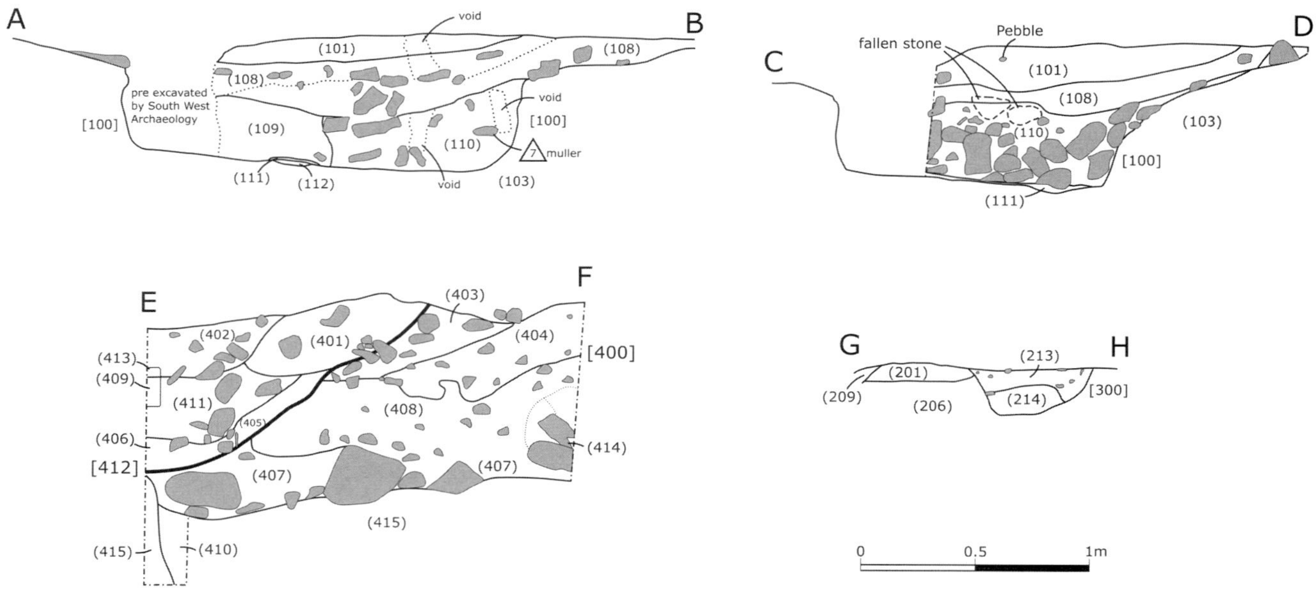

Figure 2.20: Sections through excavated pits. Pit 100, south-east facing section (left) and south-east facing section (right). Bottom South-east facing section through pits 400 and 412 (left) and north-west facing section through ditch 300 facing (right)

depression was a black charcoal-rich layer 208, which sealed a brownish black charcoal-rich silt deposit 211. Contexts 200 and 208 were in fact near identical and only barely separable.

Central pit 100

Pit 100 was a large central feature, with a rounded-rectangular plan, measuring approximately 1.8 m by 1.6 m and 0.65 m deep. It had very steep sides, a near-flat base and an eroded upper edge. The pit was largely excavated during the evaluation phase (Southwest Archaeology 2018) and it was recorded as containing a number of rapidly deposited and/or slumped deposits, including stones, clay, silt and charcoal bands. In 2018 the section was redrawn and allocated context numbers 10, 108, 109, 110, 111 and 112 (see Lawson-Jones 2019). This same basic sequence of fills was again recorded when the section was cut back in line with the main 2018 baulk in preparation for sampling (Figs 2.20 & 2.21).

The upper fill 101 consisted of a series of thin bands and lenses of redeposited silt, clay and powdery charcoal which clearly marked the final silting up of the backfilled pit. It was up to 0.15 m deep. Fill 108 was a very clear, 0.14 m deep band of soft, black, slightly greasy charcoal-powder-rich silt. The bulkiest deposit, fill 110, was an apparently rapidly dumped deposit, up to 0.4 m deep. It consisted of 80 per cent angular stones within mid-grey loose silty/gritty clay. There were few artefacts, although amongst the angular stones was a waterworn cobble muller SF 7 of Bronze Age type, a small broken/used cobble with traces of micropolish on its surface, a white quartzite pebble SF 6 and a broken pebble split by heat (Chapters 3 and 4). Initially the stones in 110 looked like they had been partially placed against the northern edge of the pit, but on further investigation this was found not to be the case. Interestingly, stones were also present in pit 400, but aside from the cist complex 228, not elsewhere on site. Their presence might suggest that a further cist complex/structure, platform or cairn had been present in the middle of the site, which had been displaced by the digging of the pits. This, however, is conjectural and the reason for the stones' presence on the site is uncertain. At the base of the pit was a 0.06 m deep layer of dark orange gritty/sandy silt 111, which in places overlay a basal 0.05 m deep black silty charcoal-rich deposit 112.

It is likely that the pit was opened and then rapidly backfilled with surrounding stones and upcast material. This is suggested by the character of the alluvial natural 103 into which the pit was cut; the absence of waterborne silt in the pit's bottom; the lack of erosion to the pit sides; and the fact that much of the pit was filled by a bulk deposit.

The pit's central location within the centre of the barrow suggests that it is of Bronze Age date; the original fieldwork report by Southwest Archaeology (2018) stated as much, and argued that it post-dated the construction of the barrow. An earlier Middle Bronze Age radiocarbon date SUERC-78031, 3169±29 BP, 1500–1400 cal BC was obtained on *Alnus* charcoal from context 111, a lower fill of the pit (*ibid.*, 26; Chapter 7), and a Bronze Age stone muller SF 7 was found in the pit. The pit fills, however, looked very mixed and the pit's stratigraphical relationship with the barrow mound, now dated to the Late Bronze Age (see below), lends support to the idea that the pit may have cut the mound. Indeed, it is probable that, in common with the other larger pits in the north-eastern part of the site (pits 400 and 412, below), the central pit is of post-medieval date, and that the charcoal on which the radiocarbon determination was obtained and the muller represent residual, redeposited material associated with a Middle Bronze Age phase of activity. If this interpretation is correct then the pit may be an undated clay extraction pit, or even an undocumented exploratory excavation into the remnant mound. Either way, it post-dates the construction of the barrow, by centuries, if not millennia.

The barrow mound

The mound was identified as comprising two components, an inner charcoal-rich black circuit layer 200 and an outer stony grey-brown deposit 106 (Fig. 2.22), which were both visually distinct from the surrounding clay.

Figure 2.21: Central pit 100 half excavated and in section. The jumble of stones can clearly be seen beneath the upper fills

Outer stony mound 106

The outer mound material was numbered 106. It was a heaped up deposit of grey brown slightly silty clay up to 0.25 m thick with angular, possibly sorted 'fist' sized stones which averaged 0.05 m to 0.08 m in size. The stony mound deposit varied slightly across the barrow area and had been spread by ploughing. It had also been cut and disturbed by later pit-related activity on the eastern side of the barrow (as discussed below). Additional damage and potential spreading associated with digging of three ditched field boundaries on the immediate southern and eastern sides of the barrow will also have contributed to the mound's spread beyond the ditch circuit (Lawson-Jones 2019). No artefacts were recovered from the outer mound which meant

Figure 2.22: East facing section across the barrow showing: ditch 218, ditch 216, 106, 200, cist complex 228 (top), pit 100, ditch 119 (a part of ditch 300), and ditch 123 (bottom)

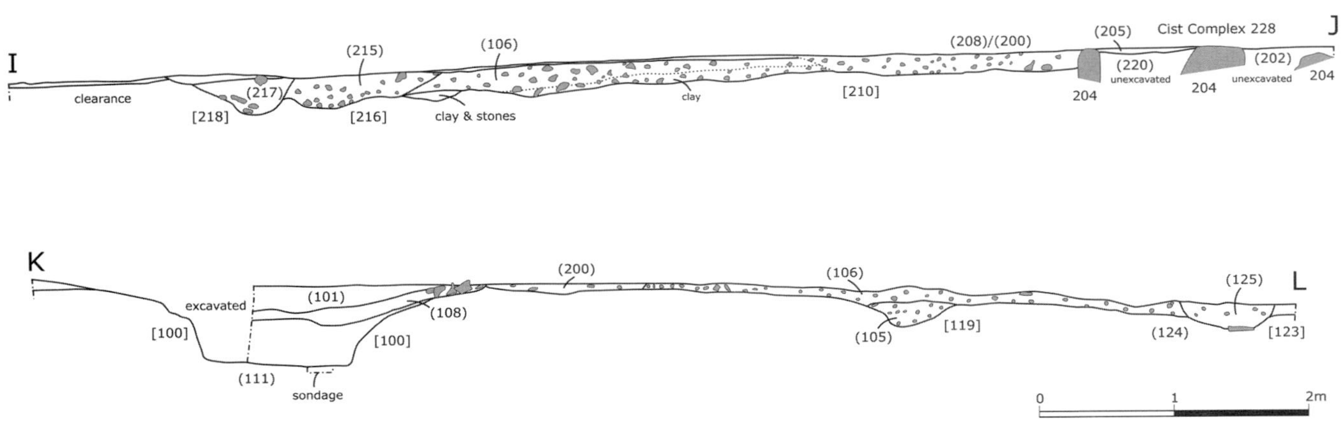

Figure 2.23: Looking north-east across quadrant 2 prior to excavation, showing inner black mound material 200 and outer stony mound material 106 (foreground). Note that the pale band separating the black and the brown on the left of the photograph is the inner bank (201)

that it is not securely dated beyond a broadly Bronze Age assignation (Fig. 2.22 and 2.23).

Inner charcoal-rich mound 200

The inner barrow mound 200 was a striking looking, near black, patchy clayey silt with small angular stones (Figs 2.12, 2.19, 2.22, 2.24 & 2.25). It was a relatively thin deposit, surviving to a thickness of up to 0.15 m. The original height of the mound is, however, uncertain as it had clearly been waterlogged at times and is likely to have been truncated by agricultural activity. Mound 200 overlay the alluvial layer 103 before merging with, and probably partially overlying, the inner edge of the peripheral brown mound material (context 106).

Much of the mound 200 comprised black powdery charcoal, as well as frequent pieces of twigs and sticks; the organic component of some of the latter had been partially replaced by mineralisation. This mineralisation is likely to reflect frequent waterlogging in the period since the barrow was constructed (Lawson-Jones 2019). The charcoal assemblage included gorse, oak and willow, which may have been derived from small scrubby trees (Chapter 7), as well as a small quantity of charred cereal grains and grasses. The assemblage would be consistent with pyre material and, with the exception of the willow, is not dissimilar to the charcoal from cist 207 (Chapter 6). The deposit (context 200) also contained heat-fractured stones.

A very small fragment of unidentified burnt bone was recovered from context 200 but it was not possible to determine whether this was human or animal. No artefacts were identified. A radiocarbon determination, SUERC-47293, 2714±27 BP, 910–810 cal BC, was obtained on *Ulex* charcoal from the mound material. This is Late Bronze Age in date and near-contemporary with the determination from cist 207, and as such it may have been derived from an associated event or events. Given that the deposit was extremely charcoal-rich, and the charcoal is vitreous and brittle, the temperature of the fire must have been high.

Figure 2.24: Quadrant 2 prior to excavation, showing inner black mound material 200 and outer mound 106. Note that the stones of the central cist complex 228 are emerging in the section (upper left-hand side of the picture)

This is supported by the fact that the stones under mound 200 also showed signs of heating. It therefore seems likely that, rather than representing material deposited onto the site from elsewhere, the mound was actually produced by one or more *in situ* burning event/s within the barrow site.

Beyond the barrow mound: ditch 216 and later ditch 218

Three sections were dug through a double-ditch alignment 216/218 at the extreme southern end of quadrant 2. The east-facing baulk section (Figs 2.14 & 2.22) clearly shows that ditch 218 cut, and thereby post-dates, ditch 216.

Ditch 216

The outer ditch 216, like the inner ditch 218 (Figs. 2.10, 2.11 & 2.22), is indicated on the geophysical survey; however, unlike the inner ditch, which was clearly curvilinear and appeared to contain and define the barrow, it did not appear concentric with it; no evidence could be seen for ditch 216 running around the western side of the site, and it did not appear within the quadrants investigated by Southwest Archaeology (quadrants 3 and 4).

The depth of ditch 216 varied from 0.23 m to 0.4 m and the maximum width was 1.5 m. It had shallow, nearly straight sides and an undulating base. Its dark brown clay/silt fill 215 included frequent angular stones, and was very similar to outer mound context 106, which is likely to have slumped into the ditch from the north when it was still open. The fill 215 produced a worked flint (SF 5) and two smoothed pebbles, one of quartz (SF 3) and another grey coloured (SF 4), from the base of the ditch (Chapter 4). Interestingly, this mirrors the position of pebbles found within the inner barrow ditch fill and is therefore potentially significant.

Ditch 218

The later inner ditch 218 may represent a recutting of 216. It had a stepped southern edge and moderately steep, straight northern edge with a nearly flat base (Figs 2.10, 2.11 & 2.22). The cut was clearest below the slumping and/or plough-spread mound material 106. The ditch fill 217 was a variable mid-brown redeposited clay with occasional stones. The stones were notably larger than those recorded in ditch 218 or mound material 106. They are most likely to represent stone from the former flanking boundary bank.

The date of these ditches is uncertain and they need not be contemporary with one another or with the barrow. Ditch 216 was initially interpreted as an outer barrow ditch and the artefacts might support this hypothesis, but this is uncertain and it is possible that it could belong to the east to west running field boundary, which had been shown on the earlier geophysical survey (AOC Archaeology 2017). Likewise, ditch 218 could be associated with the barrow as it appears to be concentric with the barrow. Alternatively, it could be a much later boundary, merely running around the edge of an existing mound.

Disturbing the barrow: pits 400, 412, ditch 121 and unstratified artefacts

Two large pits, initially thought to be associated with the barrow, were found to post-date it by several centuries. In addition a number of potentially prehistoric artefacts were recovered from the post-barrow topsoil. These are suggestive of later disturbance to prehistoric, potentially barrow-associated contexts.

Pits 400 and 412

Pits 400 and 412 were located in the north-eastern part of the barrow and largely excavated in 2017, when they were recorded as containing some particularly large stones (Southwest Archaeology 2018). They formed part of a larger group of intercutting pits extending beyond the barrow which contained rapidly dumped stones, mixed clay, rubble deposits and some burnt or charcoal-rich deposits. As with pit 100, pits 400 and 412 both revealed evidence for rapid infilling and minimal, if any, basal silting. This suggests that the pits, despite their large size, were only open for a very short time before they were backfilled.

Both pits were covered by post-infilling layers. A series of four dumped deposits were recorded dropping down in turn from west to east across the top of both pits. These appeared to represent patchy levelling. Overlying pit 400 were deposit 404, a mixture of black and mid-grey compact silty/gritty clay with stones, and 403, a dark blackish grey compact silty clay, while overlying pit 412 were deposits 401, dark black to grey compact silty clay loam, and 402, dark grey to black compact silty clay with powdery charcoal. These four deposits appeared broadly contemporary, post-dating the backfilling of both pits.

Pit 412

Pit 412 contained deposits 411, 405 and 406 (Fig. 2.20). The uppermost bulk deposit 411 was 0.3 m deep mid-brownish grey silty clay with many angular stones and some charcoal flecking. Running up the western side of the cut and merging with the fill basal 406 was layer 405. Deposit 405 was a 0.1 m deep, dark friable gritty tip-line, which sloped down from west to east and contained dark gritty heat-fractured stone. The basal fill 406 was a 0.13 m deep mid-dark grey silty grit and stone deposit. The apparent amassing and possible rearrangement of pushed-in stones from the western side of pit 400 may indicate that these were derived from a destroyed earlier feature, such as a cist or a cairn. However, as with the stones in pit 100 (see above), it is impossible to determine whether this is the case.

Visible in the baulk were deposits 413 and 409, which may represent either a continuation of pit 400, or perhaps a different pit. Fill 413 was a thin, 0.03 m to 0.05 m deep, black charcoal-rich band overlying dense mid-grey sticky clay 409. The clay was 0.1 m deep and extended into the sampled section for 0.05 m from the northern adjoining baulk, as did 413.

Pit 400

Pit 400 contained fills 408, 414 and 407. A large dump of pale redeposited clay 408 made up much of its fill. This was overlain by levelling deposits 403 and 404. Large tumbled stones 414 underlay 408 and sloped down into the pit from the west (Figs 2.11 & 2.20). The basal pit fill 407 was mid-grey to yellow silty clay with angular stones and occasional charcoal. It was a wet deposit with variable hard and soft silty clay lumps between the stones. It had formed around a particularly large stone, positioned between the bases of pit 400 and 412. The stone was removed prior to the photograph being taken, but was recorded in the drawn section (Fig. 2.20).

There were few artefacts from the pits. A flint waste flake, thought to be residual, was recovered from pit 400 (Chapter 4) and the basal fill produced a Middle Bronze Age radiocarbon determination SUERC-78030, 3081±29 BP, 1420–1280 cal BC on *Alnus* charcoal (Southwest Archaeology 2018, 27; Chapter 7). However, iron was also found within pit 400, and it seems very unlikely that the pit is prehistoric in date. Reinvestigation of pit 412 in 2018 (Lawson-Jones 2019) revealed that it cut the larger, and thereby earlier pit 400. It is, however, considered likely that these pits do not differ significantly in date. They could represent a single season of activity or a series of short-term events, all of which post-dated the barrow. It is now thought that the two pits were extractive features of much later date than the barrow.

Ditch 121

A shallow northern ditch 121 ran along part of the outer northern edge of the probable inner ditch 119 in the northern quadrant 1. The full extent of this feature is unknown as the ditch cut did not extend into the east-facing baulk section (Figs 2.10 & 2.11). The cut was filled by context 122, a dark charcoal-rich deposit with what appeared to be redeposited mound material 106. The date of the ditch is unknown but it is interpreted as representing later disturbance to the barrow site.

Unstratified prehistoric artefacts

The topsoil, which covered and extended beyond the barrow, was found to contain a number of artefacts which are potentially of prehistoric date and/or were originally associated with the barrow. Disturbance to the site is potentially indicated by three flints, including a thumbnail scraper and a burin found in the topsoil over the barrow, and by pebbles which were also recovered in the topsoil, although the latter could have entered the field at any point in time, and may be related to the use of seaweed as a soil improver (Lawson-Jones, Chapter 4). A few small abraded sherds of undiagnostic prehistoric pottery, all of which were recovered from the evaluation, were unstratified, and all but one were found beyond the barrow site.

Several unstratified stone objects which were thought to have the potential to have been worked were also recorded from the area of the barrow, and were therefore subjected to further study (Chapter 3). These included the following pieces: a partially formed cobble with a damaged area; the end of a longitudinal vein quartz cobble from which had potentially been used on a soft material and been deliberately broken (quadrant 1); a lump of stone, apparently somewhat water-rolled, with a possible deliberate detachment from one end and some other irregularities; a flat triangular cobble, which could have been used as rubber; and two pieces which appeared to be unworked or used.

The ceramic fragments included a gabbroic rimsherd from the topsoil and five small crumbs to the north-west of the ring ditch (Southwest Archaeology 2018; Chapter 3). These sherds may have been derived from Bronze Age vessels, perhaps displaced during the excavation of the large pits or of the later field boundary ditches.

After the barrow: features 114, 123 and 115

Three features, two pits and a stone-lined gully were uncovered in the excavation area which certainly post-dated the barrow and are of post-medieval date.

Feature 114

This was a shallow, rather amorphous pit measuring 1.2 m long and 0.09 m deep. It overlay and may have removed the potential northern portion of the original inner barrow ditch. It contained dark greyish black compact silty clay 104, approximately 50 per cent of which consisted of small, angular, burnt or heat-cracked stone with charcoal. The date of the feature is uncertain; however, it is possible that pit 114 was contemporary with large pits 400 and 412 and potentially with central pit 100. In common with the large pits within the barrow, it certainly post-dated the barrow.

Stone-lined culvert 123

This slightly curved, straight-sided stone-lined feature had a flat base and was aligned north-west to south-east (Figs 2.11 & 2.22). It measured 5 m long by 0.55 m wide and 0.25 m deep. The cut was lined and partially covered with stone slabs 124, and contained a 0.3 m depth of mid-grey brown silty clay 125. It extended further east and west of the excavated section and was seen extending north-west.

Culvert 123 was possibly too elaborate for field drainage, although in the absence of a better interpretation this seems the most likely explanation.

Rubbish pit 115

Pit 115 was located to the north east of the barrow. This small, near circular, steep-sided pit had a conical profile, tapering down to a concave base. In plan it measured 0.6 m by 0.5 m and was 0.4 m deep. It was filled with 116, a dark greyish brown, friable silty clay, which included two glass bottles, charcoal flecks, pebbles and modern metalwork. Pit 115 is easily interpreted as a modern rubbish pit. It represents the latest feature identified on site, post-dating all other phases of activity recorded during the excavations. The geoarchaeological auguring programme identified similarly dated layers associated with Penzance's domestic rubbish disposal and landscaping activity (Chapter 6).

Stratigraphical summary and observations

An interpretative discussion of the barrow will be presented in Chapter 13. However, a summary of the site sequence, and a few observations based on the stratigraphy, are given here. Outline phasing was suggested by both the results from the evaluation and the excavation (Southwest Archaeology 2018; Lawson-Jones 2019). The suggested sequences from the evaluation and initial excavation reporting were broadly comparable and complexity was recognised, although the large pits in the eastern side of the site they were thought by the former to be Bronze Age in date and the charcoal-rich mound and cist complex were only identified by the later fieldwork. In light of the analysis and radiocarbon dating (Chapter 7) it is now possible to refine the stratigraphical sequence a little further and offer a revised chronological order for what has been revealed to be a small but long-lived and complex barrow site.

Given the lack of evidence for a buried soil beneath the mound it seems probable that the ground had been stripped of vegetation. The potential reasons for the choice of the locale for the site are discussed in Chapter 13. However, it is worth noting here that the colluviation suggests that it was probably located on a low knoll at the bottom of an area which had been cleared and potentially cultivated some time before the barrow's construction (Chapter 6). No contemporary settlement has been identified in the immediate vicinity dating to Neolithic or Bronze Age periods, either in terms of structural remains or by proxy in the form of lithic scatters. In other words, the barrow was located on the margins of an occupied landscape, above wetter ground and overlooking St Michael's Mount and the open sea beyond. The clearing of the site and exposing of the alluvium would, however, have created a very visually distinctive white space in an otherwise vegetated and wet landscape (see Chapters 13 and 14).

Following the removal of the soil from the site, the first phase of the barrow seems to have comprised a shallow oval ring dich 300 with a low internal bank 201. The radiocarbon determination from the ditch suggests that this event occurred during the later part of the Early Bronze Age, around the 17th to 18th centuries cal BC. The original form of the barrow appears to have been an enclosure barrow, which is broadly comparable with other sites, such as Davidstow Moor barrow 8 or Caerloggas I (Miles 1975; Christie 1988), which are found elsewhere in Cornwall and are of Early Bronze Age date. In common with several other enclosure barrows and ring cairns both in the south-west region and elsewhere in Britain there was no evidence for the deposition of human remains within the defined space (Miles 1975; Lynch 2000, 133; Jones 2005; Jones & Quinnell 2014). Some caution, however, is needed as subsequent disturbance to the site may have removed any interment or deposits of human remains, and the prevailing acidic soil conditions mean that only cremated bone would have survived.

Comparatively little evidence for activity was found within the enclosed area. Selected pebbles and a chert flake were recovered from the bottom of the ring ditch 300 encircling the barrow (SF 1, SF 2 and SF 8). Pebbles are found in association with several barrow sites in the south west region in a wide range of contexts (eg, Miles 1975; Jones 2009–10; Tilley 2017), and those deposited into the ditch at Penzance appear to have been deliberately selected (Chapters 4 and 13). As such they can be seen as placed deposits associated with the marking of the barrow perimeter (Chapter 13). However, comparatively few internal features were found within the space enclosed by the ring ditch and none can be assigned to the Early Bronze Age (see below).

Hints of a Middle Bronze Age phase are, however, given by radiocarbon determinations from pits 100 and 400 and potentially by one of the artefacts. The radiocarbon determinations are, however, from ambiguous contexts. The earliest date SUERC-78029 was from the central pit 100. This feature also produced SF 7, a stone muller, with traces of grinding, potentially associated with plant fibres, on its surface along with secondary traces of harder percussive use, possibly from striking minerals (Chapter 3). The stone muller would be consistent with a date in the Bronze Age. Mullers are found on Middle Bronze Age and Late Bronze Age settlement sites (eg, Nowakowski 1991; Jones and Taylor 2010, 23; Gossip 2021), and in common with saddle querns they have been found in association with cairns in Cornwall (Christie 1988; Jones 2004–5). Pit 100, however, appeared to contain a jumbled fill and the relationship with the mound was uncertain. It is therefore quite likely that it is a much later feature, or an earlier one that had been heavily disturbed by a subsequent intrusion.

Disturbance to the site is potentially indicated by the discovery of three flints, worked stones and a small number of heavily abraded sherds of prehistoric pottery, which were recorded as being unstratified or coming from the topsoil that clearly post-dated the barrow. Pebbles similar to those from the ditch and cist were also recovered from the topsoil; however, these could have entered the field at any point in time. Pit 400, which produced a Middle Bronze Age determination, is undoubtedly much later and certainly belongs to a phase of disturbance to the site (as discussed below). The presence of structures, or perhaps a central a cairn existing within the barrow ring ditch, is also suggested by the substantial deposits of large stones which were found redeposited in pits 100 and 400. However, the original form of any removed features, along with their phasing within the barrow sequence, has been completely lost.

The low outer mound 106 is certainly prehistoric and stratigraphically predates the subsequent Late Bronze Age mound material 200. The earlier outer mound could, however, be Early, Middle or Late Bronze Age in date. Smaller barrows with low covering mounds are known from the Early Bronze Age in Cornwall and include sites at Davidstow Moor on Bodmin Moor and at Trelowthas, near Probus (Christie 1988; Jones *et al.* 1997). Smaller barrow sites are very typical of the Middle Bronze Age period in southern England and the south-west region (White 1982; Entwistle 2001; Bradley & Fraser 2010; Jones 2012; Caswell & Roberts 2018). In Cornwall, recent re-excavation of a barrow on a headland at Godrevy revealed that a small site covered by a low mound dates to the middle centuries of the 2nd millennium cal BC (Gossip & Jones, forthcoming). In common with the Penzance Heliport barrow there were few finds from the Godrevy barrow, although three fragments of unidentifiable cremated bone were recovered from Godrevy.

Figure 2.25: Mound 200 and ditch 300 under excavation

The next certain phase associated with the Penzance Heliport barrow dates to the Late Bronze Age and comprises the cist complex and the covering charcoal-rich mound. The two cists within the complex were small, and could not have held articulated inhumations. Deposits of disarticulated unburnt bone could have been placed inside the cists; these would not have survived, however, although cremated bone would have done. Currently the latest comparable cists in Cornwall are of later Middle Bronze Age date, for example the recently-dated one found below the rampart at Gunwalloe, with its deposit of cremated bone (Wood 2015). In common with other parts of Britain (eg, Brück 1995; Caswell & Roberts 2018; Johnston 2020, 105–106), formalised later Bronze Age funerary sites of any form are rare both in Cornwall and across the wider south-west peninsula, where only small quantities of bone have been found (eg, Wainwright 1980; Brunning 1997). Currently the small amount of cremated bone from a pit at Quintrell Downs, near Newquay (Jones & Smith 2015) represents the best example for the deposition of human remains in Cornwall.

The larger of the cists 207 did, however, contain what can be described as a structured deposit. This deposit took the form of a wrapped ingot fragment, and a single sherd of Beaker pottery. Both objects can be viewed as fragments of things, *pars pro toto*, and this aspect of the assemblage will be discussed in Chapter 13. By contrast, the small cist 219 was associated with pebbles. The upper fill contained a number of quartzite pebbles which, given the frequent association between barrows and cists in Cornwall with quartz (eg, Dudley 1960; Miles 1975; Jones 2009–10), may well represent deliberately introduced material into the cist. At the bottom of the cist was a single pebble which becomes distinctly blood red in colour when wet. The juxtaposition of selected blood red and white stones is of potential significance and will be discussed in Chapter 13.

The inner charcoal-rich mound 200 was confirmed by radiocarbon dating to be broadly the same date as cist 207. It seems to have been formed as a result of a series of conflagrations close to or on top of the site, as suggested both by the burnt stones on top of the alluvial clay beneath the barrow mound, and by the heat fractured stones in the mound itself. This *in situ* formation of the mound contrasts with the situation at other barrows and cairns in the south west region and in Wales, where charcoal was bought to sites for inclusion within pits or as part of burial-related contexts (eg, Wainwright *et al.* 1979; Lynch 1984; Jones 2016a), thereby representing material which had been deposited onto the site after being burnt elsewhere.

The low knoll of the barrow may have been associated with gatherings of people, and this might also be indicated by the presence of the small quantity of charred cereal grains which were identified both with the mound material 200 and cist 207 (Chapter 6). The original height of the mound is, however, uncertain as it has been subject to waterlogging and drying, which led to mineralisation and degradation of the charcoal. The site has also been subject to later truncation. The surviving height of the inner mound is therefore very unlikely to represent its original height in the Late Bronze Age.

Interestingly, the formation of mounds or heaps of material in the Late Bronze Age is not without parallel. In Cornwall, the cist at Gunwalloe was covered by a substantial midden deposit of broadly the same date as the Penzance barrow mound (Wood 2015, 37) and in Wessex and elsewhere large mounds were formed by depositional events during the Late Bronze Age and Early Iron Age (Lawson 2000; Madgwick & Mulville 2015; Gwilt *et al.* 2016; Waddington *et al.* 2019; Brück 2019, 153; Johnston 2020). The mound at Penzance of course differed in that it was the result of burning event(s) that were sited in a liminal zone between the higher situated dryland and the sea. As was noted in relation to the whiteness of the alluvial clay beneath the barrow, the burning of fires would have created a visual sensory effect with people from the land and sea seeing a column of smoke rising from the coastal strip (eg, Thomas 2007). This aspect of the formation of the site as a mound barrow will be discussed in Chapter 13.

The covering of the barrow by a charcoal-rich mound in the Late Bronze Age represents the last phase of the excavated features that that can, with any reliability, either be stratigraphically or artefactually assigned to the prehistoric period. The outer ditches 216 and 218 may well represent a redefining of the barrow on its southern side and the placing of pebbles in ditch 216 might support this hypothesis (Chapter 4). However, it is also possible that they are later in date and unrelated to the barrow.

The large pits, 400 and 412 in quadrant 4, the north east part of the site, are clearly later in date, despite the Middle Bronze Age radiocarbon determination from pit 400. These features may have been associated with extractive activities, probably in the medieval or later post-medieval periods and the radiocarbon date is likely to have resulted from the redepositing of disturbed material from the damaged part of the barrow.

3

The pottery and worked stone

Henrietta Quinnell and Christina Tsoraki
with petrographic comment by Roger Taylor

The pottery

Henrietta Quinnell with petrographic comment by Roger Taylor

The prehistoric pottery assemblage from Penzance Heliport barrow was exceedingly small and consists of seven sherds; six from the 2017 evaluation and only one from the subsequent 2018 excavation (Southwest Archaeology 2018; Lawson-Jones 2019). All the recovered sherds are small and abraded, and only the sherd from cist 207 was obtained from a securely stratified archaeological context. The pottery from the evaluations was reported on in the evaluation archive report (Southwest Archaeology 2018) and a summary extracted from that report is given in this chapter. A full description of the sherd from the excavation is given below.

The pottery from the 2017 evaluations (extracted from Southwest Archaeology 2018)

Six sherds of prehistoric pottery weighing 27 g were recovered from the evaluation of the barrow. A single sherd, weighing 11 g, came from topsoil. It is a small fragment of rim from a large vessel, oxidised throughout and in a gabbroic fabric. This appears to be from a Bronze Age vessel, but it is not possible to reconstruct its style and form.

The other five sherds, weighing 16 g, were recovered on the outside edge of the enclosing ring ditch on the north-west side of barrow. These five sherds all appear to come from the base of the same vessel, in a fine fabric with iron (limonite) and fine muscovite inclusions; it also contained burnt-out organic inclusions. The limonite indicates that the clays were sourced from a boggy environment, which may also account for the organic inclusions. The muscovite would be derived from a granitic source, and the edge of the Lands' End granites is located *c.* 1.2 km to the north. These factors point to a local source for the base clay. The character of the fabric suggests the sherds are not Iron Age in date, and the absence of gabbroic clay/temper might point to an earlier Bronze Age date. The condition of the pottery and the lack of diagnostic forms make greater precision difficult.

The sherd from the 2018 excavations

A single body sherd weighing 10 g came from 203, the lower fill of cist 207 (Fig. 3.1). The sherd is 6–7 mm thick and is fairly fresh except for one edge which was moderately abraded. It is a reduced dark grey 5YR 4/1 with both surfaces oxidised 5YR 6/2 pinkish grey. Both colours are probably due to burning before breakage.

Figure 3.1: The burnt sherd of Beaker pottery found within cist 207, fill 203

Figure 3.2: Cobble with bevelled end and traces of anvil use (left). Double sided muller SF 7 from pit 100, fill 110, on granite cobble, with depressions on both sides from subsequent anvil or hammerstone use (right). (Photograph: Gary Young)

Petrology: Feldspar – plagioclase as soft white altered sub-rounded and translucent less altered sub-angular grains, some showing traces of twinning, 0.3–0.4 mm. *Amphibole* – probably tremolite/actinolite, translucent colourless elongated grains, 0.2–0.3 mm. *Magnetite* – a scatter of black glossy magnetic grains, 0.2–0.8 mm. *Quartz* – a scatter of transparent to translucent mainly angular and some rounded grains, 0.2–0.4 mm, rarely 1.2 mm. *Rock* – slate, medium grey, sparse tabular fragments, 1.5 mm and 2 mm. *Matrix* – Silty finely sandy with grains of the main tempering minerals with some fine mica. *Comment.* A generally fine-grained gabbroic fabric with a few included slate fragments.

This sherd is unusually fine for a gabbroic fabric and contains non-gabbroic inclusions and possibly clay. While it is impossible to be certain, the most likely ceramic to which this belongs is Beaker, and from its thickness probably domestic Beaker. Beaker gabbroic admixture fabric occurs occasionally, for example fabric 7 in the assemblage from Boscaswell in West Penwith (Quinnell & Taylor 2006).

The worked stone assemblage

Henrietta Quinnell

The very small stonework assemblage consists of 17 pieces of stone; seven from the 2017 evaluation and 10 from the subsequent 2018 excavation (Southwest Archaeology 2018; Lawson-Jones 2019). The descriptions of the stonework assemblage given here should be read in conjunction with the detailed microwear analysis (presented below).

Evaluation trenching 2017

Unstratified in evaluation trench opened up over the barrow. Cobble with bevelled end, 152 × 59 × 44 mm, 567 g (Fig. 3.2, left). Cobble has one bent side forming a good grip. The bevelled end has a double facet, one more worn than the other. There are three small patches of anvil use, two on the illustrated face, one on the other face. If a bevelled pebble of Late Mesolithic date, the cobble used is wider and thicker than the norm (eg, Jones *et al.* 2018; 2019). In addition, four other whole or broken cobbles of different materials without apparent use also unstratified in the barrow evaluation trench, also broken flat cobble from interface between the bottom of the mound and the alluvium 103 in Quadrant 3 and a small flat pebble from the covering topsoil. The assemblage of small pebbles is discussed in Chapter 4 (below).

Excavations in 2018

SF 7, context 110 in pit 100 (Fig. 3.2, right). Muller on flat granite cobble, *c.* 200 × 160 × 65 mm, *c.* 3650 g. Probably no original cobble surface remaining. Both flat surfaces worn smooth, one more than the other. Both also have depressions, suggestive of anvil working. The whole perimeter has been pecked/dressed/used so that this is rough. Tsoraki (below) confirms a two-stage use, first for grinding plant materials and then for processing a medium hard material. Comparable mullers have been found on barrow sites, as well as frequently on Middle and Late Bronze Age settlements (eg, Quinnell 2004–5;

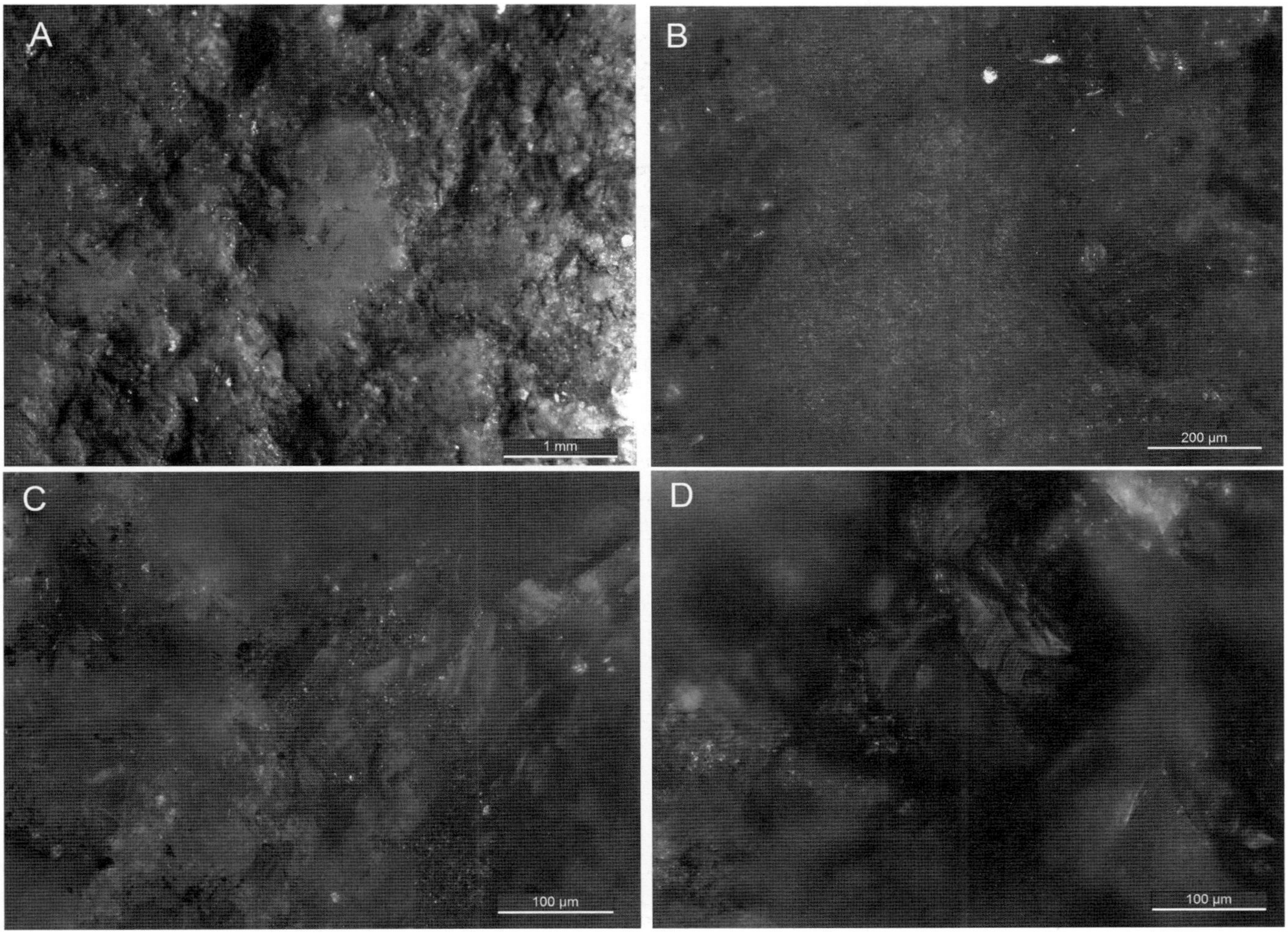

Figure 3.3: Microwear traces on the use-face of grinding tool PZH18 SF7: A) overview of microrelief and levelling of crystal grains, grey-coloured residue is visible on the levelled crystal grain at the centre of the micrograph; B) plant micropolish (100× magnification), C: flat, smooth-textured micropolish (200× magnification), D) conchoidal microfractures (200× magnification)

2010; Jones & Kirkham 2021). It is unclear how far the radiocarbon result 1500–1400 cal BC (3169±29 BP, SUERC-78031) relates to the muller (see Chapter 2, above).

Unstratified: Cobble, 109 × 77 × 37 mm, 343 g. No obvious use wear but a small damaged area. See the microwear analysis, below.

Unstratified Quadrant 1: End of longitudinal cobble of vein quartz, 32+ × 54 × 26 mm, 90 g. Possibly deliberately broken. The flatter parts of the cobble have a natural smooth surface, on one face enhanced by possible use on soft materials. See the microwear analysis, below.

Unstratified: Lump of stone, 190 × 120 × 80 mm, 2000+ g, apparently somewhat water-rolled. Possible deliberate detachment from one end and some other irregularities could be anthropogenic. See the microwear analysis, below.

Unstratified: Flat triangular cobble, 126 × 118 × 36 mm, one side very smooth and could be due to use as a rubber.

Unstratified: Five pieces including, a small vein quartz cobble, a fractured rough cobble and a small cobble all appear unworked or used.

PZ18 Microwear analysis of stone objects

Christina Tsoraki

Four stone objects were subjected to detailed microwear analysis, an analytical technique that entails the analysis of microscopic traces that form on the surface of objects during the stages of production and use including the handling of objects, but also through post-depositional processes (Van Gijn 2010). Microscopic observations were conducted at low (up to 100×) and high (100× and 200×) magnifications. The optical microscopes employed in this study include a stereomicroscope (Leica M80) with an external, oblique light source and with a coaxial illumination unit (Leica M80 LED5000 CXI, magnifications up to 230×), and an incident light microscope (Leica DM1750M) used for observations at 100× and 200×. Micrographs were taken with a Leica MC120HD camera and Z-stacks were created with the Helicon Focus software. Following well-established methodologies (Adams *et al.* 2009; Dubreuil *et al.* 2015; Hamon 2008) recorded wear patterns included grain edge rounding, levelling, grain extraction, micropolish features, texture and development, microstriations, microfractures, and the presence of residues. The microwear patterns observed on the archaeological tools were interpreted in relation to the reference collection of experimentally used tools housed at the Laboratory for Material Culture Studies at Leiden University as well as published data (eg, Adams *et al.* 2009; Hayes *et al.* 2018; Li *et al.* 2018; Santiago-Marrero *et al.* 2021).

Results

PZH18 SF 7, pit 100, context 110: A complete ovate grinding tool that has two flat use-faces; at the centre of each flat use-face a shallow concavity (hollow) is present suggesting that the tool had two distinct episodes of use (sequential use). Grain extraction across the flat surfaces suggests that the use-faces were pecked prior to use. At low magnification, modifications of the microrelief include levelling of crystal grains and rounding at their edges, while small plateaus created by coalescing crystal grains form across the use-face. A possible grey-coloured residue is visible on a localised area on one of the flat use-faces and is found in association with a levelled crystal grain (Fig. 3.3a). At high magnifications, a fine, granular, reflective micropolish can be seen across the surface (Fig. 3.3b) on the higher elevations of the microtopography, and is distributed across the use-face with a longitudinal directionality. A similar type of micropolish is observed on the opposing side though wear development is more limited on this surface. The relief of the topography inside the central hollows is irregular, while the individual crystal grains show edge rounding and occasional impact fractures with a pointed morphology. At high magnifications, a flat, smooth-textured micropolish of localised distribution accompanied by conchoidal microfractures is visible (Figs 3.3c & 3.3d). The wear traces across the flat use-faces are consistent with contact with plant material, while wear traces in the interior of the central hollows suggest contact with a medium-hard material. This suggests that the object was originally used for grinding plant materials and was then re-used to process a medium hard material, possibly of mineral origin, using a percussive motion.

PZH18 Unstratified E cobble: cobble that shows a possible attempt to create a notch on one margin, but no micropolish or other diagnostic microwear traces are visible on the surface of the cobble.

PZH18 Unstratified Quadrant 1: waterworn small-sized quartz cobble broken in half with no wear traces. All surfaces are natural.

PZH18 Unstratified C: burnt slab with irregular topography. Part of one end seems to have been deliberately removed. No wear traces associated with an abrasive or percussive motion are visible on the surface.

4

Flint, chert and small pebble assemblage

Anna Lawson-Jones

The flint and chert assemblage

The worked flint assemblage consists of eight pieces: six from the 2017 evaluation and two from the subsequent 2018 excavation (Southwest Archaeology 2018; Lawson-Jones 2019) (Table 4.1). In common with many Cornish flint assemblages (eg, those found along the north Land's End pipeline, Lawson-Jones 2013), most of the pieces are made from flint pebbles which are readily available locally on Cornwall's beaches (Rogers 1923). Five of the eight flints have remnant pebble cortex strongly suggesting an immediately local beach origin – today the nearest beach is only 400 m to the south. Of the remaining three non-corticated pieces, two probably also had a local beach origin, but the pale cherty burin appears different and may have either been made from a more carefully selected pebble or been brought to the site from further afield. The majority of the pieces fit well within a broadly Early to Middle Bronze Age date range. Given their stratigraphic position within, or apparent focus on the barrow and their generally fresh appearance, they are likely to be contemporary with the barrow's construction and use. None is strongly diagnostic of the Bronze Age, with the exception of a probable thumbnail scraper blank. The burin, however, could be earlier and has a probable Late Neolithic date.

Flint and chert from the evaluation

A very dark probable thumbnail scraper blank from the topsoil is the most diagnostically Bronze Age piece of the assemblage. It is fresh, dark and slightly speckled with abrupt scars around its thickest edge. Its ventral face has had a single flake removed to form a slightly wedge-shaped, thumbnail-sized flake 20 mm long. It has no tool-specific retouch and no use wear. It may have been either discarded or lost. One cortical flake has minimal use as a simple, unmodified cutting flake. This was found sealed beneath the barrow mound on the natural alluvium 103. It is 42 mm long with a 25 mm long, nearly straight working edge which shows tiny, neat removals along much of its length. This was a handheld tool with a corticated dorsal side and comfortable forefinger position for controlled use. The complete, pale chert burin from the topsoil above the barrow is 43 mm long. Slight damage of its tapered point suggests minimal use while the wear on both long sides suggests hafting or binding for handheld use. This is considered likely to be the earliest piece in the assemblage. It suggests that other material from the immediate site, including some of the pebble assemblage discussed below, may have a pre-barrow origin.

In addition, there were three unused waste flakes. A fresh and very faulted Greensand chert secondary flake from the topsoil may have been smashed as opposed to deliberately knapped. A small cortical flake from beneath the barrow mound could be residual and suggests on-site core preparation. The small, fresh, misshapen tertiary flake from a fill within pit 400, which cut the barrow, is in a residual context. It represents either onsite tool manufacture or debitage, or just possibly post-depositional damage from when the pit was in use.

Figure 4.1: Flint SF 8 from the barrow ditch 119, fill 117

One very pale, poor-quality chert flake (SF 8), probably used expeditiously as a cutting flake, was found in fill 117 at the base of barrow ditch 119 (Fig. 4.1). It is fresh and unabraded and shows a very brief use of its 30 mm sharp edge. Its domed corticated dorsal surface allowed handheld, if short-term, use.

Flint from the excavation

One flake (SF 5) with miscellaneous use at tapered or nosed end, suggesting chisel or gouge-like usage. Some backing or softening of sharp edges around much of the domed corticated dorsal surface would have enabled comfortable handheld use. It was found at the base of the outer barrow/field ditch 216/215.

The pebble assemblage

The 93 pebbles comprising the assemblage include: 26 white quartz pebbles, 27 quartzite pebbles, 21 flint/chert pebbles, 12 dark green/grey pebbles (including several of probable greenstone), 3 gritstone pebbles, 2 halves of a small split pebble, 1 smooth red/brown pebble, and 1 haematite pebble. All were found during the 2018 excavation (Lawson-Jones 2019; Table 4.2). Of the 93 pebbles, 28 have an identified/secure context. Of these, six are small finds, nine are from soil samples and 13 are excavated finds. The remaining 65 pebbles came from the mechanically stripped topsoil which included a mix of topsoil, ploughsoil and pebbles which were from the 2017 evaluation that had been reburied when the site was reinstated.

Stratified assemblage

Of the 28 stratified pebble excavation finds, 14 are directly related to the barrow and its use. Ten of these were associated with central cist complex 228. Three overlay the cist and were found in 205 – one quartz and two flint/chert pebbles. Six quartzite pebbles of varying size came from cist 219 fill 226 (Fig. 4.2); and

Table 4.1: The worked flint/chert assemblage from the 2017 evaluations (PJW17) and the 2018 excavations (PZH18)

Project code/ quad	*Context*	*Sample/ small find*	*Form/use*	*Description*	*Weight (g)*
PJW17 U/S	Topsoil over barrow	–	Waste flake	Greensand chert pebble flake. Secondary cortex. Heavily faulted	18.2
PJW17 U/S	Topsoil over barrow	–	Scraper blank	Small v. dark piece. No cortex. Probable unfinished, lost or unused blank for thumbnail scraper	2.1
PJW17 U/S	Topsoil over barrow	–	Burin	Complete, long, off-white burin. Minor lateral damage. No cortex	4.9
PJW17 Quadrant 3	Layer 103 at base of barrow mound	S 102	Cutting flake	Large cortical, smooth pebble flake. Faulted, mottled grey-brown flint. No retouch. Limited edge use	17.5
PJW17 Quadrant 3	Layer 103 at base of barrow mound	S 102	Waste flake	Small pale brown cortical pebble flake. Unused	2.8
PJW17	Pit 400, post-barrow feature	–	Waste flake	Small, pale grey, fresh/sharp, misshapen waste flake. No cortex	1.8
PZH18 Quadrant 2	Fill 215 of outer barrow/field ditch 216	SF 5	Miscellaneous tool	Cortical reddish-brown pebble flake with some ventral thinning. Tapered end battered from gouging use	33
PZH18 Quadrant 1	Barrow ditch 119, fill 117	SF 8	Cutting flake?	Split poor quality, v. pale chert pebble. Small removals show light cutting use on 1 edge	32.3

from the same cist a small, smooth, complete dark reddish-brown pebble came from 227, which when found damp appeared blood-red and had probably been deliberately placed within the cist (Fig. 4.2). None of the other cist-associated pebbles appeared 'special' in character, but all six in the cist are smooth and a milky white coloured quartzite. White pebbles and quartz are commonly associated with cists and barrows (eg, Darvill 2002; Jones 2009–10), and as such the six pebbles may have been deliberately included within the fills. Four further pebbles directly associated with the barrow came from quadrant 2. Two pebbles were found in barrow ditch 300, fill 214 and two came from outer barrow/possible field ditch 216, fill 215. None suggested use or appeared significant or different enough to suggest deliberate deposition. However, all four came from an original ditch fill deposit and all four were lying on (as opposed to near) the base of the ditches. As such it seems possible that they had been deliberately deposited into the barrow ditch(es). Two are of quartz, one of flint and the fourth is grey in colour. As noted above, quartz and other distinctive pebbles are frequently associated with pits and barrows in the south-west region (eg, Jones *et al.* 2012; Tilley 2017; Jones & Lawson-Jones 2020).

Of the pebbles found in the post-barrow dated features 11 came from later pit features which cut through the barrow deposits and contained redeposited Bronze Age material. The central pit 100 produced 10 pebbles from the excavated remaining half of the pit following the 2017 evaluation. It is uncertain whether these pebbles, like the flint and the stone muller (Chapter 2), had been deliberately introduced to the site in prehistory. A further pebble came from the recleaned section of large peripheral pit 400, and if introduced to the site in the Bronze Age, was in a residual context. A further three pebbles came from the raised beach deposit 410, unexpectedly found beneath pit 400.

Unstratified assemblage

The 65 unstratified pebbles, with the exception of two (described in the Note below and see Table 4.2), are neither modified nor utilised (see Chapter 3, for discussion of the worked stone assemblage). They are varied in size, although predominantly small and less than 700 mm long. They also vary in colour, texture and stone type, the latter including white quartz, gritstone, greenstone and variably coloured flint and chert pebbles. All suggest either an on-site or very local, probable beach source.

Some of these pebbles will be the result of past disturbance to and exposure of the underlying pebble and gravel raised beach deposits (for example, as recorded beneath pit 400). Others are likely to be present as a result of the importation of seaweed and sand to improve drainage and bolster soil fertility, as suggested by the post-barrow field ditches which may have used the barrow's raised ground as a focal point. The smallest pebbles may even have been 'blown in' as can be found elsewhere around Cornwall (eg, Hayle, Gwithian, Newquay and Lelant). The remaining pebbles, although unstratified, and unfortunately inseparable from the other material, will be prehistoric introductions to the site, and associated with or related to the barrow.

No clear pattern, however, has been found that can distinguish barrow context pebbles from unstratified pebbles. There was, for example, no bias in the assemblage for white quartzite pebbles, which might suggest an association with a layer (eg, paving) or structured deposits. Likewise, the unknapped flint and chert pebbles cannot be linked with caches or placed deposits. This lack of patterning may simply be a reflection of the ubiquitous presence of locally sourced pebbles within the immediate and wider setting, and subsequent disturbance to the site.

Note

Included within the 65 unstratified pebbles are two which appear to show use or modification

Figure 4.2: Pebbles from the barrow site. Pale grey and white pebbles from cist 219, fill 226 (top) and 'blood red pebble SF 16 from Cist 219, fill 227 (bottom)

(listed at the end of Table 4.2, below). Both came from the northern part of the site and were found during topsoil stripping. One had been repeatedly broken. The other was a complete, flat discoidal piece showing patchy percussive damage, parallel scratches and possible etched lines.

Table 4.2: The pebble assemblage from the Penzance Heliport excavations

Small find/ sample	*Context*	*Pebbles*	*No.*	*Use*	*Description*	*Weight (g)*
SF 1	Barrow ditch 300 base of fill 214	Flint/chert	1	–	Slightly amorphous. Complete	71.9
SF 2	Barrow ditch 300 base of fill 214	Quartz	1	–	Complete	63.7
SF 3	Outer barrow/field ditch 216 base of fill 215	Quartz	1	–	Complete	54.1
SF 4	Outer barrow/field ditch 216 base of fill 215	Grey pebble	1	–	Complete grey pebble	34.3
SF 6	Pit 100 fill 110	Quartzite pebble	1	–	Complete. 1 smooth flat surface	65
SF 16	Cist 219, fill 227. Structured deposit	Pebble	1	–	Small, smooth. Dark brown when dry, blood-red when wet	14
–	Pit 100 fill 101	Pebble	2	–	Broken, heated split pebble	16
–	Pit 115 fill 116	Quartz	6	–	V. small.	9.5
–	Pit 115 fill 116	Haematite	1	Possible	Splitting/heated?	4.5
–	Under pit 400 layer 410	Pebbles	3	–	From underlying raised beach	114.1
–	Layer 205 overlay cist complex 228	Quartz	1	–	Rounded square. With some flat smooth faces	53.5
	Layer 205 overlay cist complex 228	Flint/chert	2	–	1 with possible residue?	33.8
S 38	Cist 219 fill 226	Quartzite	6	–	4 small, 2 larger. Complete	122.9 & 22.5
S 14	Pit 412 fill 402	Flint/chert	1	–	1 flat very smooth face	23
		Unstratified, but with general location detail				
–	Q1 – U/S topsoil	Quartzite	2	–	Complete small white. Complete small black	18.7
–	U/S topsoil	Quartz	2	–	Complete	87.8
–	U/S topsoil	Flint/chert	4	–	Complete	25.5
–	U/S topsoil	Flint/chert	1	–	Angular with 2 natural flat smooth surfaces – 90° angle	6.2
–	Central – U/S topsoil	Quartzite	15	–	7 small, 8 larger. 1 smooth/yellow. Complete	167 and 33
–	Central – US topsoil	Flint/chert	1	–	Complete	22. 8
–	Central – U/S topsoil	Dark green pebbles	5	–	4 complete, 1 broken. Different sizes/ shapes. 1 greenstone?	342.5
–	North – U/S topsoil	Quartz	15	–	Different sizes, shapes. Complete.	321.7
–	North – U/S topsoil	Flint/chert	11	–	Different sizes, shapes, colour. Complete	125.6
–	North – U/S topsoil	Dark green pebbles	5	–	Quartzite/greenstone. Hard, smooth. Varied sizes, shapes	244.7
–	North – U/S topsoil	Dark pebble	1	–	Complete dark, slightly triangular, greenstone? Several flat smooth faces	66.9
–	North – U/S topsoil	Stone	1	–	Small flattish gritstone	7.2
–	North – U/S topsoil	Stone	1	Yes	Complete, flat, discoidal gritstone. Patchy damage around thin convex edge – small percussive-chisel scars. Parallel scratches near edge. Occasional etched lines	84.2
–	North – U/S topsoil	Stone	1	Yes?	Broken, abraded gritstone. 3 breaks. Small break earliest	33.7

5

The copper alloy ingot

Anna Tyacke with Jens Andersen

Description

Anna Tyacke

A fragment of a cast copper alloy ingot, found within cist 207 (Lawson-Jones 2019) (Figs 5.1–5.4). The ingot would have originally been circular in plan and plano-convex in profile, but this fragment is rectangular in plan and in section and triangular in profile, with the internal edge at 12 mm in height tapering to 3 mm in height/thickness at the original outer edge. This extant part of the outer edge, which runs for about 38 mm along one side of the fragment, retains part of the slight curvature of the plano-convex ingot. The surface of the ingot is pitted where air bubbles formed during the casting process and the sides of the fragment have cavities typically seen in these bun ingots. There are several circular bubble vesicles and a large spherical aperture at one edge suggests that a large bubble formed to create that cavity. But there is also a rectangular cavity which may have been left by either a wholly-decayed socketed metal implement with a rectangular aperture that had melted into the ingot, or by another object, such as an angular stone, which had left an impression and then fallen out after the ingot was cast. At the side of this cavity there is also a rectangular object protruding from the section which is 9 mm wide (but could have originally continued beyond the broken edge), and 5 mm in height/thickness. One of the flat faces of the ingot has a light green surface where bronze disease has been active before conservation (Fig. 5.1), and the opposite face has a crust of orange iron oxide adhering to the surface (Fig. 5.2), which has been suggested to have been part of a mineralised organic wrapping (Ratcliffe-Warren; Appendix 1).

Dimensions: length: 44 mm, width: 30 mm, height: 12 mm, weight: 55.47 g.

The ingot was compositionally analysed by Jens Andersen, as described below.

The composition of the ingot

Jens Andersen

Two surface analyses of each side of the ingot were undertaken using an X-ray fluorescence

Figure 5.1: The upper side of the copper alloy ingot

Figure 5.2: The lower side of the copper alloy ingot, with brown orange crust, potentially a mineralised organic wrapping, adhering to it

(XRF) spectrometer. Some highlights: The brown side is a crust of iron oxide. The green side is copper-rich. The bronze has no Co, Ni, Mo, Cd or Sb but carries As and Sn. There is also a small Pb signal (Table 5.1). Thorium was identified on one side of the ingot. One would not expect, from a metallurgical point of view, that thorium would partition into bronze. As the signal was only present on one side of the artefact this suggests that it derived from the soil where the artefact was buried, rather than being a signature of the metal's provenance or production. There are some geological 'hot spots' (that is to say, thorium-rich areas) around Constantine and in West Penwith between Newbridge and Morvah, so it is indeed likely that the thorium relates to the object's microenvironment.

Table 5.1: Composition of the ingot

	Brown side	*Brown side*	*Green side*	*Green side*
Mg	2.36	2.32	2.69	2.36
Al	4.17	4.07	2.71	2.36
Si	6.5214	6.4853	4.1667	4.7478
P	1.103	1.0889	0.2454	0.2556
S	0.0829	0.0746	0.1105	0.1328
K	0.2134	0.1816	0.1465	0.1913
Ca	0.6527	0.6144	0.2368	0.2976
Ti	0.0386	ND	ND	ND
Fe	43.02	44.59	1.8458	3.8164
Co	ND	ND	ND	ND
Ni	ND	ND	ND	ND
Cu	14.64	20.73	79.34	79.51
Zn	0.1205	0.1086	ND	ND
As	0.0694	0.0599	0.006	0.0083
Mo	ND	ND	ND	ND
Ag	ND	ND	0.0112	0.0056
Cd	ND	ND	ND	ND
Sn	0.0686	0.0104	0.0133	0.0159
Sb	ND	ND	ND	ND
W	ND	ND	0.0405	0.035
Pb	0.0081	0.0127	0.027	0.0275
Th	ND	ND	0.2263	0.1705
U	ND	ND	ND	ND

The X-ray fluorescence spectrometer is an energy-dispersive spectrometer and it works with two different X-ray energies. The higher energy X-rays at 40 kV are used for minor elements, including thorium, while the lower energy X-rays, at 15 kV, are used for detecting major elements. The thorium would be measured on the $L\alpha$ line at 12.97 keV. It would be possible to get thorium signals also on bismuth ($L\alpha = 10.84$ keV, $L\beta 2 = 12.97$ keV), which could be present in the metal. Bismuth, as lead, would have an affinity to metal and I have found it quite often in the ores of the Redruth-Camborne area.

Since the analyses were undertaken on the oxidised surface of the artefact, rather than on a drilled or cut sample from the subsurface, the results cannot be taken as an accurate representation of the composition of the bronze. The surface's composition will include, in addition to the bronze, a record of the changes that the material has undergone during oxidation, as well as material from the soil that has adhered to the oxidised surface. During corrosion, as the copper oxidises, there can be greater loss of copper than of tin or lead.

Discussion

Anna Tyacke

Plano-convex ingots like this one were created and used in the metalworking process, typically during the Late Bronze Age, *c.* 1000–700 cal BC. Similar ingot fragments have been found in Late Bronze Age metalworkers' hoards in Cornwall (eg, Knight 2021, 101–103; Chapter 12, this volume), including one recently found at St Levan (Treasure number 2016 T20; PAS record number CORN-E8DF11) and another from St Buryan (Treasure number 2012 T570; PAS record number CORN-37D710). In both cases the hoards included socketed axeheads that date from the Ewart Park phase (*c.* 950–850 BC) of the Late Bronze Age. The ingot fragment was found in layer 203 at the base of cist 207. The layer has been radiocarbon dated to the Late Bronze Age, SUERC-47292, 2734±27 BP, 930–810 cal BC, so this ties in very well with the ingot typology (as discussed in Chapter 7). Comparable copper alloy ingots have also been identified in Devon: Pearce illustrates similar ingots with rectangular profiles from Mountbatten, Plymouth (Pearce 1983, 451, plate 36, no. 281t), which were found with other Late Bronze Age metalwork, and Knight *et al.* illustrate a similar plano-convex ingot from Churston Ferrers in Devon (Knight *et al.* 2015, 79, plate 6, no. 123b; recorded in DEV-D9F1E2 (2011T441)) which dates to the Ewart Park phase of the Late Bronze Age.

The St Levan hoard contains several ingot fragments where objects have been melted down to form composite ingots, but the purity of the copper within the copper alloy still remains high despite these additions. The results of analyses carried out by Peter Northover on the St Levan ingots nos. 17, 18, 27 and 45 which, potentially like the Heliport ingot, also have fragments of formed tools melted back into them, show that they are still almost pure copper (between 85 per cent and 99 per cent) with the only other elements occurring in appreciable quantity being antimony (which does not show up at all in the Heliport specimen), arsenic and sulphur, which are more prevalent than tin. This could be due to the use of lumps of metal that were rich in those elements – either reused Chalcolithic copper that had been found, or else objects imported from the Continent, high in those elements and low in tin, which were being melted down during the Late Bronze Age (Peter Northover, pers. comm.). It should be noted, however, that Northover's work consisted of electron probe microanalysis with wavelength dispersive spectrometry using cut samples from the interior of the St Levan ingots. This method produced more accurate results than the surface XRF analysis of the Heliport ingot fragment as they are not affected by surface contamination by corrosion products or by anomalies such as gasses.

Another ingot from the Penzance area (PAS record CORN-F4B411) that was previously analysed by Jens Andersen using XRF produced the following readings:

65%	copper (but probably quite pure as 30% of the reading was recorded as anomalies which include gasses and not inclusions)
7.36%	iron
0.16%	antimony
0.04%	zinc
0.03%	tin

These are typical of readings that had been taken from the surface of other individual Late Bronze Age ingots, before Northover's more detailed analyses of the hoards had occurred.

Figure 5.3: A side of the copper alloy ingot, with the remnant brown orange crust or mineralised organic wrapping visible in places

Figure 5.4: A side of the copper alloy ingot, with circular aperture close to the edge visible

6

Palaeo-environmental and palaeo-economic evidence

Michael J. Allen, with A.J. Clapham, Nigel Cameron, C.T. Langdon and R.G. Scaife

Palaeo-environment and palaeo-economy: the data sets and sampling

Michael J. Allen

The geoarchaeology of the site has been discussed above (Chapter 2) and was defined by a series of 19 boreholes recorded in the field and three cores removed for further, more detailed examination. Those cores provided samples for pollen and diatom analysis, and for radiocarbon dating of the stratigraphic and palaeo-environmental evidence. These together provide the long record of land-use history from at least the Late Mesolithic (4230–4060 cal BC) to after 2580–2460 cal BC, with the upper humose sediments encompassing the period of the Bronze Age barrow construction and re-use of the cist. Although these Bronze Age events are not specifically identified by radiocarbon dates in the cored stratigraphy, we think that these points are identified by changes in the land-use history in the pollen record.

The plant remains and charcoal recovered from contexts in, and associated with, the Bronze Age barrow are charred (burnt by fires created by human communities) and are fuel, crop waste and other waste by products discarded into the fire. In contrast to the pollen and diatoms which provide evidence of the local landscape, land-use and lived-in environment, these plant macrofossils generally provide information about the human economy and activities. The charred plant remains can potentially inform on the varieties of crop grown, the location of cultivated areas, harvesting (methods and time) and processing (for storage, sowing, redistribution or consumption), while the wood charcoal can indicate the species of wood selected for burning (domestic fires vs pyres), woodland management practices (coppicing, pollarding) and the choice of wood used for construction and objects (artefacts). Both the charcoal and plant remains have then been burnt either purposefully as tinder or fuel, or accidentally/incidentally as waste (eg, construction timbers, chaff and artefacts).

Consequently this chapter considers these two lines of evidence – the palaeo-environmental and the palaeo-economic – separately, with the former evidence being derived from pollen, diatoms and geoarchaeology (Chapter 2) and the latter from the charred plant and wood charcoal remains. Of course there is some overlap between these sets of data. Evidence of human economy and activity such as woodland clearance, tillage, cereal cultivation and pasture-related practices might be evident in the pollen data, while information on the nature of the local soils, geology and environments might also be obtained from charred weed seeds and the species of trees in the wood charcoal assemblages. Such themes are pulled together and drawn out with the geoarchaeological evidence in the discussion and conclusion sections of this chapter, and provide the basis for much wider interpretations of the social use of the changing landscape in later chapters (Chapters 10 & 14).

Palaeo-environment

The palaeo-environmental evidence is derived from pollen and diatom data from the cores, along with geoarchaeological data. Three cores (T1/3, T1/5 and T2/11) were selected, retained and described in detail, and subsampled for pollen, diatoms and radiocarbon dating.

Review of the geoarchaeology: summary of the stratigraphy

Michael J. Allen

The geoarchaeological evidence, presented in detail in Chapter 2, is summarised here from core T1/3 as it provides the context for the pollen (Scaife & Langdon) and diatom (Cameron) evidence. The 4 m of sediments recorded probably embrace Pleistocene and Holocene deposits, the age of which is not yet determined. The onset of local 'alluviation' (Unit 3), peat formation (Unit 2) and colluviation (Unit 1) may be driven to a greater or lesser extent by human activities such as deforestation, ground preparation, and tillage. The main sedimentary units not only provide access to pollen and diatom data, but themselves are a proxy for human activities (cf. French 2003; 2015).

Made ground: Up to 1.1 m of made ground was identified, which was found to contain modern and recent artefacts (including plastic items, Victorian pottery and modern clothing). Much of this relates to the decommissioning of the former heliport and construction of the retail park to the south of Jelbert Way. No made ground was sampled for palaeo-environmental data.

Holocene colluvium (Unit 1): A stony yellowish-brown to greyish-brown silt loam, probably colluvium resulting from human activity (clearance, tillage) upslope, was not represented in core T1/3; it may relate to activity associated with the barrow, or to post-barrow cultivation.

Humose/peat deposits (Units 2.1 and 2.2): The most significant deposits in terms of geoarchaeological and palaeo-environmental potential are the humose/peat deposits. The upper portion (Unit 2.1, 110–131 cm) was a very dark brown to dark brown humic almost stone-free silt loam, possibly a highly humified peat. Below 131 cm to 155 cm (Unit 2.2) it became a very dark grey humified stone-free silty peat.

'Alluvium' (Unit 3): Here a stiff greenish-grey silt loam to silty clay loam with few stones over the basal colluvium and beneath the humose layer. It is fine-grained, and well-sorted and humic, suggesting fluvial, slow water.

Basal colluvium (Unit 4): A strong brown (7.5YR 5/6) dense silty sand loam with some small stones, becoming stonier with depth, and at 332–334 mm contains a dark reddish-brown sand of sand. This basal colluvium is considered a largely a result of mass movement and may even be Pleistocene Head and overlays Sand deposits. Pollen does not survive in these deposits.

Sand (Unit 5): A greenish yellow stone-free wet medium sand probably representing sand blow and dunes against the footslope. Pollen was absent from this deposit. Could be Pleistocene.

Core samples and subsampling

Michael J. Allen

Palaeo-environmental subsampling; pollen and diatoms

Following description (Appendix 2.1 core T1/3) and photography (Appendix 2.2), samples were taken from all three cores. These included one full sequence (T1/3) and one section of the best expressions of humose/humified peat (T1/5 1–2 m), and the thickest humose profile (T2/11 1–3 m). Subsamples were removed at 10 mm bandwidth and at 40 mm intervals for pollen (except in the colluvium or Head where this was increased to 80 mm) and at wider, typically 80 mm intervals, for diatoms (except in the

Unit	Core T1/3 Pollen	Core T1/3 Diatoms	Core T1/3 ^{14}C	Core T1/5 Pollen	Core T1/5 Diatoms	Core T1/5 ^{14}C	Core T2/11 Pollen	Core T2/11 Diatoms	Core T2/11 ^{14}C
1 Colluvium	–	–	–	–	–	–	–	–	–
2 Humose layer	12 (10)	3 (1)	3	5	3	2	15	8	4
3 'Alluvium'	8 (5)	4	–	9	5		5	3	–
Undefined	3	1	–	–	–	–	–	–	–
4 Basal colluvium	6	3	–	–	–	–	8	4	–
5 Sand	3	2	–	–	–	–	–	–	–

Note: a number of samples were assessed from all layers below the upper colluvium from core T1/3 (pollen and diatoms) but microfossils were absent or poorly preserved in many deposits

Table 6.1: Subsamples of 10 mm bandwidth taken from the cores. Samples in parentheses are the numbers of samples that were progressed to analysis. Note: a number of samples were assessed from all layers below the upper colluvium from core T1/3 (pollen and diatoms) but microfossils were absent or poorly preserved in many deposits

colluvium or head where this was increased to 160 mm). In all, 118 subsamples (78 for pollen and 40 for diatoms) were taken, comprising 37 pollen and 17 diatom subsamples from 2.76 m of the profile in core T1/3, and a further 15 pollen and 8 diatom subsamples from the humose sediments in core T1/5 (1–2 m), and 26 pollen and 15 diatoms from T2/11 (Appendix 2.1).

Sampling for absolute dating

Material was removed for radiocarbon dating. From core T1/3 this included short-lived fine roundwood twigs (×1), but where these did not survive small soil samples for humin acids were removed (×2). No organic plant matter survived in the core from T1/5 so two samples were removed for humin acids. For the longest humose sequence (T2/9) two samples of plant matter and two sample for humin acid dating were taken (see Appendix 2.1 & Table 6.1). A series of three samples from core T1/3 were submitted for AMS radiocarbon dating (as discussed below; see also Table 6.2).

Assessment

Core T1/3 was selected for detailed assessment as it contained the longest, deepest and most representative stratigraphy. Importantly the humose layer was well represented in this core, and it was hoped that this might equate to the activity associated with the barrow's construction and use. A series of 37 pollen, 17 diatom and three radiocarbon samples were taken from the core (Table 6.1), and 14 pollen and six diatom samples were selected for assessment. Pollen assessment by Scaife & Langdon (in Allen 2019b) showed that while well-preserved pollen was present in the alluvial levels and in the overlying humose sediment, all samples below 1.8 m in depth in the basal colluvium and sand were completely devoid of pollen. A suite of 15 samples were then progressed to analysis from these upper deposits (Table 6.1). Similarly the diatoms were assessed by Nigel Cameron but were only present in a single sample from the top of the humose deposits. No further analysis was conducted but that assessment is presented below.

Radiocarbon dating of the cores and palaeo-environmental sequence

In order for the geoarchaeological sequences (Chapter 2) and any palaeo-environmental sequence to complement usefully the archaeological record it is essential to provide a chronology with which to compare with the archaeological narrative. Consequently, samples of waterlogged plant remains – and failing that, small bulk samples for humin acid dating, were taken. Three samples were taken from core T1/3 (Table 6.1); these comprised a small roundwood twig at the top of deposits (@ 114 cm), and humin acid samples from the contact/boundary *within* the thick humose layer (@ 131 cm at the boundary between the upper humose layer Unit 2.1 and the lower humose layer Unit 2.2), and a basal humic acid sample (@ 155 cm). These were complemented by six further small bulk samples for humin acid dates from the top and bottom of the humose layer in T1/5 at 102 cm and 110 cm respectively. From the longer, but root-intruded, sequences in T2/11 two samples of plant matter (@178 cm ×2) and two for humin acids (@180 cm and 196 cm) were also taken.

Three samples were submitted for AMS radiocarbon dating from core T1/3 to date the start and end of the formation of the humose

Table 6.2: Radiocarbon results from the top and bottom of the humose layer (Unit 2)

Sample depth cm	*Deposit*	*Material*	*Lab no*	*Result BP*	*δC[13] ‰*	*Cal BC*
114	Top Unit 2.*1*	Dicot stem (twig)	SUERC-87220	1.2995±0.0038	–28.0	modern
131	Boundary 2.1/2.1	Humic acid	SUERC-95372	4006±27	–28.7	2580–2460
155	Base Unit 2.1	Humose deposit	SUERC-87224	5321±23	–28.0	4230–4060

layer (Unit 2), and a single sample from the boundary between the two humose layers, namely:

114 cm dicotyledonous stem near top of the peat/humose layer (2.1)
131 cm 'peat'/humin acid boundary of peat/humose layer (2.1/2.2)
155 cm 'peat'/humin acid at the base of the peat/humose layer (2.2)

Details of sample processing and calibration are given in Chapter 7.

Consideration of the results

The dicotyledonous stem at 114 cm was obviously modern material dragged down with the core and not recognised as such by either the geoarchaeologist nor the environmental archaeologists and archaeobotanist identifying the material. The base of the humose layer ('peat') Unit 2 is firmly dated to the Late Mesolithic period (4230–4060 cal BC). This shows not only the onset of 'peat' formation over alluvium (that is, drying out) at 4230–4060 cal BC), but gives a date just prior to vegetational change (pollen assemblage zone 2; Fig. 6.1), described below by Langdon and Scaife. The result at 131 cm provides a Chalcolithic date in the middle of humose layer. Unfortunately no result was obtained from the top of humose layer.

Pollen assessment analysis from core T1/3

R.G. Scaife and C.T. Langdon

Previous pollen studies include those of the peat and mineral sediments at Mount's Bay, Prah Sands (French 1983), Marazion Marsh (Healy 1996a), the Camel Estuary (Healy 1996b) and Penzance Harbour (Scaife 2006). These and other regional sequences also provide critical data on Holocene eustatic

Figure 6.1. Probability distribution of radiocarbon results in the Penzance and west Cornwall locale, with the base of humose layer (Unit 2) marked as a grey bar

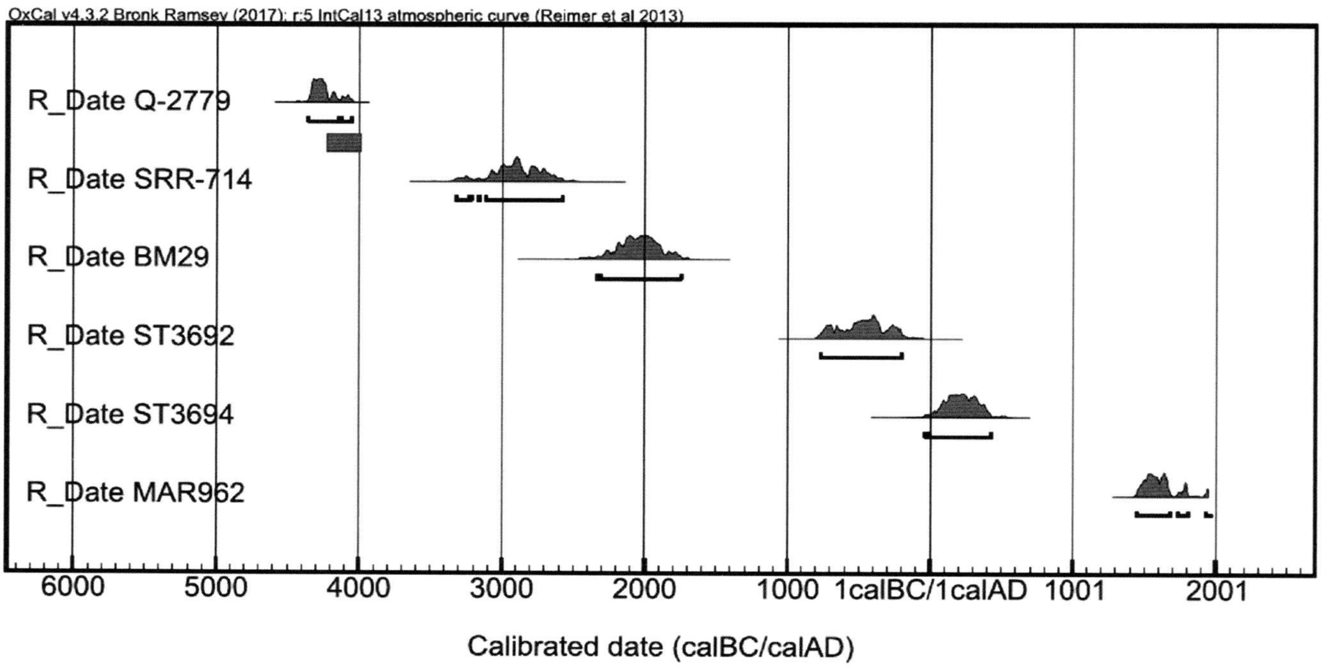

change (Heywood & Kidson 1982; Healy 1993; 1995; 1999a). These existing data clearly show the potential for understanding in detail the past vegetation and environment, especially in relation to past sea-level change and human impact. An assessment (Langdon & Scaife 2019) demonstrated the potential of the Heliport site for reconstructing the local vegetation and environment, especially in relation to the late prehistoric period, adding to the existing palaeo-ecological database. This would be especially pertinent to the study of the adjacent, excavated Bronze Age cairn. Well-preserved pollen has been recovered from the lower alluvial levels and in the overlying humic sediment, although samples below 1.8 m were found to be completely devoid of pollen.

Pollen procedures

Samples of 1–2 ml volume were processed using standard techniques for the extraction of the sub-fossil pollen and spores (Moore & Webb 1978; Moore *et al.* 1992). A pollen sum of up to 400 pollen grains of was counted for each level where preservation permitted. All pollen of marsh taxa (largely Cyperaceae), fern spores and miscellaneous taxa (liverworts, pre-Quaternary palynomorphs, etc.) were also counted for each of the samples analysed. A standard pollen diagram (Fig. 6.2a–b) has been presented using Tilia and Tilia Graph with percentages calculated as follows:

Sum = % total dry land pollen
Marsh/aquatic
= % tdlp + sum of marsh/aquatics
Spores = % tdlp + sum of spores.
Misc. = % tdlp + sum of misc. taxa.

Pollen taxonomy, in general, follows that of Moore & Webb (1978), modified according to Bennett *et al.* (1994) for pollen types and Stace (1992) for plant descriptions. It should be noted that the very high values of *Alnus* within the sum zones PENZ: 1 and PENZ: 2 will have reduced the relative percentages of other taxa from the surrounding region of drier soils (Janssen 1969). Thus, the importance of *Quercus* and *Corylus* in the pollen assemblages is under-represented in percentage terms. This is taken into account during discussion. An extensive modern comparative collection was available for any critical identifications. These procedures were carried out in the Palaeoecology Laboratory of the Department of Geography and Environmental Science, University of Southampton.

The pollen data

There is a very clear break in pollen preservation around 1.80 m. This is coincident with a stratigraphical change from coarser sediment (colluvium) and overlying alluvium and humic peat/silt. While the former is devoid of pollen, the latter was found to be pollen-rich. The changing stratigraphy relates to significant change in the depositional environment. Overall, the pollen data are dominated by trees and shrubs except for the uppermost levels above *c.* 1.30 m which have higher values of herbs; largely Poaceae, including occasional cereal pollen. Throughout most of the profile, *Alnus* with a phase of *Salix* (willow which is under-represented in pollen assemblages) are the dominant wetland/mire taxa. Non-wetland taxa are dominated by *Quercus* and *Corylus avellana* with sporadic records of other taxa. The changing palynological record from *c.* 1.30 m shows a marked reduction in the importance of the tree and shrub pollen and a corresponding increase in herb pollen numbers. Three local pollen assemblage zones have been recognised (l.p.a.z. PENZ: 1 – PENZ: 3). These are described from the base of the profile where pollen preservation begins at *c.* 1.80 m upwards to the top of the profile at 1.20 m.

Zone PENZ: 1: 1.80 m to 1.48 m. This lower zone spans the alluvium and its transition into an upper more humic/peaty silt. Trees and shrubs are important with high values whereas herbs are minimal. *Alnus* is dominant, peaking to 80% with *Quercus* (to 20%) and *Corylus avellana* type (av. 20%). There are few herbs with slightly higher and more diverse assemblages in the lower levels. These include Poaceae (9% in the basal level at 1.78 m and 1–2% above), and occasional Apiaceae, Scrophulariaceae and Asteraceae types (*Bidens* type, *Anthemis* type and Lactucoideae). Marsh/fen taxa consist primarily of Cyperaceae throughout (to 8%) and occasional *Typha angustifolia*/*Sparganium* type. Spores of ferns comprise primarily *Dryopteris* type and *Polypodium* and sporadic moss (*Sphagnum*).

Summary: Pollen is absent below 1.80 m into the underlying colluvial layers. From 1.80 m, pollen preservation occurred, as conditions became wetter. This provided a suitable habitat for colonisation by alder and

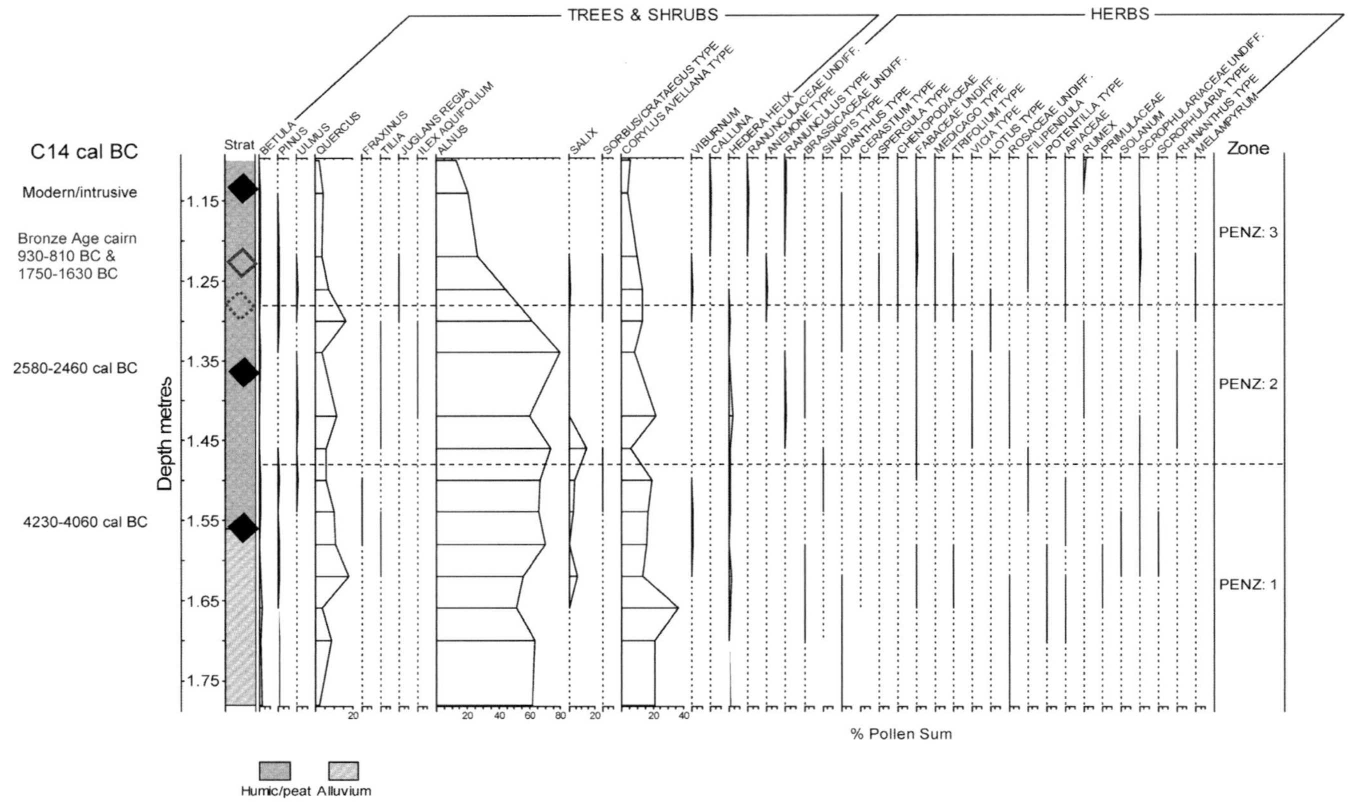

Figure 6.2a: Penzance Heliport site core T1/1 pollen percentage diagram; trees shrubs and herbs.

willow and consequent accretion of humic sediment. The on-site ground flora of this alder carr (Alnetum) comprised typical grasses, sedges, bulrush/bur reed and marsh ferns and probably ivy. *Polypodium* was probably saprophytic on the trees. The surrounding, drier soils supported dominant oak and hazel woodland. The dominance of alder has reduced the apparent, statistical importance of other taxa (Janssen 1969).

Zone PENZ:2: 1.48 m to 1.28 m. This local pollen assemblage zone is defined by an expansion of on-site *Salix* and importantly the incoming of *Plantago lanceolata* although the latter is in low numbers. There appears to have been an expansion of Cyperaceae at this time although *Alnus* remained important and attains its highest values (80%) along with high *Salix* values (to 17%). The latter is ephemeral and dies out in quantity from *c.* 1.45 mm subsequently with only sporadic occurrences. *Quercus* and *Corylus* remain dominant in the surrounding pollen catchment. *Hedera* incoming at the top of zone 1 remains consistent in low numbers throughout this zone. This zone is also characterised by the first occurrence of some herbs including Fabaceae (legumes, vetches, etc.), Brassicaceae, *Rumex* and *Plantago lanceolata*. Spores of *Dryopteris* type become important, peaking to 67% (sum + fern spores) with occasional *Polypodium*.

Summary: This zone appears to show the first impact of human activity on the woodland of the fluves. Oak and hazel remained important in the surrounding drier zone with alder and willow dominant at the base of slope, so existed as a ribbon of alder carr (Alnetum/Salicetum) at the footslope at 10 m OD where it is damper, but above the real coastal deposits. Ribwort plantain (*Plantago lanceolata*) is a clear indication of the first human influence from the Late Mesolithic dated to 4230–4060 cal BC (5321±23 BP, SUERC-87224) at the base of this phase.

Zone PENZ: 3: 1.28 m to 1.10 m. The uppermost zone shows a marked transition from arboreal to herb-dominated pollen assemblages. Poaceae, especially, become important (to 66% at top of profile) with Cereal pollen present for the first time in this zone. Other herb taxa include small numbers of Chenopodiaceae (goosefoot

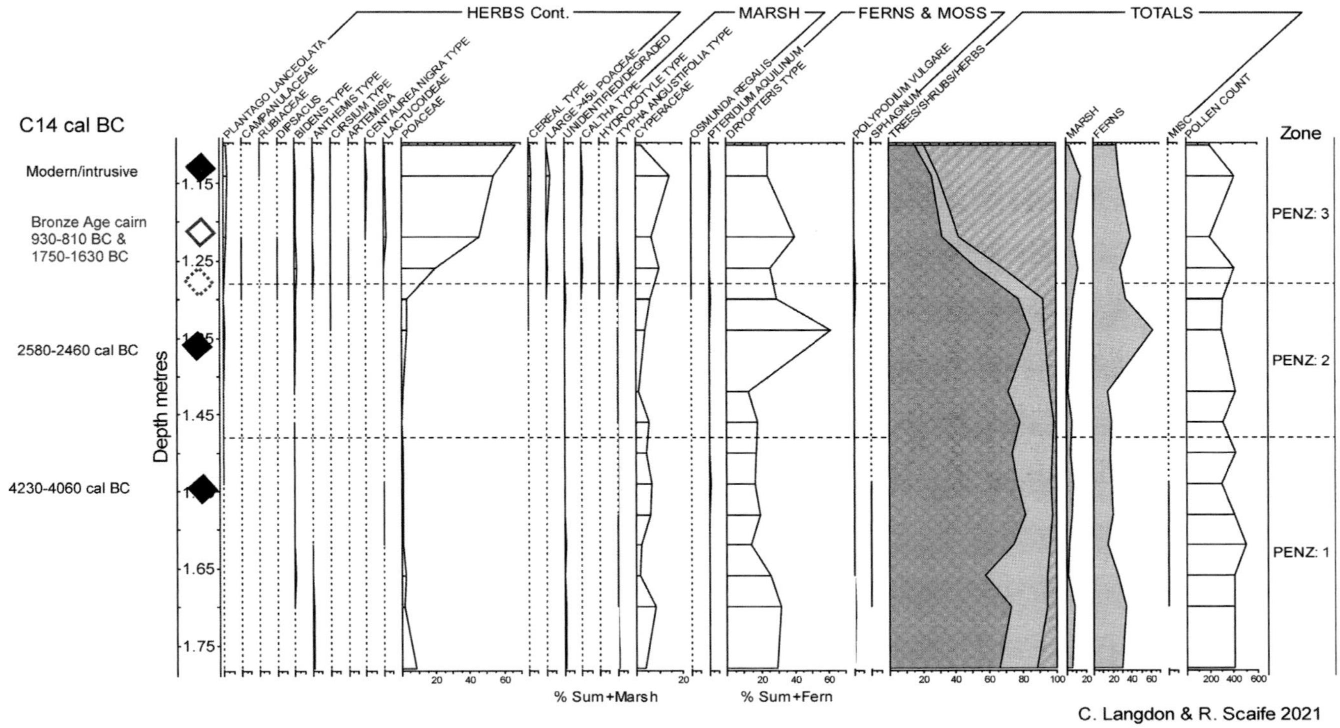

Figure 6.2b: (continued from previous page) herbs (cont.), marsh, ferns and mosses.

and oraches), Fabaceae, Caryophyllaceae, *Filipendula*, *Rumex* and *Plantago lanceolata* (3%) and Asteraceae types. Tree and shrub pollen decrease correspondingly with *Alnus* to 14%, *Quercus* (to 5%), *Corylus* avellana type (to 6%) and *Salix* to absence. There are traces of *Calluna*.

Summary: This upper zone shows a clear opening of the environment with change from woodland both on the site and in the surrounding drier zone. Grassland, possibly pasture, became dominant. There is, however, also evidence of arable cultivation (cereal pollen). The small increase in Chenopodiaceae (goosefoot, orache and samphire) may be halophytes and be an indication marine brackish conditions. This is, however, speculative as such taxa are also typical of agricultural habitats.

Discussion

It should be noted that the very high values of *Alnus* within the sum zones 1 and 2 will have reduced the relative percentages of other taxa from the surrounding region of drier soils. Thus, the importance of *Quercus* and *Corylus* in the pollen assemblages is particularly underrepresented. It is very probable that there is a strong relationship between the depositional environment, the associated pollen assemblages and Holocene sea-level change. Here, there appears to be a hydroseral succession from probably fen through to on-site alder and willow carr woodland. This sequence was transgressional from what appears to have been an alluvial environment to a detrital humic peaty-silt, the latter accumulating under a more stable floodplain (alder) regime. Whilst it is possible that this change is directly related to a decline in relative sea-level due to sediment accrual in relation to neotectonic activity, it is also likely that local factors such as barrier bar formation/destruction may have been responsible.

Two radiocarbon dates have been obtained which demonstrate that the sediments started to accrue during the Late Mesolithic (that is, middle Holocene; Flandrian II–Atlantic) period before 4230–4060 cal BC (5321±23 BP, SUERC-87224) and extend into the Chalcolithic with a date of 2580–2460 cal BC (4006±27 BP, SUERC-95372) at the change from l.p.a.z. PENZ: 1 and l.p.a.z. PENZ: 2.

These dates are comparable with other sequences from this region. French (1985) has listed radiocarbon dates from a number of submerged forest sites which similarly span the late prehistoric period. He also notes that the variability may be a function of such local geomorphological processes. Other, more recent analysis at Marazion Bay (Healy 1995; 1996b; 1999b) includes absolute dates from the following sites:

Penzance, Newlyn
 2470–1640 cal BC (3656±150 BP, BM 29)
Penzance
 3080–2700 cal BC (4280±100 BP, SRR-714)
Penzance Harbour
 4960–770 cal BC (6000±35BP, NZA-25945)
Portmellin
 770–190 cal BC (2345±100 BP, ST 3692)
Prah Sands
 cal AD 600–900 (1290±70 BP, MAR 962)
Prah Sands
 50 BC–AD 420 (1805±100 BP, ST 3694)
Marazion Bay
 5560–4040 (5420±60 BP, Q-2779)

These and further dates are discussed more fully in Chapter 11.

Scaife (2006) also examined a truncated peat sequence from within Penzance Harbour (discussed in Chapter 9) and overall, the data he obtained resemble the results obtained here.

Middle Holocene/Late Mesolithic environments
This site produced a radiocarbon date of 4230–4060 cal BC (5321±23BP, SUERC-87224) at 1.55 m suggesting that the lower levels of the profile may be attributed to the middle Holocene, Atlantic period (Flandrian II), that is, Late Mesolithic (l.p.a.z.1). Typical for this period in the south-west of England, drier areas of this wetland zone and the interfluves supported dominant *Quercus* and *Corylus* woodland possibly with some *Ulmus.* Higher values of Poaceae and Cyperaceae in the basal levels suggest that initially, a grass-sedge fen may have developed prior to colonisation by *Alnus (glutinosa)* which became dominant (Alnetum).

Human influences
Of particular relevance to this this study was the need to ascertain the impact of the nearby Bronze Age activity on the local woodland habitat. The first indications of such disturbance come at 1.5–2 m with incoming of *Plantago lanceolata* (ribwort plantain) and the date of 4230–4060 cal BC (5321±23 BP) places this arrival during the Late Mesolithic and marks the first evidence of probable clearance although here, there is little evidence for woodland removal. There is no associated cereal pollen or taxa which can definitely be attributed to such activity and as ribwort plantain is anemophilous this arrival of ribwort plantain probably represents localised areas of grassland/clearance at some distance from the site.

It is only in the upper levels of the profile (l.p.a.z. 3) that there is any strong evidence of human activity. The start of this significant environmental change has been dated to the Chalcolithic period, 2580–2460 cal BC (4006±27 BP, SUERC-95372) at 1.31 m. Thus, it is suggested that the overlying sediment of zone 3 may be attributed to the Bronze Age and relates to the adjacent archaeological evidence.

In the upper zone (PENZ: 3), there is evidence of cereal cultivation associated with a decrease in woodland with clearance of the local dominant oak and hazel woodland. There may, however, be taphonomic factors with this pollen evidence responding to the depositional environment which became less densely wooded with change from alder carr to a more open fen habitat and wider pollen catchment. It is also probable that these factors are interrelated and result from the impact of the Bronze Age activity on the drier, adjacent area. Removal of woodland will have raised the local ground water table through a reduction in evapotranspiration rates and increased surface run-off. This increased waterlogging would have had a detrimental effect on alder which may also have been felled at this time. French (1983) at Prah Sands also recorded a phase of woodland clearance by fire with decreases in oak and alder and development of heathland. Radiocarbon dates previously obtained by Heyworth & Kidson (1982) of cal AD 250–540 (1805±100 BP) and Scourse and Kemp (1999) of 40 cal BC–cal AD 530 (1680±50 BP, Q-2372) and cal AD 250–540 (1570±50 BP, Q-2373) show a possible Roman/early historic age (but remaining late prehistoric in character) which may correlate with the forest clearance data obtained here.

Sample & depth (cm)	*Sediment unit*	*Diatoms*	*Diatom nos*	*Quality of preservation*	*Diversity*	*Assemblage type*	*Potential for % count*
D1 110	2.1 'peat'	+	low	very poor	low	fw aero	low
D2 154	2.2 'peat'	–	–	–	–	–	none
D3 162	3 alluvium	–	–	–	–	–	none
D4 186	3 alluvium	–	–	–	–	–	none
D5 202	3 alluvium	–	–	–	–	–	none
D6 330	4 colluvium	–	–	–	–	–	none

(+ present; – absent; fw freshwater; aero aerophilous)

Table 6.3: Summary of diatom evaluation results Penzance Heliport samples showing correlation between sample number and depth/sediment unit (+ present; - absent; fw freshwater; aero aerophilous)

Sea-level change

Many of the peat and alluvial sequences found in Mount's Bay have been controlled primarily by sea-level change and the secondary consequences of barrier bar formation and/or destruction. Here, however, due to altitude, there is no direct evidence of marine or brackish conditions during the period represented by the pollen (middle Holocene, later Mesolithic to Bronze Age) although small numbers of Chenopodiaceae in zone 3 may be attributed to longer distance transport from the coastal zone.

It appears that the on-site community was an established fen carr at this time although it is possible that post-glacial rising relative sea-level will have initiated the damper valley conditions favourable for alder colonisation. It is probable that marine/brackish transgression occurred subsequently. Healy (1995; 1996a 1999a; 1999b) investigated the palaeo-environmental record for Marazion Marsh, Mount's Bay. This is one of the most important coastal sequences examined in this region, providing data on palaeo-environmental information extending back to 4450–4040 cal BC (5420±60 BP, Q-2779). It is possible that the data obtained here may be correlated with the periods of standstill or relative sea-level retrogression as identified by Healy and in the more regional studies by Kidson and Heyworth 1973, Heyworth and Kidson (1982), Healy (1995; 1996a; 1999a; 1999b) and Waller and Long (2003). French (1985) has noted that there is much variation in the dates obtained from the coastal sites, possibly due to the formation and/or destruction of barrier bars.

Summary and conclusion

This study proved successful and has produced useful information on the past vegetation and environment spanning the late middle Holocene, Late Mesolithic and Bronze Age periods. Three local pollen assemblage zones have been recognised which define the character of the Late Mesolithic and Neolithic (4230–4060 to 2580–2460 cal BC) woodland and its replacement by grassland and agriculture. The onsite vegetation saw the development of an alder carr (*Alnetum*) from an initial grass-sedge fen which in part (Neolithic) included a dominant onsite willow community (probably *Salicetum*). The surrounding dryland zone supported oak and hazel woodland during the Late Mesolithic (middle Holocene/Atlantic) and Neolithic. This landscape character is typical of the later Holocene for this region. This woodland was removed during the Chalcolithic period and was subsequently replaced by grassland, also with some evidence of arable cultivation. Although the local hydrology of the coastal zone will have been controlled by changes in relative sea-level, there is no palynological evidence for marine or brackish conditions, due to the altitude of the site. It is thought that the habitat was a mature and stable alder carr fen community which may have been transgressed at a later date. The data obtained are comparable with a number of other past studies undertaken in this region of Cornwall. These other studies indicate that the character and age of such peat sequences varies markedly.

Diatom assessment (core T1/3)

Nigel Cameron

Core T1/3 was selected for detailed sampling. It was hoped (prior to radiocarbon dating) that this core covered the longest chronological sequence. At the time the samples were submitted for assessment the date of the sequence was unknown; however, two samples submitted for radiocarbon dating indicated the

Table 6.4: Diatoms from sample at 110 cm (2.1 'peat'): abunance scale
1 – present
2 – common
3 – more common

Taxon	*D1 110 cm*
Achnanthes lanceolata	1
Amphora libyca	1
Chrysophyte cysts	3
Cymbella sp.	1
Diploneis sp.	2
Gomphonema sp.	1
Hantzschia amphioxys	2
Navicula elginensis	1
Pinnularia major	1
Pinnularia sp.	2
Pinnularia obscura	1
Unknown Naviculaceae	1

deposits were of at least Late Mesolithic (4230–4060 cal BC) and younger than Chalcolithic (2580–2460 cal BC) date, with the upper humose deposits probably representing the Bronze Age palaeo-environment. Six samples from the T1/3 sequence were selected for diatom assessment. The corresponding sample depths of the diatom samples chosen for assessment are shown on the summary table below (Table 6.3). The diatom assessment of each sample takes into account the numbers of diatoms, the state of preservation of the diatom assemblages, species diversity and diatom species environmental preferences.

Methods

Diatom preparation followed standard techniques (Battarbee *et al.* 2001). Two coverslips were made from each sample and fixed in Naphrax for diatom microscopy. A large area of the coverslips on each slide was scanned for diatoms at magnifications of ×400 and ×1000 under phase contrast illumination.

Diatom floras and taxonomic publications were consulted to assist with diatom identification; these include Werff and Huls (1957–1974), Hartley *et al.* (1996), Krammer and Lange-Bertalot (1986–1991).

Results and discussion

The results of the diatom evaluation are summarised in Table 6.3 and diatom species data are represented in Table 6.4.

Diatoms are absent from the five samples assessed from between 330 cm to 154 cm covering the alluvium, colluvium and base of the humose layer. The exception was in a sample near the top of the alluvium at 162 cm (sample D3) where a single, very poorly preserved pennate diatom fragment was recorded. This small fragment may be derived from the freshwater aerophile *Pinnularia major*. There is no further potential for diatom analysis of these samples. The absence of diatoms from the samples from this section of the T1/3 core can be attributed to taphonomic processes (Flower 1993; Ryves *et al.* 2001). This may be the result of diatom silica dissolution and breakage caused by factors such as extremes of sediment alkalinity or acidity, the under-saturation of sediment pore water with dissolved silica, cycles of prolonged drying and rehydration, or physical damage to diatom valves from transport and abrasion.

Diatoms are, however, present in the top sample from the top of the humose (humified peat) layer at 110 cm (sample D1). Diatoms in this are present in relatively low numbers; the quality of valve preservation is very poor with much fragmentation and dissolution of silica. Diatom diversity is low and the potential for percentage diatom analysis is low (Table 6.3). However, this diatom assemblage does provide some environmental evidence. The diatoms present here are all shallow water, non-planktonic species. These are attached or benthic diatoms; planktonic, open water taxa are absent. The freshwater diatoms represented also include species tolerant of ephemeral aquatic or damp terrestrial environments. These aerophilous taxa are able to withstand periods of desiccation. The existence of an aquatic habitat subject to periods of drying is also supported by the abundance of chrysophyte stomatocyts. These cysts are formed by chrysophytes, another group of siliceous algae, often in response to environmental stress such as drying of the aquatic environment.

The aerophilous diatom taxa include *Hantzschia amphioxys, Pinnularia major* and *Pinnularia obscura*. Freshwater non-plankton include *Amphora libyca, Achnanthes lanceolata* and *Navicula elginensis* (Table 6.4). The poor quality of diatom preservation is reflected in the fragmented nature of the diatom valves and consequently the number of taxa identifiable only to the level of genus. Aside from the shallow water depth and freshwater nature of the waterbody, the diatoms do not show any evidence for high rates of water flow or aquatic nutrient enrichment for example.

Summary and conclusions

1. Microscope slides were prepared for diatom

assessment from six samples taken from Core T1/3.
2. Diatoms are absent from the lower five samples, with the exception of a small fragment noted at 162 cm (2.2 'peat'). The absence of diatom assemblages from the samples is attributed to taphonomic processes. Percentage diatom analysis is not possible for these five samples.
3. Diatom assessment of the top sample indicates a diatom assemblage comprised of a mixture of aerophilous-freshwater and freshwater diatom taxa. These are non-planktonic diatoms that are associated with shallow water, ephemeral aquatic or wet terrestrial habitats. There is no evidence from this diatom assemblage for high rates of water flow or for aquatic nutrient enrichment.
4. The presence of relatively high numbers of chrysophyte stomatocysts provides supporting evidence of environmental stress such as periodic drying out of the aquatic environment.
5. There is low potential for further diatom analysis of the top sample from 110 cm (2.1 'peat').
6. No further analysis was undertaken.

Waterlogged wood and plant remains

Michael J. Allen

After description, photography, subsampling and examination for artefacts, three bulk small samples of 0.7 to 0.9 litres were removed from core T1/3 from the humose layer for examination for waterlogged plant remains (110–118 cm, and 118–121 cm from unit 2a, and 133–145cm (Unit 2b).

The samples were processed by washover bucket flotation in the AEA laboratory facilities. The flot was decanted onto a 300 µm mesh sieve and the residues passed through a nest of 2 mm, 1 mm, 0.5 mm and 300 µm mesh. Despite the presence of waterlogged wood in the core (equivalent to sample 100–118 cm) little waterlogged material was present in any sample. A few fine roundwood and small pieces of larger wood fragments were present, especially in the upper sample. The flots contained very little (>30 ml) of fine organic detritus with few recognisable plant remains and virtually no seeds or seed cases. The deposit was largely a fine silt and dark minerogenic sand. In fact, the greater decomposition at the base with some surface plant remains is typically of humose terrestrial soils; an azonal moist ranker. This confirmed the highly humified nature of the 'peaty' humose layer.

Palaeo-economy

Bulk samples were taken from key deposits during the excavation of the barrow by the excavators. Flots from two key contexts – (a black fill of the mound, context 200, and the lower fill of the north cist, context 203) – were selected for analysis and identification of the charcoal and charred plant remains (Clapham, below). These provide the basis of some comment on the palaeo-economy of the society that built the barrow, as well as activities related to the barrow and its use. These identifications also facilitated the section of suitable material for radiocarbon dating (Chapter 7).

Charred plants and charcoal from the barrow

A.J. Clapham

Two samples of charred material, one from the almost black inner mound deposit 200 and one from the lower fill of the northern cist 207, fill 203 were analysed for charred plant remains and charcoal. Although the two samples were full of charred material, charred plant remains were limited in both numbers and diversity. Charcoal was present in great quantities, but the number of taxa present was small.

Methods

The samples of 30 and 40 litres were processed using standard flotation techniques by Cornwall Archaeological Unit (CAU) with the flot being collected on 0.3 mm mesh. The flots, once dried, were then sieved through a series of mesh sizes: 4 mm, 2 mm and 0.3 mm.

For charred plant remain analysis each flot was sorted using a low-powered (×7–×56) stereomicroscope and the plant remains picked out were identified using the author's own modern seed reference collection and Cappers *et al.* (2006).

For charcoal identification 25 pieces from each sample were selected randomly and examined under a high-powered (×14–×112)

Table 6.5: Charred plant remains identified from the two barrow samples (contexts 200 and 203)

Species	Common name	*Sample* 3	6
	Context	200	203
	Feature	*mound material*	*lower fill of cist 207*
Hordeum vulgare grain	barley	4	–
Cereal grain indet. frags	Misc. cereal grain	–	6
Pteridium aquilinum pinnule frags	bracken	–	2
Medicago sp./*Melilotus* sp.	medick/melilot	–	1
Trifolium sp.	clover	–	1
Persicaria maculosa	redshank	–	1
Polygonum aviculare	knotgrass	1	–
Fallopia convolvulus	black bindweed	–	2
Chenopodium album	fat hen	–	6
Luzula campestris	field wood-rush	1	–
Poaceae (non-cereal) culm internodes	grass	8	3
Poaceae (non-cereal) culm bases	grass	2	–
Cenococcum geophilum sclerotia	soil fungus	10	–

Table 6.6: Charcoal identified from fill of the cist 207 and mound material 200

Taxon	Common name	*Sample* 3	6
	Context	200	203
Fabaceae (*Ulex* sp.)	gorse	11rw: 1hw	15rw: 6hw
Quercus sp.	oak	6rw: 1hw	3rw
Salix sp.	willow	4rw	–
Unidentifiable		2kw	1kw
Total		25	25

(rw = roundwood; hw = heartwood; kw = knotwood)

stereomicroscope. Each piece was examined in all three dimensions to obtain the most accurate identification. Identification was aided by Hather (2000). Where possible, annual growth rings were counted. Where roundwood was noted the diameter was recorded. All nomenclature follows that of Stace (2019). The results are shown in Tables 6.5 and 6.6 and Figures 6.3a and 6.3b.

Results

All plant remains were preserved by charring. The quality of preservation was at best poor, especially the charcoal. Most of the charcoal from both contexts was encrusted in clay and mineral impregnation (iron oxide) was evident. The charcoal had a vitreous/lustrous quality to it and was very friable/brittle, breaking into small pieces when fractured to produce a clean surface for identification. Once under the microscope it was noted that the charcoal fragments showed signs of distortion and rupturing. This, along with the vitreous/lustrous appearance, suggests that the wood used in the pyres was subjected to high temperatures.

The charred plant remains and charcoal (Tables 6.5 & 6.6)

The numbers of plant remains in both samples were low in both samples as was species diversity. Charcoal dominated the remains and in both samples was mostly of twig-like material.

Inner mound deposit 200

The sample from deposit 200 of the central mound material consisted of a dark black clay silt with patches of small angular stones and powdery, twiggy charcoal. The depth of the deposit varied from 0.05 m to 0.15 m in the south of the mound. The higher central/northern portion of the deposit was possibly truncated by ploughing/machine clearance. The deposit overlies the natural clayey silt 206 (Lawson-Jones 2019; Chapter 2).

The charred plant remains present in this sample consisted of four barley (*Hordeum vulgare*) grains and single examples of knotgrass (*Polygonum aviculare*) and field club-rush (*Luzula campestris*). Other remains identified included those of non-cereal grasses (Table 6.5). It is most likely that the plant assemblage represents a background flora, or the remains of a turf used in the pyre.

The charcoal (Table 6.6) consisted of three taxa: Fabaceae, most likely gorse (*Ulex* sp.), oak (*Quercus* sp.) and willow (*Salix* sp.).

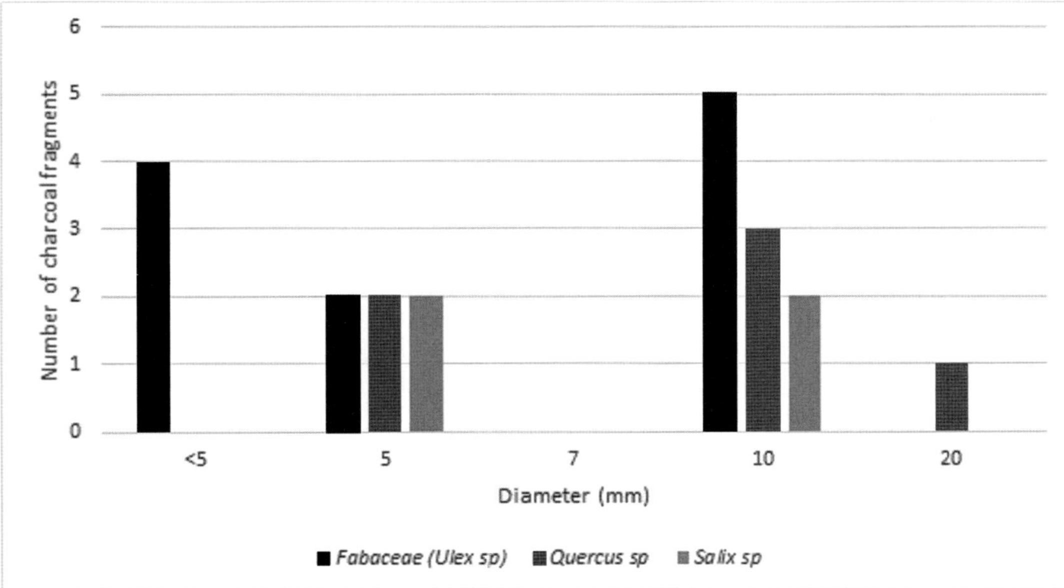

Figure 6.3a: Distribution of diameter (mm) of roundwood identified from mound fill 200

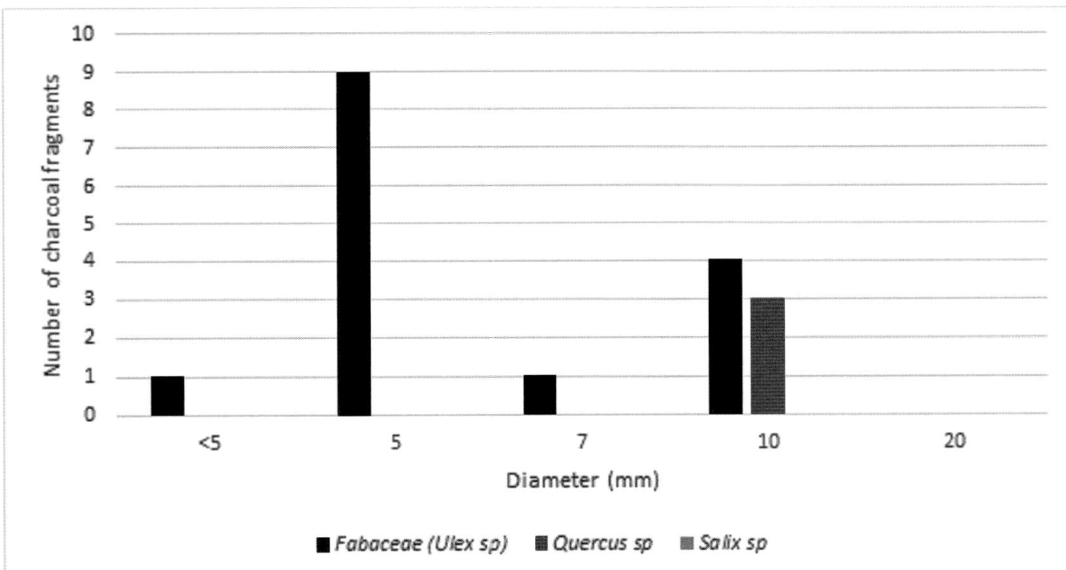

Figure 6.3b: Distribution of diameter (mm) of roundwood identified from lower fill 203 of cist 207

The commonest find was that of Fabaceae (*Ulex* sp.). Assignment of Fabaceae charcoal to a species is difficult due to the variation encountered, not between species but within the same species (Hather 2000). Given the local conditions at Penzance it is most likely that the Fabaceae charcoal is that of gorse (*Ulex* sp.), probably common gorse (*Ulex europaeus*). Due to the variable nature of Fabaceae wood, annual ring counts can also be difficult as they can vary both in size and they may not be complete, or else they produce false rings (Hather 2000). Annual rings were visible in some of the Fabaceae fragments (4 pieces) and ranged from 4 to 5 rings. The diameter of the roundwood ranged from 10 mm to less than 5 mm (Fig. 6.3a).

Oak (*Quercus* sp.) was the second commonest charcoal taxon with seven fragments being identified, six of which were roundwood and one of heartwood. Annual rings ranged from 15+ for the fragment of heartwood and between 4 and 8 for the roundwood. The diameter of the roundwood ranged from 20 mm to 5 mm (Fig. 6.3a). Four fragments of willow (*Salix* sp.) were identified from this sample and consisted of roundwood whose diameter ranged between 10 mm and 5 mm (Fig. 6.3a). No annual rings were discernible due to distortion of most of the pieces.

Northern cist 207, lower fill 203

This sample was of the dark, nearly black, soft loose silt fill of the northern cist 207. It contained occasional very small stones and quite frequent charcoal. It was 0.08 m deep and extended across the base of the stone-sided cist and came down on to a thin gritty rab-like deposit at the base of the cist which was of a yellow clayey silt (206). The very base of the deposit produced a copper alloy ingot (Chapters 2 & 5). Again, the charred plant remains were sparse in number and diversity (Table 6.5) and consisted of six fragments of indeterminate cereal grain, two pinnule fragments of bracken (*Pteridium aquilinum*) and single examples of medick/melilot (*Medicago* sp./*Melilotus* sp.), clover (*Trifolium* sp.), redshank (*Persicaria maculosa*), along with two black bindweed (*Fallopia convolvulus*) and six fat hen (*Chenopodium album*) seeds. Three grass stems were also recorded. The charred plant assemblage represents open disturbed habitats which may have been present around the cist or perhaps from a turf that was used on the pyre. The bracken may have been used as tinder for the pyre.

The charcoal (Table 6.6) mostly consisted of small roundwood of Fabaceae (*Ulex* sp.) with some oak roundwood. The Fabaceae roundwood had a diameter of between 10 mm and less than 5 mm with most (9 pieces) having a diameter of 5 mm (Fig. 6.3b). All the oak roundwood had a diameter of 10 mm. Annual rings of the Fabaceae charcoal fragments were difficult to discern but where they could be seen the roundwood ranged from 4–7+ rings with one larger piece showing 20+ annual growth rings. The oak roundwood annual ring count ranged from 5 to 8+ rings.

Discussion

Given the similarity in the radiocarbon dates obtained for each sample (context 200, 910–810 cal BC; 2714±27 BP, SUERC-47293; and context 203, 930–810 cal BC; 2734±27 BP, SUERC-47292), it is possible to discuss the charred assemblages together. The charred plant assemblages from both contexts contained a small number of cereal remains with barley grains. No chaff remains were found in either sample. The low numbers possibly suggests that the cereals are part of a 'background' flora along with the other plant remains identified from the samples. However, microwear wear on the cobble muller (SF 7) from pit 100 is consistent with the processing of plant material (Chapter 3) and small grain assemblages are known from other Bronze Age monuments (Jones 2004–5), which allows the possibility of small-scale consumption of food at the site. The non-cereal remains were of open/disturbed/cultivated habitats and therefore may be associated with the cereal remains. Due to the paucity of the remains, it is difficult to say whether crops were grown in the area, but the possibility cannot be ruled out. It is highly unlikely that the remains formed part of the cremation ritual.

The charcoal was limited to three taxa: Fabaceae (probably gorse), oak, and willow. Willow was not found in the lower fill 203 of the cist. Most of the charcoal consisted of small roundwood pieces ranging in size from 10 mm to less than 5 mm in diameter with a single piece measuring 20 mm in diameter (Figs 6.3a & 6.3b). Heartwood of the tree species (oak and willow) was noticeably absent. Where it was possible to count the annual rings of the woody taxa, a small range of only 4 to 8 rings was recorded. This limited number of taxa and the small size range used in the pyre may be due to the local woodland having already been cleared by the time the cist was built, with only scrub species such as gorse that could survive on poor, thin soils being present. Previous work (Healy 1995; 1996a; French 1999) has shown that the area was most likely treeless by the Late Bronze Age, therefore restricting the range of available woody species for creating a pyre. The small size of the oak and willow may suggest that the availability of large branches and trunks was limited and perhaps the local oaks and willows were small scrubby trees. This is highly probable given the exposed windy position which would have stunted tree growth and promoted the growth of scrubbier species such as gorse.

The vitreous/lustrous appearance and the brittle nature of the charcoal indicates that the temperature of the pyre must have been high. This is supported by many of the charcoal pieces exhibiting the distortion or obliteration of the diagnostic features of the charcoal. It is also possible that the distortion of the charcoal could be due to the use of green rather than dry material where the water present in the wood rapidly turns to steam and ruptures the cells obscuring their identification. There is no real evidence for woodland management within the samples analysed.

Conclusions

The charred plant remains were mainly of species which are found on disturbed/open ground and were probably growing in the area, becoming incorporated into the pyre; some grains of barley (*Hordeum vulgare*) and indeterminate cereal grain fragments were also present. Although limited in number and diversity this suggest that cereal cultivation may have been carried out in the area. The charcoal consisted of most probably gorse (*Ulex* sp.) with oak and willow. It is likely that this limited number of woody taxa was collected locally and used in the pyre (Table 6.6). The lack of diversity in wood types and the small diameter of the pieces recorded suggests that wood in the area was in short supply as the landscape had already been cleared of its woodland cover. It is likely that any expanse of wooded landscape by the Late Bronze Age was restricted to the steep-sided river valleys and other inaccessible places such as cliff faces. The vitreous/lustrous appearance and the distortion of the woody tissues suggests that high temperatures were reached in the pyre. The gorse may have been used as kindling.

7

Radiocarbon dating

Michael J. Allen and Andy M. Jones

Five radiocarbon determinations were obtained from the Penzance Heliport barrow (Table 7.1 & Fig. 7.1). Three of these were obtained during the evaluation phase (SUERC-78029, SUERC-78031 and SUERC-78030) and two more were obtained as part of the current project (SUERC-47292 and SUERC-47293). Further radiocarbon determinations were also obtained from the augering, and these have been discussed in Chapter 6.

The samples were submitted for AMS radiocarbon dating at the Scottish Universities Environmental Research Centre. They were processed at SUERC following a modified version of the pre-treatment method outlined by Longin (1971) with modification of the ultrafiltration method (Bronk Ramsey *et al.* 2004) and measurement by AMS as described by Xu *et al.* (2004).

The AMS radiocarbon dates and results are given in Table 7.1 and are quoted in accordance with the international standard known as the Trondheim convention (Stuiver & Kra 1986). They are conventional radiocarbon ages (Stuiver & Polach 1977). Calibration of the results has been performed using the data set published by Riemer *et al.* (2013) and performed using the programme OxCal v4.2.3 (www.flaha.ox.ac.uk/). Details of the algorithms employed by this program are available from the on-line manual or in Bronk Ramsey (1995; 1998; 2001; 2009). The calibrated date ranges (Table 7.1) in text are cited are those with 95% confidence and have been rounded out to the nearest 10 years (Mook 1986). The radiocarbon age given is calibrated to the calendar timescale using the Oxford Radiocarbon Accelerator Unit calibration program OxCal 4.3.2 (Bronk Ramsey 2009); date ranges have been calibrated using the IntCal13 atmospheric calibration curve (Reimer *et al.* 2013).

With the exception of the determination (SUERC-78029) from barrow ditch [300], however, none of the charcoal fragments submitted from the 2017 evaluation (Southwest Archaeology 2018) was confirmed to be related functionally to the feature from which they came, and all pieces could be incidental or residual. However, the similarity of the results from the two pits suggests contemporary or near-contemporary events, lending some weight to the argument that the charcoal fragments selected may relate to events that had taken place at the barrow.

Feature	*Context*	*Material*	*Lab no.*	*Result BP*	*δC¹³‰*	*Cal BC*
Northern cist 207	203	*Ulex* cf *europaeus*	SUERC-47292	2734±27	–23.8	930–810
Central mound 102	200	*Ulex* sp.	SUERC-47293	2714±27	–24.5	910–810
Barrow ditch 300	301	*Alunus/Corylus*	SUERC-78029	3391±29	27.6	1750–1630
Central pit 100	111	*Alnus* roundwood	SUERC-78031	3169±29	–28.0	1500–1400
Large recut pit 400	407	*Alnus* roundwood	SUERC-78030	3081±29	–27.6	1420–1280

Table 7.1: Radiocarbon determinations from the Penzance barrow

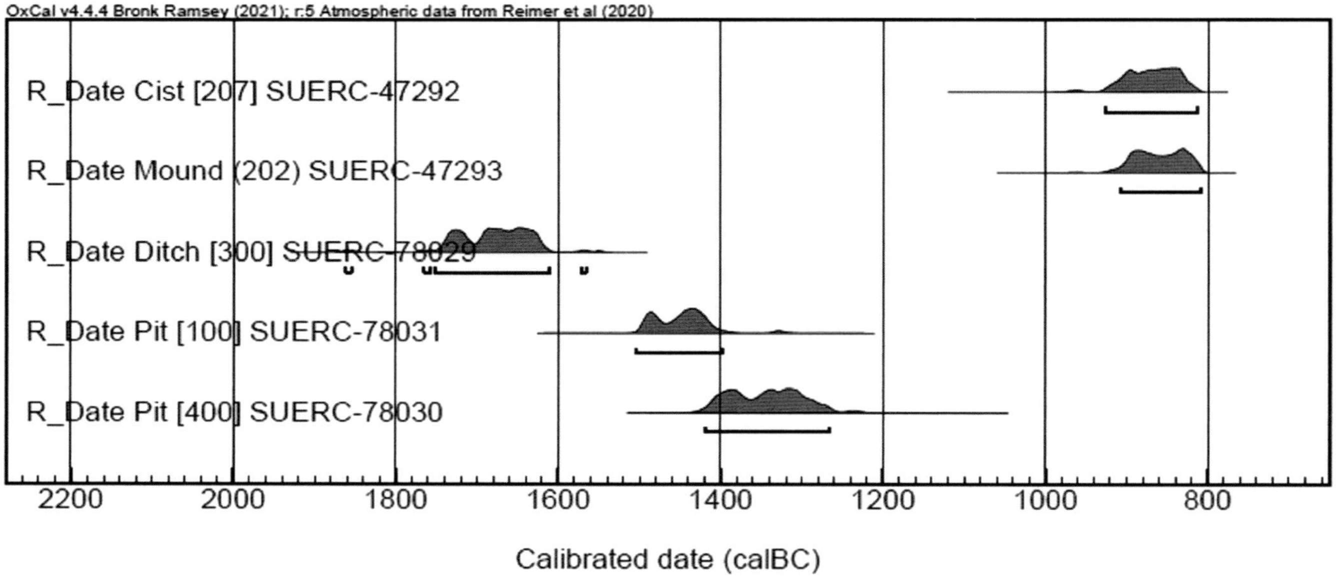

Figure 7.1: Radiocarbon determinations from the Penzance Heliport barrow

Charcoal from the 2018 excavation, however, were carefully selected to be considered to be related functionally to events associated with the barrow. Roundwood charcoal from the lower fill of central cist 207 was from a deposit with frequent charcoal, copper ingot fragment (SF 15) (Chapter 5) and a burnt sherd of Beaker pottery (Chapter 3). The charcoal was considered likely to be pyre debris (Chapter 6). The central mound deposit 200 contained abundant charcoal fragments and black powdery charcoal, and the deposit itself was black in colour (Chapter 2). The quantity of charcoal was also assumed to indicate that it was pyre-derived material, although whether the two deposits related to the same pyre event was unclear, and it is possible that a series of events took place on the site.

The dates on the charcoal were therefore intended to define whether one or more than one events were involved, and whether they related to dated charcoal from the ditch 103, central pit 100 and large recut pit 400 to the north-east of the centre of the barrow. The resulting determinations both fell in the Late Bronze Age and appear belong to events close in time, and are consistent with the date of the copper ingot fragment (Chapter 5). It therefore seems likely that the barrow had a long history with initial use associated with the cutting of ditch 300 a little before the middle of the 2nd millennium cal BC followed by later activity at the end of the millennium, when cist 207 was infilled and the charred mound raised over the site (as discussed in Chapter 13). The two Middle Bronze Age radiocarbon determinations from pits 100 and 400 suggest activity during intervening period; however, they are clearly from disturbed contexts. The dating of the cist and the mound to the Late Bronze Age represents an unique discovery and the significance of the results will be discussed in Chapter 13.

SECTION 3:

FIELDWORK AT MARAZION MARSH

8

Marazion Marsh: background and fieldwork methodology

Michael J. Allen and Andy M. Jones

Background

Andy M. Jones

The Cornwall Archaeological Unit were commissioned by Cormac consulting to undertake a programme of archaeological investigation during coastal protection works, designed to counteract the effects of rising sea-levels in the Mount's Bay area, as the line of the main London railway, the coastal footpath and cycle way, Longrock industrial estate and housing in the vicinity were considered vulnerable to the threat posed thereby. The marshes are, however, an important resource associated with significant archaeological finds and deposits including a Roman urn containing a hoard of 1000 coins and buried peats, which have been forming since the Mesolithic period. The area surrounding the Marsh also contains a large number of significant later prehistoric find-spots including those of Bronze Age hoards and metalworking deposits. These deposits form the focus for Chapter 10.

The archaeological recording was undertaken in October to December 2019 and included a watching brief undertaken by Cornwall Archaeological Unit during site works and environmental coring carried out by AEA: Allen Environmental Archaeology at the southern side of the marsh to recover palaeo-environmental material for further assessment and analysis. However, the environmental coring in the marshes revealed a long peat sequence on the southern edge of Marazion Marsh.

The initial results from the watching brief together with an assessment of the palaeo-environmental samples were presented in an archive level report (Jones 2020b). The assessment of the palaeo-environmental deposits from the coring were shown to be of national significance. While no further reporting was required for the watching brief, given the importance of the results of the palaeo-environmental sampling, it was deemed to be useful to review them, and the methods used to obtain them, here. Accordingly, this section presents the background and methods and Chapters 9 and 10 discuss the results.

Introduction

Michael J. Allen with Andy M. Jones

Marazion Marsh is a drowned embayed estuary in the shadow of St Michael's Mount with a modest inland body of brackish water (Fig. 8.1). It is separated from the sea at Mount's Bay by an ancient sand and gravel bar (Longrock) which generally prevents access to the marsh by the sea, and behind which lies the largest reed bed (16.8 ha) in Cornwall. The embayed estuary (Marazion Marsh) is dominated by *Phragmites australis* reed bed and marsh, alder scrub (*Alnus glutinosa*) with white birch (*Betula pubescens*), willow (*Salix* spp.),

Figure 8.1: (opposite page) Location map with the extent of Marazion Marsh, the Heliport barrow and St Michael's Mount

Figure 8.2: (opposite page) Location of dated peats in the area; the core reported here is the blue dot, those in Marazion Marsh recorded by Healy are the red stars to east

rushes (*Juncus* sp.), and grasses/sedges (eg, *Equisetum*, Cyperaceae and Gramineae). The *Phragmites*-dominated marsh is drained by the Red River (also known as the Marazion River), which is the present day incarnation of the submerged St Michael's channel forming part of the Mount's Bay palaeo-valley system (Ong 1966; Camm & Dominy 1998; Camm 1999). It runs through the marsh and cuts a channel (now culverted) through the barrier at its eastern end (Healy 1999b).

The marsh is an important RSPB reserve for breeding and over-wintering birds and passage migrants. It is a SSSI, carefully managed for wildlife, and the prevention of run-off from adjacent agricultural activity. The marsh is surrounded by regionally and nationally important metalwork finds of Bronze Age to Romano-British date (as reviewed in Chapter 12). These include the discovery, during drainage works in 1793, of a pot containing about 1000 copper Roman coins (thought to be of Emperor Victorinus, AD 268–271: Gilbert 1817, 193; Penhallurick 2009, 150) and in the 19th century one or two Middle Bronze Age palstaves, which were said (rather unusually) to have been deposited in an iron vessel (Pearce 1983, 400; Chapter 12, this volume).

The basal geology of Lower Devonian Mylor Slates (and locally Hornfelsed Slate and Hornfelsed Siltstone; Goode & Taylor 1988; Shail 1989) lie beneath 7–10 m of Holocene sediment. Analysis by Healy (eg, 1995; 1999b) had already demonstrated that the marsh contains an important palaeo-environmental record. The most relevant palaeo-environmental records are those located to the east, and south of the railway line (Fig. 8.2). Marine sand over sand and gravel over organic deposits were encountered and the latter analysed for pollen and diatoms and dated to *c.* cal AD 350–950 and 4450–2900 cal BC (Healy 1995; 1996b; 1996c; 1996d; 1999a; 1999b). This research concentrated on sea-level rise and identifying the impact of mining rather than palaeo-environmental and land-use reconstruction. It showed marine transgression between *c.* 4350 and 3200/2900 BC with rising water tables and sea-levels, concomitant with increased salinity sealing a basal organic-rich horizon with minerogenic deposits. It suggested an increasing marine influence, but the developing marsh was protected from direct impact from the sea by the sand and gravel spit in its southern, seaward margin, although several breaches or overwashes occurred as a result of rising sea-level.

The transition from freshwater to marine/brackish-water conditions starts in organic-rich basal sediments (4350–2900 cal BC). The main marine transgression occurred in the Neolithic after *c.* 3200 cal BC with substantial and rapid minerogenic marine sedimentation over organic-rich deposits, and similar transgression can be seen elsewhere in coastal sites (eg, Ponsandane, Prah Sands, Gulval Forest Maenporth, Trewornan) in Cornwall (Healy 1995; 1999c). Only the organic-rich deposits were examined by Healy for pollen; nevertheless, it shows increasing site wetness during its formation. The pollen record shows basal records (4450–4040 cal BC; see Table 8.1) of Mesolithic open grasslands (high herbaceous pollen), and the development of local open woodland cover with increased tree and shrub pollen. Increasing wetness ensued accompanied by lower rates of peat development, and the development of *Phrgamites* reed bed, with woodland decreasing leaving alder-dominated fen-carr and reed-marsh. This is associated with minerogenic sand-dominated sediments (with some gravels). There is a gradual transition from freshwater to brackish-water conditions in the lower peat deposits, indicating marine water ingression through the sand and gravel bar, rather than large-scale marine inundation breaching a barrier protecting the embayed estuary and marsh.

Fieldwork opportunity and aims

Michael J. Allen

A palaeo-environmental record has the potential to examine a long history of the environment and land-use, especially in relation to prehistoric activity, featuring and metalwork deposition in the area (eg, Pearce 1983; Knight *et al.* 2015; Chapter 12, this volume), to Roman activity and the deposition of one of the region's largest coin hoards on the edge of the marsh, and to medieval activity at St Michael's Mount. The environmental record could potentially establish whether the clearance of the post-landnam open woodland and the establishment of extensive pasture were associated with these activities, and provides a

Barrow site
Marazion Marsh
Penzance
St Michael's Mount
0
2km

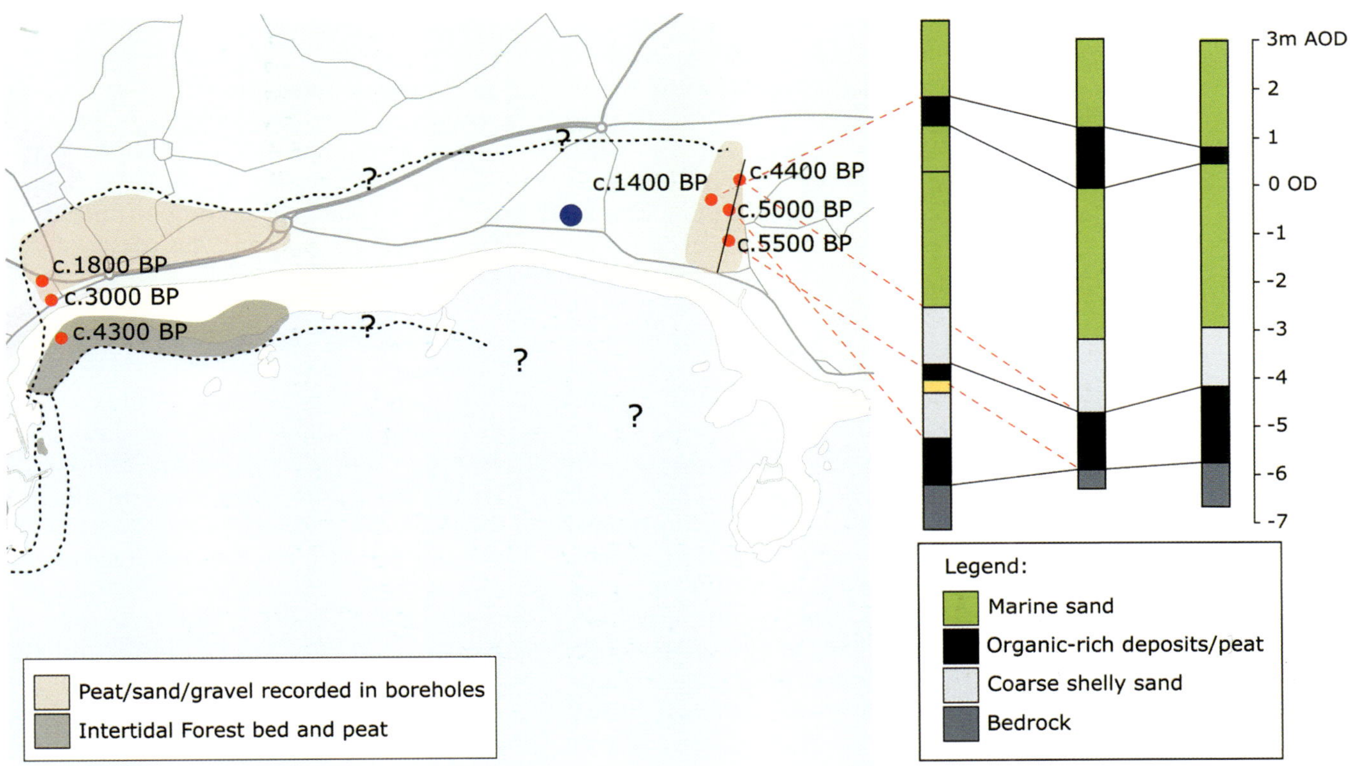
c.1400 BP
c.4400 BP
c.5000 BP
c.5500 BP
c.1800 BP
c.3000 BP
c.4300 BP
3m AOD
2
1
0 OD
-1
-2
-3
-4
-5
-6
-7
Legend:
Marine sand
Organic-rich deposits/peat
Coarse shelly sand
Bedrock
Peat/sand/gravel recorded in boreholes
Intertidal Forest bed and peat

Site	*Core*	*Grid Ref*	*OD*	*Material*	*Lab ref*	*Result BP*	*δC*^{13} *‰*	*Calibrated date*
Upper 'peat'								
Marazion Marsh	C	SW 510312	+0.88		Q-2778	1610±40		cal AD 350–550
Marazion Marsh	A	SW 512313	+0.80		Q-2775	1210±40		cal AD 680–940
Lower 'peat'								
Marazion Marsh	B	SW 513316	–4.46		Q-2776	5100±65		4040–3710 cal BC
Marazion Marsh	C	SW 513312	–4.71		Q-2780	4380±55		3330–2890 cal BC
Marazion Marsh	A	SW 512313	–5.28		Q-2774	4395±60		3340–2890 cal BC
Marazion Marsh	B	SW 513316	–5.71		Q-2777	5050±65		3980–3700 cal BC
Marazion Marsh	C	SW 513312	–6.21		Q-2779	5420±80		4450–4040 cal BC
Ponsandane	–	SW 481311	+2.21		Q-2882	680±50		cal AD 1270–1390
Ponsandane	–	SW 481311	+0.42		Q-2883	3050±65		1490–1110 cal BC
Hayle	–	SW 565380	–1.59		Q-2773	4520±50		3020–2630 cal BC
Gulval Forest	–	SW 484309	–1.60	Birch wood	SRR-714	4280±50	–24.7	3080–700 cal BC
Maeonporth	–	SW 791297	–5.53		Q-2881	6110±85		5300–4800 cal BC
Trewornan	–		–9.41		Q-2781	6460±80		5620–5610 cal BC

Calibration by OxCal v4.3.2 Bronk Ramsey (2017); r:5, and IntCal13 atmospheric curve (Reimer *et al.* 2013)

Table 8.1: Marazion Marsh ^{14}C *results from Healy 1995; 1999b; 1999c; Harkness & Wilson 1979 (calibration by OxCal v4.3.2 Bronk Ramsey (2017); r:5, and IntCal13 atmospheric curve (Reimer* et al. *2013))*

record of coastal development and formation of the lake and marsh.

A programme of coring and geoarchaeological and palaeo-environmental work was a mitigation response relating to coastal protection and allied works on the beach at Longrock, Mount's Bay and within and adjoining Marazion Marsh towards the eastern end of the Bay. In particular the coring here was specifically in relation to a proposed silt trap where the water from Marazion Marsh makes its way out of the Marsh to the sea. Coring was located at, or as near as possible to, the proposed silt trap (Figs 8.3 & 8.4). It was felt that the acquisition of dated and more detailed palaeo-environmental sequences (pollen plants and diatoms) may enable these data to be correlated with the periods of standstill or relative sea-level retrogression as identified by Healy and in broader regional studies by Heyworth and Kidson (1982) and Waller and Long (2003).

More significantly the aims were to recover a long stratified sediment sequence which could provide a dated palaeo-environmental record of the changing physical environment, resources and land-use history. This would act as the background for the important archaeological finds, and as a comparison with the prehistoric and Bronze Age palaeo-environmental data (pollen, charred plants, etc.) from the cairn at the Penzance Heliport site, and associated palaeo-environmental coring) from the higher, drier land at the heliport on the slopes above Penzance itself (Chapters 2 and 6). It would complement and significantly advance the work of Healy, whose analysis was restricted to the organic-rich deposits, but here we wished to concentrate on the potential changing human resources using the landscape and land-use record.

Background and previous work

As alluded to above, the deep (7 m+) stratified deposits in the marsh itself have been the subject of research by Healy in particular, but this is set within a backdrop of interest in submerged forests around the coasts of the South West (eg, Westward Ho!, Devon; Balaam *et al.* 1987; Heyworth 1978). A number of such forests are known around Mount's Bay from Ponsandane to Gunwalloe (Borlase 1758; Healy 1996b, French 1999, fig. 2; fig. 1), and there are dated examples along the Cornwall coastline (including the late glacial example in the St Mount's Bay palaeo-valley, dated to 12,180–11,800 cal BC (12070±80 BP, SRR 3022). Excepting that example, the submerged forests range from -5.53 m OD (5300–4800 cal BC, 6110±85, BP, Q-2881) to -1.6 m to +2.2 m with dates ranging from 2470–1660 cal BC (3656±150 BP, BM-29), to cal AD 1260–144 (680±40 BP, Q-2882), as cited in French (1999). No major palaeo-environmental work has been done on these submerged forests, however, and the term 'forest' has been questioned by Healy (1995; 1999b).

Previous work in Marazion Marsh by Healy encountered two organic/peat horizons in three cores (Fig. 8.5). An upper horizon at about +0.88–0.80 m OD was dated to cal AD 350–950, and the lower horizon from -4.46 m to -6.21 m OD was dated to 4450–2900 cal BC (Table 8.1). Minerogenic banded sediments in Marazion Marsh (eg, Healy 1996d), and relating to silts and sands higher up the core profiles profile relate to mining of metalliferous ores in the catchment area in the 18th and in particular the early 19th centuries (Dines 1956).

The peat horizon in the core here is at 1.10 m OD to -0.69 m OD suggesting that it may relate to the later peat phase recovered previously, and thus relates to the late Romano-British and early medieval activity in the area. The core, however, continues for another *c.* 5.5 m below this horizon and thus the macrofossils (pollen and diatoms) may relate to the later Mesolithic and Neolithic phases analysed by Healy (*op. cit.*).

Coring 2019

Coring was undertaken 1st and 2nd October 2019 by Cormac Ltd. Due to tidal water levels, soft sediments and the presence of fast running deep water in a channel, the rig was set up on a small platform constructed close the edge of standing water and channel on the north side of Longrock Road at the foot of the embankment and the edge of the marsh. After a platform had been constructed, stabilised and made good, a Dando terrier rig was craned in.

The precise location of the core was chosen due to accessibility (Fig. 8.3), although while the core head was positioned as far as practicable from the road embankment, it did lie within a line of rotten squared wooden posts, one of which was *c.* 11 × 9 cm and stood *c.* 0.7 m high (presumably marking the foot of the embankment). Further to the north, away from the embankment, the base of the rig would have been submerged, and engulfed by rising tidal water levels. The location is recorded at 150517.82 E, 31345.39 N, and at 2.15 m OD.

One core was undertaken and drilled to bedrock (Fig. 8.5). The vegetative mat, roots and organic mud (to 0.4 m) were cut out (and retained in part undisturbed) to enable better sample recovery. Sleeves were inserted and the cores of 117 mm diameter were recovered in a window sampler by percussion coring. The coring and core recovery was supervised by the writer who recovered the retained cores to the AEA laboratory facilities where it was sampled throughout for pollen, diatoms, waterlogged plants, shells and material suitable for radiocarbon dating.

Methods

Cores of 117 mm diameter and 1 m length were recovered using the percussion-driven Dando Terrier rig (Fig. 8.3). Cores were examined in the AEA laboratory; each was cut open (not extruded), the exposed face cleaned and undisturbed sediment described under magnified illumination following standard pedological and sedimentological terminology (eg, Hodgson 1997), and photographed (by Allen using the method described in Allen *et al.* 2019; appendix 1). The profile was subsampled at 10 mm bandwidth and at 40 mm intervals through the humified peat (Unit 3) and 80 mm and 160 mm intervals through minerogenic deposits for pollen, and at broader intervals for diatoms. Small bulk samples were taken though the entire sequence, generally in 100 mm blocks, for the recovery of waterlogged plants and shells. Samples for radiocarbon dating were sediment samples for humic acid (10 mm bandwidth) in the absence of any recognisable and locatable suitable plant remains.

The analyses

The recovery of an undisturbed sediment core 7.20 m long beneath the modern root mat and soft organic mud (to 0.4 m) enabled subsampling for pollen, diatoms, waterlogged plant remains and shells as well as humic samples for radiocarbon dating. Detailed assessment of selected samples for pollen, diatoms and shells (see Langdon and Cameron respectively in Allen *et al.* 2019) defined the sets of samples that were progressed to full analysis.

The stratigraphy

Coring on the edge of the marsh, north of Longrock Road, was at 2.15 m OD and cored through weathered bedrock (shale and silt at -4.85 m OD) and recorded bedrock at -5.35 m OD (7.50 m depth); coring continued to -6.70 m OD (8.85 m depth). The stratigraphy

Figure 8.3: The Dando terrier rig tucked in at the base of the embankment on the edge of the marsh (Photos: © M.J. Allen 2019)

comprises fine sand (to 1.10 m OD) over humified peat and organic-rich deposits (cal AD 420–A30 to 5060–4850 cal BC) to -0.45 m, over stony sand gravels fining upwards to a silt to -2.75 m, over silts and clays to bedrock at -4.85 m.

This is a major sequence which significantly expands the stratigraphic and archaeological

Figure 8.4: Approximate location of core (approximate former location of the silt trap), Healy's cores lie off the to the east of this map

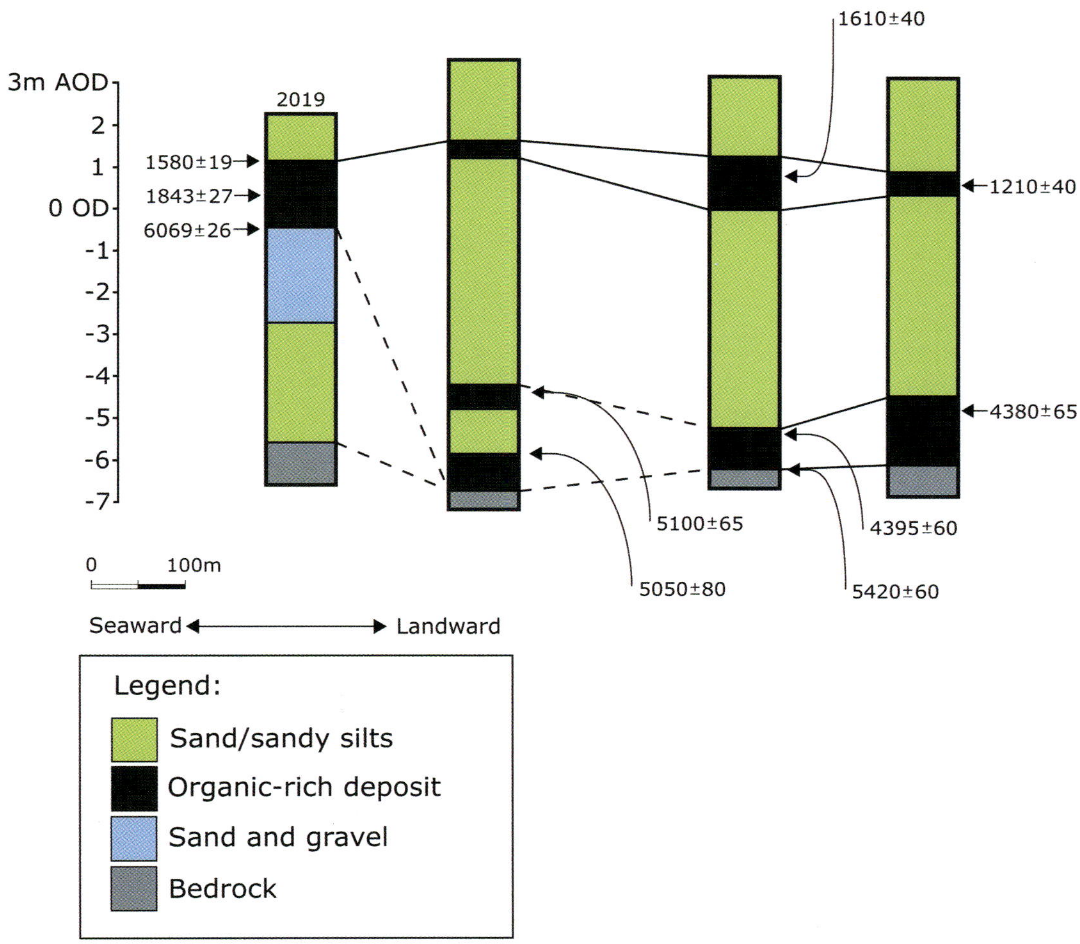

Figure 8.5: Marazion Marsh stratigraphy; Healy boreholes 1, 2 and 3 (= A, B and C) (Healy 1995) in relation to the 2019 core

record recorded previously as seen in the comparative summary stratigraphy (Fig 8.5). The new core provides a chronologically more continuous peat/organic-rich deposit over the older gravels and minerogenic silts, but all at significantly higher altitude than recorded previously (-0.67 = 5060–4850 cal BC, vs -6.21 m =4450–4040 cal BC, BH C=BH2; Healy 1995, fig. 2).

The deposits are detailed below and can be summarised as follows:

Unlike Healy's cores to the east, which show deep early organic late Mesolithic to Neolithic horizons (4500–3000 cal BC) separated from an early medieval upper organic deposit (cal AD 350–940) by up to 6 m of coarse sand and shells, occasionally with an a organic/peaty band (4000–3700 cal BC), the 2019 core has basal silts, sands and gravel, and the two peat horizons identified by Healy are amalgamated.

The sequence over weathered bedrock starts with 2.10 m of fine silts, essentially stone-free, which are dark grey becoming olive grey and slightly stony before they are superseded by sandy gravels. The gravels are dense, greenish grey compact small and medium gravels in medium sand with no, to few, inclusions of marine shell; these are marine deposits, probably the inner edge of the gravel spit forming prior to 5060–4850 cal BC.

Radiocarbon dating

Samples were taken through the peat and organic horizon for radiocarbon dating. Vertical *Phragmites* roots/stem were present throughout most of the peat/organic horizon (Unit 3), and apart from *Phragmites* stems that may have been near-horizontal in one location, no clearly defined organic remains were recognisable during sampling. All samples are, therefore, of sediment for humic acid dates, rather than individual recognisable plant remains. Samples

Table 8.2: Radiocarbon results from the core (calibration by OxCal v4.3.2 Bronk Ramsey (2017); r:5, and IntCal13 atmospheric curve (Reimer et al. *2013))*

Unit	*Depth cm*	*Pollen zone*	*Material*	*Lab. ref.*	*Result BP*	*δC¹³ ‰*	*Calibrated date*
Top 3	114	Mid 3	Humic acid	SUERC-90858	1580±19	–28.4	cal AD 420–540
Upper 3	146	2/3	Humic acid	SUERC-91998	1843±27	–28.6	cal AD 80–240
Lower 3	224	1/2	Humic acid	SUERC-92002	2576±27	–27.7	820–590 cal BC
Top 3/4	259	mid-zone 1	Humic acid	SUERC-95373	3986±27	–28.1	2580–2460 cal BC
Base 3/4	282	nr base 1	Humic acid	SUERC-90859	6069±26	–28.3	5200–4850 cal BC

Calibration by OxCal v4.3.2 Bronk Ramsey (2017); r:5, and IntCal13 atmospheric curve (Reimer *et al.* 2013)

from the top (114 cm), middle (224 cm) and base (224 cm) of Unit 3 and the bottom (282 cm) were submitted for radiocarbon dating, and the results are given in Table 8.2.

Stratigraphy

The earliest stratigraphy (pre-5200–4850 cal BC; Units 4–8) comprises 4.3 m of grey minerogenic silts (Units 7 and 8), a 0.7 m thick lens of small and medium gravel (-2.75 to -1.5 m OD; Unit 6) and minerogenic silt to -0.60 m OD (2.84 m depth, Unit 4), above which organic-rich horizons (Unit 3) occurred. The main organic-rich and humified peat horizon (with sand inwashes) occurred between 1.10 m OD and -0.69 m OD (Unit 2), and dated to between cal AD 420–540 and 820–590 cal BC, with the 0.24 m humic silt band below (Unit 3/4) dating to 5200–4850 cal BC. Although a basal organic horizon was recorded previously at -7.06 to -5.18 m and dated to 4450–4040 cal BC (formerly calibrated to 6030 cal BC, Healy 1995; 1999b; Table 8.1), this does not seem to be present here. It is probably equivalent to the thin humic silt band (Unit 3/4), where its higher altitude may be attributed to its location at the edge of the marsh, and inlet channel. Above 1.10 m OD (that is to say, 1.1 m depth) were fine sands, fine stone inwashes Unit 2) and humic silts under *Phrgamites* reed bed (Unit 1).

The results here indicate that the main humic peat/organic-rich deposits span the later Mesolithic to early post Roman period and provide one of the longest – if not the longest – dated sequences from the marsh.

Table 8.3: Processing record of the 23 small bulk samples

Depth (cm)	*Unit*	*Deposit*	*Wet wt (g)*	*>4 mm*	*>2 mm*	*>1 mm*	*>0.5 mm*	*>300 μm (wet)*
60–70	2a		1061	–	59	113	122	10
90–100	2b	Stony silty sand	1054	1	4	168	180	30
100–114	2b		1005	–	9	332	200	60
114–125	3		896	–	5	70	79	300
125–135	3		1095	1	10	137	115	300
135–145	3		1152	4	92	541	137	100
180–190	3	Humified peat	664	–	1	3	31	200
200–210	3		896	–	–	–	–	300
230–240	3		1095	–	2	1	1	250
245–255	3		906	–	–	–	–	225
265–75	3		1265	–	–	–	–	50
290–300	4	Blue silt	1011	176	55	56	44	30
330–340	5	Grey sandy gravel	1738	439	186	146	151	10
370–380	6		1708	821	105	96	85	–
410–420	6	Brown gravel	1874	528	171	164	136	–
420–430	6		1876	525	62	55	46	–
500–510	7a	Grey silt loam	1207	347	35	25	18	–
550–560	8.1		1456	225	84	71	49	–
590–600	8.1		1462	29	24	27	26	–
615–625	8.2	Weathered bedrock	1432	142	55	54	39	2
650–660	8.2		1386	41	40	37	29	+
690–700	8.3		1405	142	70	86	44	–
705–715	8.3		1537	131	80	69	59	–

Depth (cm)	*OD (m)*	*Unit*	*Pollen zone (cm)*	*¹⁴C sample at (cm)*	*Description*
0–53	2.15	1	7: 8–58		V. dark grey humic silt/*Phragmites* peat over humic sand
53–86	1.53	2a	6: 58–98		Stony lens (small & medium stones) & stony silty sand
86–114	1.29	2b	5 98–148		Fine humic sand inwash bands
114–260	1.10	3	4: 148–210 3: 210–242 2: 242–282	114 146 259 224	Dark brown a&nd greyish brown humified peat with bands of bleached sand (cal AD 420–540) (cal AD 80–240) (820–590 cal BC) (2580–2460 cal BC)
260–284	–0.45	3/4		282	Dark grey humic silt band (5200–4850 cal BC)
284–305	–0.69	4	1: 282–296		Bluish silt
305–360	–0.90	5			Greenish grey compact stony sand (loam) & gravel
360–430	–1.45	6			Dark yellowish brown gravel
430–490				NOT RECOVERED	
490–520	–2.75	7a	502–526		Olive grey stiff silty clay loam
520–535	–3.05	7b			Olive silt loam (sandy)
535–605	–3.20	8.1-8.3			Dark grey dense silty clay to silt, weathered bedrock
605–685	–3.90	8.2			Grey silty clay
685–720	–4.70	8.3			Dark greenish grey silty clay
720–750	–4.85	9.1			Mixed shale and silt, weathered bedrock
750–785	–5.35 (–6.70)	9.2			Shale bedrock

The sequence was dated with five radiocarbon assays on humic acid providing a time-frame for sedimentation from the Mesolithic (5060–4850 cal BC) to the late Saxon/early medieval period (cal AD 420–540; Table 8.2). Details of the sampling are given in Chapter 9.

The coarse fractions (especially >4 mm) of the 23 processed samples show a changing presence of clasts and geological components that may relate to offshore (marine) vs onshore (riverine and lacustrine) inclusions (Table 8.3). The initial deposits indicate low-energy fine grained sandy silt loams (Unit 7) over deeply weathered stony bedrock (Unit 8). Although described as grey silty clay, the analysis of clasts in the single sample located at 500–510 cm (Unit 7), however, indicated that it contained a moderate quantity of clasts. Above this are inwashes of marine gravels (Units 6 and 5), probably representing the very early development of the gravel spit, and the sealing of the Marazion embayment. Succeeding this are lower energy deposits comprising i) a fine-grained minerogenic deposits (bluish silt Unit 4) probably formed under low-energy standing water, and ii) the start of organic-rich deposits and development of peat (Unit 3). Cessation of peat development and organic-rich deposits is seen by the onset of inwash of fine-grained marine sands.

Samples assessed and/or analysed (regardless of microfossil content) are shown in bold; terminology follows Hodgson (1997).

Subsampling and the analyses

A total of 212 subsamples were removed: 107 pollen, 76 diatom, 23 bulk sample and 6 samples for consideration for radiocarbon dating, taken through the stratigraphy. The pollen provides the long history of vegetation change in the immediate and to a lesser extent in the wider local environs, and this is complemented by the autochthonous waterlogged plant remains of the site vegetation. These are, in turn, complemented by the more limited diatom record providing indications of salinity and fresh to marine conditions.

Preservation and survival

After processing, only 16 of the 33 bulk samples produced flots and were considered to have the potential to contain waterlogged plant remains. Assessment showed that waterlogged plant remains preservation was limited, and no samples below the organic-rich humified peat (Unit 3; 7 samples) were viable for analysis. Only two samples had good waterlogged plant preservation and these were from fine humic inwashed sand bands (Unit 2b; 90–100 cm) and the humified peat (Unit 3 at 230–240 cm).

Location 150517.82; 31345.39; 2.15 m OD

Depth (cm)	*OD (m)*	*Unit*	*Samples*			*Description*
			Pollen	*Bulk*	*^{14}C*	
0–26	2.15	1	**8** **16** **24**			V. dark greyish brown (10YR 3/2) soft humic organic silt with abundant vertical & diagonal medium fleshy roots & some large diam. (<18 mm) tubular *Phragmites* roots, clear boundary *Phragmites* peat root mat
26–43		1	**32** **40**D			V. dark greyish brown (10YR 3/2) soft humic silt, common fine fleshy & fibrous roots, some medium tubular roots (*Phragmites*), abrupt boundary *Phragmites* peat
43–53		1	**48**			V. dark grey to black (10YR 3/1–2/1) humic soft silty sand. Common fine & medium fleshy & fibrous roots, abrupt boundary Humic sand
53–62	1.53	2a	**54**D			V. dark grey (10YR 3/1) to dark grey (2.5Y 4/1) humic silt loam, common small, rounded stones, abrupt boundary Stony lens
62–86		2a	**62** **70D** **78**	60–70		Dark grey (2.5Y 4/1) silty sand with common medium/ coarse bleached sand grains, common medium, subrounded stones, rare medium fibrous roots, abrupt boundary Stony silty sand
86–96	1.29	2b	**86D** **94**	90–100		Stone-free fine sandy loam inwash 86–7 cm black humic silty sand, 87–96 cm grey (2.5Y 4/1) looks bluish grey silty sand Fine humic sand inwash bands
96–114		2b	**102D** **110**	100–114		V. dark greyish brown (10YR 3/2) soft silty (?humic) sand, many medium–coarse bleached sand grains – becoming v. dark grey (10YR 3/1) with depth, clear to abrupt boundary Humic sand
114–140	1.10	3	**114**D **118** **122D** **126** **130**D **134** 138D	114–125 125–135 135–145	**114 cm** cal AD 420–530	V. dark greyish brown (10YR 3/2) humified peat with clear vegetative matter (stems, *Phragmites* frags), & vertical & horizontal roots/stems. From 130 cm includes medium–coarse bleached sand grains, increasing markedly by 135–40 cm (ie, transition) Clear boundary Humified peat
140–146		3	**142**			Band of coarse bleached sand in grey (10YR 6/1–5/1) sand matrix, abrupt boundary Sand band (within peat)
146–160		3	**146**D **150** 154D **158**		146 cm cal AD 80–240	V. dark greyish brown (10YR 3/1) peat as above, but with band of fine sand at 156–8 cm Peat
160–180		3	162D **166** **170D** **174** 178D			Bleached light greyish brown (10YR 4/2) fine sand Sand inwash

Depth (cm)	*OD (m)*	*Unit*	*Samples* *Pollen*	 *Bulk*	 *¹⁴C*	*Description*
180–225			182 186D **190** 194D **198** 202D **206** 210D **214** 218D **222**	180–190 200–210	180 cm 190 cm	V. dark greyish brown (10YR 3/2) humified peat with some plant matter (180–90 cm) & below 190 cm less plant matter. Band of sand at 214–29 cm Clear boundary Peat
225–240			226D **230** 234D **238**	230–240	224 cm 820–590 cal BC	Dark greyish brown (10YR 4/2) soft smooth humic silt/ humified peat, rare plant matter, abrupt boundary Peaty silt
240–260			242D **246** **250**D **254** 258D	245-255	2580–2460 cal BC **259 cm**	V. dark grey to black (10YR 3/1–2/1) humified silty peat, abrupt boundary Humified peat
260–284	–0.45	3/4	**262** 266D **270** 274D **278** 282D	265–275	5060–4850 cal BC **282 cm**	V. dark grey (10YR 31) humic silt, becoming less humic (& lighter in colour) with depth, sharp boundary Humic silt
284–305	–0.69	4	**286** 288D **294D** **302**D	290–300		Greenish grey (5G 5/1) looks bluish, stiff massive silt to silty clay, becoming sandier at *c.* 3 m, clear boundary Blue silt
305–315	–0.90	5	310D			Greenish grey (5G 5/1), now looking greenish, sand loam with a few small & rear medium, rare, subangular stones, rare *Phragmites* root vertical & small horizontal elements Stony sand (loam) – transition
315–360			318D 326D 334D 342D 350D 358D	330–340		Mixed greenish grey (5G 5/1) to light greyish brown (2.5Y 6/2) compact sand/sand loam with many small & few medium subangular stones, rare vertical roots, minerogenic, (no marine shells noted), clear boundary Stony sand/gravel
360–420	–1.45	6	366D 374D 382D (389D) **390D** 398D 406D 414D	370–380 410–420		Dark yellowish brown to light olive brown (2.5Y 4/2 and 2.56 3/3) moist dense small gravel (abundant small & common medium subangular stones) in a fine/medium sand loam matrix – stones become predominately just small at 390 cm (no marine shells noted, no organic matter – minerogenic) Gravel
420–430			422D 430D	420–430		Greyish brown (2.5Y 5/2) moist/wet dense small & medium gravel in a sandy matrix Gravel
430–490						NOT RECOVERED
490–520	–2.75	7a	494D 502D 510D	500–510		Olive grey (5Y 4/2) stiff silty clay with fine sand rare small & v. rare medium stones, occasional large cobbles to 14 cm Clear boundary grading into Silty clay loam

Depth (cm)	*OD (m)*	*Unit*	*Samples*			*Description*
			Pollen	*Bulk*	^{14}C	
520–535	–3.05	7b	**518**D **526D**			Olive (5Y 5/3) silt loam to sandy silt loam, dense/compact with very large diffuse 'mottles' of olive brown (2.5Y 4/4) that look yellowish brown (aka orange), few small stones, abrupt boundary Silt loam (sandy)
535–575	–3.20	8.1	**534**D 542D 550D 558D 566D 574D	550–560		Dark grey (5Y 4/1) grading to grey (5Y 5/1) most set silty clay to silty clay loam with few small stones Grey silty clay
575–605			582D **590D** 598D	590–600		Dark grey (4/N) dense firm silt, some small stones, clear boundary Dense grey silt
605–635	–3.90	8.2	606D 614D 622D 630D	615–625		Grey (5/N) (steely grey) moist to wet stony structureless silt/silty clay, after 615 becoming essentially stone-free, massive Grey silty clay
635–685			638D 346D **654D** 662D 670D 678D	650–660		Dark greenish grey (10Y4/10Y) looks bluish steely grey, stiff silt (or silty clay) with deposition/deformation structures, otherwise homogeneous, massive & stone-free Grey silty clay
685–700	–4.70	8.3	686D **694D**	690–700		As above but small many small stones
700–720			702D 710D 718D	705–715		Dark greenish grey (4/10Y–4/5GY) as above but stone-free, clear to abrupt boundary Grey silty clay
720–750	–4.85	9.1				Greenish black (2.5/N) mixed shale & silt Weathered bedrock
750–765	–5.35	9.2				Black (2.5/N) shale dust with shale fragments Bedrock
765–785						Not recovered
785–885	(–6.70)					Black (2.5/N) shale dust with shale frags & rare large shale lumps Bedrock

D indicates diatom sample; samples assessed and/or analysed in bold

Only two other poorer plant remain samples from the humified peat (125–135 cm and 245–255 cm) contained enough waterlogged remains to even be considered for analysis.

All samples assessed for pollen from dense grey silts (Unit 8.1) below 590 cm depth (-3.75 m OD) were devoid of pollen, as too were samples from the gravels (Unit 6) at 390 cm depth (-1.71 m OD). Pollen was, however, present in these organic-rich deposits (Units 3 and 4) and the overlying fine sands (Units 1 and 2). Of nine samples selected for diatom assessment, all samples from below the organic-rich humified peat (that is, Unit 4 and below) were essentially devoid of diatoms (6 samples), and the organic-rich horizon (Unit 3) produced extremely low numbers with very poor preservation. Only the fine humic sand (Unit 2b, sample at 102 cm) contained excellent diatom preservation. Even the single sample assessed above this (Unit 2a. 70 cm) contains very low diatom numbers.

Despite the records of marine shells (*Cerastoderma edule, Littorina littorea, Scobicularia plana*) and brackish water shells (*Hydrobia ulvae*) in medium quartz-dominated sand at *c.* -4.75 to -5.15 m OD over a basal organic horizon by Healy (1996b; 1999b), no shells or shell fragments were present in the flots, nor were any noted during scanning of the 4 mm, 2 mm, 1 mm and 0.5 mm fractions of the processed bulk samples.

The preservation record was, therefore, highly varied between the different micro- and macro-fossil proxies analysed and presented below, making a balanced picture of the overall land-use history and development of the marsh challenging. What is attempted here is a much more nuanced examination of these changes than those offered by previous workers who had bold and simpler palaeographical aims (cf. Healy 1993 *et seq.*; sea-level and basic vegetation changes). The combination of these datasets used an archaeological framework allows us to examine the developing lived-in landscape and its potential to provide resources for human use as well as to contribute to the story of changing human lifeways. Further, these interpretations of community activity and engagement applies to the surrounding area, as well and the Marazion Marsh environs. The palaeo-environmental data presented in Chapter 9 provide the platform for this wider interpretation. These comprise are pollen analysis giving both local and wider vegetation history, waterlogged plant remains (local marsh history), and diatoms (watery environment and salinity).

9

A Mesolithic to modern palaeo-environmental and landscape record

Michael J. Allen
with contributions by Nigel Cameron, A.J. Clapham and C.T. Langdon

Pollen analysis: a vegetation history

C.T. Langdon

Coastal Holocene sediment sequences have long been recognised in Cornwall (Borlase 1758; Henwood 1858a; 1858b; Reid 1913). A series of 28 submerged forests or associated peat in the region has been logged (French 1983), from which there is much variation in the dates of peat inception obtained from these coastal sites, possibly due to the formation and/or destruction of barrier bars. Existing pollen studies include those of the peat and mineral sediments at Mount's Bay, Prah Sands (French 1983), Marazion Marsh (Healy 1996d), the Camel Estuary (Healy 1999c) and Penzance Harbour (Scaife 2006). These and other regional sequences also provide critical data on Holocene eustatic change (Heyworth & Kidson 1982; Healy 1993; 1995; 1999a). The analysis presented here was from the core on the southern edge of Marazion Marsh adjacent to the sand and gravel bar from which assessment indicated the potential for understanding, in detail, the past vegetation and environment, especially in relation to past sea-level change and human impact (Langdon 2019). Two diagrams are presented in this report; one shorter diagram from older, lower sediments (olive grey silt loams) from 526 cm to 502 cm (Fig. 9.1), and an extensive diagram from 296 cm to 8 cm of organic-rich deposits and humified silts (Unit 3), through the silty sands (Unit 2) and the sand and *Phragmites* marsh (Unit 1; Fig. 9.2), with a gap in the record through the sands and gravels (Units 5 and 6; 296–502 cm). This is an important coastal sequence already investigated by Healy (1995; 1996b; 1996c; 1999a; 1999b) providing data on vegetation change and relative sea-level change extending back to 4450–4040 cal BC (5420±60 BP (Q-2779). The study here is significant as it has yielded an earlier date at the site, from humic mineral sediments, of 5200–4850 cal BC (6069±29 BP, SUERC-90859) and so is potentially the longest record of vegetation change at Marazion Marsh.

Pollen procedures

Due to the very minerogenic nature of some of the samples, larger volumes of up to 5 ml were processed using standard techniques for the extraction of the sub-fossil pollen and spores (Moore & Webb 1978; Moore *et al.* 1992). The sub-fossil pollen and spores were identified and counted using a Nikon biological research microscope. A pollen sum of up to 400 pollen grains of was counted for each level, where possible. All pollen of marsh taxa, fern spores and miscellaneous taxa (pre-Quaternary palynomorphs, *Pediastrum*, etc.) were counted for each of the samples analysed. Full pollen diagrams have been plotted using Tilia and Tilia Graph and are presented in Figures 9.1 and 9.2. Percentages have been calculated as follows:

Sum = % total dry land pollen (incl. *Alnus and Salix*)
Marsh/aquatic = % tdlp + sum of marsh/aquatics
Spores = % tdlp + sum of spores
Misc. = % tdlp + sum of misc. taxa

Pollen taxonomy, in general, follows that of Moore & Webb (1978) modified according to Bennett *et al.* (1994) for pollen types and Stace (1992) for plant descriptions. An extensive modern comparative collection was available for any critical identifications. These procedures were carried out in the Palaeoecology Laboratory of the Department of Geography and Environmental Science, University of Southampton.

Pollen data

Initially 16 samples were assessed, of which four samples from the lower profile were devoid of pollen (390 cm, 590 cm, 654 cm and 594 cm). Nevertheless a further 36 samples were prepared for full pollen analysis (8 cm, 16 cm, 24 cm , 32 cm, 48 cm, 54 cm, 62 cm, 78 cm, 86 cm, 94 cm, 110 cm, 118 cm, 126 cm, 134 cm, 150 cm, 158 cm, 166 cm, 174 cm, 182 cm, 198 cm, 206 cm, 214 cm, 222 cm, 230 cm, 238 cm, 246 cm, 254 cm, 262 cm, 270 cm, 278 cm, 286 cm, 302 cm 502 cm, 510 cm, 518 cm, 534 cm) and the count was increased on 12 samples (40 cm, 70 cm, 102 cm, 114 cm, 130 cm, 142 cm, 146 cm, 170 cm, 190 cm, 250 cm, 294 cm, 526 cm), where possible. Of the new samples prepared only four (16 cm, 24 cm, 302 cm and 534 cm) were devoid of pollen or had concentrations that were too low to be viable. Full counts of 400 grains were achieved where this was possible although some samples (8 cm, 32 cm, 40 cm, 48 cm, 54 cm, 70 cm, 118 cm, 134 cm, 142 cm, 146 cm, 166 cm, 170 cm, 174 cm, 286 cm, 510 cm, 518 cm and 526 cm) yielded lower, but still informative, counts as was expected and noted would be the case in the assessment.

The lower sediments (olive to olive grey silt loams, Unit 7a–7b, 502–590 cm)

Due to the relative complacency of this pollen profile (Fig. 9.1) it is described here as a single

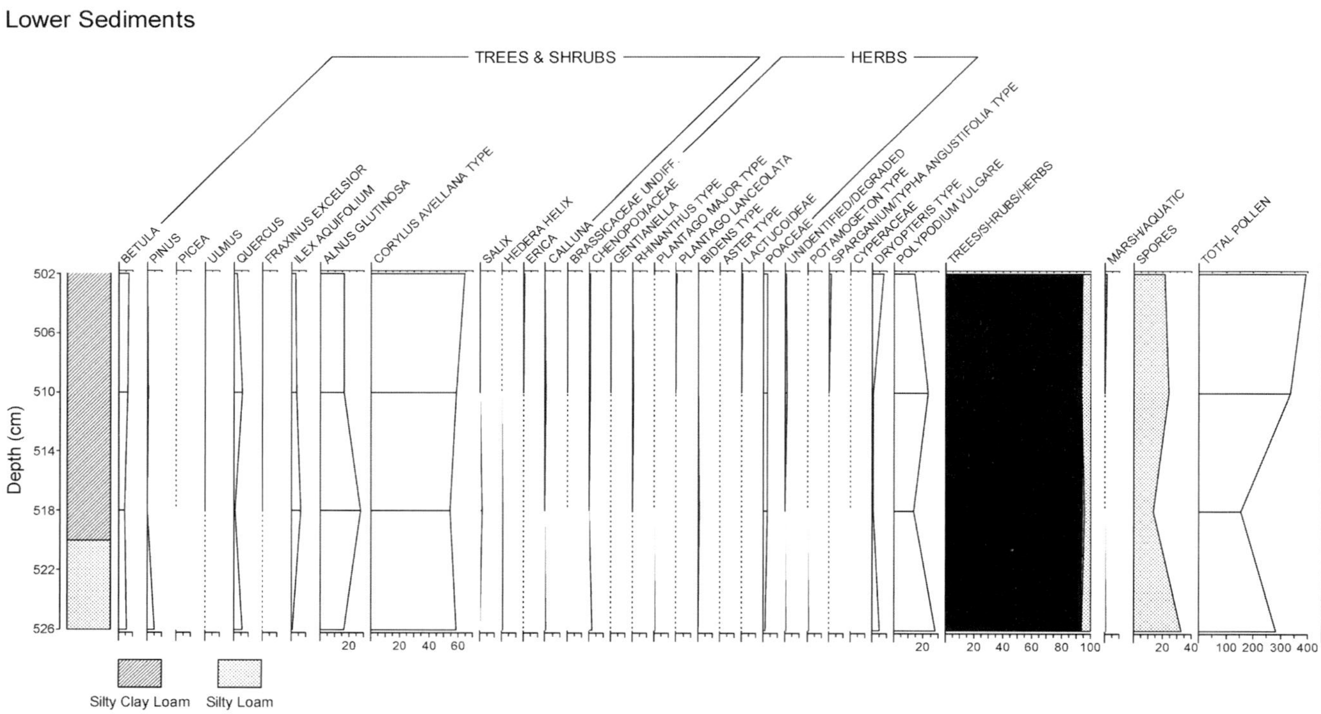

Figure 9.1: Pollen diagram for the lower sediments (units 7)

continuous zone. Dominated by *Corylus avellana* type pollen (to 60%), with some *Pinus* declining from 5% to <2%, *Alnus,* (up to 30%), *Quercus* (3%–7%) and *Betula* (5%–8%) also recorded. Notably, one *Picea* pollen grain was counted. Small numbers of *Salix*, *Erica* and *Calluna* (<3%) are noted. Some Poaceae and Chenopodiaceae are also present (<5%), whilst other herbs include *Gentianella*, *Rhinanthus* type, *Plantago lanceolata*, *Bidens* type and Lactucoideae. *Dryopteris* type spores and *Polypodium* are part of the assemblage whilst some *Sparganium/Typha angustifolia* type and Cyperaceae (<2%) are also recorded.

The upper sediments (humic silts & sands to organic-rich deposit, peat, Units 1–4, 8–296 cm)

The upper part of the cored profile contained pollen from the modern marsh horizons, through fine humic inwash sands into the organic-rich humified peat sequence dating from 5060–4850 cal BC to cal AD 420–540. This longer profile (Fig. 9.2) has been split into seven zones for ease of interpretation and discussion and are defined below. These are described from the bottom upwards.

Interpretation and discussion

The pollen data have been interpreted and described in terms of the on-site (autochthonous component) vegetation and pollen representing the surrounding area of the site (allochthonous component) and in some cases, that from more regional and long-distance sources. It is highly likely that there is a strong relationship between the depositional environment, pollen assemblages and sea-level change.

The lower sediments (olive to olive grey silt loams, Unit 7a–7b, 502–590 cm)

The lower sediments are characterised by a sandy silty loam, grading into silty clay and although pollen preservation was variable in these sediments the pollen record obtained is of importance as these data capture the earlier nature of the vegetation prior to 5060–4850 cal BC, not previously recorded at the site (eg, Healy 1999b). The pollen spectra (Fig. 9.1) are dominated by tree and shrub type pollen, mainly *Corylus* (hazel), with an understorey of some ferns, and *Alnus* (alder) the latter of which was probably growing in wetter areas. Alder and hazel are typically found in Holocene sediments in West Cornwall (Healy 1996b) and Scaife (2006) also notes that *Corylus* is the dominant mid-Holocene woodland in drier areas around Penzance Harbour. Small numbers of Chenopodiaceae type pollen (goosefoot, orache, samphire) may have derived from halophytes and be an indication of marine, brackish conditions. Some freshwater influence at the top of the profile is evident with a small amount of *Sparganium/Typha angustifolia* notable (bur-reed/bulrushes).

Quercus (oak) and *Salix* (willow) and small amounts of *Ulmus* (elm) are also evident in these lower samples with *Ilex* (holly) and some *Hedera* (Ivy) also apparent and is most likely derived from more regional sources. The presence of this more regional oak/elm/hazel woodland and a small amount of *Hedera* and *Ilex* indicate summer temperatures were warm enough to sustain growth of these types and would further imply a mid-Holocene, probably Mesolithic, date for this sequence following earlier climatic drying and warming. This is, however, speculative and dating would be required to corroborate this.

Of interest is a single incidence of a *Picea* (spruce) pollen grain. This is non-native and unusual but may be as a result of pre-Quaternary reworked pollen, contamination, or, most likely, long distance marine transport from North America. Likewise, the pine pollen here may be attributed to the typical over-representation in fluvial, especially marine sediment due to the buoyancy of the saccate pollen.

Summary: Dominated by hazel woodland, with some alder.

The upper sediments (humic silts and sands to organic-rich deposit, peat, Units 1–4, 8–296 cm)

Apart from the pollen data discussed from the lower sediments, the rest of the samples analysed sit in, or close to the humified peat and overlying sediments. Pollen preservation probably occurred here because conditions became wetter, thus providing conditions suited to the colonisation of the site by alder woodland. The taphonomy of the pollen is likely complex and the pollen zonation mirrors, to some extent, the changing depositional environments.

Pollen zone	*Description*
Zone 7: *Salix–Pinus* 58–8 cm	Zone 7 is delimited by an increase in *Salix* pollen to 45% at 40 cm, which subsequently declines as the zone progresses. There is also a continuous *Pinus* pollen signal during this phase in the diagram. Other trees & shrubs present include *Betula* (<3%), *Quercus* (*c.* 5%), *Alnus* (8%–<3%) and *Corylus* (10–5%) with the more occasional record of *Fraxinus*, *Ilex* & *Hedera* (<3%). Poaceae values decline from zone 6 but still remain between 20% & 60%, whist the herb pollen assemblage consists of Chenopodiaceae (60% at 8 cm), Lactucoideae (declining from 20% to <5% & other pollen types such as *Sinapis* type, *Filipendula*, *Potentilla*, *Armeria* 'A' line, *Calystegia*, *Plantago lanceolata*, *Bidens* type, & *Artemisia*. Some *Menyanthes*, *Myriophyllum alterniflorum*, & *Sparganium* noted, whilst Cyperaceae percentages decline from 40% to <3% by the end of the zone. Some *Dryopteris* type spores & *Sphagnum* (declining from 5% to <3%) are also present
Zone 6: Poaceae–cereal type–*Plantago lanceolata–Plantago coronopus* 98–58 cm	This zone is characterised by Poaceae values increasing from 40% to 50%. This is in conjunction with a continuous Cereal type curve with values that reach a maximum of *c.* 5% at 72 cm. *Plantago lanceolata* percentages increase to 20% at the start of the zone & remain between 10% and 20% throughout. Additionally, *Plantago coronopus* percentages rise to 10% & then decline toward the end of the zone. Percentages of trees & shrubs are generally low with *Betula* (<3%), *Quercus* (<4%), *Alnus* (<3-5%), *Corylus* (10%, declining to 5%), & *Calluna* (<3%) continually present. There is also the sporadic occurrence of *Pinus*, *Picea*, *Sorbus*, *Salix*, and *Erica* (all <3%). The herb pollen assemblage is diverse with Caryophyllaceae types, Chenopodiaceae, *Trifolium* type, Apiaceae, *Bidens* type, & Lactucoideae continually present. Other herbs present include Brassicaceae, *Filipendula*, *Rumex*, *Stachys* type, *Anthemis* type, *Urtica* type, & cf. *Cannabis* type. *Myriophyllum alterniflorum*, *Myriophyllum spicatum*, *Alisma* type, *Potamogeton* type, *Sparganium*/*Typha angustifolia* type, & Cyperaceae are also recorded (10–15%). Fern spores are recorded at <5% (*Dryopteris* type & *Polypodium*), whilst Sphagnum spores are continually present (<5%). *Pedaistrum* peaks during this phase to 40% total pollen plus misc
Zone 5: Poaceae–*Corylus avellana* type–*Plantago lanceolata* 148–98 cm (146 cm, Humic acid, cal AD 80–240; 1853±27 BP, SUERC-91998) (114 cm, Humic acid, cal AD 420–540; 1580±19 BP, SUERC-90858,)	Zone 5 is delimited by *Plantago lanceolata* pollen to 12%, an increase in *Corylus avellana* type to between 15% & 30% & relatively high values of Poaceae reaching a maximum of 60%. Other tree & shrub pollen noted at <5% includes *Betula*, *Quercus*, and *Alnus* (the latter increases to *c.* 10% by the end of the zone). *Calluna* is present throughout the zone (<4%), whilst *Pinus*, *Fraxinus*, *Fagus*, *Ilex*, *Salix*, & *Erica* also present at times at <3%. The herb pollen assemblage is diverse & includes the halophytes Chenopodiaceae, *Plantago maritima*, & *Plantago coronopus* present throughout, or nearly throughout, the zone. Other herbs present include *Rumex*, Fabaceae types, *Potentilla* type, Polygonaceae types, *Gentianella* type, *Galium*, & Asteraceae types, amongst others. Some Cereal type is recorded towards the end of the zone. A more diverse range of aquatic pollen is notable compared to zone 4 with *Myriophyllum alterniflorum*, *Menyanthes*, & *Potamogeton* type featuring. Cyperaceae values increase to a maximum of 40% at 110 cm. *Dryopteris*, *Polypodium*, & *Sphagnum* are also recorded. Numbers of the aquatic algae *Pediastrum* increase towards the end of the zone
Zone 4: Poaceae–Chenopodiaceae 210–148 cm	This zone is associated with Poaceae percentages between 50% & 80% with an increase in Chenopodiaceae type pollen to 10% & then declining to *c.* 3% by the end of the zone. Tree & shrub pollen percentages are relatively low, with *Corylus avellana* type pollen fluctuating between 10% & 30%, whilst *Alnus* pollen percentages decline from 20% to <3% by the end of this phase. *Quercus* pollen percentages also decline to <5% by the end of the zone & *Betula* percentages remain at 8% or less. Small numbers of *Pinus*, *Ulmus*, *Tilia*, *Ilex*, *Salix*, *Erica*, & *Calluna* are also notable. *Plantago lanceolata* & Lactucoideae are present throughout this zone with a diverse range of other herbs at <3% including *Plantago maritima* & *Plantago coronopus* types. Other herbs recorded sometimes at <3% include *Trifolium* type, Fabaceae, *Rumex*, *Armeria* 'B' line, *Gentianella* type, *Galium*, *Bidens* type, & *Centaurea scabiosa* type, amongst others. *Nuphar* & *Sparganium*/*Typha angustifolia* type appear sometimes whilst Cyperaceae is continually present at <10%. *Pteridium*, *Dryopteris* type, *Polypodium*, & *Sphagnum* are present in low numbers.
Zone 3: Poaceae–*Plantago lanceolata* 242–210 cm (224 cm, Humic acid, 820–590 cal BC; 2576±27 BP, SUERC-92002)	Zone 3 is delimited by an increase in Poaceae to 50% & consistent increase in *Plantago lanceolata* to 5%–6%. Values of trees & shrubs are generally lower than in zone 2 with a decline in *Betula* & *Alnus* pollen (10%–5% & 35%–*c.* 15% respectively). However, *Quercus* percentages increase slightly from 5% to 15% & *Corylus avellana* type values remain relatively stable between 15% & 25%. *Salix*, *Hedera* and *Calluna* are present at <4% throughout the zone whilst other trees and shrubs occasionally recorded include *Pinus*, *Ulmus*, *Ilex*, & *Erica*. Herbs present throughout include Chenopodiaceae, Apiaceae, *Rumex*, *Plantago maritima*, & Lactucoideae (<3%), whilst other herb pollen types recorded include Polygonaceae types, *Plantago coronopus*, *Campanula* type, *Bidens* type, & *Artemisia* (amongst others). There is the occasional incidence of *Alisma* type & *Potamogeton* type pollen, whilst Cyperaceae is continually recorded at <4%. Small numbers of *Polypodium* & *Sphagnum* spores are noted

Pollen zone	*Description*
Zone 2: *Alnus–Corylus avellana* type–*Betula* 282–242 cm (259 cm, Humic acid, 2580–2460 cal BC; 3986±27 BP, SUERC-95373)	This zone is characterised by increasing values of *Alnus* to 65% at 254 cm which subsequently decline to *c.* 50% by the end of the zone. *Corylus avellana* type declines as the zone progresses from 60% to *c.* 20% by 242 cm; *Betula* peaks at 30% at 254 cm. Other trees & shrubs present include *Quercus* (*c.* 4%–6% throughout), with sporadic occurrences of *Pinus*, *Ulmus*, *Ilex*, *Hedera*, *Salix*, & *Calluna* (all <3%). Few herbs are recorded although some Scrophulariaceae, *Plantago lanceolata*, *Succisa* type, *Aster* type, Lactucoideae, & *Artemisia* are present (all <3%). Small numbers of Cyperaceae are recorded. Spores sporadically present include *Osmunda* & *Pteridium*, with peaks in *Polypodium* at 252 cm (15% total pollen + spores) & *Sphagnum* (17% total pollen + spores) at 248 cm
Zone 1 : Poaceae–*Alnus–Corylus avellana* type 296–282 cm (282 cm, Humic acid, 5200–4850 cal BC; 6069±26 BP, SUERC-90859)	Delimited by values of Poaceae to 30%, *Alnus* to 30%, & *Corylus avellana* type to 30%. Other trees & shrubs present include *Betula* (15%), *Pinus* (<3%), *Quercus* (5%), & *Ilex* (<3%). Herbs present (4% or less) include *Plantago lanceolata*, *Succisa* type, *Bidens* type, & *Anthemis* type. Small numbers of Cyperaceae are recorded whilst *Dryopteris* type reaches 20% total pollen + spores. Some *Sphagnum* and *Polypodium* are also present

Zone 1: 296–282 cm – Late Mesolithic

This initial zone is characterised by a silty clay grading into a more humic silt with a Late Mesolithic date of 5200–4850 cal BC (6069±26 BP, SUERC-90859) at 282 cm at the end of the zone. This is earlier than that obtained by Healy (1993) who has an earliest date for ^{14}C dated material of 4450–4040 cal BC (5420±60 BP, Q-2779). If we consider that the lower sediments might also be of Mesolithic origin, then we can assume that sediment accumulation between the lower and upper profiles was particularly rapid.

The more minerogenic nature of these sediments means that pollen preservation was poorer than average, and there may be an element of differential pollen preservation. The nature of these sediments might also point to a complex pollen taphonomy in which sediment and pollen are washed in from nearby interfluves as well as those derived from more typical local and regional sources. The pollen evidence, however, suggests an on-site environment that was characterised by relatively open, possibly fen conditions with some freshwater input which would indicate high groundwater levels. It is possible that the grass pollen here is related to one or more habitats, dry pasture or most likely wet fen with the pollen perhaps derived from *Phragmites*, a large perennial reed grass found in wetlands. Similarly, Healy (1995) notes higher percentages of herbaceous pollen in the initial zone of his study of Marazion Marsh and suggests that *Phragmites* became established along the coast during this phase of development of the marsh. *Phragmites*-rich sediment has also been recorded by Healy (1999c) at Trewornan, River Amble, Camel Estuary in which an organic rich sediment was examined with a single radiocarbon date of 5220–5610 cal BC (6460±80 BP, Q-2781) as a datum. This *Phragmites*-rich sediment gives way to woody material identified as largely *Alnus* (a pattern also seen into zone 2). A small peak in *Sphagnum* (bog moss) suggests wet waterlogged conditions on-site as well as the incidence of *Sparganium/Typha angustifolia* (bur-reed/bulrush) type pollen. This high water table would allow the deposition of sediments richer in organic remains and the development of peats seen in subsequent zones (Healy 1999b). Alder woodland was also growing nearby with percentages of *Alnus* pollen indicating that it was growing locally in wetter areas.

Whilst freshwater conditions most likely prevailed trees, would have been a part of the regional vegetation mosaic more regionally with *Corylus* (hazel), *Betula* (birch), *Quercus* (oak) and *Hedera* (ivy) growing on drier interfluves with an understory of ferns such as *Dryopteris* spp. This is concurrent with other pollen evidence summarised from the Cornish coast (Scaife, forthcoming).

Zone 2: 282–242 cm – Chalcolithic

A change in sediment type to a dark humic silt occurs at the start of this zone and is associated with a date of 5200–4850 cal BC (6069±26 BP, SUERC-90859) at 282 cm as discussed previously. Another date of 2580–2460 cal BC (3986±27 BP, SUERC-95373,) is available in this zone at 259 cm, pertaining to the Chalcolithic period and is associated with a

Figure 9.2a: Pollen diagram for the upper sediments (units 1–4)

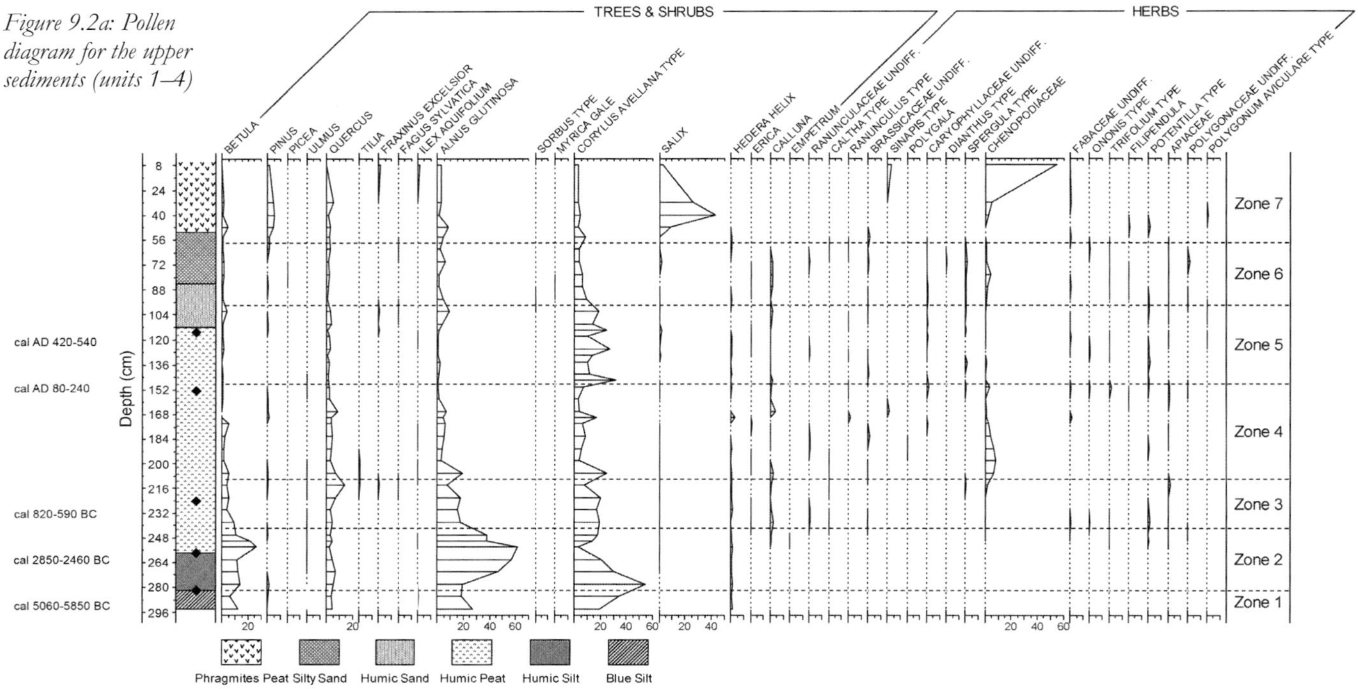

change in sedimentology to peat growth. This is considerably later than the date at 282 cm, only 23 cm below, and this disparity might be as a result of two possibilities: compaction of the sediments and very slow continuous accretion, or an hiatus as a result of an erosional event prior to peat inception. It is not clear from the stratigraphy or pollen evidence which of these might be the likely possibility. Despite this, this zone represents a phase of stabilisation with peat inception at 260 cm.

The on-site vegetation of the peat-forming community was one of alder woodland with some *Salix* (willow) and ground flora of *Dryopteris* (ferns) initially. *Alnus* (alder) most likely colonised as trees that are more susceptible to wet conditions declined, allowing the development of an alder-dominated carr and a phase of stabilisation as a result of rising sea-level, a common pattern seen is other studies in the region summarised by Scaife (forthcoming). Development of peat is also indicated during this phase by an increase in *Sphagnum* (bog moss) spores towards the end of the zone and further suggests that the water table was high allowing the development of peats to the rear of the protective coastal barrier (Healy 1996b). Drier areas of this wetland and the interfluves supported *Betula* (birch), *Quercus* (oak) and *Corylus* (hazel) woodland possibly with some *Ulmus* (elm).

Summary: A generally wooded environment dominated by alder in wetter areas and birch, oak and hazel on drier zones and interfluves, comparable to Healy (1995; 1996b; 1999a; 1999b).

Zone 3: 242–210 cm – Late Bronze Age/Early Iron Age

Dated to 820–590 cal BC (2576±27 BP, SUERC-92002) at 224 cm and characterised by the continued developed of peat, but with a notable change in the vegetation assemblage to a more open environment. On-site grass (Poaceae) becomes more dominant whilst percentages of *Alnus* (alder) decline. There is some initial evidence of ephemeral brackish influences with the first incidence of the halophytic pollen types Chenopodiaceae (goosefoot/oraches/samphire), *Plantago maritima* type (sea plantain) and *Plantago coronopus* type (bucks-horn plantain), making an initial appearance at the start of the zone. This is most likely to be as a result of an increase in relative sea-level at this time (Heyworth & Kidson 1982; Healy 1995). Healy (1995) indicated that brackish conditions at Marazion Marsh encroached gradually and has no evidence in

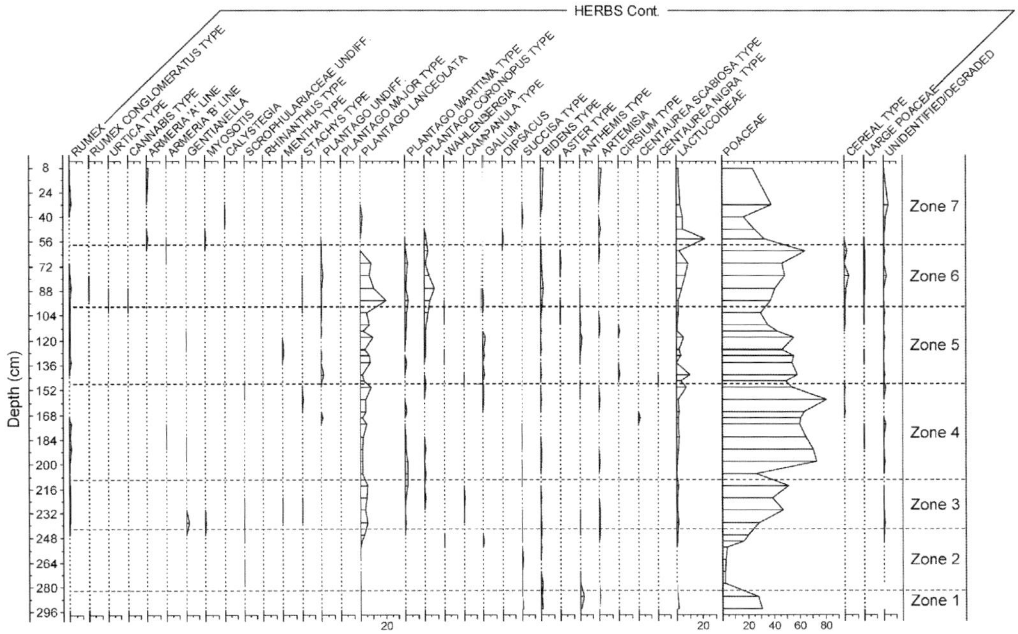

Figure 9.2b

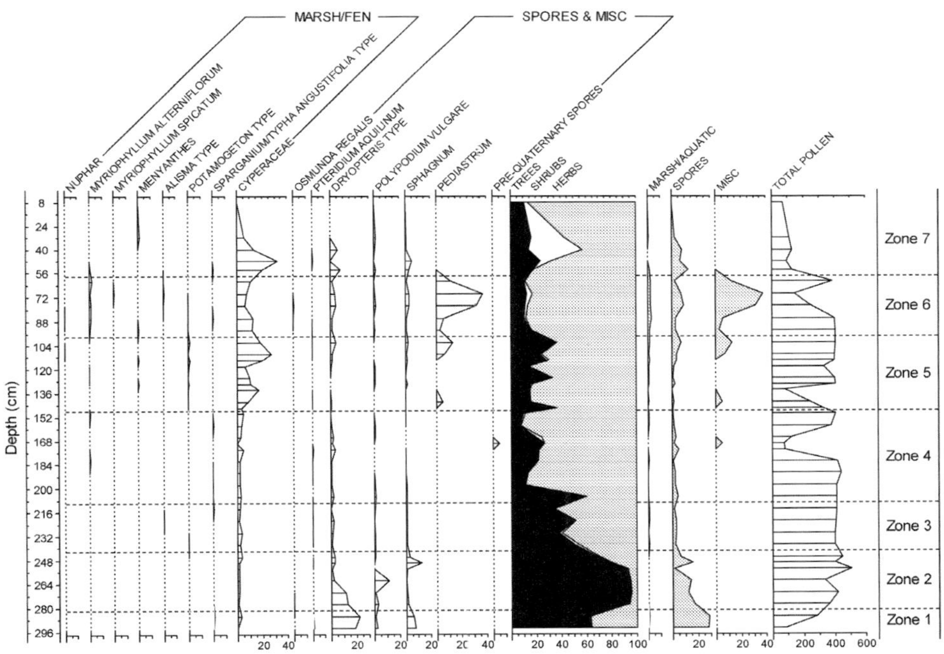

Figure 9.2c

the palaeoecological data that suggest this was a result of large-scale marine inundation, similar to the evidence here. Instead, this colonisation of more saline tolerant plant types might be as a result of marine water pulses accessing the marsh through stream channels or temporary barrier breaches.

The wider environment becomes considerably more open in zone 2 as Poaceae (grasses, some of which may have derived from *Phragmites*) dominate and values of trees decline markedly. During this phase there is a marked increase in taxonomic diversity with an increase in herbs of a pastoral affinity such as *Plantago lanceolata* (ribwort plantain) and Lactucoideae (dandelions) which suggests stronger pastoral land use in the nearby region. Burton and Charman (1995, Crift Down near Lostwithiel) interpreted a similarly large drop in tree pollen and an increase in grasses and anthropogenic 'weed' pollen during the Bronze Age as a result of clearance for agriculture. Similarly, Scaife (1996) also records an increased diversity of herbs at Chysauster (near Penzance) in which increases in *Plantago lanceolata* and Poaceae are notable during the Bronze Age. During the time-span in this zone, there are low but continuing numbers of acidophilous Ericaceae (*Calluna*) and *Sphagnum* (bog moss). These acidophilous plants may be attributable to wet and dry heath within the catchment and due to soil deterioration and acidification and possible heathland development as a consequence of the aforementioned agricultural intensification. More regionally, *Corylus* (hazel) and other deciduous trees (birch and oak) are probably growing in smaller stands around the site.

Summary: A phase of anthropogenic clearance with a strong pastoral signal. Some evidence of indirect marine influence.

Zone 4: 210–148 cm – Iron Age to Romano-British

With peat accumulation continuing during this zone there is evidence for increased marine influence in zone 4 as pollen with a brackish affinity becomes more prevalent with the representation of halophytes such as *Polygala* (milkwort), *Plantago coronopus* type (bucks-horn plantain), *Armeria* (thrift and/or sea lavender) and Chenopodiaceae (goosefoot, orache and samphire) increasing to 10% from the previous zone. These plants may have colonised dunes locally. *Polygala* is a poorly represented pollen type, typical of short turf grassland, and it might have been growing on calcareous dunes. There is also some evidence of freshwater present as some *Sparganium/Typha angustifolia* (bur-reed/bulrushes) is also recorded and *Myriophyllum alterniflorum* (water milfoil). Whilst barrier structures may have been important in controlling the evolution of the west Cornish coast, as previously mentioned Healy (1995) suggests that the transition to more marine brackish conditions happened gradually and not as a result of large-scale water inundation. The change represented here might have been as a result of a storm surge/rise in sea-level breaching the barrier and causing increased salinity (Healy 1996b) or as a result of increased ephemeral marine inundation as sea-level rose. Increased elements of sand in the stratigraphy might indicate encroachment of marine conditions closer to the site.

The herb pollen spectra show predominantly pasture with *Plantago lanceolata* and Lactucoideae increasing throughout the zone. Cereal type pollen is recorded towards the end of the zone which might indicate some arable agriculture in the region and further increased human agency. The latter are less well-represented in pollen assemblages unless in very close proximity to sampling.

Summary: Increased marine influence as saltmarsh conditions move closer to the site in relation to a likely increase in relative sea-level. A strong pastoral element to the pollen spectra with mixed agriculture evidenced towards the end of the zone

Zone 5: 148–98 cm – Romano-British and early post-Roman

Radiocarbon dates of cal AD 80–240 (1853±27 BP, SUERC-91998) at 146 cm, and cal AD 420–540 (1580±19 BP, SUERC-90858) at 114 cm from the humified peat (Unit 3) date this zone. A phase of fen development as reversed hydroseral succession takes place as the water table continues to rise. This is demonstrated by an increase in Cyperaceae (sedges) concurrent with the introduction of the freshwater aquatic algae *Pediastrum* which shows a change to a freshwater fen with sedges and other reed swamp elements (bulrush). Other pollen types associated with a freshwater affinity in this zone include *Nuphar* (water lily), *Myriophyllum alterniflorum* (water milfoil), *Menyanthes* (bogbean) and *Potamogeton* type. The latter type is present throughout this phase at low percentages and can include both pond weed and sea arrow grass and it is the latter which may have been part of the halophytic/saltmarsh habitat. Other plants with a halophytic affinity at lower percentages include *Plantago maritima* (sea plantain) and *Plantago coronopus* type (bucks-horn plantain) continually a part of the pollen assemblage. Although pollen percentages of *Salix* are low during this phase, as a low pollen producer, its continual presence would indicate that it was part of the on-site vegetation assemblage.

Some resurgence of *Corylus avellana* type (hazel) pollen is apparent during this phase, whilst other tree pollen recorded is most likely to be derived from long-distance more regional sources with birch, alder and oak part of this regional pollen rain. Locally there is a continued significant pastoral influence during this phase with an increase in *Plantago lanceolata* (ribwort plantain) from the dryland zone. Likewise Cereal type pollen is apparent in small numbers towards the end of this phase which would indicate mixed agriculture regionally.

Summary: A phase of fen development as part of a reversed hydroseral succession. Evidence for a mixed agricultural economy.

ZONE 6: 98–58 CM POST-ROMAN

Zone 6 is a phase in which numbers of freshwater fen taxa increase with a continuation of a high number of sedges and the presence of *Alisma* (water plantain), *Myriophyllum* (milfoil) and *Potamogeton* (although this taxon includes both pond weed and sea arrow grass) in conjunction with a large increase in *Pediastrum* (freshwater aquatic algae, which rarely appear in brackish water). This appears to be a continuation of the freshwater phase of transitional fen development seen in the previous zone caused by ponding back of the fluvial system by rising relative sea-level. However, there is still evidence of saltmarsh habitat in the pollen spectra with the presence of halophytes including Chenopodiaceae (goosefoot/oraches/samphire), *Spergularia* type (sea spurrey), *Plantago maritima* type (sea buckthorn) and a rise *Plantago coronopus* type (bucks-horn plantain). The latter *P. coronopus* growing on drier areas and sandy dunes concurrent with stratigraphy which suggests more sandy deposits concurrent with a change in the sediment regime to more stony silty sand. This change in the sediment budget might be as a result of on-shore movement of sandy deposits.

This pollen evidence in this zone represents a mixed agricultural economy with both evidence for increased pastoral and arable agriculture, the latter evidenced by a peak in *Cereal* type pollen at 78 cm. Burton and Charman (1995) interpret a big rise in grass and sedge pollen, the appearance of cereals and a further rise in the anthropogenic herb pollen in peats from Crift Down near Lostwithiel to medieval farmers. Of interest is the presence of *Cannabis* type pollen at the start of the zone. This taxon comprises both hemp (*Cannabis sativa*) and hop (*Humulus lupulus*). Differentiation of these two genetically similar taxa is not possible in the fossil state and recourse to ecological preference must be used. The latter (hop) is a native plant of alder-willow carr woodland. However, the presence of *Cannabis* might be as a result hemp cultivation for fibre within the agricultural environment described. The presence of *Cannabis sativa* (hemp) type is diagnostic of the Saxon-medieval periods (Godwin 1967; Bradshaw *et al.* 1981).

Tree pollen is generally low during this phase and is interpreted as being derived from long-distance/more regional sources. *Picea* here might have been the result of cultivation or as a result of long-distance fluvial transport.

Summary: Continued development of freshwater fen and strong evidence for pastoral and arable agriculture.

ZONE 7: 58–8 CM, *C.* AD 1650

Stratigraphically this phase is associated with *Phragmites* peat over humic sand with willow (*Salix*) carr becoming progressively more important. Contrasting with alder with its high pollen productivity and general over representation in pollen spectra, willow is usually poorly represented and here it was clearly important. The ground flora of the carr probably consisted of grasses (Poaceae), sedges (Cyperaceae) and some typical marsh frond ferns. Chenopodiaceae (goosefoot/oraches/samphire) becomes considerably more important at the end of this zone and suggests a marine phase and a dominant saltmarsh environment. Other plants with a halophytic affinity indicated at the end of this phase include *Armeria* 'A' line and *Armeria* 'B' line. Evidence for pastoral and arable agriculture is sparse but this may be a taphonomic effect due to the relatively low pollen count, poorer preservation and the dominance of first *Salix* and subsequently Chenopodiaceae.

Pine is sporadically present throughout the profile this may be attributed to the typical over representation in fluvial, especially marine sediment due to the buoyancy of the saccate pollen. However, the expansion in zone 7 is typical of a biostratigraphic marker seen in many pollen diagrams of the recent historic period (Long *et al.* 1999) and is attributed initially to planting of exotic conifers in parks and gardens *c.* AD 1650–1700 after popularity resulting from John Evelyn's treatise, *Sylva*. Subsequently, pine also increases in importance from forestry plantation. The pollen is anemophilous and is of regional rather than local origin in this instance.

Summary: Dated to c. *AD 1650 based on the pine rise as a biostratigraphic marker. Willow is dominant with Chenopodiaceae becoming more important latterly.*

Summary and conclusions

This study proved successful and has produced a long and comprehensive picture of the past vegetation and environment of the site. The following principal points have been made in this investigation.

- The data provide a record of vegetation development from the Mesolithic onwards with a possible hiatus/compaction in zone 6.
- The local hydrology of the coastal zone will have been controlled by changes in relative sea-level and secondary consequences of barrier bar formation and/or destruction.
- Seven pollen assemblage zones have been recognised which define diminution of woodland, progressive marine influence and the development of a fen type backwater latterly in a reverse hydroseral succession.
- Initial sediments are dominated by *Corylus* and *Alnus* with some other deciduous tree types as part of the wider landscape.
- There is significant evidence for pastoral agriculture from Zone 3 onwards, with the first evidence of arable agriculture during Zone 4.
- More significant evidence of arable farming is present in Zone 5 with some *Cannabis* type also recorded.
- The final zone is dominated by *Salix* carr locally and Chenopodiaceae.
- The data obtained are comparable with a number of other past studies undertaken in this region of Cornwall (French 1983; Healy 1995; 1996b; 1996c; 1999a; 1999b) which are also summarised by Scaife (forthcoming).

Diatom analysis

Nigel Cameron

Following assessment of nine samples (Cameron 2019) only a single sample was selected for full analysis. The assessment and analysis results are described below. The diatom-based reconstruction of salinity, total aquatic phosphorus (TP) and pH is discussed, and the assessed samples are considered in relation to the radiocarbon dating results.

Methods

Diatom preparation followed standard techniques (Battarbee *et al.* 2001). Two cover-

Table 9.1: Sediment unit descriptions with summaries of diatom evaluation results showing correlation between sample number and depth/sediment unit

Unit	*Sample/ depth (cm)*	*Diatoms*	*Diatom nos*	*Quality of preservation*	*Diversity*	*Assemblage type*	*Potential for % count*
2a: stony lens	D1/70	present	v. low	mod to v poor	mod	fw hal bk	v low
2b: fine humic sand	D2/102	present	v. high	good	high	fw acid with mar bk	excellent
3: humified peat	D3/170	present	ex low	v. poor	low	mar bk fw	none
4: bluish silt	D4/294	present	1 frag.	ex poor	–	fw aero?	none
6: gravel	D5/390	absent	–	–	–	–	none
7b: olive silt loam	D6/526	absent	–	–	–	–	none
8.1: dense grey silt	D7/590	absent	–	–	–	–	none
8.2: grey silty clay	D8/654	absent	–	–	–	–	none
8.3: grey silty clay	D9/694	absent	–	–	–	–	none

Key: fw = freshwater; bk = brackish; mar = marine; aero = aerophilous; hal = halophilous; ex = extremely; mod = moderate; frag. = fragment)

slips were made from each sample and fixed in Naphrax for diatom microscopy. Diatom counting was carried out a magnification of ×1000 under phase contrast illumination using a Leica microscope. Diatom floras and taxonomic publications were consulted to assist with diatom identification; these include Hendey (1964), Werff & Huls (1957–1974), Krammer & Lange-Bertalot (1986–1991), Hartley *et al.* (1996), Camburn & Charles (2000) and Witkowski *et al.* (2000).

Diatom species' salinity preferences are indicated using the halobian groups of Hustedt (1953; 1957, 199), these salinity groups are summarised as follows:

1. Polyhalobian: >30 g L^{-1}.
2. Mesohalobian: 0.2–30 g L^{-1}.
3. Oligohalobian – Halophilous: optimum in slightly brackish water.
4. Oligohalobian – Indifferent: optimum in freshwater but tolerant of slightly brackish water.
5. Halophobous: exclusively freshwater.
6. Unknown: taxa of unknown salinity preference.

Diatom-based total phosphorus (TP) reconstruction was carried out using the European Diatom Database (EDDI) (Battarbee *et al.* 2000) Combined TP dataset (formerly at http://craticula.ncl.ac.uk/Eddi/jsp/index.jsp). pH reconstruction was carried out using the Surface Waters Acidification Project (SWAP) diatom/lake water-chemistry data set (Stevenson *et al.* 1991). The C2 program (Juggins 2003) was used for the manipulation of data formats, taxonomic harmonisation, weighted average environmental reconstruction and for plotting graphs.

Table 9.2: Diatom assessment records for the upper four samples

Sample	*D1*	*D2*	*D3*	*D4*
Unit	*2a*	*2b*	*3*	*4*
Depth (cm)	*70*	*102*	*170*	*294*
Salinity group/diatom taxon				
Polyhalobous				
Paralia sulcata	1	2	–	–
Mesohalobous				
Amphora coffeaeformis	1	–	–	–
Bacillaria paradoxa	–	1	–	–
Diploneis interrupta	–	1	1	–
Pinnunavis elegans	–	1	–	–
Synedra pulchella	1	1	–	–
Halophilous to oligohalobous indifferent				
Diploneis ovalis	–	1	–	–
Rhoicosphaenia curvata	1	–	–	–
Oligohalobous Indifferent				
Achnanthes minutissima	–	1	–	–
Eunotia arcus	1	–	–	–
Fragilaria exiguiformis	1	3	1	–
Fragilaria pinnata	–	1	–	–
Gomphonema gracile	1	–	–	–
Navicula contenta	1	–	–	–
Navicula hungarica	–	1	–	–
Pinnularia major	cf.	–	–	–
Synedra acus	–	1	–	–
Synedra ulna	1	–	–	–
Oligohalobous indifferent to halophobous				
Eunotia pectinalis var. *minor*	1	1	–	–
Eunotia pectinalis var. *minor* fo. *impressa*	1	1	–	–
Eunotia sp.	1	1	–	–
Halophobous				
Brachysira vitrea	1	–	–	–
Cymbella gracilis	–	1	–	–
Eunotia praerupta	1	–	–	–
Frustulia rhomboides var. *saxonica*	–	1	–	–
Tabellaria flocculosa	1	1	–	–
Unknown salinity group				
Chrysophyte cysts	–	1	–	–
Diploneis sp.	1	1	–	–
Fragilaria sp.	1	–	–	–
Gomphonema sp.	–	1	–	–
Mastogloia sp.	–	1	–	–
Navicula sp.	1	1	–	–
Nitzschia sp.	1	–	–	–
Pinnularia sp.	–	1	–	cf.

Results and discussion

The results of the diatom evaluation are summarised in Table 9.1 and diatom species data are presented in Table 9.2 and Figures 9.3 and 9.4.

Diatoms are absent from the bottom six samples assessed from the core, that is to say, all deposits below 294 cm and the organic-rich rich humified peats (Unit 3). The exception is in the top sample from this section of the sequence (bluish silt, Unit 4, sample at 294 cm) where a single, eroded diatom fragment was recorded (possibly derived from the freshwater aerophilous diatom *Pinnularia major*). These sediments represent several sediment types. The bottom three samples were from silt/clay sediments (Units 8.3 to 8.1); sample at 526 cm is from a silt/sandy loam (Unit 7b), sample at 390 cm is from gravel (Unit 6), and sample at 294 cm from the bluish silt (Unit 4). There was no further potential for analysis of these samples.

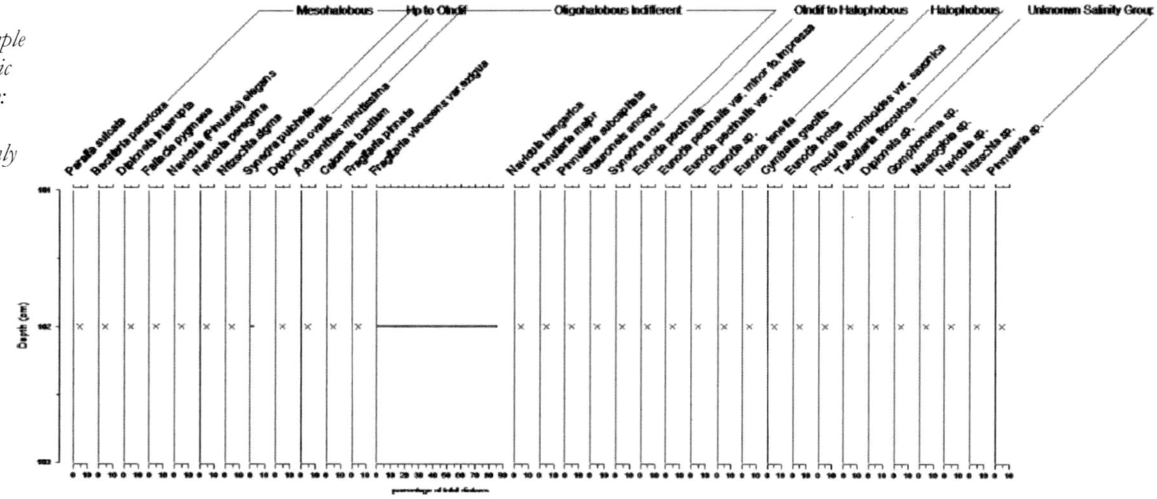

Figure 9.3: Diatom histogram of the sample at 102 cm (fine humic sand; Unit 2b) Note: Paralia sulcata *is Polyhalobous - the only species in this group*

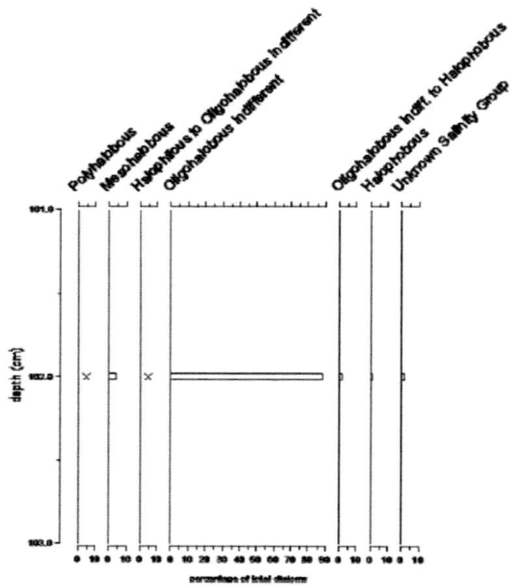

Figure 9.4: Diatom summary histogram of the sample at 102 cm (fine humic sand; Unit 2b)

The diatom sample from 170 cm depth from the humified peat with sand bands (Unit 3) contains an extremely low number of very poorly preserved diatoms. The diatom assemblage is of low diversity and is composed of a mixture of marine, brackish and freshwater diatoms. The most common diatom found in this sample is the marine planktonic species *Paralia sulcata* and this is likely to represent flood deposits (cf. sand bands). The aerophilous, brackish water, benthic diatom *Diploneis interrupta* was also recorded and also the freshwater species *Fragilaria exiguiformis* (see discussion below). No further analysis was undertaken.

Fine humic sand (Unit 2b; 102 cm)

Assessment of the sample (D3) from 102 cm depth (fine humic sand with inwash bands; Unit 2b) showed it to contain a well preserved diatom assemblage with a very high number of diatoms and high species diversity (although not an even distribution of species and an assemblage dominated by a single taxon). Further, more detailed diatom analysis was conducted of this sample. Percentage diatom analysis (Figs 9.3 & 9.4) was undertaken and a total of 520 valves were counted and 33 diatom taxa were recorded. As the assessment indicated there are traces of marine, brackish and halophilous taxa, these include *Paralia sulcata, Bacillaria paradoxa, Diploneis interrupta, Pinnunavis elegans, Navicula peregrina, Nitzschia sigma*, *Synedra pulchella* and *Diploneis ovalis*. Percentage analysis confirms that these species comprise a small component of the diatom flora and probably represent transport of allochthonous valves during flooding events. The only fully marine diatom present is the planktonic species *Paralia sulcata*. Except for *Synedra pulchella* (3%), the marine, brackish and halophilous diatom taxa occur at abundances of less than 1% and in total saline diatoms comprise 5% of the assemblage. It is also possible that some of this saline component of the assemblage may derive from reworked sediment.

Freshwater oligohalobous indifferent and halophobous taxa comprise the most important part of this diatom assemblage and a total of 19 taxa were recorded. The diatom assemblage is dominated by the non-planktonic freshwater species *Fragilaria virescens* var. *exigua (F. exiguiformis)*. This diatom is associated with acid, oligotrophic, peaty water with high levels of dissolved organic carbon levels. In the Surface Waters Acidification Project (SWAP) lakes the optimum pH distribution of *Fragilaria exiguiformis* according to weighted average estimation is pH 5.7 (Flower *et al.* 1996). The dominance of this diatom has a great influence on the reconstructed pH value for Marazion Marsh (see below). *Fragilaria virescens* var. *exigua* is widespread and common in oligotrophic freshwater, found in epilithic and surface sediment diatom communities for example. The species was for example found in 122 of 167 lakes in the SWAP training set, with a maximum abundance of 51%.

In addition to the dominance of *Fragilaria exiguiformis*, there are several other non-planktonic freshwater diatoms, notably halophobous species that are also associated with oligotrophic water with very low salinity. These diatoms include *Eunotia pectinalis*, *E. pectinalis* var *minor*, *E. pectinalis* var. *minor* fo. *impressa*, *E. pectinalis* var. *ventralis*, *E. incisa*, *E. tenella*, *Cymbella gracilis*, *Frustulia rhomboides* var. *saxonica* and *Tabellaria flocculosa*. These diatoms are unable to grow in marine or brackish environments or in freshwater with high conductivity values. Other freshwater, oligohalobous indifferent diatoms present here include *Achnanthes minutissima*, *Caloneis bacilium*, *Fragilaria pinnata*, *Navicula hungarica*, *Pinnularia major*, *Pinnularia subcapitata*, *Stauroneis anceps* and *Synedra acus*. With the exception of *Fragilaria virescens* var. *exigua* (*F. exiguiformis*), which comprises 86% of the assemblage, all of these oligohalobous indifferent and halophobous, freshwater taxa occur at abundances of less than 1%. In total freshwater taxa comprise 92% of the assemblage.

Stone lens, with silty sand matrix (Unit 2a, 70 cm)

The top sample from the core (70 cm) is from a stony lens with stony silty sand (Unit 2a). The sample (D2) contains a very low number of diatoms and the quality of diatom preservation varies from moderate to very poor. Diatom species diversity is moderate and the diatom assemblage is composed of a mixture of freshwater, halophilous and brackish water species (Table 9.2). There is very low potential for further diatom analysis of this sample. Nevertheless, the assessment shows that the assemblage contains a small number of brackish water non-planktonic diatoms *Amphora coffeaeformis* and *Synedra pulchella*, with the halophilous species *Rhoicosphaenia curvata*. Marine and brackish-marine diatoms are absent and there is no evidence for marine flooding in this sample. However, more common than the brackish and halophilous diatoms are non-planktonic (shallow water) freshwater and halophobous taxa that in many cases are associated with acid freshwater habitats with high dissolved organic carbon, low salinity and low nutrient levels. These oligotrophic freshwater diatoms include *Eunotia arcus, Fragilaria exiguiformis, Gomphonema gracile, Eunotia pectinalis* var. *minor, Eunotia pectinalis* var. *minor* fo. *impressa, Brachysira vitrea, Eunotia praerupta* and *Tabellaria flocculosa*. There is also a small component of, desiccation-tolerant, aerophilous diatoms represented by *Navicula contenta* and *Pinnularia major*.

Considering possible differences in identification criteria and in diatom nomenclature, nevertheless, the diatom assemblages investigated in the top of this sequence and in particular in sample (D2) from 13 cm differ in their diatom composition from those assemblages found in the earlier sediments researched by Healy (1995). There remains no clear evidence from the composition of diatom assemblages and the form of diatom valves found in the core for any effects on the aquatic environment of mining waste, for example from metal pollution (Falasco *et al.* 2009).

The absence or poor quality of diatom preservation in many samples from the profile can be attributed to taphonomic processes (Flower 1993; Ryves *et al.* 2001). Silica dissolution and breakage may be caused by factors such as extremes of sediment salinity, alkalinity or acidity, the under-saturation of sediment pore water with dissolved silica, cycles of prolonged drying and rehydration, or physical damage to diatom valves from transport and abrasion.

In addition to carrying out percentage diatom analysis and grouping diatom taxa by their salinity preferences, quantitative diatom-based environmental reconstruction has been carried out for the sample at 102 cm (D2) using transfer functions for TP and pH.

Table 9.3: The representation of fossil diatom taxa in diatom training sets for TP and pH, with comparison of diatom-based reconstructions of TP, and pH using different models. The fossil diatom taxa are shown to be well represented in the training sets and consistent values for reconstructed TP and pH are demonstrated between models

Total number of diatom species (minus marine taxa) in Marazion Marsh fossil sample compared with the number of these species present in the combined European TP training set; and percentage sum of diatoms in the fossil samples represented by species in the training set	
Total number of diatom species in fossil sample	27
Number of fossil diatom species present in the TP training set	23
% sum of diatoms in fossil sample present in the TP training set	97
TP reconstruction for the Marazion Marsh sample using the Combined European TP dataset. (The R^2 values for the reconstructions vary from 0.76 for the two models with tolerance downweighting and 0.71 for the models without downweighting. Standard error of prediction is about 2 μg l^{-1} for all models)	
TP (μg l^{-1}) with Inverse Regression model	8
TP (μg l^{-1}) with Classical Regression	4
TP (μg l^{-1}) with Inverse Regression model and Tolerance Downweighting	11
TP (μg l^{-1}) with Classical Regression model and Tolerance Downweighting	7
Total number of species in the Marazion Marsh fossil diatom sample, number of these species in the SWAP (modern) training set and percentage of diatoms in the sample represented by species in the training set	
Total number of diatom species in fossil sample	16
Number of fossil diatom species present in the SWAP training set	14
% sum of diatoms in fossil sample present in the SWAP training set	91
pH reconstruction using the SWAP dataset. (standard error of prediction for all samples and both models is 0.3 pH units)	
pH with Inverse Regression model	5.8
pH with Classical Regression	5.8
pH with Inverse Regression model and Tolerance Downweighting	5.8
pH with Classical Regression model and Tolerance Downweighting	5.8

Diatom-based TP reconstruction (fine human sand, sample at 102 cm)

Inferring the values of past aquatic phosphorus, or other chemical or environmental variables, from fossil diatom remains preserved in sediments involves two stages (eg, Cameron *et al.* 1999). First the relationship between diatom abundances and the contemporary environmental variable of interest is modelled using a modern training or calibration set comprised of surface sediment diatom samples and associated water chemistry. These relationships are used to derive a transfer function. The second stage is to use the transfer function to infer past values from the fossil diatom assemblages.

Diatom-based TP reconstruction was carried out for the Marazion Marsh sample using the combined European TP dataset. This training set is derived from a training set of 347 lakes across Europe (Battarbee *et al.* 2000). The diatom taxonomy of the Marazion Marsh fossil samples was first harmonised with the EDDI combined TP training set. TP reconstruction was then carried out by Weighted Averaging (WA) using both inverse and classical regression methods. Generally these regressions provide similar results for the sediment sequence with low standard errors of prediction, high r^2, and low root mean square errors (RMSE). The results of the quantitative reconstructions for TP are shown in Table 9.3.

The taxa in the fossil samples from the Marazion Marsh sample are well represented in the combined European TP dataset. Of 27 species in the fossil sample 23 species are present in the training set. A high percentage of the total fossil flora (97%) in the samples is also present in the training set (Table 9.2). The combined European TP dataset therefore provides good analogues to produce a TP reconstruction for this sample. The traces of marine and marine-brackish taxa present in the fossil samples are not present in the TP training set because this calibration set is based on samples taken from freshwater lakes. However, since the saline diatoms represent traces from flooding or reworking of sediments, these marine and marine-brackish taxa can reasonably be excluded from the diatom assemblages used for TP reconstruction.

There is a small range (7 μg l^{-1}) of predicted TP values between models for diatom-based reconstructions of TP and it is not clear here which is the most appropriate to use for the Marazion Marsh diatom assemblage. This variation is seen between Inverse and Classical regression models, with higher predicted values using Inverse Regression. There are also differences between these models and their respective variants using tolerance downweighting; where species with a wide range of nutrient tolerance (and therefore less predictive value) are given less weight in the model. However, the reconstructed TP levels are consistently low (ranging from 4 μg l^{-1} to 11 μg l^{-1}).

The diatom-inferred total phosphorus (TP) values can be compared with nutrient levels defined as follows (Smol 2008):

oligotrophic (TP < 10 μg l^{-1}), low levels of nutrients and biological productivity;
mesotrophic (TP 10 μg l^{-1} – 20 μg l^{-1}), intermediate levels of nutrient concentration and biological productivity;
eutrophic (TP> 30 μg l^{-1}), nutrient rich, highly productive

Comparison with present day and historical nutrient levels reconstructed using diatom-based transfer functions (Bennion *et al.* 1996; Cameron in Keevil 2004, 315) confirms that the values for reconstructed TP in the Marazion Marsh sample are consistently low, whichever model for reconstruction is used. The water quality predicted from three of the reconstructions (TP< 10 μg l^{-1}) indicates that the water is oligotrophic. The fourth value (11 μg l^{-1}) is at the low end of the mesotrophic range.

Diatom-based pH reconstruction

Diatom-based pH reconstruction was carried out using the SWAP diatom/lake water-chemistry data set (Stevenson *et al.* 1991). Diatom taxonomy of the fossil sample was harmonised with this training set using the C2 program (Juggins 2003) to carry out species coding changes and merges. The taxa in the fossil sample from Marazion Marsh are well represented in the SWAP training set and a high proportion of the total fossil flora (91%) in the sample is also present in the training set (Table 9.3). The SWAP dataset therefore provides good diatom analogues to produce a pH reconstruction for this sample.

The results of pH reconstruction using a Weighted Average (WA) model were produced using both Inverse and Classical regression methods with and without species tolerance down-weighting (Table 9.3). The results for the four methods are the same (pH 5.8) with low standard errors of prediction, high r^2 (0.87 or 0.88) and low root mean square errors (RMSE).

These results reflect the naturally acid, oligotrophic (low nutrient levels) diatom flora of Marazion Marsh.

Discussion and chronology

The diatomaceous levels at the top of the sequence (70 cm, 102 cm, 170 cm) lie across Unit 2a, Unit 2b and Unit 3 in the core (Table 9.1) described respectively as stony lens and stony silty sand, fine humic sand inwash bands and humified peat with sand bands. The results of radiocarbon dating (Table 8.2) place the bottom diatom sample at 170 cm that contains an assemblage of marine, brackish and freshwater diatoms, in the Iron Age to Roman period (lying between 820–590 cal BC and cal AD 80–240). The best-preserved sample, at 102 cm (fine humic sand, Unit 2b), that was analysed, is dominated by an oligotrophic freshwater diatom flora, with indication of coastal flooding, is post-Roman (post- cal AD 420–540). The top sample at 70 cm also post-dates the Roman period and may be significantly younger in age. Despite the local archaeological evidence (Allen *et al.* 2019) for human activity around Marazion Marsh throughout the time of sediment accumulation, the diatom assemblages show no clear indication of anthropogenic impact. For example, in increased nutrient levels in the freshwater marsh (high TP levels might also be anticipated with large bird populations), or for example with the impact of historic and prehistoric metalworking in the immediate area.

The contrast with the general trend of rising sea-level and marine dominated diatom assemblages seen in earlier studies at Marazion Marsh from this period of sediment accumulation (Healy 1995) is interesting. Although clear evidence for marine and brackish water diatoms is seen in the present study, the freshwater oligotrophic dominated diatom assemblage seen at 102 cm here may be explained by spatial variation across the Marsh, perhaps with isolated freshwater pools subject only to occasional saline incursion. Reworking of sediment or wind-blown diatom supply might also account for some of the saline component in a freshwater marsh environment.

In addition to lateral variation in the Marsh,

the most recent sediment levels dated in the study of Healy (1995) in cores A and C are approximately 30 cm to 65 cm lower in elevation than the diatomaceous levels in recent sediments dated in the present study. This might have an appreciable effect on the incursion of saline diatoms into an elevated part of the Marsh.

Conclusions

1. Diatom assemblages are only present in the top three samples that were assessed for diatoms (Allen *et al.* 2019). There was excellent potential to carry out percentage diatom analysis in only one sample D2 (102 cm, Unit 2b). The quality of preservation meant that it was not possible to carry out diatom analysis for samples D3 (170 cm) and D1 (70 cm).
2. Sample at 170 cm (D3, Unit 3), from a humified peat with bands of sand, contains an extremely low number of very poorly preserved diatoms. Most common in the mixture of marine, brackish and freshwater diatoms is a marine planktonic species and this may represent episodes of marine inundation (cf. sand bands) during the Iron Age and Roman period.
3. Sample from 102 cm (D2) depth was analysed and diatom species were grouped by salinity preference and in addition diatom-based environmental reconstructions have been carried out using transfer-functions for TP and pH.
4. Diatom sample from 102 cm (D2, Unit 2b) from a fine humic sand with inwash bands contained traces of marine and brackish water taxa. However, diatom analysis confirms that saline taxa represent a relatively small component of the diatom assemblage in this sample and may represent rare flooding episodes or derive from reworked sediment. Freshwater and halophobous taxa comprise the most important part of the diatom assemblage in sample D2. The diatom assemblage is dominated by a single taxon that is associated with acid (diatom-based pH reconstruction pH 5.8), oligotrophic water with high dissolved organic carbon levels. There are also a variety of other non-planktonic halophobous diatoms that are associated with oligotrophic water with very low conductivity. Consistent with these observations diatom-based pH reconstruction indicates that reconstructed TP values are within the oligotrophic range (TP $< 10\ \mu g\ l^{-1}$) or at the low end of the mesotrophic range. The sample analysed for diatoms is post Roman.
5. The top sample from the core (70 cm, D1, Unit 2a) from a stony lens with stony silty sand contains a very low number of diatoms. The diatom assemblage comprises a mixture of freshwater, halophilous and brackish water species. Marine and brackish-marine diatoms are absent and, perhaps surprisingly at this time, there is no evidence for marine inundation. The most important components of the assemblage are shallow-freshwater and halophobous taxa that are associated with acid freshwater habitats with high dissolved organic carbon, low salinity and low nutrient levels. Radiocarbon dating indicates that this sample is post-Roman.
6. The composition of diatom assemblages in the upper sediments from this sequence, particularly from sample at 102 cm (D2), contrast with an earlier, sea-level based, study where diatom assemblages show increasing numbers of polyhalobous diatoms indicating rising sea-levels (Healy 1995). Lateral variation in environments across the Marsh revealed by the different position of sediment cores between these two studies and the significantly higher elevation of the upper sediments (representing later prehistoric and historic times) in the present study show that the sedimentary environment may have been partially isolated the from the sea.
7. Percentage diatom analysis confirms that there is no evidence from the diatom assemblages for the effect of mining waste on the aquatic environment.

Bulk samples (waterlogged plant remains and shells)

Michael J. Allen

A series of 23 small bulk samples (896–1874 g) were removed for the recovery of waterlogged plant remains from especially the peat, and organic deposits (principally Unit 3), and for marine/brackish water shells after the record

Depth	Unit	Deposit	Sample wet wt (g)	Waterlogged flot	Waterlogged wet 300 µm (ml)	Plant remains analysed
60–70	2a		1061	✓	10	–
90–100	2b	Stony silty sand	1054	✓	30	✓
100–114	2b		1005	✓	60	–
114–125	3		896	✓	300	–
125–135	3		1095	✓	300	✓
135–145	3		1152	✓	100	–
180–190	3	Humified peat	664	✓	200	–
200–210	3		896	✓	300	–
230–240	3		1095	✓	250	✓
245–255	3		906	✓	225	✓
265–275	3		1265	✓	50	–
290–300	4	Blue silt	1011	✓	30	–
330–340	5	Grey sandy gravel	1738	✓	10	–
370–380	6		1708	–	0	–
410–420	6	Brown gravel	1874	–	0	–
420–430	6		1876	–	0	–
500–510	7a	Grey silt loam	1207	–	0	–
550–560	8.1		1456	–	0	–
590–600	8.1		1462	–	0	–
615–625	8.2	Weathered bedrock	1432	✓	2	–
650–660	8.2		1386	✓	+	–
690–700	8.3		1405	✓	0	–
705–715	8.3		1537	–	0	–

Table 9.4: Processing record of the 23 small bulk samples

of *Cerastoderma edule, Littorina littorea, Scobicularia plana,* and *Hydrobia ulvae* by Healy (1996b; 1999b). The samples were removed *en bloc* from the core after description and subsampling for pollen, diatoms and radiocarbon dating. Samples of 10 cm thickness were removed in totality from the core covering all units. Samples were pre-weighed (in moist condition), soaked in water, and processed by bucket washover flotation in the AEA (Allen Environmental Archaeology) laboratory facilities, in a similar fashion to the recovery of snails (Allen 2017a, 35–36). The flots were retained on 4 mm, 2 mm and 300 µm mesh sieves, and the minerogenic residues were fractioned through 4 mm, 2 mm, 1 mm and 0.5 mm mesh sieves (Table 9.4). The plant remains and shells recovered from these samples are reported below.

Analysis of the plant remains

A.J. Clapham

Four samples from the assessment stage were selected for analysis. Three of the samples were from Unit 3, a humified peat with sand bands, and one from Unit 2b, a stony silty sand with fine humic sand inwash bands. Plant remains were present in all four samples representing a variety of wetland habitats. From the analysis it is evident that there is some change in the vegetation through time linked with changes in water quality from freshwater to brackish conditions. Evidence of a heathy component was also evident in some of the samples. Radiocarbon dates for Unit 3 (humified peat) ranged from 2580–2460 cal BC (3986±27 BP, SUERC-95373) at the base (259 cm) to cal AD 420–540 (1580±19 BP, SUERC-90858) at the top (114 cm). Small fragments of charcoal which were for the main part were too small for an identification were present throughout the part of the sedimentary profile analysed suggesting continuing human activity in the area.

Methods

Four samples were selected from the original assessment (Clapham 2019) of 16 samples and are shown in Table 9.5. Small bulk samples (896–1874 g) were removed for the recovery of the waterlogged plant remains especially from the peat and organic deposits (principally Unit 3). A series of 23 bulk samples was removed from the core after description and subsampling for pollen, diatoms, and radiocarbon dating. Samples of 10 cm thickness were removed covering all units recorded. Samples were pre-weighed and processed by bucket washover

Table 9.5: Samples and sample size analysed for plant macrofossils

Depth (cm)	*Unit*	*Deposit*	*Wet weight (g)*
90–100	2b	stony silty sand	1054
125–135	3	humified peat	1095
230–240	3	humified peat	1095
245–255	3	humified peat	906

flotation in the AEA laboratory facilities. The flots were retained on 4 mm, 2 mm and 0.3 mm mesh sieves and the minerogenic residues fractioned through 4 mm, 2 mm, 1 mm and 0.5 mm sieves. Prior to analysis the samples selected were re-sieved by the author through a series sieves to flush out any humic or clay particles that had broken down during storage. This produced a cleaner sample facilitating the extraction of the plant macrofossils.

The samples were examined using a low-powered (×8–×56) stereomicroscope and the extracted plant macrofossils were identified using the author's own modern plant reference collection and a plant seed atlas (Cappers *et al.* 2006). Where charcoal fragments were deemed identifiable (especially from 245–255 cm), the pieces were examined in 3 dimensions and identified with the aid of Hather (2000). The results are recorded in Table 9.6. Nomenclature of the plant taxa follows Stace (2019).

Results

The results of the plant macrofossil analysis are shown in Table 9.6. The plant remains were extremely well preserved allowing identification to species level in many cases. Plant remains were abundant in all the samples with over 80 taxa identified. Five major types of habitat were recognised from the charred plant assemblages including general terrestrial, heathland, wetland (of various types), aquatic and those influence by maritime/brackish conditions (see Tables 9.7 & 9.8). Plant remains were preserved by waterlogging and charring with the former being the dominant mode of preservation.

Humified peat (Unit 3: 114–260 cm, 1.10 – -0.45 m OD)

Three samples from this humified peat with sand lenses unit were analysed (Table 9.6).

Four humic acid samples were provided for radiocarbon dating from this unit (Table 9.5). Although none of these dates corresponds directly with the samples analysed within Unit 3 it does provide a timescale for the changes in vegetation and hydrology exhibited in the samples.

245–255 cm (after 2580–2460 cal BC)

This sample contained many finely comminuted remains of monocotyledonous roots and stems, some of which were clearly of grass stems and grass culm nodes. Identification of these stems was not possible due to the lack of distinguishing features. Small pieces of possible birch (*Betula* sp.) bark were recorded along with some large pieces of charcoal, some of which were identifiable.

Short lengths of non-grass stems were also noted approximately 1 cm in length with a diameter of 0.5 mm. It is possible that these are the stems of common spike-rush (*Eleocharis palustris*). Several habitats were represented by the plant remains present in this sample (Table 9.6). A terrestrial component was represented by a small number of taxa (see Tables 9.8 & 9.9) and included silverweed (*Potentilla anserina*), common nettle (*Urtica dioica*), slender parsley-piert (*Aphanes australis*), common chickweed (*Stellaria media*) and mudwort (*Limosella aquatica*). A heath component was represented by the finds of bell heather (*Erica cinerea*) seeds and *Calluna/Erica* charcoal. This may have been growing on the drier exposed areas.

By far the greatest part of the plant assemblage in this sample represented the wetter environments from species usually found on the edges of waterbodies and marshy conditions such as hemp-agrimony (*Eupatorium cannabinum*), marsh pennywort (*Hydrocotyle vulgaris*) and rushes (*Juncus* sp.) along with sedges such as the yellow sedges (*Carex flava* group), and spring sedge (*Carex caryophyllea*). Taxa that are usually found either as emergent (roots below water level but stems and flowers are above water) or fringing waterbodies included, lesser marsh-wort (*Helosciadium inundatum*), three-lobed crowfoot (*Ranunculus tripartitus*), brookweed (*Samolus valerandi*) and common spike-rush (*Eleocharis palustris*). The latter species was the most common find in this sample, water purslane (*Lythrum portula*) being the second commonest. Aquatic vegetation was represented by bog pondweed (*Potamogeton polygonifolius*) and, water-starwort (*Callitriche* sp.). Some of the identified taxa could be classified as pioneers of mud exposed during the summer, these include three-lobed crowfoot,

Table 9.6: (continued on the following two pages) The plant remains

Species	*Common name*	*Depth (cm)* 90–100 *Unit* 2b	125–135 3	230–240 3	245–255 3
Waterlogged remains					
Pteridium aquilinum pinnule	bracken	–	1	1	–
Nymphaea alba	white waterlily	4	1	–	–
N. alba frags	white waterlily	10	1	–	–
Ranunculus acris/ repens/ bulbosus	buttercups	2		6	
Ranunculus flammula	lesser spearwort	5	27	172	7
R. *flammula* frags	lesser spearwort	7	–	40	–
R. *lingua*	greater spearwort	1	32	58	–
R. *tripartitus* seeds	three-lobed crowfoot	–	–	–	55
R. *tripartitus* frags	three-lobed crowfoot	–	–	–	51
R. subgen. *Batrachium*	crowfoot	–	–	10	–
R. subgen. *Batrachium* frags	crowfoot	–	–	9	–
Myriophyllum alterniflorum	alternate water-milfoil	2	–	–	–
Medicago lupulina pod	black medick	1	–	–	–
Rubus Sect *Glandulosus* whole	bramble	1	6	–	–
R. Sect *Glandulosus* half seeds	bramble	–	125	–	–
R. Sect frags	bramble	2	6	–	–
R. Sect *Glandulosus* prickles	bramble	–	3	–	–
Potentilla anserina	silverweed	–	4	–	1
Potentilla sp	cinquefoils	4	–	6	1
Potentilla sp frags	cinquefoils	2	–	5	–
Aphanes australis	slender parsley-piert	2	2	11	4
Rosaceae prickle		–	–	2	–
Urtica dioica	common nettle	5	5	2	3
Hypericum tetrapterum	square-stalked St John's-wort	–	2	5	–
H. elodes	marsh St John's-wort	–	–	1	–
Viola palustris	marsh violet	–	3	–	–
V. palustris frags	marsh violet	–	25	–	–
Salix caprea leaf base	goat willow	–	1	–	–
Salix sp leaf frags	willow	–	3	–	–
Linum catharticum	fairy flax	–	–	2	–
Lythrum salicaria	purple loosestrife	1	1	–	–
L. portula	water-purslane	–	–	13	670
Epilobium hirsutum	great willowherb	–	–	5	–
Raphanus raphanistrum ssp *maritimus*	sea radish	–	–	1	–
Persicaria maculosa	redshank	–	–	2	–
P. hydropiper	water-pepper	–	–	4	1
Polygonum aviculare	knotgrass	–	–	1	–
Rumex acetosella	sheep's sorrel	5	–	16	–
Rumex hydrolapathum	water dock	1	–	–	–
Stellaria media	common chickweed	–	–	–	2
S. alsine	bog stitchwort	–	–	–	1
S. aquatica	water chickweed	–	–	1	–
Atriplex sp	orache	–	–	1	–
Chenopodium album	fat hen	–	–	8	5
Oxybasis glauca	oak-leaved goosefoot	–	–	4	–
Suaeda maritima	annual sea-blite	2	–	–	–
Lysimachia tenella	bog pimpernel	–	–	15	1
Samolus valerandi seeds	brookweed	–	–	102	2
S. valerandi fruit frags	brookweed	–	–	1	–
Erica tetralix	cross-leaved heath	–	11	12	–
E. cinerea	bell heather	–	–	56	3
Erica sp leaf frag.	heather		1	8	–
Plantago major	greater plantain	1	–	–	–
Littorella uniflora	shoreweed	6	–	–	–
Hippuris vulgaris	mare's-tail	–	1	–	–

Table 9.6 continued

	Depth (cm)	*90–100*	*125–135*	*230–240*	*245–255*
	Unit	*2b*	*3*	*3*	*3*
Species	*Common name*				
Callitriche sp	water-starworts	–	–	6	7
Limosella aquatica	mudwort	–	25	5982	48
Prunella vulgaris	self-heal	2	1	1	–
Lycopus europaeus	gipsywort	1	5	1	–
Mentha aquatica	watermint	5	97	–	–
Carduus sp	thistle	–	–	1	–
cf *Cirsium* sp phyllary	thistle	–	–	1	–
Achillea millefolium	yarrow	–	–	–	1
Eupatorium cannabinum frags	hemp-agrimony	–	3	1	18
Hydocotyle vulgaris	marsh pennywort	5	9	159	9
Helosciadium inundatum	lesser marshwort	2	–	11	4
Baldellia ranunculoides fruits	lesser water-plantain	12	1	–	–
B. ranunculoides seeds	lesser water-plantain	48	–	–	–
Alisma sp	Water-plantain	–	–	5	2
Triglochin maritima	sea arrowgrass	–	–	–	1
Potamogeton natans	broad-leaved pondweed	–	1	–	–
P. polygonifolius fruits	bog pondweed	–	106	447	81
P.n polygonifolius lids	bog pondweed	–	5	105	11
P. berchtoldii	small pondweed	52	–	–	–
Stuckenia pectinata	fennel pondweed	1	–	–	–
Groenlandia densa	opposite-leaved pondweed	48	13	–	–
Potamogetonaceae fruit frags	pondweeds s.l.	26	–	–	–
Potamogeton sp submerged leaf frags	pondweed		–	29	26
Ruppia maritima	beaked tasselweed	27	–	–	–
R. spiralis	spiral tasselweed	41	1	–	–
Iris pseudacorus exocarp frags	yellow flag	–	1	–	–
Juncus maritimus/conglomeratus seeds	sea/compact rush	–	–	226	66
J. maritimus/conglomeratus fruit frags	sea/compact rush	–	–	43	–
Juncus sp	rushes	2	255	1852	284
Scirpus sylvaticus	wood club-rush	–	13	–	–
Schoenoplectus lacustris	common club-rush	59	–	–	–
S, tabernamontani	grey club-rush	394	3	21	1
Schoenoplectus sp frags	club-rushes	126	–	–	–
Schoenoplectus sp embryos	club-rushes	22	–	–	–
Eleocharis palustris	common spike-rush	5	1	120	1417
E. palustris frags	common spike-rush	2	–	–	315
E. palustris embryos	common spike-rush	–	–	–	24
Isolepis setacea	bristle club-rush	–	–	–	1
Cladium mariscus	great fen-sedge	5	–		–
C. otrubae nutlets	false fox-sedge	–	–	66	–
C. otrubae nutlet frags	false fox-sedge	–	–	59	–
C. echinata	star sedge	–	1	–	–
C. elongata	elongated sedge	–	60	–	–
C. panicea	carnation sedge	–	1	–	2
C. distans	distant sedge	1	–	–	–
C. flava group	yellow sedges	15	–	12	37
C. flava group frags	yellow sedges	5	–	8	59
C. caryophyllea	spring-sedge	10	8	82	7
C. caryophyllea frags	spring-sedge	–	–	44	–
C. pilulifera	pill sedge	–	63	–	–
Glyceria sp	sweet-grasses	–	3	5	–
Small Poaceae <2 mm	grasses	6	7	48	21
Poaceae stems		–	2	–	–
Poaceae culm nodes		–	10	22	13

Table 9.6 continued

Species	*Common name*	*Depth (cm)* *Unit*	*90–100* *2b*	*125–135* *3*	*230–240* *3*	*245–255* *3*
Miscellaneous waterlogged remains						
Cenococcum geophilum sclerotia	soil fungus		–	–	–	5
Characeae oogonia	Stoneworts		8	14	1	–
Sphagnum sp leaves	bog moss		–	2	1	–
Musci stem frags	indeterminate mosses		–	4	3	–
Musci buds	indeterminate mosses		–	–	1	–
Roundwood			–	5	–	–
Bark frags			–	–	–	21
Dicot & monocot leaf frag.			20	–	–	1
Monocot epidermal frags			–	5	–	–
Monocot stems			–	–	–	27
Worm cocoons			2	8	–	18
Caddis fly larval case frags			–	2	3	3
Cladoceran eggsacs	waterfleas		–	–	12	54
Copepod eggsacs			–	–	–	3
Charred remains						
Erica sp leaf frag.	heather		1	3	8	1
Calluna/Erica sp charcoal			–	–	–	4
Dicot leaf frag			1	–	–	–
Juncus effusus/conglomeratus fruit frags	soft/compact rush		–	4	–	–
J. maritimus/conglomeratus fruit frags			–	–	1	–
cf Juncaceae stem frags			–	–	–	2
Carex otrubae utricle	false fox-sedge		–	1	–	–
Potamogeton polygonifolius lids	bog pondweed		–	1	–	–
Schoenoplectus/Cyperaceae culm base			–	–	–	4
Charcoal fragments			49	293	235	350

water purslane, water pepper (*Polygonum hydropiper*), and mudwort.

A high number of small charcoal fragments were recorded from this sample, some of which were large enough to be identified. These included several fragments of heather (*Calluna/Erica*) charcoal and the charred stems of perhaps rush (*Juncus* sp.) and the charred culm bases of club-rush (*Schoenoplectus* sp.).

230–240 cm (after 2580–2460 cal BC)

This sample was also dominated by the remains of monocotyledonous stems, roots, and leaves. The plant assemblage contained within this sample was the most diverse with regards to the number of taxa recorded. Some of the waterlogged plant remains were poorly preserved than others suggesting that there may have been periods of drying out permitting oxygen into the deposits and therefore allowing some decomposition to take place prior to waterlogging again. Similar habitats to those found in the lowest sample from Unit 3 were present in this sample with the wetland component being the commonest type of habitat (Tables 9.6 & 9.8). A single taxon dominated the remains, this being mudwort (*Limosella aquatica*) of which nearly 6000 seeds were identified. This species is discussed in greater detail later. The wetland habitat can be split into several subgroups including bankside vegetation, fringing/emergent vegetation, general wetland species and bare mud, see Tables 9.7 and 9.9.

The aquatic habitat was dominated by the presence of bog pondweed. The general terrestrial habitat consisted of species of disturbed ground such as fat hen (*Chenopodium album*), knotgrass (*Polygonum aviculare*), grassland with selfheal (*Prunella vulgaris*) and wet and dry heathland/moorland by bell heather and cross-leaved heath (*Erica tetralix*). Small fragments of charcoal were recorded from this level but at a reduced level from that recorded at 245–255 cm.

Table 9.7: Habitats indicated by the plant assemblages from Marazion Marsh

Species	*Common name*
Terrestrial (general)	
Pteridium aquilinum	bracken
Ranunculus acris/repens/bulbosus	buttercups
Medicago lupulina	black medick
Rubus Sect *Glandulosus*	bramble
Potentilla anserina	silverweed
Aphanes australis	slender parsley-piert
Urtica dioica	common nettle
Linum catharticum	fairy flax
Persicaria maculosa	redshank
Polygonum aviculare	knotgrass
Rumex acetosella	sheep's sorrel
Stellaria media	common chickweed
Atriplex sp	orache
Chenopodium album	fat hen
Oxybasis glauca	oak-leaved goosefoot
Plantago major	greater plantain
Prunella vulgaris	self-heal
Achillea millefolium	yarrow
Indeterminate Poaceae	grasses
Heathland	
Erica tetralix	cross-leaved heath
E. cinerea	bell heather
Wetland	
Ranunculus lingua	greater spearwort
Ranunculus flammula	lesser spearwort
Hypericum tetrapterum	square-stalked St John's-wort
Hypericum elodes	marsh St John's-wort
Viola palustris	marsh violet
Salix caprea	goat willow
Salix sp	willow
Lythrum salicaria	purple loosestrife
L. portula	water-purslane
Epilobium hirsutum	great willowherb
Persicaria hydropiper	water-pepper
Rumex hydrolapathum	water dock
Stellaria alsine	bog stitchwort
S. aquatica	water chickweed
Lysimachia tenella	bog pimpernel
Samolus valerandi	brookweed
Limosella aquatica	mudwort
Lycopus europaeus	gipsywort
Mentha aquatica	watermint
Eupatorium cannabinum	hemp-agrimony
Hydocotyle vulgaris	marsh pennywort
Helosciadium inundatum	lesser marshwort
Baldellia ranunculoides	lesser water-plantain
Alisma sp	water-plantain
Juncus maritimus/conglomeratus	sea/compact rush
Juncus sp	rushes
Scirpus sylvaticus	wood club-rush
Eleocharis palustris	common spike-rush
Isolepis setacea	bristle club-rush
Cladium mariscus	great fen-sedge
Carex otrubae	false fox-sedge
C. echinata	star sedge
C. elongata	elongated sedge
C. panicea	carnation sedge
C. distans	distant sedge
C. flava group (*C. demissa* type)	yellow sedges
C. caryophyllea	spring-sedge
C. pilulifera	pill sedge
Aquatic	
Nymphaea alba	white waterlily
Ranunculus tripartitus	three-lobed crowfoot
R. subgen. *Batrachium*	crowfoot
Myriophyllum alterniflorum	alternate water-milfoil
Littorella uniflora	shoreweed
Hippuris vulgaris	mare's-tail
Callitriche sp	water-starworts
Potamogeton natans	broad-leaved pondweed
P. polygonifolius	bog pondweed
P. berchtoldii	small pondweed
Stuckenia pectinata	fennel pondweed
Groenlandia densa	opposite-leaved pondweed
Iris pseudacorus	yellow flag
Schoenoplectus lacustris	common club-rush
Glyceria sp	sweet-grasses
Maritime influence/brackish conditions	
Raphanus raphanistrum ssp *maritimus*	sea radish
Suaeda maritima	annual sea-blite
Triglochin maritima	sea arrowgrass
Ruppia maritima	beaked tasselweed
R. spiralis	spiral tasselweed
Schoenoplectus tabernamontani	grey club-rush

125–135 cm (Iron Age to Romano-British)

This was the uppermost sample from Unit 3 to be analysed and is 11 cm from the junction of Unit 3 with 2b. Plant remains were preserved by waterlogging and charring with the former being the dominant form of preservation. The coarser fraction (4 mm) was dominated by common reed (*Phragmites australis*) and other monocotyledonous rhizome/root material. Other smaller grass culm nodes were also recorded (Table 9.6). The number of taxa recorded from this sample was slightly fewer than that from the previous sample with the same habitats being represented, see Tables 9.8 and 9.9.

The main taxon representing the terrestrial part of the assemblage was that of bramble (*Rubus* Sect *Glandulosus*). Most of the bramble achenes (Table 9.6) were present as half achenes, which suggests that they have been eaten/gnawed by small rodents. No toothmarks were visible in the chewed seeds preventing the identification of the culprit. The presence of a greater number of bramble achenes may suggest that the land was perhaps drying out but there is no convincing evidence for trees growing locally. The presence of a single find of a goat willow (*Salix caprea*) leaf base and a few fragments of non-diagnostic willow (*Salix* sp.) leaf fragments, perhaps does indicate the presence damp woodland nearby which is supported by the finds of wood club-rush (*Scirpus sylvatica*). The moorland component of the terrestrial habitat is only represented by several cross-leaved heath seeds and leaf fragments.

The wetland component of the assemblage was still the dominant habitat represented with bankside/marshy and fringing/emergent vegetation dominating. There appears to be a decline in species which can be considered as bare mud pioneers. Indicating that water levels remains high all year. The presence of marsh violet (*Viola palustris*) lends indirect support to the presence of willow carr locally. The fully aquatic component is represented by bog pondweed, broad-leaved pondweed (*Potamogeton natans*) and somewhat surprisingly opposite-leaved pondweed (*Groelandia densa*), as this taxon is usually associated with base-rich waters, although it can be present where base-rich water flows over an acidic substrate such as peat (Preston 1995).

The beginning of a possible maritime influence is indicated by the presence of spiral tasselweed (*Ruppia spiralis*) and grey club-rush (*Schoenoplectus tabernamontani*). Similar amounts of charcoal fragments to those of the previous sample were noted (Table 9.6).

Unit 2b (86–114 cm, 1.29–1.10 m OD)

This unit comprises of fine humic sand with inwash bands. A single sample (90–100 cm) was analysed.

90–100 cm (after cal AD 420–540)

This sample contained fewer remains of finely comminuted plant remains than those from Unit 3. This sample was the poorest in terms of the number of taxa present, although there was an abundance of plant remains (see Table 9.6). Similar habitats were present in this sample as in the previous three samples from Unit 3, although there was no heathland component present (Table 9.8). There were 10 taxa that could be thought to be representative of the general terrestrial habitat (Tables 9.8 & 9.9), Wetland habitats were also well represented with 15 taxa and again included those which can be found on the banks of water bodies, emergent and fringing vegetation as well as those associated with more boggy/marshy conditions. The aquatic element is better represented in this sample with seven taxa present which includes white water lily (*Nymphaea alba*), small pondweed (*Potamogeton berchtoldii*), fennel pondweed (*Stuckenia pectinate*) and opposite-leaved pondweed and common club-rush (*Schoenoplectus lacustris)*. There is a more prominent maritime/brackish element in this sample indicating a greater influence of increased sea-level perhaps through the breaking of the seaward barrier allowing an influx of salt water. These taxa include, beaked-(*Ruppia maritima*) and spiral tasselweed, grey club-rush, annual sea-blite (*Suaeda maritima*) and the brackish water tolerant small pondweed. No pioneers of bare mud were evident suggesting that the water table was high enough all year round to prevent any drying out of the shallow pools. This sample recorded the lowest number of small charcoal fragments, but enough to suggest continued human activity in the area.

Depth (cm)	*90–100*	*125–135*	*230–240*	*245–255*	*Overall*
Unit	*2b*	*3*	*3*	*3*	
Habitat					
Terrestrial (general)	10	7	15	8	21
Heathland	0	1	2	1	2
Wetland	15	20	22	18	37
Aquatic	7	7	4	3	15
Maritime influence/ brackish water	4	2	2	2	6
Total	36	40	45	32	81

Table 9.8: Habitats and taxa represented within the plant assemblages analysed at Marazion Marsh

Discussion

Most of the plant remains were preserved by waterlogging with a minority by charring. Charcoal fragments, too small to be identified were present throughout the profile suggesting

Table 9.9: (continued on the opposite page) Presence/absence of taxa and habitats through time

Species	Common name	*Depth (cm)* / *Unit*	*90–100* / *2b*	*125–135* / *3*	*230–240* / *3*	*245–255* / *3*
Waterlogged remains						
Terrestrial (general)						
Pteridium aquilinum	bracken			■	■	
Ranunculus acris/repens/bulbosus	buttercups		■		■	
Medicago lupulina	black medick		■			
Rubus Sect *Glandulosus*	bramble		■	■		
Potentilla anserina	silverweed			■		■
Potentilla sp	cinquefoils		■		■	■
Aphanes australis	slender parsley-piert		■	■	■	■
Urtica dioica	common nettle		■	■	■	■
Linum catharticum	fairy flax				■	
Persicaria maculosa	redshank				■	
Polygonum aviculare	knotgrass				■	
Rumex acetosella	sheep's sorrel		■		■	
Stellaria media	common chickweed					■
Atriplex sp	orache				■	
Chenopodium album	fat hen				■	■
Oxybasis glauca	oak-leaved goosefoot				■	
Plantago major	greater plantain		■			
Prunella vulgaris	self-heal		■	■	■	
Carduus sp	thistle				■	
Achillea millefolium	yarrow					■
Small Poaceae <2 mm	grasses		■	■	■	■
Heathland						
Erica tetralix	cross-leaved heath			■	■	
Erica cinerea	bell heather				■	■
Wetland						
Ranunculus lingua	greater spearwort		■	■	■	
R. flammula	lesser spearwort		■	■	■	■
Hypericum tetrapterum	square-stalked St John's-wort			■	■	
H. elodes	marsh St John's-wort				■	
Viola palustris	marsh violet			■		
Salix caprea	goat willow			■		
Lythrum salicaria	purple loosestrife		■	■		
L. portula	water-purslane				■	■
Epilobium hirsutum	great willowherb				■	
Persicaria hydropiper	water-pepper				■	■
Rumex hydrolapathum	water dock		■			
Stellaria alsine	bog stitchwort					■
S. aquatica	water chickweed				■	
Lysimachia tenella	bog pimpernel				■	■
Samolus valerandi	brookweed				■	■
Limosella aquatica	mudwort			■	■	■
Lycopus europaeus	gipsywort		■	■	■	
Mentha aquatica	watermint		■	■		
Eupatorium cannabinum	hemp-agrimony			■	■	■
Hydocotyle vulgaris	marsh pennywort		■	■	■	■
Helosciadium inundatum	lesser marshwort		■		■	■
Baldellia ranunculoides	lesser water-plantain		■	■		
Alisma sp	Water-plantain				■	■
Juncus maritimus/conglomeratus	sea/compact rush				■	■
Juncus sp	rushes		■	■	■	■
Scirpus sylvaticus	wood club-rush			■		
Eleocharis palustris	common spike-rush		■	■	■	■
Isolepis setacea	bristle club-rush					■
Cladium mariscus	great fen-sedge		■			

Table 9.9 continued

Species	*Common name*	*Depth (cm)* *Unit*	*90–100* *2b*	*125–135* *3*	*230–240* *3*	*245–255* *3*
Waterlogged remains						
Carex otrubae	false fox-sedge				■	
C. echinata	star sedge			■		
C. elongata	elongated sedge			■		
C. panicea	carnation sedge			■		■
C. distans	distant sedge		■			
C. flava group	yellow sedges		■		■	■
C. caryophyllea	spring-sedge		■	■	■	■
C.pilulifera	pill sedge			■		
Aquatic (general)						
Nymphaea alba	white waterlily		■	■		
Ranunculus tripartitus	three-lobed crowfoot					■
R. subgenus *Batrachium*	crowfoot				■	
Myriophyllum alterniflorum	alternate water-milfoil		■			
Littorella uniflora	shoreweed		■			
Hippuris vulgaris	mare's-tail			■		
Callitriche sp	water-starworts				■	■
Potamogeton natans	broad-leaved pondweed			■		
P. polygonifolius	bog pondweed			■	■	■
P. berchtoldii	small pondweed		■			
Stuckenia pectinata	fennel pondweed		■			
Groenlandia densa	opposite-leaved pondweed		■	■		
Iris pseudacorus	yellow flag			■		
Schoenoplectus lacustris	common club-rush		■			
Glyceria sp	sweet-grasses			■	■	
Maritime influence/brackish conditions						
Raphanus raphanistrum ssp *maritimus*	sea radish				■	
Suaeda maritima	annual sea-blite		■			
Triglochin maritima	sea arrowgrass					■
Ruppia maritima	beaked tasselweed		■			
R. spiralis	spiral tasselweed		■	■		
Schoenoplectus tabernamontani	grey club-rush		■	■	■	■
Charred remains						
Charcoal frags			■	■	■	■

a continued human presence in the area. A range of habitats were represented by the plant assemblages; most of these were present throughout the profile. Some habitats were more prevalent in some of the samples (Table 9.8) than in others, but the overall impression is the change in hydrology from a freshwater regime to a brackish one, linked to the rise in sea-level or a breach of the seaward barrier at Marazion Marsh. With regards to individual taxa recorded within the samples, one, mudwort (*Limosella aquatica*) maybe classified as an important find as this species is now considered to be extinct from the modern Cornish flora (French *et al.* 1999).

Terrestrial habitats

A total of 21 taxa representing general terrestrial (Tables 9.7, 9.8 & 9.9). These can be split into various sub-categories of habitat types. These include woodland/shrubland as represented by bracken (*Pterdium aquilinum*) and bramble (*Rubus* Sect *Glandulosus*), and grassland by black medick (*Medicago lupulina*), self-heal (*Prunella vulgaris*), yarrow (*Achillea millefolium*) and various grasses. It is most likely, given the underlying geology of the area that the soils are acidic in nature and this is indicated by the presence of sheep's sorrel (*Rumex acetosella*). The most common terrestrial habitat represented was that of bare, open, and disturbed ground which can include cultivated ground. The presence of the terrestrial habitat declines up the profile (Tables 9.8 & 9.9) although it does remain the second most common habitat represented by the plant assemblages after those of the wetland habitat.

Heathland

There were only two taxa which could be classified as belonging to the heathland/ moorland vegetation components of the plant assemblages. Others classified under the wetland vegetation type may also be found in heath and moorland situations, such as the various sedges. The heathland component was present in all sample apart from the sample 90–100 cm in Unit 2b. Cross-leaved heath (*Erica tetralix*) tends to be found on the wetter heaths, whilst bell heather (*Erica cinerea)* is found on the drier areas. It is most likely that these taxa were part of an allochthonous component of the assemblages which may have found their way into the deposit from the surrounding higher drier land. It is also possible that these taxa were growing further back inland.

Wetland

The wetland taxa found were present in all the samples studied and in all cases was the most common habitat type. A total of 37 taxa represent this vegetation type (Table 9.8). As with the terrestrial component the wetland taxa can be divided into sub-categories. Waterside vegetation was represented by greater and lesser spearwort (*Ranunculus lingua, R. flammula*), square-stalked St John's Wort (*Hypericum tetrapterum*), marsh St John's Wort (*Hypericum elodes*), purple loosestrife (*Lythrum salicaria*), great willowherb (*Epilobium hirsutum*), gipsywort (*Lycopus europaeus*), watermint (*Mentha aquatica*), hemp-agrimony (*Eupatorium cannabinum*) and marsh pennywort (*Hydrocotyle vulgaris*). A fringing/emergent vegetation presence was indicated by water-purslane (*Lythrum portula*) – which can also survive as an aquatic, mudwort (*LImosella aquatica*), lesser water-plantain (*Baldellia ranunculoides*), water-plantain (*Alism*a sp.), rushes (*Juncus* sp.), and common spike-rush (*Eleocharis palustris*). Grey club-rush (*Scheoenoplectus tabernaemontani*) is present in large numbers in Unit 2b and although it can be classified as fringing/ emergent vegetation it is in recent times found mainly in coastal areas and indicates brackish conditions. Several of these taxa can also be considered as bare mud pioneers and will be discussed in greater detail below.

There are several sedge species in the assemblages and these all represent wet, boggy conditions, usually on acidic soils and therefore perhaps belong with the waterside vegetation. The presence of great fen-sedge (*Cladium mariscus*) in the 90–100 cm (Unit 2b) sample could be considered unusual as this species is commonly associated with fen conditions and is extremely rare in Cornwall today and restricted to a few sites on the Lizard (French *et al.* 1999). Overall, the presence of a high number of wetland taxa within the assemblages suggests a marshy/boggy environment with occasional open pools of shallow water as indicated by the aquatic taxa present. Some of the marshy/ boggy areas would have consisted of tall fen communities dominated by reeds (*Phragmites australis*) and the club-rushes interspersed with areas of low growing marsh with a creeping vegetation.

Aquatic

Aquatic plant species are present in all the samples. Fifteen taxa can be assigned to this category overall. The greatest number of aquatic species are found in the upper two samples 125–135 cm (Unit 3) and 90–100 cm (Unit 2b), (Tables 9.8 & 9.9). There is a general increase in the number of aquatics up the profile suggesting an increase in the water table due to an increasing marine influence. All the aquatics present prefer open, still, or slow-moving water. Most of the aquatic species are either calcifuges or prefer acidic waters and the nutrient status between oligotrophic and mesotrophic, although some can tolerate a wide range of conditions including eutrophic (nutrient-rich) waters (see Table 9.10). Shallow water is preferred, ranging in depth from 0.3–1.5 m but some such as shoreweed (*Littorella uniflora*), alternate water-milfoil (*Myriophyllum alterniflorum*) and broad-leaved pondweed (*Potamogeton natans*) can be found at deeper depths of up to 5.4 m (Table 9.10). Those preferring a more nutrient-rich water are found within the uppermost sample analysed (90–100 cm) in Unit 2b. This is also associated with an increase in salinity leading to brackish conditions.

Aquatic species	*Common name*	*Water flow*	*Water depth (m)*	*pH amplitude*	*Nutrient status*
Nymphaea alba	white waterlily	still/slow	0.5–1.5	wide	oligo-mesotrophic
Ranunculus tripartitus	three-lobed crowfoot	still/slow	shallow	calcifuge	oligo-mesotrophic
Myriophyllum alterniflorum	alternate water-milfoil	still/slow	0.3–3.0	acidic	oligo-mesotrophic
Littorella uniflora	shoreweed	slow	shallow (3–4)	wide	oligo-mesotrophic
Hippuris vulgaris	mare's-tail	still/slow	shallow	base-rich, tolerates saline conditions	oligo-mesotrophic
Callitriche sp	water-starworts	still/slow	shallow	wide	oligo-mesotrophic
Potamogeton natans	broad-leaved pondweed	still/slow/fast	1–2 (5.4)	wide	oligo-eutrophic
P. polygonifolius	bog pondweed	still/slow/wet terrestrial	<1.5 (3)	acidic	oligo-mesotrophic
P. berchtoldii	small pondweed	still/slow	shallow	wide	meso-eutrophic
Stuckenia pectinata	fennel pondweed	still/slow	0.5–1.5	wide (mostly acidic/neutral)	eutrophic/brackish
Groenlandia densa	opposite-leaved pondweed	still/slow/fast	shallow	base-rich (over acidic peat)	oligo-mesotrophic
Ruppia maritima	beaked tasselweed	still/slow	<0.5	wide	brackish/saline
R. spiralis	spiral tasselweed	still/slow	0.5+	wide	brackish/saline
Iris pseudacorus	yellow flag	still/slow	<0.3	wide	meso-eutrophic (brackish)
Schoenoplectus lacustris	common club-rush	still/slow	0.3–1.5	wide	oligo-eutrophic
S. tabernamontani	grey club-rush	still/slow	shallow	wide	brackish

Table 9.10: Attributes and affinities of the aquatic plant species found in the Marazion Marsh (after Preston 1995 and Preston & Croft 1997)

Maritime influence/brackish conditions

Six taxa can be considered to exhibit either a maritime influence or brackish conditions (Table 9.8). There does appear to some brackish/maritime conditions throughout the profile, although at the lower levels this appears to be at a minimum. The level/unit which has the greatest maritime/brackish influence is at 90–100 cm in Unit 2b where there is a doubling of the number of taxa (Tables 9.6 & 9.8). The presence of the tasselweeds (*Ruppia maritima* and *R. spiralis*) suggest brackish lagoons 0.5 m deep. Spiral tasselweed tolerates more saline conditions that beaked tasselweed and is found in deeper water than that of beaked tasselweed (Table 9.10). The occurrence of sea radish (*Raphanus raphanistrum* ssp. *maritimus*), annual sea-blite (*Suaeda maritima*) and sea arrowgrass (*Triglochin maritima*) may suggest the presence somewhere in the vicinity of saltmarsh although at some distance from the sampling point due to the low numbers present.

Bare mud pioneers

There are several plant taxa that can be considered as bare mud pioneers. They can thrive in other habitats but come into prominence when bare mud is exposed in dry summers. Salisbury (1970) carried out a study of those species and Table 9.11 is taken from that work. The pioneer mud species are limited to the lower samples (230–240 cm and 245–255 cm). Salisbury (1970) found that these mud species tend to be very localised and sensitive to edaphic conditions, if the mud is too dry, germination and therefore colonisation of the bare mud will not happen. He also found, that because of this restricted occurrence, it is not surprising that in any single locality only a small proportion of the plants that can colonise this habitat are encountered at any one time (Salisbury 1970).

As to be expected these mud colonising plants are annuals which are adapted to such ephemeral habitats as they need to complete their lifecycle before the winter when the bare mud is submerged by rising water levels. As these habitats are erratic in occurrence and ephemeral in nature, species dependent on their survival of the availability (or lack of) bare mud often have seeds that can remain dormant for many years such as mudwort (*Limosella aquatica*), and these species may disappear for many years. The plants of this habitat have no specialised methods of dispersal and are thought to be spread on the feet of waterfowl (Salisbury 1970). Seven taxa found in the plant assemblages studied here can be considered as being adapted to this kind of habitat (Table 9.11). In general, they flower early in the year and this flowering period can be between 4 and 5 months, giving the ability of the species to take full advantage of the right conditions. Seed is usually produced a month – 6 weeks

Table 9.11: Flowering times of the bare mud pioneer species at Marazion Marsh (after Salisbury 1970)

Species	*Common name*	*Flowering period*
Ranunculus tripartitus	three-lobed crowfoot	May–Oct.
Stellaria aquatica	water chickweed	May–Oct.
Lythrum portula	water-purslane	May–Oct.
Callitriche sp	water-starworts	June–Oct.
Persicaria hydropiper	water-pepper	June–Oct.
Samolus valerandi	brookweed	June–Oct.
Limosella aquatica	mudwort	June–Oct.

after pollination with some of the seeds germinating immediately if the conditions are right, otherwise the seeds remain dormant until favourable conditions return.

The presence of these species in the lower part of Unit 3 suggests that the water levels dropped sufficiently in summer and for a long enough period to permit the colonisation of the exposed mud. Mudwort is the only mud pioneer present higher up the column in 125–135 cm but in significantly reduced numbers (from 5982 at 230–240 cm to 25 at 125–135 cm); this suggests that conditions became more unsuitable for these pioneer species over time with fewer mud exposures perhaps linked to an increase in the local water table effected by a rise in sea-level sustaining high water levels throughout the year. The change in dominance between water-purslane (*Lythrum portula*) at 245–255 cm to that of mudwort at 230–240 cm is most likely to be due to the ephemeral nature of this habitat where at the lower level the conditions were perhaps more suitable for water-purslane while at 230–240 cm the conditions were more suitable for mudwort.

Mudwort is worth a mention on its own. This species is considered extinct in the flora of Cornwall (French *et al.* 1999) and nationally scarce by Stace (2019) where it is found in not more than 100 different 10 × 10 km grid squares in the British Isles since 1987. This may be linked to several factors, but it is most likely due to the lack of suitable habitats currently. The presence of large numbers of mudwort seeds at 230–240 cm indicates that it can be considered as part of the Cornish flora since at least the late Bronze Age. Mudwort (*Limosella aquatica*) favours wet sandy muds by waterbodies that often dry out in summer (Stace 2019). It is a member of the flora that can be found on drying mud and its occurrence can be very local. It is an annual species which can disappear for years then re-appear when conditions are favourable (Salisbury 1967).

Mudwort is a small plant in stature, but if not crowded out it can produce ancillary rosettes which extends it coverage. In situations where there is a dense sward of plants, very few or no ancillary rosettes are produced. Mudwort flowers from July to September but has been recorded as flowering as early as June and as late as October. Once pollinated a capsule is produced, the number per plant can vary between 3 and 111, with a mean of 31 capsules per plant. The number of seeds carried within each capsule can vary from a minimum of 64 to a maximum of 196, with the average number of seeds per capsule has been calculated as 116.7 (Salisbury 1967). The average seed production per plant is 3600.

There is a wide size range for individual plants which is dependent on the density of the mudwort sward as well as the time of germination. Therefore, seeds that germinate early in the season are most likely to produce larger plants than those that germinate later in the season. The timing of the seasonal drought and therefore exposure of mud, is also important in the development of the plant. The size of the plants and therefore the number of fruits produced is dependent on sunshine following exposure and the density of the sward. If there is an early drought then there are fewer plants with a greater number of secondary rosettes but if the drought is later or, there is a dense sward, then the number of rosettes is reduced and therefore the corresponding number of fruits.

Seed production is large for a species of such a small stature. The large output of seeds in relation to size is characteristic of species peculiar to the flora of bare mud (Salisbury 1967). Conditions required for the successful reproduction of these plants recur at infrequent intervals and therefore they have become opportunists with the capacity to occupy the exposed mud in large numbers very rapidly when the conditions are favourable. Seed size is small at 0.65 × 0.3 mm and they tend to fall with the finest silt which is deposited towards the surface of the mud. Dormancy is imposed by the lack of oxygen and light. The seeds are released in moist or wet conditions but if they become desiccated, they are less readily dispersed. Long distance dispersal is only thought to be by the feet of waterfowl (Salisbury 1967).

Experiments on the conditions required for the germination of mudwort seeds have shown that light is essential (Salisbury 1967). Rapid germination is exhibited when responding to sunlight and warmth that occurs when the mud exposed in exposed in summer and subjected to prolonged sunshine. The delay between the exposure of the mud and the onset of germination is related to the drying out of the mud which must reach a temperature sufficient for germination. Seeds can germinate as early as June or as late as October depending on the amount of sunlight (Salisbury 1967). Germination can take place underwater, but it is rare, and the number of seedlings produced is reduced (Salisbury 1967).

Seeds of mudwort can remain dormant in mud for many years until sufficient exposure to sunlight again raises the temperature of the mud and provides the light stimulus to bring about the resurgence of the species. This conspicuous intermittence of occurrence and striking variation of abundance is a shared trait with other species of drying mud. The presence of mudwort and the other pioneering mud species at the lower levels of Unit 3 suggests that conditions were ideal in summer for these species to thrive. Suggesting that hot, dry summers which dried out the shallow pools were common at that time.

Evidence of human activity

The presence of human activity in environmental samples is usually indicated by the presence of charred cereal remains or those plants often associated with their cultivation. This type of evidence is absent from these samples. The presence of charcoal, no matter how small, can also be an indication of human activity within the catchment area of the samples. Small charcoal fragments are present in all the samples analysed here (Table 9.6). The small size of the fragments suggests that they have been transported some distance and it is likely that most of the human activity is taking place further away on drier ground. The number of charcoal fragments declines as you reach the topmost sample at 90–100 cm in Unit 2b (see Table 9.6). In the lowermost sample some of the fragments were large enough to identify. Among the pieces that were identifiable were small stems of either *Calluna* or *Erica* (heathers) which suggests that the moorlands or drier lands were being exploited either to clear the land for cultivation or to provide a source of fuel in an area devoid of trees. Other charred remains identified included possible culm bases of sedges and stems of rushes, which may suggest more local burning events.

Therefore, evidence of human activity from the plant macrofossils is limited to fragments of charcoal which may represent the exploitation of the moorlands/heaths in the hinterland. The charcoal due to its small size may have either been blown into the deposit by the wind or been carried down by the streams coming off the higher ground. The larger pieces of the sedge culm bases may reflect a more local activity. There is little evidence of woodland in these samples suggesting that trees were not growing in the area.

Previous research in the area and its relevance to this work

Quaternary palaeosols and other organic horizon occur throughout Cornwall and offshore (French 1999). Those palaeosols which are found beneath present-day offshore sediments and in the intertidal zone of zone of most estuaries and bays have acquired the name 'Submerged Forest'. This is due to presence in many cases of fallen tree trunks and other tree remains such as acorns and nuts which were very well preserved (Table 9.12).

Submerged forest beds developed on the Holocene alluvium (Healy 1995) and in a few cases they can be traced inland, such as Marazion Marsh where they represent a seaward extension of valley bottom marshes that still occur today. Marazion Marsh is in Mount's Bay and large, extensive submerged forest deposits have been recorded historically in parts of the bay (Borlase 1758; Boase 1822; 1826; Carne 1846). The greatest expanse of submerged forest is said to occur between Marazion Marsh and Newlyn (French 1999). Reid (1913) recorded that the Mount's Bay submerged forest was rooted in soil directly on solid rock, but this is not the case at Marazion Marsh. A transect of boreholes carried out by Healy (1996b) parallel to

Table 9.12: 18th, 19th and 20th century macrofossil records from the submerged forest beds at Mount's Bay, Cornwall (after French 1999)

Species	*Common name*	*Records*
Pinus sylvestris	Scot's pine	cones by Boase 1822
Taxus baccata	yew	Boase 1826
Ulmus sp	elm	Boase 1826
Fagus sylvatica	beech	Boase 1826
Quercus sp	oak	Kitchen 1764; Boase 1826; Carne 1846; Henwood 1873; Enys 1899; Reid 1913; Thurston 1930
Betula sp	birch	Robson 1944
Alnus glutinosa	alder	Boase 1826; Robson 1944
Corylus avellana	hazel	Borlase 1758; Boase 1826; Carne 1846; Henwood 1873; Reid 1913
Salix sp	willow	Borlase 1758; Boase 1826; Ussher 1879; Reid 1913; Robson 1944
Fraxinus excelsior	ash	Boase 1826
Ranunculus flammula	lesser spearwort	Reid 1913
Rubus sp	bramble	Reid 1913
Potentilla sp	cinquefoil	Reid 1913
Prunella vulgaris	self-heal	Reid 1913

the beach demonstrated that at the base weathered rock formed two channels and the deeper parts were overlain by peat which in turn was succeeded by marine sediments. In the deeper eastern channel, a marine transgression occurred at below -4 m OD. In the higher channel this occurred at -1.5 and -2.5 m OD. A second band of peat overlies the deeper channel at above 1 m OD which topped by further sand/marine deposits. It is not known whether the any of the peat bands in Marazion Marsh correspond with the submerged forest beds. Previous radiocarbon dating of the submerged forest deposits showed that the intertidal sections are younger than 5000 BP (Healy 1995; 1996b; French 1999) but some may have begun forming much earlier as shown by a date of 12070±80 BP (SRR-3022) from Mount's Bay at -32 m OD.

Analysis of sections of the submerged forest beds in Mount's Bay shows that the sequence of events leading to the formation. Submergence and preservation of the submerged forest palaeosol varied around the bay indicating that there is no simple overall stratigraphy that can explain the submerged forest phenomenon (French 1999). In the past, there have been *ad hoc* recording of plant macrofossils from the submerged forest beds in Cornwall (see Table 9.12). These records are the obvious *in situ* tree stumps and associated nut and acorns. There have been very few (if any) systematic plant macrofossil studies of these deposits, apart from Pascoe (1970) which appears to be a very short report with little or no interpretation. Therefore, this study may well be the first thorough analyses of the plant macrofossil assemblages present within the submerged forest deposits of Cornwall.

The macrofossil evidence from these casual finds gives the impression of a well-developed woodland and other habitats within these deposits are rarely noticed apart from the work by Reid (1913) and Pascoe (1970) which suggested that boggy/marshy conditions were prevalent within the deposits. Pollen evidence from Mount's Bay (Healy 1995; 1996b; French 1999) suggests the presence of a very localised coastal alder dominated wet woodland with little indication of extensive woodland inland which, it has been suggested had already been cleared by human activity. The diatom evidence (Healy 1995; 1996b; French 1999) suggests an increasing marine influence as you move up the sedimentary column which is a response to rising sea-level. Therefore, there is an indication that there are a variety of habitats, woodland, marshland, and freshwater/brackish lagoons represented within the submerged forest beds suggesting a complicated stratigraphy.

What is evident from the current study of the plant macrofossils and the pollen record is that there is little evidence, if any, for woodland in the area. This current study suggests that there the main habitats are marshy/boggy ground with fringing vegetation of shallow open water which begins as freshwater and through time becomes more brackish. There is also evidence that at the base of the organic horizon (245–255 cm and 230–240 cm) of a drop in water level in summer exposing bare mud which is in turn colonised by the annual mud pioneers such as mudwort and water-purslane.

Macrofossils are rarely deposited more than a metre from the parent plant (Greatrex 1983) and therefore produce a picture of the immediate vegetation growing around the sampling site whilst palynology produces a picture of the extra-local and regional vegetation. Macrofossils can also demonstrate in detail the ecological dynamics of submerged forests (Clapham 1999). When a fully integrated approach is taken as demonstrated in this project (plant macrofossils, pollen, and diatom analyses) a more comprehensive picture of the palaeoecology and land use of the area can be achieved.

Conclusions

The study of the plant macrofossils from the core at Marazion Marsh has shown that the area consisted of marshy/boggy areas with tall fringing and shallow open water vegetation which in the initial stages dried out in summer allowing the bare mud to be colonised by mud bank pioneers. Through time this summer drop in water levels is lost and the water table remains high throughout the year which becomes increasingly brackish. There are drier areas where more heathland vegetation such as bell heather can grow. This may have been growing on the higher drier land in the area. There is little evidence for woodland locally. The only evidence of human activity in the area is indicated by the presence of charcoal fragments which occur throughout the profile studied, nevertheless this sparse but is continuous. The fragments of charcoal may represent the clearing of the vegetation in order to exploit the natural resources and may be connected to the Bronze Age hoards found within the area. The fact that the charcoal is present throughout the whole profile suggests that human activity continued in order to exploit the natural environment for resources such as fish.

Marine shells

Michael J. Allen

Despite the records of marine shells (*Cerastoderma edule, Littorina littorea, Scobicularia plana*) and brackish water shells (*Hydrobia ulvae*) in medium quartz-dominated sand at *c.* -4.75 to -5.15 m OD over a basal organic horizon by Healy (1996b; 1999b), no shells or shell fragments were present in the flots, nor were any noted in during scanning of the 4 mm, 2 mm, 1 mm and 0.5 mm fractions.

10

The changing environment and land-use history of the marsh environs: the environment of the St Michael's Mount hinterland

Michael J. Allen

Much previous research has been strongly focused on relative sea-level studies (cf. Healy 1993; 1995; 1996b; 1999a; French 1999); however, at Marazion Marsh, once the gravel bar formed, probably not long after 5060–4850 cal BC, the marsh became cut off from the sea and thereby was less subject to marine influences; the sediment accumulation and peat growth relate to the inland pool and are not true sea-level indices. A summary of the overall palaeo-environmental and geoarchaeological conclusions is given in the summary chart (see below).

Sea-level and the coastline

Although Healy, in particular, has used analyses at Marazion Marsh to examine seal-level rise (from which former coastlines can be crudely postulated), the work here shows that few of the dated horizons in Marazion Marsh (as presented in Table 10.1 and the summary chart below) are true index points. That is, although they are dated points with altitudinal reference within the peat, the deposits themselves are not directly related to past relative or absolute sea-level.

Sea-level index points are dated horizons that are bio-stratigraphically and/or litho-stratigraphically *directly* related to past sea-level. They are stratigraphic points that represent the position of relative sea-level in the past, and are obtained through a combination of bio-stratigraphy and/or litho-stratigraphy, dating the stratigraphy, and its current absolute altitude (Edwards & Horton 2000; Edwards 2006; Horton *et al.* 2013). To define a sea-level index point from a sediment, its age, altitude, tendency and indicative meaning – the modern counterpart height to relative sea-level – are required (Shennan 1982; Long *et al.* 1999; Edwards & Horton 2006; Gehrels 2007; Barlow *et al.* 2013; Horton *et al.* 2013), as described by Best (2016). Index points are, therefore, identified from the contacts between organic (peat) deposits and fine-grained minerogenic deposits that form high in the intertidal zone, and data from diatoms and other biological data (pollen and waterlogged plant remains) determine if they represent transgression or regressions (Gehrels 2007).

The marsh here formed behind a gravel and sand bar and is not directly related to sea-level, other than through occasional

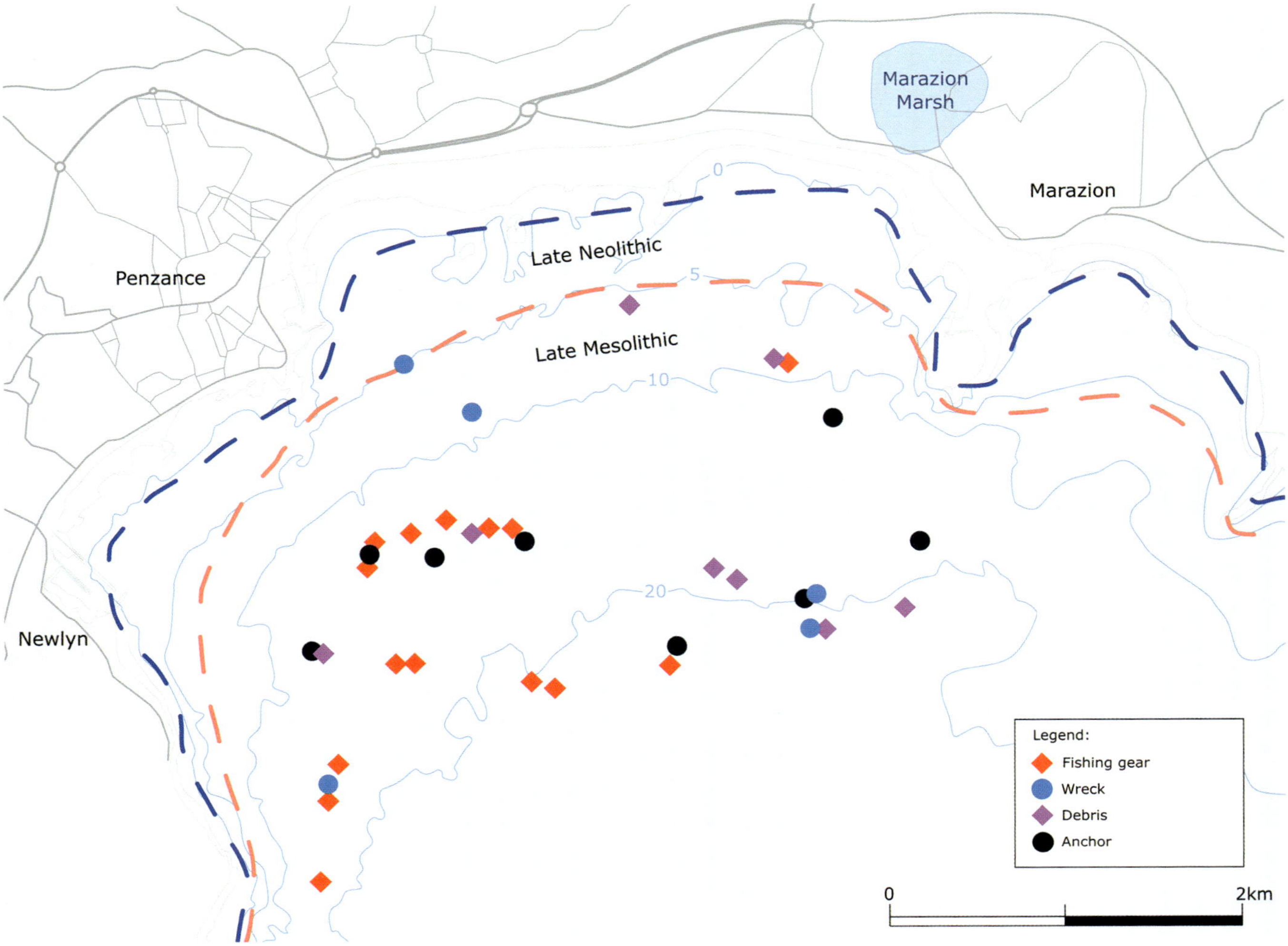

Figure 10.1: The west of Mount's Bay show approximate coastline in the later Mesolithic (5000 cal BC) and later prehistoric (c. 1000 cal BC), in relation to historic maritime finds

breaching. Although the organic accumulation may be related to eustatic groundwater fluctuations it will have a time-lag in the vegetation response. Any index points are really minerogenic sediment under or overlain by organic materials which denote change to or from a semi-terrestrial habitat depending on transgressive/regressive eustasy. Marazion is a back marsh and there would have been a substantial time-lag for the effects of rising sea-level to make their mark. If the bar moved progressively inshore the basal ages will be diachronous – but here at least we assume the bar is fairly constant in its location.

We feel, therefore, that these data cannot contribute to accurate sea-level index points. The stratigraphic and biological record is, however, undoubtedly driven by sea-level change, and the formation on the freshwater marsh can provide information on sea-level from which a general indication of the former coastline can be considered. The nature of the changing coastline from Mount's Bay to Penzance is discussed below in relation to the sites at both Penzance Heliport and Marazion Marsh.

Radiocarbon results for the 6th millennium BC at Marazion Marsh are broadly comparable with those elsewhere around the Cornish coast, in terms of the altitude from which the dated material comes (Fig. 10.1), but by the Early Bronze Age, contexts yielding radiocarbon dates at Marazion Marsh are at considerably higher altitudes than those dated elsewhere along the Cornish coast (Table 10.1) – that is, *c.* -0.4 m OD vs -1.6 m OD, thereby confirming that the sand and gravel spit had formed by the later Neolithic. This is additionally confirmed

Figure 10.2: The submerged forest at low tide at Chyandour, to west of St Michael's Mount, Mount's Bay (Photograph: Andy M. Jones)

by the palaeo-environmental evidence relating to water locked behind the gravel bar: fresh water is attested from the later Mesolithic, but it clearly becomes more fresh water in later prehistory.

Submerged forests and inland woodlands

The evidence from the early sediments here from 502–526 m (*c.* -3 m OD) suggests the former presence of an early hazel woodland (prior to 5060–4850 cal BC; Table 10.1) which tends to be non-coastal, with an understory of ferns, with alder (in wetter areas). The limited records of pine, birch and oak and traces of elm possibly suggest that there was little woodland inland (cf. French 1999, 368) during this later Mesolithic period (*c.* 5000 BC).

Detailed information about other submerged forests is surprisingly somewhat scant: even the well-known submerged forest at Mount's Bay seems to have received little academic and research attention. Nevertheless, it seems that alder, hazel and birch were common with oak and willow and low sequences of other tree and shrub pollen (Healy 1999a). Groundwater tables were high leading to wet and marshy, rather than dry-ground conditions, with herbaceous and aquatic plant pollen (Healy 1999a). Numerous submerged forest deposits exist, especially along the south-west coast of Cornwall, for example at Whitesand Bay, Lamorna Cove, Mount's Bay (Marazion Marsh/St Michael's Mount; Fig. 10.2), Prah Sands, Porthleven, Gunwalloe, Poldhu and Kenneck Sands (Fig. 10.3; French 1999, fig. 1; Bell 1997, fig. 26). In fact one of the first recorded submerged forests in the England was that at Mount's Bay where, on the 10th of January 1757 between Penzance and St Michael's Mount, William Borlase records 'the remains of wood which … covered anciently a large tract of ground on the edge of Mount's

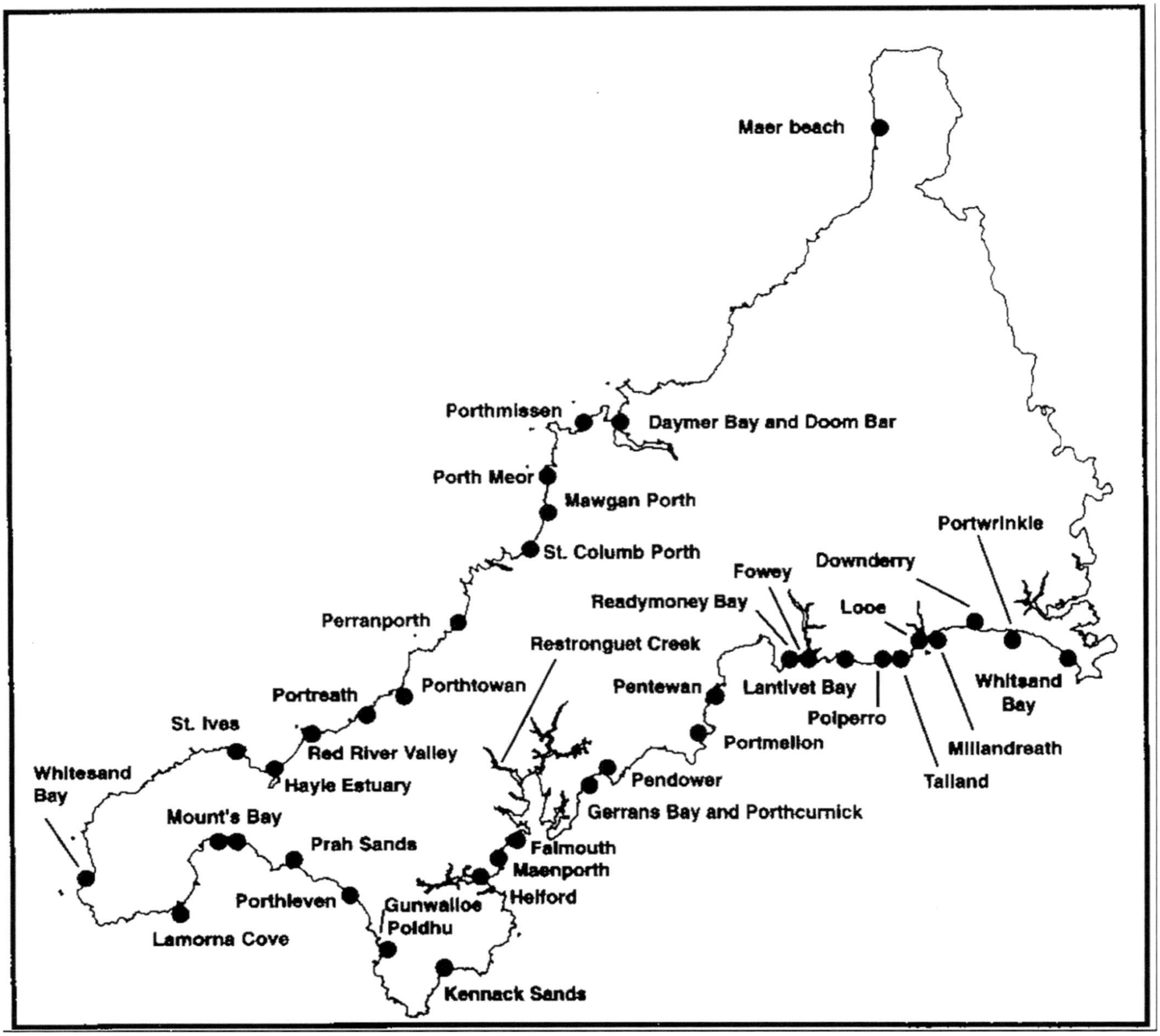

Figure 10.3: The location of submerged forest palaeosols in Cornwall, from French (1999, fig. 1; and see Bell 1997, fig. 26)

Bay…' (Borlase 1758). These all indicate near-coastal or low-lying open woodlands growing in high groundwater conditions, and contrasting with to the drier open hazel, birch and oak woodland with an open understory of ferns and herbaceous plants on the drier hinterland.

The development of the marsh

Open woodland developed on fine-grained silts of the later Mesolithic from 5.2 m (that is to say, -3.05 m OD), but gravels in the core from *c.* 4.3 m (that is, -0.90 m to -2.75 m OD) indicate that the gravel bar started to form in the embayed estuary prior to 5060–4900 cal BC. Greenish grey and bluish silts probably represent marine sediment but no diatoms or waterlogged plant remains survive to confirm this. However, by *c.* 5000 BC the presence of humic silt and *Phragmites* reed, alder and willow carr indicate the formation of a low-species diversity marsh with muddy edges set in an area of open heath, and open birch, oak hazel and elm woodland on higher ground. Deep organic deposits and humified

Site	*Grid ref.*	*OD (m)*	*Material*	*Lab ref.*	*Result BP*	*Calibrated date*
Ponsandane	SW 481311	+2.21		Q-2882	680±50	cal AD 1270–1390
Ponsandane[1]	SW 480311	+2.00			1770±40	cal AD 20–410
Prah Sands	SW 578280	–2.0		ST 3694	1805±100	50 cal BC– cal AD 420
Ponsandane	SW 481311	+0.42		Q-2883	3050±65	1490–1110 cal BC
Hayle	SW 565380	–1.59		Q-2773	4520±50	3020–2630 cal BC
Gulval Forest	SW 484309	–1.60	Birch wood	SRR-714	4280±50	3080–2700 cal BC
Maeonporth	SW 791297	–5.53		Q-2881	6110±85	5300–4800 cal BC
Trewornan		–9.41		Q-2781	6460±80	5620–5220 cal BC
Mount's Bay		–32.0		SRR-3022	12,070±80	12,180–11,830 cal BC
Larriggan*		–	Oak wood	BM	3656±150	2470–1640 cal BC
Penzance Harb		–7.22		NZA-25945	6000±35	5000–4800 cal BC
Marazion Marsh	SW 511313	+1.01	Humic acid	SUERC-90858	1580±19	cal AD 420–540
Marazion Marsh	SW 511313	+0.69	Humic acid	SUERC-91998	1843±27	cal AD 80–240
Marazion Marsh	SW 510312	+0.88		Q-2778	1610±40	cal AD 350–550
Marazion Marsh	SW 512313	+0.80		Q-2775	1210±40	cal AD 680–940
Marazion Marsh	SW 511313	–0.29	Humic acid	SUERC-92002	2576±27	820–590 cal BC
Marazion Marsh	SW 511313	–0.44	Humic acid	SUERC-95373	3986±27	2580–2460 cal BC
Marazion Marsh	SW 511313	–0.67	Humic acid	SUERC-90859	6069±26	5200–4850 cal BC
Marazion Marsh	SW 513316	–4.46		Q-2776	5100±65	4040–3710 cal BC
Marazion Marsh	SW 513312	–4.71		Q-2780	4380±55	3330–2890 cal BC
Marazion Marsh	SW 512313	–5.28		Q-2774	4395±60	3340–2890 cal BC
Marazion Marsh	SW 513316	–5.71		Q-2777	5050±65	3980–3700 cal BC
Marazion Marsh	SW 513312	–6.21		Q-2779	5420±80	4450–4040 cal BC

Table 10.1. Radiocarbon results of dated peat horizons in the Marazion Marsh environs (see Fig. 8.5)

Results from this project, and Barker & Mackay (1959, 35–6); Healy (1995; 1999b; 1999c); Harkness & Wilson (1979); French (1999); James (1990); James & Guttman (1992); [1] Taylor & Goode (1987); Wessex Archaeology (2006); *cited in de Beer (1960). Calibration by OxCal v4.3.2 (Bronk Ramsey (2017); r:5, and IntCal13 atmospheric curve (Reimer *et al.* 2013)

peats confirm the development and growth of Marazion Marsh behind the gravel bar from *c.* 2500 cal BC. Bands of bleached sand with the organic material suggest marine water ingress, and that perhaps the gravel bar was either incomplete, or occasionally breached. These conditions endured for about two millennia, with sphagnum bog developing, occasional sea-breaches and open wet muddy margins.

By AD 400 the gravel bar was both complete and high enough to prevent most marine ingression, and the presence of fine humic sands indicate the formation of freshwater river silts in a freshwater fen sedge and reed swamp. We presume that, from this period onwards, the marsh and open water behind the bar expanded to become, eventually, the species-rich, most ecologically diverse and largest reed bed in Cornwall that we know today (Fig. 10.4).

Human activity

Despite evidence of human activity on the fringes of the marsh in terms of the deposition of Late Bronze Age metal hoards and Roman coin hoards, there is little palaeo-environmental or geoarchaeological evidence for direct activity in, or intervention with, the marsh. There is fine charcoal present throughout much of the core suggesting local fires in the vicinity. At least some of this is likely to derive from the burning of the moorland and heath in the hinterland from the later Mesolithic (*c.* 5000 cal BC) onwards. It is difficult to define what this represents in terms of land use, but this could hint at some semi-formal management of moor and heathland (as discussed, for instance Allen & Scaife 1991).

There is evidence in the pollen record from humic silts and inwash bands (Unit 2b, pollen zone 5) above upper organic deposits

Depth (cm	*OD*	*Unit*	*Stratigraphy*	*Calibrated ¹⁴C result (with depth indicated)*	*Pollen zone*
0–53	2.15	1	Peat & humic silt of humic sand		7: 8–58 cm *Phragmites* peat with willow, car edges marsh, ferns – end of marine phase cultivation
53–86	1.53	2a	Fine stony lens & stony silty sand		6: 58–98 cm freshwater fen increases, ponding back, some brackish element, rising SL, mixed farming & *Cannabis*. Tree pollen low & distant
86–114	1.29	2b	Fine humic sand inwash bands		5 98–148 cm of fen development water table rise = change to fresh-water fen sedges & reed swamp. Some brackish noted. Hazel & woodland on drier land. Mixed agriculture/pasture
114–260	1.10	3	Dark brown & greyish brown humified peat with bands of bleached sand	114 AD 420–540 146 AD 80–240 224 820–590 BC 259 2580–2460 BC	4: 148–210 cm more brackish, some fw, pasture and arable 3: 210–242 cm open and pasture sphagnum bog, dry wet heath [?increase in sea level]
260–284	–0.45	3/4	Dark grey humic silt band	282 5060–4900 BC	2: 242–282 cm stabilisation (peat) alder & willow wood, but birch oak hazel ?elm on drier land
284–305	–0.69	4	Greenish grey to bluish silt		1: 282–296 cm open fen with freshwater and high groundwater tables, hazel birch oak with understory fens on higher ground
305–360	–0.90	5	Gravel		
360–430	–1.45	6			
430–490			NOT RECOVERED		
490–520	–2.75	7a	Olive grey **silt clay loam**		502–526 cm: tree and shrubs with fern understory, marine brackish conditions
520–535	–3.05	7b	Silty **silty loam** (sandy)		
535–750	–3.20	8.1-3	Dark grey dense silty clay to silt, with mixed shale **weathered bedrock**		
720–750	–4.85	9.1	Mixed shale & silt **Weathered bedrock**		
750–785	–5.35 (–6.70)	9.2	Shale bedrock		

Diatoms	*Plants*	*Charred*	*Environment*	
				freshwater
Shallow-freshwater & no evidence of marine influence	Rise in sea level		Freshwater	
102 cm freshwater & traces of marine & brackish rare/ occasional marine inundations isolated from the sea, no mining waste	90–100 cm wetter – water lily pondweed (?greater brackish marine) higher water less muddy edges (**rise in sea level**) greatest marine influences Rise in sea level	**Decline** in charcoal	↑	
	125–130 cm bankside, marsh edge of water **decline** in wetland, muddy edges, increase brambles, damp woodland			Brackish marsh edge
	230–240 cm *Phragmites* reed bankside, marsh edge of water **higher** water levels muddy edges 245–250 cm edge of water/marshy – heath	Small charcoal including heather, rush. Exploitation/burning of heather	Brackish	*Phragmites* reed, muddy edges to inland pool, hazel birch oak on higher & drier land. Gravel bar largely sealing off inland marsh
			↑ Marine	Gravel bar developing Oak and willow woodland in wider landscape Locally open hazel woodland, damp ground marine brackish conditions

Figure 10.4: Marazion Marsh from the east. (© Historic Environment, Cornwall Council, F84-136)

from 1.14 m depth and above of late cereal cultivation and of pasture and grazing on drier adjacent land from the Romano-British period onwards (cal AD 80–240). Other than this the evidence of human activity actually in and around the marsh is difficult to discern. This may in part be a result of the local marsh vegetation screening out most of the non-local pollen, as there is evidence in the archaeological record of Mesolithic activity in the vicinity, and of Bronze Age barrows (such as the one described in Chapter 2). We must also consider that from the later Mesolithic, about 1km of land existed south of the 'marsh', and even by the Middle to Late Bronze Age, when many of the metal hoards were deposited (see Jones & Knight; Chapter 12), there may have been nearly ½ km of low-lying land in what is now the sea of Mount's Bay. Evidence of human activity, and the changing nature of the landscape, are explored more fully below and in Chapter 14.

Resource potential for human communities

Despite the lack of evidence for human activity in the marsh itself and in its immediate environs, the marsh would nevertheless have provided a range of resources. These include pooling fresh water, reeds and rushes for thatching, matting, flooring and bedding and possibly basketry. The ecosystem, as today, would have attracted wildlife, some of which could have been caught and hunted, such as wild fowl. Bearing this in mind, the marsh's resources may have played a significant role in the lives of the local inhabitants from the Mesolithic to the Bronze Age, and indeed later.

Conclusions

Marazion Marsh consisted of marshy/boggy areas with tall fringing and shallow open water vegetation which, in the initial stages of the marsh's formation, dried out in summer allowing the bare mud to be colonised by mud bank pioneers. Through time this summer drop in water levels was lost and the water table remained high throughout the year, becoming increasingly brackish. There will have been drier areas where more heathland vegetation such as bell heather could grow, for example on the cliff tops. There is little evidence for woodland locally. Evidence for human activity is sparse but is continuous throughout time and is indicated by the presence of small fragments of charcoal throughout the sequence. This site is one of the few in the area to have been subjected to research featuring a wide suite of environmental techniques. As a result it is considered to be of great importance in helping us understand past changing environments and human activity in the area.

The marsh could have provided a wide range of resources (plant, animals and freshwater) for exploitation by prehistoric populations, but the impact of these people on the marsh and its environment was minimal.

SECTION 4:

THE ENVIRONMENTAL, ECONOMIC AND CULTURAL SETTING OF LANDSCAPE: EXCAVATED SITES AND THEIR WIDER LANDSCAPE CONTEXT

11

The submerging landscape from prehistory into the Anthropocene

Michael J. Allen

Of all the changes that affected the landscape in this part of Cornwall over the last 10,000 years – changes that include vegetational shifts, seen at both the regional and the site-specific scale, and fluctuations in the level of the water table at the local level at what became Marazion Marsh – the most striking is the wholesale change and loss of the land itself, and its associated resources, by the progressive rise of the sea-level. This chapter is concerned with characterising those changes and considering the impact on the people who lived in and around the area – in other words, the wider social, ideological and philosophical implications of the loss of land to the sea. These implications are discussed further in Chapter 14.

Sea-level rise and the drowning of landscapes have different physical implications and ramifications for each specific site, landscape and coastline, but the social implications may be more universal (as explored in Chapter 14). Here we discuss the physicality of sea-level change that was involved in the drowning of the landscape, and then view this from the perspective of the two sites (ie, the Heliport Bronze Age barrow and Marazion Marsh) and their associated communities.

The submersion and drowning of archaeological landscapes is a recurrent theme in the prehistory of Cornwall and the Isles of Scilly, as Charles Thomas noted in his study of the Scilly Isles (Thomas 1985), and it remains a theme of current research (eg, Charman *et al.* 2016; Barnett *et al.* 2020) on the archaeology of the Channel Islands and the study of Neolithic sites around the British and wider Atlantic coastlines (eg, Garrow & Sturt 2017; Wickham-Jones 2018; Cook *et al.* 2021). This theme is likely to become an increasing focus of archaeological research as monuments, World Heritage Sites and landscapes become threatened by sea-level rise (eg, Wickham-Jones 2015, 4; and see Chapter 14).

Mapping the drowning coast

The changing coastline is mapped, in simplistic terms, by relating the submarine topography or bathymetry against dated relative seal-level data (eg, Long & Roberts 1997; Heyworth & Kidson 1982). Sea-level changes can be driven by either variations in the masses or volume of the oceans, or by changes of the land with respect to the sea surface. Relative sea-level (RSL) change is any sea-level change that is observed with respect to a land-based reference frame. Processes such as an increase in water volume or mass due to melting ice, or the down-warping of land (when water volumes are constant) may result in changes in relative sea-level. In reality the process is more complex (Rovere *et al.* 2016), and requires the analysis of *sea-level index points* (dated items of known OD and which relate to the contemporaneous sea-level) in relation

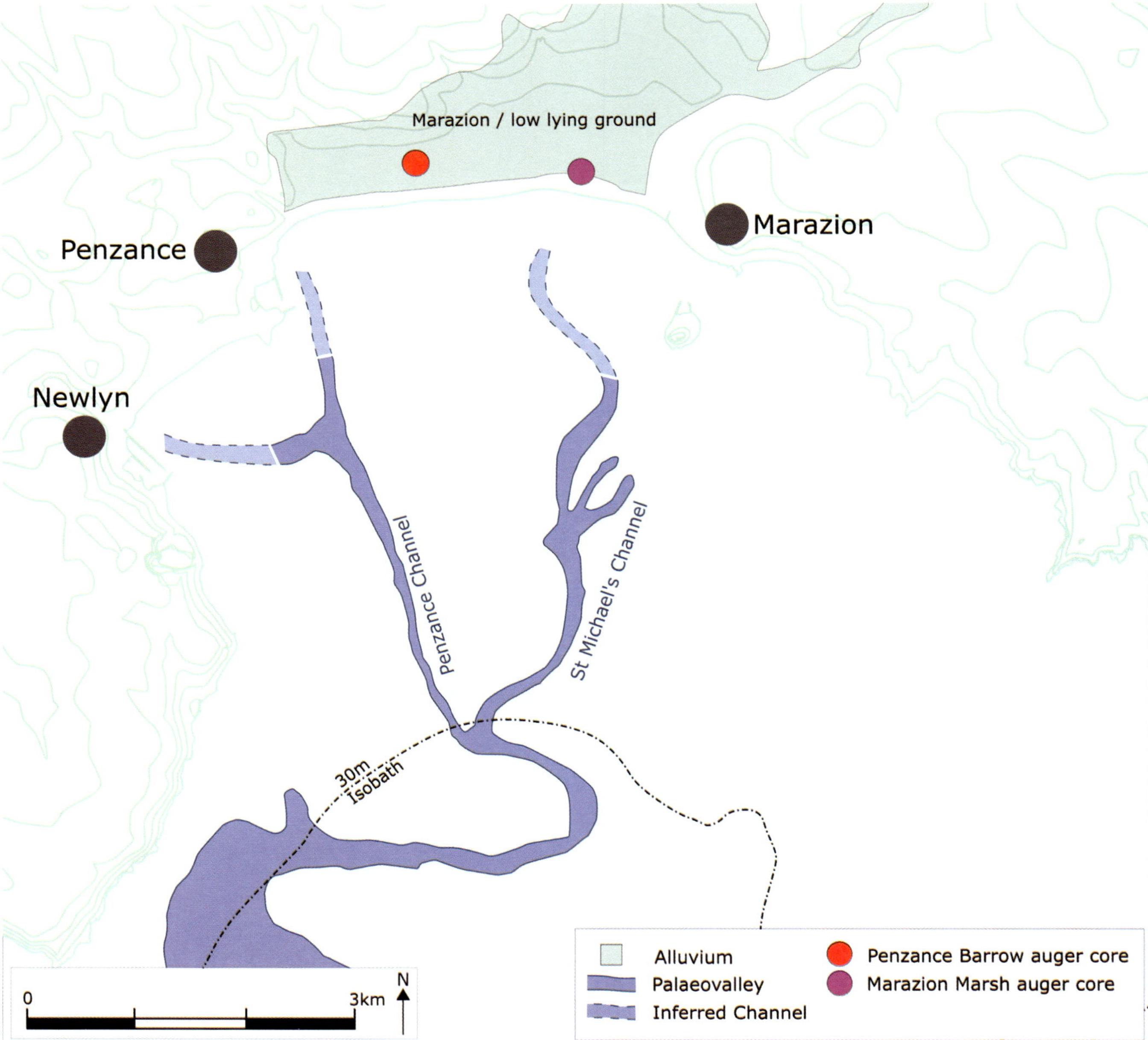

Figure 11.1: Map 1 showing the sites, and the area mapped in the coastline regression analysis (Figs 11.3–11.9)

to local and area-specific, rather than generic, RSL curves. For Mount's Bay this has been undertaken by Channon (2018) in a much more nuanced fashion, not only utilising sea-level index points (SLIP) and sea-level limiting points (SLLP; that is to say, barriers), with revised more recently relative sea-level (RSL) curves. She also employed these data with new methods (Channon 2018) to create more accurate reconstructions, specifically of the Mount's Bay Holocene coastal development, than those produced for general coastline studies. Whereas Channon used these data to understand future projections of change (Channon 2018, 16), here we use these models (Figs 11.1 to 11.9) to map and discuss past coastline changes, and to consider the impact on the communities who lived in and exploited the resources of the area. Channon used the Mount's Bay meta-analysis of recent SLIPs and SLLPs and incorporated this within Healy's (1995) data in order to extend and add precision of the history of the Holocene RSL. The primary data employed were

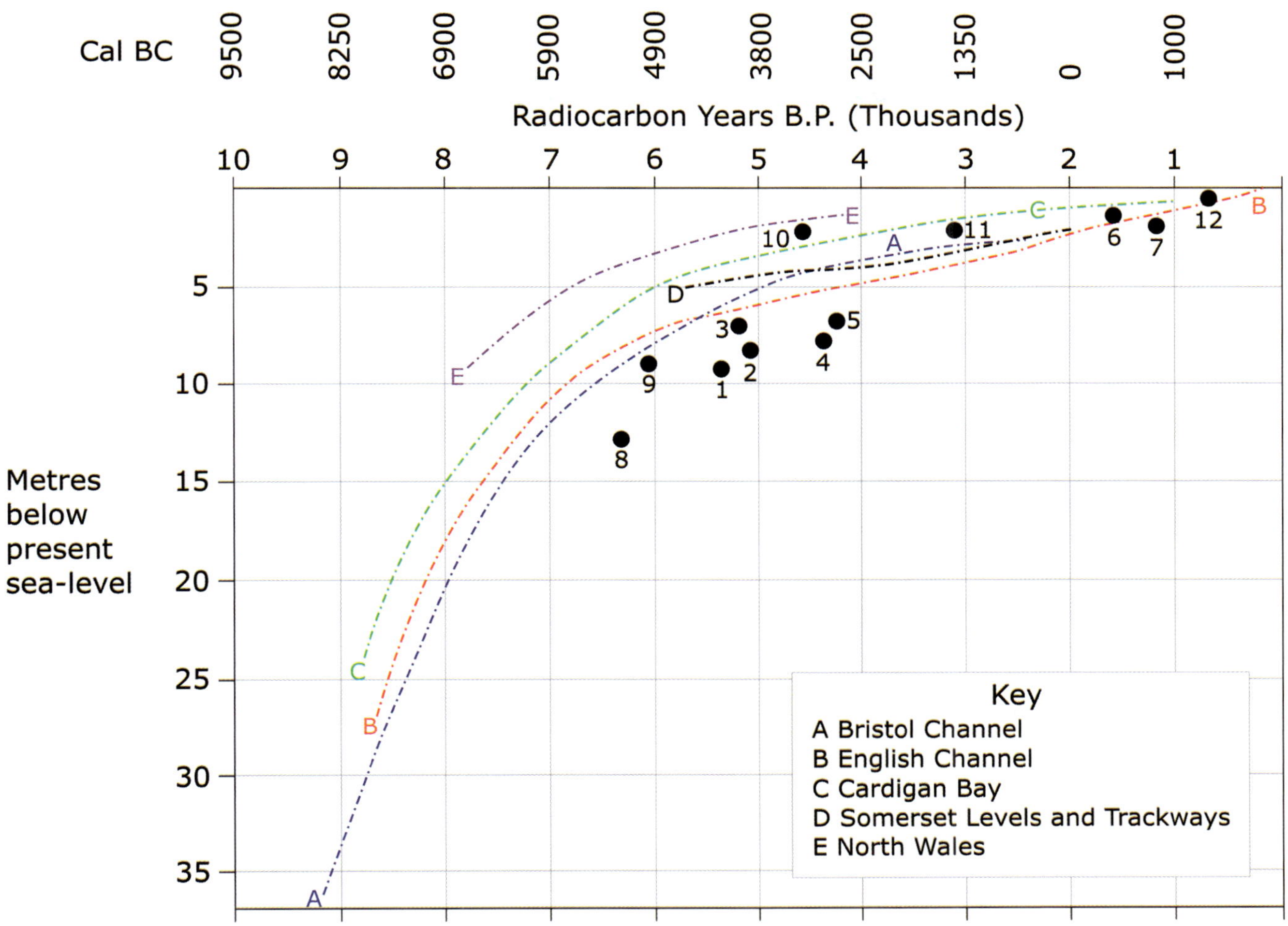

Figure 11.2: Relative sea-level curve for west Cornwall (from Healy 1995, fig. 6b), based on radiocarbon dates and SLIPS primarily from Marazion Marsh

those derived from Healy (1995) using the accepted, and additional, SLIPs within the Mount's Bay coast area. The radiocarbon dates from several different projects and sources were recalibrated to provide a unified chronology. SLLPs, although limited in their application, were obtained from several studies including those of Taylor and Goode (1987), and Heyworth and Kidson (1982). These SLLPs extended, and added precision to, the most recent RSL curve. Previous SLIPs produced from the Isles of Scilly, *c.* 60 km from Mount's Bay (Charman *et al.* 2016), and also from southern Devon (Massey *et al.* 2008) which emphasised the local variability while providing data from the south-west ranging from *c.* 7500 to 5500 cal BC. These provide some context for RSL change between Healy's (1995) and earlier SLLPs identified by Taylor and Goode (1987).

The model of palaeocoastal progression was reconstructed using bathymetric data by Channon using an updated RSL curve for Mount's Bay. Bathymetric data from Digimap's HydrospatialOne (2017) data at 5 m intervals was manipulated using QGIS software, and the BGS GeoIndex open access on/offshore (2018) and Historic England's Peat Database (2018) were incorporated to understand the distribution of peat beds within the area.

Holocene coastline development of Mount's Bay

The topography and subtidal geomorphology of Mount's Bay shows a narrow shallow rim, and beyond a couple of hundred metres on its eastern and western flanks and about 1 kilometre from the current shoreline along Longrock, the topography drops to a wide

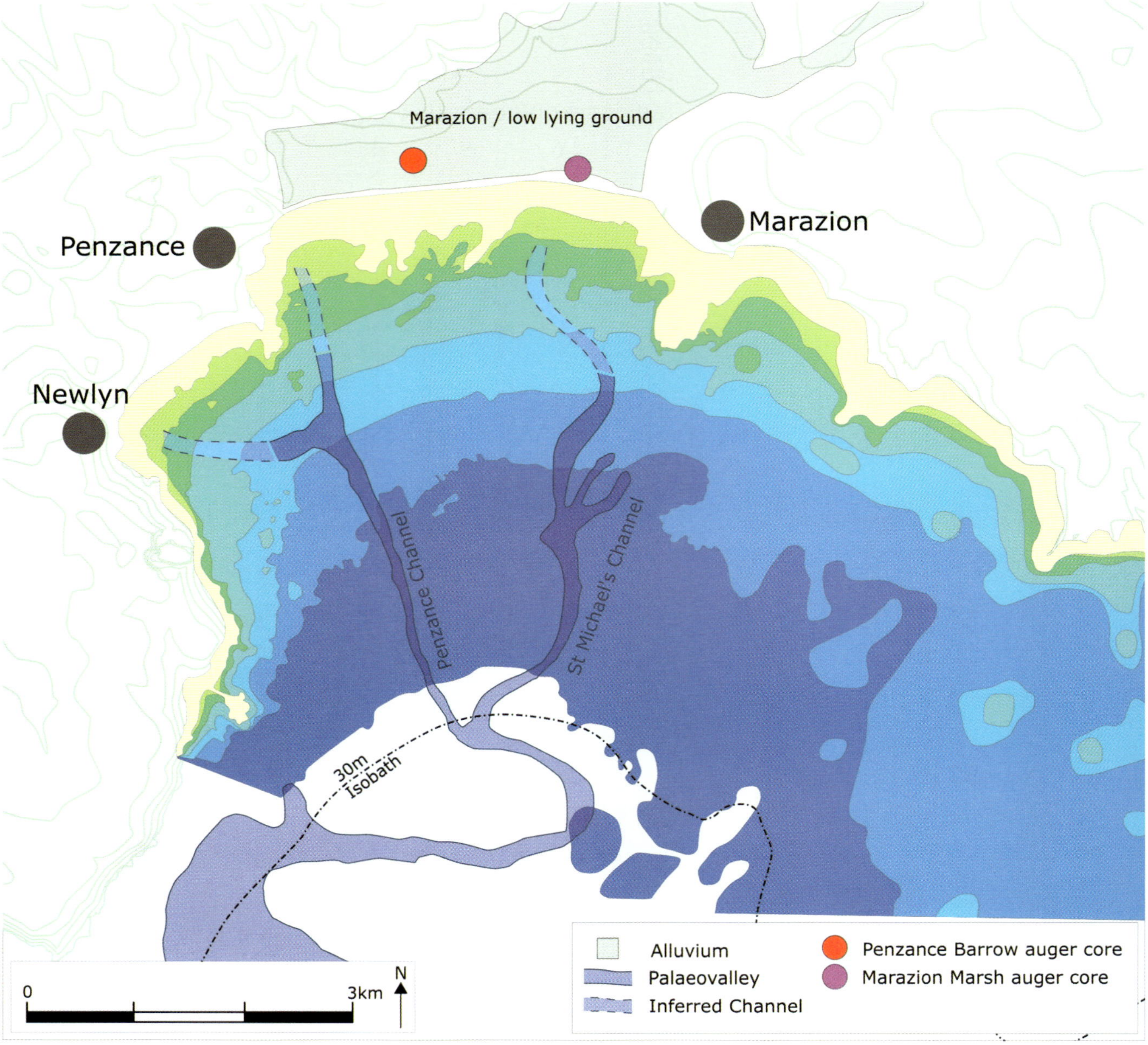

Figure 11.3: Mount's Bay; 12,000 cal BC (Scale image is 10 km wide, scale bar is 3 km)

U-shaped valley at about 30–40 m below current sea-level, with two rivers meeting and flowing out to the sea. The area of regression includes this 'landscape' extending from Mousehole in the west to beyond Perranuthnoe and Cudden Point in the east (Fig. 11.1), and covers approximately 32 km^2, the bay being some 8 km wide and 5 km deep. All of Mount's Bay was terrestrial landscape in the late Upper Palaeolithic at 12,000 cal BC (Fig. 11.3). The coastline is mapped from 12,000 cal BC (later Upper Palaeolithic) to the Late Neolithic/Chalcolithic boundary *c.* 2500 cal BC) in a series of seven steps (Figs 11.3–11.8, and 11.9), during which time the sea-level rose by 30 m (Fig. 11.2) and all 32 km^2 were lost to the sea. These changes are explained in the series of images based on those generated by Channon (2018, fig. 10).

Prior to 12,000–10,750 cal BC Mount's Bay hardly existed, but two rivers (Penzance Channel and St Michael's Channel) drained across the lowland and converged into a single channel beyond Cudden Point about 5 km from

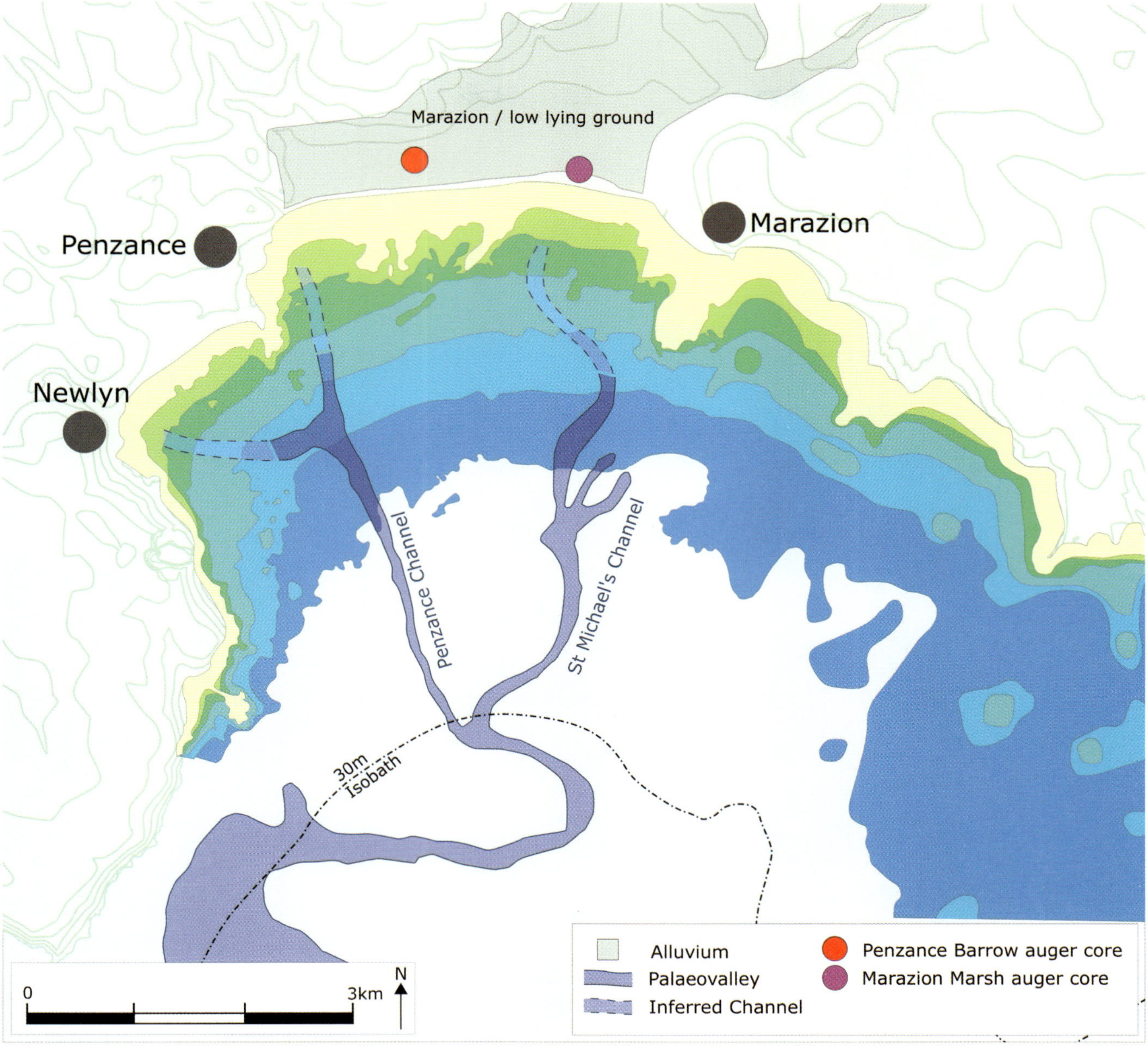

Figure 11.4: Mount's Bay; 10,750 cal BC (Scale image is 10 km wide, scale bar is 3 km)

the current shoreline (Camm 1999, fig. 13; Camm & Dominy 1998); see also Chapter 9 (and Chapter 1). A clear, almost parallel-sided embayment existed by *c.* 10,750 cal BC, and the deep valley started to become engulfed with water. By 9500 cal BC the eastern valley side had also been largely submerged, creating for the first time an indented, crescent-shaped bay. In the early postglacial period (that is, 8000–6000 cal BC) the sea-level rose rapidly by about 1 m per century (see Fig. 14.1), so by about cal 5000 BC in the Late Mesolithic period, the sea-level was about 9–10 m below OD. From this time (*c.* 5000 cal BC) the rate of sea-level rise slowed considerably, and a constant, but much slower rate of, sea-level rise is then recorded throughout prehistory to about 2 m or less below OD by the end the prehistory and the Roman invasion. In total, about 20 km^2 of low-lying land with open woodland and freshwater rivers supporting a rich and diverse plant and wildlife had been lost to the sea.

St Michael's Mount, however, was not cut

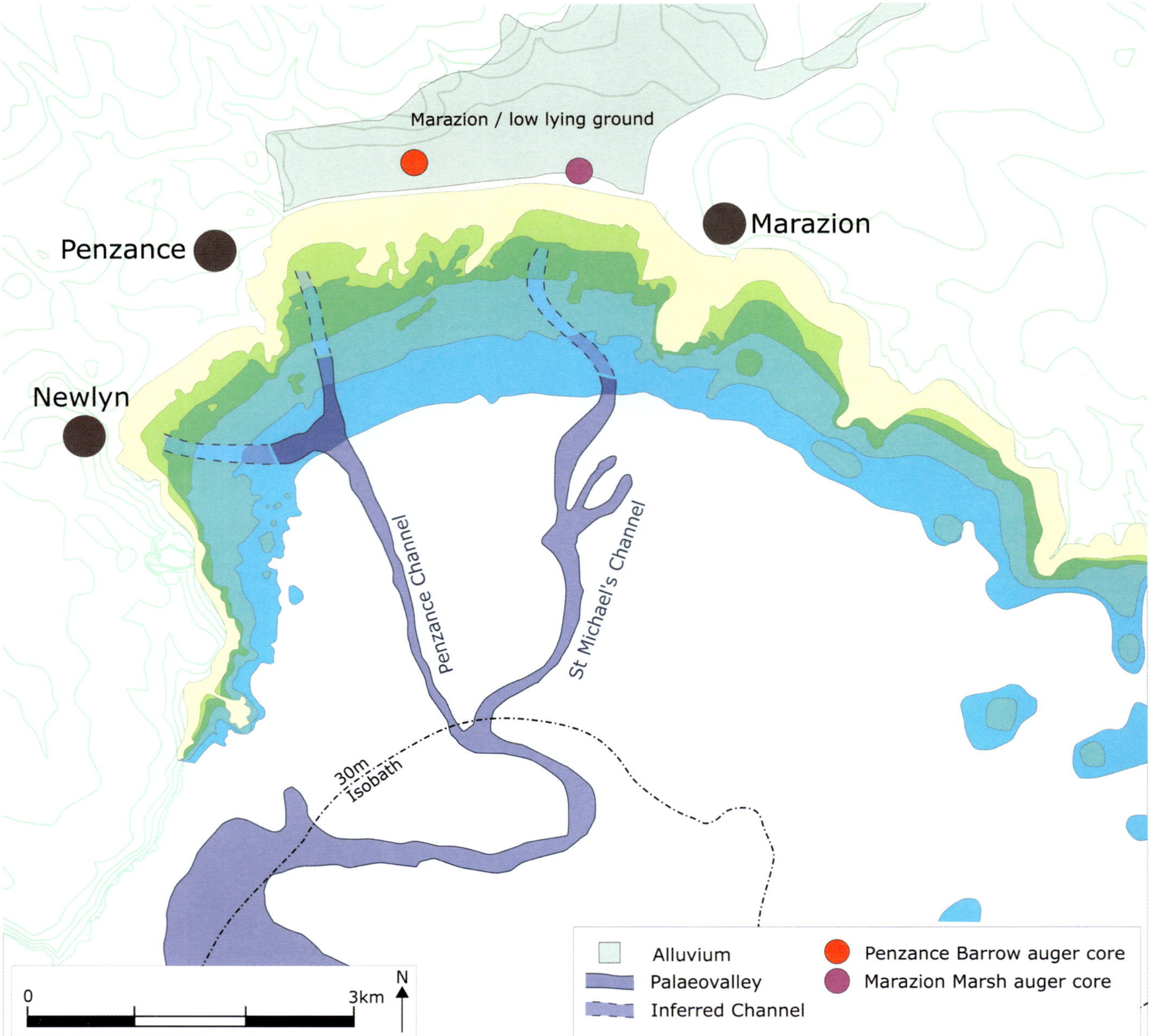

Figure 11.5: Mount's Bay; 9500 cal BC (Scale image is 10 km wide, scale bar is 3 km)

off from the mainland until post-Roman times. A selection of the regression maps are presented together in Chapter 14 (see Fig. 14.1), showing the sequence of development and the changing morphology of Mount's Bay, behind which the nature and character of Marazion Marsh was also fundamentally changed (as described in Chapter 10).

The implication of the loss of land, the changing morphology and ecological diversity, and even the eventual creation of the tidal-locked St Michael's Mount, would have had significant and profound effects on the lives of the communities living both in the area and further afield. The lowland is likely to have provided important land with a different character, ecology and potential from that of the higher and drier land surrounding it. Importantly, the valley saw the convergence of two freshwater rivers which then flowed out to the sea, forming a corridor and avenue from the sea (more than 6 km from the current coastline), inland toward the drier land. They provided freshwater fish and

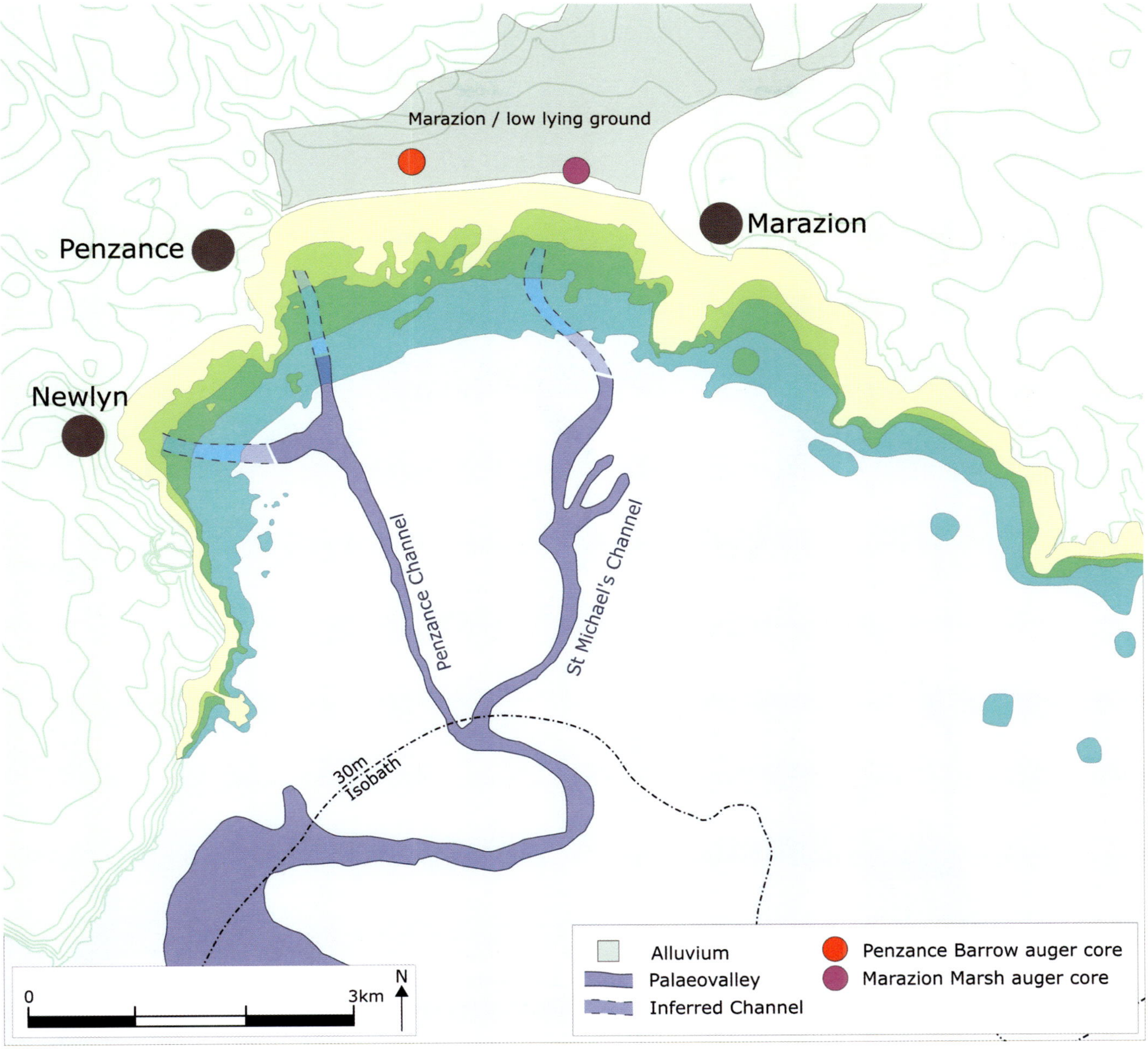

Figure 11.6: Mount's Bay; 8200 cal BC (Scale image is 10 km wide, scale bar is 3 km)

birds, reeds and other wetland resources – all valuable for people living in the surrounding landscape. They constituted a clear ecotonal location that attracted diverse wildlife which, in turn, attracted human activity and eventually occupation. The rich ecology, and in later prehistory the merging of freshwater and saltwater in a large open still pool, ringed by rushes and rich in birdlife, created a strange and distinctive landscape – and from later prehistory, at least, one that was treated in new and differing ways. These new ways of inhabiting the landscape will be the subject of the following chapters (Chapters 12, 13 & 14).

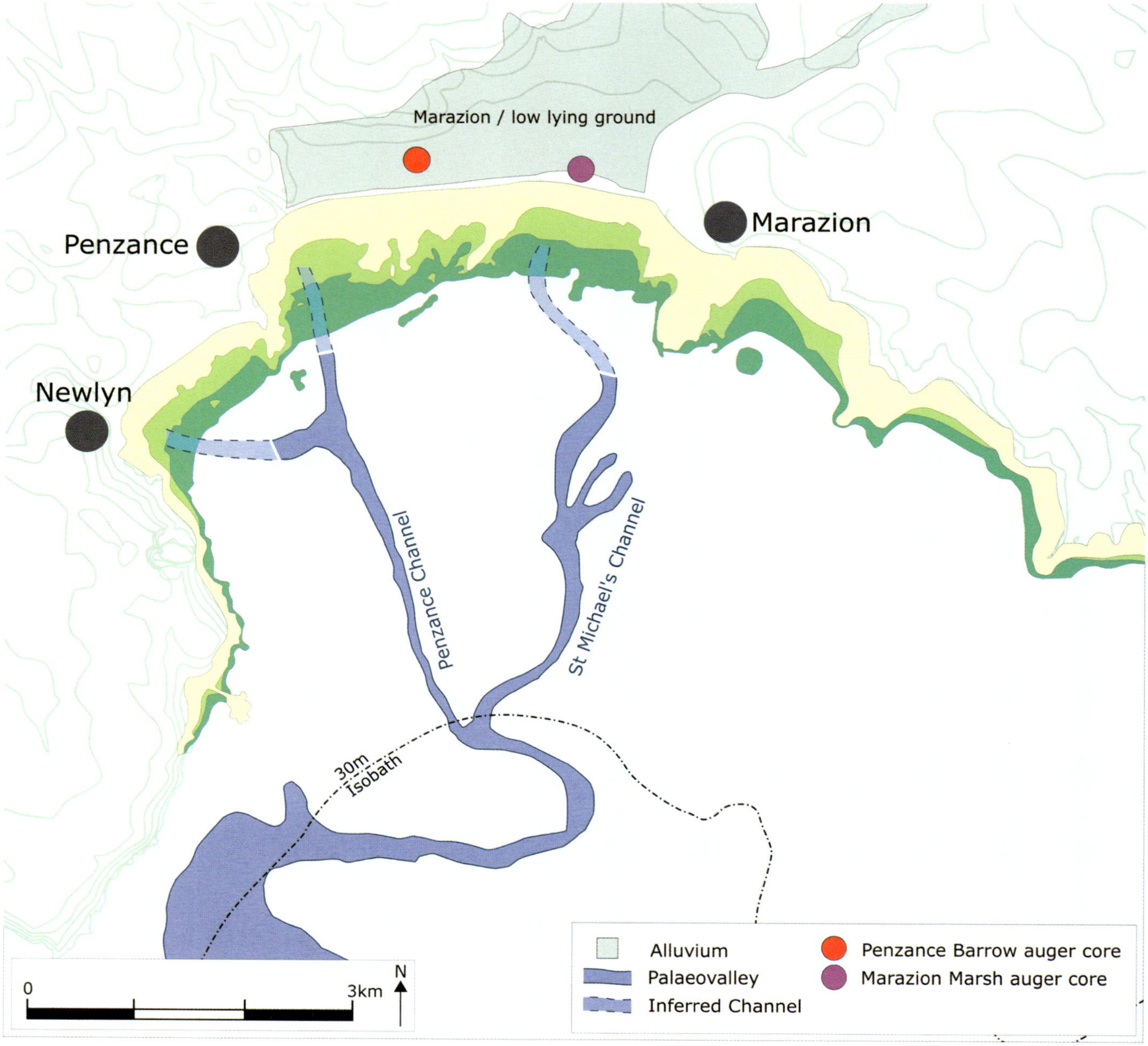

Figure 11.7: Mount's Bay; 6700 cal BC (Scale image is 10 km wide, scale bar is 3 km)

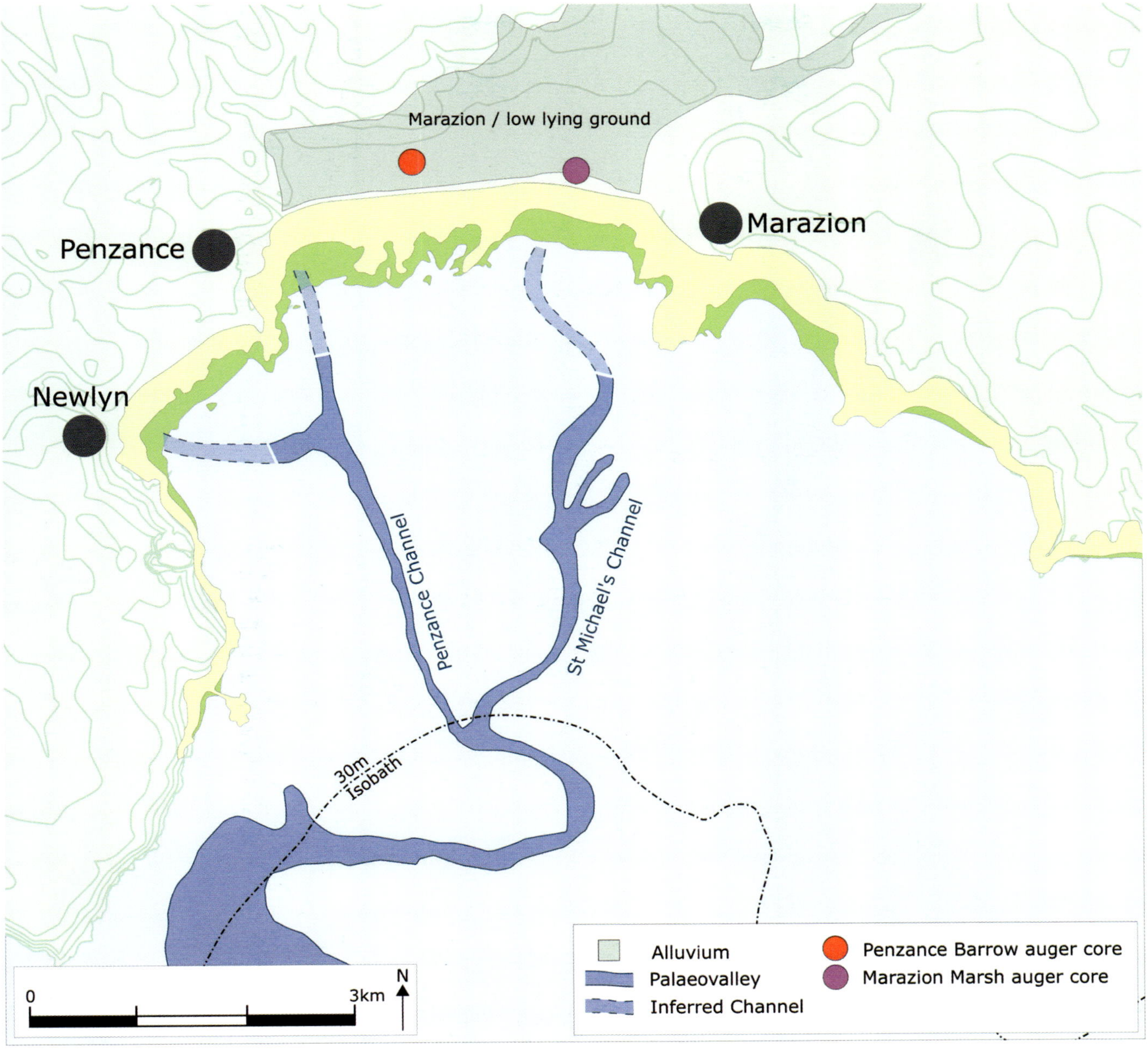

Figure 11.8: Mount's Bay; 4800 cal BC (Scale image is 10 km wide, scale bar is 3 km)

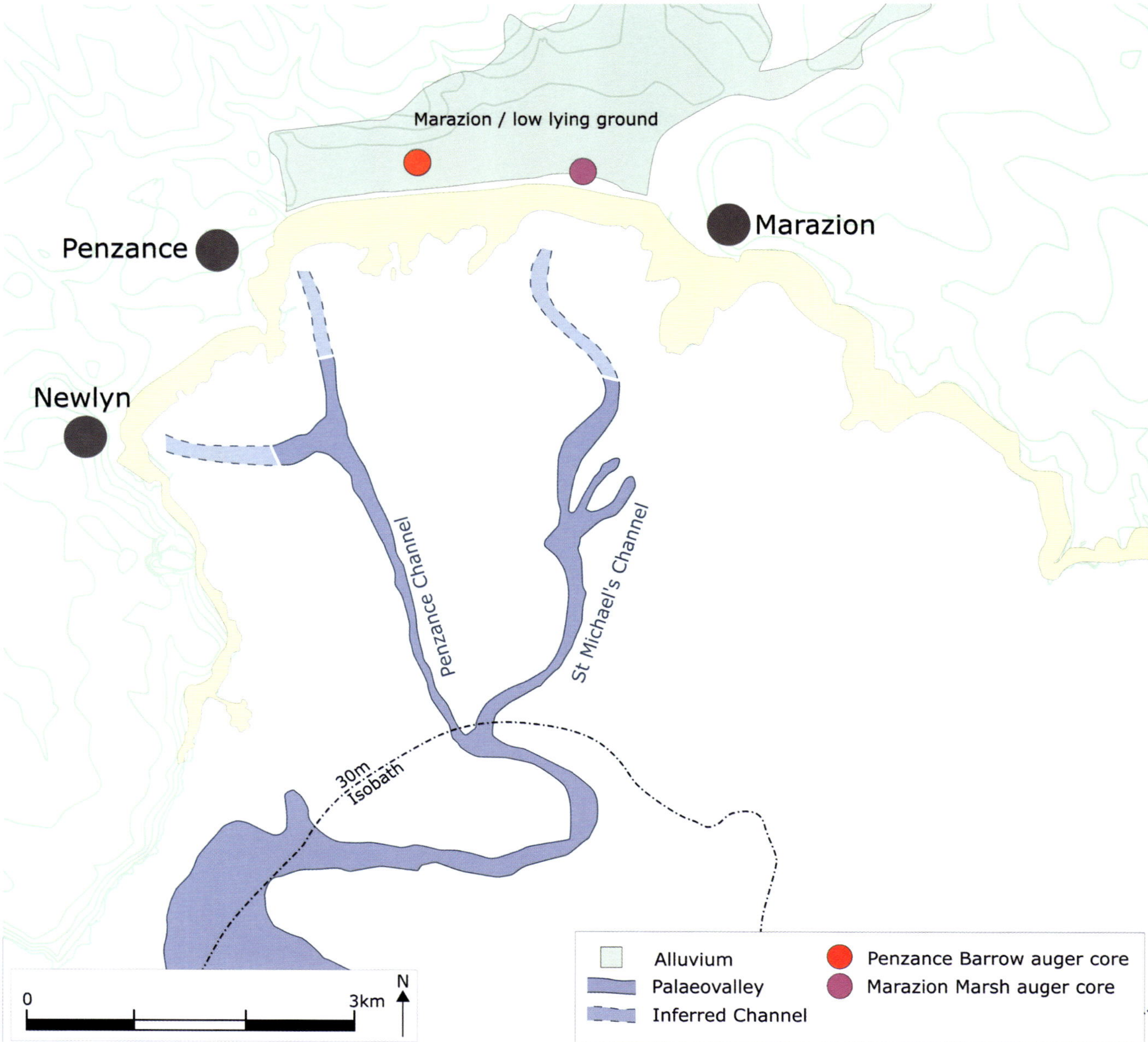

Figure 11.9: Mount's Bay; 2500 cal BC (Scale image is 10 km wide, scale bar is 3 km)

12

A landscape of deposition

Andy M. Jones and Matthew G. Knight

The Mount's Bay area has long been associated in the archaeological literature with the exchange of copper and tin. St Michael's Mount, in particular, has often been suggested to be the site of *Ictis* recorded by Pytheas the Greek in the 4th century BC (Hencken 1932, 158–188; Herring 2000, 116–118; Cunliffe 2002, 71–92). Whether the site can be considered to be *Ictis* or an *Ictis*-like site is a moot point. Nevertheless, it does seem that area is likely to have been part of an Atlantic network in the later 2nd and 1st millennium cal BC, especially during the period 1200–800 cal BC when interactions reached their peak (Henderson 2007, 57–98; Cunliffe 2009; 2015; 2021, 110–114). Mount's Bay was potentially one of a series of places of exchange located along the southern coast of England, which includes sites such as Hengistbury Head, Dorset and Mount Batten, Devon (Cunliffe 1987; 1988) (Fig. 12.1). Evidence for these exchanges includes bronze artefacts and metal ingots interpreted as cargoes from shipwrecks, as at Salcombe in Devon and Langdon Bay, Kent (Needham *et al.* 2013). The eastern end of the Bay is dominated by the Mount, while the western end is also overlooked, by Lescudjack hillfort (Kirkham, forthcoming). That site, now surrounded by development, would in the 1st millennium BC have been a dominant feature on the northern horizon, overlooking the sandy shore where boats could have been pulled up out of the water. With its broad sandy sweep and potentially easy access to the north coast (see Chapter 14) the Bay – like comparable locations in northern Britain (Bradley *et al.* 2016b; Bradley 2021) – may have provided an ideal haven and a liminal zone between land and sea for the exchange of artefacts and metal ores.

The association of metal with Mount's Bay, however, extends well beyond the Iron Age and the character of 'exchange' almost certainly represents more than just 'economic' trade between local communities and visiting traders (Helms 1988; Brück & Fontijn 2013; Brück 2019, 232; Fontijn 2019). Moreover, as Stuart Needham (2001) has noted in relation to Bronze Age hoards, there need not be a distinction between ritualised and utilitarian metalwork deposition, and most if not all deliberate deposits were 'ritual' at one level or another. The area around the Bay is associated with the deposition of metalwork, especially during the later Bronze Age but also, in a spectacular way, in the Roman period too (Gilbert 1817; Penhallurick 2009). For this reason, one of the traditional divisions in British archaeology between prehistory and the Roman period will be ignored here (cf. Bradley 2017). The area might have been regarded as a place of exchange where the liminality of the setting allowed for extended kinship networks between widely dispersed maritime communities to operate (cf. Johnston 2020); the interactions between those communities included the deposition of artefacts. These practices and their wider context will be the subject of this chapter.

Site name	*Site no.*	*Form*	*Dating*	*Context & associations*	*Principal references*
			BRONZE AGE		
Tredarvah	1	Middle Bronze Age (MBA) assemblage comprising: 1 quoit-headed pin frag., 1 disc-headed pin frag. Décorated with horizontal & oblique incisions, 4 bronze pin shaft frags, 2 copper alloy frags of an object forming a double spiral, 1 flanged axehead, 1 side-looped spearhead, 1 tanged knife in 2 pieces, 1 corroded blade & pieces of slag	MBA	Hillslope site overlooking west end of Mount's Bay. Metalwork grouped together, found within spread of charcoal-rich 'occupation' material, including sherds from 10–17 Trevisker Ware vessels, a large saddle quern & a whetstone	Pearce & Padley 1977; Pearce 1983, 422–423, no. 120
Beacon Field, Marazion 1	2	2 refitting frags of sword blade & tang	Late Bronze Age (LBA), Ewart Park?	Unstratified metal detected finds, no secure context	Knight *et al.* 2015, 34, no. 44
Beacon Field, Marazion 2	3	Frag. from a second sword	LBA, Ewart Park?	Unstratified metal detected finds, no secure context but found with above sword frags	Knight *et al.* 2015, 34, no. 45
Marazion	4	Sword blade frag.	LBA, Ewart Park?	Unstratified metal detected finds, no secure context, but said to have been found near a socketed axehead	Knight *et al.* 2015, 34, no. 46; PAS CORN-30BC82
Venton Hall, Marazion	5	Blade frag. from possible rapier	MBA	Unstratified metal detected find. Found on higher ground to E of Marazion & the same area as sword frag. above	Knight *et al.* 2015, 34, no. 47; PAS CORN-021D57
Marazion Marsh	6	Palstave, poss. 2, poss. associated with frags from 7 axeheads	MBA, but (if original description of find circumstances is correct) deposited into marsh at a later date	Located within the Marshes, said to have been found with other frags, in an iron vessel in 1882	Rowlands 1976, 300; Pearce 1983, 400; Russell 1971; Knight *et al.* 2015, 34, no. 42
Marazion, near St Michael's Mount	7	Frag. of cauldron & metalworking debris	LBA/Iron Age	Now lost but recorded as being found in stream flowing into sea near St Michael's Mount. The metalwork was found with a great quantity of ashes, charcoal, smelted ore, & slag, with grains of tin embedded in it below several metres of sand. Indicative of a metalworking site on the shore	Edmonds 1849; Hencken 1932, 165
St Michael's Mount	8	Hoard including frags of 48 weapons, tools, & ingots including 7 socketed axeheads, 1 socketed gouge 5 sword/ blade frags, 1 chape, 1 buckle/fitting, 2 frags copper alloy plate, 1 casting jet, 22 copper ingots, & 7 uncertain frags or pieces of metallurgical debris	LBA	Located in a cavity under a rock on the W side of the Mount	Knight *et al.* 2015, 34, no. 43; Knight 2022
St Michael's Mount	9	Broken copper ingot	LBA	Ingot associated with Plain Ware pottery & saddle quern found in platform for a probable roundhouse at S end of island	Herring 2000, 17

Site name	*Site no.*	*Form*	*Dating*	*Context & associations*	*Principal references*
St Michael's Mount	10	Damaged copper ingot	LBA	Found in 2002 during vegetation clearance on NW slopes of the Mount. Findspot appeared to be a levelled subcircular platform cut into the hillside, poss. for a roundhouse but not excavated. Potential chisel marks can be seen where the ingot has been spilt into pieces	Unpublished; this volume, Fig. 12.10
St Michael's Mount	11	Hoard, said to have included spearheads, axeheads, & swords	LBA	Hoard discovered near bottom of the Mount. The objects had been wrapped in linen	Evans 1881, 31
Penzance Heliport	12	Copper ingot frag.	LBA. Radiocarbon dated 930–810 cal BC (2734±27 BP, SUERC-47292) mound above cist 910–810 cal BC (2714±27 BP, SUERC-47293) cist fill 203 associated with ingot frag.	Barrow site associated with later cist & covered by low mound of charred material. Frag. copper alloy found in cist 207 with single sherd of LBA pottery & a red pebble	This volume, Chapter 5
			ROMAN		
Marazion Marsh	13	Roman coin hoard. Over 1000 coins found in a pot	Surviving coins are of late 3rd century date	Recovered from Marazion Marsh during digging of a drainage trench in the late 18th century. The coins had been deposited in a ceramic vessel. Other coins may have been found in the vicinity	Penhallurick 2009, 150
St Michael's Mount	14	Roman coin findspot	Tetricus I (AD 271–274)	Roman bronze coin found on the slipway in 1905	Anon 1970, 92

Table 12.1: Recorded metalwork in the Mount's Bay area. See also Figures 12.2, 12.8 & 12.9

Places and character of deposition

The low-lying area between Penzance and Marazion contains relatively few documented occupation sites aside from St Michael's Mount and Lescudjack and only a small number of monuments, such as round barrows (Chapter 1). There are, however, a significant number of identified metalwork findspots (hoards and single artefacts), including 12 dating to the Bronze Age and one or possibly two of the Roman period (Fig. 12.2). Most of these are located on the lower ground, especially in the vicinity of St Michael's Mount and Marazion (Table 12.1). This concentration is all the more remarkable given the limited chances for discovering ancient artefacts in the mosaic of marshy areas and deep sandy expanses on the one hand, and large areas of post-medieval industrial disturbance associated with extractive industries, landfill and railway infrastructure on the other. In other words, there are not only areas where the natural environment makes discovery difficult, but also others where large-scale human-made changes to the landscape have occurred at a time when any archaeological documentation was dependent on antiquarian recording.

The concentration of finds is also notable for its relatively tight timespan which, with one major later exception, is focused upon the later 2nd to early 1st millennium BC. No Chalcolithic/Early Bronze Age metalwork finds, in barrows or as hoards or single findspots, are recorded in the vicinity of the project area. The association of some of the Late Bronze Age artefacts with the deposition of ingots and potentially also metalworking debris is also noteworthy, as are the artefacts themselves; the practice of depositing metal objects into or near bodies of water is very

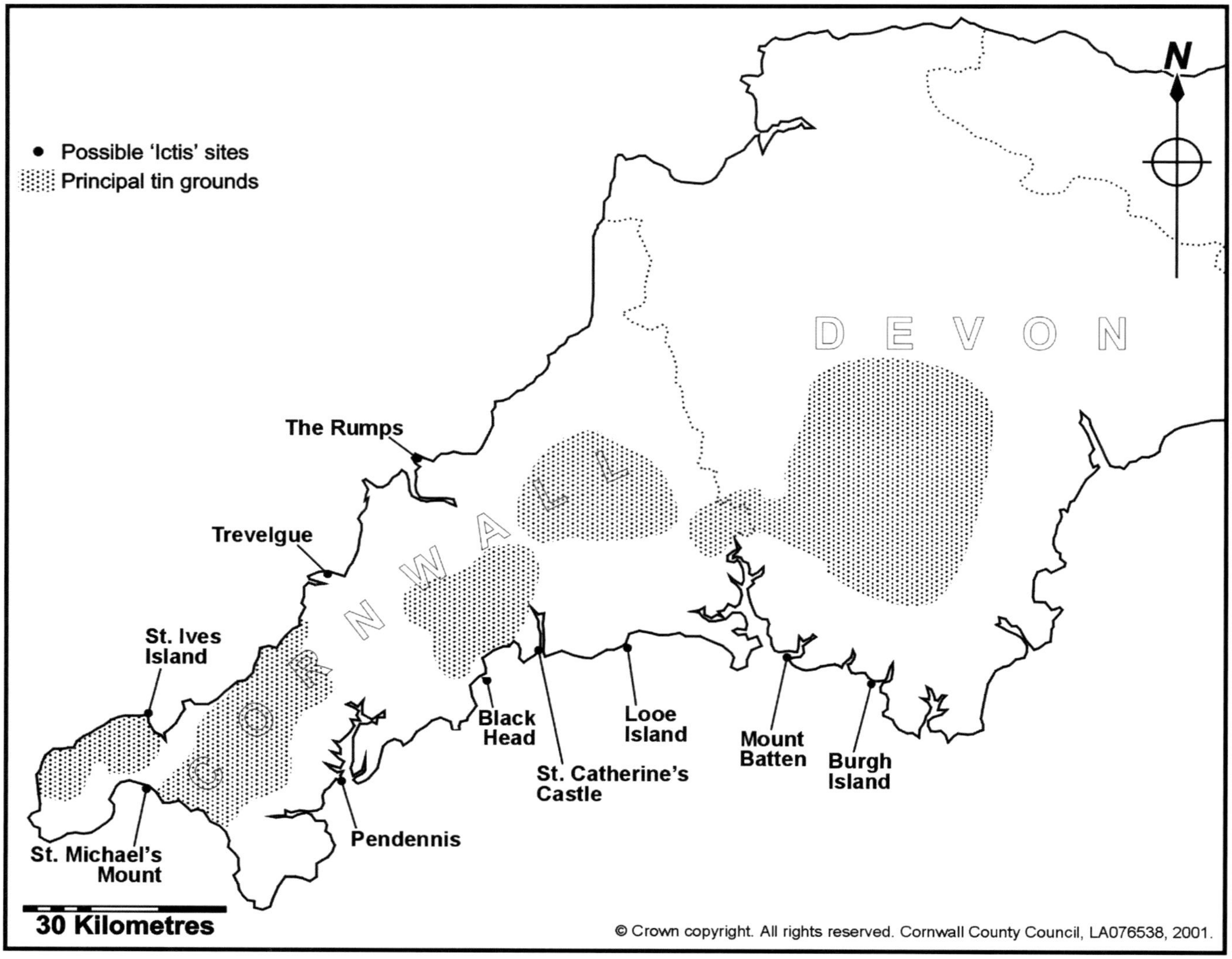

Figure 12.1: Map showing location of possible places of later prehistoric exchange along the coast of Devon and Cornwall in the, and principal tin grounds (after Herring 2000)

widespread, being attested across Britain and western Europe (Bradley 1990; Fontijn 2019; Webley *et al.* 2020).

As noted above, an interesting factor in the pattern of metalwork finds in the area is the potentially non-random nature of its distribution in the local landscape (cf. Yates & Bradley 2010a). This non-randomness arguably becomes more apparent when chronological factors are also taken into consideration.

Middle Bronze Age

Of the 12 Bronze Age metalwork findspots, three are of Middle Bronze Age date (*c.* 1500–1000 cal BC). These comprise the Tredarvah hoard, a possible rapier fragment from Venton Hall, Marazion and a palstave(s) potentially associated with a metal vessel and other fragmented objects from Marazion Marsh. The sample is too small to draw hard and fast observations, but it is notable that two of the three findspots are located in dry, rather than wet, places and even the objects found in Marazion Marsh may have been deposited in special circumstances.

The Tredarvah hoard was a collection of copper alloy objects which had been gathered for deposition with 'occupation material' in a place which was a dryland site overlooking Mount's Bay and the sea to the south (Pearce & Padley 1977) (Fig. 12.2). Susan Pearce (1983, 423) recorded a further three findspots from the Penzance area. Two of these artefacts

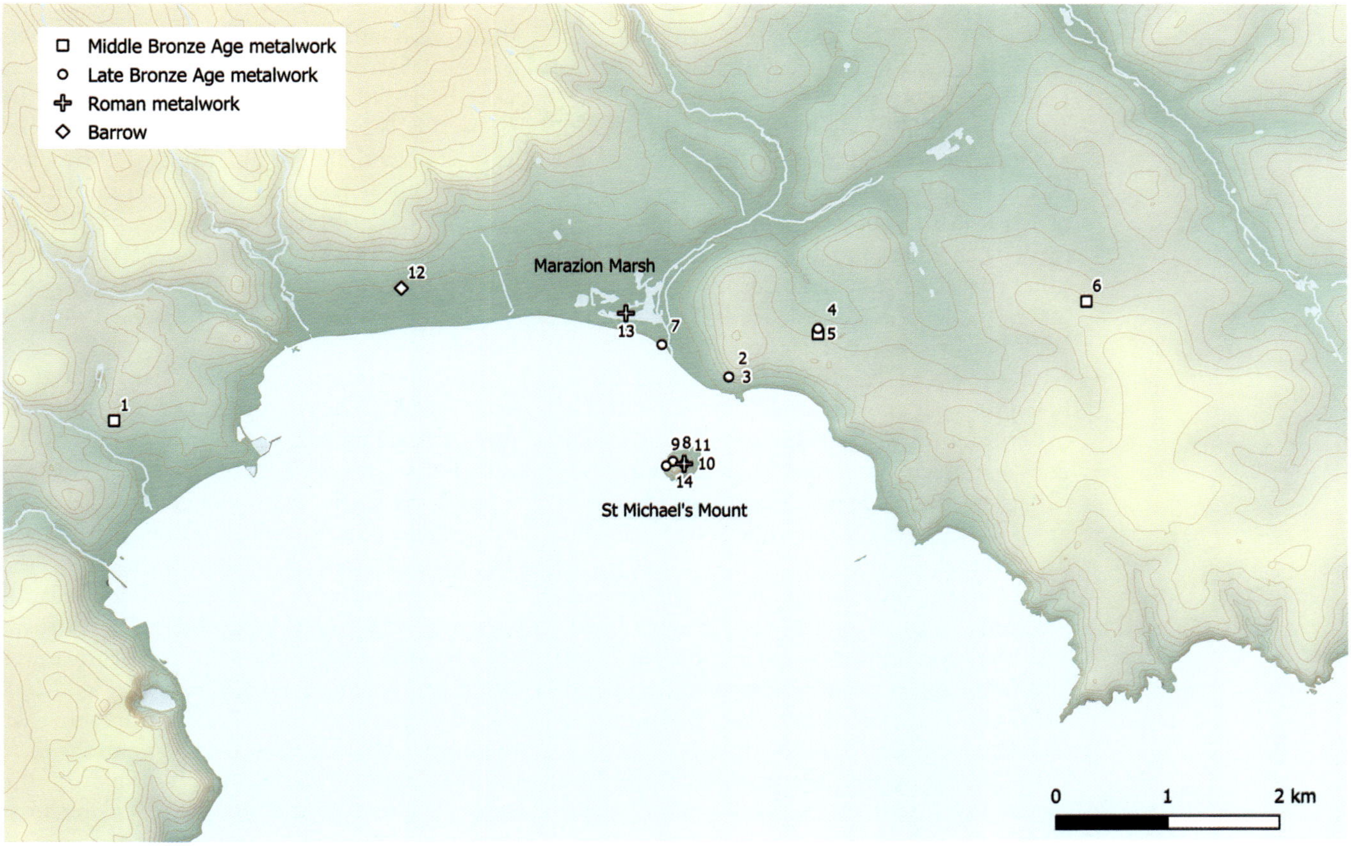

Figure 12.2: Finds of metalwork from around Marazion/Mount's Bay area. Numbers correspond to Table 12.1. Contains OS data © Crown copyright and database right 2021

are Middle Bronze palstaves and the third is an unidentifiable potential axe blade, which Pearce considered to be a chiselled flat axehead, so it may date to earlier during the Bronze Age. The precise findspots are unknown, but potentially these too were locations away from and overlooking the littoral. Venton Hall, on the eastern side of Marazion, is less elevated but is certainly situated away from the coast, and whilst the context of the deposition of metalwork is uncertain it lies within an area of enclosures of potential prehistoric date.

By contrast with the dryland character of the other sites in this area Marazion Marsh, with its palstave(s), was a wetland findspot. The Marazion Marsh findspot bears further consideration, as the artefact(s) is/are said to have been found within an iron vessel. If this really was the case and the original description of the discovery is correct, then the palstave(s) must have been many centuries old when they were deposited, potentially during the Iron Age or Roman period. As such, when deposited they would have been ancient artefacts which, in common with other old objects found in later mixed period hoards, 'were out of time' (eg, Hingley 2009; Knight 2019a). This makes it likely that either the palstave(s) had first been deposited in a dryland location and then possibly recovered through chance, or else had been curated/in circulation for a very long time prior to being deposited into the marshes. In either scenario, the palstave(s) could have been regarded as being magically charged, and associated with ancestral or supernatural beings (eg, Davies 2019). Interestingly, however, the palstave(s) were still treated in a manner that was consistent with the deposition of other metalwork finds in the Iron Age and Roman periods in Cornwall (eg, Jones 2019a, 115–145). In other words, the act of depositing the palstave(s) might have occurred at a point in time when wetland deposition was the appropriate place for artefacts in the local landscape.

Late Bronze Age

Nine of the recorded findspots date to the Late Bronze Age (*c.* 1000–800 cal BC) (Fig. 12.2). The finds include single objects, often recorded by metal detectorists, as well as hoards and finds from secure contexts. This increase in the number of Late Bronze Age metalwork finds and hoards is in step with other parts of Britain and Europe (eg, Bradley 2013: Bradley *et al.* 2015; Milcent 2015; Fontijn 2019; Costa *et al.* 2020; Dunkin *et al.* 2020). Nonetheless, it is of interest that all these findspots, bar one example, come from the eastern side of Mount's Bay, and the one which does not, from the Penzance Heliport barrow (Chapters 2 and 13) was located on a low rise in what may have been a liminal zone between dryland and the sea.

Starting at the eastern end of the bay are the finds from Marazion and Beacon Field. The Marazion findspot is not recorded in detail beyond being an unstratified sword fragment, although a socketed axehead fragment is said to have been found nearby (Knight *et al.* 2015, 34). Moreover, the possible rapier was apparently found in the same area (Tyacke 2008), so this findspot was more inland. The Beacon Field finds are also unstratified fragments. More, however, is known about their location, as the field is situated on a slope overlooking St Michael's Mount, which lies 800 m to the south south-west. This means that the original place of deposition is likely to have had a direct visual relationship with the Mount, where the majority of other Late Bronze Age findspots occur.

Two of the metalwork deposits on St Michael's Mount are hoards. Although their discoveries are separated by several hundred years there are similarities in the descriptions of their locales. The first hoard, which was mentioned by Leland in the 16th century (Evans 1881, 31), was said to have contained axeheads, spearheads and swords wrapped in linen. The position of the hoard is not precisely known but it was recorded as being near the bottom of the Mount, possibly on the western side of the island, although given the survival of the linen some commentators prefer Marazion Marsh as the actual findspot for the hoard (Penhallurick 1986, 216; Herring 2000, 116). Assuming that the Mount is the correct place, a similar location was chosen for the large hoard of Late Bronze Age artefacts that was discovered in 2009. Here the artefacts were buried under a rock at the bottom of the slope (Fig. 12.3). Both hoards were therefore associated with the Mount, the most distinctive topographical feature in the local landscape, and situated not far from the edge of the sea. Two single ingot finds have also been recovered from the Mount and again there are similarities between the two findspots, and indeed with the hoard sites.

The first ingot fragment was located in a probable Late Bronze Age roundhouse platform, situated on the south-east part of the island (Herring 2000, 17). Again, the situation is low-lying as the settlement lies at the foot of the granite outcrop which forms the Mount. The second ingot findspot was located on the north-west side of the island. The findspot appeared to be a levelled subcircular platform for a roundhouse, cut into the side of the lower slope (information Carl Thorpe) (Fig. 12.4). As with the first ingot findspot and that of the hoards, the metalwork came from the base of the granite of the Mount, not far from the water's edge and at the foot of one of the most distinctive landscape features in the region.

The location of the hoards and the ingots in the study area therefore bears similarities with that of other metalwork deposits, both those which are in or adjacent to water and those associated with liminal and stunning topography (eg, Bradley 1990; Yates & Bradley 2010b; Johnston 2020, 99; Webley *et al.* 2020, 114). In the south-west peninsula, it is notable that hoards of metalwork and related material have been recovered from topographically distinctive places, including hills, prominent stones and outcrops, as well as beside or within watery contexts (Pearce 1976; Penhallurick 1986). At Carn Brea, socketed axeheads were deposited on the hillside, and at both Breage and St Erth, two fragmentary hoards were recovered from the same hilltop (Borlase 1769, 281–287; Knight *et al.* 2015, 29, 31, nos 5–6, 21–22; Knight 2022, 107–108, 135). At St Buryan, a hoard of socketed axeheads, ingots and a flint flake was recovered from the top of a hill on a coastal headland and hoards were recovered in relation to prominent stones at Viaduct Farm, Higher Roseworthy and Helsbury (Cornish 1880–81; Needham 1981; Knight 2022, 135). At Bloody Pool on Dartmoor, a hoard was recovered from a marshy location, and there are concentrations of deposits along river valleys in south Devon and Cornwall, often close to the coast (Tucker 1867; Greeves 2019; Knight 2022, 96–108; Fig. 12.9).

The final findspot in the immediate vicinity of St Michael's Mount was located at the Marazion end of the causeway area, near to a stream, and is of a rather different character. This site was buried beneath the sand and is poorly understood (Edmonds 1849), but traces of activity associated with metallurgy were clearly evident. The site is only datable by the identified fragments from a large bronze vessel, probably a cauldron, which is suggestive of a Late Bronze Age date. Nonetheless, it appears to be either a site associated with the smelting and making of non-ferrous objects and/or perhaps a place where the residues from such events were gathered together. The proximity of the Mount, the sea and a source of running water may have made it an ideal place to smelt tin and copper ready for exchange. However, like other findspots of non-ferrous metalworking residues (eg, Webley *et al.* 2020, 69–125), it is situated in a striking liminal setting, and this should also be taken into account in interpreting the significance of the deposit. The site would have been located beyond settled areas where roundhouses are situated, in a locale where metalworking events could take place in a space which would have been open to wider kin groups and more distant communities (eg, Johnston 2020). It is possible that the material forming the deposit was intended to be visible and could have been heaped up. Such a mound would have made very obvious visual statements about the community and its connections, and in the case of the Mount's Bay findspot, it spoke of particular activities (see below).

A similar point can be made about the location of the one site which is located to the west of St Michael's Mount. The Penzance Heliport ingot fragment was recovered from a cist which had been constructed within an older barrow site that had been constructed on a low clay knoll close to the edge of dry land with views out over the Bay and St Michael's Mount (this volume, Chapters 2 and 6). The cist, which did not contain any (surviving) human remains, was mounded over with a deposit which was extremely charcoal-rich, and it is possible that one or more large fires had been lit here. In other words, like the deposit associated with the cauldron fragments, the edge of the wetland might have been involved with events that were visually distinctive, and spatially between open water and the drier, higher ground to the north.

By contrast with the Middle Bronze Age, it is possible that the late 2nd and 1st millennium BC witnessed a shift from dryland/settlement

Figure 12.3: Photograph showing the St Michael's Mount hoard site after excavation. Note the site is located under a large rock at the base of the granite forming the Mount

Figure 12.4: Photograph of the location of the 2002 copper ingot. The findspot appeared to be situated within a platform close to the base of the granite forming the Mount

locales as places for deposition, towards the referencing of the water's edge and St Michael's Mount. The potential reasons for this will be discussed below (Chapter 13); suffice it to say here that this shift in depositional practice reflects increasing contact and establishment of more extensive kinship networks on the one hand, but also the changing relationship with the water's edge as the trees died, the coastline became a 'hard' sandy edge and the Mount an even more liminal place rising out of the deepening waters, on the other hand.

Roman period

Two locales are associated with Roman metalwork. One of these is associated with Roman period settlement activity which is known on the Mount (Herring 2000); here, the coin of Tetricus that was found requires no further discussion as it was a possible chance loss. The second findspot does, however, need consideration as it was located in Marazion Marsh. Here, around 1000 coins of the later 3rd century AD were found; this represents one of the largest coin hoards known from Cornwall. This pattern is matched elsewhere in the United Kingdom where there is a significant number of votive coin hoard depositions in wet locales (eg, Bland *et al.* 2020, 102, 195–197). A recent review of deposition Roman artefacts in Cornwall (Jones 2019a, 115–145) revealed that there was a frequent association between wet or watery edge locales and 'offertory' acts which are likely to have had their origins in later prehistory. In Cornwall, comparable Roman period coin hoard deposits from creek-side locations are known from a significant number of locations, including St Michael Caerhays, Malpas, Condurrow (on the Helford), a creek in Constantine, Tywardreath, Turnaware and Lerryn (Penhallurick 2009, 36–7, 109–115, 141, 192–209 & 247–251). Additional finds have also been made by metal detectorists in recent years: for example, 1091 radiates were found in a pot beside a creek at Ethy, St Winnow (Penhallurick 2009, 42). A particularly notable coin hoard is that from the creek-side location at Hayle Causeway. Here the coin hoard was highly unusual in that 'probably some thousands' of coins were buried in a copper vessel. Many of the surviving coins seem to be copies and could be considered to be 'mock money', made for ceremonial purposes (*ibid.* 50–51). The Hayle find is also of interest because it was located at the opposing eastern end of the Penwith peninsula from Marazion, in an area that was also associated with exchange and which had a comparable history of metalwork deposition in the Bronze Age (eg, Pearce 1983).

Content, treatment and context

The content and treatment of the recovered artefacts provide another means of understanding the patterns of deposition in the study area. As with the consideration of the locale, rather more information can be gleaned from the Late Bronze Age finds, since only the Middle Bronze Age hoard from Tredarvah has any kind of context recorded from that period, and most of the Roman coin hoard from Marazion Marsh has been lost.

The Tredarvah hoard was made up of a group of bronze objects which were placed together within a deposit of 'occupation' material that included large numbers of sherds from Trevisker Ware vessels and worked stone objects. The hoard included a flanged axehead and a spearhead, but many of the items (including pins and a double spiral object) can be regarded as being personal ornaments which are typical of the period (eg, Roberts 2007) (Fig. 12.5). The detailed context of the find is uncertain given that the finds were salvaged (Pearce & Padley 1977), but they are of interest as they are in some ways reminiscent of the kinds of deposit associated with the abandonment of roundhouses during the Middle Bronze Age (Nowakowski 2001; Jones *et al.* 2015), and indeed the site was initially interpreted as a house (Pearce & Padley 1977). No structure was identified, however, and a major difference is the quantity of metalwork in particular, which exceeds any associated with a roundhouse (Jones *et al.* 2015). The ceramic assemblage is also larger than those recovered from most infilled roundhouse sites. Nonetheless, it seems likely that the spread of material had been generated by occupation events and it is possible that these had led to the formation of a mound, into which the metalwork had subsequently been inserted. It is also notable that the majority of the metalwork items comprising the hoard were fragmented or damaged. Some of this damage is the result of corrosion, but in other cases it is

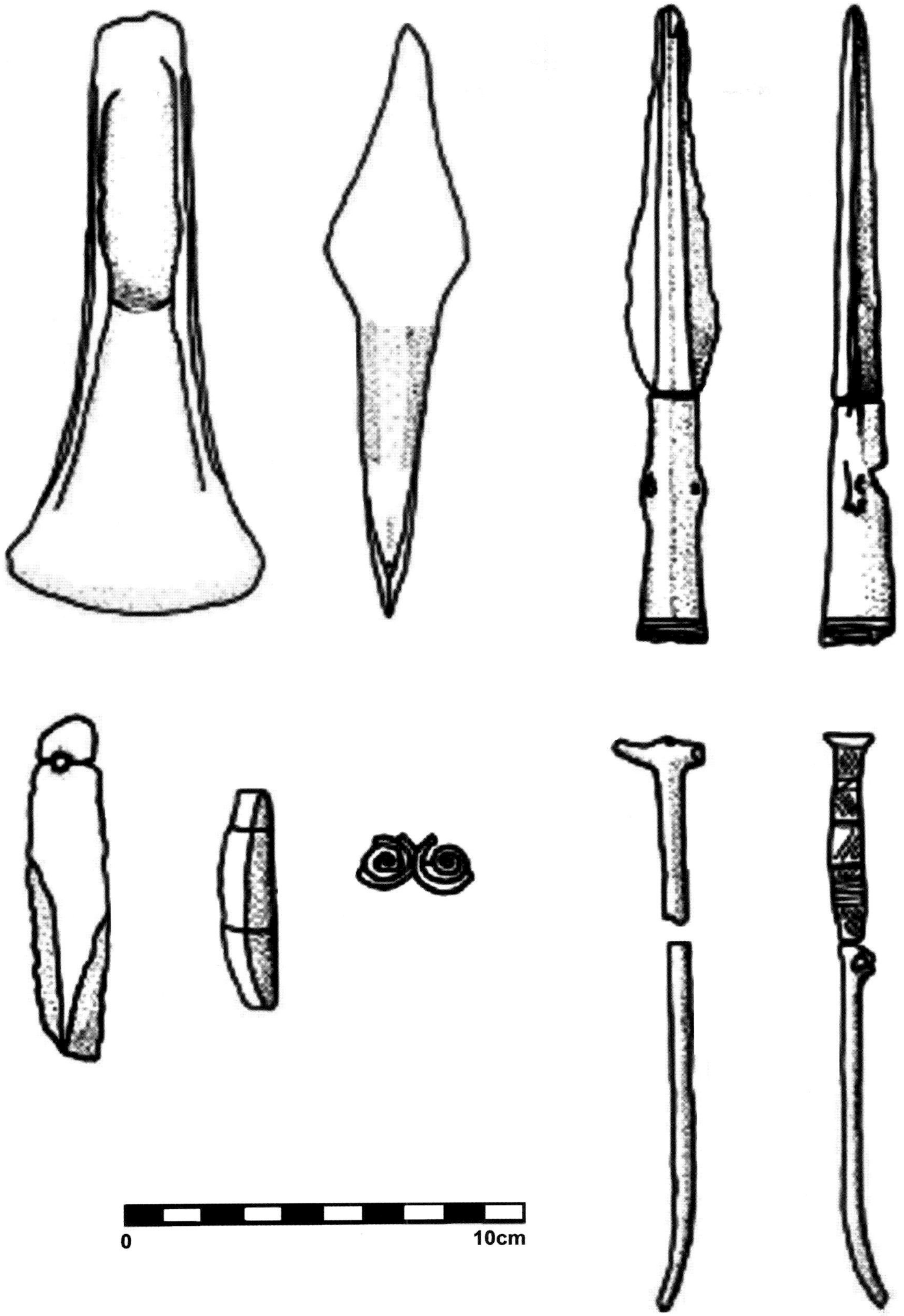

Figure 12.5: The bronze artefacts comprising the Tredarvah hoard. Upper row; palstave and spearhead. Lower row; tanged knife, blade, spiral fragment and pin fragments (after Pearce & Padley 1977)

Figure 12.6: Late Bronze Age sword blade fragment from Marazion (site 4 in Table 12.1). PAS CORN-30BC82. (Photograph: Anna Tyacke)

genuinely ancient, being accidental, use-related or possibly deliberate. The complete axehead bears evidence of use and resharpening, and the spearhead had broken across the blade-socket junction, a weak point that suggests breakage through use; similarly, a decorated Picardy-style pin is bent towards its broken tip, again probably the result of wear. Several of the pins survive in multiple fragments, possibly from their deliberate breakage and a fragmented tanged and riveted knife shows signs of having been burned. The practice of depositing used and fragmented Middle Bronze Age metalwork, particularly in association with occupational contexts, has been recognised in Cornwall and elsewhere in the south-west region. The histories of the objects are likely to have influenced the way they were treated and may explain why they were incorporated. The Middle Bronze Age witnessed an increasing focus on the settlement and the household as a focus of group identity and the deposit comprising residues from occupation, personal possessions and items associated with the transformation and storage of food may represent the linkages between people, households and shared kinship. (For a discussion of this, see for example Jones *et al.* 2015; Brück 1999; 2019, 115–162; Johnston 2020).

The Late Bronze Age sees both points of commonality and of contrast with the Middle Bronze Age. A particular point of similarity between the two periods is the treatment of artefacts. In common with the Tredarvah hoard, the majority of the surviving metalwork finds recovered from the project area have been used and damaged. All of the unstratified finds from Beacon Field were probably broken by heating and striking the blade (cf. Knight 2019b; 2022) and the same is true of many of the pieces that were found in the St Michael's Mount hoard, and at all three of the ingot findspots (see below). As noted above, this is a feature of many objects recovered from hoards of the later Bronze Age (Brück 2019, 91–96).

A major difference from the Tredarvah hoard is in the contents of the material deposited. Although the Tredarvah hoard included an axehead and a spearhead, most of the items were small personal trinkets, such as pin shaft fragments. By contrast, during the later Bronze Age, in common with elsewhere (Coombs 1975; Needham 1982; Bradley 1990; Fontijn 2019; Knight 2019b), there was a shift to depositing axeheads, weapons (Fig. 12.6) and ingots. At Beacon Hill, for example, all the metalwork finds were fragments from swords and the antiquarian find from St Michael's Mount comprised axeheads, spearheads and swords.

The most recently discovered hoard from the Mount (Table 12.1) has a similar character, and offers insights into its accumulation, treatment and formation and broader connections. Of the 48 pieces, most are incomplete and at least 39 show signs of deliberate fragmentation or damage. These included fragmentary ingots, sword blades and tools, as well as two incomplete socketed axeheads plugged with fragments of other objects (Fig. 12.7), a practice found elsewhere in Britain and Ireland during the Late Bronze Age (eg, Dietrich & Mörtz 2019). There are no refitting pieces within the hoard, suggesting either a selective collection of pieces or a randomised accumulation as a result of multiple fragmentation events over time with pieces added and taken away (cf. Needham 2007; Wiseman 2018). Metallurgical waste found with the hoard may suggest that these fragmentation processes were linked with recycling and recasting processes. Nonetheless, the conspicuous absence of certain object types (eg, spearheads) indicates that this represents a selective repertoire of material that was deemed suitable for deposition.

Only three objects were deposited complete or largely intact: a south Welsh-type socketed axehead, a bag-shaped chape and a decorated buckle or fitting, possibly for a harness or scabbard. These pieces are intriguing as they suggest broader connections that extend beyond Cornwall. South Welsh-type axeheads were in production and circulation in south-west England (Needham 1981) but, as their name suggests, they were most commonly deposited in south Wales; they were less often buried in Cornwall. The chape is the only example from Cornwall and south-west England more broadly, and the buckle/fitting appears to be unique in Britain, though it comprises stylistic elements of other object forms (Juddery & Roberts 2010; Knight 2022). In addition to these objects, a fragment of a carp's tongue sword and a broken hog's-back knife were also included; together these represent components more typical of the Late Bronze Age carp's tongue/Boughton-Vénat complex in south-eastern England and Atlantic France (Briard 1965, 199–239; 1991; Coffyn *et al.* 1981; Boulud & Fily 2009; Turner 2010; Brandherm & Moskal-del Hoyo 2014). In these areas, similar accumulations of fragmentary material, including weapons, tools, ingots and occasionally ornaments were gathered for deposition. The hoard deposited on St Michael's Mount is thus indicative of cross-Channel connections during the Late Bronze Age with shared ideologies between communities in Cornwall and north-western France (Knight 2022, 103–8).

We can consider this further in relation to other contemporary hoards deposited in Cornwall, which primarily comprise fragmentary axeheads, swords and ingots, but which

Figure 12.7: The bronze artefacts comprising the St Michael's Mount hoard. (Photograph: Jim Parry)

Figure 12.8: Findspots of Late Bronze Age metalwork from western Cornwall. Numbers correspond to Table 12.1. Contains OS data © Crown copyright and database right 2021

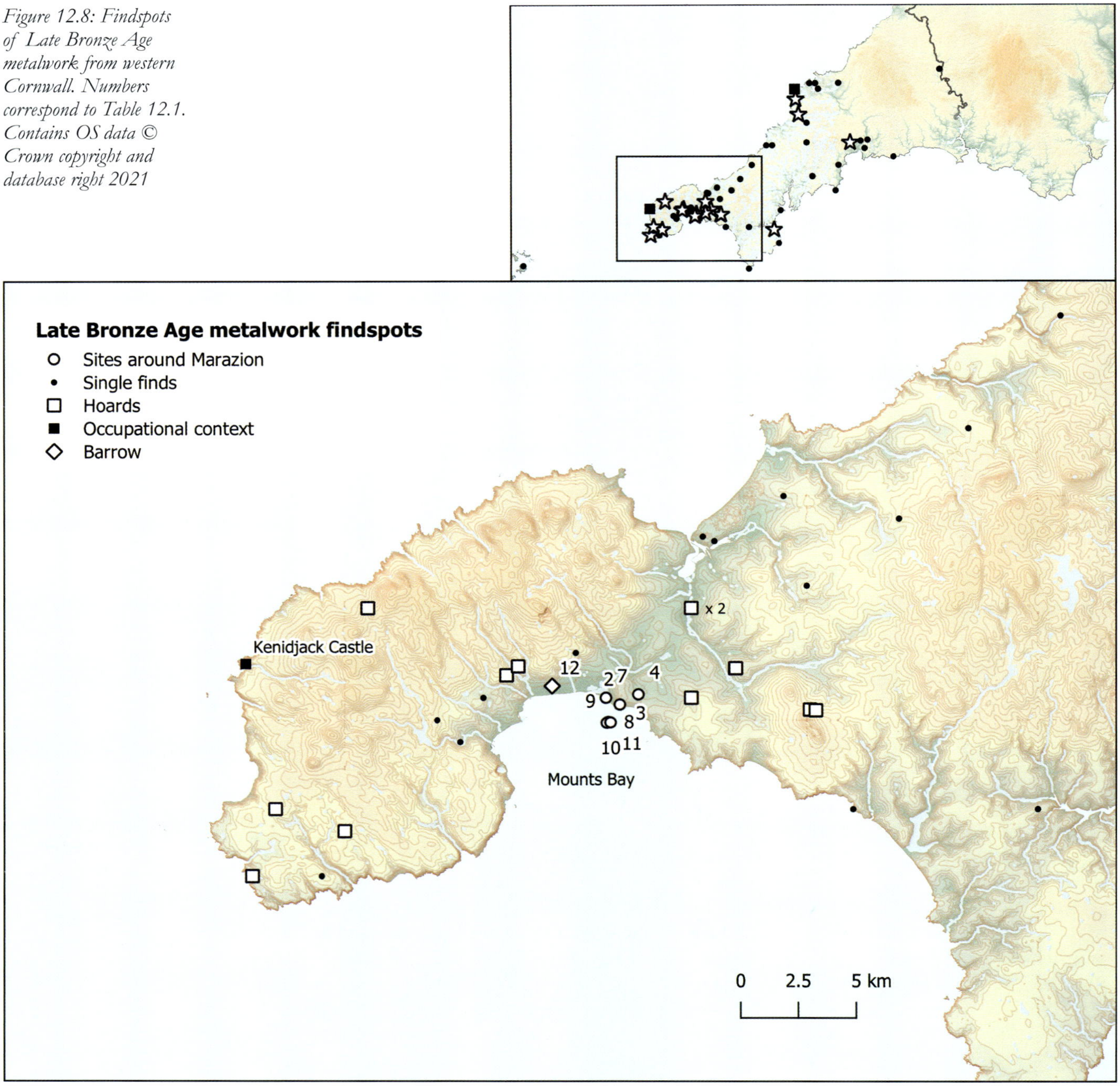

occasionally hint at these wider connections (Knight 2022, 103–8). A hoard from Breage parish contained a socketed axehead plugged with fragments of a sword, a socketed tool, a torc and a hog's-back knife as well as ingots and metallurgical waste. A second hoard found nearby included fragments of an axehead, several ingots and two sword blades, one of which was a carp's tongue type. Similarly, at St Erth, an end-winged axehead – another object type indicative of cross-Channel connections – was the only complete object deposited with 16 ingot fragments. These examples, and others, are largely concentrated in western Cornwall towards the Penwith peninsula, where 15 of the 20 currently known Cornish Late Bronze Age hoards are located (Fig. 12.8), with no comparable hoards further

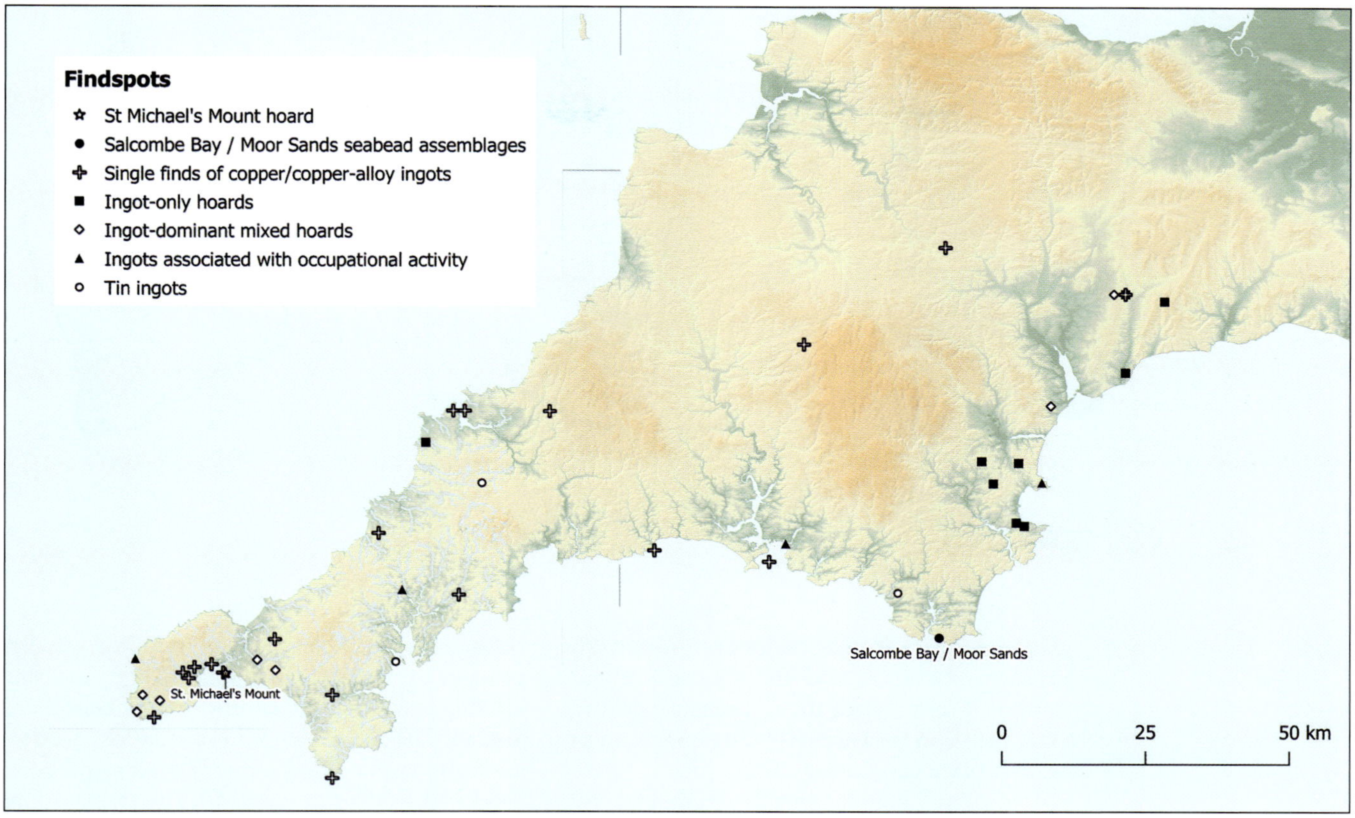

Figure 12.9: Deposits of Late Bronze Age ingots in south-west England. All ingots are copper/copper alloy unless otherwise stated. The Salcombe Bay/ Moor Sands assemblages contain 280 copper and 40 tin ingots. Contains OS data © Crown copyright and database right 2021

east. Whilst we should not forget that this may represent recovery bias, it seems there was a genuine depositional practice in this region, of which the St Michael's Mount hoard was an example, which reflected known expressions of how hoards should be gathered, treated and deposited. In many cases, the objects and imported items were destined for fragmentation and perhaps recycling; however, the extensive breakage (which must have been the result of repeated fragmentation events involving fire), and their eventual deposition in a location such as the Mount, hint at a technical and embedded practice that was part of the way in which the social reproduction of communities was achieved in and around the area (Knight 2022).

As well as the ingots from the St Michael's Mount hoard, there are three single artefact finds in the study area. The ingot finds are comparable with those found elsewhere in the immediate area and in the wider south-west region (Knight 2022). Indeed, as indicated above, the gathering and fragmenting of ingots, both in hoards and as single deposits, has been identified as a particular practice in the south-west peninsula, concentrated in western Cornwall and south Devon (Knight 2022). Many of the deposits, like those in the study area, are located close to the coast and/ or waterways, for example at Mount Batten and near Dawlish in Devon, or at Gillan Creek on the south side of the Helford River in Cornwall (Tylecote 1967; Cunliffe 1988, 56–58; Knight 2022) (Fig. 12.9). In Devon, multiple deposits of ingots are known around Tor Bay, with particular concentrations recovered around the estuaries and valleys of the Exe and Otter rivers. Depositions may have been made in relation to the route by which material was travelling into or out of the region (McGrail 1993; Bradley 2019, 259–60; Knight 2022, 101–3). Moreover, similarities in the treatment and findspot locations of isolated and hoarded ingots suggests a scaled practice, whereby deposition was governed by similar guiding principles (Knight 2017; 2018, 393–402; 2021). In this sense we may consider even single finds as selectively deposited and imbued with some meaning. The size of the deposit may thus

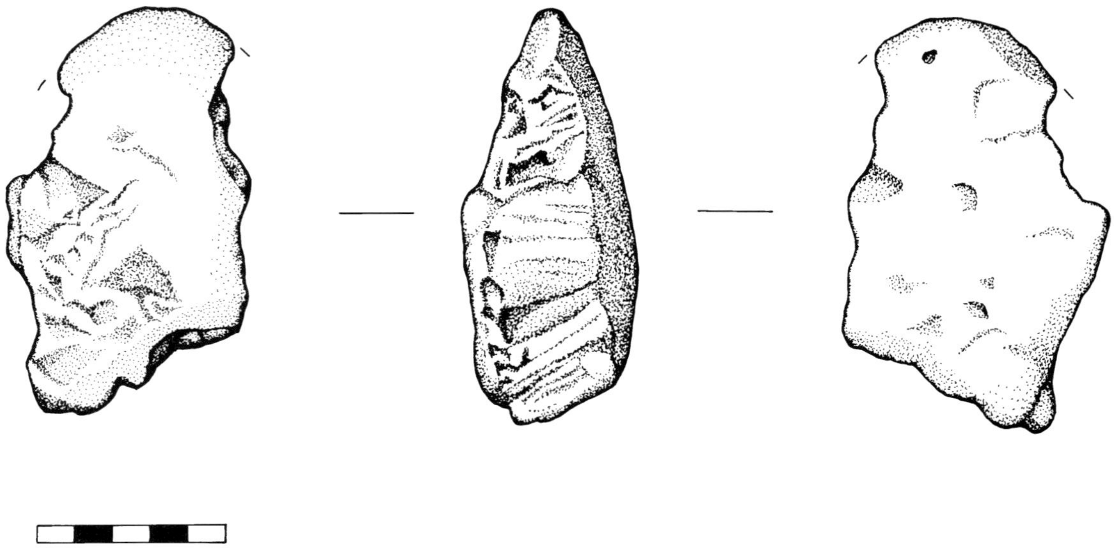

Figure 12.10: The 2002 copper ingot from St Michael's Mount. Note evidence for deliberate damage on the surface of the ingot

relate to the numbers of people involved, access to resources and the value of metal itself, or it may reflect the importance of the social situation that necessitated deposition in the first place (cf. Becker 2013).

Two of the ingots from the study area are single finds located on the Mount, seemingly associated with probable house platforms. Their contexts are not fully understood, however. The previously published ingot, which survived as a small lump of metal, was recovered from a layer within a suggested roundhouse, behind defensive lines on the south side of the Mount. It was associated with a saddle quern and Plain Ware pottery sherds which were dated to the earlier part of the 1st millennium BC (Herring 2000). The object was broken, probably deliberately reduced in size, and it has breaks/cut scars on three of its four sides. It appears to be a chip from the end of a plano-convex ingot, its top being flat and its bottom convex. This breakage happened in prehistory, and it is possible that the ingot had been fragmented during rites of abandonment of the house. Although Late Bronze Age roundhouses are still comparatively rare in Cornwall, there is good evidence for the structured abandonment of houses during the Middle Bronze Age (Nowakowski 2001; Jones 2015). Rather than just signifying that the occupant house was associated with the trading of metal (as Herring 2000 had argued), the inclusion of the fragment of ingot might also have symbolically represented the links between people who were involved in the process of working metal, exchange, and the kinship events that bound them together. Sociality and connectedness may of course have also applied to the quern used to prepare food and to the pots used for the preparation or serving of food.

The second ingot find may also be from a house platform (Fig. 12.4) although its context is less well documented. The ingot does, however, show very clear signs of being deliberately damaged (Fig. 12.10), with pieces being removed from it. Potential ingot fragments have also been recovered from another structure in west Cornwall although their context is not well dated. Between 20 and 30 'pieces of copper' were found within a 'small square hut' beyond the wall of the cliff castle at Kenidjack, in St Just-in-Penwith in the 19th century (Hencken 1932, 87–89). This site is also of interest in relation to this discussion as multiple axeheads were recovered there, including a South Welsh-type socketed axehead and a winged form, again signalling broader connections (Pearce 1983, 411).

The third ingot within the study area is the find from the cist at the Heliport site barrow (Chapter 2). Intriguingly the cist did not contain human remains as would probably have been the case in the earlier Bronze Age (eg, Jones 2012; 2016a), but the ingot was instead deposited with a single sherd of pottery and a red water-rolled pebble. The ingot, like the pottery sherd, once again represents a small fragment from a larger item. Jo Brück (2006; 2019) has drawn attention to the transformation and fragmenting of both deceased people and substances in the Bronze Age as a means of circulating them to maintain significant relationships between people and objects. The contents of the cist might therefore reflect a desire to make and remake connections at a site which, in previous generations, would have more explicitly referred to human remains. As noted above, the barrow is located on a slight knoll and radiocarbon dating indicates that soon after the deposition of the ingot into the cist, a fire was set on the covering mound. Fire would have been associated with transformation, including the change associated with the production of metal, the cooking of food and the cremation of human remains (Brück 2019, 230; Webley *et al.* 2020). A tiny fragment of burnt bone was in fact found in amongst the charcoal but it was too small to be identified. Whatever transformation was involved, the conflagration on the edge of dryland would have been a memorable event(s) (Noble 2007; Thomas 2007).

The potential metalworking site near to St Michael's Mount is not well documented and the artefacts are now lost (Pearce 1983, 416). However, it seems reasonable to assume that the antiquary who reported on the find would have been familiar with non-ferrous metalworking and would be able to recognise cauldron fragments (Edmonds 1849). As noted above, the cauldron was incomplete and, like the other artefacts discussed here, had been fragmented. The scale of the deposit, if it dates to the Bronze Age, appears to be unusual given the paucity and small-scale nature of non-ferrous metalworking sites in the south-west region and beyond (Jones *et al.* 2015; Webley *et al.* 2020; Jones & Kirkham 2021). One possibility is that a series of smelting activities occurred on or near to the place where the discovery was made and that they were gathered together to create a visible mound on the edge of the seashore. Mounds of Late Bronze and Iron Age date, containing midden and other waste material including metalwork, are known from elsewhere in southern Britain including those at Potterne and East Chisenbury in Wiltshire (eg, Lawson 2000; Waddington *et al.* 2019). Several mounds have been investigated in Wessex, but it is also notable that collections of material were also heaped up in coastal places in the south-west peninsula, as at Mount Batten, and also in Wales at Llanmaes, where metalwork was also incorporated with midden material (Cunliffe 1988, 100–103; Gwilt *et al.* 2016). A particular concentration of at least eight Late Bronze Age–Earliest Iron Age midden sites has been noted around the Isle of Purbeck in Dorset. At these sites were found butchery remains, broken pottery, shale working debris and metalworking evidence these as sites of communal craft production and feasting (Roberts *et al.* 2015; Ladle 2018). Such midden deposits may have been intended to mark places associated with communities, kin and gatherings for exchange, and if casting was also involved, with spectacular events that would have inspired awe in the onlookers (Sörman 2019; Fontijn 2019, 111).

Deposition of the Roman coin hoard in Marazion Marsh is also likely to have been a spectacular event. The deposition of more than a thousand coins may have represented an amassing of coinage by the community. The weight of the coins might have prevented it being carried very far and could imply that this event took place at the edge of the marsh (eg, Bland *et al.* 2020, 68) and it is likely to have been undertaken with the intention of making them unrecoverable (eg, Bland 2015). As noted above, coins that were obtained through engagement with the Roman economy – especially those found in or near watery contexts – continue to be discovered in significant numbers (eg, Tyacke 2011; Borlase 2020, 119). In common with Marazion Marsh the majority of these coins are found in ritualised contexts such as hoards in or near to streamworks or bodies of water (Jones 2019a, 116–117), and they may not have been used in day-to-day exchange. Instead, it is arguable that they represent a form of continuity of local practices and understandings from the Iron Age, and long-term engagement with particular places for deposition (as discussed, for example, by Farley 2015; 2021). The Marazion coin hoard is therefore unlikely to be a chance loss, and can be viewed as a votive offering made in a watery locale, which by the Roman period is may very well have accrued a numinous significance (cf. Herriott 2005).

Summary

To conclude, the area of Mount's Bay, especially the eastern end closest to the Mount itself, appears to have been the focus for the deposition of both metalwork and residues associated with non-ferrous metalworking. This arguably has its origins in the Middle Bronze Age but reached a peak in the Late Bronze Age, when frequent but mostly small-scale depositional events occurred. These, however, may have been influenced and connected with cross-Channel traditions. The significance of the area may well have continued into the Iron Age and Roman period when potentially the palstave(s) and certainly coins were deposited into the waters of Marazion Marsh.

The significance of the Mount may have developed from its role as a place of exchange and kinship and epic voyages between distant communities linked by the sea (eg, Helms 1988; Needham 2000; 2009; Van de Noort 2013). Indeed, the relatively large number of fragmented ingots, for example, may have spoken of those connections and relationships. The Mount's topographically distinct nature is also likely to have made it a focal point for deposition and perhaps the increasingly wet nature of the ground may also have inspired reactions (eg, Pryor 2001) to the increasingly liminal waterlogged low-lying ground and the deepening tidal separation of the Mount from the land (Chapters 10 & 11).

13

Bronze Age engagements with a liminal space

Andy M. Jones

This chapter is concerned with drawing upon and synthesising the excavated and environmental data from the previous sections and other published works, placing them within a narrative that makes human and non-human relationships, ontologies, and engagement with a changing liminal landscape central to the story which is being presented here. The main focus for this narrative will be the knoll upon which the barrow is set and the Bronze Age, the period to which much of the excavated evidence relates. It will also consider wider environmental changes that had taken place, which are considered here to have influenced the siting of the barrow. The chapter will, however, commence with the pre-Bronze Age background into which the barrow was set, as long-term human relationships with the area are also likely to have shaped perceptions of it.

Before the Bronze Age barrow

The Mount's Bay area is, as noted in Chapter 1, dominated by St Michael's Mount, which also provides some of the best, if albeit very sparse, evidence for both Mesolithic and Neolithic activity in the low-lying land comprising the project area (Herring 2000, 114). Flintwork of Mesolithic date has been found on the Mount, as has an Early Neolithic leaf-shaped arrowhead (*ibid.*). As discussed in Chapter 1, the majority of occupation sites of both prehistoric and Roman date, from artefact scatters to enclosed settlements, tend to be found on the better-drained land to the north. Aside from a comparatively small number of non-metal artefacts and the deposition of later Bronze Age metalwork (as discussed in Chapter 12), there are scant tangible traces of human activity in the coastal strip, which in the Neolithic is likely to have comprised a mosaic of wet woodland with open spaces and marshier areas (Chapters 6, 9 & 10). This apparent picture of an empty landscape devoid of human interest is, however, very likely to be misleading (Chapter 14). It is arguably better to consider the area as a component of a larger taskscape featuring interconnected but shifting relationships between human, non-humans, materials and places (eg, Ingold 2000; van den Berg 2021).

Today areas such as Marazion Marsh are rich in wild resources and, as research in the Severn Estuary and in Langstone Harbour, Hampshire has shown, low-lying landscapes (Bell 2007, 327–334; 2013, 314–340; Allen & Gardiner 2000, 199–220) tend to be high in biodiversity, teeming with resources which made them attractive to humans (see Chapter 14). The mosaic of habitats in Mount's Bay would have provided a diverse and abundant range of food sources including fish, shellfish, marine animals and seabirds, and fruits and nuts (eg, Rackham 1989, 80; Pollard 1996), which doubtless would have been exploited during the Mesolithic and Neolithic periods, although it remains to be seen whether the Neolithic inhabitants ate fish and shellfish. During the Neolithic it is likely that domestic animals, including cattle, would have been grazed here too (eg, Bell 2013). In this context it is worth noting that an Early Bronze Age tooth belonging to a neonatal cow was recovered from an intertidal peat deposit on the Isles of Scilly (Charman *et al.* 2016, 205), which suggests the use of wetland areas for the grazing of animals.

In addition to supplying food, the animals, plants and trees which were found in this zone would have been important for myriad other purposes. Timber, for example, would have been used for constructing buildings and making wooden tools and containers, while plant fibres could have been used to make clothing and a wide range of other organic artefacts that seldom survive in the archaeological record (as discussed, for example, by Hurcombe 2014; see also Chapter 14). The area was far from being an unoccupied wilderness: grazing animals, harvesting and the hunting of wild resources would have been among the activities undertaken by communities who inhabited and travelled around the local area. The colluvium below the Penzance barrow site is certainly indicative of human activity on the slopes above it (Chapters 2 & 6). In west Cornwall connections between the coast and inland areas have also been shown by the distribution of lithic finds that were obtained from coastal locations and carried inland to large occupation sites, including Clodgy Moor which lies a couple of kilometres inland to the south-west of Mount's Bay (Jones *et al.* 2013; 2015; 2018; 2019). These routines of movements and activities would not have stood in isolation from one another but will have been integrated into long-term patterns of occupation connected with the more 'tangible' evidence for settlement activity on the higher ground.

Movement to the coast from inland and across the sea would, as several scholars have noted, have been important forms of wayfaring, allowing communities to communicate with each other and to establish social relations over long distances (Cooney 2004; Edmonds 2004; Cummings 2007; Robinson 2007a, 114–115; 2007b; Garrow & Sturt 2017). As outlined in Chapter 1, the sea was not a barrier and communities in Cornwall and especially West Penwith were in contact with far-flung communities from at least the Neolithic period. Inter-community gatherings on the shore, in a place distinct from the higher ground, may have established patterns which continued into the Bronze Age (Kirkham 2011; Jones, forthcoming b). In the Neolithic, axeheads made from stone that had been collected from a variety of sources across West Penwith (Jones *et al.* 2017) were widely distributed across Britain (eg, Clough & Cummins 1988). With a memorable topographical landmark marking one end of the bay and its liminal setting beyond the settled high ground, Mount's Bay might have been viewed as a 'neutral' maritime haven in which these axeheads could have been exchanged. There is certainly both anthropological and archaeological evidence for communities using such places for gatherings (cf. Malinowski 1922; McKinley *et al.* 2014, 232–234; Bradley *et al.* 2016b; Bradley 2021, 45–78; O'Brien 2021). If this was the case, the establishment of Mount's Bay as a place of maintaining social relations could have created a landscape role that extended down the millennia.

The coastal littoral, as well as being a place of resources and a neutral 'in between' place for communities to gather, is also an environment which is subject to constant change. It is a place where dryland extending towards the Mount appears and disappears. Twice a day the sea rises and falls, linked to the cycle of the moon, and when bodies of water lie to the south as at Mount's Bay, both the solstitial suns and the major and minor standstill moons that rise and set in the north travel over the water and set on the other side of the Bay. The rising and setting sun in midwinter often flanks the body of water; the moon at the southern major standstill would do the same. In the winter the sun travels nearer to the water and the same is true for the moon (Higginbottom 2020, 79). Viewed from the land, the Mount would have been framed by such celestial events. The connection between the heavens, the seas and the land would have been part of the rhythm of life for the people who inhabited this environment and it is likely that their cosmology drew together people, the land, the sky and the sea. Such cosmologies are well documented in relation to coastal and other communities in the anthropological literature of northern Europe and North America (Walens 1981, 118–119; Terebikhin 1993), and it is possible that broadly comparable cosmologies could have existed in

Britain and along the Atlantic Façade during the Neolithic period and beyond (eg, Bradley 2000a, 12; Scarre 2002a; 2002b; Higginbottom 2020).

The visually distinct Mount may have been one of those places in the landscape which drew people together. Artefactual evidence is sparse, although this is not surprising given the later development and settlement on the island, which has left few undisturbed places. Indeed, the site may have been an Early Neolithic tor enclosure (Herring 2000, 115) comparable to well dated excavated examples at Carn Brea and Helman Tor (Herring 2000; Mercer 1981; 1997; Oswald *et al.* 2001; Whittle *et al.* 2011). In the Early Neolithic period the Mount would have been situated in an area of trees, open spaces and marshes, and as such would have been a distinctive natural place set within a liminal zone. Topographically distinct natural locales such as these could become the focal points for human activity. Anthropological studies have demonstrated the importance of unmodified natural features such as rock formations in sacred cosmologies and the rocks may be seen as being animate or being the homes of spirits (Mulk 1994; Äikäs 2017; Kõivupuu 2020). In the Neolithic period, such beliefs could have led to various forms of human engagement with distinctive outcrops, including enclosure and structured deposition (eg, Bradley 1998; 2000a; Tilley 2010). In Cornwall distinctive hills such as Carn Brea, Helman Tor, Roche Rock, Rough Tor and in West Penwith, Carn Galva and Trencrom all became the focal points for occupation, monuments, artefact deposition and/or enclosure during the Neolithic and Early Bronze Age periods (Herring 1999; Cole & Jones 2002–3; Jones 2004–5; 2016b; 2019a; 2019b; Davies 2010). The importance of these outcrops and tors for local landscape cosmologies and potentially kinship networks is also indicated by the fact that they are referenced by ceremonial monuments of Neolithic and Bronze Age date. It therefore seems likely that, given its distinctive shape and setting, the Mount was a significant place in Neolithic (and later) landscape cosmologies.

It is, however, also worth remembering that rocky outcrops were not the only focal places for activity in the Neolithic, nor the only features which are likely to have been of significance. Although timber monuments such as Seahenge in East Anglia (Brennand & Taylor 2003) reveal both the importance of trees in Bronze Age rituals and the presence of monuments in a low-lying setting (as discussed below), it is also the case that certain trees themselves can be venerated without modification, either within groves or individually (eg, Houlbrook 2015; Sen & Bhakat 2021). Trees are frequently revered and anthropologists have found that rituals marking human life cycles make use of trees which, through their longevity, growth and natural cycles, can become loaded with symbolism and themselves can be conceived as being alive, or containing non-human spirits, or as having metaphorical analogies with the human body (Bonnemere 1998; Rival 1998; Taylor 2020). Moreover, as Cummings and Whittle (2004, 71) noted, their presence can add to the experience of monument settings, just as tree cover during the summer months of the year can obscure views to prominent landscape features such as the Mount.

Just as the areas of woodland would have created shadowy spaces and dark places, the fissures in the rocks of the Mount will have been shadowy recesses. Shadowy spaces such as fissures and caves are known to have been significant places in prehistory (Bradley 2000a; Rose 2000–1; Tilley 2010, 427–458; Dowd 2015), associated with transformations and regarded as a boundary between worlds. At least one of the Late Bronze Age metalwork hoards from the Mount was buried in a space beneath such a fissured outcrop (Chapter 12, Fig. 12.3). The same liminal qualities are true for bodies of water, which in this area would have structured experience of place and carried particular associations (Bradley 2000a, 26). The changing extent and qualities of the local water sources, from fresh to brackish to saline across the Mount's Bay area and over time, may have led to perception of them having numinous characteristics (eg, Herriot 2005; Fowler 2013, 193; Brück 2019, 175–177) – characteristics that may have informed the choice of places for depositing artefacts during the Bronze Age (as discussed in Chapter 12).

The gradual rise in water levels around Mount's Bay and the effects of the water's increasing salinity by the Iron Age period at least onwards would have irrevocably altered the environment, with trees slowly dying and looking skeletal, and former areas of grazing disappearing. The old paths would have vanished, and the ground would have

Figure 13.1: (opposite page) An outcropping rock on the top of Watch Croft, in West Penwith enhanced by a cairn of small stones. (Photograph: Andy M Jones)

Figure 13.2: (opposite page) Photograph of the low yellow clay covered bank in the entrance area of the Caerloggas I enclosure barrow. The clay demarcated the correct approach to the site (Photograph: Henrietta Quinnell)

become treacherous underfoot. By contrast, however, the new shoreline would have been sandier and harder, a defined edge separating the sea from the inhabited landscape to the north. The Mount would have remained as the last fixed point in a shifting, increasingly submerged landscape. The changes would have engendered responses, some practical and others relating to beliefs and memories, from the local community, especially during the Mesolithic when sea-level rise is likely to have been at its greatest and the Late Neolithic and Bronze Age, when the hard shoreline started to develop. Grazing and movement to the south would have become increasingly restricted and old relationships and entanglements with places and with the non-humans who occupied them, and had shaped human experience of the world, disappeared forever (eg, Basso 1996; Kohn 2013). The biography of the landscape, and the social memories associated with it, would have slowly become mythologised, and these myths would have influenced the behaviour of the living communities (as discussed in Chapter 14; cf. for example, Connerton 1989; Basso 1996; Jones, forthcoming b).

The Bronze Age barrow

Although findspots of artefacts in the project area are, as previously noted, quite sparse, by the later Early Bronze Age (*c.* 1700–1600 cal BC) when the Penzance Heliport barrow was constructed, the landscape already had a long biography of inhabitation. The barrow was probably built in a period of flux as sea-levels continued to rise, changing the character and position of the coast, which is likely to have developed a harder sandy shoreline (Chapter 6). In the wider area, the expanses of wet woodland, marshy ground and the diverse habitat mosaic that were still present when the barrow was built had disappeared by the Late Bronze Age. In some places the ground would have been marshier by the later Bronze Age. In the Marazion Marsh core, the pollen evidence suggests that trees had declined and that there were cleared areas used for pasture in the near vicinity of the marsh, at the same time as the water there changed from brackish to freshwater (Chapters 9 & 10). In the intertidal zone, trees may have become skeletal stumps sticking up at low tide as poignant reminders of a lost land, which would have led credence to and reinforced local myths and stories. By contrast, in other areas, the ground behind the beach was becoming drier during the Bronze Age as a result of colluviation (Chapter 2). This happened in the area of the Penzance barrow site, which was situated close to a fresh spring water source issuing from the base of the slope (Chapter 6). The barrow on its low knoll would have had extensive views towards the new sparkling waters of Marazion Marsh and over the sea to the south and the Mount.

The knoll

The knoll was of course partly formed as an unintended consequence of earlier human activity: cultivation upslope had led to the movement downslope of white colluvium, which gathered to form a low mound or 'barrow-like' swelling at the foot of the slope above an area of marshier ground. This natural mound formation may have informed the choice of location for constructing a barrow, because of its resemblance to barrow mounds (eg, Ingold 2010). Elsewhere in Britain other forms of 'barrow-like' mound, including periglacial features and sandy knolls, are known to have been the focus for activity, which included burying the dead during the Bronze Age (eg, Wymer & Healy 1996; Mullin 2001; Downes & Card 2002).

Comparable examples of natural features becoming the foci for burials and mounds are also found in the south-west peninsula. During the Early Bronze Age on Dartmoor, the Whitehorse Hill cist was set into a natural peat mound which might have appeared to be 'barrow-like', and at Headon Down a natural rise associated with pits may have been enhanced by a low mound to create an apparent low barrow (Dyer & Quinnell 2013; Jones 2016a). Within West Penwith a comparable process can be seen with the natural 'cairn-like' outcrops, as at Watch Croft and at Boscregan which were purposefully incorporated into Bronze Age cairns (Tilley 2010, 450; Jones 2016b) (Fig. 13.1). Natural outcrops, mounds and swellings may have been considered to be the work of the ancestors or ancient mounds. Making use of them as places for gathering or for activities such as burial may have been considered to be extensions of earlier practices, and indeed a means of making connections with the past (cf. Bradley 2002).

A second attraction of the knoll may have been its colour. As noted in Chapter 2, the lack of evidence for a buried soil beneath the mound makes it likely that, in common with other barrow sites (eg, Griffith 1984; Christie 1988; Jones 2005), the ground had been stripped of vegetation. The white colluvium is visually distinctive and, once cleared of soil, would have stood out from the surrounding landscape, which would have been a muted combination of green vegetation and dark brown soils (as shown in Chapter 2, Fig. 2.12) The deployment of coloured clays in mounds and over banks and soils is known at many other barrow sites in the south-west region (Borlase 1872; Miles 1975; Christie 1988) as at Caerloggas I (Miles 1975) (Fig. 13.2), and several writers have argued that distinctive colours played a key role in structuring the experience of a site through their physical and metaphorical or symbolic properties. Yellow clays in particular have been linked by some

commentators to solstitial events or to stages within the life of the barrow (Owoc 2001a; 2001b; 2002; Jones 2005). By contrast, the white clay at the Penzance barrow was not an addition to the site, but was instead revealed by the act of digging on the knoll. Its localised presence may have helped make it recognisable as a special place.

Finally, water may have had a role in the barrow siting. The barrow was close to a source of fresh spring water, which seasonally may have appeared as a stream issuing from the foot of the hillslope, a phenomenon giving the locale particular significance. Springs, waterholes and streams could certainly be foci for monuments and for the deposition of artefacts during the Bronze Age (eg, Tilley 2009; Gossip & Jones, forthcoming; Bradley *et al.* 2015; Davies 2022). At Jacob's Well, at Woodbury Common in east Devon, for example a mound of pebbles, cracked stones and charcoal was constructed near to near to a spring (Tilley 2009). Radiocarbon dating of this site placed activity in the Early and Middle Bronze Age, suggesting that it had a prolonged period of use. At the Penzance barrow, the issuing of clear water during a certain time of the year may have been considered a magical occurrence, the place of which was marked by the barrow.

The view to the sea, the water, the freshwater pool at Mount Marsh and the Mount may also have given the barrow site significance too. Ceremonial monuments and barrows are recorded in coastal locations in various parts of Britain and Europe (eg, Lageras 2002; Papworth 2013; Wickham-Jones 2018). In eastern England, for example, timber monuments during the Early Bronze Age were constructed close to the shore at Holme-next-the-Sea ('Seahenge'), Norfolk (Brennand & Taylor 2003; Evans 2015; Robertson *et al.* 2016), and in south-east England some barrow groups may have been false-crested so that they were visible from the sea (eg, Field 1998). Early Bronze Age burials and barrows are also known from several of the special coastal places identified by Richard Bradley (2021, 75–77, 86) including Dundrum in County Down and Hengistbury Head in Dorset.

In Cornwall there are concentrations of barrow sites along the coast. Notable clusters occur on the north Cornish coast and especially in Harlyn Bay area as at Tom Parsons' Cairn (Fig. 13.3). Like Mount's Bay, Harlyn Bay is likely to have been a focal point for long-distance exchange (Christie 1985; Jones *et al.* 2011; Jones, forthcoming a). Several clusters of barrows and cairns also occur within West Penwith, including at Boscregan, where the sea might have provided a spectacular backdrop for barrow-associated activity (Jones 2016b).

However, unlike many barrows that may have been located so as to be visible from certain locations and to help guide movement across the landscape (for example, as has been argued for barrow groups in east Cornwall (Frieman & Lewis 2021), the Penzance barrow was never monumental and instead its location may have been chosen as a place from where to look out. Indeed, it is quite possible that all the characteristics of the locale mentioned above combined to create a special place, situated between the settled land to the north and the shore and sea to the south.

The barrow (enclosure barrow)

The first phase of the barrow, which dates to the latter part of the Early Bronze Age (1750–1630 cal BC; 3391±29 BP, SUERC-78031), can in no way be considered as making a monumental statement in the landscape. Following the removal of the turf, this phase of the barrow seems to have involved the digging of a shallow oval ring ditch 300 with the upcast being used to create a low internal bank 201 – in other words, an enclosure barrow (Fig. 2.13). The intention does not appear to have been to create a major barrier and there was no evidence for a primary mound. The substantial deposits of sizable stones which were found in the large later pits 100 and 400 may represent redeposited stone from a destroyed internal cairn, comparable to small cairns found within other sites (as discussed below). However, the existence and original form of any cairn, or its phasing within the barrow sequence, is purely conjectural. The site was, however, subsequently covered by the low outer mound 106 (see below).

Mound-less enclosure barrows and cairns are in fact a fairly common in the south-west peninsula and further afield in Britain. In lowland parts of Britain, such as the Wessex chalklands, they can take the form of earthen ring barrows, and other variants such as pond and saucer barrows (Miles 1975; Christie 1988; 2012; Jones 2012; Jones & Quinnell 2014), while

Figure 13.3: Tom Parson's cairn on the north Cornish coast. This coastal platform barrow is located close to the cliff edge and has extensive views out to sea

in upland areas including Dartmoor, Bodmin Moor and Wales they occur as stony ring cairns (eg, Wainwright *et al.* 1979; Lynch 1984; 2000, 133–136; Butler 1997; Jones 2004–5).

The Penzance barrow in its original form, a shallow ring ditch with an internal bank, has features in common with a number of Cornish enclosure barrows. Barrows defined by low banks and/or shallow ditches include sites such as the primary phase of Caerloggas I, although there the bank and ditch were significantly more substantial and the site enclosed a small rocky outcrop (Miles 1975). At Davidstow site 8 a circular site, 10 m in diameter, was defined by a ditch with an internal bank; both were relatively slight and comparable to the Penzance barrow. Few features were found inside the Davidstow site, although a small low quartz cairn was constructed near to the centre of the enclosed space, which was later covered by a low mound (Christie 1988; Jones 2005). Finds were limited to a few flints and a quern. These elements have similarities with the Penzance barrow site, where artefacts and features were also scarce, and in common with Penzance, the Davidstow site was subsequently covered by a low mound. A third comparable site is the Highgate enclosure barrow, found during excavations along the route of the A30 (Nowakowski & Johns 2015, 83–94) (see Fig. 13.4). At this site, an oval enclosure was defined by lengths of segmented ditches. In common with the Penzance barrow, these ditch segments were shallow and there were few features within the enclosure. There was, however, an off-centre pit which contained a deposit of cremated human remains within a Collared Urn. Unlike the Penzance barrow, where mound 106 was constructed, there was no sign of subsequent mounding and the Highgate enclosure is several centuries earlier, dating nearer to the start of the 2nd millennium cal BC. In addition to these, there are numerous sites across the south-west region which have been recorded as ring ditches and it is possible that many were not mounded but may in

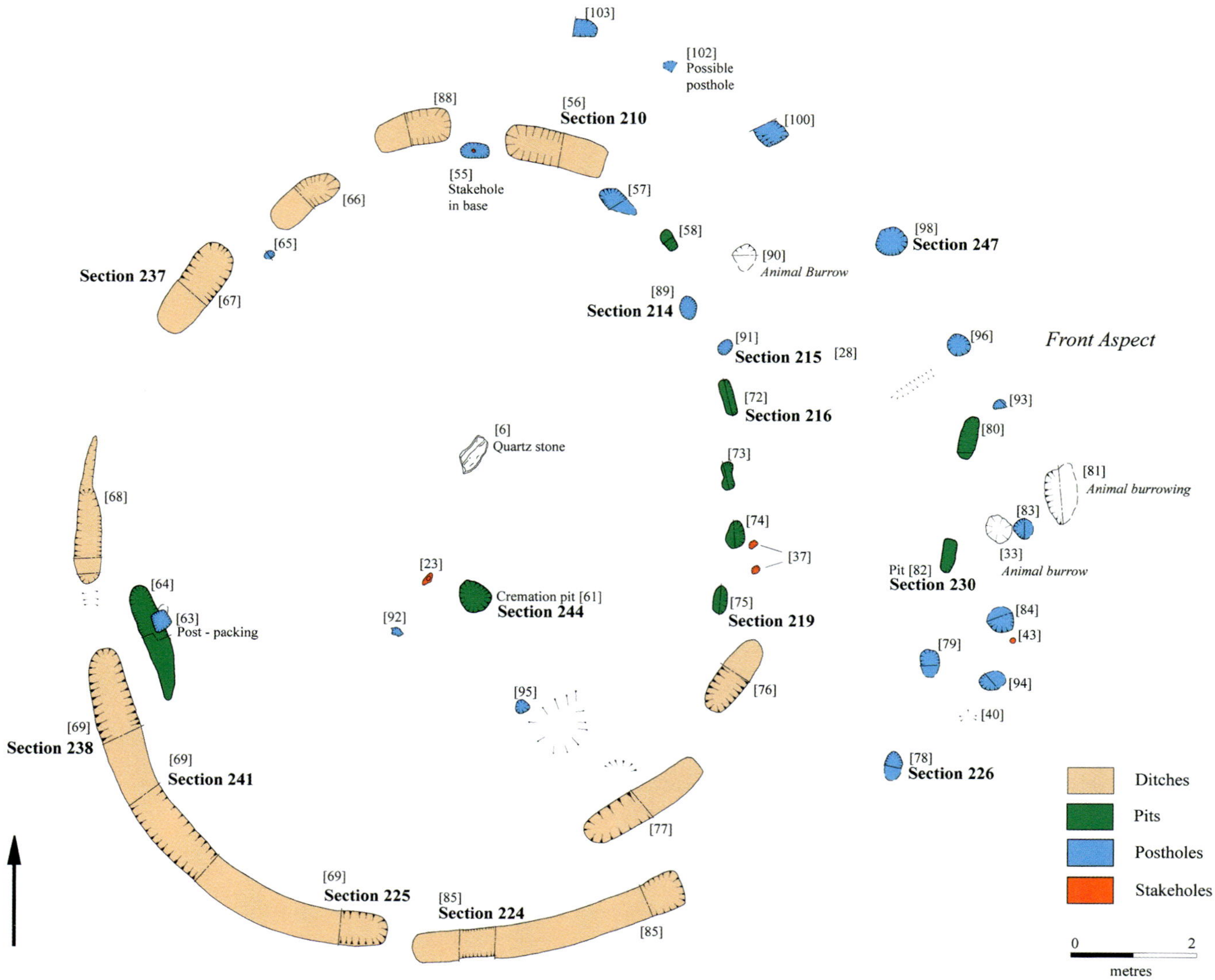

Figure 13.4: The Early Bronze Age Highgate ritual enclosure, an oval area, enclosed by shallow and segmented ditches

fact have been enclosure barrows (Henrietta Quinnell, pers. comm.).

Some enclosure barrows and especially ring cairns do frequently contain features such as small pits (Lynch 1972; 1993, 134–143; Jones 2012) – which, at Shaugh Moor, were charcoal-filled (Wainwright *et al.* 1979) – or token amounts of cremated bone. In common with the sites described above, however, features within the Penzance enclosure barrow were few. None of the internal features can be confidently assigned to the Early Bronze Age and those of prehistoric date that were found, such as the cist complex 228, are of Late Bronze Age date. The presence of a further cist (see below), or perhaps a small central cairn, comparable to those found at Davidstow barrows 3 and 8 (Christie 1988), remains a distinct possibility, although this is conjectural.

It is also the case that other excavated enclosure barrows have produced little in the way of either features or artefacts: for example, Stannon site 10 was entirely devoid both of features and of artefacts (Jones 2004–5). Similarly, Davidstow site 3a was enclosed by a bank but no features were found within it; the same is true of Davidstow site 3, where a bank and ditch encircled a space which, in its early phases, was free of any features (Christie 1988; Jones 2005, 105–107). The ditch around Davidstow site 3 did, however, become the focus for the deposition of two wooden objects and quartz blocks.

The ditches of other barrows in Cornwall also became the focus for the deposition of artefacts, although few have been completely excavated. Sites with notable concentrations of finds in ditches include the barrows at Tregulland, Watch Hill and Trelowthas (Fig. 13.5) (Ashbee 1958; Jones & Quinnell 2006a; Nowakowski 2007). This is also the case with the Penzance barrow, where selected pebbles and a chert cutting flake (SF 1, SF 2 and SF 8) were recovered from the bottom of the ring ditch 300 which enclosed the barrow.

The pebble assemblage from the Penzance barrow ditch 300 is of interest as pebbles are found in association with several barrow sites in Cornwall and the wider the south-west region, as well as more widely across Britain (eg, Cooper *et al.* 2021, 131–133). Contexts include the pebble cairns of east Devon, where study of the cairns revealed the deliberate selection of certain pebbles (Tilley 2017, 130–152), and at the Godrevy Barrow white pebbles were found to have been spread on the barrow mound (Gossip & Jones, forthcoming).

Two of the three pebbles found in the Penzance barrow ditch were of quartz (Chapter 4), which may have been deliberately selected. Quartz has a widespread association with prehistoric monuments, both in Cornwall and much more widely (Dudley 1964; Darvill 2002; Neighbour 2005; Cummings 2009, 110–12). In some cases quartz pieces, blocks and pebbles were incorporated into burial contexts, such as the quartz pebbles found in the Constantine Island cist (Jones 2009–10). Elsewhere in Cornwall they were deposited into ditch fills, as at the Watch Hill barrow (Miles 1975) and at Treliske barrow II, where quartz blocks were found in the ditch (Dudley 1960). Beyond Cornwall, on Exmoor there is evidence to suggest that quartz was deliberately extracted in the Early Bronze Age, potentially for incorporation within ceremonial monuments (Juleff & Bray 2007). Given its triboluminescent properties (as described, for example, in Bradley 2005a, 112), quartz is likely to have been considered to be a magical substance. There is widespread anthropological evidence for the use of quartz in First Nations rituals and in the Americas and Australia (Lewis-Williams & Pearce 2005, 256–260; Taçon 1991). The Turkana Indian shamans of the Amazon, for example, include quartz crystals inside their 'healing wands'; when shaken during rituals, these wands produce smoke and sparks which are associated with male fertility and creation (Reichel-Dolmatoff 1997, 128–129). These properties are very likely to have been recognised by people in prehistoric Britain too. Quartz also appears in the Late Bronze Age contexts on the Penzance barrow as well (as described below).

Figure 13.5: The Trelowthas barrow under excavation. The shallow re-cut barrow ditch showing in the picture became the focus for deposits of pottery

The chert cutting flake, too, may have carried associations. The flake appeared to be fresh and little used. Flint and chert tools are commonly associated with barrows across the south-west region as a whole (Dudley 1964; Pollard & Russell 1969; Miles 1975; Christie 1988; Butler 1997, appendix 3). In some instances these artefacts could be taken to be 'grave goods', for example the plano-convex flint knife accompanying the cremated remains at Pentire Glaze (Patchett 1950). In the majority of cases, however, the relationship is much more ambiguous. For example, at the Watch Hill barrow on the St Austell granite, many flints came from the turf stack which formed the mound (Jones & Quinnell 2006a). These may have been derived from occupation activity preceding the mounding of the barrow. Other flints are likely to have been deposited as part of funerary-related activities, such as feasting around the barrow. This can be seen for example, at Constantine Island on the north Cornwall coast (Jones 2009–10), where the pieces of flint had been casually knapped and quickly discarded after use onto the barrow site.

Although the chert flake from the Penzance barrow might easily be overlooked and viewed as a mundane artefact (cf. Lemonnier 2012), it could have been associated with a particular individual and, like the quartz, have had its own biography and significance (Spector 1991; Gosden & Marshall 1999). Alternatively (or additionally), it could have been deposited after a particular one-off act such as the preparation of food for a funerary feast or the cutting up of objects – a literal severing of ties between persons – within the enclosure. Either way, it could have carried a 'vibrancy' which may have stimulated a social memory and encouraged a particular response(s).

The quartz pebbles and the chert flake from the Penzance barrow ditch therefore fit a wider pattern of artefactual associations in barrow ditches that has been found in the south-west region. These can be seen as part of a broader tradition of placing deposits to mark the barrow perimeter. These deposits could have helped make the act of ditch cutting more memorable and the boundary less permeable by linking it with objects associated with particular people, places or the perceived properties of the objects (eg, Nowakowski 2007; Leary *et al.* 2013, 209–210; Jones, forthcoming b).

The perimeter of the barrow may have been subsequently re-inscribed: the outer ditches 216 and 218 may well represent redefining of the barrow on its southern side. Shallow multiple ditches are known at other barrow sites in Cornwall including at Davidstow Moor (Christie 1988) and the placing of worked flint SF 5 and smoothed pebbles SF 3 and SF 4 in ditch 216 is similar to deposits associated with ring ditch 300 (Chapter 4). However, the dating of both ditches is uncertain, and it is possible that they are later in date and unrelated to the barrow.

Another feature of enclosure barrows and ring cairns, both in the south-west region and elsewhere in Britain, is that they frequently contain either no or minimal, tokenistic evidence for the deposition of human remains within the defined space (Miles 1975; Lynch 2000, 133; Jones 2005; Jones & Quinnell 2014). For example, none of the ring cairns at Stannon Down on Bodmin Moor produced any evidence for burial, even though cremated bone would have survived (Jones 2004–5) and the same is true of Littlejohns and Gaveriggan barrows, and many of the barrows on the St Austell Granite including the enclosure barrow at Trenance (Miles 1975; Johns 1994; Jones 2005; Nowakowski & Johns 2015, 57–101). This paucity of evidence for burial appears to also be the case with the Penzance barrow. Here, however, some caution is needed as there is the potential for later disturbance of the barrow, including the excavation of large pits within the centre of the site that may have removed any deposits of human remains.

The first phase of the Penzance barrow therefore has resonances with enclosure barrows found elsewhere in the wider south-west region, and Cornwall in particular, namely the defining of a space for activities which were not necessarily associated with the disposal of human remains.

A Middle Bronze Age barrow?

In the wider area there is more evidence for later Bronze Age activity to the north of the barrow site (as discussed in Chapter 14). In West Penwith, as in other parts of Cornwall, the Middle Bronze Age sees the appearance of the first permanent roundhouse settlements and field systems, and in Penzance the first hoard of metalwork appears at Tredarvah (Pearce & Padley 1977; Nowakowski 2016a; Jones & Kirkham 2021). The higher ground to the immediate north of the barrow will also have been used for grazing and agriculture and have contained roundhouses. These, however, are likely to lie beneath the current Anciently Enclosed Land (land that has been enclosed by at least the medieval period, Cornwall County Council 1996) which has seen little excavation, and no settlements of this period are currently known (Chapter 1).

Activity on the barrow site during the centuries between the digging of the ditch in the earlier Bronze Age and the construction of the cist complex after *c.* 1000 cal BC is uncertain. There is, however, some evidence to support a Middle Bronze Age phase, in the form of two radiocarbon determinations, one from the near-central pit 100, of 1500–1400 cal BC (3169±29 BP , SUERC-78031) and the second from the large pit 400 of 1420–1280 cal BC (3081±29 BP, SUERC-78030). The radiocarbon determinations are, however, from redeposited contexts that may incorporate residual material and as such they cannot be relied upon to date the features from which they came. Pit 100 also produced a stone muller SF 7, with traces of grinding, potentially associated with plant fibres,

Figure 13.6: The enclosure barrow at Trenance, defined by a low ring of stones. (Photograph: Henrietta Quinnell)

and of subsequent mineral crushing (Chapter 3). Other unstratified pieces of stone from the barrow were also found, including one which had possibly been used as a rubber and another which had potentially been deliberately broken. Mullers are found on both Middle and Late Bronze Age settlement sites (eg, Nowakowski 1991; Jones & Taylor 2010, 23; Gossip 2021). Querns, rubbers and mullers have been found in association with barrows and cairns in Cornwall, including Davidstow Moor site 8 and the recently excavated platform cairn in Constantine Bay, where a lightly used quern and rubbing stone were placed purposefully beside one another and incorporated into the matrix of the cairn (Christie 1988; Jones 2004–5; forthcoming c; Watts 2014, 72–101). In both settlement and barrow contexts there is evidence that querns were not casually deposited and were part of structured deposits. In common with the flints and the pebbles, the muller may have been associated with an individual or with tasks performed within the enclosure barrow, for example with the grinding of cereals for food.

Unfortunately, the fills within pit 100 appeared to be disturbed and the relationship with the mound was uncertain. It is therefore likely that it is a much later feature, or just possibly an earlier one that had been heavily disturbed by a subsequent intrusion (Chapter 2). Disturbance to the site, especially in quadrant 4, was suggested by the discovery of three flints and a small assemblage of tiny, abraded sherds of prehistoric pottery in the topsoil (Chapters 3 and 4).

The low outer mound 106 could also be of Middle Bronze Age date, as stratigraphically it pre-dates the charcoal-rich Late Bronze Age mound 200. In the absence of secure dating it could be of Early, Middle or Late Bronze Age in date. Smaller barrows with low covering mounds and platform barrows are known from the Early Bronze Age in Cornwall (Miles 1975; Johnson & Rose 1994, 40; Jones 2005, 40–72) and include several of the sites at Davidstow Moor (Christie 1988) and the Trelowthas barrow (Fig. 13.5), the latter of which appears to have started as an enclosure barrow that was subsequently covered by a low platform (Christie 1988; Jones *et al.* 1997). As we have already seen, this sequence also occurred at Davidstow Moor site 8, at Trenance (Fig. 13.6), and at the Gaverigan barrow (Miles 1975; Christie 1988; Nowakowski & Johns 2015). A cycle of enclosure followed by mounding is a feature of many barrows in the

Figure 13.7: The small Middle Bronze Age ring cairn at, Shallowmead on Exmoor (Photograph: Henrietta Quinnell)

south-west region generally (Jones & Quinnell 2006a; Jones 2012; forthcoming a), and may have been a way of cutting off access to the enclosed space and drawing activities on the site to a close.

Small barrows are, however, more typical of the Middle Bronze Age in southern England, where they are often associated with deposits of cremated remains and Deverel-Rimbury pottery and are frequently sited relatively close to settlements (White 1982; Entwistle 2001; Bradley & Fraser 2010; Caswell & Roberts 2018). Small barrows are also found in the south-west region (Jones 2012). However, Deverel-Rimbury ceramics are not common in the region and are absent from Cornwall (Quinnell 2012). Another notable difference between the south-west peninsula and elsewhere in southern England is that in the peninsula, the presence of large amounts of cremated remains, seen at sites such as Simon's Ground in Dorset (White 1982), is a rare occurrence.

Other forms of monument continue to be constructed with minimal deposition of human remains, albeit on a much reduced scale, as for example the small ring cairn at Shallowmead, Exmoor (Quinnell 1997) (Fig. 13.7). This can be seen in Cornwall, too. On Constantine Island a Middle Bronze Age cist was set into an existing mound, and the recent re-excavation of a barrow on a headland at Godrevy revealed that a small site covered by a low mound dated to the middle centuries of the 2nd millennium cal BC (Jones 2009–10; Gossip & Jones, forthcoming). Neither of these sites, nor the Penzance barrow, produced many finds, although the Constantine Island cist contained inhumed remains and the Godrevy barrow produced a small amount of cremated bone, albeit not definitely identifiable as being human.

The character of the Middle Bronze Age phase of activity at the Penzance barrow remains uncertain, but activity of some sort is nevertheless indicated by radiocarbon dating, as described above. As we have seen, however, the material that was dated may be residual and need not relate directly to activity on the site. What we can say is that the site underwent transformations which are echoed at other barrow sites, namely those from an open enclosure to a mounded barrow. By contrast, the subsequent Late Bronze Age period represents a clear phase of activity, but with far fewer contemporary parallels.

The Late Bronze Age barrow

In the wider area around the barrow, there is increasing evidence for human activity during the Late Bronze Age. As discussed in Chapter 12, much of this evidence takes the form of metalwork deposition, although house platforms are known on St Michael's Mount, and in West Penwith the excavation of stone-walled roundhouses at Bosiliack has revealed evidence of occupation in the Late Bronze Age (eg, Jones & Quinnell 2011b). It is also possible that, as in Ireland, the nearby enclosed hilltop sites which overlook the project area at Castle-an-Dinas, Ludgvan and Lescudjack could have been first enclosed in the later Bronze Age (eg, Jones 2016b; O'Brien & O'Driscoll 2017; Kirkham, forthcoming), although none of these sites has been excavated.

Activity at the barrow site during the Late Bronze Age comprises the construction of a cist complex and a charcoal-rich mound which covered the site, thereby sealing the earlier features.

The cist complex

Cist complex 228 comprised two conjoined north–south aligned cists 207 and 219, with a short linear arrangement of stones 222 extending from the eastern side. Neither cist contained any human bone, although this would not have survived the acidic soils. Cremated remains, however, would have survived the soil conditions.

A radiocarbon determination on charcoal from 103, the lower fill of cist 207 of 930–810 cal BC (2734±27 BP, SUERC-47292) attests to activity in the Late Bronze Age at a time when, with a few exceptions (for example, as at Plas Gogerddan in Dyfed and at Rylstone in Yorkshire: Murphy *et al.* 1992; Melton *et al.* 2016), barrows had ceased to be constructed both in the local area and elsewhere in Britain (eg, Lambrick with Robinson 2009, 194; Tellier 2018, 121). Bronze Age and Iron Age round barrows are, however, known outside of Britain (Fontijn *et al.* 2011; Leonard 2015, 93–96) and these will be discussed in relation to the mound below. Activity at the Penzance Heliport site was also broadly contemporary with the deposition of Late Bronze Age metalwork in the Mount's Bay area, and arguably closely related to the increase in long-distance relations which were evident during this period (Chapter 12).

The unexpected date of the construction of the cist raises important questions about the character and interpretation of the site, especially since by the Late Bronze Age the enclosure barrow must have been an ancient, albeit a relatively small-scale, monument in the local landscape.

Numerous Early Bronze cists are known from West Penwith, as well as western Britain and Ireland (eg, Butler 1997; Jones 2016a; 2016b; Cleary 2016). An obvious function of cists is the interment of human remains, although the acidic environment at the Penzance barrow site precludes the survival of unburnt bone. Neither cist was large enough to have held an articulated unburnt body, although disarticulated bones could have been accommodated. Deposits of cremated bone would have survived inside the cist, although currently the latest securely dated cists containing human remains in Cornwall are of Middle Bronze Age date, for example the recently dated cremated remains from the cist below the rampart at Gunwalloe (Wood 2015, 37), and the cist on Constantine Island referred to above, which held inhumed remains (Jones 2009–10).

Although a small number of later Bronze Age inhumation graves are known in southern England, for example from Snail Down, Wiltshire and the Isle of Thanet, Kent (eg, Thomas 2005, 86; McKinley *et al.* 2014), across Britain there had been a shift away from formal burial in barrows by the Late Bronze Age, as noted above. Instead, where human remains are recovered, they are found, usually fragmented, in a variety of contexts which include settlements, rivers and other wetland locations (eg, Brück 1995; Pryor 2001, 330–349; Schulting & Bradley 2013; Caswell & Roberts 2018; Johnston 2020, 105–106).

Any form of later Bronze Age burial is a rarity both in Cornwall and in the wider south-west region, especially in contexts such as within graves or below barrows. Instead, fragments of bone recovered from a variety of contexts are more typical of the very limited number of instances. For example, at Rose Ash in Devon a deposit of cremated bone from an adult dating to the later part of the Middle Bronze Age was placed within a plain vessel, thereby denoting a formalised burial (Wainwright 1980). By contrast, at Greylake in Somerset, fragments of human and animal bone, pottery and white quartz pebbles were found in association with a waterlogged wooden structure dated by dendrochronology to 963 BC and 942 BC (Brunning 1997). Currently no example of a formalised human burial is known from Cornwall and the small amount of cremated bone found within a pit at Quintrell Downs and dated to (1010–830 cal BC (2775±27 BP, SUERC-60205; Jones & Smith 2015) is the only Late Bronze Age cremation deposit. This is broadly contemporary with the Penzance barrow and represents the best Late Bronze Age example of the ritualised deposition of a token amount of human remains in Cornwall. Despite the huge increase in instances of metalwork deposition during the Late Bronze Age in the region, there are no known graves with artefacts during this period, which suggests that individual status was not being marked. It is therefore possible that as Brück and Davies (2018) have argued, there may have been less autonomy and room for individualistic competitive gain in the Late Bronze Age than is often suggested.

Cists need not contain human remains at all, of course, and activities involving human remains may not have been central to all barrow sites, where engagements with non-humans might instead have been paramount, and where objects such as pottery or stone or metal artefacts could have been substituted for human bones (Cooper *et al.* 2021, 241). In fact numerous earlier Bronze Age examples across the south-west region appear to have been too small to hold articulated burials (eg, Jones 2013a; 2016a), although the possibility that they could have held disarticulated unburnt remains should not be ruled out, as the prevailing acidic soil conditions will have destroyed unburnt bone. It could be argued that such cists might be better thought of as boxes or 'wrappings' (cf. Douny & Harris 2014), containers for a range of materials, which could include curated objects or heirlooms and human remains. Anthropological recording provides potential analogies: for example, the Kwakiutl, on the north-west coast of America, conceive boxes to be metaphorical places of birth and containers for the dead, as well as holders of sacred objects (Walens 1981, 45). In Bronze Age Britain some cists show evidence for being re-opened by later generations (Fowler 2013, 245; Booth & Brück 2020; Brück & Booth 2022), revealing that they and their contents could be revisited. Late Bronze cists are rare but the practice of inserting human remains into Early Bronze Age cists is attested, for example at Broomlands, Kelso in Scotland, where the unburnt remains of two individuals dating to the Late Bronze Age were inserted into such a cist (McLaren & Wilson 2015).

The potential for artefacts or bone to be added to or retrieved from the Penzance cist complex after its construction was, however, restricted by its covering with a charcoal-rich mound 102, also dating to the Late Bronze Age, which did not appear to have been disturbed. Objects were recovered from both cists. The larger cist 207 contained a structured deposit, consisting of a copper ingot fragment, which had been broken and then wrapped within an organic material that had become mineralised on its surface (Chapter 5 and Appendix 1). A single, burnt sherd that has been identified as possibly belonging to a domestic Beaker pot (Chapter 3) was also recovered from the cist and is discussed below. The charcoal in the fill of the cist may have been derived from a pyre (Chapter 6) and could be interpreted as evidence for the deliberate infilling of the cist. On Dartmoor, in the Early Bronze Age, there is evidence that some cists were backfilled with soil as, for example, at Chagford 4, Peter Tavy 39 and Walkhampton 17, and at Chagford 3 a cist had been filled with a 'black soil' (Baring Gould 1898; Burnard 1897; 1899). Pits infilled with charcoal are also known on Dartmoor (eg, Dyer & Quinnell 2013) and Cornwall, for example at Tresavean, where pits were filled with identified pyre material dating to the Middle Bronze Age (Jones & Thorpe 2014). A similar infilling event could have occurred at the Penzance barrow, although material could have entered the cist from the overlying charcoal-rich mound.

Both of the objects in cist 207 can certainly be viewed as representing the deliberate fragmentation of artefacts. Deliberate breaking and fragmenting of artefacts and of human remains is of course well documented throughout the Bronze Age of Britain and Ireland (Brück 2019; Knight 2019b; 2022; Johnston 2020). Three of the most recent publications on the Bronze Age of Britain and Ireland argue that the fragmentation of objects during this period was not about commodification but the fact that objects had biographies and histories (Brück 2019, 233; Johnson 2020; Knight 2022, 161), and in the case of metalwork fragmentation this may have been a practical way of severing links associated with artefacts and enabling exchange of metals between kinship groups (Knight 2022, 161; Johnston 2020, 113). This would have facilitated the maintenance and regeneration of kinship networks through the circulation of fragments, which enabled some group members to recycle and create new objects made from known objects with biographies, and others to place fragments into votive deposits. As regards why a fragment of a copper ingot should have been placed within a cist, as Cooper *et al.* (2021, 27) comment, not all 'mortuary material culture' need be associated with a corpse at all. As we have seen in Chapter 12, around the time that the cist was constructed metalwork was being deposited in the local landscape on a larger scale than hitherto in a variety of contexts, often in a deliberately fragmented condition.

With cist 207, it is arguable that there are potentially two scales of remembrance at work. The Beaker sherd was clearly already several centuries old when it was burnt, and it belonged to an ancestral time long before either the ring ditch or the cist was constructed. Although it could be argued to be a residual find, it's location in lower cist fill close to the ingot, suggests otherwise. As such it was an 'out of time object' (cf. Knight *et al.* 2019a). It is conceivable that the sherd was associated with the earliest Bronze Age activity on the knoll and therefore had a link to the site or was perhaps recognised as being part of an ancient vessel belonging to ancestor from a mythological time. Either way, given the relatively frequent occurrence of sherds as opposed to complete Beakers and other ceramics in Cornish cists and barrows (eg, Jones & Quinnell 2006a; 2006b), its burial in cist 207 in the 'old way' may therefore have been an appropriate way of treating what might have been considered to be an inalienable possession of the ancestors.

By contrast, the copper ingot appears to have been fairly fresh when fragmented and deposited in the cist. Its burial can, as outlined above, be seen as the deliberate fragmentation of an object, part of which was deposited as a votive offering, perhaps to maintain human and non-human relations. Other fragments may have been shared between members of the kinship group, with some being used to make new bronze objects and others deposited in hoards. The latter point is of interest as although examples of formal burial are uncommon in the Late Bronze Age, and shared metalwork associations between hoards and graves rarer still (Cooper *et al.* 2021, 75–110), ingots and ingot fragments are a particular feature of metalwork hoards in south-west England (Chapter 12; Knight 2022, 101–103). In short, the ingot fragment in the cist may represent part of a web of social relations, relating to the correct way of exchanging metal. As with the burial of the Beaker sherd, there could also have been an element of being seen to respect ancient traditions of cist construction. Although no human remains were present in the cist, the ingot fragment was embedded in social relations and would have related to particular Bronze Age ontologies relating to personhood. As such it could have been treated in a similar way to that used for human remains in the previous centuries.

The small cist 219 did not contain any artefacts but it was associated with selected pebbles. The upper fill contained a number of white quartzite pebbles. As noted above in relation to the ring ditch 300, quartz is likely to have been considered to possess magical properties and there is a frequent association between this material and Early Bronze Age barrows and cists in Cornwall. Quartz pebbles and pieces were also found in the Middle Bronze Age cist at Constantine Island (Jones 2009–10). Quartz pebbles are also found in Late Bronze Age ritual contexts in the south-west, for example, as noted above, at Greylake in Somerset where white quartz pebbles were associated with the human remains (Brunning 1997) and at Quintrell Downs, where quartz cobbles were recovered from pits adjacent to the one containing human cremated remains (Jones & Smith 2015). This association also continues into the Iron Age, with quartz being associated with cist graves and ceremonial monuments (eg, Bullen 1912; Jones & Taylor

2015; Jones 2019a, 113–114; Cooper *et al.* 2021, 185–218).

By contrast with the quartz, a single pebble had been placed at the bottom of the cist, which when wet becomes distinctly blood red in colour. This contrast in colour may have been deliberate. Elsewhere in Britain and Ireland it has been noted that a distinction may have been made between red and white stones in the construction of monuments, including stone circles and chambered cairns during both the Neolithic and Bronze Age periods (eg, Lynch 1998; Jones 1999; Bradley 2000b, 126–128). Given the long association between ochre and burials and red stones in funerary monuments (Tilley 1996; Scarre 2002c), the pebbles in the Penzance barrow cist were perhaps drawing on long-held colour symbolisms and associations. If interpreted in this way, a colour distinction may have been at play between white luminous quartz and the blood red of the wet stone. As with the artefacts in cist 207 these stones may have been linked to Bronze Age ontologies.

The mound

The second Late Bronze Age component of the site was the mound 200, charcoal from which was radiocarbon dated to 910–810 cal BC (SUERC-47293, 2714±27 BP). This determination is very close in time to that from the cist complex and the mound is likely to have been deposited over the site very shortly after the cists had been constructed.

As noted above, although Late Bronze Age monuments such as ring barrows in Ireland or smaller mounds in the Low Countries are known (Cooney & Grogan 1994, 145; Bourgeois 2013; 103; De Reu & Bourgeois 2013; Leonard 2015), the creation of a mounded barrow in the south-west of Britain during this period would have represented an exceptional and therefore memorable event.

The inner mound at the Penzance barrow would have been unforgettable in several senses. By contrast with typical earlier barrows and cairns which had mounds of earth or stone, mound 200 was largely composed of charcoal, comprising large quantities of probable gorse, willow and oak (Chapter 6). Oak has a recurrent association with barrows in both the south-west region and Wales and was frequently used in funerary pyres (Lynch 1984; Jones 2004–5; Tilley 2010). Oak charcoal is found on sites even in areas which were a long way from the nearest available oak tree (eg, Jones 2016a). This suggests that oak was considered to be important for the transformation of persons, from the recently deceased to 'ancestral' bone. Unlike the charcoal assemblages from Early Bronze Age barrows and cairns where the charcoal had been burnt off site and had cooled prior to burial (eg, Wainwright *et al.* 1979; Jones 2016a), the Penzance barrow charcoal assemblage seems to have been formed as a result of one or a series of conflagrations either close to or on top of the site. Localised burning is also suggested by the burnt stones which were found on top of the alluvial clay beneath the barrow mound, and by the heat-fractured stones in the layer itself. While the conflagrations may represent pyres, however, only one small fragment of charred bone was found, and this was too small to be identified as human. A non-funerary interpretation of the charcoal-rich mound is therefore possible.

Whether human remains were burnt on the site or not, as with the cist complex the formation of mound 200 harked back to earlier practices both in Cornwall and elsewhere in Britain. This is not an entirely unknown phenomenon, as the later Bronze Age and Iron Age sometimes witnessed the reinvention of older monument forms. At Rylstone in Yorkshire, for example, a log coffin burial in a barrow was carried out centuries after the last interment of that type had been made in the area (Melton *et al.* 2016). Within other barrows in Britain and Europe there is there is of course evidence for the adding of later burials and the re-use of sites (eg, Barclay & Halpin 1999, 309; Thomas 2005; van Beek & Louwen 2013), and in the Iron Age of Cornwall there are indications that an attempt was made to re-imagine and create circular monuments resembling ancestral sites such as cairns, barrows and hengiform monuments, such as those found at Scarcewater near St Stephen-in-Brannel, Camelford and Nansledan, Newquay (Jones & Taylor 2010, 84; 2015; Rainbird & Pears 2017). As John Barrett (1999) pointed out, Early Bronze Age barrows are likely to have become mythical places in the landscape by the Iron Age, and it seems probable that this was true of the Penzance barrow. By the Late Bronze Age it would have been a place associated with myth and memory.

Another point to consider here is that during the Late Bronze Age burial traditions were not the only features associated with the creation of mounds and the transformation of substances. During this period other forms of mound, associated with the activities of the living, were forming. These mounds were principally connected with cooking: burnt mounds were not just the by-product of hot-stone cooking, but were also a way of marking the landscape with memories of social gatherings, some of which are likely to have been on a large-scale.

These cooking or burnt mound sites lie at the smaller end of later Bronze Age mounding practices. Such sites are found across Britain and Ireland and were in use throughout the Bronze Age and beyond (eg, Buckley 1990; Lambrick with Robinson 2009, 179–181; Hawkes 2013). Burnt mound sites typically consist of three components: a pit or large trough, a mound of burnt stone and charcoal, and a hearth or fire pit, located close to a source of water, which was used to fill the troughs. The associated mounds are made up of large heaps of fire-cracked stones. The stones are likely to have cracked by being heated in a fire before being immersed in the water within the trough to bring it to the boil. Later Bronze Age burnt mounds are still, however, comparatively rare in the south-west of Britain. In Devon, two burnt mounds at Burlescombe in east Devon were excavated and radiocarbon dated to the Middle Bronze Age (Best & Gent 2007), and at Jacob's Well on Woodbury Common in Devon a mound of pebbles and charcoal beside a spring has been radiocarbon dated to the Early to Middle Bronze Age (Tilley 2009). In Cornwall, two features within a Late Bronze Age enclosure at Tremough provide the best contemporary evidence for heating of stones and the marking of sites by low cairns. The first, pit 124, had been filled with charcoal and large quantities of burnt stone, which had probably been used for cooking. In addition, fragments from moulds, including one for the tip of a sword, were found along with a cushion stone used for shaping copper alloy objects plus sherds of Late Bronze Age pottery from a large cooking vessel (Jones *et al.* 2015, 121–122). Together these are suggestive of a linked event involving the production of metalwork and the social consumption of food. No mound was associated with this feature; however, stones were found beyond the pit, and these may have belonged to a displaced cairn (*ibid.*). The second feature at Tremough, pit 119, was also found to contain a large number of burnt stones and charcoal was sealed beneath a cairn of stones 205, which contained sherds of Late Bronze plainware pottery. It was suggested that the cairn may have marked the site of significant feasting activity (Jones *et al.* 2015, 221). Both examples reveal a focus on the preparation, cooking, and sharing of food in communal gatherings.

No trough or fire pit was discovered at the Penzance barrow site, although it was located close to a seasonal spring, and mound 200 contained burnt stones as well as charcoal. The small quantity of charred cereal grains present within the sampled the mound material and the cist (Chapter 6), and potentially the small amount of burnt bone, could represent the residues from cooking and food preparation or of small offerings made during rites carried out on the site. The stone muller SF 7, which bore traces of grinding found in it 100, could, as noted above, also date to the Late Bronze Age and have been associated with the preparation of food and potentially with the processing of minerals. The consumption/offering of small amounts of food is found on several earlier barrow sites in Cornwall. At Stannon Down (Jones 2004–5), small quantities of charred grain were associated with the cairn group, and as noted above querns, mullers and flints are also associated and deposited in ritualised contexts on barrow sites. The processing of minerals can of course be linked with metalworking and, as we have seen, this could be connected with the broken ingot found in the cist as well as to sites in the wider area (Chapter 12). This suggests that there may have been an interest in memorialising events through social memory (cf. Connerton 1989).

Social events and large gatherings may have also been commemorated by the formation of immense midden mounds which were being created elsewhere in Britain and on the Continent during the Late Bronze Age (Bradley *et al.* 2016a, 239–241). In Britain, these mounds have been identified in Wales, the Thames Valley and most notably in Wessex (eg, Lawson 2000; Lambrick with Robinson 2009, 339; Madgwick & Mulville 2015; Waddington *et al.* 2019). At Llanmaes, in the Vale of Glamorgan, for example, an extensive midden of Early Iron

Age date was found to cover roundhouses belonging to the Late Bronze Age to Earliest Iron Age period (Gwilt *et al.* 2016). The midden deposit contained very large quantities of bone, mostly derived from animals but also some human; over 300 metal artefacts, mostly of copper alloy; and over 1000 sherds of pottery. In Wessex substantial large, mounded middens were created during the Late Bronze Age and Early Iron Age, as at All Cannings Cross where the mound covers three hectares and is in excess of 3 m thick (Field & McOmish 2017, 103). These immense heaped-up spreads of midden material incorporated pottery, vast quantities of animal and some human bone, worked stone and items of metalwork (Sharples 2010, 52–53). These activities involved the collection of fragmented material which is likely to have been brought to these locations by kin groups and communities and merged together (Johnston 2020, 357). They represented places where people gathered for a variety of purposes, including feasting exchange and rituals (Brück 2019, 153). Over time they undoubtedly became highly visual statements which may have memorialised people, events and places.

With the exception of the promontory midden site at Mount Batten, in Plymouth, Devon (Cunliffe 1988), there is less evidence for very large-scale mound formation in the south-west region. At Mount Batten excavations revealed evidence for an extensive midden which produced ceramic and metalwork finds of Bronze Age and Iron Age date, as well as animal bone. Cornwall has not, to date, produced a comparable coastal site. Nonetheless, there is evidence that since the Middle Bronze Age mounds were being created in Cornwall, albeit on a smaller scale. As discussed in Chapter 12, at Tredarvah, Penzance (Pearce & Padley 1977), a spread of Middle Bronze Age occupation material, which included Trevisker pottery, worked stone artefacts, charcoal and metalwork was uncovered that was initially thought to be associated with a roundhouse. Salvage investigation of the site suggested that although the layer was derived from occupation-related activity it was not directly associated with a structure, and may instead have represented a heap of material into which the metalwork had been deposited. On the Lizard peninsula, at Higher Polcoverack, St Keverne, a low mound covering an area containing Bronze Age pottery was found to cover a series of pits and postholes (Harris & Smyth 1983). The features did not form a structure and the mound did not appear to be a barrow, but the covering mound did seem to have been deliberately deposited suggesting the marking of a place associated with earlier activity. Interestingly, the aforementioned Middle Bronze Age coastal cist at Gunwalloe (Wood 2015, 71–72) was covered by a substantial midden deposit of Late Bronze Age date, broadly contemporary with the Penzance mound 200. In the vicinity of Mount's Bay, it is also possible that a mound associated with metalworking may have existed on the coast close to Marazion (see Chapter 12), but the context of this site is uncertain as it was documented in the 19th century.

Returning to the Penzance barrow, there are elements of the Late Bronze Age mound that invite comparisons with burnt mounds and with other forms of mound that developed during this period. At the same time, the association of the mound with the cist complex suggests that a connection was also being made with the barrow mounds of the past. The mound at the Penzance barrow of course differed from 'traditional' barrow mounds of earlier Bronze Age date in that, rather than being composed of earth and stone, it had been formed as a consequence of at least one burning event. In many societies, fire is considered to be sacred and/or magical and essential for ritual performance (eg, Layard 1942, 45; Yates 1989; Reichel-Dolmatoff 1997, 134–136; Vitebsky 2005, 85–90). The significance of the burning event(s) at the Penzance barrow may have been heightened by the fact that the barrow was situated in a liminal zone between the dryland and the sea, which it overlooked, within an area associated with long-distance exchange and the deposition of metalwork. The burning of fires in this special place would not only have been memorable events (eg, Thomas 2007; Xygalatas *et al.* 2013), but will also have entailed distinct sensory effects. Close to the barrow, the smell of burning wood would have held connotations associated with transformation, for example of people to bone, the raw to the cooked and of ore into metal objects. The smoke itself may have also had supernatural properties of its own: in North America, for example, the Kwakiutl people see fires as being transformative and consider smoke to provide

Figure 13.8: The site of the Penzance barrow, a distinct knoll at the bottom of the hillslope, which rises to the north. (Photograph: Andy M. Jones)

a means of communication with the spirits; and across the Americas, smoking was often considered to be part of a sacred, rather than recreational act (Walens 1981, 11; Schultes & Hofmann 1992, 62; von Gernet 2007; Godlaski 2013). The act of burning wood would have created smoke visible for miles, far beyond the visual envelope of the barrow site itself. People from the land and sea would have been able to see a column of smoke arising from the coastal strip, and this will have reminded them of the special nature of the place (eg, Susmann 2021).

Conclusion: creating and transforming space

Taken through time, the narrative of the Penzance barrow may demonstrate a place which, during the Bronze Age, enabled the performance and (re)production of ontologies; that is to say a place where the interweaving and making of connections between people, non-human spirits, place and the deep past occurred. In the Early Bronze Age a special, natural white barrow-like knoll was uncovered within a changing landscape, where clear waters magically sprang from the ground on a seasonal basis. Beyond the knoll, the sea crept closer, drowning an old landscape of diverse habitats, no doubt believed to be populated by a variety of non-humans, and of places, stories of which could have been inspired by the decaying trunks of ancient tree stumps, exposed at low tides. The white knoll was encircled and inscribed by a low bank and ditch. People assembled, left offerings of lithics that had been gathered from the surrounding landscape, and looked out over the sea and the sparkling waters of the marshes (Fig. 13.8).

By the Late Bronze Age, the encircled knoll of the barrow would have been regarded as an old or traditional place in the landscape, associated with memories and gatherings of people. The addition of cists to this ancient monument would serve to re-make connections to past generations through the undertaking of 'traditional' rites at this ancient place. Objects were fragmented and buried in the 'old way', enclosed within a stone chest set into the 'white place', thereby maintaining connections between kin and other beings in an appropriate way. Finally, a mound was raised from fires burnt on this special spot, the smoke from which rose skyward, alerting communities to the activities taking place there and inscribing them in the landscape.

14

Inhabiting a changing landscape: response and reflection

Andy M. Jones and Michael J. Allen

The historian Priya Satia (2020, 1) recently wrote that historians are '...storytellers, custodians of the past, repositories of collective memory and poetic interpreters of what it is to be human'. The same is also of course true of archaeologists, who are custodians of deep time, and who use a range of analytical techniques and theoretical approaches to record change and create evolving narratives, which are relevant to the present and the future. As Cipolla (*et al.* 2021) suggest, as a discipline, we are also in a perfect situation to reveal 'the nomadic, the minoritarian, and the non-western'. To this we can also an ability to working at multiple scales from the 'bottom up' as opposed to top down (Black Trowel Collective 2016). This in turn allows us to reconfigure archaeology as a discipline which is 'future oriented, committed to a reshaping of our discipline where the pasts we compose from materials in the present have stories that help inform and shape the future' (Cipolla *et al.* 2021). At the same time it is acknowledged that other narratives exist, and the past emerges to inform other responses to the landscape and changes to it (Chapter 15).

This is particularly true of the landscape considered in this volume, one that has not only witnessed dramatic, if long-term, change in prehistory (Fig. 14.1 and Chapter 11) but continues to do so. Due to global warming it is likely to see significant change in the future. In the long term we may well see the loss to the sea of the coastal strip that forms the focus for this volume, and the breaching of Marazion Marsh which may eventually become part of a channel stretching to the Hayle Estuary, thereby creating the 'Isle of West Penwith'.

The submergence of such an area will, like the drowning of Mount's Bay in prehistory, result in changes to resources, creating both a sense of loss, and changes to the way people live their lives. In the future, as in the past, responses will be required from communities that are of a social and practical nature. In no sense, however, should this area be seen as being (or having been) a marginal zone, as studies of other wetland/marshy areas have shown. In the Severn Estuary and Langstone Harbour or the Humber wetlands, for example, perceptions of wetlands in prehistory are likely to have differed significantly from those of today and they are likely to have been inhabited and engaged with for a variety of purposes, which will have developed and changed over time (eg, Allen & Gardiner 2000; Locock 2001; Gardiner *et al.* 2002; Van de Noort 2004, 60–69; Bell 2007; 2013).

As we have considered in Chapters 12 and 13, there is increasing evidence for the use of the area in the later Bronze Age, as a place of metalwork deposition, and as a place of ceremony at the barrow site. As discussed in the preceding chapters, this is likely to have been a

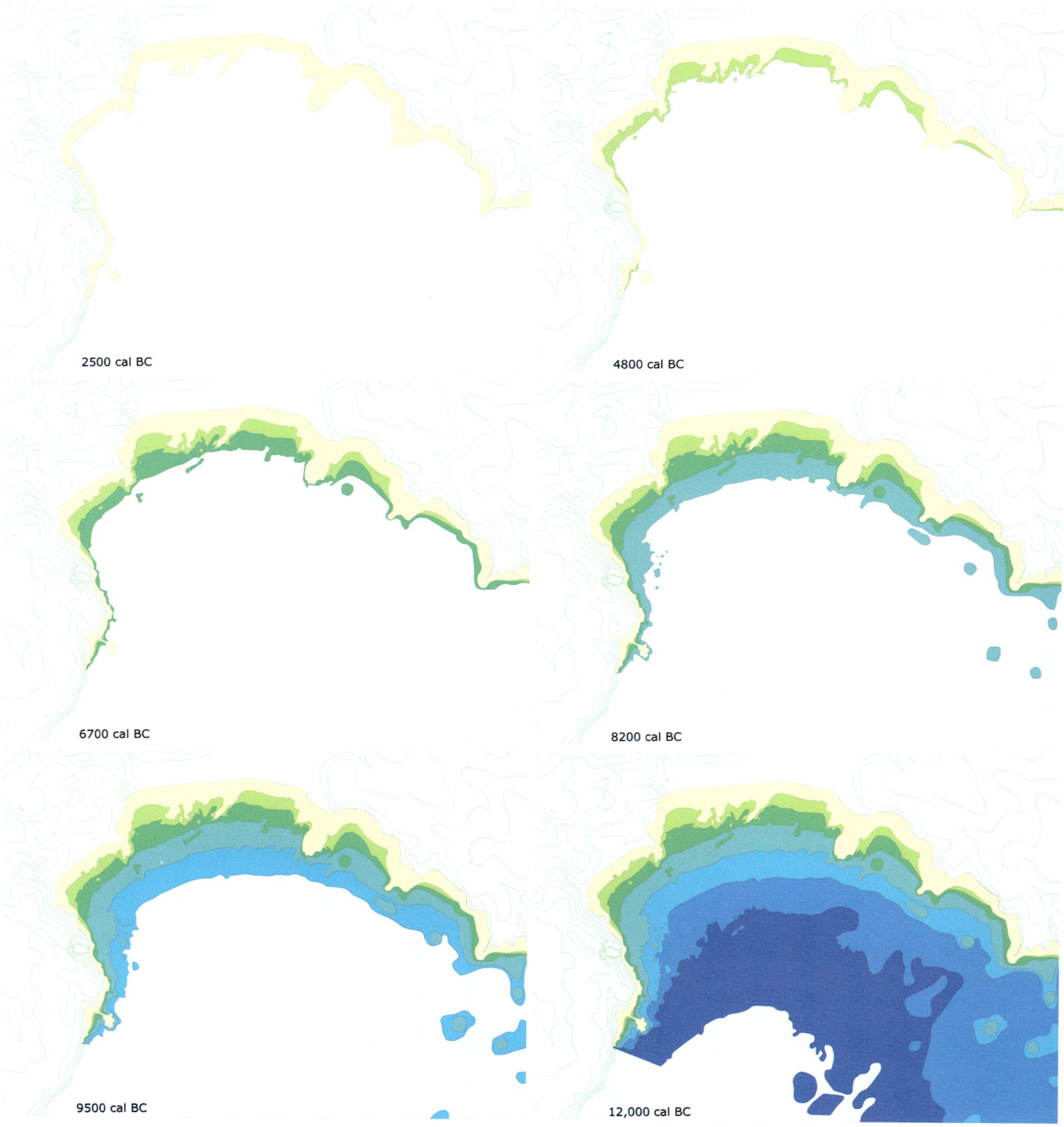

Figure 14.1: Regression analyses of 12,000 years of the coastal development of Mount's Bay (images after Channon 2018, fig. 10)

result of the area's setting on the edge of the land and its evolving character and landscape biography that have led to it being considered to have liminal qualities. This is, however, only one aspect of the way it would have been viewed or occupied in the past. As Richard Bradley (2005b) has pointed out, the 'ritual' and the 'domestic' elements of life would have been closely interrelated in the past, an observation that has been made by anthropologists for contemporary societies too (eg, Humphrey & Laidlaw 1994). Indeed, it is by inhabiting an environment that communities are able to comprehend and make sense of the world (Kohn 2013). In other words, the project area is unlikely to have been set aside purely for the deposition of metalwork in a liminal space. Instead, it is likely to have been valued and used for a range of reasons and as a place of resources, and consequently can be regarded as a taskscape (cf. Ingold 1993; 2000) of interrelated activities. Given the area's dryland maritime location, these activities will have included exchanges with diverse groups (eg, Bradley *et al.* 2016b; Äikäs *et al.* 2021; Bradley 2021), the nature of which would have shifted over time due to changing conditions. It is also worth remembering here that the coastal strip we see today is not that which existed in prehistory, and that what did exist then was not isolated, detached from the higher ground to the north or, given Mount's Bay's maritime setting, from connections with more distant places.

This chapter provides an overview of our current state of knowledge regarding human activity and the changing landscape in West Penwith from the Mesolithic to the Roman period. It goes on to discuss aspects of environmental change in more detail and to consider the possible responses to that change by the communities who lived in and around this part of Cornwall, including in the realm of memories and myth-making. It finishes with suggestions for further work that needs to be undertaken in the area, and with some general comments about the contemporary relevance of the archaeology of drowned landscapes, as communities around the world face similar challenges as climate change affects sea-levels.

Chronological review

Mesolithic

As noted in Chapters 1 and 13, there is very little direct evidence for Mesolithic activity within the Mount's Bay area, being limited to a few flints (Herring 2000, 114) and the palaeo-environmental evidence from Marazion Marsh and elsewhere in the Bay, which informs us about the character of the landscape and the extent of available dryland. Many sites, such as Marazion Marsh, for instance, are currently coastal, but in the Mesolithic would have been many kilometres from their shoreline, so any marine, littoral and shoreline reference today needs to be carefully verified in the archaeological record.

The palaeo-environmental information reveals that during the Mesolithic the area was a rich mosaic of different habitats that would have provided an abundant range of food sources including fish, shellfish, sea mammals, seabirds and their eggs (Jacobi 1979; Pollard 1996; Jones *et al.* 2019). In fact the west coast of the Lizard, which faces onto Mount's Bay, is noted for its breeding population of grey seals (Jacobi 1979; Smith 2020). In addition to sources of meat and fish the area also contained plant resources, edible nuts and berries, grasses and trees, as well as other materials (bark, resins and mosses, etc.) which would also have had a variety of purposes including for clothing, cordage, basketry, glues and structures, as well as medicinal uses (cf. Rackham 1989; Deakin 2008; Hurcombe 2014). The Mesolithic foreshore, too, would have provided flint and pebbles such as greywacke, which were not available inland and could be collected and used to make tools.

The landscape and environmental context of the area were very different in the Mesolithic (a period of five millennia, from around 9000 BC to around 4000 BC) from the present. Marazion Marsh and Penzance were far from coastal; the sea was 1–2 km from the current bay and St Michael's Mount was a wholly terrestrial knoll at the head of a valley with two rivers draining off into the sea. The palaeo-environmental evidence we have is largely recovered from the silts in what is now Marazion Marsh, but the early Mesolithic Mount's Bay existed as an open low-lying landscape cut by two rivers descending steeply over 2 km into a lowland basin surrounded by a mosaic of open willow woodland, with open hazel woodland on the drier slopes both within what is now Mount's Bay and extending past Marazion Marsh and Penzance itself. This mirrors the oak, ash and hazel woodland on the Isles of Scilly in the later Mesolithic (Scaife 1984; Ratcliffe & Straker 1996), as well as that at Trewaronan on the River Amble in the Camel estuary (Healy 1993), at Porthallow on the Lizard (Tinsley 1999, quoted in Wilkinson & Straker 2008, 70), and the hills above Penzance. Adjacent to the lowland rivers in what is now Mount's Bay, damper and more maritime conditions prevailed locally, just as at Trewornan where reed swamp and succeeding alder carr were present (Healy 1999c).

Many of the organic resources would of course have had seasonal availability, and Roger Jacobi (1979) suggested that the coastal areas of Cornwall and Devon would have been of greatest value to Mesolithic communities during spring, summer and autumn, with peaks of productivity in March/April and August/November. As noted above, although direct evidence for occupation in the project area is lacking and the area to the immediate north has seen little investigation, it is clear that occupation within Mount's Bay would have been part of a much wider pattern of coastal and riverine resource exploitation involving different types of settlement in terms of scale and character (eg, Allen & Gardiner 2000, 199–220; Bell 2007, 327–334; Jones *et al.* 2018).

Beyond the project area and the hills to the immediate north, the number of Mesolithic flint scatter sites increases dramatically (eg, Berridge & Roberts 1986; Jones *et al.* 2018; Conneller 2022, 337). On the western side of the Bay, fieldwalking at Clodgy Moor identified large lithic scatters, probably associated with repeated visits (Jones *et al.* 2013), whilst more extensive investigations on the Lizard peninsula to the east have revealed several significant scatters, including those at Poldowrian and Windmill Hill (Smith & Harris 1982; Smith 1987; 2020). Fifteen kilometres to the north-east are the very large number of scatters in the Gwithian area (which was not coastal then), at least one of which appears to have been the associated with the production of Group XIX greywacke tools, which were distributed around Cornwall (Jones *et al.* 2018; forthcoming). Situated at the southern end of the lower ground between the Hayle Estuary/Gwithian area, Mount's Bay would have been ideally located for groups moving between the two coasts.

No evidence has been found in the West Penwith area for longer distance connections, including maritime ones, and more generally evidence for the movement of lithics in Mesolithic Britain is scarce, in contrast with the Neolithic period (Thomas 2013, 210; Jones *et al.* forthcoming). However, given the evidence for long-distance movement of Portland chert (Stewart 2012) and possibly also for Group VI Langdale tuff (Brown *et al.* 2019; Topping 2021, 10) during the Mesolithic, and even for contact with the Continent by people at St Martins on Scilly (on the basis of the style of flintwork: Anderson-Whymark *et al.* 2015; Garrow & Sturt 2017), we cannot altogether rule out the possibility that the Mesolithic inhabitants of West Penwith and Mount's Bay were in long-distance contact with other groups of hunter-fisher-foragers.

In comparable coastal wetland and estuarine areas elsewhere, footprints representing groups of young and adult people have been discovered, demonstrating human engagement with these zones during the Mesolithic period, and confirming their importance to Mesolithic communities (Bell 2007, 298; Walker 2016; Burns 2021). While no such footprints have been found in what is now Mount's Bay or in the area of Marazion Marsh, nevertheless we can envisage groups of people, women, men and children travelling into the Bay from the surrounding areas at different times of year to hunt, harvest and collect different resources as they became available.

Neolithic

In the Neolithic, a gravel bar offshore helped to create and maintain a high coastal inland pool of brackish water, surrounded locally by *Phragmites* reed bankside marsh at Marazion, with open hazel, birch, and oak on higher land and extending onto the drier ground beyond Marazion, both seawards across the edge of the valley of what is now Mount's Bay, as well as inland. Elsewhere in Cornwall we have sparse palaeo-environmental evidence, but at Porthallow, Tinsley (1999) describes oak with an understorey of hazels, which we might expect on the hills rising above Penzance.

In terms of direct evidence for human activity in the study area, the Early Neolithic record is similar to that for the Mesolithic, being limited to a few flint objects, with the larger scatters being found on the higher ground (Fig. 1.2). Areas of clearance on the drier ground to the north seem likely but there is little evidence for direct human impact before the Chalcolithic. As with the Mesolithic period, land would have extended out to the Mount during the Early Neolithic and there would have been a diverse range of resources in the open woodland. The shared locations of some later Mesolithic and Neolithic lithic scatter sites in the wider area, for example, at Poldowrian on the Lizard and Clodgy Moor to the west (Smith & Harris 1982; Jones *et al.* 2013), might support some form of continuity with the grazing of animals also being undertaken (during the Neolithic), as in other comparable areas, such as the Severn Estuary (eg, Bell 2013, 319–322). As in other parts of the south-west there is very limited evidence for cultivation in West Penwith and, with the exception of a large rectangular house and a smaller domestic structure at Penhale Round in mid Cornwall (Nowakowski & Johns 2015), settlement activity is largely defined by deposits in pits, typically containing pottery, flint, charred hazel nutshells, charcoal and more rarely small amounts of charred grain (eg, Cole & Jones 2002–3; Jones & Lawson Jones 2018; Taylor 2022). On the whole, the contents of these pits do not, with the exceptions of the pottery and the occasional grains, differ significantly from those of the Mesolithic. As with other regions in Britain, there were significant changes in the vicinity to patterns of inhabitation, which are indicative of considerable change.

During the Early Neolithic the first tor enclosures and chamber tombs appear in the wider south-west region and three potential tor enclosures are located within West Penwith (Oswald *et al.* 2001; Whittle *et al.* 2011), in recently created local woodland clearings. The first of these potential Neolithic enclosures, as noted in Chapter 13, is situated within the project area on St Michael's Mount (Herring 2000). The evidence is, as discussed, extremely limited, although the Mount would provide an ideal locale for communal gatherings, being a distinctive place in a liminal setting. The other two potential enclosure sites are also located on very distinctive hills: Trencrom, a flat-topped hill that marks the eastern landward 'gateway' into Penwith, and the 'keel' shaped hill at Carn Galva, close to the north coast. Unfortunately, dating evidence for these sites is limited to flints, although both certainly became the foci for later prehistoric activity (Herring 1999; Jones 2016b; 2019b). All three sites would have made good places for communal gatherings at distinctive hilltops in the Neolithic and, judging by the concentration of later monuments around them, they were significant places in the landscape in later prehistory. Although there is no accompanying palaeo-environmental evidence, we would expect that these enclosures were in areas that had been cleared of open woodland, with the trees probably cleared far enough away from the enclosure banks to enable the occupants to see over the treeline and then survey the surrounding countryside – just as has been postulated for the causewayed enclosures on the chalkland of Wessex and southern England (Allen 2017b).

In contrast to the relative paucity of enclosure sites, West Penwith has the highest concentration of Early Neolithic chamber tombs in the south-west peninsula, where some six or seven examples have been documented (Kytmannow 2008; Herring 2016b; Jones 2016b; 2020a). As with the possible enclosures, these structures will have represented a wholly novel phenomenon in the south-west when they were constructed, totally alien to the Mesolithic lifestyle and its associated practices. While most of these monuments are too ruined for their original form to be discerned, one (Zennor Quoit) is a portal tomb, an Early Neolithic monument type with an Irish Sea distribution, predominantly found in Ireland (Jones 2020a, fig. 8; cf. Sheridan 2004; Lynch 2014; Darvill & Wainwright 2016), while another (Chun Quoit) may be a closed chamber of the type known from the Morbihan area of Brittany, along Britain's Atlantic façade, and around the coast of the northern half of Ireland, again of Early Neolithic date (Alison Sheridan, pers. comm.). These monuments speak of long-distance contacts by sea. Sadly, given the general non-survival of unburnt bone in Cornwall's acid soils, it has not been possible to obtain any isotopic or aDNA evidence that might endorse the idea of such contacts and movements, unlike elsewhere (eg, Wysocki & Whittle 2000; Neil *et al.* 2017; 2020; Cassidy *et al.* 2020).

A further practice which will have been wholly alien to the Mesolithic way of life in the south-west peninsula was the exploitation of the metagabbro or 'greenstone' outcrops in Penwith, including in Mount's Bay where detached pieces can also be collected as cobbles from the seashore and in the streams. (The exploited rock has been given the label 'Group I' by the formerly-named Implement Petrology Committee: Clough & Cummins 1988, 7.) No interest seems to have been shown in these rocks during the Mesolithic, probably because they are hard to work, requiring pecking and grinding. However, from the beginning of the Neolithic Group I rock was used to make distinctive green coloured axeheads, which were distributed widely across Britain (Clough & Cummins 1988; Markham & Floyd 1998; Jones *et al.* 2017). An axe-making site has recently been recorded at Clodgy Moor just beyond the western side of Mount's Bay (Jones *et al.* 2013). The recovered greenstone artefacts comprised cobbles and detached pieces, some of which could potentially come from the Mount's Bay area. No finished axeheads were recovered from the Clodgy Moor site (Jones *et al.* 2013), however, and it seems likely that they were taken away for exchange elsewhere. Large numbers of Neolithic polished axeheads from Penwith, for example, were found within the tor enclosure at Carn Brea (Mercer 1981), and it is possible that finished axeheads from the Mount's Bay area were exchanged between groups at communal enclosures. It certainly the case that beyond Cornwall 'greenstone' axeheads have been found on enclosure sites, including Hembury in Devon, Hambledon Hill in Dorset and Windmill Hill in Wiltshire (Liddle 1932; Whittle *et al.* 1999, 240; Mercer & Healy 2008, 632) and the overall distribution of Group I axeheads extends as far as northern England (Clough & Cummins 1988, maps 2 and 3). It is also tempting to see St Michael's Mount as a nodal and inviting place in the lowland landscape, as well as a potential place of exchange, perhaps like the neighbouring foreshore, which may have been a haven for travellers approaching Penwith by sea (Bradley *et al.* 2016b).

Increased evidence for human impact on the environment is detectable in the palaeo-environmental record during the later Neolithic period. The land in Mount's Bay that had vanished beneath the sea would have been noticeable to communities, who would have lost access to valuable habitats and pasture for grazing. At Marazion Marsh a sand and gravel spit was forming which cut the marshland off from the sea. The shore nearby might have been a focal point for the mooring of boats. As with the earlier part of the Neolithic, however, there are no traces of settlement, either in the coastal strip or in the hinterland on the higher ground. There are no certain Late Neolithic structures or monuments in West Penwith as a whole, although one cannot rule out the possibility that some of the stone circles may date to this period (Jones 2016b). As is the case in the rest of Cornwall, Grooved Ware forms the most substantive evidence for the Late Neolithic period (Jones & Quinnell 2011a; Taylor 2022). Most of the Grooved Ware from West Penwith is derived from surface collection from just one site at Clodgy Moor (Jones *et al.* 2013), rather than from pits (although the assemblage is likely to be derived from ploughed out features, such as pits). The presence of Grooved Ware indicates contact with the wider world, since this type of pottery, long-lived and invented in Orkney, has an extensive distribution across Britain and Ireland (cf. for example, MacSween *et al.* 2015; Carlin 2017; Parker Pearson *et al.* 2020).

From the foregoing discussion it seems likely that for much of the Neolithic Mount's Bay continued to be visited to make use of a range of resources. In the Early Neolithic, advantage may have been taken of the areas of grassland, with cattle being grazed. Flint would have continued to be collected by women and men from the shore, but it is likely that this was now supplemented by the collection of waterworn 'greenstone' cobbles which were fashioned into axeheads. By the end of the period, loss of land would have changed access to resources, narrowing the range of those resources and their geographical availability. Lithic resources would still have been available for collection on the shore but the environment would have become less diverse, and patterns of grazing and hunting changed. The formation of sandy spits and beaches, however, might have provided safe havens 'in-between' zones where exchange, including of axeheads, with more distant communities could have taken place. It is, however, in the Bronze Age that we see the most significant evidence for wider contacts both in Mount's Bay and the wider West Penwith area.

Chalcolithic/earlier Bronze Age

The Chalcolithic is marked, in Britain, by the appearance of Beaker pottery and metal use, among other novelties (eg, Needham 2012; Parker Pearson *et al.* 2019). None of Beakers in the south-west is of the earliest, Continental forms (Quinnell 2003; Jones & Quinnell 2006b) and the only Beaker from Mount's Bay is the single, burnt sherd of domestic ware found within the Late Bronze Age cist at the Penzance Heliport barrow site (Chapter 3). In

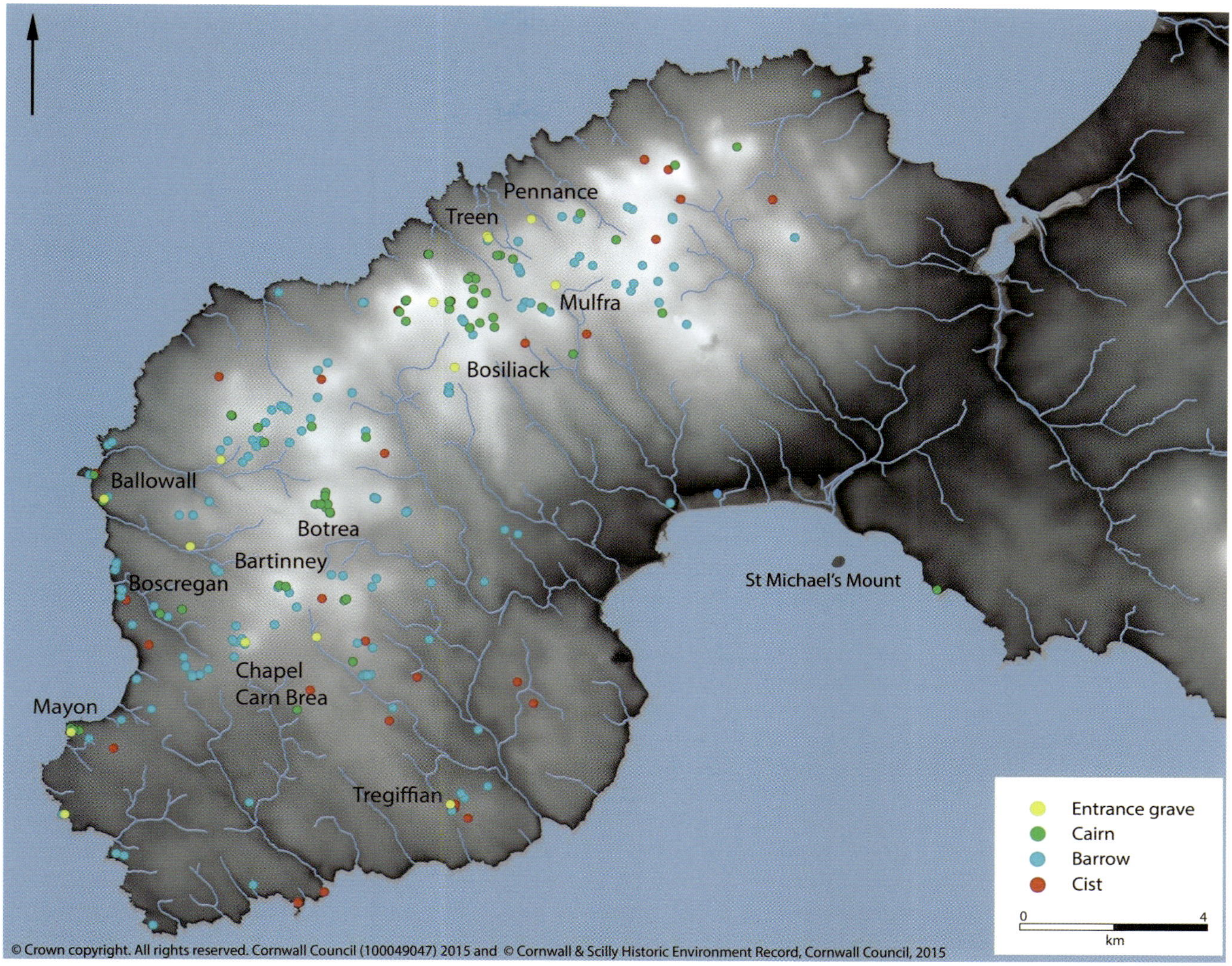

Figure 14.2: Map showing the location of Early Bronze Age entrance graves, cairns, barrows and cists. The figure shows the spread of ceremonial monuments across the Penwith landscape, especially to the north of Mount's Bay

the broader West Penwith area several Beaker-associated sites are known, and they represent a significant concentration in the wider south-west peninsula (Jones 2016b). By themselves, Beakers do not necessarily prove evidence for long distance communications and again there is no aDNA evidence available either to support or to refute models of population replacement which have been posited for other parts of Britain (eg, Olalde *et al.* 2018). Crucially, however, at the western end of the peninsula near Zennor a domestic Beaker structure was uncovered. Radiocarbon dating revealed occupation dated to *c.* 2300–2100 cal BC and the character of the architecture suggested that the use of the structure was probably short-lived (Jones *et al.* 2012). Of considerable significance is the fact that recent work on the stonework assemblage associated with the structure has revealed evidence for the processing of cassiterite pebbles to produce tin (Carey *et al.* 2022). In Britain tin was first mixed with copper to make bronze, using tin from south-west Britain, around 2200 BC (Fontijn 2009; Haustein *et al.* 2010; Bray & Pollard 2012; Radivojević *et al.* 2018), and the new evidence from Sennen suggests that some of this tin is likely to be from West Penwith. As with the earlier Neolithic axeheads, a potential place where tin could be exchanged is Mount's Bay, a place which, in the later Bronze Age, certainly has a strong connection with metallurgy (Chapter 12).

No Early Bronze Age settlements (*c.* 2200–1500 cal BC) have been identified either in the project area or within West Penwith as a whole, although just to the east, at Gwithian on the north Cornish coast, a roundhouse structure and areas of cultivation dating to this time have been identified, preserved within blown sand (Nowakowski *et al.* 2007). Cultivation is indicated on the land above the Penzance Heliport site and pasture was established in the vicinity of Marazion Marsh. The chief evidence for human activity in the Early Bronze Age comes in the form of cists, barrows, cairns and entrance graves (Fig. 14.2), and unstratified finds of lithics. Virtually all of these sites and finds are located on the higher ground to the north and west of Mount's Bay; the Penzance Heliport barrow is the only known example situated within the lower-lying coastal strip (although other unrecorded sites might exist).

Regarding Early Bronze Age funerary monuments, barrows have already been discussed in Chapter 13. Entrance graves are a megalithic form of funerary monument, featuring a small chamber encased within a small round cairn with large kerbstones (Jones & Thomas 2010). Once thought to be of Neolithic date, it is now firmly believed that they were constructed and used during the Early Bronze Age (Jones & Thomas 2010; Jones & Quinnell 2022). As with the much earlier, Early Neolithic portal tombs, they have a distinctive Irish Sea distribution, with West Penwith being the only place on the south-west peninsula where they have been found. Concentrations are known from the Isles of Scilly and the Tramore area of south-east Ireland, while one probable example is known from Ballakelly on the Isle of Man and other, similar monuments are known from the Channel Islands (Jones & Thomas 2010; Kirkham 2011; Sawyer 2015; Lynch & Davey 2017, 84). The entrance graves of West Penwith thus reflect contacts with the wider world (Jones, forthcoming a), potentially via the harbour given the comparative safety of the haven, with people mooring their boats in the Mount's Bay area.

The Bronze Age

The Bronze Age saw the greatest changes to the landscape. There is evidence for the clearance of trees during the Early Bronze Age and the Penzance Heliport barrow was constructed on colluvium that was derived from earlier upslope cultivation. A hard beach edge may also have formed and at Marazion Marsh the sand and gravel spit was well established. At Marazion Marsh there is less evidence for direct human impact, although in the later Bronze Age the palaeo-environmental record suggests that the surrounding area comprised an open environment used for pasture. As we have seen and demonstrated (Chapters 12 & 13), much of the direct human activity relates to metalwork deposition and ceremonial activity in the Bay.

By the later Bronze Age the Mount's Bay area would certainly have been settled, with some parts being cultivated and others used for grazing. Open areas of rough grassland would have provided valuable pasture. From the Middle Bronze Age the drier parts are likely to have been dotted with the dispersed roundhouse settlements which are known from across Cornwall. Lithic resources are likely to have declined in importance during the Bronze Age: there is, for example, little interest in the greenstones which had been so widely worked and exchanged to distant communities throughout the Neolithic.

Whilst the environment and landscape had become more managed, with open areas for grazing and the establishment of field systems, at Marazion more subtle changes were afoot. By the mature Bronze Age we can start to see the retardation of the brackish influences in the Marazion pool. Although it retained muddy edges, brambles increased and damp woodland developed on its margins, but the water mass itself became less brackish and more strongly freshwater. The consequence was to leave brighter, clearer water, in contrast to other briny coastal pools in Cornwall which were dulled by the halocitic content. Was it this bright water that attracted the deposition of so many metalwork hoards (see Fig. 12.1, and below)?

Unlike the preceding periods there is also a clear division in the character of human activity between the Chalcolithic/Early Bronze Age (*c.* 2500–1600 cal BC) and the later Bronze Age from around 1600 cal BC to 800 cal BC.

Middle and Late Bronze Age

The Middle and Late Bronze Age of West Penwith, like most areas of Britain, witnessed a decline in ceremonial monument construction but an increase in the construction of houses (eg, Brück 2000; Johnston 2020, 164). More widely in Cornwall the middle centuries of the 2nd millennium BC saw the development of widespread settlements which, in the uplands, featured stone-walled houses (eg, Johnson & Rose 1994; Nowakowski 2016a; Jones & Kirkham 2021) and in the lowlands, featured a distinctive form of roundhouse which was set within a hollow (eg, Nowakowski 1991; Jones *et al.* 2015). In West Penwith as a whole, no hollow-set roundhouses have been identified to date, and the Middle Bronze Age settlement that is known is largely found in the upland areas to the north of Mount's Bay (Fig. 14.3). Evidence for Middle Bronze Age activity within the vicinity of the study area is limited to activities at the Heliport barrow site and some metalwork finds including the hoard from Tredarvah (Pearce & Padley 1977). However, it is very likely that the area was fully settled in the Middle Bronze Age, with small groups of roundhouses being scattered throughout areas of cultivation and pasture.

As for Late Bronze Age activity, it is during this time that we see the first evidence for occupation on St Michael's Mount (which by now was on its way to becoming an island), in the form of house platforms and Plain Ware ceramics (Herring 2000). The form of the houses is, however, unknown as the platforms have not been fully excavated. Elsewhere in lowland Cornwall the few known Late Bronze Age houses are defined by post-rings, which were no longer set in hollows (eg, Jones & Taylor 2010; Gossip 2021). Across the rest of West Penwith the identified examples of Late Bronze Age occupation take the form of the reuse of older Middle Bronze Age stone-walled roundhouses, as at Bodrifty and Bosiliack (Dudley 1956; Jones & Quinnell 2011b; Nowakowski 2016b) (Fig. 14.3).

Returning to Mount's Bay, the settlement on St Michael's Mount could arguably have arisen because the eastern end of the bay was becoming increasingly used as a place to moor boats, close to an area where tin and copper could be obtained. Metalworking and the deposition of metalwork certainly play a significant part in the activities taking place in Mount's Bay during the Late Bronze Age. As we have seen, bronze and copper from various sources would have been essential to make Cornish tin at this time. No Bronze Age boats are known from Cornwall but elsewhere, discoveries of sewn plank vessels dating to the Middle Bronze Age (in the case of the Dover Boat) and the Early Bronze Age (in the case of the boats from North Ferriby in the East Riding of Yorkshire) would have been capable of sailing along the coast and across open water (Wright *et al.* 1989; Clark 2004; Van de Noort 2006). Cargoes of bronze artefacts from suspected wrecked vessels found Langdon Bay in Kent and Salcombe Bay in Devon (Needham *et al.* 2013) certainly demonstrate movement of metalwork, and the St Michael's Mount hoard shares characteristics with those in south-east England and Atlantic France (Knight 2022, 123). Moreover, recent chemical and isotopic analysis of tin and copper ingots and bronze artefacts from the Salcombe Bay shipwrecks (Berger *et al.* 2022) indicates the use of tin from the south-west and copper from much more diverse Continental sources. This points to the ore-rich regions of Cornwall and Devon playing a key role in the Late Bronze Age circulation of tin around (and possibly even beyond) Europe. It therefore seems likely that, during the Late Bronze Age there were a series of established places to come ashore along the south coast of Britain (eg, Cunliffe 1987; 1988). Although the bulk transportation of material, as suggested by the Salcombe and Langdon Bay finds, does point towards some form of organised commerce, the exchange of metals in the Bronze Age is likely to have differed significantly from modern conceptions of trade and economy, being deeply embedded in social relations rather than a form of modern capitalism (Kristiansen & Larsson 2005, 48–51; Brück & Fontijn 2013). Such exchanges may, to some extent, have been linked with extended kinship networks (such as might be identified through stable isotope and aDNA evidence, were unburnt human bone to survive in the area: cf. McKinley *et al.* 2014, 93–144; Patterson *et al.* 2022). It could be that some voyages were undertaken to obtain and exchange gifts which were probably considered to be supernaturally charged (Helms 1988; Wilkin & Vander Linden 2015; Johnston 2020).

The Iron Age/Roman period

There are no known open settlements of Iron Age or Roman date within the project area and little of the palaeo-environmental information gathered by the project directly relates to these periods. However, as was the case in the Late Bronze Age, it is likely that settlements did exist on the better-drained land, possibly in locations which were enclosed and

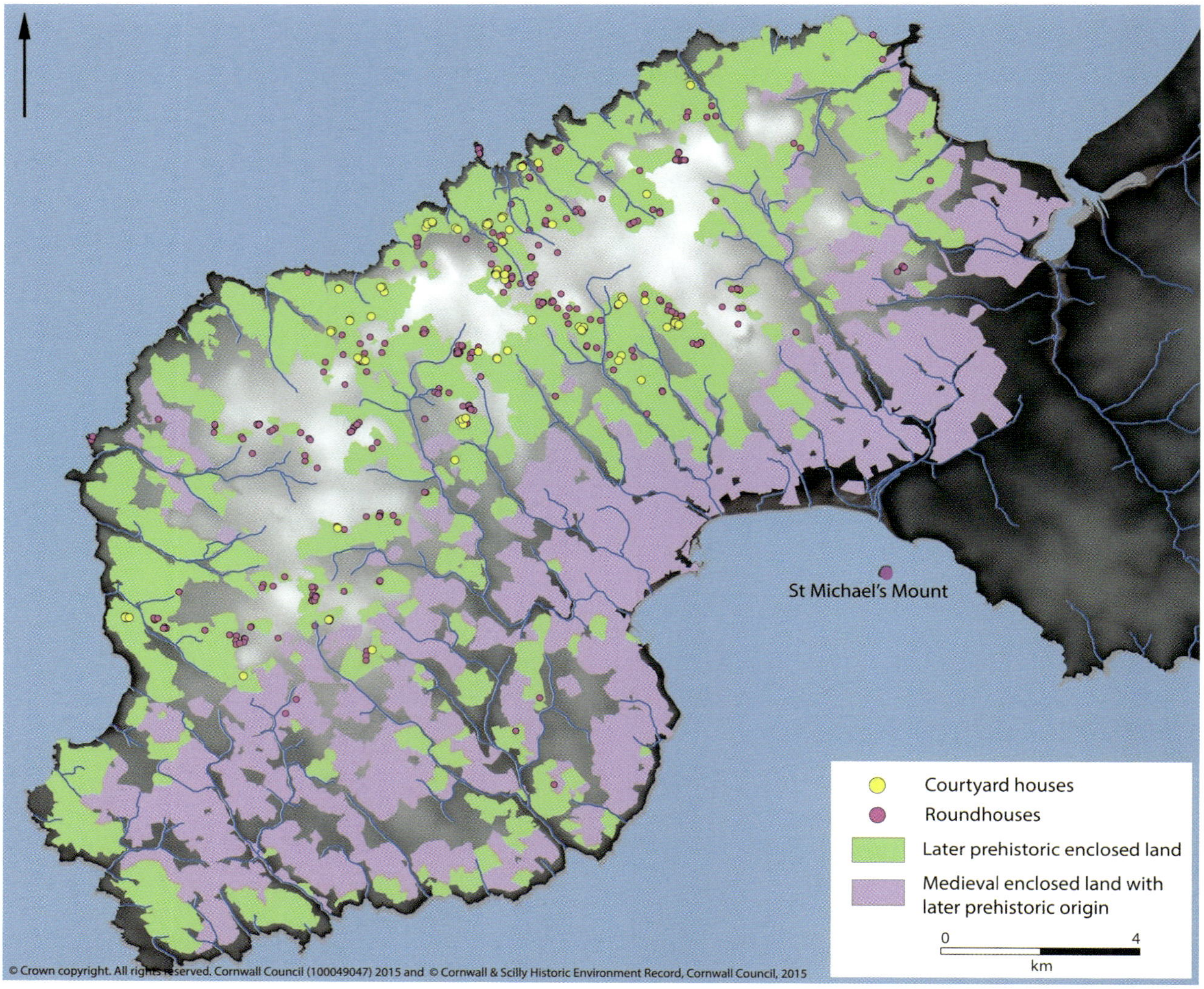

Figure 14.3: Map showing the location of prehistoric enclosed land (Bronze Age, Iron Age and Roman periods) and distribution of known roundhouses and courtyard houses

which subsequently became settlements in the medieval period. It is also certain that the area would have been farmed throughout the Iron Age and Roman periods (see Fig. 14.3). This assertion is supported by archaeological work undertaken elsewhere in West Penwith. To the north of the project area in the higher lying parts of West Penwith, survey has identified extensive areas of ancient fields (Nowakowski 2016b). Recent OSL dating of field boundaries at Bosigran has revealed a chronology starting in the Middle Bronze Age and continuing through the Iron Age and beyond (Vervust *et al.* 2020). Likewise, the excavations, albeit rather limited, of roundhouses at Bodrifty and Bosiliack (Dudley 1956; Jones 2013b) have produced similar results, with evidence for structures being reused in the Iron Age. The landscape continued to be more open and farmed, colluvium occurred locally and at Marazion Marsh brackish water started to recede and much of the Marazion pool would have been freshwater.

The Iron Age and Roman period was one of one of increasing enclosure, albeit of different types. Although it is possible that the hilltop enclosures which appear in the south-west peninsula, like those in Ireland or parts of western Britain, may have had their origins in the Late Bronze Age (cf. Brown 2009; Jones 2010; O'Brien & O'Driscoll 2017), current dating would suggest an earlier Iron Age date for their construction with a decline in the Late Iron Age (Sharples 2010, 70–75; Pope *et al.* 2020). Two or three sites – Castle-an-Dinas, Lescudjack, and potentially St Michael's Mount

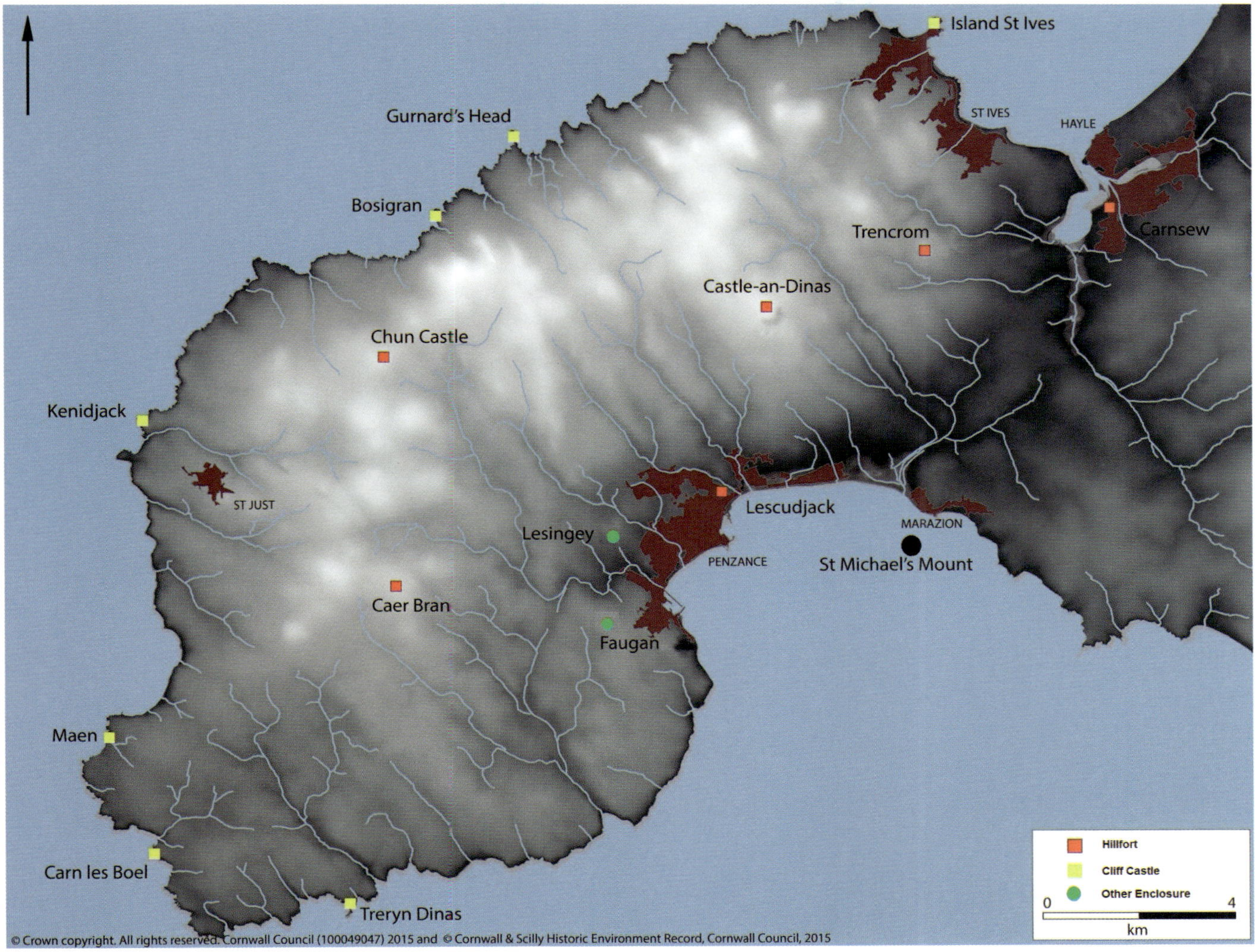

Figure 14.4: Map showing the location prehistoric hilltop enclosures in West Penwith

– have been identified within, or close to, our study area (Fig. 14.4). Two further enclosure sites on the western side of Penzance, Lesingey and Faugan, have also sometimes been referred to as hillforts. There is, however, little to distinguish them from later enclosures, such as rounds (Kirkham, forthcoming) which are ubiquitous in the landscape during the Roman period.

In the Iron Age the project area was overlooked by the three aforementioned hilltop enclosure sites. The first, Castle-an-Dinas, Ludgvan, lies to the north of the coastal strip but has good views over the project area. The hillfort is undated but it may be the earliest of the three hilltop enclosures in the surrounding area, and is potentially comparable to other circular enclosures which have been argued to have later 2nd to earlier 1st millennium BC origins (Jones 2010; 2016b). Castle-an-Dinas is a circular multivallate site containing the remains of a possible cairn. The enclosure is unexcavated, although possible 'huts' and an infilled well were recorded by Borlase (1769, 346–347) within in the interior.

The second major hilltop enclosure, at Lescudjack, lies at the western end of Mount's Bay and might have been sited to dominate approaches into the Bay. Today the enclosure lies within Penzance and is now part of the urban landscape, being surrounded by houses and partly covered by allotments (Fig. 14.5). Limited geophysical survey and small-scale test pitting revealed little in the way of dating evidence but, in common with Castle-an-Dinas, it has commanding views over the Bay and it is possible that the ramparts were designed to be impressive from the sea (Kirkham,

Figure 14.5: Lescudjack hillfort. This enclosure has been absorbed into the eastern edge of modern-day Penzance (Photograph: Historic Environment, Cornwall Council)

Figure 14.6: St Michael's Mount on a winter's day. Its identification as an Iron Age cliff castle is uncertain, however, it would have been a dominant feature at the eastern end of the bay with a harbour (Photograph: Andy M. Jones)

forthcoming), and of course to travellers entering the bay aboard sea-going vessels.

The last and most famous potential enclosure site is St Michael's Mount (Fig. 14.6), which overlooks and dominates the eastern end of the Bay. This site has been suggested to be an Iron Age cliff castle (eg, Nowakowski 2016b, 185). However, there are no securely identified earthworks or artefacts of later Iron Age date known from the island. The Mount has often and long been described as being *Ictis* or an *Ictis* site, the place where overseas voyagers came to obtain tin and copper. It seems likely that tin in particular would have continued to be important. However, more distant contacts are, in fact, less well attested in the Iron Age of Cornwall than in other parts of southern Britain. Although a few finds of pre-Roman Conquest amphorae are known (Fitzpatrick 2013; Gossip 2021), Breton pottery is scarce in Cornwall as a whole in comparison to Hengistbury Head, and pre-Roman coinage is also rare (Penhallurick 2009, 272). It may be, therefore, that either many of the vessels entering Mount's Bay came along the coast (Cunliffe 2009), or else that ceramics were not a medium for exchange and perishable materials such as fine textiles worth their weight in gold were preferred (Randsborg 2011) in exchange for tin and copper. As has been argued for another Iron Age coastal port at Poole in Dorset, where few imported ceramics are found in the surrounding hinterland (Wilkes *et al.* 2021), it is possible that communities and individuals each acted in a local social sphere, with those on the coast being linked with more distant communities to form a far wider network.

Behind the hard shoreline people would have continued to farm, with spaces potentially becoming bounded by ditch-defined fields. Towards the end of the Iron Age small enclosures started to appear in the Cornish landscape (Quinnell 2019; Jones & Kirkham 2021, 333–345), a trend which certainly increases after the Roman Conquest. Although direct settlement evidence in the project area is scanty in the Roman period, on the surrounding areas of higher ground there are numerous 'round' type enclosures similar to those found elsewhere in Cornwall (eg, Quinnell 2004) and the distinctive courtyard house settlements, such as Chysauster, which are unique to West Penwith on the Cornish mainland (Hencken 1933; Nowakowski 2016b) (Fig. 14.7). Within Penzance itself, archaeological recording at the Penzance College site revealed settlement evidence associated with a round (an enclosed settlement) and a field system of Late Iron Age to Roman date (Gossip 2010). The available evidence strongly suggests that, as in other parts of Cornwall, there was increasing evidence for settlement activity in West Penwith, of both an enclosed and open type, as well as an increasing number of ditched field systems off the moorland areas (Quinnell 2019; Jones & Kirkham 2021). The number of coins, both as stray finds and especially in hoards, also dramatically increases, such as those found in Marazion Marsh (Penhallurick 2009; Bland *et al.* 2020). As discussed in Chapter 12, deposition of the coins at Marazion is likely to have been votive in nature, rather than relating to commercial exchange or the hiding of personal wealth.

St Michael's Mount is likely to have continued to be a focal point for seafaring travellers, perhaps hinted at by the discovery of a Roman coin on the island. Communities in the area are still likely to have had strong maritime connections but potentially such connections increasingly occurred at centres along the coast which, after the Conquest, would have been subject to Roman control and taxation. The imposition of Roman control and taxation undoubtedly had repercussions for local social organisation and identity. New settlement types (for example courtyard houses) and more localised forms of artefact appeared (Jones 2021; Thomas 2021; Frieman *et al.* 2022).

Living with a drowning landscape: response and reflection

From the preceding section and the earlier chapters, it is clear that Mount's Bay was a dynamic landscape in terms of its changing environmental conditions and the resources it offered. As time moved on, the changing character of the land altered people's relationships with their environment, and its non-human inhabitants changed too. It is also clear that activities in and around Mount's Bay did not occur independently of those that happened elsewhere in the south-west peninsula; the project area was integrated into wider patterns of inhabitation. Likewise, at various times the opportunities for longer-distance travel by sea were clearly exploited. Far from being a marginal place on the edge of Atlantic Europe, then, Mount's Bay (and West Penwith more generally) was involved in much wider networks of interaction, featuring (among other things) kinship ties and reciprocal exchange.

Naturally, the loss of land through submergence will have presented challenges and opportunities to communities. The tangible archaeological evidence tends to reflect the latter, with for example the development of Mount's Bay as a probable centre for exchange activities during the Late Bronze Age arguably relating to improved access for boats occasioned by the development of a sand and gravel spit (as discussed below). The 'other side of the coin' would, however, have been one of emotional separation from old areas of grazing and the inability to visit 'old' remembered places which had become inaccessible. In

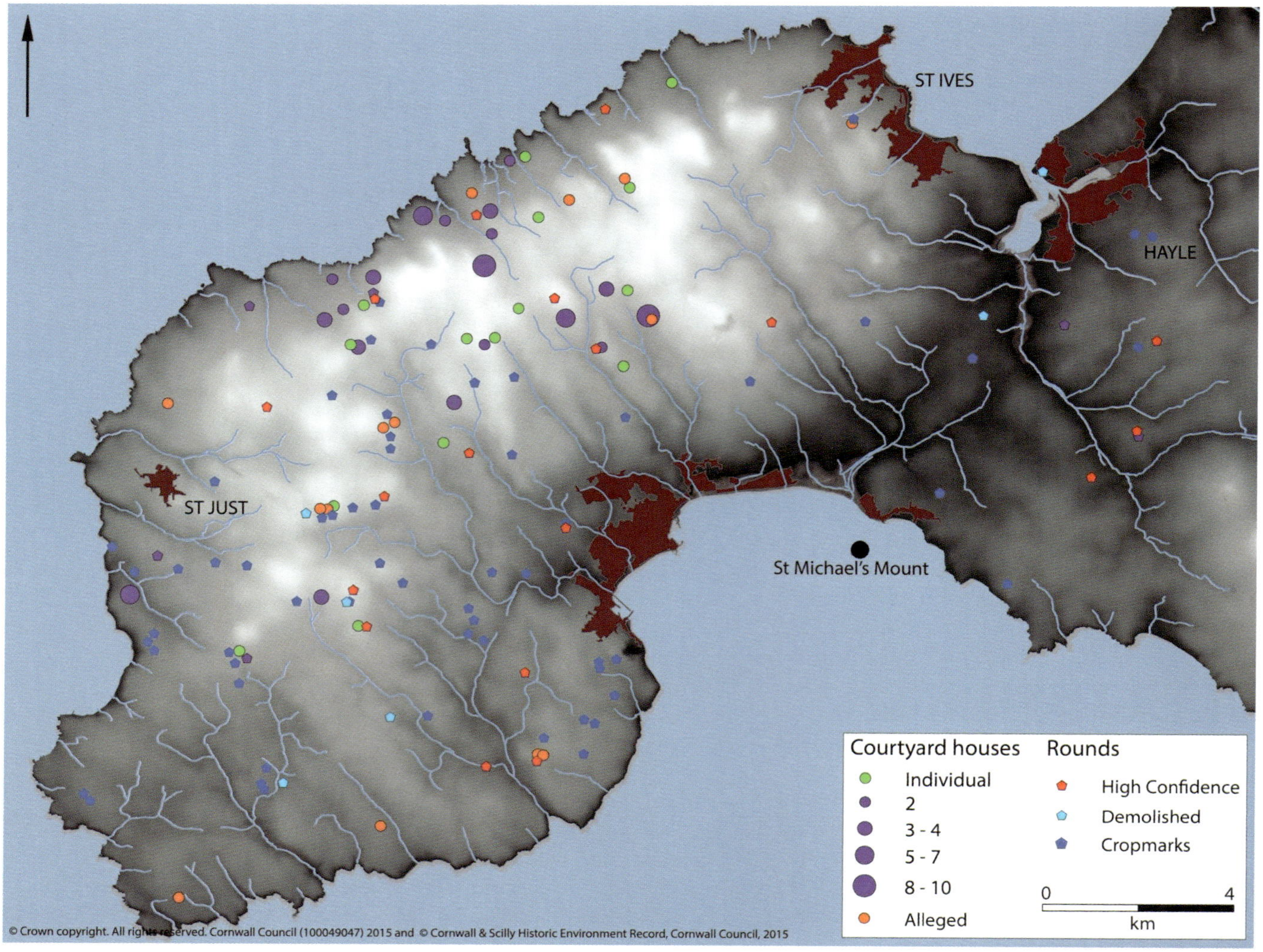

Figure 14.7: Map showing the distribution of rounds and courtyard house settlements in West Penwith

certain ways, memories and stories of those lost landscapes will have continued to linger, with the remains of the ancient tree stumps of the submerged forests, exposed by winter storms, providing a reminder (Figs 10.3, 14.8 & 14.9; Chapter 15).

We now turn to consider ecological changes and the social responses to them.

Rising sea-levels

Although a rise in sea-level can occur quickly, especially when perceived from an archaeological timescale, on a personal timescale it can vary from being imperceptible, to be noticeable as a gradual change over the course of a lifetime or even a generation (*c.* 25 years) (Wickham-Jones 2018, 21). Although rising sea-level, and ultimately the drowning of the landscape, does entail flooding and submergence, the process need not necessarily involve rapid flooding and a rapid transformation from dry land or coastal margin to a submerged landscape, such as may be occasioned by the breaching of a barrier. It may be gradual, and may take the form of changes in groundwater levels, flood events, and, significantly, in the salinisation of bodies of water in the lower courses of rivers and streams.

Flooding, topography and access

Here we briefly consider the potential effects on land and society of the more gradual, almost imperceptible change that we think occurred at Mount's Bay, and many other archaeological landscapes. Inundation is not as simple as

Figure 14.8: The submerged forest at low tide at Mount's Bay with St Michael's Mount in the distance. All the dark lumps are tree stumps of the former forest (Image © Gregory Martin, Cornwall Live)

just the loss of former coastal, near-coastal, and low-lying land. Submergence of inland waterways, low-lying pastures and valleys can shape topography and perceptions of the landscape, making access to areas that were formerly on well-trodden pathways difficult or impossible. Locations can become isolated and separated as points in the landscape and may become more significant topographically as blocks of landscape around them are removed by the sea. Rivers widened as valley floors became inundated. Consequently, flow rates in rivers and waterways decreased, resulting in increased sedimentation infilling channels, pools and lagoons, while the tidal range extended further inland, introducing saline water further upstream. This potentially led to a wholesale change in the perception of the landscape and territory, and of how it articulated and could be utilised. Mobility and long-established pathways and routes to and from, and across, the land may have had to be renegotiated and reset, and links and systems redesigned and rebuilt. The advancing sea was likely to have been attributed agency and identity; it became necessity to build a new relationship with the land.

The cumulative effect of the loss of land, loss of resources and changing hydrology would arguably have been a restructuring of communities within and across the landscape. This may have entailed social re-organisation and the re-establishment (or new creation) of mobility patterns and routes across the landscape, as well as the development of new regimes of land use and exploitation. Reduction in land and territory could have resulted in increased social interaction of various kinds (including violence or by contrast co-operation) and could have led to changes in social organisation, material culture, monuments and settlement structures. Finally, it was not all about inundation; increases in groundwater, higher moisture, dampening soils and the accumulation of water in groundwater pools all potentially resulted in significant changes.

Figure 14.9: Tree stump in the Mount's Bay submerged forest (Image © Gregory Martin, Cornwall Live)

Environmental change

Coastal systems are dynamic, complex and non-linear; small changes can have large implications. But environmental change is not an external force 'out there' (Leary 2015, 45); it is an inseparable part of community life, which can be entangled with social structure, economy, location and ritual. The impact of rising sea-levels can thus be much wider than merely the loss of land and a change in the coastline, as Charman *et al.* (2016, figs 9.4–9.8) have elegantly documented for the Isle of Scilly. Sea-level rise has a number of implications, several of which have been rehearsed previously (eg, Clark 1960; Smith *et al.* 1989) and summarised by Leary (2015, 46). These include:

- Submergence and loss of land.
- Erosion of deposits.
- Increased flooding and storm damage.
- Saltwater ingression into aquafers and waterways.
- Rising groundwater tables.
- Changing tidal regimes.
- Changes to river and estuary morphology.
- Reduced (or changing) territories.
- Loss or change of resources including food resources.

Some of these are explored in more detail below.

Salinisation

Barely perceptible changes in the groundwater and tidal reaches in rivers will have resulted in salinisation of previous fresh drinking water, turning it sour and undrinkable for both humans and animals. Freshwater fish, river life and adjacent vegetation would have been killed and eradicated from parts of the landscape, changing the ecology and resource potential permanently. However, just as significant, salinisation can result in loss of winter pasture, loss of woodland, change in ecology of the woods, and change in many freshwater and ground plants. Dramatic changes can occur in the ground plant ecology without massive changes in water levels or inundation, yet these are still a direct consequence of rising sea-levels. Salinisation can have a considerable effect on the potential food resources of the landscape, such as through the loss and changing distribution of some fruits, berries, nuts and edible fungi. The loss of some plants may also have diminished the range of wild animal species in the area (wild boar, deer and small wild herbivores, etc), and may also have changed their migration patterns (eg, Brisset & Fernández López de Pablo 2022). Salinisation will also have affected browsed, grazed land and pasture, especially that used for winter grazing. Such changing grazing and browsing patterns will, in turn, have had consequences for the ecology, the combined effect of which could be a dramatic change in the vegetation cover of the low-lying land, despite only subtle changes to the obvious or readily visible ground conditions – perhaps wetter moister ground locally, and larger pools of shallow ground water in the winter.

Unlike inundation and transgression, which can be rapid flood events transforming the landscape 'overnight' and ejecting population from a region, the salinisation and increases in groundwater will have been more gradual processes, occurring over a generational or centurial scale, or longer. They will have had the potential to reshape and resculpture the dynamics and distribution of societal activity, to transform aspects of food procurement strategies (hunting, gathering, crop growing and animal husbandry), and even to have repercussions for societal organisation, ritual and religion and burial. It may have taken time for people to perceive the environmental changes, and reactions to these changes will have varied according to the resilience of the inhabitants (Readman 2005; Bergström 2018; Rashidian 2021). The embedded traditions of organised social activities and practices, including routines involved in subsistence strategies, will no doubt have created a degree of inertia in the process of change.

Ecologies

Changing ecology is not just loss of species, but changes in species composition and species populations, some of which can be profound (Spikins 1999; Macklin *et al.* 2000; Tipping 2004; Tipping & Tisdall 2004). In Mount's Bay over time we can see a decrease and loss in some dryland species and an increase in halophytes, and changes in the woodland ecology in terms of species composition, density, openness and ground fauna. Where woodland had formerly existed, its traces remained as wooden stumps left residing in shallow waters off the coast, as ghostly reminders of the past. The loss of woodland will have meant a loss of firewood – probably the most utilised resource – and also of timber for dwellings, structures and fences, and (importantly for coastal communities) for boat building. While this may be a loss of economic resources, it may be a gain in stories, myth and legend.

Community resilience

Some of the changes in the environment – the drowning of the landscape, changes in salinity and ecologies – will have had a profound effect on the ecosystems and on the resource potential of the land, and thus directly on the communities who lived in, and off, the land and seascape. As the landscape changed and its potential changed, the communities residing here and utilising this landscape could have responded by either moving out and moving on or, as recent analysis of Late Bronze Age data from Ireland suggests (Armit *et al.* 2014), by being resilient, and adapting their lifestyles, their food procurement strategies and their rituals to the new and changing circumstances. People's memories of the past could have become woven into myths and legends about the past.

The themes of gradual change and human responses to it that are addressed here with regard to the Penzance landscape have a wider resonance for any (prehistoric) drowned landscape, such as the Isles of Scilly, the Channel Islands, the Severn Estuary or the Humber Estuary. We are dealing with change that cannot be discerned from one year to the next, nor one decade to the next, but over the course of a lifetime, with memories of that change being passed down from one generation to the next. The resulting myths and memories could have been retold, altered, embellished and misremembered. The changes detailed here will not only have affected the people living in Mount's Bay and utilising its changing suite of resources, but also *any* communities that may have used any of the resources that that landscape offered. Thus, the social and economic effects of the changing landscape throughout prehistory will have affected a wider area than Mount's Bay alone.

Resilience and perception

Despite changes in the ecologies and landscape, and in spite of increased difficulties in procuring or producing food as a result, societies have a tendency to 'stick with it' beyond the point of economic sense because of tradition, organisation, social cohesion and belonging, and this resilience may typically be seen in landscapes under gradual and developmental change. An enduring sense of place, ownership, identity and belonging is likely to delay the inevitable requirement to move, regroup and restructure. For communities, it was not a case of simply moving, translocating and creating the same way of life anew in a slightly different location. They will have had a long and profound connection with that landscape; their traditional way of life was long-lived and familiar, and giving it up will not have been easy (eg, Arenstam Gibbons & Nicholls 2006 on the abandonment of an island by its community in Chesapeake Bay, America). Translocation often results in a loss of identity and the loss of traditions and rituals (Leary 2015, 65); social cohesion can decline and traditional structures of power and authority may be challenged as new practices are adopted. The same community can consequently look archaeologically different in terms of its material culture and the design and layout of its settlements and other structures: new tools and toolkits might need to be developed, while old tools fall into disuse, for example (Torry 1978; Few *et al.* 2004). In such circumstances, then, it is no wonder that the remembrance of landscape form and past societies often leads to storytelling and myth of ancient lands lost to the sea, as has been shown by recent study of Australian Aboriginal oral stories, which have been passed down over many generations (eg, Nunn & Cook 2022). In a south-west context, there is of course the myth of the submergence of the land of Lyonesse.

Shadows of past landscapes, and the evocative ghostly stumps of former forests (Figs 10. 3 & 14.8), are key ingredients of stories and myths and show that inundation is not just a simple loss of land closing the door on former landscapes and taskscapes. Over time the changes will have constituted the loss of a remembered world and possibly the loss of a sense of place for the community, and of its ancestors, who will have needed to be 'accommodated' in the new location and in the new, changed lifestyle.

Resilience and connectivity in the later Bronze Age

As discussed above, the increasing salinisation and the eventual loss of terrain had detrimental implications for the management of, and access to, land and resources by communities who used the Bay for generations. However, one development in the later Bronze Age could have enabled some communities around the Bay area to become more deeply engaged in the extensive exchange networks that existed at the time. This was the formation of a gravel and sand spit to the north of St Michael's Mount in the later Bronze Age, creating a long sandy beach forming seaward of the gravel spit and making the Bay a suitable place to beach heavy wooden vessels (cf. Van de Noort *et al.* 2014) that could have been used to transport the tin and other metals that may have been exploited in West Penwith. Prior to the later Bronze Age, the approach to the Bay would have been a shallow muddy expanse that was less than inviting for seagoing vessels. The formation of the sand spit meant that the Mount's Bay area had the potential to become a place of exchange. The Mount may have provided a prominent navigational focal point for seagoing vessels, akin to those suggested to have existed along the coasts of the south-west peninsula (eg, Griffith & Wilkes 2006). It may be no coincidence that it was at this time that we see evidence for the first house platforms being constructed on St Michael's Mount and the ceremonial and depositional activities discussed in Chapters 12 and 13 being undertaken.

Furthermore, as Hencken (1932, 182) noticed long ago, the low-lying ground on the eastern side of the Bay would have been partly navigable at this time, thereby providing the shortest and easiest overland portage route to the Hayle Estuary and thence to the northern part of the Atlantic façade (that is to say, the Irish Sea zone), including Wales and Ireland. Along this 6 km route, cargoes and/or boats could have been transported without the need to travel around the treacherous Land's End peninsula to the west. Evidence for the importance of this route can be seen in the many Bronze

Age metalwork finds already documented at Marazion Bay and also in smaller numbers of findspots in the area around Hayle and in the vicinity of the potential cross-country route (Fig. 12.8). Notable deposits of later Bronze Age metalwork have, for example, been found at Ludgvan, Lelant and St Earth (Hitchins 1806; Pearce 1983; 405, 406, 413; Knight *et al.* 2015, 31, 33). Interestingly, however, the hoards located to the north of Mount's Bay do not include ingots, possibly suggesting the movement or exchange of different categories of artefact northwards.

It is, therefore, perhaps unsurprising that the formation of the beach enabled Mount's Bay and West Penwith to become increasingly drawn into the extensive Atlantic network of contacts (as documented, for example, in Cunliffe 2015), extending into Continental Europe. Mount's Bay and West Penwith thus effectively became part of what Stuart Needham has referred to as a 'maritory' (Needham 2009), and the Bay became one of a series of 'special' places which were located along the southern British coastline in the Late Bronze Age (Bradley 2021, 117–146). This was no doubt in part due to the proximity of the area to sources of tin and copper. As the waters rose and the shoreline hardened, the sandy expanse of Mount's Bay behind the spit provided ideal conditions for seagoing vessels to come ashore. For the first time, the coastal strip here became a central focus for communal practices on a scale greater than that witnessed hitherto, and long-distance maritime social relations came to the fore.

Freshwater pools and metalwork deposition

Many Cornish rivers were saltwater during the Mesolithic and earlier Neolithic periods, including the rivers at Marazion, fed by the deep channel running through buried channels in Mount's Bay (Camm 1999) which are now offshore and 35–40 m below OD. This channel enabled the ingress of salty water and brackish conditions upstream past what was to become Marazion Marsh, despite the horizontal distance and vertical altitude difference between land and sea. At Marazion, however, sedimentation and silting in the valley occurred faster than sea-level rose and, combined with the offshore sand bar, this prevented the development of the brackish conditions seen in many other rivers. In fact, while the tidal head (ie, maximum extent of the tide upriver) was moving up many rivers during the Middle to Late Bronze Age, it was probably moving down the river flowing into the Marazion pool or bay, increasing the body of freshwater rather than lessening it, because of spit and bar formation. And while coastal pools of water were becoming brackish, cloudy and sandy, that at Marazion was becoming clearer and brighter freshwater (open pools of fresh, rather than brackish water). Saline and salt-laden water is duller, greyer and reflects less light than freshwater, which is often described as bright and sparkly. Such differences would not have been lost on past communities.

It was around the time when we see the change to a much more significant body of freshwater at Marazion that the by now ancient enclosure barrow on the Heliport site was enhanced by the addition of a charcoal-rich mantle, covering cists that are of Late Bronze Age date (Chapter 13). By comparison with many Bronze Age funerary and ceremonial monuments in Britain, its location is somewhat unusual; it is not atop a hill, nor situated to be false-crested or seen from a location on the horizon (except perhaps from the lowland to the shore-line of what is now Penzance). The barrow is sited at the foot of the rising hillside, and at the back, not front, edge of a weakly defined terrace running behind what is now Penzance. Why is the barrow here? The answer might lie with water, for two reasons. Firstly, the barrow was situated close to a source of fresh spring water, which may have appeared, seasonally, as a stream issuing from the foot of the hillslope. This may have given the locale a particular magical significance. Secondly, from the vantage point of the barrow, not only can one see over Mount's Bay (and the Mount), but this is one of the best and nearest locations from which to look over and into Marazion Marsh – a pool of water that may have been bright, shimmering in the sun, in stark contrast to the grey sea and the other pools of salty, or muddy water in the area. So, Marazion would have shone out as, perhaps as a significant body of water, just as the water at Must Farm (Knight *et al.* 2019b) would have done during the Late Bronze Age in East Anglia. It is precisely at this time that we see the deposition of hoards of metalwork in and around Marazion Marsh (Fig. 12.2). A coincidence of timing with cultural practices, or is this one of the reasons for hoard deposition? Did the bright sparkling water attract this attention?

The making of myths

As the sea-level rises, we might expect to see the tidal reach of many streams to move upstream, affecting the adjacent riverbank environments and ecology and possible land-use. These changes, even in times of rapid sea-level rise (during the Mesolithic to earlier Neolithic, as shown in Fig. 11.2), would not have been perceptible at an annual scale and barely at a decadal scale, but would be recognised at a generational and longer scale, and this could have changed the histories, stories and myths as they were passed down from one generation to another. Especially strong, or significant, would be the three-generational span, that is to say grandparent to grandchild. The memories or myths held by a community encompass a longer timescale than that of the individual or even a single, family unit. They will, however, become inadvertently or purposely misremembered and used as a way of commentating on the contemporary situation, for the current community (as discussed, for example, by Connerton 1989; Gosden 1994; Bradley 2002, 112–124; and Jones 2013a; forthcoming b). This might have perpetuated embedded cultural (including ritual) practices, long after their original rationales had been forgotten. Thus, the recounting of myths and legends will have enabled the continuation of traditional practices. Many such myths, including that of Lyonesse, the story of a submerged land which once connected Mount's Bay with the Isles of Scilly (Reid 1913, 100; Thomas 1985, 264–294; Charman *et al.* 2016), are tied to the sea, or relate to sites lost to the sea. The regular re-emergence of ghostly stumps of ancient woodlands rising from the sea at low tide in Mount's Bay will have been a potent reminder of former 'lands of the ancestors', and no doubt featured in the myths and legends concerning the drowned landscape of the ancestors.

The future: recording the rising tide

The low-lying landscape of the coastal zone has, of course, not stopped changing. Sea-levels continue to rise and the Marazion Marsh project was undertaken as a response to changes that may well take place in the near future. In the longer term, barriers may not be enough to prevent coastal change, and we may well witness changes like the ones experienced by our distant forebears.

The study of climate change and rising sea-levels is, without doubt, a global issue that has ramifications far beyond Mount's Bay or the south-west peninsula. Both human and non-human communities around the world will be affected by the predicted climate change-related alterations to environments caused by sea-level rise, which will involve the dislocation of people from their inhabited spaces and the cutting off of communities from their traditional, socially valued places. Furthermore, from a disciplinary perspective, climate change, rising waters and storm surges in coastal areas will lead to unpredictable unprecedented levels of damage, destruction and eventual submergence of archaeological sites and palaeo-environmental deposits across the globe (Wickham-Jones 2015, fig. 24; Hollesen 2022; Matthiesen *et al.* 2022; Vousdoukas *et al.* 2022).

Indeed, globally, it has been suggested that sea-levels could rise by up to 1 m by 2100 (IPCC 2022). In the case of Cornwall, it is predicted by Climate Central (2021) that by 2050, with the continuing rises in sea-level, much of the low ground between Penzance and Hayle will be below the annual flood water level. In the longer term it is even possible that West Penwith could eventually become an island, the Marazion Marsh finally being subsumed, becoming part of a body of water linking Mount's Bay with the Hayle Estuary. For this to be avoided there will need to be major changes in human behaviour or else – in common with communities in the past – future populations will have to accept change and engage with a different landscape. As other studies have shown (eg, Barnatt *et al.* 2020; Ward & Barnatt 2020), the way in which people have responded in the past and continue to respond in the present is unpredictable and varied, but understanding the cultural perspectives of coastal communities, both past and present, should be at the very heart of future responses to rising sea-levels.

One of the major developments of recent years has been the identification of a new epoch, known as the Anthropocene, which has resulted from human activity (eg, Graeber & Wengrow 2021, 258). Unsurprisingly, many archaeologists and anthropologists have become concerned with how the discipline can study and contribute to understanding of climate change and the Anthropocene (eg, Latour 2014; Shaw 2016; Pétursdóttir 2017), although opinions differ as to what the best archaeological approaches should be. Whilst the wider question of the contribution that archaeology can make to the Anthropocene is being debated, the charting of the process of sea-level rise and its effects on societies can be examined through combining locally available palaeo-environmental data and the archaeological record, as has been undertaken in this volume. Indeed, highly important results have been achieved in other parts of Britain including Orkney, the Isle of Wight and Scilly, which have revealed that, against the broader background of sea-level rise, there can be significant local variation (eg, Momber *et al.* 2011; Bates *et al.* 2013; Charman *et al.* 2016; Wickham-Jones 2018, 151–166; Wickham-Jones *et al.* 2018).

Looking forward

Greater understanding of the process of sea-level rise and its effects on the landscape, sites and past human responses over time is, therefore, highly desirable and further local and regional studies around Britain, Ireland and Continental Europe represent the best way of advancing knowledge. As the late Caroline Wickham-Jones (2018, 156) has pointed out, broadscale overviews are best when supported with data from multiple techniques obtained as part of focussed local research projects.

The combination of archaeological and palaeo-environmental data undertaken by this project has certainly revealed much about natural processes and human responses to change in the area of Mount's Bay. It was, however, not the outcome of a planned research exercise but was instead the result of taking an unexpected opportunity to study the palaeo-environmental and archaeological record, much of which had gone without synthesis before. In other words, the project has been able to synthesise the evidence from the two locations in our project and from previous work in West Penwith. Some biases in the results have been inevitable, as the data tended to be concentrated in the Marazion Marsh area at the eastern end of Mount's Bay and the methods and resolution used for previous recording were not within our control. In particular, we know very little about the submarine forest which, although long documented, is neither well-dated nor mapped. Consequently, whilst some of the biases might usefully be resolved, much remains to be done.

Within Mount's Bay itself, further multi-disciplinary projects should be undertaken which could be expanded to other coastal areas in Cornwall and the wider south-west region where similar deposits survive (Fig. 10.2) that could be linked with the archaeological record. In turn, these local and regional studies could build up a much higher resolution picture of the changing coastline. Further targeted work in Mount's Bay should include:

- Accurate mapping of the submerged forest, including species identification, which surprisingly has seen little work since Reid (1913).
- Detailed palaeo-environmental work on the few remaining peat and former land surfaces associated with the submerged forests; such deposits have a wealth of information only available or preserved in these contexts (cf. Clapham 1999; French 1999), Westward Ho! (Balaam *et al.* 1987), Prah Sands (French 1983), Marazion Marsh (Healy 1996c), the Camel Estuary (Healy 1999c) and Penzance Harbour (Scaife 2006).
- High-precision radiocarbon dating of the tree stumps and associated peat surfaces, and sampling of the trees to assess their potential for dendrochronological dating.
- The targeting of further sites around Mount's Bay for further palaeo-environmental sampling and radiocarbon dating to produce higher resolution modelling.
- Diving and surveying in the Bay to recover evidence for structures and the recovery of artefacts and identification of materials for sampling.
- Moving beyond, to extend the methods used in Mount's Bay to other submerged forests and shorelines in Cornwall and the south-west.

Conclusions

In this chapter we have offered an overview of the evidence for human activity and for palaeo-environmental and landscape change in West Penwith from the Mesolithic to the Iron Age/ Roman period, and have explored the possible effects of the latter on the communities who lived in this part of Cornwall. Our broader consideration of the social, as well as practical responses to the loss of land through sea-level rise is relevant not only to other areas that have experienced this kind of change in the past, but also to communities who today face similar challenges as sea-level rises through climate change.

As we have argued, some ways in which the record for West Penwith may reflect such changes, especially during the Late Bronze Age when the establishment of a hard sandy shore in Mount's Bay may have provided resilient, adaptive communities with better opportunities to engage in long distance exporting of tin and copper than hitherto. The formation of the Bay as we would recognise it today, and its proximity to the low-lying strip of land linking the north and south coasts of Cornwall, would have provided easier access to the Hayle Estuary than sailing around the coast. This would have enabled communities in Mount's Bay to enjoy a much greater connectivity with the Atlantic interaction network than would have been possible with the muddy, marshy foreshore that had existed before. Indeed, this might explain why there is no evidence for attempts to hold back the rising tide: there are no obvious banks, barriers, embankments, dykes or ditches as seen in the inner Severn Estuary, especially in Romano-British and historic times (Allen 1986; Allen & Fulford 1990a; 1990b; 1992). (That said, there have been no systematic attempts to look for such features and, if they had existed, they could have been removed by tidal erosion, or submerged beneath both sea and mud).

We therefore recommend an approach that considers patterns of artefact deposition, land use and inhabitation from the perspective of the changing landscape and environment. Such an approach might usefully be applied (and in some cases, has been) to other locations around Britain that have witnessed significant landscape change such as, for instance, the Severn Estuary (Bell 2007; 2013; Bell *et al.* 2000); Langstone Harbour (Allen & Gardiner 2000); the Humber wetlands (van de Noort 2004), Luce Sands and Culbin Sands (Bradley *et al.* 2016b; Bradley 2021, 69–73).

An important point to emphasise in our consideration of landscape change is that, just because we as archaeologists can look back over centuries and millennia of such change, that does not mean that the prehistoric communities who lived in south-west Cornwall will necessarily have been aware of, or experienced, that change over the short term. Sea-level rise and its attendant changes can be slow, occurring over generations rather than individual lifetimes. It may have been recognised through the medium of inter-generational story-telling, with myths about the sunken landscapes of old developing in the community, with the stumps of submerged forests providing a visual reminder. The Lyonesse myth, about the stretch of land that once linked West Penwith with the Isles of Scilly, may well have developed in such a way (Charman *et al.* 2016). It is thus important for archaeologists to consider the tempo of landscape change and to understand communities' responses over the course of generations and centuries.

The impact of current climate change on human communities is a worldwide concern, and therefore, evidence for past responses to change is of national and international interest. The results of our archaeological excavation at the Penzance heliport and our geoarchaeological recording in Marazion Marsh have greatly enhanced our understanding of the Mount's Bay landscape. No doubt further research, including coring, will further refine the story of the Bay and its submergence, but for the first time all the available evidence has been drawn together to create a narrative, one which also has relevance for the future.

15

Gwelen: a drowned landscape reimagined

Emma Smith

In 2021 a new artwork *Gwelen* was produced by artist Emma Smith for the coastal path between Penzance and Marazion, inspired by the submerged forest in Mount's Bay[1].

The artwork took as starting point the correlation between the establishment and submergence of the forest and the evolution of the human brain. Well before the time the forest became submerged, humans had developed the ability to imagine it.

The title Gwelen refers to the Cornish words for viewing, a *field* of view, as well as sticks, posts and poles. The artwork is made up of a series of *seeing sticks* that offer leaning posts as rest points along the coastal path from which to imagine the submerged forest.

Each post takes its form from a local tree and is tailor made to the poses and measurements of local residents who contributed ideas on their ideal resting positions for using the imagination.

The works are made of oak in reference to the species found in the forest and markings on each sculpture make subtle reference to the varied geology of the bay over which they look.

The works are clustered as sporadic copse in reference to the dispersed and biodiverse nature of the submerged forest that included a lot of other species as well as trees.

The works are an invitation to all to stop and consider the extraordinary geology of the bay, to connect to this landscape physically through the oak, and together to use the power of imagination to conjure up the forest!

A Practice for Conjuring the Forest in Mount's Bay:

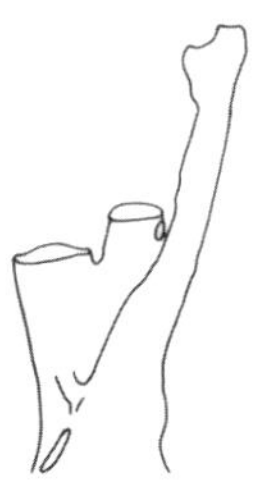

Lean and rest
Close your eyes
Open your ears
Listen to the air
It blows through trees

Seek the smallest sound
It is the grass swaying
Clock a bird
It circles to find its nest

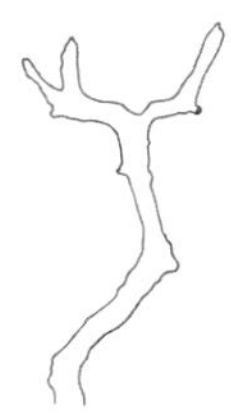

Note a sound that moves at speed
It is an insect
Recognise a voice
A forager gathers food

Hear water
Seep into pools
A stray knock
The mud cracks

A repetition
Of butterfly wings
A call
To whom?

Feel the wind in your face
It has been here all this while
Emma Smith

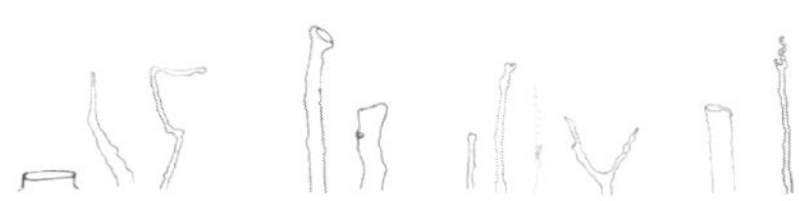

Gwelen

The following reflections on the submerged forest hidden in Mount's Bay have been assembled and contributed to this publication as part of Gwelen: an artwork by Emma Smith with residents of West Penwith. The following quotations are from the Gwelen podcast series created in collaboration with Storyline (Storylines.org.uk).

We all knew it was there
It's been well known that the fossilised forest was there
But very rarely seen
on very, very low spring tides
which only happened 2 or 3 times a year
You could see the tree stumps
and you could walk amongst them
James Wheeler

When diving off Marazion
Not far from a wreck that was called the Warspite
the battleship which went down there in 1940s
stranded on the side of St. Michael's Mount
And the petrified forest goes out almost as far as the wreck
and it was beautiful to swim on because you had these lovely tree stumps
with the roots protruding through the sand
James Wheeler

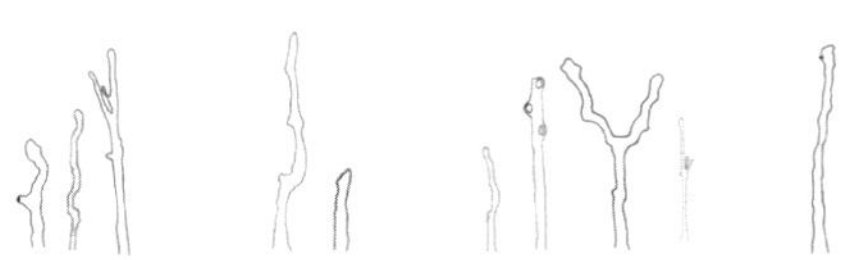

So St. Michael's Mount
In my family
Was always explained as being this place which had been submerged in the forest
So it was like a
passing down of this knowledge almost
rather than something you read about or was scientific
It was like a legend
that's like in a lot of places in Cornwall
is half true, half not
and you're not sure
But you just go along with because it's a nice story

And then similarly with the name in Cornish
So that's Karrek Loos yn Koos
Which means the grey rock in the woods
In the forest
We're not sure if that's an original name that's been passed down
from a long, long time ago
Or was introduced 5,600 years ago
When the community would have been speaking Cornish
And would be describing things around them
So it was interesting that that was the name that was given then
And really conveys that whole story
of it being a rock in the woods
Very different to how it is now

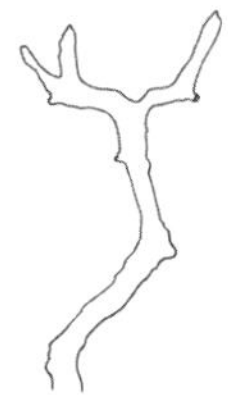

Mark Trevethan

I've always known about it
And I don't know whether or not it's true but
I've always known it as being part of Lyonesse
So when the sea apparently
submerged the land between us and the Isles of Scilly
There were villages down there
and this massive forest
And what we see now on Long Rock beach
is the remnants of that

Constance Morris

I heard they appeared
So I went down to find them
and little rockpools had formed around some of the tree stumps
So that was quite special to see
Because you could see where the roots were coming out of the stumps
going into what would have been the earth
It's part of history
And not many people have
seen or touched them

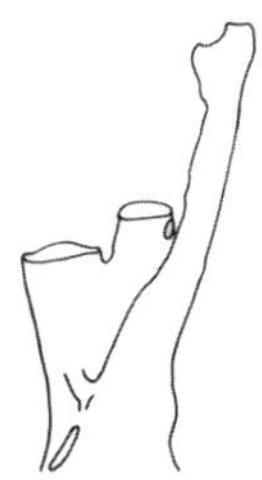

Constance Morris

I remember at primary school
being told about it
I was always told it was the hoar rock in the wood
They say grey now

Stephen Matthews

A few years ago
there was a section that was well exposed
And the thing that struck me most
where the sand had washed back there was an area of peat
and in amongst the peat there were small stones
and this is well down the beach in an area that would normally be covered by sea water
and these stones had
just been uncovered
for the first time in thousands of years
and they're sharp and angular
they'd never been subjected to the action of the sea
I just find that
the most astounding thing
Stephen Matthews

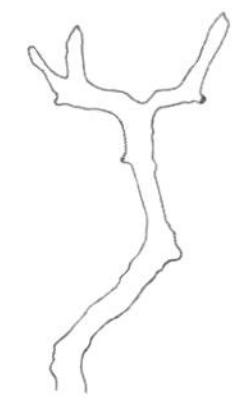

You see whole trees
and tree roots
and they're petrified
It's not often they're exposed
but when they are you can really see that
it's the remains of a forest
Jo Esra

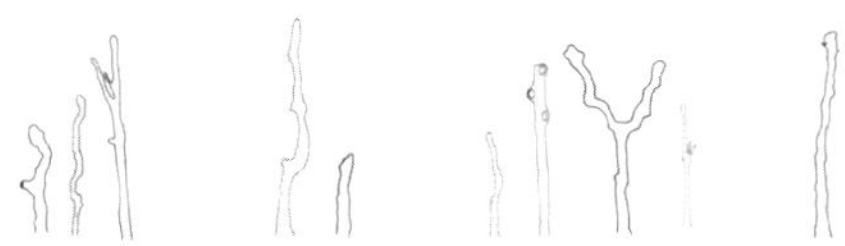

On the boat tours
we've got a depth sounder
and you can see how deep the sea is
and the ridges in it as well
So to have the cliffs that would have been there
covered in forest
I bet it would have been amazing
Constance Morris

I have such stories of this submerged forest in my head
sometimes it's hard to bring together
the images I have an in my mind
and the reality
For me that world is
at the moment
the biggest trees we've got in that environment are the kelp
what's sometimes known as the kelp forest
But that wouldn't have been there
Rachel Lambert

For more information on *Gwelen* please visit: https://newlynartgallery.co.uk/gwelen/

End Note

1. The project was commissioned by Cornwall Council as part of the EXPERIENCE project which promotes experiential tourism and sustainable economic growth during October–March. The project is co-funded by the European Regional Development Fund (ERDF) through the Interreg France (Channel) England Programme under the Natural and Cultural Heritage funding category.

The images are artist sketches for the sculptural art installation Gwelen installed along Penzance – Marazion coastal zone inspired by the submerged forest in Mount's Bay.

Emma Smith 2021

Bibliography

Adams, J., Delgado, S., Dubreuil, L., Hamon, C., Plisson, H. & Risch, R. 2009. Functional analysis of macrolithic artefacts: a focus on working surfaces. In Sternke, F., Eigeland, L. & Costa, L.J. (eds), *Non-flint raw material use in prehistory: old prejudices and new directions*, 43–66. Oxford: British Archaeological Report S1939

Äikäs, T. 2017. Sámi sacred places in ritual taskscapes. In Rajala, U. & Mills, P. (eds), *Forms of dwelling: 20 Years of taskscapes in archaeology*, 62–84. Oxford: Oxbow Books

Äikäs, T., Seitsonen, O. & Salmi, A-K. 2021. Kolari marketplace in a multicultural landscape between Sámi, Swedes and Finns. *Meta Historiskarkeologisk Tidskrift* 2021, 121–142

Allen, J.R.L. 1986. A short history of salt-marsh reclamation at Slimbridge Warth and neighbouring areas. *Transactions of the Bristol & Gloucestershire Archaeological Society* 104, 139–155

Allen, J.R.L. & Fulford, M.G. 1990a. Romano-British and later reclamations on the Severn salt-marshes in the Elmore area, Gloucestershire. *Transactions of the Bristol & Gloucestershire Archaeological Society* 108, 17–32

Allen, J.R.L. & Fulford, M.G. 1990b. Romano-British wetland reclamations at Longney, Gloucestershire, and evidence for the earlier settlement of the inner Severn Estuary. *Antiquaries Journal* 70, 288–326

Allen, J.R.L. & Fulford, M.G. 1992. Romano-British and later geoarchaeology at Oldbury Flats: reclamation and settlement on the changeable coast of the Severn Estuary. *Archaeological Journal* 149, 82–123

Allen, M.J. 1991. Analysing the landscape: a geographical approach to archaeological problems. In Schofield, A.J. (ed.), *Interpreting artefact scatters; contributions to ploughzone archaeology*, 39–57. Oxford: Oxbow Books

Allen, M.J. 2017a. The geoarchaeology of context: sampling for land snails. In Allen, M.J. (ed.), *Molluscs in Archaeology; methods, approaches and applications*, 30–47. Oxford: Studying Scientific Archaeology 3

Allen, M.J. 2017b. The southern English chalkands: Molluscan evidence for the nature of the post-glacial woodland cover. In Allen, M.J. (ed.), *Molluscs in Archaeology; methods, approaches and applications*, 144–164. Oxford: Studying Scientific Archaeology 3

Allen, M.J. 2018a. Penzance Heliport, Cornwall: geoarchaeology coring: method statement. Codford: unpublished AEA report AEA 387.01.01, 4 November 2018

Allen, M.J. 2018b. AEA 387: Penzance Heliport ~ rapid site résumé. Codford: unpublished AEA interim report, 29 November 2018 (ver 1.3)

Allen, M.J. 2019a. AEA 387: Penzance proposed Heliport site, off Jelbert Way, Penzance, Cornwall; geoarchaeology 1: deposit and sample records (centred on NGR 149166, 031497). Codford: unpublished report for Cornwall Archaeological Unit, report AEA 397.02.02, 12 March 2019

Allen, M.J. 2019b. AEA 387: Penzance proposed Heliport site, off Jelbert Way, Penzance, Cornwall; palaeo-environmental assessment: geoarchaeology, pollen and diatoms (centred on NGR 149166, 031497). Codford: unpublished report for Cornwall Archaeological Unit, report AEA 397.03.01, 7 June 2019

Allen, M.J. & Gardiner, J. 2000. *Our changing coast: a survey of the intertidal archaeology of Langstone Harbour, Hampshire*. York: Council for British Archaeology Research Report 124

Allen, M.J. & Scaife, R.G. 1991. The exploitation of the flora and fauna and its impact on the natural and derived landscape. In Cox, P.W. & Hearne, C.M. *Redeemed from the heath; the archaeology of the Wytch Farm Oilfield (1987–90)*, 216–220. Dorchester: Dorset Natural History & Archaeological Society Monograph 9

Allen, M.J., Clapham, A.J., Cameron, N. & Langdon, C.T. 2019. AEA416: Marazion Marsh, Mount's Bay, Penzance, Cornwall: palaeo-environmental assessment: geoarchaeology, pollen and diatoms. Codford: unpublished report for CAU, report AEA 416.04.04, 18 December 2019

Anon. 1970. Gifts and additions to the art gallery and museum, 1970. *Journal of the Royal Institution of Cornwall* 6, 92

AOC Archaeology Group. 2017. Penzance Heliport Ltd, Penzance proposed heliport, land at Jelbert Way, Penzance, Cornwall – archaeological geophysical survey. London: unpublished report, AOC Archaeology Group

Anderson-Whymark, H., Garrow, D. & Sturt, F. 2015. Microliths and maritime mobility: a continental European-style Late Mesolithic flint assemblage from the Isles of Scilly. *Antiquity* 364, 954–971

Antoine, P., Catt, J.A., Lautridou, J-P. & Somme, J. 2003. The loess and coversands of northern France and southern England. *Journal of Quaternary Science* 18, 309–318

ApSimon, A.M., Donovan, D.T. & Taylor, H. 1961. The stratigraphy and archaeology of the Late-Glacial and Post-glacial deposits at Brean Down, Somerset. *Proceedings of the University of Bristol Spelaeological Society* 9, 67–136

Arenstam Gibbons, S. & Nicholls, R. 2006. Island abandonment and sea-level rise: an historical analogue from the Chesapeake Bay, USA. *Global Environmental Change* 16, 40–47

Armit, I., Swindles, G.T., Becker, K., Plunkett, G. & Blaauw, M. 2014. Rapid climate change did not cause population collapse at the end of the European Bronze Age. *Proceedings of the National Academy of Sciences* 111, 17045–17049

Ashbee, P. 1958. The excavation of the Tregulland barrow, Treneglos parish, Cornwall, *Antiquaries Journal* 38, 174–196

Balaam, N.D., Bell, M.G., David, A., Levitan, B., Macphail, R.I., Robinson, M. & Scaife, R. 1987. Prehistoric and Romano-British sites at Westward Ho! Devon: archaeological and palaeoenvironmental surveys in 1983 and 1984. In Balaam, N.D., Levitan, B. & Straker, V. (eds), *Studies in palaeoeconomy and environment in south west England*, 163–264. Oxford: British Archaeological Report 181

Barclay, A. & Halpin, C. 1999. *Excavations at Barrow Hills, Radley, Oxfordshire*. Oxford: Oxford Archaeology

Barclay, G.J. & Brophy, K. 2021. 'A veritable chauvinism of prehistory': nationalist prehistories and the 'British' Late Neolithic mythos. *Archaeological Journal*, 178, 330–360.

Baring Gould, S. 1898. Seventeenth barrow report, *Transactions of the Devonshire Association* 30, 77–79

Barker, H. & Mackay, C.J. 1959. British Museum natural radiocarbon measurements 1. *American Journal of Science Radiocarbon Supplement* 1, 81–861

Barker, L. 2020. Introducing the historic environment and climate change in Wales Sector Adaptation Plan. *Archaeology in Wales* 60, 3–6

Barlow, N.L.M., Shennan, I., Long, A.J., Gehrels, R.W., Saher, M.H., Woodroffe, S.A. & Hillier, C. 2013. Salt marshes as late Holocene tide gauges. *Global and Planetary Change* 106, 90–110

Barnett, R.L., Charman, D.J, Johns, C., Ward, S.L., Bevan, A., Bradley, S.L., Camidge, K., Fyfe, R.M., Gehrels, W.R & Gehrels, M.J. 2020. Nonlinear landscape and cultural response to sea-level rise. *Science Advances* 6 [DOI: 10.1126/sciadv.abb6376]

Barrett, J. 1999. The mythical landscapes of the British Iron Age. In Ashmore, W. & Knapp, A.B. (eds), *Archaeologies of landscape*, 253–268. Oxford: Blackwell

Basso, K, 1996. *Wisdom sits in places: landscape and language amongst the western Apache*. Albuquerque NM: University of New Mexico Press

Bates, M.R., Nayling, N., Bates, R., Dawson, S., Huws, D. & Wickham-Jones, C. 2013. A multi-disciplinary approach to the archaeological investigation of a bedrock-dominated shallow-marine landscape: an example from the Bay of Firth, Orkney, UK. *International Journal of Nautical Archaeology* 42, 24–43

Battarbee, R.W., Jones, V.J., Flower, R.J., Cameron, N.G., Bennion, H.B., Carvalho, L. & Juggins, S. 2001. Diatoms. In Smol, J.P. & Birks, J.J. (eds), *Tracking environmental change using lake sediments volume 3: terrestrial, algal, and siliceous indicators*, 155–202. Dordrecht: Kluwer

Battarbee, R.W., Juggins, S., Gasse, F., Anderson, N.J., Bennion, H. & Cameron, N.G. 2000. European Diatom Database (EDDI). An information system for palaeoenvironmental reconstruction. European Climate Science Conference, 1–10, Vienna City Hall, Vienna, Austria, 19–23 October 1998, 1–10

Becker, K. 2013. Transforming identities – new approaches to Bronze Age deposition in Ireland. *Proceedings of the Prehistoric Society* 79, 225–263

Bell, M. 1983. Valley sediments as evidence of prehistoric land-use on the South Downs. *Proceedings of the Prehistoric Society* 49, 119–150

Bell, M. 1990. *Brean Down Excavations 1983–1987*. London: English Heritage Archaeological Report 15

Bell, M. 1997. Environmental archaeology in the coastal zone. In Fulford, M., Champion, T. & Long, A. (eds), *England's coastal heritage; a survey for English Heritage and the RCHME*, 56–73. London: English Heritage and RCHME

Bell, M. 2007. *Prehistoric coastal communities: the Mesolithic in western Britain*. York: Council for British Archaeology Research Report 149

Bell, M. 2013. *The Bronze Age in the Severn Estuary*. York: Council for British Archaeology Research Report 172

Bell, M. & Brown, A. 2008. *Southern regional review of geoarchaeology: windblown deposits*. Swindon: English Heritage Research Department Report 005/2009

Bell, M., Caseldine, A. & Neumann, H. 2000. *Prehistoric intertidal archaeology in the Welsh Severn Estuary*. York: Council for British Archaeology Research Report 120

Bender, B. & Winer, M. (eds), 2001. *Contested landscapes: movement, exile and place*. Oxford: Berg

Bender, B., Hamilton, S. & Tilley, C. 2007. *Stone worlds: narrative and reflexivity in landscape archaeology*. Walnut Creek CA: Left Coast Press

Bennett, K.D., Whittington, G. & Edwards, K.J. 1994. Recent plant nomenclatural changes and pollen morphology in the British Isles, *Quaternary Newsletter* 73, 1–6

Bennion, H., Juggins, S. & Anderson, N.J. 1996. Predicting epilimnetic phosphorus concentrations using an improved diatom-based transfer function and its application to lake eutrophication management. *Environmental Science and Technology* 30, 2004–2007

Berger, D., Wang, Q., Brügmann, G., Lockhoff, N., Roberts, B.W. & Pernicka, E. 2022. The Salcombe metal cargoes: new light on the provenance and circulation of tin and copper in later Bronze Age Europe provided by trace elements and isotopes. *Journal of Archaeological Science* 138, 1–28

Bergström, J. 2018. An archaeology of societal resilience. *Safety Science* 110(C), 31–38

Berridge, P. & Roberts, A. 1986. The Mesolithic period in Cornwall. *Cornish Archaeology* 25, 7–34

Best, J. & Gent, T. 2007. Bronze Age burnt mounds and early medieval timber structures at Town Farm Quarry, Burlescombe Down, Devon. *Archaeological Journal* 164, 1–79

Best, L.A. 2016. Late Holocene relative sea-level change and the Implications for the groundwater resource, Humber Estuary, UK. Unpublished PhD thesis, University of York

Black Trowel Collective. 2016. Foundations of an anarchist archaeology: a community manifesto. *Savage Minds/Anthro{dendrum}* [http://savageminds.

org/2016/10/31/foundations-of-an-anarchist-archaeology-a-community-manifesto/]

Bland, R. 2015. Hoarding in Britain from the Bronze Age to the 20th century. In Naylor, J. & Bland, R. (eds), *Hoarding and the deposition of metalwork from the Bronze Age to the 20th century: a British perspective*, 1–20. Oxford: British Archaeological Report 615

Bland, R., Chadwick, A., Ghey, E., Haselgrove, C., Mattingley, D.J., Rogers, A. & Taylor, J. 2020. *Iron Age and Roman coin hoards in Britain*. Oxford: Oxbow Books

Boase, H.S. 1822. Observations on the Submersion of part of the Mount's Bay; and on the inundations of marine sand on the north coast of Cornwall, *Transactions of the Royal Geological Society of Cornwall* 2, 129–144

Boase, H.S. 1826. On the sandbanks of the northern shores of Mount's Bay. *Transactions of the Royal Geological Society of Cornwall* 3, 166–191

Bonnemere, P. 1998. Trees and people: some vital links. Tree products and other agents in the life cycle of the Ankave-Anga of Papua New Guinnea. In Rival, L. (ed.), *The social lives of trees: anthropological perspectives on tree symbolism*, 113–132. Oxford: Berg

Booth, T. & Brück, J. 2020. Death is not the end: radiocarbon and histo-taphonomic evidence for the curation and excarnation of human remains in Bronze Age Britain. *Antiquity* 94(377), 1186–1203

Booth, T., Brück, J., Brace, S. & Barnes, I. 2021. Tales from the supplementary information: ancestry change in Chalcolithic–Early Bronze Age Britain was gradual with varied kinship organization. *Cambridge Archaeological Journal* 31(3), 379–400

Borlase, M. 2020. *Cornwall's trans-peninsular route: Socio-economic and cultural continuity across the Camel/Fowey corridor – AD 43 to AD 700*. Oxford: British Archaeological Report 653

Borlase, W. 1758. *Natural History of Cornwall*. Oxford: W. Jackson

Borlase, W. 1769. *Observations on the antiquities historical and monumental, of the county of Cornwall. Consisting of several essays on the first inhabitants, druid-superstition, customs, and remains of the most remote antiquity, in Britain, and the British Isles*. Oxford: W. Jackson

Borlase, W.C. 1872. *Naenia Cornubiae: a descriptive essay, illustrative of the sepulchres and funereal customs of the early inhabitants of the county of Cornwall*. London: Longmans, Green, Reader & Dyer

Boulud, S. & Fily, M. 2009. Les dépôts métalliques de l'extrême fin du Bronze final en Bretagne: nouvelle évaluation des données à la lumière des découvertes récentes. In. Roulière-Lambert, M.J., Daubigney, A., Milcent, P.-Y., Talon, M. & Vital, J. (eds), *De l'âge du Bronze à l'âge du Fer en France et en Europe occidentale (Xe–VIIe siècle av. J.-C.). La moyenne valleée du Rhône aux âges du Fer. Actes du XXXe colloque international de l'A.F.E.A.F., co-organisé avec l'A.P.R.A.B. (Saint-Romain-en-Gal, 26–28 mai 2006)*, 283–298. Dijon: Revue archéologique de l'Est supplément 27

Bourgeois, Q. 2013. *Monuments on the horizon. The formation of the barrow landscape throughout the 3rd and 2nd millennium BC*. Leiden: Sidestone Press

Bowen, E.G. 1972. *Britain and the western seaways*. London: Thames & Hudson

Bradley, R. 1990. *The passage of arms. An archaeological analysis of prehistoric hoards and votive deposits*. Cambridge: Cambridge University Press

Bradley, R. 1998. Ruined buildings, ruined stones: enclosures, tombs and natural places in the Neolithic of south-west England. *World Archaeology* 30, 13–22

Bradley, R. 2000a. *An archaeology of natural places*. London: Routledge

Bradley, R. 2000b. *The good stones*. Edinburgh: Society of Antiquaries of Scotland

Bradley, R. 2002. *The past in prehistoric societies*. London: Routledge

Bradley, R. 2005a. *The moon and the bonfire. An investigation of three stone circles in north-east Scotland*. Edinburgh: Society of Antiquaries of Scotland

Bradley, R. 2005b. *Ritual and domestic life in prehistoric Europe*. London: Routledge

Bradley, R. 2007. *The prehistory of Britain and Ireland*. Cambridge: Cambridge University Press

Bradley, R. 2013. Hoards and the deposition of metalwork. In Fokkens, H. & Harding, A. (eds), *The Oxford handbook of the European Bronze Age*, 121–139. Oxford: Oxford University Press

Bradley, R. 2017. *A geography of offerings: deposits of valuables in the landscapes of ancient Europe*. Oxford: Oxbow Insights in Archaeology 3

Bradley, R. 2019. *The Prehistory of Britain and Ireland* (2nd edn). Cambridge: Cambridge University Press

Bradley, R. 2020. *A comparative study of rock art in later prehistoric Europe*. Cambridge: Cambridge University Press

Bradley, R. 2021. *Maritime archaeology on dry land: special sites along the coasts of Britain and Ireland from the first farmers to the Atlantic Bronze Age*. Oxford: Oxbow Books

Bradley, R. & Fraser, E. 2010. Bronze Age barrows on the heathlands of southern England; construction, forms and interpretation. *Oxford Journal of Archaeology* 29, 15–34

Bradley, R., Green, C. & Watson, A. 2018. The placing of Early Bronze Age metalwork deposits: new evidence from Scotland. *Oxford Journal of Archaeology* 37, 137–145

Bradley, R., Lewis, J., Mullin, D. & Branch, N. 2015. 'Where water wells up from the earth': excavations at the findspot of the Late Bronze Age hoard from Broadward, Shropshire. *Antiquaries Journal* 95, 21–64

Bradley, R., Haselgrove, C., Vander Linden, M. & Webley, L. 2016a. *The later prehistory of north-west Europe: the evidence from development-led fieldwork*. Oxford: Oxford University Press

Bradley, R., Rogers, A., Sturt, F., Watson, A., Coles, D., Gardiner, J. & Scott, R. 2016b. Maritime havens in earlier prehistoric Britain. *Proceedings of the Prehistoric Society* 82, 125–159 [doi:10.1017/ppr.2015.22]

Bradshaw, R.H.W., Coxon, P., Greig, J.R.A. & Hall, A.R. 1981. New fossil evidence for the past cultivation and processing of hemp (*Cannabis sativa* L.) in eastern England. *New Phytologist* 89(3), 503–510

Braje, T.J. 2016. Evaluating the Anthropocene. Is there something useful about a geological epoch of humans? *Antiquity* 90, 504–512

Brandherm, D. & Moskal-del Hoyo, M. 2014. Both sides now: the carp's tongue complex revisited. *Antiquaries Journal* 94, 1–47

Briard, J. 1965. *Les dépôts Bretons et l'Âge du Bronze Atlantique*. Rennes: Travaux du Laboratoire d'anthropologie préhistorique

Briard, J. 1991. Le groupe de l'épée en langue de carpe en

Armorique: une revision. In Chevillot, C. & Coffyn, A. (eds), *L'âge du Bronze atlantique, ses faciès de l'Écosse à l'Andalousie et leurs relations avec le Bronze continental et la Méditerranée, Actes du colloque de Beynac*, 125–144. Beynac-et-Cazenac: Association des Muse´es du Sarladais

Brisset, E. & Fernández López de Pablo, J. 2022. Impacts of sea-level rise on prehistoric coastal communities: land use and risk perception during the Mesolithic–Neolithic transition in central Mediterranean Spain. *Journal of Maps* [DOI: 10.1080/17445647.2022.2071649]

Brennand, M. & Taylor M. 2003. The survey and excavation of a timber circle at Holme-next-the-Sea, Norfolk, 1998–9. *Proceedings of the Prehistoric Society* 69, 1–84

Bronk, C., Higham, T., Bowles, A. & Hedges, R. 2004. Improvements to the pretreatment of bone at Oxford. *Radiocarbon* 46, 155–163

Bronk Ramsey, C. 1995. Radiocarbon calibration and analysis of stratigraphy: the OxCal program. *Radiocarbon* 37, 425–430

Bronk Ramsey, C. 1998. Probability and dating. *Radiocarbon* 40, 461–474

Bronk Ramsey, C. 2001. Development of the radiocarbon calibration program OxCal. Radiocarbon 43, 355–363

Bronk Ramsey, C. 2009. Bayesian analysis of radiocarbon dates. *Radiocarbon* 51, 337–360

Bronk Ramsey, C. 2017. Methods for summarizing radiocarbon datasets. Radiocarbon 59(2), 1809–1833

Brown, F., Dickson, A. & Evans, H. 2019. Crossing the divide: raw material use in the north-west of the British Isles in the late Mesolithic and Neolithic. In Teather, A., Topping, P. & Baczkowski, J. (eds), *Mining and quarrying in Neolithic Europe: a social perspective*, 149–162. Oxford: Neolithic Studies Group Seminar Papers 16

Brown, I. 2009. *Beacons in the landscape. the hillforts of England and Wales*. Oxford: Windgather Press

Brück, J. 1995. A place for the dead: the role of human remains in Late Bronze Age Britain. *Proceedings of the Prehistoric Society* 61, 245–277

Brück, J. 1999. Houses, lifecycles and deposition on Middle Bronze Age settlements in southern England. *Proceedings of the Prehistoric Society* 65, 245–278

Brück, J. 2006. Fragmentation, personhood and the social construction of technology in Middle and Late Bronze Age Britain. *Cambridge Archaeological Journal* 16, 297–315

Brück, J. 2019. *Personifying prehistory: relational ontologies in Bronze Age Britain and Ireland*. Oxford: Oxford University Press

Brück, J. 2000. Settlement, landscape and social identity: the Early–Middle Bronze Age transition in Wessex, Sussex and the Thames Valley. *Oxford Journal of Archaeology* 19, 273–300

Brück, J. & Booth, T. 2022. The power of relics: the curation of human bone in British Bronze Age burials, *European Journal of Archaeology* 25(4), 440–462

Brück, J. & Davies, A. 2018. The social role of non-metal 'valuables' in Late Bronze Age Britain. *Cambridge Archaeological Journal* 28(4), 665–688

Brück, J. & Fontijn, D. 2013. The myth of the chief: prestige goods, power and personhood in the European Bronze Age. In Fokkens, H. & Harding, A. (eds), *The Oxford handbook of the European Bronze Age*, 197–215. Oxford: Oxford University Press

Brunning, R. 1997. Two Bronze Age wooden structures in the Somerset moors. *Archaeology in the Severn Estuary* 8, 5–8

Buckley, V. 1990. *Burnt offerings: international contributions to burnt mound archaeology*. Bray: Wordwell

Bullen, R.A. 1912. *Harlyn Bay and the discoveries of its prehistoric remains*. Harlyn Bay: Colonel Bellers

Burnard, R. 1897. Sixteenth barrow report. *Transactions of the Devonshire Association* 29, 66–71

Burnard, R. 1899. Eighteenth barrow report. *Transactions of the Devonshire Association* 31, 94–100

Burns, A. 2021. The Mesolithic footprints retained in one bed of the former saltmarshes at Formby Point, Sefton Coast, north west England. In Pastoors, A. & Lenssen-Erz, T. (eds), *Reading prehistoric human tracks*, 295–316. Cham: Springer

Burton, P.F. & Charman, D.J. 1995. Vegetation change in lowland Cornwall: preliminary results from Crift Down near Lanlivery and Hoggs Moor near Lostwithiel. *Cornish Archaeology* 34, 74–79

Butler, J. 1997. *Dartmoor atlas of antiquities. Volume 5: the second millennium B.C.* Tiverton: Devon Books

Camburn, K.E. & Charles, D.F. (eds), 2000. *Diatoms of low alkalinity lakes in the northeastern United States*. Philadelphia: Academy of Natural Sciences of Philadelphia Special Publication 18

Cameron, N. 2019. Diatom assessment. In Allen, M.J., Clapham, A.J., Cameron, N. & Langdon, C.T., AEA416: Marazion Marsh, Mount's Bay, Penzance, Cornwall: palaeo-environmental assessment: geoarchaeology, pollen and diatoms. Codford: unpublished report for CAU, report AEA 416.04.04, 18 December 2019

Cameron, N., Birks, H., Jones, V., Berges, F., Catalan, J., Flower, R., Garcia, J., Kawecka, B., Koinig, K. & Marchetto, A. 1999. Surface-sediment and epilithic diatom pH calibration sets for remote European mountain lakes (AL: PE Project) and their comparison with the Surface Waters Acidification Programme (SWAP) calibration set. *Journal of Paleolimnology* 22, 291–317

Camidge, K. & Randall, L. 2009. *An archaeological survey of Mount's Bay*. Penzance: CISMAS

Camm, G.S. 1999. Palaeovalley systems in Mount's Bay, west Cornwall. In Scourse, J.D. & Furze, M.F.A. (eds), *The Quaternary of west Cornwall, field guide*, 46–57. London: Quaternary Research Association

Camm, G.S & Dominy, S.C. 1998. Palaeovalley systems in Mount's Bay and St. Austell Bay, south coast of Cornwall. *Proceedings of the Ussher Society* 7, 328–330

Cappers, R.T.J., Bekker, R.M. & Jans, J.E.A. 2006. *Digital seed atlas of the Netherlands*. Groningen: Groningen Archaeological Studies 4

Carey, C., Tsoraki, C., Jones, A.M., Harris, O.J.T., Crellin, R.J. & Lyons, P. 2022. Beaker and Early Bronze Age tin exploitation in Cornwall, UK: cassiterite processing identified through microwear and pXRF analyses. *Journal of European Archaeology*, 1–21 [doi:10.1017/eaa.2022.30]

Carlin, N. 2017. Getting into the groove: eExploring the relationship between Grooved Ware and developed passage tombs in Ireland *c.* 3000–2700 cal BC. *Proceedings of the Prehistoric Society* 83, 155–188

Carne, J. 1846. Notice on the remains of submarine forest in the north-eastern part of Mount's Bay. *Transactions of the Royal Geological Society of Cornwall* 6, 230

Cassidy, L., Ó Maoldúin, R., Kador, T., Lynch, A., Jones, C., Woodman, P.C., Murphy, E., Ramsey, G., Dowd, M., Noonan, A., Campbell, C., Jones, E.R., Mattiangeli, V. & Bradley, D.G. 2020. A dynastic elite in monumental Neolithic society. *Nature* 582, 384–388 [doi: 10.1038/s41586-020-2378-6]

Caswell, E. & Roberts, B.W. 2018. Reassessing community cemeteries: cremation burials in Britain during the Middle Bronze Age (*c.* 1600–1150 cal BC). *Proceedings of the Prehistoric Society* 84, 329–357

Catt, J.A. & Staines, S.J. 1982. Loess in Cornwall. *Proceedings of the Ussher Society* 5, 368–376

Channon, A.H. 2018. A palaeoenvironmental reconstruction of the Mount's Bay coastline, south-west Cornwall: implications and applicability towards understanding current trends and future projections of sea-level rise. Unpublished BA dissertation, University of Plymouth

Charman, D., Johns, C., Camidge, K., Marshall, P., Mills, S.F., Mulville, J., Roberts, H.M & Stevens, T. 2016. *The Lyonesse project: a study of the coastal and marine environment of the Isles of Scilly*. Truro: Cornwall Archaeological Unit

Christie, P. 1985. Barrows on the north Cornish coast: wartime excavations by C.K. Croft Andrew 1939–1944. *Cornish Archaeology* 24, 23–122

Christie, P. 1988. A barrow cemetery on Davidstow Moor, Cornwall: wartime excavations by C.K. Croft Andrew. *Cornish Archaeology* 27, 27–169

Cipolla, C.N., Crellin, R.J. & Harris, O.J.T. 2021. Posthumanist archaeologies, archaeological posthumanisms. *Journal of Posthumanism* 1, 5–21

Clapham, A.J. 1999. The characterisation of two mid-Holocene submerged forests. Unpublished PhD thesis, Liverpool John Moores University

Clapham, A.J. 2019. An assessment of the waterlogged plant remains from the Marazion Marsh, Mount's Bay, Penzance, Cornwall (AEA 416). In Allen, M.J., Clapham, A.J., Cameron, N. & Langdon, C.T., AEA416: Marazion Marsh, Mount's Bay, Penzance, Cornwall: palaeo-environmental assessment: geoarchaeology, pollen and diatoms. Codford: unpublished report for CAU, report AEA 416.04.04, 18 December 2019

Clark, J.G.D. 1960. Excavations at the Neolithic site at Hurst Fen, Mildenhall, Suffolk (1954, 1957 and 1958). *Proceedings of the Prehistoric Society* 26, 202–245

Clark, P. 2004. The Dover Boat ten years after its discovery. In Clark, P. (ed.), *The Dover Bronze Age Boat*, 1–12. Oxford: Oxbow Books

Cleary, K. 2016. Burial practices in Ireland during the Late 3rd millennium BC – connecting new ideologies with local expressions. In Koch, J.T. & Cunliffe, B. (eds), *Celtic from the West 3: Atlantic Europe in the metal ages – questions of shared language*, 139–178. Oxford: Oxbow Books/Celtic Studies Publications

Climate Central. 2021. *Land projected to be below annual flood level in 2050* [https://coastal.climatecentral.org/map/12/-5.4041/50.1587/

Clough, T.H. McK. & Cummins, W.A. 1988. *Stone axe studies volume 2*. London: Council for British Archaeology Research Report 67

Coffyn, A., Gomez, J. & Mohen, J.-P. 1981. *L'apogeé du Bronze atlantique: le dépôt de Vénat.* Paris: L'âge du Bronze en France 1, Picard

Cole, R. & Jones, A.M. 2002–3. Journeys to the Rock: archaeological investigations at Tregarrick Farm, Roche, Cornwall. *Cornish Archaeology* 41–42, 107–143

Conneller, C. 2022. *The Mesolithic in Britain: landscape and society in times of change*. London: Routledge

Connerton, P. 1989. *How societies remember.* Cambridge: Cambridge University Press

Cook, I., Johnston, R. & Selby, K. 2021. Climate change and cultural heritage: a landscape vulnerability framework. *Journal of Island and Coastal Archaeology* 16, 553–571

Coombs, D. 1975. Bronze Age weapon hoards in Britain. *Archaeologia Atlantica* 1, 49–81

Cooney, G. 2004. Neolithic worlds: islands in the Irish Sea. In Cummings, V. & Fowler, C. (eds), *The Neolithic of the Irish Sea*, 145–159. Oxford: Oxbow Books

Cooney, G. & Grogan, E. 1994. *Irish prehistory, a social perspective*. Dublin: Wordwell

Cooper, A., Garrow, D., Gibson, C., Giles, M. & Wilkin, N. 2021. *Grave goods: objects and death in later prehistoric Britain*. Oxford: Oxbow Books

Cornish, T. 1880–81. Bronze celts. *Penzance Natural History and Antiquarian Society* 1880–81, 75

Cornwall County Council. 1996. *Cornwall: a landscape assessment 1994*. Truro: Cornwall County Council

Costa, K., Brun, P. & Mille, B. 2020. Late Bronze Age archaeometallurgical hoards surveys from France (1350 to 800 BCE). *Materials and Manufacturing Processes* 35, 149–150

Crawford, O.G.S. 1927. Lyonesse revisited: the early walls of Scilly. *Antiquity* 1, 5–14

Cummings, V. 2007. Megalithic journeys: moving around the megalithic landscapes of Neolithic western Britain. In Cummings, V. & Johnston, R. (eds), *Prehistoric journeys*, 54–63. Oxford: Oxbow Books

Cummings, V. 2009. *A view from the west: the Neolithic of the Irish Sea zone*. Oxford: Oxbow Books

Cummings, V. & Whittle, A. 2004. *Places of special virtue: megaliths in the Neolithic landscapes of Wales*. Oxford: Oxbow Books

Cunliffe, B. 1987. *Hengistbury Head, Dorset. Volume 1: the prehistoric and Roman settlement, 3500 BC–AD 500*. Oxford: Oxford University Committee for Archaeology Monograph 13

Cunliffe, B. 1988. *Mount Batten Plymouth, a prehistoric and Roman port*. Oxford: Oxford University Press

Cunliffe, B. 2001. *Facing the ocean: the Atlantic and its peoples, 8000 BC to AD 1500*. Oxford: Oxford University Press

Cunliffe, B. 2002. *The extraordinary voyage of Pytheas the Greek*. London: Penguin

Cunliffe, B. 2009. Looking forward: maritime contacts in the first millennium BC. In Clark, P. (ed.), *Bronze Age connections, cultural contact in prehistoric Europe*, 12–37. Oxford: Oxbow Books

Cunliffe, B. 2015. Facing the northern ocean: The British Late Bronze and Iron Ages in their Continental perspective. In Hunter, F. & Ralston, I. (eds), *Scotland in later prehistoric Europe*, 5–17. Edinburgh: Society of Antiquaries of Scotland

Cunliffe, B. 2021. *Bretons and Britons: the fight for identity*. Oxford: Oxford University Press

Darvill, T. 2002. White on blonde: quartz pebbles and the

use of quartz at Neolithic monuments on the Isle of Man and beyond. In Jones, A. & MacGregor, G. (eds), *Colouring the past*, 73–92. Oxford: Berg

Darvill, T. & Wainwright, G. 2016. Neolithic and Bronze Age Pembrokeshire. In Darvill, T., James, H., Murphy, K. Wainwright, G. & Walker, E.A. (eds), *Pembrokeshire County History, Volume I, prehistoric, Roman and early medieval Pembrokeshire*, 55–222. Haverfordwest: Gomer Press

Davies, A. 2019. The devil or the divine? Supernatural objects and multi-period hoards in later prehistory. In Knight, M., Boughton, D. & Wilkinson, R. (eds), *The past in the past: investigating the significance of the deposition of earlier objects in later contexts*, 60–76. Oxford: Archaeopress

Davies, A. 2022. Unusual deposition on Bronze Age and Iron Age settlements and hillforts in the upper and middle Thames Valley. *Oxford Journal of Archaeology* 41, 63–84

Davies, S.R. 2010. The Early Neolithic tor enclosures of southwest Britain. Unpublished PhD thesis, University of Birmingham

Deakin, R. 2000. *Waterlog: a swimmer's journey through Britain*. London: Vintage.

Deakin, R. 2008. *Wildwood: a journey through trees*. London: Penguin

de Beer, G. 1960. Itkin. *Geographical Journal* 126, 160–167

De Reu, J. & Bourgeois, J. 2013. Bronze Age barrow research in Sandy Flanders (NW Belgium): an overview. In Fontijn, D., Louwen, A.J., van der Vaart, S. & Wentink, K. (eds), *Beyond barrows. Current research on the structuration and perception of the prehistoric landscape through monuments*, 155–194. Leiden: Sidestone Press

Dietrich, O. & Mörtz, T. 2019. Sockets full of scrap? Remarks on deliberate fragmentation in Late Bronze Age metal deposits in south-eastern and north-western Europe. In Brandherm, D. (ed.), *Aspects of the Bronze Age in the Atlantic archipelago and beyond. Proceedings from the Belfast Bronze Age Forum, 9–10 November 2013*, 28–297. Hagen: Archaeologia Atlantica Monograph 3

Digimap HydrospatialOne 2017. SHAPE Geospatial Data: Scale 1:25000, Tiles: nw55000055, nw55000060, seazone: EDINA Marine Digimap Service. Accessible from: https://digimap.edina.ac.uk/ (accessed 11 July 2017)

Dines, H.G. 1956. *The metalliferous mining region of south-west England*. London: Economic Memoir of the British Geological Survey

Douny, L. & Harris, S. 2014. Wrapping and unwrapping, concepts and approaches. In Harris, S. & Veldmiejer, A.J. (eds), *Wrapping and unwrapping material culture: archaeological and anthropological perspectives*, 15–40. Walnut Creek CA: Left Coast Press

Dowd, M. 2015. *The archaeology of caves in Ireland*. Oxford: Oxbow Books

Downes, J. & Card, N. 2002. Knowes of Trotty, Orkney (Birsay and Harray parish), Bronze Age barrow cemetery. *Discovery and excavation in Scotland* 3, 87

Dubreuil, L., Savage, D., Delgado-Raack, S., Plisson, H., Stephenson, B. & de la Torre, I. 2015. Current analytical frameworks for studies of use-wear on ground stone tools. In Manuel Marreiros, J., Gibaja Bao, J.F. & Ferreira Bicho, N. (eds), *Use-wear and residue analysis in archaeology*, 105–158. New York: Springer

Dudley, D. 1956. An excavation at Bodrifty, Mulfra, near Penzance. *Archaeological Journal* 113, 1–32

Dudley, D. 1960. Treliske, Truro, Cornwall: area hospital site emergency excavation, May 5th–17th 1958. *Journal of the Royal Institution of Cornwall* (supplement), 14–26

Dudley, D. 1964. The excavation of the Carvinnack barrow, Tregavethan, near Truro, Cornwall. *Journal of the Royal Institution of Cornwall* 4, 414–451

Dunkin, D., Yates, D. & Bradley, R. 2020. The findspots of Bronze Age metalwork in lowland England: a new field study. *Oxford Journal of Archaeology* 39, 67–88

Dyer, M. & Quinnell, H. 2013. Excavation of a group of Early Bronze Age monuments on Headon Down, Sparkwell. *Proceedings of the Devon Archaeological Society* 71, 55–80

Edmonds, E. 2004. *The Langdales: landscape and prehistory in a Lakeland valley*. Stroud: Tempus.

Edmonds, R. 1849. On the fragments of a bronze furnace (supposed to be Phoenician) discovered near St Michael's Mount – the Itkin of Diodorus Siculus. *Transactions of the Penzance Natural History and Antiquarian Society* 1, 347–351

Edwards, R.J. 2006. Mid- to late-Holocene relative sea-level change in southwest Britain and the influence of sediment compaction. *The Holocene* 16(4), 575–587

Edwards, R.J. & Horton, B.P. 2000. Reconstructing relative sea-level change using UK salt-marsh foraminifera. *Marine Geology* 169, 41–56

Ehser, A., Borg, G. & Pernicka, E. 2011. Provenance of the gold of the Early Bronze Age Nebra Sky Disk, central Germany: geochemical characterization of natural gold from Cornwall. *European Journal of Mineralogy* 23, 895–910

Entwistle, R. 2001. A Bronze Age round barrow and Deverel Rimbury cremation cemetery at Zionshill Copse, Chandler's Ford, Hampshire. *Proceedings of the Hampshire Field Club and Archaeological Society* 56, 1–20

Enys, J.D. 1899. The Anniversary Address of the President. *Transactions of the Royal Geological Society of Cornwall* 12, 193–204

Evans, C. 2015. Wearing environment and making islands: Britain's Bronze Age inland North Sea. *Antiquity* 89(347), 1110–1124 [doi:10.15184/aqy.2015.99]

Evans, J. 1881. *The Ancient bronze implements, weapons and ornaments of Great Britain and Ireland*. London: Longmans, Green & Co

Falasco, E., Bona, F., Badino, G., Hoffmann, L. & Ector, L. 2009. Diatom teratological forms and environmental alterations: a review. *Hydrobiologia* 623, 1–35

Farley, J. 2015. Coins and conquest: coin hoarding in the Late Iron Age and early Roman period in the north Thames and east midlands regions. In Naylor, J. & Bland, R. (eds), *Hoarding and the deposition of metalwork from the Bronze Age to the 20th century: a British perspective*, 41–66. Oxford: British Archaeological Report 615

Farley, J. 2021. The Hallaton ingot: Silver in Iron Age Britain. *Oxford Journal of Archaeology* 40, 87–104

Few, R., Ahern, M., Matthies, F. & Kovats, S. 2004. Floods, health and climate changes; a strategic review. Unpublished University of East Anglia (Tyndall Centre for Climate Change Research) working paper 63

Field, D. 1998. Round barrows and the harmonious landscape: placing Early Bronze Age burial monuments in south-east England. *Oxford Journal of Archaeology* 17, 309–326

Field, D. & McOmish, D. 2017. *The making of prehistoric Wiltshire: life, ceremony and death from the earliest times to the Roman invasion.* Stroud: Amberley

Findlay, D.C., Colborne, G.J.N., Cope, D.W., Harrod, T.R., Hogan, D.V. & Staines, S.J. 1984. *Soils and their use in south west England.* Harpenden: Soil Survey of England and Wales Bulletin 14

Fitzpatrick, A.P. 2013. Roman amphorae in Iron Age Cornwall: pre-Roman, Roman or post-Roman? *Cornish Archaeology* 52, 233–238

Fitzpatrick, A.P., Butterworth, C.A. & Grove, J. 1999. *Prehistoric and Roman sites in east Devon: the A30 Honiton to Exeter improvement DBFO Scheme, 1996–9.* Salisbury: Wessex Archaeology

Flower, R.J. 1993. Diatom preservation: experiments and observations on dissolution and breakage in modern and fossil material, *Hydrobiologia* 269/270, 473–484

Flower, R.J., Jones, V.J. & Round, F.E. 1996. The distribution and classification of the problematic *Fragilaria (virescens* v.) *exigua* Grun./*Fragilaria exiguiformis* (Grun.) Lange-Bertalot: A new species or a new genus? *Diatom Research* 11(1), 41–57

Fontijn D.R. 2009. Land at the other end of the sea? Metalwork circulation, geographical knowledge and the significance of British/Irish imports in the Bronze Age of the Low Countries. In Clark P. (ed.), *Bronze Age connections: cultural contact in prehistoric Europe*, 130–149. Oxford: Oxbow Books

Fontijn, D. 2019. *Economies of destruction: how the systematic destruction of valuables created value in Bronze Age Europe, c. 2300–500 BC.* London: Routledge

Fontijn, D., Bourgeois, Q. & Louwen, A.J. 2011. *Iron Age echoes. Prehistoric land management and the creation of a funerary landscape – The 'Twin Barrows' at the Echoput in Apeldoorn.* Leiden: Sidestone Press

Fowler, C. 2013. *The emergent past. A relational realist archaeology of Early Bronze Age mortuary practices.* Oxford: Oxford University Press

Fox, C. 1938. *The personality of Britain.* Cardiff; National Museum of Wales

French, C. 2003. *Geoarchaeology in action: studies in soil micromorphology and landscape evolution.* London: Routledge

French, C. 2015. *A handbook of geoarchaeological approaches for investigating landscapes and settlement sites.* Oxford: Studying Scientific Archaeology 1

French, C.N. 1983. The Prah sands loam, *Quaternary Newsletter* 40, 14–23

French, C.N. 1985. *Cornish Biological Records* 8. Redruth: University of Exeter, Institute of Cornish Studies

French, C.N. 1999. The 'submerged forest' palaeosols of Cornwall. *Geoscience in south-west England* 9, 365–369

French, C., Murphy, R. & Atkinson, M. 1999. *Flora of Cornwall. Atlas of the flowering plants and ferns of Cornwall with notes on some species recorded on the Isles of Scilly.* Camborne: Wheal Seaton Press

Frieman, C.J., Jones A.M., & Lewis, J. 2022. Worlds within worlds: embanked enclosures and transforming identities during the Romano-British period in Cornwall. In Ibsen, T., Ilves, K., Maixner, K., Messal, S. & Schneeweiß, J. (eds), *Fortifications in the natural and cultural landscape; from organising space to the creation of power*, 267–284. Schloss Gottorf: Center for Baltic and Scandinavian Studies

Frieman, C.J & Lewis, J. 2021. Bronze Age wayfaring and monumentalised landscape. In Gibson, C.D., Cleary, K. & Frieman, C.J. (eds), *Making journeys: archaeologies of mobility*, 95–106. Oxford: Oxbow Books

Fyfe, R. 2018. Appendix 8: assessment of humose sediments. In Southwest Archaeology, Penzance Heliport Replacement, Jelbert Way, Penzance, Cornwall: results of an archaeological evaluation. North Molton: Unpublished report, Southwest Archaeology

Fyfe, R., Newton, T. & Head, K. 2017. *Sampling and assessment of peat at Eastern Green, Penzance.* Plymouth: University of Plymouth

Gardiner, J., Allen, M.J., Hamilton-Dyer, S., Laidlaw, M. & Scaife, R.G. 2002. Making the most of it: late prehistoric pastoralism in the Avon Levels, Severn Estuary. *Proceedings of the Prehistoric Society* 68, 1–40

Garrow, D. & Sturt, F. 2017. *Neolithic stepping stones; excavation and survey with the western seaways of Britain 2008–2014.* Oxford: Oxbow Books

Gehrels, W.R. 2007. Microfossil reconstructions. In Elias, S. (ed.), *Encyclopedia of Quaternary science* 3015–3024, 3576. Oxford: Elsevier

Gilbert, C.S. 1817. *An historical survey of the county of Cornwall.* Plymouth and London: J Congdon

Godlaski, T.M. 2013. Holy smoke: tobacco use among Native American tribes in North America. *Substance Use & Misuse* 48, 1–8 [https://doi.org/10.3109/10826084.2012.739490]

Godwin, H. 1967. Pollen analytic evidence for the cultivation of *Cannabis* in England. *Review Palaeobotany and Palynology* 4, 71

Goode, A.J.J. & Taylor, R.T. 1988. Geology of the country around Penzance. *Memoir of the British Geological Survey* Sheets 351 & 358 (England & Wales). London: HMSO

Gosden, C. 1994. *Social being and time.* Oxford: Blackwell

Gosden, C. & Marshall, Y. 1999. The cultural biography of objects. *World Archaeology* 31, 169–178

Gossip, J. 2010. Penwith College, Penzance, Cornwall. Archaeological recording in advance of redevelopment: Archive report. Truro: Unpublished Historic Environment Projects

Gossip, J. 2021. Life outside the round – Bronze Age and Iron Age settlement at Higher Besore and Truro College, Threemilestone, Truro. In Jones, A.M. & Kirkham, G. (eds), *Later prehistoric settlement in Cornwall and the Isles of Scilly: evidence from five excavations*, 147–280. Oxford: Archaeopress

Gossip, J, & Jones AM. forthcoming. The Godrevy barrow revisited. In Jones, A.M. (ed.), *Close to the Edge: excavations of Cornish coastal barrows.* Oxford: Archaeopress

Graeber, D. & Wengrow, D. 2021. *The dawn of everything: a new history of humanity.* London: Allen Lane

Greatrex, P.A. 1983. Interpretation of macrofossil assemblages from surface sampling of macroscopic plant remains in mire communities. *Journal of Ecology* 71, 773–791

Greeves, T. 2019. Dartmoor's sacred pools. Design in the prehistoric landscape. *Dartmoor Magazine* 137, 24–26

Griffith, F.M. 1984. Archaeological investigations at Colliford Reservoir, Bodmin Moor 1977–78. *Cornish Archaeology* 23, 47–140

Griffith, F.M. & Wilkes, E.M. 2006. The land named from the sea? Coastal archaeology and place-names of Bigbury Bay, Devon. *Archaeological Journal* 163, 67–91

Gwilt, A.T., Lodwick, M., Deacon, J., Wells, N., Madgwick, R. & Young, T. 2016. Ephemeral abundance at Llanmaes: exploring the residues and resonances of an Earliest Iron Age midden and its associated archaeological context in the Vale of Glamorgan. In Koch, J. & Cunliffe, B. (eds), *Celtic from the West* 3, 277–303. Oxford: Oxbow Books/ Celtic Studies Publications

Hamon, C. 2008. Functional analysis of stone grinding and polishing tools from the earliest Neolithic of north-western Europe. *Journal of Archaeological Science* 35, 1502–1520

Harkness, D.D. & Wilson, H.W. 1979. Scottish Universities Research and Reactor Centre radiocarbon measurements III. *Radiocarbon* 21(2), 228–229

Harris, D. & Smyth, G. 1983. Excavation of a barrow (?) at Higher Polcoverack, St Keverne. *Cornish Archaeology* 22, 93–99

Harris Stone, J. 1912. *England's Riviera: a topographical and archaeological description of Land's End Cornwall and adjacent pots of beauty and interest.* London: Kegan Paul, Trench Trubner & Co.

Hartley, B., Barber, H.G, Carter, J.R. & Sims, P.A. 1996. *An atlas of British diatoms.* Bristol: Biopress

Hather, J.G. 2000. *The identification of the northern European woods: a guide for archaeologists and conservators.* London: Archetype Publications

Haustein, M., Gillis, C. & Pernicka, E. 2010. Tin isotopy – a new method for solving old questions. *Archaeometry* 52, 816–832

Hawkes, A. 2013. The beginnings and evolution of the fulacht fia tradition in early prehistoric Ireland. *Proceedings of the Royal Irish Academy* 114C, 1–51

Hayes, E., Pardoe, C. & Fullagar, R. 2018. Sandstone grinding/pounding tools: use-trace reference libraries and Australian archaeological applications. *Journal of Archaeological Science Reports* 20, 97–114

Healy, M.G. 1993. Holocene coastal evolution and relative sea-level Change in west Cornwall, U.K. Unpublished PhD thesis, National University of Ireland

Healy, M.G. 1995. The lithostatigraphy and biostratigraphy of a Holocene coastal sediment sequences in Marazion Marsh, West Cornwall, UK, with reference to sea-level movements. *Marine Geology* 124, 237–252

Healy, M.G. 1996a. Holocene coastal evolution at Marazion Marsh and Hayle Copperhouse, West Cornwall. In Healy, M.G. (ed.), *Late Quaternary coastal change in west Cornwall*, 46–59. Durham: Environmental Research Centre, Department of Geography, University of Durham, IGCP Project 367

Healy, M.G. 1996b. Late Quaternary coastal change in west Cornwall. In Healy, M.G. (ed.), *Late Quaternary coastal change in west Cornwall*, 1–10. Durham: Environmental Research Centre, Department of Geography, University of Durham, IGCP Project 367

Healy, M.G. 1996c. Holocene coastal evolution at Marazion Marsh and Hayle Copperhouse, West Cornwall. In Healy, M.G. (ed.), *Late Quaternary coastal change in west Cornwall*, 46–59. Durham: Environmental Research Centre, Department of Geography, University of Durham, IGCP Project 367

Healy, M.G. 1996d. Metalliferous mine waste in West Cornwall: the implications for coastal management. In Jones, P.S, Healy, M.G. & Williams, A.T. (eds), *Studies in European coastal management*, 147–155. Cardigan: Samara Publishing.

Healy, M.G. 1999a. Holocene relative sea-level change in west Cornwall. In Scourse J.D. & Furze, M.F.A. (eds), *The Quaternary of west Cornwall, field guide*, 58–61. London: Quaternary Research Association

Healy, M.G. 1999b. Marazion Marsh (pollen record). In Scourse, J.D. & Furze, M.F.A. (eds), *The Quaternary of west Cornwall, field guide*, 74–80. London: Quaternary Research Association

Healy, M.G. 1999c. Trewornan, River Amble, Camel Estuary. In Scourse, J.D. & Furze, M.F.A. (eds), *The Quaternary of west Cornwall, field guide*, 199–203. London: Quaternary Research Association

Helms, M. 1988. *Ulysses' sail: ethnographic odyssey of power, knowledge and geographical distance.* Princeton NJ: Princeton University Press

Hencken, O'Neill, H. 1932. *The archaeology of Cornwall and Scilly*. London: Methuen

Hencken, O'Neill, H. 1933. An excavation by H M Office of Works at Chysauster, Cornwall, 1931. *Archaeologia* 83, 237–284

Henderson, J. 2007. *The Atlantic Iron Age: settlement and identity in the first millennium BC.* London: Routledge

Hendey, N.I. 1964. *An introductory account of the smaller algae of British coastal waters. Part V. bacillariophyceae (diatoms).* London: Ministry of Agriculture Fisheries and Food Series IV

Henwood, W.J. 1858a. Notice of the submerged forest near Padstow. *Reports of the Royal Institute of Cornwall* 3, 17–19

Henwood, W.J. 1858b. Notice of the submarine forest near Padstow. *Royal Institute Cornwall* 3, 17-19

Henwood, W.J. 1873. On the detrital tin ore of Cornwall. *Journal of Royal Institute of Cornwall* 4, 191–254

Herring, P. 1993. *An archaeological evaluation of St Michael's Mount.* Truro: Cornwall Archaeological Unit

Herring, P. 1999. Trencrom, Lelant, historical and archaeological assessment. Truro: unpublished report, Cornwall Archaeological Unit

Herring, P. 2000. *St Michael's Mount, Cornwall, reports on archaeological works, 1995–8* Truro: Cornwall County Council

Herring, P. 2016a. Medieval West Penwith (*c.* 400–1540 AD). In Herring, P., Johnson, N., Jones, A.M., Nowakowski, J.A., Sharpe, A. & Young, A., *Archaeology and landscape at the Land's End, Cornwall*, 216–237. Truro: Cornwall Council

Herring, P, 2016b. A tomb for the living: Grumbla cromlech, the Giant's Chair, Sancreed. *Cornish Archaeology* 18, 119–135

Herring, P., Johnson, N., Jones, A.M., Nowakowski, J.A., Sharpe, A. & Young, A. 2016. *Archaeology and landscape at the Land's End, Cornwall*, 216–237. Truro: Cornwall Council

Herriott, C. 2005. The numinous aquatic: water cult and society in Irish prehistory. Unpublished PhD thesis, University of Bristol

Heyworth, A. 1978. Submerged forests around the British Isles: their dating & relevance as indicators of post-glacial land & sea level changes. In Fletcher, J. (ed.), *Dendrochronology in Europe. Principles, interpretations & applications to archaeology & history* 1, 279–288.. Oxford: British Archaeological Report S5/National Maritime Museum, Greenwich, Archaeological Series 4/

Research Laboratory for Archaeology & History of Art, Oxford University Publication 2

Heyworth, A. & Kidson, C. 1982. Sea-level changes in south-west Britain and Wales. *Proceedings of the Geologists' Association* 93, 91–111

Higginbottom, G. 2020. The World ends here, the World begins here: Bronze Age megalithic monuments in western Scotland. *Journal of World Prehistory* 33, 25–134

Hingley, R. 2009. Esoteric knowledge? Ancient bronze artefacts from Iron Age contexts. *Proceedings of the Prehistoric Society* 75, 145–165

Historic England 2018. Peat Database Cornwall Results [https://content.historicengland.org.uk/content/docs/research/peat-database-cornwall.pdf]

Hitchins, M. 1806. Account of antiquities discovered in Cornwall. *Archaeologia* 15, 118–121

Hodges, H. 2000. *Artifacts. An introduction to early materials and technology.* London: Duckworth

Hodgson, J.M. 1997. *Soil survey field handbook*. Silsoe: Soil Survey and Land Research Centre

Hollesen, J. 2022. Climate change and the loss of archaeological sites and landscapes: a global perspective. *Antiquity* 96(390), 1382–1395

Horie, C.V. 1987. *Materials for conservation: organic consolidants, adhesives and coatings (conservation and museology).* London: Butterworths

Horton, B.P., Engelhart, S.E., Hill, D.F., Kemp, A.C., Nikitina, D., Miller, K.G. & Peltier, W.R. 2013. Influence of tidal-range change and sediment compaction on Holocene relative sea-level change in New Jersey, USA. *Journal of Quaternary Science* 28(4), 403–411

Houlbrook, C. 2015. The Wishing-Tree of Isle Maree. In Houlbrook, C. & Armitage, N. (eds), *The Materiality of Magic: an artifactual investigation into ritual practices and popular belief*, 123–142. Oxford: Oxbow Books

Humphrey, C. & Laidlaw, J.A. 1994. *The archetypal actions of ritual: a theory of ritual illustrated by the Jain rite of worship.* Oxford: Clarendon

Hurcombe, L. 2014. *Perishable material culture in prehistory: investigating the missing majority*. London: Routledge

Hustedt, F. 1953. Die Systematik der Diatomeen in ihren Beziehungen zur Geologie und Okologie nebst einer Revision des Halobien-systems. *Svensk Botanisk Tidskrift* 47, 509–519

Hustedt, F. 1957. Die Diatomeenflora des Fluss-systems der Weser im Gebiet der Hansestadt Bremen. *Abhandlungen herausgegeben vom Natuwissenschaftlichen Verien zu Bremen* 34, 18–440

Ian Farmer Associates 2017. Penzance Heliport ground investigation report. Coventry: Unpublished Report ref. C60983

Ingold, T. 1993. The temporality of the landscape. Conceptions of time and ancient society. *World Archaeology* 25, 152–174

Ingold, T. 2000. *The perception of the environment: essays in livelihood, dwelling and skill.* London: Routledge

Ingold, T. 2010. The round mound is not a monument. In Leary, J., Darvill, T. & Field, D. (eds), *Round mounds and monumentality in the British Neolithic and beyond*, 253–260. Oxford: Neolithic Studies Group Seminar Papers 10

IPCC. 2022. Sea level rise and implications for low lying islands, coasts and communities. In IPCC (eds), *The ocean and cryosphere in a changing climate: special report on the ocean and cryosphere in a changing climate*. Cambridge: Cambridge University Press

Jacobi, R.M. 1979. Early Flandrian hunters in the south-west. *Proceedings of the Devon Archaeological Society* 37, 48–94

James, H.C.L. 1990. Post-glacial site at Ponsandane, near Penzance. *Proceedings of the Ussher Society* 7, 299–300

James, H.C.L & Guttman, E.B. 1992. Late Holocene vegetational development at Chyandour, near Penzance, west Cornwall. *Proceedings of the Ussher Society* 8, 60–63

Janssen, C.R. 1969. *Alnus* as a disturbing factor in pollen diagrams. *Acta Botanica Neerlandica*. 8, 55–58

Johns, C. 1994. Littlejohns Barrow: the damage and reprofiling of the round barrow west of Hensbarrow, Roche. *Cornish Archaeology* 33, 22–35

Johnson, N. & Rose, P. 1994. *Bodmin Moor; an archaeological survey, Volume 1*. London: RCHME

Johnston, R. 2020. *Bronze Age worlds: a social prehistory of Britain and Ireland.* London: Routledge

Jones, A. 1999. Local colour: megalithic architecture and colour symbolism in Neolithic Arran. *Oxford Journal of Archaeology* 18, 339–350

Jones, A.M. 2004–5. Settlement and ceremony; archaeological investigations at Stannon Down, St Breward, Cornwall. *Cornish Archaeology* 43–44, 1–140

Jones, A.M. 2005. *Cornish Bronze Age ceremonial landscapes* c. *2500–1500 BC*. Oxford: British Archaeological Report 394

Jones, A.M. 2009–10. Excavation of a Bronze Age barrow on Constantine Island, St Merryn, Cornwall. *Cornish Archaeology* 48–49, 67–98

Jones, A.M. 2010. Misplaced monuments?: a review of ceremony and monumentality in first millennium cal BC Cornwall. *Oxford Journal of Archaeology* 29, 203–228

Jones A.M. 2012. Going west: ceremony, barrows and cairns in the south west peninsula. In Britnell, W. & Silvester, R.J. (eds), *Reflections on the past, essays in honour of Frances Lynch*, 172–194. Welshpool: Cambrian Archaeological Association

Jones, A.M. 2013a. Memory, myth, place and landscape inhabitation: a perspective from the south-west peninsula. In Chadwick, A. & Gibson, C. (eds), *Memory, myth, place and long-term landscape inhabitations*, 55–75. Oxford: Oxbow Book

Jones, A.M. 2013b. Archaeological excavations at Bosiliack, Madron, Cornwall, 2011. *Cornish Archaeology* 53, 135–169

Jones, A.M. 2015. Ritual, rubbish or everyday life? Evidence from a Middle Bronze Age settlement in mid Cornwall. *Archaeological Journal* 172, 30–51

Jones, A.M. 2016a. *Preserved in the peat: an extraordinary Bronze Age burial on Whitehorse Hill, Dartmoor, and its wider context*. Oxford: Oxbow Books

Jones, A.M. 2016b. Early landscape and ceremony. In Herring, P., Johnson, N., Jones, A.M., Nowakowski, J.A., Sharpe, A. & Young, A., *Archaeology and landscape at the Land's End, Cornwall*, 112–137. Truro: Cornwall Council

Jones, A.M. 2019a. *Excavation of later prehistoric and Roman sites along the route of the Newquay Strategic Road Corridor, Cornwall.* Oxford: Archaeopress

Jones, A.M. 2019b. Excavations at Carn Galva and Bosporthennis Quoit, West Penwith, in 2009. *Cornish Archaeology* 58, 27–49

Jones, A.M. 2020a. Investigations at Trethevy Quoit 2019: the anatomy of a Cornish portal dolman. *Cornish Archaeology* 59, 49–76

Jones, A.M. 2020b. Longrock and Marazion Marsh coastal protection works. Archaeological recording: archive report. Truro: unpublished report, Cornwall Archaeological Unit

Jones, A.M. 2021. From Beaker pits to living in the round: some themes. In Jones, A.M. & Kirkham, G. (eds), *Later prehistoric settlement in Cornwall and the Isles of Scilly: evidence from five excavations*, 333–345. Oxford: Archaeopress

Jones, A.M. forthcoming a. The Early Bronze Age in the south west: long-distance contacts and local identities In Jones, A.M. &. Quinnell, H. (eds), *Sourcing prehistoric materials – new perspectives.* Oxford: Archaeopress

Jones, A.M. forthcoming b. Remembering and forgetting: reusing stones and bones, and making and unmaking monuments. In Gibson, C., Brown, D. & Pyzel, J. (eds), *Gone…but not forgotten. Forgotten … but not long gone. Mundane memories, artificial amnesia and transformed traditions.* Oxford: Archaeopress

Jones, A.M. forthcoming c. Excavations at Tom Parsons' Barrow, Constantine Bay. In Jones, A.M. (ed.), *Close to the edge; excavations of Cornish coastal barrows.* Oxford: Archaeopress

Jones, A.M. & Kirkham, G. 2013. From landscape to portable art: the changing settings of simple rock art in south-west Britain and its wider context. *European Journal of Archaeol*ogy 16, 636–659

Jones, A.M. & Kirkham, G. (eds), 2021. *Later prehistoric settlement in Cornwall and the Isles of Scilly: evidence from five excavations.* Oxford: Archaeopress

Jones, A.M. & Lawson-Jones, A. 2018. Pits and flints: archaeological recording along the A30 to Higher Carblake road scheme, Cornwall. *Cornish Archaeology* 57, 1–33

Jones, A.M. & Lawson-Jones, A. 2020. Beneath the sands: a placed Beaker pit deposit at Tyringham Road, Lelant, Cornwall. *Cornish Archaeology* 59, 145–158

Jones, A.M. & Mikulski, R. 2015. After the storm: an Early Bronze Age cist burial at Harlyn Bay, Cornwall, 2014. *Cornish Archaeology* 54, 139–156

Jones, A.M. & Quinnell, H. 2006a. Redating the Watch Hill barrow. *Archaeological Journal* 163, 42–66

Jones, A.M. & Quinnell, H. 2006b. Cornish Beakers: new discoveries and perspectives. *Cornish Archaeology* 45, 31–70

Jones, A.M. & Quinnell, H. 2011a. The Neolithic and Bronze Age in Cornwall, *c.* 4000 cal BC to *c.* 1000 cal BC: an overview of recent developments. *Cornish Archaeology* 50, 197–229

Jones, A.M. & Quinnell, H. 2011b. Bosiliack: a later prehistoric settlement in Penwith, Cornwall. *Archaeological Journal* 168, 96–132

Jones, A.M. & Quinnell, H. 2014. Saucer barrows: places for ritual within Wessex Early Bronze Age chalkland barrow cemeteries. *Oxford Journal of Archaeology* 33, 339–359

Jones, A.M. & Quinnell, H. 2022. The Tregiffian project: analysis of an entrance grave. *PAST* 101, 1–2

Jones, A.M. & Smith, R.P. 2015. A Late Bronze Age pit, burnt bone and stones at Quintrell Downs, Newquay, Cornwall. *Cornish Archaeology* 54, 193–204

Jones, A.M. & Taylor, S.R. 2010. *Scarcewater, Pennance, Cornwall, archaeological excavation of a Bronze Age and Roman landscape*. Oxford: British Archaeological Report 516

Jones, A.M. & Taylor, S.R. 2015. Archaeological investigations of Late Iron Age settlement at Sir James Smith's Community School, Camelford, Cornwall, 2008–9. *Cornish Archaeology* 54, 1–87

Jones, A.M. & Thorpe, C. 2014. Pits and pyre debris at Tresavean, Lanner, Cornwall. *Cornish Archaeology* 54, 157–169

Jones, A.M. & Thomas, A. 2010. Bosiliack and a reconsideration of entrance graves. *Proceedings of the Prehistoric Society* 76, 271–296

Jones, A.M., Gossip, J. & Quinnell, H, 2015. *Settlement and metalworking in the Middle Bronze Age and beyond: new evidence from Tremough, Cornwall.* Leiden: Sidestone Press

Jones, A.M., Lawson-Jones, A. & Quinnell, H. 2019. Excavations at the North Cliffs 2016: investigating Mesolithic flint scatters in Hudder Field. *Cornish Archaeology* 58, 1–26

Jones, A.M., Nowakowski, J.A & Thorpe, C. 1997. Archaeological investigations along the Probus Bypass, Cornwall, archive and assessment report. Truro: unpublished report, Cornwall Archaeological Unit

Jones, A.M., Quinnell, H. & Taylor, R.T. 2017. Cornish axe groupings, not Cornish axe factories: new work on the sourcing of Neolithic stone axes in Cornwall. In Shaffrey, R. (ed.), *Written in stone: papers on the function, form, and provenancing of prehistoric stone objects in memory of Fiona Roe*, 35–53. Southampton: Highfield Press

Jones, A.M., Quinnell, H. & Taylor, R.T. forthcoming. Recent work on the Group XIX artefacts from the North Cliffs: reconsidering the use of Cornish greywacke. *Lithics*

Jones, A.M., Taylor, S.R. & Sturgess, J. 2012. A Beaker-associated structure and other discoveries along the Sennen to Porthcurno SWW pipeline. *Cornish Archaeology* 51, 1–67

Jones, A.M., Lawson-Jones, A., Quinnell, H. & Tyacke, A. 2013. Landscapes of stone: contextualising greenstone working and lithics from Clodgy Moor, West Penwith, Cornwall. *Archaeological Journal* 170, 2–29

Jones, A.M., Marley, J., Quinnell, H. & Hartgroves, S. 2011. On the beach: new discoveries at Harlyn Bay. *Proceedings of the Prehistoric Society* 77, 89–110

Jones, A.M., Lawson-Jones, A., Quinnell, H., Tyacke, A. & Taylor, R.T. 2018. The North Cliffs Project. *Mesolithic Miscellany* 25(1), 23–48

Jones, D.A. 1992. *Principles and prevention of corrosion.* Hoboken NJ: Prentice Hall

Juddery, M. & Roberts. B.W. 2010. Report to H.M. Coroner for Cornwall 2009 T557. Available at: https://finds.org.uk/database/artefacts/record/id/270750

Juggins. S. 2003. *C2 User guide. Software for ecological and palaeoecological data analysis and visualisation.* Newcastle upon Tyne: University of Newcastle [http://www.campus.ncl.ac.uk/staff/Stephen.Juggins/software/C2Home.htm]

Juleff, G. & Bray L.S. 2007. Minerals, metals, colours and landscapes: Exmoor's Roman Lode in the Early Bronze Age. *Cambridge Archaeological Journal* 17, 285–296

Keevill, G. 2004. *The Tower of London Moat. Archaeological Excavations 1995–9.* Oxford: Historic Royal Palaces Monograph 1

Kitchen, T. 1764. *England illustrated. Cornwall I.* London: R & J. Dodsley

Kirkham, G. 2011. Something different at the Land's End. In Jones, A.M. & Kirkham, G. (eds), *Beyond the core:*

reflections on regionality in prehistory, 101–111. Oxford: Oxbow Books

Kirkham, G. forthcoming. 'That notable treble entrenchment of earth': recent work at Lescudjack hillfort, Penzance. *Cornish Archaeology*

Knight, M.G. 2017a. The deliberate destruction of Late Bronze Age socketed axeheads in Cornwall. *Cornish Archaeology* 56, 203–224

Knight, M.G. 2017b. There is method in the fragments: a damage ranking system for Bronze Age metalwork. *European Journal of Archaeology* 24(1), 48–67

Knight, M.G. 2018. The intentional destruction and deposition of Bronze Age metalwork in South West England. Unpublished PhD thesis, University of Exeter

Knight, M.G. 2019a. Doubtful associations? Assessing Bronze Age 'multi-period' hoards from northern England, Scotland and Wales. In Knight, M., Boughton, D. & Wilkinson, R. (eds), *The past in the past: investigating the significance of the deposition of earlier objects in later contexts*, 19–41. Oxford: Archaeopress

Knight, M.G. 2019b. Going to pieces. Investigating the deliberate destruction of Late Bronze Age swords and spearheads. *Proceedings of the Prehistoric Society* 85, 251–272 [doi:10.1017/ppr.2019.3]

Knight, M.G. 2022. *Fragments of the Bronze Age: the destruction and deposition of metalwork in south-west Britain and its wider context*. Oxford: Prehistoric Society Research Papers 13

Knight, M.G., Boughton, D. & Wilkinson, R. 2019a. *The past in the past: investigating the significance of the deposition of earlier objects in later contexts*. Oxford: Archaeopress

Knight, M.G., Ormrod, T. & Pearce, S. 2015. *The Bronze Age metalwork of south western Britain. A corpus of material found between 1983 and 2014*. Oxford: British Archaeological Report 610

Knight, M., Ballantyne, R., Robinson Zeki, I. & Gibson, D. 2019b. The Must Farm pile-dwelling settlement. *Antiquity* 93(369), 645–663

Kohn, E. 2013. *How forests think: toward an anthropology beyond the human*. Berkeley CA: University of California Press

Kõivupuu, M. 2020. Tradition in landscape, landscape in tradition: discourse of natural sanctuaries in Estonia. *Time and Mind* 13, 267–281

Koskinen-Koivisto, E. & Seitsonen, O. 2019. Landscapes of loss and destruction: Sámi elders' childhood memories of the Second World War. *Ethnologia Europaea* 49(1), 24–40 [doi:10.16995/ee.816]

Krammer, K. & Lange-Bertalot, H. 1986–1991. *Bacillariophyceae*. Stuttgart: Gustav Fisher

Krause, R., Breuer, L., Korolnik, S., Pernicka, E., Schorer, B., Spatzier, A., Stein, V. & Bofinger, J. 2021. An Early Bronze Age burial with a golden spiral ring from Ammerbuch-Reusten, southwestern Germany. *Praehistorische Zeitschrift*, 1–10. [https://doi.org/10.1515/pz-2021-0010]

Kristiansen, K. & Larsson, T.B. 2005. *The rise of Bronze Age society: travels, transmissions and transformations*. Cambridge: Cambridge University Press

Kytmannow, T. 2008. *Portal tombs in the landscape, the chronology, morphology and landscape setting of the portal tombs of Ireland, Wales and Cornwall*. Oxford: British Archaeological Report 455

Ladle, L. 2018. *Multi-period occupation at Football Field, Worth Matravers, Dorset. Excavations 2006–2011*. Oxford: British Archaeological Report 643

Lageras, K.E. 2002. Visible intentions? Viewshed analysis of Bronze Age burial mounds in western Scania, Sweden. In Scarre, C. (ed.), *Monuments and landscape in Atlantic Europe. Perception and society during the Neolithic and Early Bronze Age*, 179–191. London: Routledge

Lambrick, G. with Robinson, M. 2009. *The Thames through time: the Thames Valley in late prehistory 1500 BC–AD 50*. Oxford: Oxford Archaeology

Langdon. C.T. 2019. Pollen assessment analysis. In Allen, M.J., Clapham, A.J., Cameron, N. & Langdon, C.T., AEA416: Marazion Marsh, Mount's Bay, Penzance, Cornwall: palaeo-environmental assessment: geoarchaeology, pollen and diatoms. Codford: unpublished report for CAU, report AEA 416.04.04, 18 December 2019

Langdon, C.T. & Scaife, R.G. 2019. Pollen assessment analysis. In Allen, M.J., Cameron, N., Langdon, C.T. & Scaife, R.G., AEA 387: Penzance Proposed Heliport Site, Off Jelbert Way, Penzance, Cornwall; palaeo-environmental assessment: geoarchaeology, pollen and diatoms. unpublished report for CAU, report AEA 387.03.02, dated 7 June 2019

Latour, B. 2014. Agency at the time of the Anthropocene. *New Literary History* 45, 1–18

Lawson, A.J. 2000. *Potterne, 1982–5: animal husbandry in late prehistoric Wiltshire*. Salisbury: Wessex Archaeology

Lawson-Jones, A. 2013. Discoveries along the North Land's End pipeline. *Cornish Archaeology* 52, 197–222

Lawson-Jones, A. 2019. Penzance Heliport, Cornwall Phase 2: archaeological barrow excavation. Truro: unpublished report, Cornwall Archaeological Unit

Layard, J.W. 1942. *Stone men of Malekula*. London: Chatto & Windus

Leary, J. 2015. *The remembered land, surviving sea-level rise after the last ice age*. London: Bloomsbury Academic

Leary, J., Field, D. & Campbell, G. 2013. *Silbury Hill: the largest prehistoric mound in Europe*. Swindon: English Heritage

Lehoërff, A. & Talon, M. 2017. *Movement, exchange and identity in Europe in the 2nd and 1st millennia BC: beyond frontiers*. Oxford: Oxbow Books

Lemonnier, P. 2012. *Mundane objects: materiality and non-verbal communication*. Walnut Creek CA: Left Coast Press

Leonard, K. 2015. *Ritual in Late Bronze Age Ireland*. Oxford: Archaeopress

Lewis-Williams, D. & Pearce, D. 2005. *Inside the Neolithic mind*. London: Thames & Hudson

Li, W., Tsoraki, C., Lan, W., Yang, Y., Zhang, J. & van Gijn, A. 2019. New insights into the grinding tools used by the earliest farmers in the central plain of China. *Quaternary International* 529, 10–17 [https://doi.org/10.1016/j.quaint.2018.10.005]

Liddell, D. 1932. Report of the excavations at Hembury fort Devon, third season. *Proceedings of the Devon Archaeological Exploration Society* 1, 162–190

Locock, M. 2001. A later Bronze Age landscape in the Avon Levels: settlement, shelters, and saltmarsh at Cabot Park. In Brück, J. (ed.), *Bronze Age landscapes: tradition and transformation*, 121–128. Oxford: Oxbow Books

Long, A.J. & Roberts, D.H. 1997. Sea-level change. In Fulford, M., Champion, T. & Long, A. (eds), *England's coastline heritage; a survey for English Heritage and the*

RCHME, 25–49. London & Swindon: English Heritage and RCHME

Long, A.J., Scaife, R.G & Edwards, R.J. 1999. Pine pollen in intertidal sediments from Poole Harbour, UK; implications for late-Holocene sediment accretion rates and sea-level rise. *Quaternary International* 55, 3–16

Longin, R. 1971. New method of collagen extraction for radiocarbon dating. *Nature* 230, 241–242

Lynch, F. 1972. Ring cairns and related monuments in Wales. *Scottish Archaeological Forum* 4, 61–80

Lynch, F. 1984. Moel Goedog I: a complex ring cairn near Harlech. *Archaeologia Cambrensis* 133, 8–50

Lynch, F. 1993. *Excavations in the Brenig Valley: a Mesolithic and Bronze Age landscape in north Wales*. Bangor: Cambrian Archaeological Association

Lynch, F. 1998. Colour in prehistoric architecture. In Gibson, A. & Simpson, D. (eds), *Prehistoric religion and ritual*, 62–67. Stroud: Sutton

Lynch, F. 2000. *Prehistoric Wales*. Stroud: Sutton

Lynch, A. 2014. *Poulnabrone: an Early Neolithic portal tomb in Ireland*. Dublin: Wordwell

Lynch, F. & Davey, P. 2017. *The chambered tombs of the Isle of Man: a study by Audrey Henshall 1969–1978*. Oxford: Archaeopress

Macfarlane, R. 2019. *Underland: a deep time journey*. London: Hamish Hamilton

Macklin, M., Bonsall, C., Davies, F.M. & Robinson, M. 2000. Human-environment interactions during the Holocene: new data and interpretations from the Oban Area, Argyll, Scotland. *The Holocene* 10, 109–121

MacSween, A., Hunter, J., Sheridan, J.A., Bond, J., Bronk Ramsey, C., Reimer, P., Bayliss, A., Griffiths, S. & Whittle, A. 2015. Refining the chronology of the Neolithic settlement at Pool, Sanday, Orkney: implications for the emergence and development of Grooved Ware. *Proceedings of the Prehistoric Society* 81, 283–310

Madgwick, R. & Mulville, J. 2015. Feasting on forelimbs: conspicuous consumption and identity in later prehistoric Britain. *Antiquity* 345, 629–44

Malinowski, B. 1922. *Argonauts of the western Pacific*. London: Routledge

Markham, M. & Floyd, P.A. 1998. Geochemical fingerprinting of west Cornish greenstones as an aid to provenancing Neolithic axes. *Geoscience in Southwest England* 9, 218–223

Marsden, P. 2019. *The Summer Isles: a voyage of the imagination*. London: Granta

Massey, A.C., Gehrels, R.W., Charman, D.J., Milne, G.A., Peltier, R.W., Lambeck, K. & Selby, K.A. 2008. Relative sea-level change and post-glacial isostatic adjustment along the coast of south Devon, United Kingdom. *Journal of Quaternary Science* 23, 415–433

Matthiesen, H., Brunning, R., Carmichael, B. & Hollesen, J. 2022. Wetland archaeology and the impact of climate change. *Antiquity* 96(390), 1412–1426

Mattingly, J., Marley, J. & Jones, A.M. 2009. Five gold rings? Early Bronze Age gold lunulae from Cornwall. *Journal of the Royal Institution of Cornwall* 48, 95–114

McGrail, S. 1993. Prehistoric seafaring in the Channel. In Scarre, C. & Healy, F. (eds), *Trade and exchange in prehistoric Europe*, 199–210. Oxford: Oxbow Monograph 33

McKinley, J.I., Leivers, M., Schuster, J., Marshall, P., Barclay, A. & Stoodley, N. 2014. *Cliffs End Farm, Isle of Thanet, Kent: a mortuary and ritual site of the Bronze Age, Iron Age and Anglo-Saxon period with evidence for long-distance maritime mobility*. Salisbury: Wessex Archaeology

McLaren, D. & Wilson, D. 2015. The excavation of two short cist burials at Broomlands, Kelso. *Scottish Archaeological Journal* 36–37, 147–161

McOmish, D., Field, D. & Brown, G. 2010. The Late Bronze Age and Early Iron Age midden site at East Chisenbury, Wiltshire. *Wiltshire Archaeological and Natural History Magazine* 103, 35–101

Melton, N., Montgomery, J., Roberts, B.W., Cook, G. & Harris, H. 2016: On the curious date of the Rylstone log-coffin burial. *Proceedings of the Prehistoric Society* 82, 383–392

Mercer, R.J. 1997. The excavation of a Neolithic enclosure complex at Helman Tor, Lostwithiel, Cornwall. *Cornish Archaeology* 36, 5–63

Mercer, R.J. 1981. Excavations at Carn Brea, Illogan, Cornwall 1970–73. *Cornish Archaeology* 20, 1–204

Mercer, R. & Healy, F. 2008. *Hambledon Hill, Dorset, England. Excavation and survey of a Neolithic monument complex and its surrounding landscape*. Swindon: English Heritage

Milcent, P-Y. 2015. Bronze objects for Atlantic elites in France (13th–8th century BC). In Hunter, F. & Ralston, I. (eds), *Scotland in later prehistoric Europe*, 19–46. Edinburgh: Society of Antiquaries of Scotland

Miles, H. 1975. Barrows on the St. Austell Granite. *Cornish Archaeology* 14, 5–81

Momber, G., Tomalin, D.J., Scaife, R.G., Satchell, J. & Gillespie, J. 2011. *Mesolithic occupation at Bouldnor Cliff and the submerged prehistoric landscapes of the Solent*. York: Council for British Archaeology Research Report 164

Mook, W.G. 1986. Business meeting: recommendations/resolutions adopted by the twelfth International Radiocarbon Conference. Radiocarbon 28, 799

Moore, P.D. & Webb, J.A. 1978. *An illustrated guide to pollen analysis*. London: Hodder & Stoughton

Moore, P.D., Webb, J.A. & Collinson, M.E. 1992. *Pollen analysis* (2nd edn). Oxford: Blackwell Scientific

Mudd, A. & Joyce, S. 2014. *The archaeology of the south-west reinforcement gas pipeline, Devon; investigations in 2005–7*. Cirencester: Cotswold Archaeology

Mulk, I.M. 1994. Sacrificial places and their meaning in Saami society. In Carmichael, D., Hubert, J., Reeves B. & Schande, A. (eds), *Sacred sites, sacred places*, 121–131. London: Routledge

Mullin, D. 2001. Remembering, forgetting and the invention of tradition; burial and natural places in the English Early Bronze Age. *Antiquity* 289, 533–588

Murphy, K., Caseldine, A.E., Dresser, Q., Williams, G., Wilkinson, J.L. & Crowther, J. 1992. Plas Gogerddan, Dyfed: a multi-period burial and ritual site. *Archaeological Journal* 149, 1–38

Needham, S. 1981. *The Bulford–Helsbury manufacturing tradition: the production of Stogursey socketed axes during the later Bronze Age in southern Britain*. London: British Museum Press

Needham, S. 1982. *The Ambleside hoard: a discovery in the Royal Collections*. London: British Museum Press

Needham, S. 2000. Power pulses across a cultural divide: cosmologically driven acquisition between Armorica and Wessex. *Proceedings Prehistoric Society* 66, 151–208

Needham, S. 2001. When expediency broaches ritual

intention: the flow of metal between systemic and buried domains. *Journal of the Royal Anthropological Institute* NS7, 275–298

Needham, S. 2007. Bronze makes a Bronze Age? Considering the systemic of Bronze Age metal use and the implications of selective deposition. In Burgess, C., Topping, P. & Lynch, F. (eds), *Beyond Stonehenge: essays on the Bronze Age in honour of Colin Burgess*, 278–287. Oxford: Oxbow Books

Needham, S. 2009. Encompassing the sea: 'maritories' and Bronze Age interactions. In Clark, P. (ed.), *Bronze Age connections, cultural contact in prehistoric Europe*, 12–37. Oxford: Oxbow Books

Needham, S. 2012. *Case and place for the British Chalcolithic*. In Allen, M.J., Gardiner, J. & Sheridan, A. (eds), *Is there a British Chalcolithic? People, place and polity in the late 3rd millennium*, 1–26. Oxford: Prehistoric Society Research Papers 4

Needham, S., Parham, D. & Frieman, C. 2013. *Claimed by the sea: Salcombe, Langdon Bay, and other marine finds of the Bronze Age*. London Council for British Archaeology Research Report 173

Neighbour, T. 2005. Excavation of a Bronze Age kerbed cairn, at Olecote, Breasclete, near Calanais, Isle of Lewis. *Scottish Internet Reports* 13, 1–77 [https://doi.org/10.9750/issn.2056-7421.2005.13]

Neil, S., Evans, J., Montgomery, J. & Scarre, C. 2020. Isotopic evidence for human movement into central England during the Early Neolithic. *European Journal of Archaeology* 23, 512–529

Neil, S., Montgomery, J., Evans, J., Cook, T. & Scarre, C, 2017. Land use and mobility during the Neolithic in Wales explored using isotope analysis of tooth enamel. *American Journal of Physical Anthropology* 164, 371–393

Newman, P. 2011. *The field archaeology of Dartmoor*. London: English Heritage

Nicolas, C. 2016. *Flèches de pouvoir à l'aube de la métallurgie*. Leiden: Sidestone Press

Noble, G. 2007. *Neolithic Scotland: timber, stone, earth and fire*. Edinburgh: Edinburgh University Press

Nowakowski, J.A. 1991. Trethellan Farm, Newquay: the excavation of a lowland Bronze Age settlement and Iron Age cemetery. *Cornish Archaeology* 30, 5–242

Nowakowski, J.A. 2001. Leaving home in the Cornish Bronze Age: insights into the planned abandonment process. In Brück, J. (ed.), *Bronze Age landscapes tradition and transformation*, 139–148. Oxford: Oxbow Books

Nowakowski, J.A. 2007. Digging deeper into barrow ditches: Investigating the making of Early Bronze Age memories in Cornwall. In Last, J. (ed.), *Beyond the grave: new perspectives on barrows*, 91–112. Oxford: Oxbow Books

Nowakowski, J.A. 2016a. Prehistoric settlement – roundhouses and fields, 2nd to 1st millennia BC. In Herring, P., Johnson, N., Jones, A.M , Nowakowski, J.A., Sharpe, A. & Young, A., *Archaeology and landscape at the Land's End, Cornwall*, 138–159. Truro: Cornwall Council

Nowakowski, J.A. 2016b. Remarkable landscapes of ancient fields – the later prehistoric and Romano-British legacy. In Herring, P., Johnson, N., Jones, A.M., Nowakowski, J.A., Sharpe, A. & Young, A. (eds), *Archaeology and landscape at the Land's End, Cornwall*, 160–190. Truro: Cornwall Council

Nowakowski, J.A. & Johns, C. 2015. *Bypassing Indian Queens. Archaeological excavations 1992–1994. Investigating prehistoric and Romano-British settlement and landscapes in Cornwall*. Truro: Cornwall Archaeological Unit, Cornwall Council & Highways Agency

Nowakowski, J.A., Quinnell, H., Sturgess, J., Thomas, A. & Thorpe, C. 2007. Return to Gwithian: shifting the sands of time. *Cornish Archaeology* 46, 13–76

Nunn, P. & Cook, M. 2022. Island tales: culturally-filtered narratives about island creation through land submergence incorporate millennia-old memories of postglacial sea-level rise. *World Archaeology* 54, 29–51

O'Brien, Y. 2021. The role of persistent places and landmarks in navigation. In Gibson, C.D., Cleary, K. & Frieman, C.J. (eds), *Making journeys: archaeologies of mobility*, 17–26. Oxford: Oxbow Books

O'Brien, W. & O'Driscoll, J. 2017. *Hillforts, warfare and society in Bronze Age Ireland*. Oxford: Archaeopress

Olalde, I., Brace, S. Allentoft, M.E., Armit, I., Kristiansen, K., Booth, T., Rohland, N., Mallick, S., Szécsényi-Nagy, A., Mittnik, A., Altena, E., Lipson, M., Lazaridis, I., Harper, T. K., Patterson, N., Broomandkhoshbacht, N., Diekmann, Y., Faltyskova, Z., Fernandes, D. & Reich, D. *et al.* 2018. The Beaker phenomenon and the genomic transformation of northwest Europe. *Nature* 555, 190–196

Oldfather, C.H. 1933. *Diodorus of Sicily*. London: Heinemann

Ong, P.M. 1966. Geochemical investigation at Mount's Bay. Unpublished PhD. thesis, University of London

Oswald, A., Dyer, C. & Barber, M. 2001. *The creation of monuments: Neolithic causewayed enclosures in the British Isles*. Swindon: Historic England

Owoc, M. 2001a. 'The times, they are a changin': experiencing continuity and development in the Early Bronze Age funerary rituals of southwestern Britain' In Brück, J. (ed.), *Bronze Age landscapes tradition and transformation*, 207–216. Oxford: Oxbow Books

Owoc, M. 2001b. Bronze Age cosmologies: the construction of time and space in south-western funerary/ritual monuments. In Smith, A.T. & Brookes, A. (eds), *Holy ground: theoretical issues relating to the landscape and material culture of ritual space*, 27–38. Oxford: British Archaeological Report S956

Owoc, M., 2002. Munselling the mound: the use of soil colour as metaphor in British Bronze Age funerary ritual. In Jones, A. & MacGregor, A. (eds), *Colouring the past*, 127–140. Oxford: Berg

Papworth, M. 2013. Excavations at Thorncombe Beacon, Doghouse Hill and Golden Cap on the Golden Cap Estate, West Dorset. *Proceedings of the Dorset Natural History and Archaeological Society* 134, 205–247

Parker Pearson, M., Chamberlain, A., Jay, M., Richards, M.P. & Sheridan, A. (eds), 2019. *The Beaker People: isotopes, mobility and diet in prehistoric Britain*. Oxford: Prehistoric Society Research Papers 7

Parker Pearson, M., Pollard, P., Richards, C., Thomas, J., Tilley, C. & Welham, K. 2020. *Stonehenge for the ancestors. Part 1: Landscape and monuments. The Stonehenge Riverside Project Volume 1*. Leiden: Sidestone Press

Pascoe, C. 1970. Peat remains at Portmellon and Maenporth. *Journal of Camborne-Redruth Natural History Society* 2(2), 18–21

Patchett, F. 1950. Cornish Bronze Age pottery, part II. *Archaeological Journal* 107, 44–65

Patterson, N., Isakov, M., Booth, T., Büster, L., Fischer, C.-E., Olalde, I., Ringbaurer, H. *et al.* 2022. Large-scale migration into Britain during the Middle to Late Bronze Age. *Nature* 601, 588–594 [https://doi.org/10.1038/s41586-021-04287-4]

Pearce, S.M. 1976. The Middle and Late Bronze Age of the south-west and its relationship to settlement. *Proceedings of the Devon Archaeological Society* 34, 136–145

Pearce, S.M. 1983. *The Bronze Age metalwork of south western Britain*. Oxford: British Archaeological Report 120

Pearce, S.M. & Padley, T. 1977. A Bronze Age find from Tredarvah, Penzance. *Cornish Archaeology* 16, 25–41

Penhallurick, R.D. 1986. *Tin in antiquity: its mining and trade throughout the ancient world with particular reference to Cornwall*. London: Institute of Metals

Penhallurick, R.D. 2009. *Ancient and early medieval coins from Cornwall and Scilly*. London: Royal Numismatic Society

Pétursdóttir, Þ. 2017. Climate change? Archaeology and Anthropocene. *Archaeological Dialogues* 24, 175–205

Phillips, A. 2007. Landscape: the settings to our lives. In Barber, J., Clark, C., Cressy, M., Crone, A., Hale, A., Henderson, J., Housley, R., Sands, R. & Sheridan, A. (eds), *Archaeology from the wetlands: recent perspectives. Proceedings of the 11th WARP conference, Edinburgh 2005*, 5–16. Edinburgh: Society of Antiquaries of Scotland

Pollard, M.A. & Heron, C. 1996. *Archaeological chemistry*. Cambridge: Royal Society of Chemistry

Pollard, S. & Russell, P. 1969. Excavation of round barrow 248b, Upton Pyne. *Proceedings of the Devon Archaeological Society* 27, 49–74

Pollard, T. 1996. Time and tide: coastal environments, cosmology and ritual practice in prehistoric Scotland. In Pollard, T. & Morrison, A. (eds), *The early prehistory of Scotland*, 198–213. Edinburgh: Edinburgh University Press

Pope, R., Mason, R., Hamilton, D., Rule, E. & Swogger, J. 2020. Hillfort gate-mechanisms: a contextual, architectural reassessment of Eddisbury, Hembury and Cadbury hillforts. *Archaeological Journal* 177, 339–407

Preston, C.D. 1995. *Pondweeds of Great Britain and Ireland*. London: Botanical Society of Britain & Ireland Handbook 8

Preston, C.D. & Croft, J.M. 1997. *Aquatic plants in Britain and Ireland*. Colchester: Harley Books

Price, N. 2020. *Children of ash and elm: a history of the Vikings*. London: Penguin Books

Pryor, F. 2001. *The Flag Fen Basin: archaeology and environment of a fenland landscape*. London: English Heritage

Quinnell, H. 1997. Excavations of an Exmoor barrow and ring cairn. *Proceedings of the Devon Archaeology Society* 55, 1–38

Quinnell, H. 2003. Devon Beakers: new finds, new thoughts. *Proceedings of the Devon Archaeological Society* 61, 1–20

Quinnell, H. 2004. *Trethurgy; excavations at Trethurgy Round, St Austell: community and status in Roman and post-Roman Cornwall*. Truro: Cornwall Archaeological Unit

Quinnell, H. 2004–5. Worked stone, 43–44, in Jones, A.M., Settlement and ceremony; archaeological investigations at Stannon Down, St Breward, Cornwall. *Cornish Archaeology* 1–140

Quinnell, H. 2010. The artefacts. In Jones, A.M. & Taylor, S.R., *Scarcewater, Pennance, Cornwall, archaeological excavation of a Bronze Age and Roman landscape*, 93–119. Oxford: British Archaeological Report 516

Quinnell, H. 2012. Trevisker pottery: Some recent studies. In Britnell, W. & Silvester, R.J. (eds), *Reflections on the past: essays in honour of Frances Lynch*, 146–171. Welshpool: Cambrian Archaeological Association

Quinnell, H. 2019. Twenty years after Trethurgy: revisiting Roman period settlement in Cornwall. *Cornish Archaeology* 58, 107–128

Quinnell, H. & Taylor, R.T 2006. Pottery and stonework. In Jones, A.M. & Quinnell, H., Cornish Beakers; new discoveries and perspectives. *Cornish Archaeology* 45, 40–49

Rackham, O. 1989. *The last forest: the story of Hatfield Forest*. London: Dent

Radivojević, M., Roberts, B., Pernicka, E., Stos-Gale, Z., Rehren, T., Bray, P. & Broodbank, C. 2018. The provenance, use, and circulation of metals in the European Bronze Age the state of debate. *Journal of Archaeological Research* 26, 1–55

Rainbird, P. & Pears, B. 2017. The excavation of an Iron Age site at Nansledan, Newquay. *Cornish Archaeology* 56, 85–114

Randsborg, K. 2011. *Bronze Age textiles: men, women and wealth*. London: Bristol Classical Press

Rashidian, E. 2021. The resilience concept in archaeology; a critical consideration. *Academia Letters* (February), 1–6

Ratcliffe, J. & Straker, V. 1996. *The early environment of Scilly; palaeoenvironmental assessment of cliff-face and intertidal deposits 1989–1993*. Truro: Cornwall County Council

Redman, C.L. 2005. Resilience theory in archaeology. *American Anthropologist* 107(1), 70–77

Reichel-Dolmatoff, G. 1997. *Rainforest shamans: essays on the Tukano Indians of the northwest Amazon*. Dartington: Themis Books

Reid, C. 1913. *Submerged forests*. Cambridge: Cambridge University Press

Reimer, P.J., Bayliss, A., Beck, J.W., Blackwell, P.G., Bronk Ramsey, C., Buck, C.E., Cheng, H., Edwards, R.L., Friedrich, M., Grootes, P.M., Guilderson, T.P., Haflidason, H., Hajdas, I., Hatté, C., Heaton, T.J., Hoffman, D.L., Hogg, A.G., Hugen, K.A., Kaiser, K.F., Kromer, B., Manning, S.W., Niu, M., Reimer, R.W., Richards, D.A., Scott, E.M., Southon, J.R., Staff, R.A., Turney, C.S.M. & van der Plicht, J. 2013. Intcal13 and marine13 radiocarbon age calibration curves, 0–50,000 years cal BP. *Radiocarbon* 55, 1869–1887

Riley, H. & Wilson-North, R. 2001. *The field archaeology of Exmoor*. London: English Heritage

Rival, L. 1998. Trees, from symbols of life and regeneration to political artefacts. In Rival, L. (ed.), *The social lives of trees: anthropological perspectives on tree symbolism*, 1–38. Oxford: Berg

Roberts, B.W. 2007. Adorning the living but not the dead: understanding ornaments in Britain *c.* 1400–1100 cal BC. *Proceedings of the Prehistoric Society* 73, 135–167

Roberts, B.W. 2013. Britain and Ireland in the Bronze Age: farmers in the landscape or heroes on the high seas? In Fokkens, H. & Harding, A. (eds), *The Oxford handbook of the European Bronze Age*, 531–549. Oxford: Oxford University Press

Roberts, B.W., Boughton, D., Dinwiddy, M., Doshi, N., Fitzpatrick, A.P., Hook, D., Meeks, N., Mongiatti, A., Woodward, A. & Woodward, P.J. 2015. Collapsing commodities or lavish offerings? Understanding massive metalwork deposition at Langton Matravers, Dorset, during the Bronze Age–Iron Age transition. *Oxford Journal of Archaeology* 34, 365–395

Robertson, D., Taylor, M., Tyers, I., Cook, G. & Hamilton, W. 2016. A second timber circle, trackways, and coppicing at Holme-next-the-Sea Beach, Norfolk: use of salt and freshwater marshes in the Bronze Age. *Proceedings of the Prehistoric Society* 82, 227–258

Robinson, G. 2007a. *The prehistoric island landscape of Scilly*. Oxford: British Archaeological Report 447

Robinson, G. 2007b. Journeys through the seascapes of Scilly. In Cummings, V. & Johnston, R. (eds), *Prehistoric journeys*, 110–120. Oxford: Oxbow Books

Robson, J. 1944. The recent geology of Cornwall. A review. *Transactions of the Royal Geological Society of Cornwall* 17, 132–163

Rogers, W. 1923. *The shingles and sands of Cornwall*, Royal Cornwall Polytechnic Society 5, 45–50

Rose, P. 2000–1. Shadows in the imagination: encounters with caves in Cornwall, *Cornish Archaeology* 39–40, 95–129

Rovere, A., Stocchi, P. & Vacchi, M. 2016. Eustatic and relative sea level changes. *Current Climate Change Reports* 2, 221–231

Rowlands, M.J. 1976. *The production and distribution of metalwork in the Middle Bronze Age in southern Britain*. Oxford: British Archaeological Report 31

Russell, V. 1971. *West Penwith survey*. St Austell: Cornwall Archaeological Society

Ryves, D.B., Juggins, S., Fritz, S.C. & Battarbee, R.W. 2001. Experimental diatom dissolution and the quantification of microfossil preservation in sediments. *Palaeogeography, Palaeoclimatology, Palaeoecology* 172, 99–113

Salisbury, E.J. 1967. The reproduction and germination of *LImosella aquatica*. *Annals of Botany* NS 31(121), 147–162

Salisbury, E.J. 1970. The pioneer vegetation of exposed mud and its biological features. *Philosophical Transactions of the Royal Society of London. Series B, Biological Sciences* 259(829), 207–255

Santiago-Marrero C.G., Tsoraki, C. Lancelotti, C. & Madella, M. 2021. A microbotanical and microwear perspective to plant processing activities and foodways at Neolithic Çatalhöyük. PLoS ONE 16(6): e0252312 [https://doi.org/10.1371/journal.pone.0252312]

Satchell, J., Momber, G., Tidbury, L., Daire M.Y., Dupont, C., Missiaen, T., Jongepier, I. & Vos, P.C. 2015. *Arch-Manche: archaeology, art and coastal heritage: tools to support coastal management*. Southampton: Arch-Manche Technical Report [www.archmanche-geoportal.eu]

Satia, P. 2020. *Time's monster: history, conscience and Britain's empire*. London: Penguin

Sawyer, K. 2015. *Isles of the dead? The setting and function of the Bronze Age chambered cairns and cists of the Isles of Scilly*. Oxford: Archaeopress Archaeology

Scaife, R.G. 1984. A history of Flandrian vegetation in the Isles of Scilly: palynological investigations of Higher Moor and Lower Moor peat mires. *Cornish Studies* 11, 33–47

Scaife, R.G. 1996. Pollen analysis of the Bronze Age cairn and a peat profile, 203–209 in Smith, G., MacPhail R.I., Mays, S.A., Nowakowski, J., Scaife, R.G., Sharpe, A., Tomalin, D.J. & Williams, D.F., Archaeology and environment of a Bronze Age cairn and prehistoric and Romano-British Field system at Chysauster, Gulval, near Penzance, Cornwall. *Proceedings of the Prehistoric Society* 62, 167–219

Scaife, R.G. 2006. Penzance Harbour (62490): an assessment of the pollen and diatom content. Unpublished report for Wessex Archaeology

Scaife, R.G. Forthcoming. The Pleistocene and Holocene Environment of Southern England: a review of pollen studies with particular reference to archaeology. Portsmouth: Historic England

Scarre, C. 2002a. Coast and cosmos: the Neolithic monuments of northern Brittany. In Scarre, C. (ed.), *Monuments and landscape in Atlantic Europe. Perception and society during the Neolithic and Early Bronze Age*, 84–102. London: Routledge

Scarre, C. 2002b. A pattern of islands: the Neolithic monuments of north-west Brittany. *European Journal of Archaeology* 5, 24–41

Scarre, C. 2002c. Epilogue: colour and materiality in prehistoric societies. In Jones, A. & MacGregor, G. (eds), *Colouring the past*, 227–242. Oxford: Berg

Schultes, R. & Hofmann, A. 1992. *Plants of the gods: their sacred, healing, and hallucinogenic powers*. Rochester NY: Healing Arts Press

Schulting, R. & Bradley, R. 2013. Of human remains and weapons in the neighbourhood of London: new AMS 14C dates on Thames 'river skulls' and their European context. *Archaeological Journal* 170, 30–77

Scourse, J. & Kemp, R.A. 1999. Prah Sands. In Scourse, J.D. & Furze, M.F.A. (eds), *The Quaternary of west Cornwall, field guide* 156–163. London: Quaternary Research Association

Scourse, J.D. & Furze, M.F.A. (eds), 1999. *The Quaternary of west Cornwall, field guide*. London: Quaternary Research Association

Seitsonen, O. 2021. Rain, reindeer, digging and tundra: children's visual perception of an archaeological expedition to Northernmost Sápmi (Finnish Lapland). *Time and Mind* 14, 431–457 [https://doi.org/10.1080/1751696X.2021.1951563]

Sen, U.K. & Bhakat, R.K. 2021. Conservation of resources by religious and social prohibitions by Santal communities in south west Bengal, India. *Time and Mind* 14, 3–32 [https://doi.org/ 10.1080/1751696X.2021.1865641]

Shail, R.K. 1989. Gramscatho-Mylor facies relationships; Hayle, south Cornwall. *Proceedings of the Ussher Society* 7, 125–130

Sharpe, A. 2017. Penzance Park and Ride, Cornwall Archaeological watching brief. Truro: unpublished report, Cornwall Archaeological Unit.

Sharples, N. 2010. *Social relations in later prehistory: Wessex in the first millennium BC*. Oxford: Oxford University Press

Shaw, J. 2016. Archaeology, climate change and environmental ethics: Diachronic perspectives on human: non-human: environment worldviews, activism and care. *World Archaeology* 48, 449–465

Shennan, I. 1982. Interpretation of Flandrian sea-level data from the Fenland, England. *Proceedings of the Geologists' Association* 93, 53–63

Sheridan, A. 2004. Neolithic connections along and across the Irish Sea. In Cummings, V. & Fowler, C. (eds), *The Neolithic of the Irish Sea, materiality and traditions of practice*, 9–21. Oxford: Oxbow Books

Sheridan, A. & Shortland, A. 2004. '... beads which have

given rise to so much dogmatism, controversy and rash speculation': faience in Early Bronze Age Britain and Ireland. In Shepherd, I.A.G. & Barclay, G.J. (eds), *Scotland in ancient Europe*, 263–282. Edinburgh: Society of Antiquaries of Scotland

Smith, A.G., Whittle, A., Cloutman, E.W. & Morgan, L.A. 1989. Mesolithic and Neolithic activity end environmental impact on the south-east fen-edge in Cambridgeshire. *Proceedings of the Prehistoric Society* 55, 207–249

Smith, G. 1987. The Lizard project: landscape survey 1978–1983. *Cornish Archaeology* 26, 13–68

Smith, G. 2020. A later Mesolithic activity area at Windmill Farm, Predannack Downs, the Lizard, Cornwall. *Cornish Archaeology* 59, 1–48

Smith, G. & Harris, D. 1982. The excavation of Mesolithic, Neolithic and Bronze Age settlements at Poldowrian, St Keverne, 1980. *Cornish Archaeology* 21, 23–66

Smol, J.P. 2008. *Pollution of lakes and rivers. A palaeo-environmental perspective* (2nd edn). Oxford: Blackwell

Sörman, A. 2019. Casting in the longhouse: the organization of metalworking in Late Bronze Age settlements in south-eastern Sweden. *Current Swedish Archaeology* 27, 143–189

Southwest Archaeology. 2018. Penzance Heliport replacement, Jelbert Way, Penzance, Cornwall – results of an archaeological evaluation. North Molton: unpublished report, Southwest Archaeology

Southwest Archaeology. forthcoming. Land at Eastern Green, Penzance: results of archaeological monitoring and recording. North Molton: Unpublished report, Southwest Archaeology

Spector, J. 1991. What this awl means: towards a feminist archaeology. In Gero, J. & Conkey, M. (eds), *Engendering archaeology: women and archaeology*, 388–405. London: Blackwell

Spikins, P. 1999. *Mesolithic northern England: environment, population and settlement.* Oxford: British Archaeological Report 283

Stace, C. 1992 *New flora of the British Isles*. Cambridge: Cambridge University Press

Stace, C. 2019 *New Flora of the British Isles* (4th edn). Middlewood Green: C. & M. Floristics

Standish, C.D., Dhuime, B., Hawkesworth, C.J. & Pike, A.W.G. 2015. A non-local source of Irish Chalcolithic and Early Bronze Age gold. *Proceedings of the Prehistoric Society* 81, 149–177

Stevenson, A.C., Juggins, S., Birks, H.J.B., Anderson, D.S., Anderson, N.J., Battarbee, R.W., Berge, F., Davis, R.B., Flower, R.J., Haworth, E.Y., Jones, V.J., Kingston, J.C., Kreiser, A.M., Line, J.M., Munro, M.A.R. & Renberg, I. 1991. *The Surface Waters Acidification Project palaeolimnology programme: modern diatom/lake-water chemistry data-set*. London: Ensis

Stewart, R.J. 2012. The role of chert in later prehistoric lithic industries with specific reference to south-west England. *Geoscience in South-West England* 13, 123–130

Stone, J.F.S & Wallis, F.S. 1951. Third report of the sub-committee of the South-Western Group of Museums and Art Galleries on the petrological determination of stone axes. *Proceedings of the Prehistoric Society* 17, 99–158

Strong, V. 1997. *Uncommon ground: cultural landscapes and environmental values*. Oxford: Berg

Stuiver, M. & Kra, R.S. 1986. Editorial comment. *Radiocarbon* 28(2B), ii

Stuiver, M. & Polach, H.A. 1977. Reporting of ^{14}C data. *Radiocarbon* 19, 355–363

Susmann, N.M. 2021. Moving down the mountain: pathways for sacred landscape transformation at ancient Epidaurus and Nemea. *Time and Mind* 14, 73–109 [https://doi.org/10.1080/1751696X.2021.1891367]

Taçon, P. 1991. The power of stone: Symbolic aspects of stone use and tool development in western Arnhem Land, Australia. *Antiquity* 247, 192–207

Taylor, B. 2020. Plants as persons: perceptions of the natural world in the North European Mesolithic. *Time and Mind* 13, 307–330 [https://doi.org/10.1080/1751696X.2020.1815292]

Taylor, R.T. & Goode, A.J.J. 1987 Late Pleistocene and Holocene radiocarbon dates from the Penzance district, Cornwall. *Proceedings of the Ussher Society* 6, 599

Taylor, S.R. 2022. *Down the bright stream: the prehistory of Woodcock Corner and the Tregurra Valley*. Oxford: Archaeopress

Tellier, G. 2018 *Neolithic and Bronze Age funerary and ritual practices in Wales, 3600–1200 BC*. Oxford: British Archaeological Report 642

Terebikhin, N.M. 1993. Cultural geography and cosmography of the Sami. *Acta Borealia* 10, 3–17

Thomas, A. 2021. *On the edge of Empire: society in the south-west of England during the first century BC to fifth century AD*. Oxford: British Archaeological Report 667

Thomas, C. 1985. *Exploration of drowned landscape; archaeology and history of the Isles of Scilly*. London: B.T. Basford

Thomas, J.S. 2007. *Place and memory. Excavations at the Pict's Knowe, Holywood and Holm Farm, Dumfries and Galloway, 1994–8*. Oxford: Oxbow Books

Thomas, J.S. 2013. *The birth of Neolithic Britain: an interpretative account*. Oxford: Oxford University Press

Thomas, N. 2005. *Snail Down, Wiltshire. The Bronze Age barrow cemetery and related earthworks, in the parishes of Collingbourne Ducis and Collingbourne Kingston: Excavations, 1953, 1955 and 1957*. Devizes: Wiltshire Archaeological & Natural History Society

Thurston, E. 1930. *Trees and shrubs of Cornwall*. Cambridge: Cambridge University Press

Tilley, C. 1996. *An ethnography of the Neolithic: early prehistoric societies in southern Scandinavia*. Cambridge: Cambridge University Press

Tilley, C. 2009. Jacob's Well, Black Hill: a Bronze Age water shrine on Woodbury Common. *Proceedings of the Devon Archaeological Society* 67, 23–38

Tilley, C. 2010. *Interpreting landscape: geologies, topographies, identities*. Walnut Creek CA: Left Coast Press

Tilley, C. 2017. *Landscape in the* longue durée*: a history and theory of pebbles in a pebbled heathland landscape*. London: University College London

Timpany, S. 2009. *Geoarchaeological regional review of marine deposits along the coastline of southern England*. Swindon: English Heritage.

Tinsley, H. 1999. Pollen assessment of samples from buried peat from Porthallow, Cornwall. Bristol: unpublished report, University of Bristol

Tipping, R. 2004. Interpretive issues concerning driving forces of vegetation change in the early Holocene of the British Isles. In Saville, A. (ed.), *Mesolithic Scotland and its neighbours; the early Holocene prehistory of Scotland in its British and Irish context, and some northern perspectives*, 45–54. Edinburgh: Society of Antiquaries of Scotland

Tipping, R. & Tisdall, E. 2004. Continuity, crises and climate change in the Neolithic and Early Bronze Age periods of north west Europe. In Shepherd, I.A.G. & Barclay, G. (eds), *Scotland in Ancient Europe: the Neolithic and Early Bronze Age of Scotland and their European context*, 71–82. Edinburgh: Society of Antiquaries of Scotland

Topping, P. 2021. *Neolithic stone extraction in Britain and Europe: an ethnoarchaeological perspective*: Oxford: Prehistoric Society Research Papers 12

Torry, W. 1978. Natural disasters, social structure and change in traditional societies. *Journal of Asian and African Studies* 13, 167–183

Tucker, C. 1867. Antiquities of bronze found in Devonshire. *Archaeological Journal* 24, 110–122

Turner, L. 2010. *A re-interpretation of the Late Bronze Age metalwork hoards of Essex and Kent*. Oxford: British Archaeological Report 507

Tyacke, A. 2008.*CORN-021D57: A Bronze Age rapier*. available at: https://finds.org.uk/database/artefacts/record/id/222103

Tyacke, A. 2011. The work of the Portable Antiquities Scheme in Cornwall. *Cornish Archaeology* 50, 71–76

Tylecote, R.F. 1967. Metallurgical examination of a socketed axe and three lumps of bronze from St Gillan, St Anthony-in-Meneage. *Cornish Archaeology* 6, 110–111

Ussher, W.E.A. 1879. Pleistocene geology of Cornwall IV: submerged forests and stream tin gravels. *Geological Magazine* NS Decade II 6, 251–263

Valdez-Tullett, J. 2019. *Design and connectivity: the case of Atlantic rock art*. Oxford: British Archaeological Report S2932

van Beek, R. & Louwen, A. 2013. The centrality of urnfields. Second thoughts on structure and stability of Late Bronze Age and Early Iron Age cultural landscapes in the Low Countries. In Fontijn, D., Louwen, A.J., van der Vaart, S. & Wentink, K. (eds), *Beyond barrows. current research on the structuration and perception of the prehistoric landscape through monuments*, 81–112. Leiden: Sidestone Press

van den Berg, M. 2021. A borderland on the edge of materiality: ancient remains, storied landscapes, and community narratives from the arm of Finland. *Time and Mind* 14, 371–395 [https://doi.org/10.1080/1751696X.2021.1951558]

Van de Noort, R. 2004. *The Humber wetlands; the archaeology of a dynamic landscape*. Macclesfield: Windgather Press

Van de Noort, R. 2006. Argonauts of the North Sea. A social maritime archaeology for the 2nd millennium BC. *Proceedings of the Prehistoric Society* 72, 267–288

Van de Noort, R. 2013. Seafaring and riverine navigation in the Bronze Age of Europe. In Fokkens, H. & Harding, A. (eds), *The Oxford handbook of the European Bronze Age*, 382–397. Oxford: Oxford University Press

Van de Noort, R., Cumby, B., Blue, L., Harding, A., Hurcombe, L., Hansen, T., Wetherelt, A., Wittamore, J. & Wyke, A. 2014. Morgawr: an experimental Bronze Age-type sewn-plank craft based on the Ferriby boats. *International Journal of Nautical Archaeology* 43(2), 292–313 [https://doi.org/10.1111/1095-9270.12058]

Van Gijn, A. L. 2010. *Flint in focus. Lithic biographies in the Neolithic and Bronze Age*. Leiden: Sidestone Press

van Heeringen, R.M. & Theunissen, L. 2007. Archaeological monitoring of (palaeo)wetlands in the Netherlands: from best practice to guidelines sites. In Barber, J., Clark, C., Cressy, M., Crone, A., Hale, A., Henderson, J., Housley, R., Sands R. & Sheridan, A. (eds), *Archaeology from the wetlands: recent perspectives. Proceedings of the 11th WARP conference, Edinburgh 2005*, 49–65. Edinburgh: Society of Antiquaries of Scotland

Vervust, S., Kinnaird, T., Herring, P. & Turner, S. 2020. Optically stimulated luminescence profiling and dating of earthworks: the creation and development of prehistoric field boundaries at Bosigran, Cornwall. *Antiquity* 94(374), 420–436

Vitebsky, P. 2005. *Reindeer people: living with animals and spirits in Siberia*. Chicago IL: University of Chicago Press

von Gernet, A.D. 2007. Nicotian dreams: the prehistory and early history of tobacco in eastern North America. In Goodman, J., Lovejoy, P.E. & Sherratt, A. (eds), *Consuming habits: drugs in history and anthropology*, 65–85. London: Routledge

Vousdoukas, M.I., Clarke, J., Ranasinghe, R., Reimann, L., Khalaf, N., Duong T.M., Ouweneel, B., Sabour, S., Iles, C.E., Trisos, C.H., Feyen, L., Mentaschi, L. & Simpson, N.P. 2022. African heritage sites threatened as sea-level rise accelerates. *Nature Climate Change* [https://doi.org/10.1038/s41558-022-01280-1]

Waddington, K., Bayliss, A., Higham, T., Madgwick, R. & Sharples, N. 2019. Histories of deposition: creating chronologies for the Late Bronze Age–Early Iron Age transition in southern Britain. *Archaeological Journal* 176(1), 84–133

Wainwright, G. 1980. A pit burial at Lower Ashmore Farm, Rose Ash Devon. *Proceedings of the Devon Archaeological Society* 38, 13–16

Wainwright, G.J., Fleming, A. & Smith, K. 1979. The Shaugh Moor Project: first report. *Proceedings of the Prehistoric Society* 45, 1–34

Walens, S. 1981. *Feasting with cannibals. An essay on Kwakiutl cosmology*. Princeton NJ: Princeton University Press

Walker, E.A. 2016. The Palaeolithic and Mesolithic hunter-gatherers of Pembrokeshire. In Darvill, T., James, H., Murphy, K., Wainwright, G. & Walker, E.A. (eds), *Pembrokeshire County History, Volume I, Prehistoric, Roman and early medieval Pembrokeshire*, 1–54. Haverfordwest: Gomer Press

Waller, M.P. & Long, A.J. 2003. Holocene coastal evolution and sea-level change on the southern coast of England: a review, *Journal of Quaternary Science* 18, 351–359

Ward, S. & Barnatt, R. 2020. Prehistoric communities off the coast of Britain embraced rising seas – what this means for today's island nations. *The Conversation* 4 November [https://theconversation.com/prehistoric-communities-off-the-coast-of-britain-embraced-rising-seas-what-this-means-for-todays-island-nations-147879]

Watts, S. 2014. *The structured deposition of querns; the contexts of use and deposition of querns in the south-west of England from the Neolithic to the Iron Age*. Southampton: The Highfield Press

Webley, L., Adams, S. & Brück, J. 2020. *The social context of technology: non-ferrous metalworking in later prehistoric Britain and Ireland*. Oxford: Prehistoric Society Research Papers 11

Webster, C.J. (ed.) 2008. *The Archaeology of south west*

England; resource assessment and research agenda. Taunton: Somerset County Council

Werff, A. Van Der & Huls, H. 1957–1974. *Diatomeenflora van Nederlands*. Utrecht: Abcoude's-Gravenhage

Wessex Archaeology, 2006. Penzance Harbour, Cornwall: final technical report, palaeoenvironmental and geotechnical assessment. Salisbury: unpublished report, Wessex Archaeology

White, D.A. 1982. *The Bronze Age cremation cemeteries at Simons Ground, Dorset*. Dorchester: Dorset Natural History & Archaeology Society Monograph 3

Whittle, A., Pollard, J. & Grigson, C. 1999. *The harmony of symbols: the Windmill Hill causewayed enclosure, Wiltshire*. Oxford: Oxbow Books

Whittle, A., Bayliss, A., Healy, F., Mercer, R., Jones, A.M. & Todd, M. 2011. The south-west peninsula. In Whittle, A., Healy, F. & Bayliss, A. (eds), *Gathering time: dating the Early Neolithic enclosures of southern Britain and Ireland*, 476–509. Oxford: Oxbow Books

Wickham-Jones, C.R. 2015. *Between the wind and the water, World Heritage Orkney* (2nd edn). Oxford: Windgather Press

Wickham-Jones, C.R. 2018. *Landscape beneath the waves: the archaeological investigation of underwater landscapes*. Oxford: Studying Scientific Archaeology 4

Wickham-Jones, C. R., Bates, R., Dawson, S., Dawson, A. and Bates, M. 2018. The changing landscape of prehistoric Orkney. In Persson, P., Reide, F., Skar, B., Breivik, H.M. & Jonsson, L. (eds), *The ecology of early settlement in northern Europe*, 393–414. Sheffield: Equinox Publishing

Wilkes, E., Pitman, D., Randall, C. & Brown, A. 2021. Think global, act local: multi-scalar connections of Iron Age communities in Poole Harbour, Dorset, England. *Archaeological Journal* 178, 32–52

Wilkin, N. & Vander Linden, M. 2015. What was and what would never be: changing patterns of interaction and archaeological visibility across north-west Europe from 2500 to 1500 cal BC. In Anderson-Whymark, H., Garrow, D. & Sturt, F. (eds), *Continental connections: exploring cross-Channel relationships from the Mesolithic to the Iron Age*, 99–121. Oxford: Oxbow Books

Wilkinson, K. & Straker, V. 2008. The Neolithic and Early Bonze Age environmental background. In Webster, C.J. (ed.), *The archaeology of south west England; south west archaeological research framework: resource assessment and research agenda*, 63–74. Taunton: Somerset County Council

Wiseman, R. 2018. Random accumulation and breaking: the formation of Bronze Age scrap hoards in England and Wales. *Journal of Archaeological Science* 90, 39–49

Witkowski, A., Lange-Bertalot, H. & Metzeltin, D. 2000. *Diatom flora of marine coasts I*. Königstein: Iconographia Diatomologica, Annotated Diatom Micrograph 7

Wood, I.I. 2015. *Gunwalloe through the ages: Middle Bronze Age to the 12th century AD, Lizard Peninsula, Cornwall*. Exeter: National Trust

Woodward, A. 2002. Beads and Beakers: heirlooms and relics in the British Early Bronze Age. *Antiquity* 294, 1040–1047

Wright, E.V., Hutchinson, G.R. & Gregson, C.W. 1989. A fourth boat-find at North Ferriby, Humberside. *Archaeological Journal* 146, 44–57

WYG Group Ltd. 2017a. Penzance Heliport Ltd. Penzance proposed Heliport, land at Jelbert Way, Penzance; archaeology desk based assessment. Leeds: unpublished report A09450-3, WYG Group, December 2017

WYG Group Ltd. 2017b. Penzance Heliport Ltd. Penzance proposed heliport, land at Jelbert Way, geoarchaeological and palaeo-environmental assessment. Leeds: unpublished report, job no A094051.2, WYG Group, July 2017

WYG Group Ltd. 2018a.Proposed heliport, Jelbert Way, Penzance (PA/16/09346); response to consultation comments from Cornwall Council Historic Environment Team submitted 08 June 2018. Leeds: unpublished consultation document, WYG Group

WYG Group Ltd. 2018b. Barrow excavation, Penzance Heliport Replacement, Cornwall; Overarching Written Scheme of Investigation for archaeological excavation and geoarchaeological analysis. Leeds: unpublished report, job no A109662 1, WYG Group, July 2018

Wymer, J.J. & Healy, F. 1996. Neolithic and Bronze Age activity and settlement at Longham and Beestone with Bittering. In Wymer, J.J. (ed.), *Barrow excavations in Norfolk, 1984–88*, 28–53. Dereham: Norfolk Museums Service

Wysocki, M. & Whittle, A. 2000. Diversity, lifestyles and rites: New biological and archaeological evidence from British earlier Neolithic mortuary assemblages. *Antiquity* 285, 591–601

Yates, D. & Bradley, R. 2010a. Still water, hidden depths: the deposition of Bronze Age metalwork in the English Fenland. *Antiquity* 324, 405–415

Yates, D. & Bradley, R. 2010b. The siting of metalwork hoards in the Bronze Age of south-east England. *Antiquaries Journal* 90, 41–72

Yates, T. 1989. Habitus and social space: Some suggestions about meaning in the Saami (Lapp) tent *c.* 1700–1900. In Hodder, I. (ed.), *The meanings of things. Material culture and symbolic expression*, 249–262. London: Harper Collins

Xu, S., Anderson, R., Bryant, C., Cook, G.T., Dougans, A., Freeman, S., Naysmith, P., Schnabel, C. & Scott, E.M., 2004. Capabilities of the new SUERC 5MV AMS facility for 14C dating. *Radiocarbon* 46, 59–64

Xygalatas, D., Schjødt, U., Bulbulia, J., Konvalinka, I., Jegindø, E., Reddish, P. & Roepstorff, A. 2013. Autobiographical memory in a fire-walking ritual. *Journal of Cognition and Culture* 13, 1–16

Appendix 1:
Conservation of the copper ingot fragment

Laura Ratcliffe-Warren

Lab No:	1820
Object:	Ingot Fragment SF 13
Material:	Copper alloy
Age:	Late Bronze Age
Date Started:	29.11.18
Date Completed:	16.12.18
Conserved by:	Laura Ratcliffe-Warren
Description:	
Size:	Width 31 mm Length 46 mm Thickness 8 mm
No. pieces:	1

Smallish heavy sub rectangular lump of what has been confirmed to be copper (Chapter 5) from the excavations at PZH18 small find number SF 13, context 203 in cist 207 (Fig. A1). The item was kept damp from site in soil from the surrounding context and the object appeared largely stable despite some powdery green surface material suggesting copper corrosion.

Figure A1: Copper ingot prior to treatment

Condition

Major Structural:	N/A
Surface damage:	unknown
Accretions:	Soil adherent
Chemical:	Some active corrosion possible

Treatment

Slow air drying of the piece to prevent active corrosion from advancing and prepare for cleaning. The item is heavy suggesting a lot of metal present under the surface corrosion. Mechanical removal of the soil from the piece revealed a firm but uneven surface pitted with large air bubbles suggestive of a piece of a crude ingot or cast lump. One edge appears to be straighter than the rest possibly indicative of a break surface where the piece was removed from a larger object at some point prior to deposition (Fig. A1). This edge is not sharp or crisply defined as with a new clean break edge though despite corrosion so could have been broken at any time during the objects' lifespan. One side and this same edge appears to be covered in a layer of rotten organic matter which has been left in place as it may represent the preserved remains of a wrapping or organic material against which the piece was resting in the burial environment.

No chemical treatments have been applied to the object in case samples are to be taken of this organic layer. Stabilisation of the copper alloy can be managed by low humidity micro-climating. The ingot is discussed in Chapter 5.

Guidelines followed during the conservation work: (Hodges 2000; Horie 1987; Jones 1992; Pollard & Heron 1996).

Appendix 2: Borehole logs from Penzance Heliport site

Michael J. Allen

Transect 1

T1/1 149098.818 31592.481 8.81 m OD

Depth (cm)	*Unit*	*Description*
0–5	Ah	Dark brown humic silt many roots, under grass
50–60	A	Brown (10YR 4/3) silt loam, rare stones, mixed clear boundary
60–95	1. Colluvium	Dark brown (10YR 3/3) loose silt loam, rare small stones, abrupt boundary
95–100	1. Colluvium	Stony yellowish brown silty clay loam
100–120	1. Colluvium	Dark brown (10YR 3/3) loose silt loam, rare small stones, abrupt boundary
120–145	2. 'Peat'	Very dark greyish brown (10YR 3/2) stone-free humic silt loam, rare very small stones
145–165	3. ?Alluvium	Dark grey (10YR 4/1) stiff silty clay, gradual boundary
165–195	3. Alluvium	Mixed light grey dense silty clay with strong brown mottles, few small stones but increasing with depth
195–300	4. Colluvium	Yellowish brown to reddish brown (10YR 5/8–5YR 5/8) silt loam and rare medium stones, some fine sand
300+	4. Colluvium	Becoming sandy silt – dark yellowish brown (10YR 4/6) @ 285 cm becoming stonier; common small stones

T1/2 149093.297 31569.827 8.08 m OD

Depth (cm)	*Unit*	*Description*
0–5	Ah	Dark brown humic silt many roots, under grass
5–35	0. MG	Brown (10YR 4/3) silt loam, almost stone-free, Made Ground
35–50	0. MG	Very dark brown humic silty sand with modern inclusion, sharp boundary
50–85	1. Colluvium	Light brown to greyish brown minerogenic mixed silt to silty clay, with light grey clay and sand lenses – band of yellowish red sand at base
85–100	1. Colluvium	Dark silt loam to silty sand loam
100–230	3. Alluvium	Greyish blue (Gley 1) with dark greenish hues, stiff silt loam
230–245	4. Colluvium	Yellowish brown sandy clay loam, rare small stones
245–400+	4. Colluvium	Yellowish brown silt loam, rare stones @ 370–385 cm zone of stonier deposit
385–400+	5. Sand	Dark manganese stained sand

T1/3 sleeved 149086.997 31550.763 7.23 m OD

Depth (cm)	*Unit*	*Description*
0–30	A	Brown (10YR 4/3) silt loam, rare stones, mixed clear boundary
30–120	0. ?MG	Dark brown (10YR 3/3) loose silt loam, rare small stones, abrupt boundary
120–150	2. 'Peat'	Humose silt
150–200+	3. Alluvium	Grey silt – alluvium

Core T1/3		149086.997		31550.763 7.23 m OD
Depth (cm)	*Unit*	*Sample pollen*	*diatom*	*Description*
0–16	Ah			Very dark greyish brown (10YR 3/2) humic silt loam, stone-free, large crumb structure, many fine fleshy roots, clear boundary @ 11 cm glazed porcelain pottery
16–36	A			Very dark brown to dark brown (10YR 3/2–3) humic silt loam, weak small blocky structure, becoming greyer with depth, abrupt sloping boundary @ 26–36 cm almost grey/greyish brown
36–90	0. MG/dump			Mixed stiff greyish brown (10YR 3/2) to grey (10YR 6/1) with dark grey (10YR 5/1) patches, silty clay, almost stone-free, some medium stones, mixed gradual boundary @ 68 cm glass @ 70–80 cm very dark greyish brown silt silty clay admixed deposit @ 80–90 cm grey (2.5YR 6/1) looks greenish) dense coarse silt to silty loam
90–110	0. Mixed			Greenish brown and brown dense silty clay loam, rare small stones, clear boundary @ 105–110 cm becoming soft greenish silty loam
110–131	2. 'Peat'	110 114 118 122 126 130	110 114	Very dark brown to dark brown (10YR 3/2–3/3) humic silt loam (?highly humified peat), stone-free, clear to abrupt boundary @ 114 cm ^{14}C plant stem [modern]
131–155	2. 'Peat'	134 138 142 146 150 154	154	Very dark grey (10YR 3/1) humified silty peat, clear boundary @ 131 cm ^{14}C humin acids [2580–2460 cal BC] @ 155 cm ^{14}C humin acids [4230–4060 cal BC]
155–205	3. Alluvium	158 162 166 170 178 186 194 202	158 162 170 186 202	Stiff greenish grey silt loam to silty clay loam, with some darker grey patches @ 160–176 cm many vertical roots (avoided in sampling)
205–233		210 218 226	218	Mixed yellowish brown (10YR 5/6) with greenish silt and sandy silt patches, becoming denser and more yellowish brown with depth
233–267	4. Colluvium	234 242 250 258 266	234 250 266	Strong brown (7.5YR 5/6) silty sand loam, some small stones, dense and compact @ 255–267 cm becoming stonier

(continued)

(Core T1/3 continued)

Depth (cm)	*Unit*	*Sample pollen*	*diatom*	*Description*
267–300				not recovered – missing
300–350	4. Colluvium (continued)	306 314 322 330 338 346	 314 330 346	As above, abrupt boundary @ 322–334 cm dark reddish brown medium sand band
350–376+	5. Sand	354 362 370	 362 375	Greenish yellow medium sand, stone-free and wet

A total of 37 pollen, 17 diatom and three ^{14}C samples were removed

T1/4 149081.336 31530.116 6.62 m OD

Depth (cm)	*Unit*	*Description*
0–8	Ah	Dark grey humic silt loam
8–28	A	Dark brown silt loam, stone-free
28–50	1. Colluvium	Yellowish brown (5YR 5/3) silt loam many fine stones
50–105	1. Colluvium	Light grey (10YR 5/2) silt loam, rare stones @ 88–98 cm large stone
105–125		Grey silt – stone-free – alluvium
125–148	2. ?'Peat'	Dark greyish brown (10YR 4/2) dark brown silt, humic silt
148–200	3. Alluvium	Grey to dark grey stone-free silt – alluvium @ 180 cm porcelain white glaze pottery
200–215	3. Alluvium	Light grey silty sand loam, coarse grits
215–240	4. Colluvium	Stony yellowish brown firm silty sand loam
240+		Lost – not recovered

T1/5 149076.149 31511.999 6.10 m OD

Depth (cm)	*Unit*	*Description*
0–48	Ah	Brown stone-free humic silty loam
48–85		Dark brown humic loam, including medium stones, abrupt indurated boundary
85–95	0. MG	Mixed grey and light yellowish brown silt loam, few small stones, rare medium stones
95–105	0. MG	Dark brown to very dark brown humic loose silt with @ 100 cm willow pattern pottery
105–200	Alluvium	Grey silt loam
110–130	2. 'Peat'	humic silt/'peat'
130–210	3. Alluvium	Grey to greyish brown (2.5Y 5/1–2) silt, stone-free alluvium @ 150 cm reed stem
210–300+	4. Colluvium	Brownish yellow (10YR 6/8) sandy silt loam, rare small stones

Core T1/5 (1–2 m)		149076.149		31511.999 6.10 m OD
Depth (cm)	*Unit*	*Sample* pollen	diatom	*Description*
100–120	2. 'Peat'	102 106 110 114 118	102 110 118	Very dark greyish brown (10YR 3/2) humic silt/silty clay loam, more organic (humified) at the top (100–106 cm), becoming less organic and more minerogenic with depth, indurated clear boundary ^{14}C samples @ 102 cm humin acids @ 118 cm humin acids
120–188	3. ?Alluvium	122 126 130 146 154 162 170 178 186	 126 138 154 170 186	Greenish grey silt with dark brown inclusions (from above) to 40 mm across, clear mixing to 140 cm, large vertical woody roots to 14 mm ∅, to fibrous roots, clear boundary
188–195+	4. Colluvium	194		Brownish yellow heterogeneous firm silt loam to silt sand loam, common very small and small stones

A total of 15 pollen, eight diatom and two ^{14}C samples were removed

T1/6		149070.349 31493.891 5.66 m OD
Depth (cm)	*Unit*	*Description*
0–10	Ah	Brown to dark brown soft humic silt loam s
10–40	0. MG	Brown mixed
40–85		Mixed grey silt and yellowish brown silt loam
85–95		Light grey firm compact silt loam
95–113	2. ? 'Peat'	Very dark brown humic compact silt loam
113–148	3. Alluvium	Very stiff grey silt, some small stones; alluvium
148–156	'Peat'	Dark brown humic silt – mixed
156–205	3. Alluvium	Grey stiff silt
205–230	3. Alluvium	Light grey silt loam, common very small and small stones, clear boundary
230–300+	4. Colluvium	'Orange' stiff sandy clay loam, some stones, rare medium stones

T1/7		149064.496 31475.583 5.36 m OD penultimate in T1
Depth (cm)	*Unit*	*Description*
0–5	Ah	Brown to dark brown soft humic silt loam soil
3–35	A	Brown silt loam, stone-free
35–60		Greyish brown and yellowish brown mixed silt loam, stone-free
60–63	0. MG	Red cloth – sleeve of a jumper
63–130		Mixed grey to bluish grey and yellowish brown stiff stone-free silt loam
130–146	0. MG	Very dark brown humic, stone-free silt, with land drain, clear boundary @ 130 cm willow pattern pottery and glass vessel
146–218	3. Alluvium	Grey mottled silt and fine sand loam/silty loam, clear boundary
218–300	4. Colluvium	Yellowish brown stiff sandy silt loam

No humose layer noted

T1/8	149061.075	31455.952 4.76 m OD *c.* 6 m from hedge
Depth (cm)	*Unit*	*Description*
0–12	Ah	Dark greyish brown to greyish brown (10YR 4-3/2) sandy silt loam
12–82	0. MG	Mixed very pale brown (10YR 7/4) and grey (10YR 4/1) stiff silt loam, some coal/coke, rare small stones, abrupt boundary @ 45 cm plastic bag @ 60 cm drain sherd @ 70–82 cm many small stones
82–95		Very dark brown humic silt, some gleying evident
95–120	0. MG	Very dark grey crumbly silt loam Ah with field drain and brick red pottery
120–200	0. MG	Large stone – then not recovered
200–260	3. Alluvium	Dark grey (10YR 4/1) silt, becoming light brownish grey (10YR 6/2) and denser with depth, clear to gradual boundary
260–280	3. Alluvium	Grey sandier loam
280–300+	4. Colluvium	Yellowish brown (10YR 6/8) <u>sand</u> with some silt
		Repeat/re-core 1–2 m
100–120	0. MG	Very dark grey crumbly silt loam Ah with Victorian pottery sherd
120–147	3. Alluvium	Greyish brown humic silt
147–218	3. Alluvium	Grey silt slight stony
218–290	3. Alluvium	Grey sandy loam and many fine grits
290–300+	4. Colluvium	Transition to yellowish brown (10YR 6/8) <u>sand</u> with some silt

Transect 2

T2/9	149108.604	31470.654 5.01 m OD 20 m from hedge
Depth (cm)	*Unit*	*Description*
0–15	Ah	Very dark brown humic silt, stone-free
15–40	B	Brown silt loam
40–105	0. MG	Mixed blueish grey and dark brown silts
105–135	0. MG/peat	Dark brown humic crumbly silt (?'peat unit), sharp boundary'
135–148		Blueish grey dry silt, sharp boundary
148–175	0. MG	Dark brown humic soil rare medium pebbles @ 161 cm glass (bottle) @ 165 cm complete Victorian ink well pot
175–200+	3. ?Alluvium	Blueish grey homogeneous stone-free silt

T2/11	149110.618	31517.082 6.36 m OD 40 m N of T2/9
Depth (cm)	*Unit*	*Description*
0–12	A	Dark greyish brown (10YR 4/2) humic stone free silty Ah
12–28	A	Dark brown (10YR 4/3) silt loam, rare small stones many fine roots, clear/abrupt boundary
28–50		Brown, stone-free
50–76	0. ?MG	Dark yellowish brown (10YR 4/4) dry silt loam, many small and medium stones
76–100	0. MG	Grey sandy loam @ 95 cm cut slate (44 × 70 mm)
100–122		Greyish brown stone-free silt
122–205	2. 'Peat'	Dark brown humic, humified peat
205–235	3. Alluvium	Grey clay to silty clay, stone-free
235–300+	4. Colluvium	Yellowish brown stiff sandy silt loam

Core T2/11 (1–3 m)		149110.618		31517.082	6.36 m OD
Depth (cm)	*Unit*	*Sample pollen*	*diatom*	*Description*	
100–109	2. 'Peat'			Very dark brown to dark brown (10YR 1/2–3/3) humic silt loam, common medium flints, abrupt to clear boundary	
109–118				Greenish grey silty clay, common medium stones, abrupt boundary	
118–138	2. 'Peat'	138	138	Very dark brown (10YR 3/2) humic peat silt/humifed peat, common medium stones, abrupt to sharp diagonal boundary	
138–152	2. 'Peat'	142 146 150	 146	Very dark brown (10YR 3/2) humic peaty silt/humified peat, rare roots (to 6 mm ∅), essentially stone-free	
152–181	2. 'Peat'	154 158 162 166 170 174 178	154 158 174 178	Very dark brown 910YR 2/2) to black (10YR 2/1) humified peaty silt, stone-free, homogeneous ^{14}C samples @ 178 cm plant remains × 2	
181–197	2. 'Peat'	 182 186 190 194	182 190	Very dark greyish brown (10YR 3/2) humic silt, some rare organics present, horizontal wood (twig) at 185 cm, sharp/abrupt boundary ^{14}C samples @ 180 cm humic acids @ 196 cm humin acid	
197–228	3. Alluvium	198 202 206 214 222	198 206 222	Greenish grey (Grey 1 10Y 6/1) silt loam to sandy silt loam, rare stones, large vertical roots present, abrupt boundary	
228–290+	4. Colluvium	230 238 246 254 262 270 278 286	 238 254 270 286	Reddish yellow (7.5YR 6/8) and strong brown (7.5YR 5/6) sandy silt loam, common small stones, rare medium stones, patches of light olive brown (2.5Y 5/6) (ex greenish grey) silty loam, heterogeneous @ 250 cm+ becoming denser and stonier	

26 pollen samples, 15 diatom samples and four sample for radiocarbon dating

T2/12		149114.264	31563.289	7.88 m OD	@ 75 m
Depth (cm)	*Unit*	*Description*			
0–25	A	Dark brown (10YR 4/3) humic silt loam			
25–40	B	Dark brown (10YR 4/3) humic silt loam, few stones			
40–50		transition			
50–95	0. MG	Creamy silt (imported material)			
95–210	3. Alluvium	Greenish (blue) grey silt loam, stone-free alluvium, clear mixed boundary			
210–230		– mixed in core- grey silt loam and creamy silt			
230–200+	4. Colluvium	Yellowish brown (10YR 5/8–6/8) stiff silt loam with many fine stones			

T2/13		149118.358	31602.675	9.23 m OD
Depth (cm)	*Unit*	*Description*		
0–28	A	Dark brown (10YR 4/2) humic silt loam, essentially stone-free		
28–98	0. MG	Dark yellowish brown (10YR 4/6) firm silt loam, common very different medium stones		
98–110	0. MG	Transition – becoming greyer – mixed rare large stones		
110–300+		Yellowish brown (aka 'orange') stiff silt loam, some stones @ 130 cm yellowish brown and grey but stiff (same matrix)		

In south east of field

2/10 149153.422 31539.589 6.75 m OD 75 m from T2/9 (off line

Depth (cm)	*Unit*	*Description*
0–12	Ah	Dark brown to very dark brown humic silt, stone-free
12–37	B	Brown, crumbly silt loam
37–98		Mixed grey silt loam, rare small/medium round stones @ 77–81 cm dark brown lens
98–119		Light grey stiff silty clay
119–181	0. MG	Dark grey (10YR 4/1) to greenish brown silt loam @ 140 cm black plastic tube
181–121	3. ?Alluvium	Bluish grey dense silt loam, few fine fleshy/fibrous roots
212–240		Mixed (heterogeneous) dark grey (10YR 4/1) silt with few Mn nodules
240–300+	4. Colluvium	Yellowish brown stiff sandy silt loam, Mn nodules and staining to 270 cm, wet at base

No humose unit

14 149137.813 31506.46 5 6.13 m OD extra in SE

Depth (cm)	*Unit*	*Description*
0–34	0. MG	Dark brown soft stone-free silt loam, inclusions
34–76	0. MG	Very dark brown to dark greyish brown loose silty loam, very loose
76–98	0. A+MG	Dark grey to dark greyish brown firm humic silt loam, mixed
98–110		Grey to greyish brown 910YR 4/2) silt loam, with fine strong brown mottles
110–210	3. Alluvium	Grey to bluish grey (Gley 2 5B 5/1) stiff silt to silt loam alluvium, some light brown large diffuse mottles, rare small black stones
210–250		Becoming more heavily/strongly mottled with dark yellowish brown (?Mn) mottles
250–300+	4. Colluvium	Yellowish brown stiff silt loam with large inclusions of grey 'alluvium'

15 149166.5 31497.303 5.748 m OD SE of field

Depth (cm)	*Unit*	*Description*
0–15	A	Brown and dark brown humic silt loam
15–108	0. MG	Mixed with grey/greyish brown firm silt loam, some yellowish brown mottles @ 98 cm willow pattern pottery × 2
108–130	2. 'peat'	Very dark grey humic (not humose layer), includes large dry *Phragmites* stem, clear to abrupt boundary
130–242	3. Alluvium	Blueish grey firm stone-free silt (alluvium)
242–270+	4. Colluvium	Yellowish brown silt loam, almost stone-free
270–300+		Not recovered

16 149061.719 31556.168 7.27 m OD

Depth (cm)	*Unit*	*Description*
0–18	Ah	Dark brown (10YR 3/3) humic crumbly slit loam
18–100		Mixed grey and light grey compact silt loam, common very small and small stones
100–165	3. ?Alluvium	Greenish grey silt, common brown mottles, some Fe mottles
165–185		transition
185–200+	4. Colluvium	Yellowish brown silt loam, almost stone-free

Transect 3

T3/17 149012.36 31554.186 7.52 m OD

Depth (cm)	*Unit*	*Description*
0–24		Brown to greyish brown humic silt loam, gradual boundary
24–100		Light yellowish brown (10YR 5/4) silt, stone-free, diffuse large brown mottles
100–200		Not recovered except medium to large stones
Recore		
100–200+	4. Colluvium	Yellowish brown silt loam, almost stone-free

T3/18 149014.117 31507.648 5.71 m OD

Depth (cm)	*Unit*	*Description*
0–40	A	Brown (10YR 4/3) humic silt to silt loam, atone-free gradual boundary – well developed brown earth
40–60		A/C
60–115		Grey (2.5Y 6/1) medium silt well-sorted compacts, stone-fee, rare medium diffuse yellow mottles, clear to gradual boundary
115–190	4. Colluvium	Yellowish brown almost stone-free silty clay loam, but with many 'grits'
190–195		Stone

T3/19 149014.751 31471.924 4.84 m OD

Depth (cm)	*Unit*	*Description*
0–30	A	Dark brown (10YR 3/2–4/2) humic silt loam, abrupt boundary
30–145	3. ?Alluvium	Grey (2.5Y 6/1) to bluish grey silt, getting firmer with depth @ 100–145 cm few small stones
145–215		Greyish and yellowish brown silt – transition
215–230	4. Colluvium	Yellowish brown silt loam to sandy silt loam, stone-free
230–300+	4. Colluvium	Mixed light grey/grey and yellowish brown silt loam

INDEX

Numbers in *italics* denote pages with figures, numbers in bold denote pages with tables.

Places are in Cornwall unless stated otherwise.